A NAVAL HISTORY OF
WORLD WAR I

A NAVAL HISTORY OF WORLD WAR I

PAUL G. HALPERN

NAVAL INSTITUTE PRESS

ANNAPOLIS, MARYLAND

Library of Congress Cataloging-in-Publication Data
Halpern, Paul G. 1937–
   A naval history of World War I / Paul G. Halpern.
        p.   cm.
   Includes bibliographical references and index.
   ISBN 0-87021-266-4 (hc) (alk. paper)
   ISBN 1-55750-352-4 (pb) (alk. paper)
   1. World War, 1914–1918—Naval operations. I. Title.
D580.H34 1994
940.4′5—dc20   93-24265

CONTENTS

LIST OF MAPS

PREFACE

The first question any reader of this study might legitimately ask is, why do we need yet another history of the First World War at sea? There are a number of excellent histories; however, historians, like naval or aviation designers, often produce similar products when faced with the same requirements. A writer naturally analyzes where and what the most important events were, where the most modern and innovative weapons were used, and what the most important decisions were. But such analysis leads to books centered on events in the North Sea and the waters around the British Isles, with some mention of the Dardanelles and, of course, the distant battles off Coronel and the Falklands in the early months of the war. The books focus to a great extent on the activities of the Royal Navy.

This is as it should be—there is no denying that the British home waters and the North Sea were the center of gravity, and no matter what angle the war is studied from, the Royal Navy played a major role. A writer who has only a certain amount of space understandably concentrates on these areas. Staff colleges also tend to emphasize these events. The picture of the war that emerges, though, is not complete, for by concentrating on the North Sea and the British Isles, there is an assumption that nothing much from a naval point of view—with a few obvious exceptions—happened elsewhere. The study of these secondary campaigns is relegated to specialized and fairly narrowly focused studies, and some are gradually forgotten. The role of the smaller navies also is glossed over and gradually forgotten.

The aim of this study, as a glance at the table of contents will show, is to shift the focus and present a very broad picture of the war, for this was indeed a world war, and naval operations took place throughout the world and were conducted by many navies. There is a penalty for this. Just as an aircraft or naval designer must sacrifice some feature to accentuate another, in a broad study of this sort within a single volume, operational detail will have to be sacrificed. The reader will not find an in-depth analysis of naval battles such as Jutland. We already have some excellent studies of that battle, and here depth and detail have had to be sacrificed somewhat for breadth. It appears almost foolhardy to attempt a study of this scope, for it cannot be encyclopedic and include everything. The reader may find one of his pet subjects missing; as I write this, I can think of a few subjects I have not been able to include, such as shipbuilding and logistics, or the controversial role of the large *K*-class British submarines. It was not possible, lest the manuscript grow too long, to have a detailed examination of the naval aspects of the peace settlements in 1919. One can only hope that the notes will point the interested reader in the right direction.

The notes are an aid; they are not essential. They are included to show what material portions of an account are based on and to indicate where one might find further information on a subject of interest. There are those who dislike the "spots and dots" all over a page, but they need not worry. With only a few exceptions I have tried to limit the notes strictly to citations. The extended discussions that sometimes make the notes of a scholarly book or article more interesting than the text are omitted; the reader who is so inclined can safely ignore them.

In writing a study of this sort, one soon realizes how much opportunity remains for naval historians of the First World War. The Russian navy is a prime example, for there are major discrepancies in Russian, émigré, and German accounts of the same operations. One hopes that recent political developments will permit historians who have the ability to use the Russian language to mine Russian archives. There is also a need for studies of national navies, particularly those of France and Italy, that integrate naval affairs with domestic concerns. Even in the case of the United States, where we have excellent studies on aspects on the American naval role in the war, there is really nothing approaching the study on the navy as a whole similar to what the late Professor Marder did for the Royal Navy.

There is an old joke that the one thing that distinguishes the history of naval operations from the history of military operations on land is *ships sink*. We usually know what happened—it's hard to disguise the fact that a ship sank—but it is much more difficult to determine why a ship was used (or not used) in the way she was. In general there often seems to be more information about the ship's technical specifications and design.

In a topic as broad as this study, it would be unwieldy to follow strict chronological lines. I have therefore divided the work into theaters or geographical areas and, inevitably, there will be some going backward and forward in time. Geographical names are always a problem, and I have tried to use those most familiar to the people at the time, rather than those a modern linguistic purist would employ. Most of the places named in the text are on the maps accompanying the volume. The reader is no doubt aware that many names have changed and the current place name will not necessarily coincide with the one in use in 1914–18. Russian ship names were a particular problem.

I have attempted to standardize them based on both *Conway's All the World's Fighting Ships* and Anthony J. Watt's *The Imperial Russian Navy*, which usually, but not always, coincide.

I should like to thank for their assistance: David Brown, Robert Coppock, and the staff of the Naval Historical Branch, Ministry of Defence, London; Roderick Suddaby, Keeper, Department of Documents, and the staff of the Imperial War Museum, London; Dr. R. A. Morris and the staff of the manuscripts division, National Maritime Museum, Greenwich; Nicholas Rodger and the staff of the Public Record Office, London; Contre-Amiral Chattel, Chef, and Pierre Waksman, Conservateur en chef, and the staff of the Service Historique de la Marine, Vincennes; G. J. A. Raven, Director of Naval History, Royal Netherlands Navy; and Dr. Evelyn Cherpak, Naval Historical Collection Division, and the staff of the Library, Naval War College, Newport, Rhode Island.

For their advice and assistance I would also like to thank: Professor Jon Sumida; Professor Holger Herwig; Professor Charles H. Fairbanks; Professor Robert M. Grant; Dr. David Trask; Dr. John N. Westwood; Dr. Norman Friedman; Mr. Erwin Sieche of the Arbeitsgemeinschaft für Österreichische Marinegeschichte, Vienna; Ing. Erich Heyssler and Mrs. Nicholas Baker; and Capitano di fregata (CP) Ezio Ferrante. Ms. Carolyn Reynolds and the Inter-Library Loan Office of Strozier Library, Florida State University, performed wonders in tracking down obscure titles, in addition to the extra work caused by the unknown individual who stole the library's entire set of *Der Krieg zur See* some years ago.

For permission to quote from copyright or unpublished material I should like to thank: the Trustees of the National Maritime Museum (Papers of Admirals Beatty and Limpus), Mr. Thomas Troubridge (Papers of Admiral E. C. T. Troubridge), Commander Richard A. Phillimore (Papers of Admiral Richard F. Phillimore), and Mrs. Margaret Munro (Papers of Commander G. M. Eady). I should also like to apologize to any holders of copyright I have been unable to trace.

Documents that are Crown Copyright appear by permission of the Controller, Her Majesty's Stationery Office.

The maps of the Mediterranean, the Aegean, the Adriatic, the Aegean coast of Asia Minor, Sabbioncello and the Dalmatian coast, the Mediterranean patrol zones, and the Otranto barrage appear by permission of Routledge. Mr. Peter Krafft, Director of Cartography, and his staff at the Florida Resources and Environmental Analysis Center prepared all other maps.

PAUL G. HALPERN
Tallahassee, Florida

A NAVAL HISTORY OF
WORLD WAR I

1

THE NAVAL BALANCE IN 1914

The First World War was preceded by a generation of navalism, for perhaps never before or since have naval affairs been of such interest to the citizens of the great powers. This attention was fueled by the popular press, which tended to present warships as the most advanced product of the science and technology of the machine age. The public also was fascinated with more peaceful applications of maritime technology, as evidenced by the cult of the ocean liner, in which interest in the Blue Riband of the Atlantic—the award for the fastest crossing—was strong. Ocean liners were considered potential auxiliary cruisers in wartime, and their silhouettes appeared in naval annuals. Both warships and ocean liners were symbols of national pride and subjects for national competition. In the first decade of the twentieth century, this competition was keenest between the British and the Germans.[1]

For roughly a century—the Pax Britannica—the British Empire appeared to be the largest and wealthiest in the world, and the Royal Navy was assumed to have enjoyed supremacy. Like all sweeping generalizations, this supposition must be qualified; for the closer one examines the subject, the more complicated things become. British predominance was challenged, and there were periodic naval scares in the nineteenth century, when British naval supremacy may have been more apparent than real. The French were frequently more innovative, introducing, for example, the ironclad *Gloire* in 1859 and submarines in the latter part of the nineteenth century. The development of the torpedo gave the French new opportunities, and the theories of the Jeune École concerning commerce warfare against British maritime trade posed a real challenge to the Royal Navy. There were times when the French were a more creditable threat than many have realized. In the 1890s, however, the French for a variety of reasons fell behind, and by the time of the Fashoda crisis in 1898, the French navy was no match for the British.[2]

By the beginning of the twentieth century, the traditional British rivalry with France and Russia had been replaced by a far more serious challenge—that of Imperial Germany. The belated unification of Germany and its rapid industrialization is one of the great success stories of the nineteenth century. Unfortunately, by the end of the century there had been a gradual cooling of relations and a growing trade rivalry between Great Britain and Germany.[3] The fact that the German economy was outstripping the British economy meant that the Germans had the potential to be a far more serious maritime rival. The Germans were in a position to dominate the Continent both militarily and economically, and their decision to challenge the British at sea created a new and revolutionary situation in international affairs. The Anglo-German naval race was one of the most important features of the prewar period, but it is important to remember that the powerful modern warships being built by other countries also did much to erode that perceived British supremacy.

The German naval challenge to Great Britain is usually linked to the ideas of one man, Admiral Alfred von Tirpitz. Tirpitz, a torpedo officer who had commanded the German squadron in the Far East, became state secretary of the Imperial Naval Office, or Reichsmarineamt (RMA), in June 1897. Under German naval organization, the state secretary of the RMA was responsible for administration and, of particular importance, for naval building programs. The Admiralstab, created in 1899 to replace the former chief of the high command of the navy (Oberkommando), was responsible for operational planning. The chief of the Imperial Naval Cabinet completed what might be termed the triad of the German naval hierarchy and was certainly of equal importance, for he was close to the kaiser and served as a vehicle of influence for admirals with a grievance. The arrangement seemed almost designed to encourage rivalries; each department might check the others, and Tirpitz operated in a highly politicized environment. He was always, and remains, an extremely controversial figure.[4]

Tirpitz outlined the program for his well-known theory of deterrence, *Risikogedanke* (doctrine of risk), in a memorandum of 15 June 1897 entitled "General Considerations on the Constitution of our Fleet according to Ship Classes and Designs." Germany must choose its ship designs with the greatest threat to its sea power in mind, Tirpitz asserted, for there was not enough money to meet every threat. Tirpitz considered England to be Germany's most dangerous enemy, against which "we most urgently require a certain measure of naval force as a political power factor." Because numerous British overseas bases made commerce raiding against the British "hopeless," the German fleet should be constructed to "unfold its greatest military potential between Helgoland and the Thames." A fleet of this type would be adequate to deal with France and Russia, who could be disregarded for the moment in the determination of ship classes. Tirpitz argued that the military situation against England demanded "battle-ships in as great a number as possible." Technical factors, such as the capacity of German dockyards, as well as personnel and training, would limit their objectives, at least for the moment. Thus the goal for 1905 would be two squadrons of eight battleships each, a fleet flagship, and two reserve battleships—a total of nineteen ships. Tirpitz cautioned that

Germany would have to concentrate its efforts at home and keep overseas commitments within "strict limits," for "only the main theatre of war would be decisive."[5]

Tirpitz's program is highly controversial; indeed, the reason for the entire naval program has been a matter of controversy in German historiography. There is a popular view that much of the program was developed primarily for reasons of internal policy, an attempt to win over the working class and benefit the shipbuilding industry by eliminating cycles and guaranteeing regular orders. It also was intended that the fleet play an important role in social integration. In 1895 Tirpitz explained that the expansion of the navy was necessary, because "the great patriotic task and the economics to be derived from it will offer a strong palliative against educated and uneducated Social Democrats."[6]

Tirpitz's naval law had distinct advantages from the bureaucratic point of view, for it lessened the interference of a potentially meddlesome parliament by not only fixing the number of ships but also providing for their automatic replacement after a certain number of years. In the 1898 naval law, battleships and cruisers would be replaced after twenty-five years of service. The elusive goal of Tirpitz was the so-called *Marineaeternat*, or "iron budget," with the number of ships to be laid down each year a matter of law.

Tirpitz, whatever his faults, was a skilled propagandist. His creation of a "news bureau" was a master stroke, designed to tap the potential support of the legislature and people. At a time when the Royal Navy prided itself on being the "silent service," Tirpitz and his associates, in liaison with the Flottenverein—the naval league generously supported by the steel interests—conducted a masterful campaign that struck a responsive cord among the German middle classes. The membership of the Flottenverein—240,000 at the end of November 1899—was far beyond the paltry few thousand of the Navy League in England, let alone similar organizations in France and Italy.[7]

Whatever the implications of the naval program for German internal politics, the creation of the powerful battle fleet was something the British could not ignore. Furthermore, they would have been most unwise to do so: despite bland assurances from Germany about the defensive nature of the fleet, it obviously was directed primarily against Great Britain. Tirpitz informed the kaiser in September 1899 that after the completion of the German fleet, the British "would have lost, for general political reasons and because she [England] will view the situation from the purely sober standpoint of a businessman, all inclination to attack us." Instead, Tirpitz stated, the British would "concede to Your Majesty, such a measure of maritime influence which will make it possible for Your Majesty to conduct a great overseas policy."[8] The German navy would be a deterrent, but there inevitably would be a "danger zone" through which the Germans would have to pass before their fleet was strong enough to constitute a true "risk fleet," and German diplomacy would have to take this into account. Remembering the history of the Napoleonic Wars, Tirpitz warned they would have to guard against the danger of being "Copenhagened"—a reference to the preemptive strikes by the British against the Danish fleet.

Germany's initial naval law was therefore deceptively mild, but the scope of the Tirpitz program was revealed in the Second German Naval Law of June 1900—passed, incidentally, while the British were preoccupied with the Boer War and a substantial portion of the world sympathized with the Boers. The law declared that the German navy would be increased to 38 battleships, 20 armored cruisers, and 38 light cruisers. There would be 2 fleet flagships, 4 squadrons of 8 battleships each, and 4 battleships in reserve. Tirpitz used supplementary naval bills in attempts to increase the total, and advancements in naval technology changed the authorized ship types to dreadnoughts and battle cruisers. Tirpitz's goal was a 2:3 ratio with the Royal Navy, for naval experts held that a weaker fleet had to be at least two-thirds the size of its stronger opponent before it had any chance of victory. He aimed at the *dreier tempo,* that is, laying down three capital ships a year. If pursued consistently over a twenty-year period, the German fleet would number over sixty dreadnought-type battleships and battle cruisers, and the British would have to increase their fleet to ninety capital ships to match it. Tirpitz did not believe they could do this. Aside from financial considerations, they could not find the manpower. The Germans could stand the naval race better than the British, who, because of their navy's larger size, could not increase their fleet at the same rate. The British also could not compete with the advantage conscription gave the Germans, for a portion of each year's conscripts automatically went to the navy. The British had to rely on volunteers. Additionally, the British had to meet their imperial commitments beyond the North Sea, although it was in the North Sea that they were most vulnerable.

Tirpitz at times went beyond questions of mere deterrence. He appears to have believed he could defeat the British. In September 1899 he informed the kaiser that thanks to Germany's geographical position, system of military service, mobilization, torpedo boats, tactical training, systematic organizational structure, and—added no doubt for the benefit of the kaiser—uniform leadership by the monarch, "we shall no doubt have a good chance against England." Tirpitz was realistic enough to realize, however, that they could not hope to keep the sea lanes to the Atlantic open without a victorious battle.[9]

From a technical point of view, Tirpitz's scheme might have been plausible. In a broader sense, though, it had momentous consequences, for more than any other factor it moved the British from their traditional policy of splendid isolation to a Continental commitment. The entire Tirpitz scheme had a fundamental flaw: it assumed the British would not do what they had to do to maintain the necessary margin for the security at sea that was so vital for them. The British met the challenge, and Tirpitz's "danger zone" became an ever-lengthening one. Tirpitz's dreier tempo proved impossible to maintain, and it was the German government itself that refused his request for a supplementary naval law in 1913. By then, however, immense diplomatic damage had been done. The British reached an agreement with the Japanese in the Far East in 1902, and in 1904 concluded an agreement with their historic rivals, the French. The Anglo-French Entente, or Entente Cordiale, was definitely not an alliance, but an "understanding," a sweeping away of old grievances in some cases dating back to the eighteenth century. It also was a *cordial* understanding, and the Entente Cordiale came to have more inherent strength and value than the formal and presumably binding alliances of Germany's Triple Alliance partners, Italy and Austria-Hungary.

In 1907 the British reached a similar entente with their traditional Russian rivals. The Anglo-Russian Entente was never as cordial or comprehensive as its Anglo-French equivalent, but the Germans could now truly complain of "encirclement." What is even more important, under the stimulus of Germany's threatening behavior in the Moroccan crisis of 1905, the British and French began the unofficial and nonbinding staff talks that ended by creating an intangible but very real bond between them. The Anglo-French staff conversations contributed to the feeling that the British had at least a moral obligation toward the French and could not leave them in the lurch if war came.[10]

Tirpitz's confident assumptions of victory were based on the situation as it appeared in 1899. The Royal Navy of 1914 was, however, a very different service. Long years of peace may have bred a certain complacency, but all of this changed with the German challenge. Much of this change can be associated with Tirpitz's equally controversial contemporary, Admiral of the Fleet Sir John Fisher, First Sea Lord from October 1904 to January 1910.[11] Fisher is credited with revitalizing the navy and turning it into an organization better suited to the needs of modern war. He gave full support to the revolution in gunnery, particularly the work of Captain Percy Scott, which culminated in the introduction of director (centralized) control for firing by the outbreak of the war.[12] Fisher scrapped large numbers of obsolete warships and began the process of concentrating the major portion of the fleet and the newest and best ships in home waters, as opposed to in the Mediterranean or other foreign stations. Fisher was not infallible; he could be ruthless and his methods questionable. The Royal Navy was not always a happy place during his tenure, but he made his mark.

Fisher is perhaps best known for the introduction in 1905 of HMS *Dreadnought*, the all-big-gun warship. He was roundly criticized for this, because the revolutionary warship rendered existing battleships obsolete and, in effect, canceled the Royal Navy's large advantage by wiping the slate clean and giving the Germans the opportunity to catch up. His decision to build the battle cruiser HMS *Invincible* and two sister ships, completed in 1908, was even more controversial. The battle cruiser represented a new type of large, fast, armored cruiser with a dreadnought's armament but scant protection.[13]

There is evidence that the battle cruiser rather than the *Dreadnought* was actually at the heart of Fisher's scheme. By the turn of the century, foreign building made it financially impossible to build warships in adequate numbers. Fisher therefore hoped to build ships that would be qualitatively superior to their foreign rivals and tried to combine battleships and first-class cruisers in a single type, the battle cruiser. He placed great emphasis on high speed, but it was possible to achieve this without exorbitant expense only by reducing the scale of armor protection. Fisher was confident the battle cruiser's speed would enable it to impose battle and hit at long range, which would prevent the enemy from taking advantage of its relative lack of protection. The battle cruiser never replaced the battleship, largely because by the time the *Dreadnought* entered service, the diplomatic situation had altered, thereby reducing the need for combining battleship and armored cruiser in a single type. France was friendly, and the Russian navy had been crippled in the Russo-Japanese War (1904–5). Germany now represented the most likely potential adversary. Unlike the French and Russian fleets, the German fleet had relatively few armored cruisers or overseas bases and was proportionately much stronger in battleships. The British thus continued to build battle cruisers, but concentrated on battleships.[14]

As for the argument that the radical new ship negated the British advantage at sea, Fisher was convinced that the superiority of the new design outweighed the disadvantages and was confident of Great Britain's ability to outbuild its German rival and maintain the lead. This confidence was justified: at the outbreak of war the British had maintained their advantage. There were twenty-one dreadnoughts and four battle cruisers in the Grand Fleet (plus another five at other locations), compared with thirteen dreadnoughts and five battle cruisers (including the hybrid *Blücher*) in the High Sea Fleet. It is important to remember that the new warships evolved out of the necessity of finding an economical means to face the old rivalry with France and Russia, not out of the new rivalry with Germany.[15]

The new types presupposed the ability of British gunnery to hit accurately at long ranges. Fisher was overconfident the British had solved the problem, underestimating the difficulties, particularly when the range between ships on converging courses was constantly changing. The Royal Navy might well have solved the problem had it adopted the system of fire control developed by Arthur Pollen. For a variety of reasons the British instead opted for an inferior system, and this may have cheated them of decisive results in the war's actions.[16]

Next to Fisher the best-known figure associated with the Royal Navy in the period immediately before the war is undoubtedly Winston Churchill, first lord of the Admiralty from October 1911 to May 1915. As civilian head of the navy, Churchill was regarded as a brash young man, fully as controversial as Fisher. He brought dynamism and eloquence to the navy's cause, was the central figure in important strategic changes reflected in the navy's redeployment of 1912, and was responsible for the decision to switch to oil fuel.[17]

The strategic redeployment of 1912 continued Fisher's policy of concentrating in home waters. By this time the Anglo-French Entente had been tested by the Moroccan crises of 1905 and 1911. The Mediterranean fleet, reduced from fourteen battleships in 1902 to eight in 1904 and six in 1906, was shifted from Malta to Gibraltar. It could, in theory, operate in either the Mediterranean or Atlantic, but the understanding was that it would be brought home in time of war. The battleship squadron stationed at Gibraltar would return to home waters. Initially Churchill intended to leave merely a cruiser force at Malta, which meant, in effect, the abandonment of the Mediterranean by British capital ships in time of war. The French in turn transferred the only battleship squadron they had left in the north from Brest to the Mediterranean. This seemed a startling demonstration of the Entente Cordiale at work, and the press was full of assured speculation that it had been the result of prior agreement, the British leaving the guarding of the Mediterranean to the French. In fact the decision had been reached independently by both navies, and both were responding to necessity brought on by technical factors. For the French the growth of the German navy meant that the remaining battleship squadron at Brest, composed of old predreadnoughts, would have had little chance of survival should the German fleet have arrived off the French coast and public opinion forced it to sortie. The French in reality had already made the decision to concentrate in the Mediterranean by sending their newer and best battleships there. The British were disturbed by the growth of the Italian and Austro-Hungarian navies, rivals themselves but also allies of Germany in the Triple Alliance. The decision of both Italy and Austria-Hungary to build modern and powerful dreadnoughts meant that the predreadnoughts the British had retained at Malta would be outclassed by potential adversaries. Furthermore, Churchill argued that the crews were needed to man newer vessels at home.

The decision to "abandon" the Mediterranean was opposed strongly by the Foreign Office and the War Office, and in the end Churchill had to compromise. The Admiralty agreed to leave sufficient force in the Mediterranean so that, joined with the French, it would assure superiority over the combined Austrian and Italian fleets. For this purpose the Admiralty chose battle cruisers, which in theory were strong enough to fight and fast enough to run away when necessary. The Admiralty intended to provide a squadron of dreadnoughts for the Mediterranean in the future, but only when it was consistent with an appropriate margin of safety in home waters.[18] In March of 1912 Churchill revealed in Parliament that Great Britain had quietly abandoned the old "two-power standard" and was building against one power and one power alone—Germany—and that the margin of superiority was 60 percent. There were periodic attempts to dampen or slow down the naval race; for example, Churchill's proposal for a "naval holiday," during which each country would forego laying down its planned number of capital ships for that fiscal year. The most striking attempt was the visit of Lord Haldane to Germany in February 1912 in an effort to get the Germans to table their planned *Novelle*, or supplementary naval law. The effort did not succeed, largely because the Germans wanted a political agreement assuring British neutrality in the event of a Continental war *before* any naval agreement, whereas for the British the naval agreement was paramount. Both sides were speaking past each other. There is no space for a detailed account of the diplomatic aspects of the prewar naval race here, but after 1912 both sides settled in for the long haul. The march of technology meant that by the outbreak of war, the navies were dealing with superdreadnoughts, with 15-inch instead of 12-inch guns and with similar improvements in speed and protection. The British were determined to, and did, maintain their lead.[19]

British superiority is demonstrated by the number of dreadnoughts and battle cruisers in service or under construction at the beginning of the war:

	British	German
Dreadnoughts in service[a]	22	15
Dreadnoughts under construction[b]	13	5
Battle cruisers in service[c]	9	5
Battle cruisers under construction	1	3

[a] Includes two Turkish ships requisitioned by the Admiralty.
[b] Includes one ship under construction for Chile requisitioned by the Admiralty and one German dreadnought never completed.
[c] Includes one in Australian service.

The British advantage is even more marked in terms of predreadnoughts, cruisers, destroyers, and submarines, although here numerical tables are debatable, for it is not always clear what to include in terms of age and types. Given these qualifications, however, the following is a rough estimate of ships in service at the beginning of the war:

	British	German
Predreadnoughts	40	22
Coast-defense ships	NA	8
Armored cruisers	34	7
Protected cruisers	52	17
Scout cruisers	15	NA
Light cruisers[a]	20	16
Destroyers	221	90
Torpedo boats	109	115
Submarines	73	31

[a]Includes three in Australian service.

Mere lists of numbers tend to be meaningless without innumerable qualifications as to age and type of ship, which might offset some of the apparent German inferiority. The worldwide commitments of Great Britain inevitably caused British warships to be scattered throughout the world to a far greater degree, and the Germans had to detach forces to match the Russians in the Baltic. The author of the standard work on British destroyers (who credits them with only 207) points out that however impressive the number might look on paper, over half were fit solely for coastal duties, whereas the speed of many of the latest classes was only slightly more than that of the battle cruisers they would have to screen.[20]

On the other hand, the British benefitted immensely from their superiority in older types of warships. Obsolescent ships, particularly cruisers that could not be employed in a major fleet action in the North Sea, performed invaluable work in the exercise of sea power in distant waters. The large British merchant marine, which included vessels of virtually every conceivable type, also provided a source for auxiliaries that after conversion performed tasks scarcely dreamed of before the war.

The British superiority in numbers also must be qualified by the generally better protection afforded German warships and by the excellence of German gunnery and optical systems. Nevertheless German warships tended to have a shorter range than their British counterparts. Newly commissioned warships on both sides were in the process of "working up" at the beginning of the war and nowhere near the peak of efficiency. Mere "bean counting" is therefore a more complicated business than at first sight.[21]

A realistic estimate of the best and most modern forces likely to be employed at the outbreak of war by the most important British and German forces, the Grand Fleet and the High Sea Fleet, respectively, would give the following results:

	Grand Fleet	High Sea Fleet
Dreadnoughts	21	13
Predreadnoughts	8	8
Battle cruisers	4	3
Armored cruisers	NA	1
Light cruisers	11	7
Destroyers	42	90

These are maximum theoretical figures, particularly for destroyers, and take no account of ships unavailable because of refits, accidents, or other detachments. For example, in a flotilla of twenty destroyers, usually 20 percent would be absent, having their boilers cleaned or undergoing minor repairs.[22] Ships are also by their nature mobile, and their numbers (particularly of armored cruisers) change at short notice as units are recalled from other stations or entered into service as they are brought out of the reserve.[23]

There is also the question of quality. How did the British and German navies compare with each other in terms of men and matériel? The subject has been closely examined. Speaking in broad generalities, British warships tended to have larger caliber guns and greater range than their German contemporaries. British destroyers had more guns but fewer torpedo tubes than German destroyers, and they usually enjoyed a larger radius of action. The big German warships were generally better protected both above and below water. They were harder to sink, with more extensive underwater compartmentation, and they were beamier because, for reasons of economy, the beam of British warships was limited by the size of docking facilities.

British gunnery was improved immensely by the introduction of director control for firing, but at the outbreak of war, only eight battleships incorporated this innovation. The Germans had excellent stereoscopic range finders, better than their British counterparts, and displayed a high standard of gunnery. The Royal Navy, as mentioned, missed the opportunity to employ on a wide scale the truly revolutionary system of range plotting developed by Arthur Pollen. British shells also suffered from a hidden defect revealed by the test of war: they were relatively ineffective and tended to break up on contact with enemy armor. British propellant was less stable than that used by the Germans, and their ammunition hoists were not protected from flash. The problem was aggravated by the practice in action of leaving the doors to magazines open in order to speed the rate of fire. All of this, when added to the unstable cordite, proved disastrous to the battle cruisers at Jutland. German torpedoes and, particularly, mines also were more effective. In fact the Royal Navy did not have a truly effective mine until it copied a German example later in the war.[24]

The British also suffered from a disadvantage in terms of naval bases, because traditional naval bases such as Plymouth and Portsmouth dated from the days of naval rivalry with France. Except for Chatham, too far to the south, the British did not have a first-class naval base on the east coast to face the new challenge from Germany. The development of new bases proceeded very slowly; shipbuilding had a much higher priority. The Admiralty had designated Rosyth on the Firth of Forth as a major base as early as 1903, but little work had been accomplished there by the outbreak of war. Cromarty, farther to the north, had been designated as a second-class base but had no protection against submarines, and the anchorage at Scapa Flow in the Orkneys was virtually unprotected. In contrast the German North Sea bases, notably Wilhelmshaven and Cuxhaven, had elaborate defenses supplemented by the heavily fortified offshore island of Helgoland. The Germans also had the use of the Kiel Canal, recently enlarged for dreadnoughts, to shift warships from the Baltic to the North Sea without the necessity of sailing around the Danish Peninsula.

What of personnel? Here the British enjoyed the advantage of a volunteer service composed of those who had enlisted for long periods of service. The German navy was to a large extent composed of three-year conscripts, which meant that at all times a sizable portion of the service was new to naval life. The Germans were thoroughly drilled and trained, but the fact remained that officers and men of the Royal Navy spent far more time at sea. The Royal Navy possessed that indefinable something, call it confidence, that came from its long tradition of naval supremacy and constant navigation in all seas and under all conditions. The Germans were the newcomers at sea, worried about proving themselves. Unfortunately not all the British in high positions had the imagination or brilliance to match that seamanship, and the war demonstrated that the quality of staff work left much to be desired. Tactical training tended to be unimaginative, training in antisubmarine warfare was largely nonexistent, and the Grand Fleet was bound by extensive and rigid battle orders that left little scope for the initiative of individual commanders. There were those who argued that the changed conditions of warfare necessitated this. The commander in chief of the Grand Fleet, Admiral Sir John Jellicoe, fifty-five years old at the outbreak of the war, was highly competent and possessed the full confidence of his officers and men. He was, however, a great centralizer, reluctant to delegate authority. The Germans had their problems too, not the least being the great social gulf between officers and men, and on the whole they were less successful in the question of man management than the British, as the final collapse in 1918 demonstrated only too clearly.[25]

It is always important to remember, however, that because the British and Germans were the leading contenders, their navies have received the greatest amount of scrutiny, and their faults have been mercilessly exposed. Still, when compared with other navies in the world, they set the standard. Whether it was sea keeping, gunnery, the amount of time spent in port compared with time at sea, or the experience of war, in a host of naval matters, the French, Austrians, Italians, Russians, and even the Americans, until they gained the necessary experience, were a cut below.

The Anglo-German naval race had by 1914 settled down to a long haul in which the British did what they had to do to maintain the necessary lead. Some of the edge seemed to have been taken off the competition by the spring of 1914 and, perhaps symbolic of this, a British naval squadron was actually invited to visit Kiel for the traditional regatta week in June, with each British vessel paired with a German "chummy" ship acting as host. The image of men soon to be at war with one another fraternizing has always had a certain fascination, and especially in this case, for it was in the midst of the regatta that the news of Archduke Franz Ferdinand's assassination arrived, setting off the train of events that led to war. Perhaps this indicates that the Anglo-German naval race was less dangerous by this time, if only because it was predictable. This was not true of the other and less well-known naval races then going on. These were far more volatile—particularly in the Mediterranean and, even more so, in the Aegean.

The French navy was the leading Mediterranean power. For a long time second only to the British, the French had been eclipsed by the German fleet by 1905, completing at sea what had been evident on land since the Franco-Prussian war. The French navy without British assistance stood virtually no chance against the Germans in the north and had tacitly recognized this by concentrating its newest and best forces in the Mediterranean. Here the French hoped to maintain their superiority over the Italian and Austrian fleets, allies in the Triple Alliance.

Command of the sea from the very beginning of the war was essential to the French, because of the necessity of repatriating troops from North Africa for what were assumed to be the decisive battles on the French frontier. The fact that Italy and Austria were rivals, perhaps more likely to be fighting against each other than together as allies, certainly was known to the French. But they could not assume Italy would not be against them. At least initially the French had to prepare for the "worst case," which for them became even worse in the first decade of the twentieth century. Both the Italians and Austrians sought to improve their fleets and began construction of dreadnought-type warships. The two were really building against each other, but as their fleets grew it became apparent that should they combine, they might actually have a chance of wresting control of the sea from the French. This new opportunity was the result of two major factors. The first was the relative decline of the French navy and the delay in its building programs, brought about to a large extent by the ideological shenanigans of the radical governments of the early twentieth century. The second factor was the decision by the Austro-Hungarian government to construct modern dreadnoughts, converting what had been essentially a coast-defense force into a blue water navy that could not be disregarded. Austro-Hungarian naval development was in many ways the truly revolutionary event in the Mediterranean.[26]

The French navy had emerged from the nineteenth century with what was contemptuously dubbed "a fleet of samples," the reflection of a confused naval policy resulting from the constant turmoil caused by politics or surrounding the debate over the theories of the Jeune École. The French had seemed on the road to recovery with the passage of the naval law of 1900, which would have provided for a fleet of 28 battleships, 24 armored cruisers, 52 destroyers, 263 torpedo boats, and 38 submarines.[27] The law appeared to establish a firm plan for the future, including the construction of homogeneous classes. Unfortunately the minister of marine from June 1902 to January 1905 in the government of the noted radical Emile Combes was Camille Pelletan, another radical who revived the controversies of the late nineteenth century in his attempt to democratize the navy. Pelletan retarded construction of the battleship program, for he was another believer in "cheaper" naval means, such as torpedo boats and submarines. Submarines may have been the weapon of the future, but they were no substitutes for a balanced fleet, and Pelletan played havoc with the naval program at the very moment the dreadnought-type warship was to come into service. French construction fell far behind in both quantity and quality of capital ships. The French built six semidreadnought *Danton*-class battleships while the other navies were building real dreadnoughts. The first French dreadnoughts were not laid down until 1910, which was not only well after the British and Germans but after the first dreadnoughts of their Mediterranean rivals as well.

The French navy returned to the proper course with a pair of able naval ministers, Vice Admiral Augustin Boué de Lapeyrère and Théophile Delcassé, and the naval law of 1912 provided for a French fleet by 1920 of 28 first-class battle ships, 10 scout cruisers, 52 destroyers, 10 ships for overseas stations, and 94 submarines. The French accelerated this program in 1913 with newer and larger dreadnought classes, but none were ever completed. When war broke out, the French had only two dreadnoughts in service and two still completing their trials. Eight more had been laid down, of which only three were completed. The French had a relatively large number of armored cruisers, but these were big, vulnerable targets, expensive to man, too slow for real cruiser work, and too weak to stand up to real battleships. The program's scout cruisers also had not been laid down yet—they were scheduled for 1917—and the French suffered severely from lack of this type, which proved invaluable to the British and Germans in the North Sea. Lapeyrère, who followed his term as minister by commanding the 1ère Armée Navale—the major French fleet in the Mediterranean—from 1911 to 1915, also complained of the quality of the destroyers. And many of the submarines were outmoded, their achievements during the war a disappointment despite the gallantry of their crews. To compound their difficulties, the French had the problem of unstable powder, which caused the loss of two battleships before it was solved. The Austrians and Italians had a real chance to catch up, at least on paper. On the other hand, the French retained an advantage in older classes of warships.

On the eve of the war the French navy numbered:

Dreadnoughts	2 (plus 2 on trials)
Semidreadnoughts (*Danton*-class)	6
Predreadnoughts	14
Coast-defense ships	1
Armored cruisers	19
Protected cruisers	9
Destroyers	81
Large torpedo boats	17
Small torpedo boats	170
Submarines	67–75

Many of the older ships or smaller torpedo boats or submarines were of little value, suitable only for local defense. In realistic terms, in a fleet action the major French force in the Mediterranean—the 1ère Armée Navale—would probably include:

Dreadnoughts	2–4
Semidreadnoughts (*Danton*-class)	6
Predreadnoughts	9
Armored cruisers	7
Protected cruisers	1–8
Destroyers	24

Once again it is difficult to predict how many of the older battleships and protected cruisers would actually have been included.[28]

The Italian navy—the Regia Marina—had a tradition in the late nineteenth century for technical innovation, introducing battleships such as the *Dandolo* or *Italia*, which placed it at least temporarily in the vanguard of naval design. Unfortunately the resources devoted to maintenance of the fleet were not always adequate, and Italian ambitions did not always match the means of the Italian kingdom. Nevertheless the Italians laid down their first dreadnought in June 1909, a year before their French or Austrian rivals. The ship, the *Dante Alighieri*, was designed with the then-novel triple-gunned turrets. The execution of the Italian building program proved to be much slower than anticipated, partially due to the inadequacies of the Italian steel industry. Nonetheless the Italians did build extremely powerful warships, and by the outbreak of the European war they had three dreadnoughts in service and another three in varying stages of completion. They were planning another class—never to be completed—of four superdreadnoughts. Vice Admiral Paolo Thaon di Revel, capo di stato maggiore (chief of naval staff) in 1913, wanted a fleet at least 60 percent that of the French and with a 4:3 margin of superiority over the Austrians. In July 1914 the Italians had:

Dreadnoughts	3
Predreadnoughts	6–8
Armored cruisers	7
Protected cruisers	11
Light cruisers	3
Destroyers	33
Torpedo boats	71–85
Submarines	20–22

Italian predreadnoughts tended to be more lightly protected and/or armed than their rivals, although faster, and it is questionable whether some should even have been counted as battleships at all. There also were questions on the state of Italian training, and during the war British officers discovered that Italian practices in gunnery and fire control left much to be desired, even on the most imposing of the new dreadnoughts.[29]

The navy of Austria-Hungary, the k.u.k. Kriegsmarine, was probably one of the most interesting of the world's navies at the time. At the close of the twentieth century, it is difficult to realize that Austria was once a naval power, but in 1914 the Dual Monarchy controlled much of the eastern shore of the Adriatic, with major ports at Trieste and Fiume and naval bases at Pola and in the Gulf of Cattaro. The k.u.k. Kriegsmarine had a tradition of victory, notably in the Battle of Lissa in 1866, which the Italian navy dreamed of avenging. The navy reflected the multinational composition of the Habsburg monarchy. The majority of officers were German or Hungarian; German was the service language, but ships' companies were mixed, unlike the army, in which entire regiments were of the same nationality.

The k.u.k. Kriegsmarine essentially had been a small coast-defense force. The decision after the turn of the century to build large modern warships had a significant effect on the Mediterranean balance of power. The expansion of the fleet began when Vice Admiral Rudolph Graf Montecuccoli was Marinekommandant (1904–13). The old emperor, Franz Joseph I, had never been terribly interested in the navy, but his nephew and heir to the throne, the ill-fated Archduke Franz Ferdinand, was an enthusiastic supporter. The Austrians made a clear break with tradition when they started to build three ships of the semidreadnought *Radetzky*-class in 1907. In 1910 they laid down the first two of a class of four true dreadnoughts. By the time the first, the *Viribus Unitis*, was completed in October 1912, the k.u.k. Kriegsmarine had to be taken seriously. The ship, with triple-gunned turrets, was more powerful than any of the predreadnoughts the British had at Malta. Moreover, Austria-Hungary was far more likely than Italy to be an ally of Germany in the event of war. In 1914 the Austrians were planning to lay down a second class of four dreadnoughts, the *Ersatz Monarchs*. There was a common assumption in England and France that the Austrians were merely acting as surrogates for the Germans. This was wrong; the Austrians had their own interests, and their major rivals were their ostensible allies the Italians.[30] On the outbreak of war Austrian strength was:

Dreadnoughts	3
Semidreadnoughts (*Radetzky*-class)	3
Predreadnoughts	6
Coast-defense ships	3
Armored cruisers	2
Protected cruisers	3
Light cruisers	2
Destroyers	18
Torpedo boats	21–30
Torpedo boats (coastal)	40
Submarines	5

The Austrian navy by itself was obviously little threat to the French, but as the Austrians and Italians built against each other, the sum of their fleets opened new prospects. The initiative for a Triple Alliance naval understanding came from the Italians. The Italo-Turkish War (1911–12) had, at least temporarily, brought Italy closer to the Triple Alliance, especially when the Italian navy was involved in various maritime incidents with the French. Without getting into the diplomatic details of Italy's ambiguous position, suffice it to say that the Italian navy realized how terribly vulnerable an unsupported Italy would be to Anglo-French sea power. The Italian naval authorities were ignorant of the exact nature of Italy's diplomatic obligations toward its Triple Alliance allies—they never saw the text of the treaty—and did not realize how strictly defensive it was in scope. They therefore had to plan for their own worst case, and as Austrian naval strength grew, the logic behind the move toward an agreement with Austria-Hungary seemed overwhelming. The Italians began their overtures in 1913, with the Germans acting as enthusiastic midwives. In late 1912 the Germans had established a permanent naval presence in the Mediterranean as a result of the Balkan Wars (1912–13). The Mittelmeerdivision, consisting of the new battle cruiser *Goeben* and the fast light cruiser *Breslau*, would have been a powerful addition to any Triple Alliance naval force. There was nothing in the French navy that was powerful enough to both catch and fight the *Goeben*.

These considerations prompted the Triple Alliance Naval Convention of October 1913. To obtain Austrian participation, the Italians even agreed to an Austrian commander in chief, Admiral Anton Haus, for the Austro-Italian force, which planned to assemble with German forces then in the Mediterranean at Augusta, on the east coast of Sicily, after the outbreak of war. The Italians collected coal stocks here, and the three allies prepared the *Triple Codex*, a code book for use by their combined fleets. At one point Haus and Thaon di Revel even met secretly and incognito in Zurich to discuss their plans.[31]

In July 1914 the potential Austro-Italian force was six dreadnoughts and three semidreadnoughts against only two dreadnoughts and six semidreadnoughts for the French. It is easy to see why the British were so anxious to maintain a few battle cruisers in the Mediterranean to provide the margin of superiority for an Anglo-French force. Naturally there were many variables involved, and it is doubtful how effectively the Austrian and Italian naval forces would have worked together. The Triple Alliance Naval Convention never lost its air of unreality, but it did exist and had to be guarded against. The Italian decision to remain neutral when the war began ended any prospect of a major surface action in the Mediterranean and insured that the British and French would have an overwhelming superiority in surface warships.

If the prewar naval balance in the Mediterranean was delicate, the situation in the Aegean was even more volatile. The Greeks and Turks, traditional enemies, had just engaged in the Balkan Wars, in which the Turks had lost most of their remaining territories in Europe. The Turkish navy had, however, a powerful dreadnought under construction in Great Britain. In late 1913 they acquired another extremely powerful ship when the Brazilians for financial reasons put the *Rio de Janeiro*, also under construction in England, up for sale. The South American navies were a source of instability for the European powers. The Brazilians had two dreadnoughts in service, the Chileans and the Argentines each had two on order. The prospect that nearly completed capital ships such as these could change hands on short notice was alarming. Churchill complained of the Latin American naval activities, "It is sport for them, it is death for us." The implication that only the great powers should have dreadnoughts is debatable, but in the summer of 1914, the fact that the Turks might have two extremely powerful dreadnoughts was disturbing.

Relations between Greece and Turkey were very tense in the early part of 1914, and it is generally forgotten that many observers expected the war to break out there rather than where it actually did. There was talk of a preemptive strike by the Greeks, who searched frantically for major warships to match the Turks. The Greeks were forced to order a dreadnought in France as a condition of a loan from the French, but the ship would not be ready for some time. The same was true of a battle cruiser ordered in Germany. The Greeks finally obtained two predreadnoughts that the U.S. Navy found ill-suited to its requirements. President Wilson was persuaded to sell them to the Greeks to preserve the balance of power. The older ships were no match for the Turkish dreadnoughts, but, presumably, the psychological implications of the sale played a role. The Turkish ships were taken over by the Admiralty on the outbreak of war, probably a wise move, because the Turks had offered to send the ships to Germany after the conclusion of a Turkish-German alliance in August 1914.[32] Greece and Turkey at this time were fertile fields for the salesmen of other naval armaments, and both sides had received or ordered smaller warships from different European yards. Prior to the fictitious sale of the *Goeben* and *Breslau* to the Turks, the naval balance between Greece and Turkey was:

	Greece	Turkey
Predreadnoughts	2	2
Coast-defense ships	3	1
Armored cruisers	1	NA
Protected cruisers	1	2
Destroyers	14	8
Torpedo boats	17	9
Submarines	2	NA

Ironically, once the submarine war became serious, it was the fate of the Greek light craft that would most preoccupy the British and French.

The Russians were a land power of great importance in the European balance of power. Their strength at sea was nowhere near their strength on land, but their potential was significant. Unfortunately their problems were serious. The Russian navy was still in the process of recovery from the disastrous Russo-Japanese War. Geography compelled the Russians to divide their navy into at least three parts, with separate forces for the Baltic, the Black Sea, and the Far East. They had little hope of seriously contending with the Japanese in the Pacific or matching the German fleet ship for ship in the Baltic, but they could realistically hope to dominate the Black Sea once their dreadnoughts entered service. The big question was how much of the German fleet might they divert to the Baltic from its position facing the British in the North Sea. The question obviously had significant strategic importance, but in dealing with the Russians in the prewar period, the emphasis must always be on the word *potential*.

The Russians were certainly ambitious. In April 1911 Vice Admiral Ivan K. Grigorovitch, an unusually capable and energetic officer, became minister of marine and obtained funds for laying down four dreadnoughts for the Baltic and three dreadnoughts for the Black Sea. This was the first part of a long-range program that would have created by 1920 a Baltic fleet of 8 dreadnoughts and battle cruisers, 20 cruisers, 36 destroyers, and 12 submarines; and a Black Sea fleet one and one-half times the combined forces of Turkey, Bulgaria, and Romania. This demanding program met bitter resistance in the Duma and elsewhere, with charges that money spent on the larger fleet would have been wasted. The Left preferred that the money be spent on social reform; the Octobrists wanted a fleet of small units, suitable for coastal defense. Nevertheless in June 1912, the Duma approved what was known as the Small Shipbuilding Program, which provided funds for the construction from 1912 to 1917 of 4 battle cruisers, 8 light cruisers, 36 destroyers, and 18 submarines. With the exception of two light cruisers and six submarines for the Black Sea and two light cruisers for the Far East, the ships were destined for the Baltic. In April 1914, with the prospect of the Turks acquiring dreadnoughts, Grigorovitch obtained the authorization of the Duma to build an additional dreadnought, two cruisers, and eight destroyers for the Black Sea.

There was a big difference in Russia between paper projects and actual accomplishments. Despite (or perhaps because of) foreign participation, the program proceeded much more slowly than anticipated; there were charges of bureaucratic corruption and bungling at the yards, and by the war's beginning, none of the dreadnoughts had been completed. The battle cruisers would never be. The potential was there; among the smaller ships, the large, fast destroyers the Russians were building would have been among the best in the world.

The Russian navy faced more than material problems: there was a big question mark over the personnel of the fleet that had experienced the famous *Potemkin* mutiny in the Black Sea in 1905. In 1912 there had been unrest in the Baltic fleet, reportedly over poor food and treatment, and a serious plot also was uncovered at Sebastopol, which led to the trials of 142 men and seventeen executions. Foreign observers were frequently critical of the attitude of the Russian naval officer corps, although the corps must have faced special difficulties turning generally illiterate inland conscripts into seamen, particularly with the long northern winters hampering training. As the Russians had a tradition of overcoming immense difficulties and the country was in the process of industrialization, it is interesting to speculate what, given time, the Russian potential at sea might have been.[33]

At the outbreak of the war, the Russians had the following in service:

	Baltic	Black Sea
Predreadnoughts	5	5
Coast-defense ships	NA	1
Armored cruisers	6	NA
Protected cruisers	4	2
Destroyers	21	4
Torpedo boats	48	24
Gunboats	7	5
Submarines	15	7

The Russians also had the Siberian Flotilla in the Far East, which included 2 cruisers, 17 destroyers, 3 torpedo boats, 1 gunboat, and 4 submarines; but these ships were all old.

Of the European maritime powers remaining neutral in the war—Spain, the Netherlands, Sweden, Norway, and Denmark—only the Spanish had dreadnought-type warships. They had one small dreadnought in service and another two under construction, but the remainder of their fleet—an ancient battleship, two armored cruisers, and a handful of protected cruisers and destroyers—did not count for much.

The other navies were essentially coast-defense forces, with the exception of the Netherlands, which had its colonies in the East Indies to defend. The Dutch debated building five battleships for the Far East, plus four for home waters, but had reached no decision by the war's outset. The neutrals were not linked to any of the rival alliance systems and thus were unlikely to enter the war on their own. The most appropriate question, perhaps, was whether they had the strength, or will, to enforce their neutrality. On the whole their neutrality would be of more value for the belligerents than their participation in a war. The naval forces of Portugal, which did join the war on the side of the Entente, were negligible.[34]

From a naval point of view, the United States and Japan were the two most important non-European powers. Argentina, Brazil, and Chile, the South American states with the most significant navies, competed against each other, but of the three, only Brazil would finally enter the war in 1917 and send two scout cruisers and four destroyers to European waters. They arrived only at the very end of the war. The Japanese, in contrast, could not be ignored. They had proven their ability in the Russo-Japanese War, had been allies of the British since 1902, and in naval matters were predominant in the Far East. They did, in fact, enter the war very quickly, but the majority of their naval forces were employed against German possessions in the Far East. They eventually sent twelve badly needed destroyers to the Mediterranean at the height of the submarine crisis in 1917, and the performance of this force won a good deal of praise. The Japanese fleet also contained a number of prizes taken from the Russians, by the war's outbreak generally obsolete. In August 1914 Japanese naval forces included:

Dreadnoughts	2
Battle cruisers	1
Predreadnoughts	10
Coast-defense ships	4
Armored cruisers	12
Protected cruisers	15
Light cruisers	6
Destroyers	50
Submarines	12

A second large battle cruiser was completed in early August, and an additional two dreadnoughts and two battle cruisers were under construction. The Japanese called four of their armored cruisers "battle cruisers," but, although armed with 12-inch guns, by North Sea standards they were not considered true battle cruisers. Moreover, very few of the Japanese destroyers at this time could be considered modern, and the Japanese commenced a sizable destroyer-building program after the outbreak of war.[35]

The United States was not linked to any of the belligerents at the outbreak of the world war, but given its wealth, both real and potential, it was obviously the great prize among neutrals. The modern U.S. Navy was a relatively recent creation, after years of neglect following the American Civil War. The brief war against Spain in 1898 did not really provide much experience, particularly against a powerful or technologically advanced enemy. The famous cruise of sixteen American battleships around the world in 1907–1909—the "Great White Fleet"—was supposed to symbolize the renaissance of the navy but may also have demonstrated its relative backwardness. The Americans would learn; they certainly had the resources and determination. Nevertheless the fitting word for the United States Navy in the summer of 1914 was *potential*. A large building program was not approved until 1916. In this respect there were similarities between the American and Russian navies, but the potential of the Americans was far greater, and they enjoyed immense political and social advantages that the Russians lacked.[36]

The United States Navy in the summer of 1914 included:

Dreadnoughts	10
Predreadnoughts	23
Armored cruisers	12
Protected cruisers	22
Destroyers	50
Torpedo boats (old)	23
Submarines	18

The Americans had another four powerful dreadnoughts under construction and eighteen large destroyers authorized or under construction. However, sixteen of the destroyers in service were very old and fragile, and only three of the cruisers could be considered modern. There were an additional nine very old submarines, suitable only for local defense, in the Philippines.[37]

This chapter can only paint the world naval balance in 1914 in fairly broad brushstrokes, concentrating on battleships and dreadnoughts, which, because most expected a decisive naval encounter similar to Trafalgar, were the accepted standard of the time. Any discussion of other types of vessels, such as minelayers or seaplane carriers, must also be foregone. The interested reader should refer to the various naval annuals, either originals or reprints, or modern works such as *Conway's All the World's Fighting Ships, 1906–1921* for further information. The British and Germans were the major contenders, and most expected the North Sea to be the decisive area. The other navies had important roles to play, however, and considerable naval activity took place beyond the North Sea. As the war progressed, other types of warships became as important, if not more important, than capital ships. This was especially true of submarines and their antidotes—destroyers and sloops. The relative proportions of different types of ships in the fleets of 1918 were very different from what they had been in 1914.

2

Northern Waters: The First Six Months

W hen the war broke out, the generation that had experienced the Anglo-German naval race, read widely popular spy stories such as Erskine Childer's *The Riddle of the Sands,* and remembered the sudden Japanese attack on the Russian base at Port Arthur a decade earlier fully expected a major battle within a short period of time, coupled, perhaps, with a German raid or even an invasion. A young British officer in the light cruiser *Southampton* reported that 60 percent of the officers in his wardroom were certain they would be in battle within forty-eight hours.[1] This did not occur; there was not a major battle in the North Sea for nearly two years, and encounters that took place in this major theater of the naval war were often more in the nature of glancing blows. The reasons for this may be found in the prewar strategy of both the British and the Germans.

The development of mines, submarines, torpedoes, and long-range coastal artillery made the traditional close blockade of the enemy coast impractical, if not suicidal, and in his war orders to the Channel Fleet in 1908, Admiral of the Fleet Sir John Fisher stipulated that each night the blockading fleet would retire at least 170 miles from the nearest German destroyer base. Smaller craft about 30 miles off the coast would provide warning of German fleet movements. In 1911 the redoubtable Admiral Sir Arthur K. Wilson, then First Sea Lord, returned to a close blockade of the Helgoland Bight, using two destroyer flotillas supported by three cruiser squadrons. Unfortunately Wilson's plan was too dangerous, and as far as the destroyers were concerned, relatively impracticable. The destroyers had to return to port every three or four days, and because the nearest British port was 280 miles away, they needed three reliefs, with one on patrol, one in transit, and one in port. All of this required twice the number the Royal Navy possessed, and the blockading force was still vulnerable to a sudden overwhelming attack. By mid-1912 the close blockade was gone for good, replaced by an "observational blockade" of the Bight. A line of cruisers and destroyers was established from the southwest coast of Norway to a point halfway between England and Germany on the latitude of Newcastle-on-Tyne and then southward to the island of Texel and the Dutch coast. The British battle fleet would keep well to the west of this line; German trade would be cut off, and should the German battle fleet move against either the cruisers or the British coast, it would be brought to battle.

British naval maneuvers soon demonstrated that the observational blockade also was impractical. The line was close to 300 miles long and could be neither watched effectively by day and night nor adequately supported against concentrated German attacks. Any serious attempt to do so would have drained far too many destroyers and cruisers from the battle fleet. In the war orders issued at the beginning of July 1914, the observational blockade was abandoned in favor of a distant blockade to block the exits from the North Sea. The most powerful force—the Grand Fleet—was now off the Scottish coast, stationed at Scapa Flow in the Orkneys, whereas the Channel Fleet blocked the Channel off Dover in the south. There was a line of cruisers from the Shetlands to Norway, but the Grand Fleet itself exercised its domination of the sea by frequent sweeps in the area between the fifty-fourth and fifty-eighth parallels. The object was to convince the Germans they could not hazard their fleet far from its bases without the serious risk of running into overwhelming force.[2]

During the Agadir crisis in August 1911, the Royal Navy lost the debate over how to use the British army in the event of war. A. K. Wilson viewed the army traditionally, as a "projectile to be fired by the British Navy," and wanted military forces to create a diversion by capturing one or more islands off the German coast. Regular troops would also have to be held at home to guard against an invasion. The War Office, eloquently represented by General Sir Henry Wilson, the director of military operations, favored the concept of a Continental commitment, with the British Expeditionary Force rushed to France to fight alongside the French army. This was the policy adopted. Great Britain would pursue what was essentially a Continental rather than traditional maritime strategy. As for the threat of invasion, a subcommittee of the Committee of Imperial Defence concluded in April 1914 that the maximum invading force likely to avoid interception by the navy would total seventy thousand, and if an expeditionary force were sent overseas, at least two regular divisions should be left at home.[3]

These changes in British strategic thought explain why the Grand Fleet did not appear off the German coast seeking battle and establishing a close blockade shortly after war was declared. The prospect of a distant blockade posed new problems for the Germans, because their plans traditionally had rested on the prospect of a close blockade, which would afford opportunities for their light craft. By 1914 the Admiralstab's observations and analysis of what they could learn of British naval maneuvers had led them to conclude that the traditional form of permanent close blockade was now extremely dangerous for the blockading force. The war game played by the German North Sea station early in 1913 had demonstrated the difficulties the British would have had in maintaining a close blockade of the Bight. The Admiralstab therefore expected the

British would alternate between close and distant blockades according to the situation. The close blockade was most likely at the beginning of the war, when the British might expect an offensive German sortie, or when transport of the British Expeditionary Force was in progress.[4]

In the German war game of March 1914, the leader of the "Yellow" (Anglo-French) side had established a distant blockade of the German coast, closing with only light forces, and determined that a close British blockade would be very improbable and that the bulk of the British fleet would be placed far to the north at Scapa Flow. Admiral Hugo von Pohl, chief of the Admiralstab, concluded that the existing balance of strength between the German and British fleets would not permit the Germans to make an offensive thrust that far to the north, and that the distant blockade could best be countered by sending out submarines and minelayers while the German fleet acted energetically against British forces guarding the Bight. This would force the British to reinforce them, and facilitate the erosion of British strength to the point where the High Sea Fleet might meet them on equal terms. A historian who has closely studied German naval plans points out that this recommendation overlooked the fact, demonstrated by the maneuvers, that the British might not leave any forces to guard the Bight. The Admiralstab consequently failed to meet the challenge posed by the distant blockade. Furthermore, the kaiser, although agreeing to the war game's conclusions, assigned great value to the cooperation of submarines with the battle fleet and expressed the wish that in all defensive plans the offensive idea not be dropped. Therefore one might argue the Germans approached the war without any definite plans for operations against the British.[5]

According to the war orders approved at the end of July 1914, the German navy would seek to wear down the blockading forces with mines, destroyers, and submarines. The mine and U-boat offensive might even extend to the British coast, but the bulk of the fleet would only give battle under favorable circumstances, that is, after the power relationship had been balanced. These final orders, however, seemed directed primarily against the prospect of a close blockade; they failed to deal with the problem of a distant blockade in which the British would not obligingly present targets to be "worn down" in the Helgoland Bight.[6] Tirpitz himself had raised the question in May 1914 when he asked the commander of the High Sea Fleet, "What will you do if they do not come?" Reportedly neither Tirpitz nor Admiral Friedrich von Ingenohl, commander of the High Sea Fleet, had a satisfactory answer.[7]

The commander in chief of the Grand Fleet, the major British naval force, was not a likely man to put his head into the noose and make things easy for the Germans. Admiral Sir John Jellicoe, fifty-five years old, had only been named to his command on 4 August, replacing Admiral Sir George Callaghan, whom Churchill considered too old and whose health might not stand the strain of war. Callaghan had trained the fleet for war and was heartbroken, but the potentially awkward situation was handled with tact by all concerned. Despite some apprehension over "changing horses in midstream," the appointment was generally considered to be a wise one.

In his memoirs Jellicoe explained his ideas on the uses and purposes of the Royal

Navy, which centered on four major points: (1) it was absolutely vital for the navy to ensure the unimpeded use of the seas for British ships, because Britain as an island nation was not self-sufficient; (2) in the event of war the navy should bring steady economic pressure on the enemy by denying him the use of the sea; (3) the navy should cover the passage and assist any army sent overseas and protect its communications and supplies; and (4) the navy should prevent the invasion of Great Britain and its overseas dominions by enemy forces. Jellicoe argued that the quickest and surest means of achieving these objectives was to destroy the enemy's naval forces. This must be the first objective, for, as he stated quite simply, "The Fleet exists to achieve victory."[8]

But how could this be achieved if the German fleet, weaker in numbers, stayed in port? Jellicoe readily dismissed the prospect of a close blockade as impossible under modern conditions. The British would therefore block Germany's access to the high seas with their two major forces, the Channel Fleet in the south and the Grand Fleet in the north. The Grand Fleet from its strategic position in the North Sea would support the cruiser squadrons carrying out sweeps to the south in search of enemy vessels, and would be favorably placed to bring the German High Sea Fleet to action if it put to sea.[9]

The initial British deployment reflected this strategy. The Grand Fleet with its twenty dreadnoughts and four battle cruisers was stationed at Scapa Flow. To the north there were (once reservists had been mobilized for the elderly ships) the northern patrols carried out by the Sixth Cruiser Squadron (four *Drake*-class armored cruisers) and the Tenth Cruiser Squadron (eight old *Edgar*-class cruisers). In the south the major heavy force was Vice Admiral Sir Cecil Burney's Channel Fleet, with eighteen predreadnoughts and four light cruisers. There were also sizable forces at Harwich, notably Commodore Reginald Tyrwhitt's two light cruisers and thirty-five destroyers, later known as the Harwich Force, and the Eighth (Overseas) Submarine Flotilla (sixteen *D*- and *E*-class submarines) under Commodore (S) Roger Keyes. Keyes also commanded the Sixth Submarine Flotilla (six older *C*-class boats) at the Humber. These light forces were supported by "Force C," five old *Bacchante*-class armored cruisers. The commanders in chief of the home ports controlled additional forces: at the Nore (the Thames estuary and adjacent coast), 12 old destroyers, 20 torpedo boats, and 6 *C*-class submarines for coastal defense; at Portsmouth, 6 destroyers and 23 torpedo boats; and at Devonport, 4 destroyers and 8 torpedo boats. There were also substantial light forces (generally old) distributed along the east coast that were not directly attached to the fleets or under the control of the commanders in chief of the home ports. Their principal base was at Dover, and they were under an officer known as the admiral of patrols—Rear Admiral George Ballard. Ballard also had four old *Majestic*-class predreadnoughts for the defense of the Humber, but the primary concern of his approximately four light cruisers, twenty old destroyers, and fourteen small submarines was the protection of the shipping lanes between England and France.

The Royal Navy also had a number of cruisers on commerce patrols in the south: "Cruiser Force G," with four old *Talbot*-class cruisers patrolling the Channel, and "Cruiser Force E" (Eleventh Cruiser Squadron), with five old cruisers patrolling the southern entrances to the Irish Sea.[10]

The majority of the cruisers at sea in the Channel and in western areas were actually French. The role of the French navy in northern waters is often overlooked, but the numbers involved were not negligible: approximately 14 cruisers, 31 destroyers and torpedo boats, and 23 submarines. The principal French force was the 2eme escadre légère, consisting of six armored cruisers commanded by Contre-amiral Rouyer. These ships were, however, old and weakly armed, no match for the High Sea Fleet or even a powerful raider. The French, as previously explained, had made the strategic decision to concentrate their newest and strongest forces in the Mediterranean, but because no alliance existed between France and Great Britain, they had to make some provision for the north. They still did not expect the German fleet to institute a close blockade of the French coast in the event they had to fight Germany without British assistance. The same considerations about mines, torpedoes, and submarines would, after all, work against a close German blockade. The French did, however, reckon with the possibility of bombardments by heavy ships of French ports such as Cherbourg to disrupt the French mobilization and act on public opinion. They expected that any movement by the big German ships would be preceded by a mass of light cruisers, destroyers, and minelayers to neutralize the French flotillas. The French defenses in the Straits of Dover consisted of submarines, with destroyers scouting ahead of the submarines and cruisers positioned behind them for support.

French and British staff conversations before the war resulted in 1913 in an agreement between them as to the respective roles their navies would play in a war, but only *if* they were allies. Roughly, the French (joined by four British cruisers) would take the responsibility for defending the western part of the English Channel between the Cotentin Peninsula and the English Coast, whereas the British would take the responsibility for defending the Dover Strait with the flotillas based on Dover. French torpedo boats and submarines would participate, mostly in the area between the Varne and Cape Gris-Nez and inside the banks along the French coast.

The French Navy did not yet know that the British would join the war when Rouyer received a series of cables on 2 August ordering him to sail the following morning. He was informed that two German battle squadrons had passed the Kiel Canal going from east to west, and he was ordered to block the passage of the German fleet. The French navy had few illusions about the real balance of strength between itself and the High Sea Fleet, and French naval literature has always stressed the grim aspect of these obsolete ships sailing to what most of the officers and men considered certain death. The French minister of marine had been assured already by Churchill that the Germans, regardless of British neutrality, would not be permitted to operate in the Channel, but the minister rather callously failed to inform Rouyer of this fact; consequently, there was no cause for the very real anxiety.[11]

The British were also in the process of mobilizing or requisitioning sizable numbers of merchant ships, trawlers, and drifters for auxiliary forces. By the end of August, they had commissioned twenty-one armed merchant cruisers to assist in blockade duties, and the number of trawlers involved totaled more than 200. By the beginning of 1915, the Admiralty had a grand total of 827 minor vessels of all sorts in the auxiliary patrol, and by the end of the war the number had risen to more than 3,700. The French eventually followed the British example as the submarine threat developed, and in February 1915 they began requisitioning and fitting out sixty trawlers to patrol the Channel south of the line Colbart-Cherbourg.[12] As the war went on without a major battle and the submarine and mine dangers increased, the importance of these auxiliary craft grew.

The initial German deployment is easier to describe. The main German naval force, the High Sea Fleet under the command of Admiral Ingenohl in the *Friedrich der Grosse*, was concentrated in the North Sea. The First Squadron (the older dreadnoughts—four *Helgoland* and four *Nassau* class) and the Third Squadron, in the process of being formed with the latest dreadnoughts (four *König* class, with two to join) were anchored at the mouth of the Jade River, accompanied by the four battle cruisers of Rear Admiral Franz Hipper, senior officer of the scouting groups. The Second Squadron, composed of the most modern predreadnoughts (eight *Deutschland* class), was anchored at the mouth of the Elbe between Cuxhaven and Brunsbüttel, where the Germans considered that these ships, lacking torpedo nets, could be better protected by the floating boom off Cuxhaven. A cruiser and a torpedo-boat flotilla protected the mouth of the Ems, while other light forces were deployed to protect the estuaries of the Jade, the Elbe, and the Weser. Two U-boat flotillas—nineteen submarines—were attached to the High Sea Fleet. There were other German squadrons being mobilized, but they were made up of old predreadnoughts, more likely to be used in the Baltic than in any encounter with the Grand Fleet. The Baltic was a separate command under the kaiser's brother Prince Heinrich of Prussia, who initially had seven cruisers of different types and ages, fourteen torpedo boats, four U-boats, and four minelayers. His task was essentially defensive (see chapter 7), but he was authorized to make frequent sweeps and raids to keep the Russians off balance and prevent them from using their (at this stage) numerical superiority.[13]

What were the forces the Grand Fleet and High Sea Fleet could actually employ against each other? The authorities tend to agree on the major points. At first twenty British dreadnoughts would have faced thirteen German dreadnoughts, and four British battle cruisers would have faced three German battle cruisers. In the early stage of the war, each side would have made use of eight predreadnoughts (*King Edward VII* class versus *Deutschland* class). It is more difficult to reconcile the different estimates of what cruisers and destroyers might have been involved, particularly when the number of ships unavailable due to refits is considered. In August 1914 Jellicoe estimated the Grand Fleet had 9 armored cruisers to 2 for the High Sea Fleet, but only 12 light cruisers to 15 for the Germans. His situation in terms of destroyers was even more disadvantageous, for the Grand Fleet had only 42 against 88 for the Germans. Would all those destroyers really have been with the High Sea Fleet? The German official history subdivides German destroyers into 42 "newer" and 46 "older" craft, whereas at Jutland in 1916 the Germans engaged only 61. The evaluation of the numbers and the fighting value of ships can be a very complex subject. Perhaps it is sufficient to say that Jellicoe believed he was at a considerable disadvantage in destroyers. It was, in fact, a constant source of worry during the war. Jellicoe later wondered why the Germans did not use their "superfluity" of destroyers in making an attack on Scapa Flow during the early months of the 1914–15 winter. The destroyer situation also reinforced his disinclination to risk the Grand Fleet too close to the German shore. After little more than a fortnight of war, he wrote the First Sea Lord that when they did meet the High Sea Fleet, "I believe we shall give a very good account of ourself. Only I want to fight them fairly, not with a great superiority in T.B.D.'s and mines in their favor together with what may well be a scheme for, viz. a locality adjacent to some of their submarines."[14]

For some time after the war began, the British expected the Germans would come out to do battle. The Germans, for their part, expected the British would fall on the German fleet the moment it exposed itself and never expected, at least according to the future German commander in chief Admiral Scheer, that the Grand Fleet would fall back on the distant blockade and run few risks. However, the war orders issued to the commander in chief of the High Sea Fleet clearly specified that he should not risk the fleet in battle until there was a probability of victory, and this would not occur until equality had been reached by wearing down the Grand Fleet through damage inflicted while it was engaged in a close blockade of the German Bight. If a favorable opportunity for battle presented itself earlier, it was to be exploited.[15] Because neither side would rationally seek battle under unfavorable circumstances and both the British and Germans were unlikely to believe simultaneously that the situation favored them, a major encounter between the Grand Fleet and High Sea Fleet was improbable except by accident.

As a result of these considerations, the naval war in the major theater developed in a very different manner than most had expected. It was a war of sweeps, minelaying, sudden sharp clashes between relatively small numbers, and, of course, "ambushes" in the form of submarine attacks. The first clash came on 5 August when the cruiser *Amphion* and destroyers *Lance* and *Landrail* of the Third Flotilla of the Harwich Force encountered the auxiliary German minelayer *Königin Luise*. The small ship had been a prewar excursion boat, hastily taken into naval service, painted to resemble a Great Eastern Railway steamer, and then sent to lay mines off Harwich. The destroyer *Lance* fired the first shot of the Anglo-German naval war, and the *Königin Luise* was sunk. But the next day, on returning from the sweep, the dead reckoning of the Third Flotilla proved faulty and the *Amphion* ran over a German mine and sank, the first British casualty of the war.[16]

In the north, acting on rumors the Germans would attack, and in order to prevent German armed merchant cruisers from breaking out, the Grand Fleet on 4 August swept to within 100 miles of the Norwegian coast, establishing a pattern of what was to be numerous fruitless sweeps during the war. One armed merchant cruiser, the *Kaiser Wilhelm der Grosse*, did break out at this time, but her fate will be described in another chapter. The British were troubled by persistent rumors of German activities in

Norway; for example, that off the Lofoten Islands merchant ships were being fitted out as auxiliary raiders. On 7 August British cruisers and destroyers even violated Norwegian territorial waters to look for them. The British later formally apologized to the Norwegian government, but for a time Jellicoe diverted forces in extensive searches around the Norwegian coast for either potential German raiders or parent ships for submarines, and a cruiser also was dispatched to check the Danish-owned Faeroe Islands.

The kaiser had been fond of cruising in the magnificent Norwegian fjords in his yacht the *Hohenzollern*, and in the years before the war portions of the German fleet had undertaken regular summer cruises to Norwegian waters. The Norwegians were determined to remain neutral. They had heaved a sigh of relief when the German warships quickly returned to their safe bases in Germany as the diplomatic situation turned critical. The Norwegians were aware that their geographical position made a base on the Norwegian coast attractive for both sides, and on 1 August precautionary measures were taken on an official level, manning coastal fortifications and placing the Norwegian navy on alert. On the diplomatic front, the Norwegian government joined the governments of Denmark and Sweden in a declaration of intent to remain neutral in the war between Austria-Hungary and Serbia. On 2 August the Norwegians ordered full mobilization of their navy (including four coast-defense ships armed with 8.2-inch guns, four destroyers, thirty-one torpedo boats of varying ages, and one submarine) and reinforcements for their coastal defenses. The big question was whether they *could* remain neutral in an Anglo-German war. The answer in this war would be yes, if only because of the strategies of the major belligerents.[17] On the whole it was German rather than British actions—mining international waters and unrestricted submarine warfare—that would harm Norway and her large merchant fleet the most, although British enforcement of the blockade resulted in a certain amount of friction, and certain Norwegian captains had what amounted to an adversarial relationship with the British blockaders.

The first of the major British naval objectives—the transport of one cavalry and four infantry divisions of the British Expeditionary Force to France—began on 7 August. There were no convoys or escorts, and the transports sailed independently or in pairs as they filled up. To guarantee their safety, covering squadrons sealed both entrances of the Channel from raids and the Grand Fleet sailed to a position where it might attack the German fleet if it tried to interfere. The bulk of the transport began on the 12th and was substantially completed on the 18th. The Germans could do little to stop it. Shortly before the war they had concluded they might delay such a transport by energetic attacks on the British blockading force, thereby creating a climate of insecurity at sea. But when that British blockading force failed to appear close inshore, the Germans realized that only by employing the battle fleet could they have any effect.

The German naval leaders appeared sensitive to the reproach the expensive fleet did little to help the army's offensive. Admiral Scheer, then commanding the Second Squadron, dismissed the possibility of interfering with British supply lines by calling it a "totally impossible demand," with losses out of all proportion to any advantage that might be derived. Ships held up by the presence of the German fleet simply would sail after it had departed. Moreover, an incursion into the English Channel by way of the Dover Strait would place the fleet in a poor tactical position, with no room to maneuver against torpedoes and mines. The radius of action of German destroyers would only just reach that far and, lacking fuel, they would be compelled to return. The fleet would then have to either return with them or take the unacceptable risk of doing without their protection. Scheer described a German fleet in the English Channel as being placed "as if it were corked in a bottle."[18]

The Germans at this stage of the war were still expecting a major attack by the Grand Fleet, and they were uncertain of either the fleet's or the blockade line's location. On 6 August they sent ten submarines of the First Submarine Flotilla into the North Sea as far as the line between Scapa Flow and Hardanger Fjord on the Norwegian coast. One submarine disappeared without a trace, and another, U.15, was rammed and sunk with all hands on 9 August by the cruiser *Birmingham*, which had been part of the cruiser screen 30 miles ahead of the Grand Fleet. The news was highly alarming to Jellicoe, for the preceding day the dreadnought *Monarch* had reported being attacked by a submarine while detached for gunnery practice. Keyes, then Captain (S), would later write that the fact the *Monarch* was performing such a task within 500 miles of Helgoland was an example of the navy's general ignorance of submarine powers and limitations. As early as 1910 a British submarine had operated successfully over 500 miles from her base, and Keyes wondered why the Germans were not given credit for similar enterprise. But Jellicoe, if not the Admiralty, was very aware of the danger, and as soon as the immediate need to cover the British Expeditionary Force's crossing had ended, withdrew the fleet to northwest of the Orkneys. He was also worried by the lack of defenses at Scapa Flow and ordered Loch Ewe on the west coast of Scotland to be prepared as a secondary base. Future sweeps into the North Sea were accomplished as fast as possible; the big ships did not linger.[19]

Jellicoe actually felt safer at sea than he did in Scapa Flow, and in the early months of the war, the fleet stayed there no longer than was necessary to fuel. There were also panics, jokingly referred to as the first and second "Battles of Scapa" (1 September and 16 October), when a submarine was reported in the anchorage, and Jellicoe was willing to take the risk of getting the fleet to sea in a hurry in bad weather or at night. The Grand Fleet used Loch Ewe on the northwest coast of Scotland as an anchorage, and when this seemed too exposed in the second half of October, moved to Loch na Keal farther to the south on the Scottish coast. Jellicoe even went as far as Lough Swilly on the north coast of Ireland. The danger was not purely imaginary. On 23 November the submarine U.18 did manage to penetrate Hoxa Sound, one of the entrances to the anchorage at Scapa Flow, before it was rammed by a trawler and eventually forced to scuttle itself. The battle cruiser anchorage on the east coast of Scotland in Cromarty Firth was considered "fairly secure" by 26 October, but the work at Scapa Flow went more slowly, and the first line of obstructions at the Hoxa entrance was only completed on 29

December, the first line in Switha Sound on 12 January 1915, and those of Hoy Sound, the remaining entrance, by 19 February 1915.[20]

British submarines also had been active in the Helgoland Bight since the beginning of the war. Commodore (S) Roger Keyes was a fiery officer who frequently went out with his submarines in the destroyers *Lurcher* and *Firedrake*, scouting ahead for them or serving as a wireless link. The attempt to "work" submarines from surface warships appears quaint today, but in the early stages of the war it did not seem unusual, particularly for passing on wireless messages. The idea that submarines could work in conjunction with the battle fleet died hard in the Royal Navy, and later in the war it led to the unsuccessful experiment with the large and fast (but unhandy) *K*-class, steam-driven submarines.[21]

British submarines did bring back valuable intelligence on German patrols in the Helgoland Bight, and Keyes began agitating for an attack to "mop up" the German destroyer patrols. This could give the British submarines a shot at any German cruisers that might come out in support. "When are we going to make war and make the Germans realize that whenever they come out . . . they will be fallen on and attacked?" he wrote the director of operations. On 23 August he submitted a plan for the attack, securing the equally aggressive Tyrwhitt's support, and when the War Staff seemed preoccupied with other matters, managed to interest Churchill in the project. The result was the first significant naval encounter of the war. Unfortunately the Admiralty staff work was poor and nearly contributed to a disaster. The scheme called for Tyrwhitt to lead his First and Second Flotillas (each with sixteen destroyers) and their leaders, the light cruisers *Fearless* and *Arethusa*, in the attack on the patrols. Keyes's submarines would be deployed in two lines: an inner line to attack any German cruisers that might sortie, and a second line to surface and draw German destroyers away from Helgoland and out to sea. There would be another pair of British submarines off the mouth of the Ems. Rear Admiral Sir Archibald Moore with the battle cruisers *New Zealand* and *Invincible* would cruise to the north as heavy support in case they were needed. The old *Bacchante*-class armored cruisers would be off Terschelling as a reserve.

The Admiralty failed to notify Jellicoe promptly of the impending operation and then gave him few details. Jellicoe offered assistance, but Vice Admiral Sir F. Doveton Sturdee, chief of staff, informed him that the entire Grand Fleet was not necessary. However, he could support the operation with battle cruisers if convenient. Jellicoe accordingly sent Vice Admiral David Beatty with the battle cruisers *Lion*, *Queen Mary*, and *Princess Royal*, accompanied by the First Light Cruiser Squadron of Commodore William E. Goodenough (six town-class light cruisers), to join Moore. Beatty put to sea with very little information about the operation. Unfortunately, Keyes and Tyrwhitt never received the news Beatty would be at sea, apparently because they had already sailed and were out of wireless range. Consequently, when Goodenough's light cruisers arrived on the scene, they created a certain amount of confusion. Tyrwhitt quickly discovered their identity as he was beginning his sweep, but Keyes at first reported them as hostile. Keyes eventually realized his mistake, but what about the British submarines?

They had been instructed that beyond the *Arethusa* and *Fearless*, any cruisers encountered in the Bight should be considered as hostile. Goodenough's light cruisers therefore ran the considerable danger of being attacked by their own submarines, and one British submarine actually was prepared to fire when her commander noticed the red cross of Saint George in a cruiser's ensign. *E.6* actually fired at the *Southampton*, which, assuming she was being attacked by a U-boat, attempted to ram—fortunately without success.[22]

The Helgoland action of 28 August was a most confusing encounter; the track charts of the action are possibly the most difficult to follow of any battle during the war. All reports describe ships dashing in and out of the fog and haze that worked to the disadvantage of both sides. It prevented, for example, the German coastal batteries at Helgoland from effectively taking part in the action. The Germans had nine destroyers on the outer patrol line in the Bight and a similar number of minesweepers on an inner line. In theory the Germans had four cruisers, two torpedo-boat flotillas, and a minesweeping division allotted for defense of the Bight by day, and five small cruisers and three torpedo-boat flotillas by night.[23] The Germans had approximately seven additional cruisers to support the patrols, but they were in port and would have to raise steam. Most important of all, low water prevented German capital ships from crossing the Jade bar during the morning.

The sweep began with the German destroyers fleeing into the mist, which hampered the effectiveness of the British fire. Tyrwhitt's flagship, *Arethusa*, had only been commissioned two days earlier, and as German cruisers joined the action, her deficiencies became clear. Two of her guns jammed, and a shell from the cruiser *Frauenlob* reduced her speed. More and more German cruisers began to emerge from the harbors. Fortunately for the British, Rear Admiral Leberecht Maas, commander of the Second Scouting Group and senior officer of the torpedo boats, was very aggressive and extremely anxious to engage. Consequently he committed his cruisers piecemeal instead of waiting to concentrate.

The British had not done as well as they had anticipated when Tyrwhitt began his withdrawal to the west. They had sunk only the destroyer *V.187* and were still on the doorstep of the German bases with heavy ships likely to appear at any time. The damaged *Arethusa* and the British destroyers were hotly engaged. German cruisers appeared and disappeared into the mist, and the British were lucky the German attacks were not concentrated or well coordinated. The flotillas requested support, and Beatty, some 40 miles to the north, was faced with a difficult decision. He had not heard from the flotillas for some time, they now seemed to have made little progress, and with the German bases so close there was the possibility of a grave disaster. He did not think Goodenough's light cruisers would be sufficiently strong to deal with the situation quickly enough. Beatty decided to intervene decisively and with crushing strength, despite the low visibility and unknown dangers from possible submarines and mines or enemy capital ships. Captain Ernle Chatfield, his flag captain, described how Beatty turned to him on the bridge of the *Lion* and said, "I ought to go and support Tyrwhitt, but if I lose one of these valuable ships the country will not forgive me." Chatfield, admitting he was unburdened by responsibility, replied that surely they must go. "It was all he needed," Chatfield stated, "but whatever I had said would have made little difference. We steamed towards Tyrwhitt at twenty-five knots. . . ."[24]

The intervention of first Goodenough's and then Beatty's force was decisive. By the time the British withdrew, three German light cruisers, the *Mainz*, *Ariadne*, and Admiral Maas's flagship, the *Köln*, had been sunk or were sinking. Maas did not survive. Hipper's battle cruisers did not arrive until well after the British had left. The *Arethusa* and two damaged British destroyers had to be towed in the final stages of the return home. The Germans by all accounts fought bravely and well. A British officer who had been in the *Southampton* that day wrote after the war: "The Germans fought well. They have always fought well whenever I have seen them fight at sea, and they were beaten on this day because they were overwhelmed by a greatly superior force; and the side which can achieve this state of affairs will, other things being equal, always win in war."[25]

The British had won a naval victory, their first of the war, and they had won it right on the doorstep of the enemy. Tyrwhitt reported how Churchill "fairly slobbered" over him when he came aboard the battered *Arethusa*. Keyes was more modest; he wrote Goodenough, "I think an absurd fuss was made over that small affair [28 August], except in regard to the gallant conduct of the *Arethusa* and *Fearless*." He added, "It makes me sick and disgusted to think what a complete success it might have been but for, I won't say dual, but—multiple control." Keyes maintained that if they had been given the support he and Tyrwhitt wanted at the beginning—that is, Goodenough's light cruisers inshore with the *Fearless* and *Arethusa*—they might have sunk at least six cruisers.[26]

The action had important psychological repercussions on the German side. The kaiser, who was quick with his reproaches, was confirmed in his defensive inclination. Tirpitz, whose position as state secretary of the Reichsmarineamt excluded him from operational matters, was beside himself. He could not understand why at the approach of the British the entire fleet had not been ordered to sea with every vessel they had, for there would have been nothing better for the Germans than a battle so close to their own ports. Hipper, who was responsible for the defense of the Bight, did make certain changes. He decided that the German cruisers had advanced too rapidly at the signal the enemy were approaching and that in the future they were to fall back under the guns of Helgoland. Furthermore, at least four capital ships would be stationed *outside* the Jade bar for the remainder of the war, all capital ships would be at two hours' notice for steaming, and two large minefields were to be laid west of Helgoland. Perhaps most important of all, 28 August strengthened the defensive attitude of the German leaders. The kaiser was afraid that what had happened to the cruisers in the Bight might happen to his precious battle fleet. Regardless of Tirpitz's growls, the kaiser now insisted that the commander in chief of the High Sea Fleet should wire for his consent before engaging in a fleet action.[27]

The British tried another sweep into the Helgoland Bight on 11 September but achieved no success. The newly laid German minefields made such moves very dangerous; in fact, that day the Third Destroyer Flotilla narrowly missed a minefield and certain loss. The Germans continued *Kleinkrieg*, the guerrilla war waged by mines and submarines. The latter were now used much more aggressively in seeking out the British fleet and soon achieved successes that diminished much of the psychological advantage the British enjoyed after 28 August. On 5 September *U.21*, commanded by Kapitänleutnant Otto Hersing, torpedoed and sank the scout cruiser *Pathfinder*, leader of the Eighth Destroyer Flotilla (Firth of Forth) off Saint Abb's Head. This was the first British warship to be lost to a submarine during the war.

The British evened the score on 13 September when *E.9*, commanded by Lieutenant Commander Max Horton (who would later command Western Approaches in World War II), sank the old cruiser *Hela* 6 miles off Helgoland. Horton also sank the destroyer *S.116* off the Ems on 6 October. But it would be the Germans who would achieve the most spectacular success on 22 September. Kapitänleutnant Otto Weddigen, in the old submarine *U.9*, torpedoed and sank the cruisers *Cressy, Aboukir,* and *Hogue* on the Broad Fourteens, the name given to the area they patrolled off the Dutch coast. Three cruisers, sixty-two officers, and 1,397 men (most middle-aged reservists, but some young cadets mobilized directly from the Royal Naval College at Dartmouth) were lost in a little more than an hour. The submarine had given a striking demonstration of its power. Actually, both Keyes and Tyrwhitt had repeatedly tried to get the old *Bacchante*-class armored cruisers removed from the Broad Fourteens. They were sardonically known as "the live bait squadron," because the old ships stood little chance against a powerful surface raider. Sturdee, however, insisted that they, rather than destroyers, remain to guard against German raids or minelaying activities. He did not believe that destroyers could maintain a patrol in heavy weather. The old *Bacchantes* had to stay until they could be replaced by light cruisers. According to Keyes, Sturdee dismissed his arguments to withdraw the cruisers with the contemptuous remark that Keyes did not know history, particularly that of the Dutch Wars, if he did not understand the necessity for a Broad Fourteen patrol to keep the Scheldt open.[28]

The submarine had now eclipsed the High Sea Fleet as the greatest threat to the Royal Navy's control of the seas. Submarine sightings became frequent, there were unsuccessful attacks on British warships, and the navy realized how extremely difficult it was to counter the new menace. On 15 October Weddigen's *U.9* sank the old cruiser *Hawke* off the Scottish coast. Jellicoe moved the fleet's anchorage from Loch Ewe farther south to Loch na Keal and to Lough Swilly on the north coast of Ireland.

Lough Swilly was not as safe as Jellicoe hoped. In mid-October the Germans sent out three minelayers, two directed to the Firth of Forth and the third to the River Clyde. The east coast operation proved abortive, but the west coast operation was successful. Captain Hans Pfundheller, commanding the minelayer *Berlin* (17,300 tons), a converted North German Lloyd liner, decided he would not be able to reach the Clyde. He did what he considered the next best thing and laid two hundred mines on the night of 22–23 October in the shipping lanes off Tory Island to the northwest of Lough Swilly. He apparently had no idea the Grand Fleet was nearby, and after cruising without further success as far as Iceland, eventually brought his ship into the Norwegian port of

Trondheim to be interned. The minefield claimed a merchantman on the 26th, and on the morning of the 27th, the dreadnought *Audacious*. The *Audacious*, one of the most modern dreadnoughts, had been at sea with the Second Battle Squadron for firing practice. There were desperate efforts to save the ship. The large White Star liner *Olympic* responded to the distress calls and attempted to take her in tow, but after twelve hours of struggle the dreadnought sank. Jellicoe now believed that his real advantage over the Germans was eroding, and with operations in Belgium at a crucial point, asked that the loss of the *Audacious* be kept secret. The loss could hardly be kept secret for long, if only because there had been a number of American passengers in the *Olympic*, and the Germans were certain about its loss in less than a month. Nevertheless, until the end of the war the Admiralty clung to the fiction that the *Audacious* had only been damaged.[29]

Mine warfare was another aspect of the naval war that had been neglected by the British despite the considerable losses mines had inflicted on the Japanese during the Russo-Japanese War. For the majority of officers, mine warfare lacked the interest, glamour, and (probably) chances for promotion and distinction that were associated with gunnery in the big ships or flotilla work with destroyers. As one British officer graphically put it, before the war those in the minesweeping service were looked on as "no better than lavatory attendants." The Royal Navy began the war with what Jellicoe admitted was a totally inadequate force of minesweepers. There were only ten old torpedo gunboats, fitted with sweeps, and thirteen trawlers used primarily for training. The Admiralty may have been lulled into a false sense of security by the 1907 Hague Convention against indiscriminate use of mines in international waters. Unfortunately the Germans by the end of the war had laid more than 43,000 mines, 25,000 of them in the North Sea and around the British Isles. The attitude toward minesweeping changed drastically; minesweepers tied up alongside battleships, their crews allowed to use the canteens. The Admiralty laid down whole classes of minesweepers, and converted hundreds of trawlers, and at the end of the war, 726 craft were involved in the minesweeping service. Minesweeping was a slow process, and it was not practical for battleships and cruisers to follow the sweepers at sea. In the spring of 1915, the device known as the paravane, which cut mine moorings, was developed, but it took until 1917 before the entire fleet could be fitted.

Churchill and two successive chiefs of staff, Admirals Sturdee and Oliver, were reluctant to employ mines, either offensively or defensively. They feared mines would hamper the operations of British warships or submarines more than they would harm the Germans. The objection to offensive mining was that the goal was to make the German fleet come out and fight, not be mined in. The first British minefields in the Helgoland Bight were not laid until 1915. Even then the influence of the Foreign Office served as a conservative brake on mining so as not to offend neutrals. The British also had neglected their own mines and did not have a really efficient or reliable mine until 1917, when they developed the H.II, copied from a captured German mine. The minelaying force, both warship and mercantile conversions, expanded to about one hundred craft.[30]

There was steadily rising discontent with the Admiralty in October 1914. A frequent question was, What is the navy doing? The question was a particularly painful one as the losses of the army mounted. The British Expeditionary Force was obviously fighting—was the navy? Churchill's expedition to Antwerp, an attempt to prevent the city's falling into German hands, was a failure, and the Germans pushed along the Belgian coast to Ostend and Zeebrugge, which they later would develop into bases. This posed a direct threat to the communications with France. The new situation resulted in the Admiralty removing the Dover Strait from the control of the admiral of patrols and making it a separate command under Rear Admiral the Honorable Horace Hood, who held the title "rear admiral commanding the Dover Patrol and senior naval officer, Dover." Hood controlled four light cruisers, twenty-four destroyers of the Sixth Destroyer Flotilla, thirteen old B- and C-class submarines, plus trawlers and other auxiliary craft. His responsibilities also increased when General Joffre, chief of the French general staff, asked for assistance to the Belgian and French forces defending the Channel ports of Nieuport and Dunkirk. The British provided it, sending three monitors and, eventually, old battleships and a motley collection of old, if not ancient, craft, including torpedo gunboats, gunboats, and sloops. This demonstrated that even vessels that would never have been used in any real naval encounter were valuable assets for duties such as these. Hood also had four French destroyers under his command at Dunkirk, and on 30 October conducted operations from the French destroyer *Intrépide*. A French historian claimed this was the first time a British admiral flew his flag in a French warship in battle. Hood and his ships had a hot time, which cannot be described in detail here, before the German advance along the coast was stopped.

The Germans sought to take advantage of the situation by sending four large (315-ton) torpedo boats of the Ems patrol, *S.115, S.117, S.118,* and *S.119,* under the command of Korvettenkapitän August Thiele, to lay mines at the mouth of the Thames. The Germans were intercepted off Texel Island on 17 October by Captain Cecil Fox in the light cruiser *Undaunted*, with the destroyers *Lance, Lennox, Legion,* and *Loyal* of the Harwich Force. The four German ships were sunk, and valuable intelligence was later recovered from the wrecks. Unfortunately, this victory was counterbalanced on the 31st by the loss of the old cruiser *Hermes*, then serving as a seaplane carrier, to an attack by the submarine *U.27* 8 miles off Calais. The loss caused the Admiralty to withdraw the old battleship *Venerable*, which had been supporting the coastal operations. In the future no vessel larger than a destroyer, or in exceptional cases a scout cruiser, was to cross the Channel east of the meridian of Greenwich during daylight hours.[31]

On 28 October the First Sea Lord Prince Louis of Battenberg submitted his resignation. There had been a nasty public clamor about his German birth, and the unfair insinuations are usually given as the primary reason for his resignation. There is some evidence, however, that he was also criticized for being too passive in the face of Churchill—"Churchill's dupe" was the unflattering term used—and he was also criticized for his apparent lack of energy from the beginning of the war. One historian even maintains that he was asked to resign and that the initiative for resignation came from the cabinet.[32]

Battenberg was replaced by Admiral of the Fleet Lord Fisher, who was recalled from retirement. Fisher was seventy-four, but as Beatty wrote his wife, "He still has fine zeal, energy, and determination, coupled with low cunning, which is eminently desirable just now. He also has courage and will take any responsibility." No one could accuse Fisher of lack of energy. Keyes recalled that at a meeting with Admiralty officials on the subject of future submarine construction, Fisher turned to the superintendent of contracts and said that "he would make his wife a widow and his house a dunghill, if he brought paper work or red tape into the business; he wanted submarines, not contracts."[33]

Fisher believed that the war was going to be a long one and with that ruthless energy embarked on a vast building program that eventually included 5 battle cruisers; 2 light cruisers; 5 flotilla leaders; 56 destroyers; 65 submarines; more than 33 monitors of various sizes; 24 sloops (for antisubmarine work); 50 antisubmarine motor launches; and 200 large and 60 small landing barges, protected by steel shields for landings under fire. He also was instrumental in bringing into service the first squadron of nonrigid airships (generally referred to as *blimps*), which proved very useful for antisubmarine patrols near the coast. Elements of Fisher's program were controversial, notably the light-draft battle cruisers *Glorious, Courageous,* and *Furious,* with their high speed, small number of very large guns, and meager protection. They were condemned as costly "white elephants," and the three were converted later into aircraft carriers. Whatever the debate over parts of his program or methods, on balance Fisher's achievements were real. Unfortunately the Churchill-Fisher combination was highly volatile, and, as we shall see, Fisher would resign over the Dardanelles campaign, shortly before Churchill too would be forced from office.[34]

In the autumn of 1914, a period of discontent and unease over the performance of the navy, the British were developing a priceless advantage over the Germans, but one that had to be kept a strict secret: through a combination of circumstances the Admiralty was gaining the ability to read much of the German wireless traffic. The British actually had three windfalls. The best known came from the Russians. On 26 August the German light cruiser *Magdeburg,* on reconnaissance in the Gulf of Finland, ran aground on the island of Odensholm off the Estonian coast. The ship could not be refloated, and the intervention of Russian warships prevented the effective destruction of the ship and, apparently, the proper disposal of confidential books. The Russians were able to recover three copies of the SKM (*Signalbuch der Kaiserlichen Marine*) with the current key. They offered one copy to their British allies if the British would send a ship to a north Russian port to collect it. The British complied, and on 13 October two Russian naval officers arrived at the Admiralty with the precious book. The second windfall came from Australia, where the HVB (*Handelsverkehrsbuch*), the code book used for communications between the Admiralstab and German merchantmen as well as in the High Sea Fleet, was found in a German steamer seized at the beginning of the war. This, after perhaps inexcusable delay, reached the Admiralty by the end of October. The third windfall was truly amazing, coming from a lead-lined chest apparently jettisoned by the senior officer of the four German torpedo boats sunk off the Dutch coast on 17 October. The chest was dragged up in the nets of a British trawler fishing off Texel on 30 November and reached the Admiralty on 3 December. There was a copy of the VB (*Verkehrsbuch*) code in the chest, a code used at sea, mostly by flag officers. It is not clear if the code breakers provided any advance information on the thwarted German minelaying raid of 17 October, but the incident of the VB book was usually referred to by those involved in code breaking as "the miraculous draught of fishes."[35]

The cryptographers who worked with these codes were under the direction of Sir Alfred Ewing, the former director of naval education. The code-breaking organization was commonly known by where it was installed in early November—Room 40 on the first floor of the old Admiralty building. Room 40 and its work also would become closely linked with Captain (later Rear Admiral) Reginald Hall. "Blinker" Hall (as he was nicknamed because of his habit of constantly blinking his eyes) became director of the Intelligence Division in November 1914 and would later become one of the legends of the First World War. But in October 1914 all of this was far in the future. It took time before the full potential of Room 40 could be realized. At first the cryptographers were inexperienced and did not always understand naval procedure or terminology. Some staff officers, in turn, looked down on the cryptographers who had come from civilian backgrounds. The usual problem with such an intelligence source was how to use it in a manner that would not alert the enemy it existed. The Admiralty may have carried secrecy to an excessive degree. Admiral Oliver, that indefatigable workhorse and chief of staff from November 1914 to May 1917, was a great centralizer and drafted almost every signal from Room 40 in his own hand. Until 1917 Hall merely had access to, but not control of, material. This concentration of the dissemination of intelligence in a very few hands meant that the commander in chief might not receive all available information in time for it to be of use. As a result Room 40 would not reach its peak of efficiency and become a true intelligence center until much later in the war.[36]

The loss of the *Audacious* only served to heighten Jellicoe's concern that his real margin of superiority over the High Sea Fleet in a fleet action was not large. On 30 October he informed the Admiralty of the conditions under which he would give battle. He expected the Germans to try to make the fullest use of mines, torpedoes, and submarines. The Germans could not count on having their greatest number of submarines, minelayers, or aircraft present unless the battle was fought in waters chosen by them, which would be in the southern portion of the North Sea. Jellicoe's objective therefore would be to fight a fleet action in the northern portion of the North Sea, which would be nearer the British bases, thereby giving damaged British ships a better chance of reaching home. It would work in the opposite way for the Germans: the British would have a better chance of destroying damaged ships. A battle in the northern portion of the North Sea would also hamper a night destroyer attack by the Germans before or after an action, whereas it would favor a concentration of British cruisers and destroyers with the battle fleet.

On a tactical level, Jellicoe declared that if the German battle fleet were to turn away from his advancing fleet, "I should assume that the intention was to lead us over mines and submarines, and should decline to be so drawn." He did not want the Admiralty to think this was a refusal of battle, though it might result in failure to bring the enemy to action as soon as expected. Nevertheless it was in his opinion the proper course to defeat and annihilate the enemy, for if he made a false move it was quite possible half the battle fleet could be disabled by underwater attack before the guns opened fire. In an action Jellicoe planned to guard against submarines by moving the battle fleet at very high speed to a flank before deploying or opening fire, so that the encounter would take place off the ground on which the enemy wanted to fight. The Germans might refuse to follow him, but if the fleets remained in sight of each other, the high speed would force submarines to surface if they wished to follow, and Jellicoe felt that after an interval at high speed he could safely close.[37]

Beyond "underhanded" weapons such as the submarine and mine, and in terms of surface ships in the sort of classic encounter that the Grand Fleet ardently desired, Jellicoe was less confident than many might have supposed. His concern over the shortage of destroyers compared to what he might expect to face was an old story. But capital ships? What had happened to the initial 20:13 advantage? It had been whittled down. The *Audacious* had been lost, the *Ajax* and *Iron Duke* (Jellicoe's flagship) had developed condenser trouble, the *Orion* had suspected defects in her turbine supports, the *Conqueror* was refitting, and the battle cruiser *New Zealand* was in dock. Although the *Erin* and *Agincourt*, former Turkish dreadnoughts taken over by the Admiralty at the beginning of the war, had joined the fleet, Jellicoe did not regard these newly commissioned ships as efficient. Jellicoe estimated that two dreadnoughts and a battle cruiser had joined the German fleet since the beginning of the war. The ratio in terms of efficient dreadnoughts was now 17:15; in battle cruisers 5:4.

Things became worse in November. Admiral Maximilian Graf von Spee's German Asiatic Squadron defeated a British force off the Chilean coast on 1 November, and Fisher quickly dispatched the battle cruisers *Inflexible* and *Invincible* to the South Atlantic and the *Princess Royal* to the West Indies. Turkey entered the war on the side of Germany, and the battle cruisers *Indefatigable* and *Indomitable* remained off the Dardanelles. Beatty had only four battle cruisers (the *Lion*, *Queen Mary*, *New Zealand*, and *Tiger*) to meet Hipper's four German battle cruisers plus the hybrid *Blücher*. Moreover, the *Tiger* had only just joined and was not fully efficient, and the dreadnought *King George V*, just back from refitting, was disabled by condenser defects.

December brought no real relief. The new dreadnoughts *Benbow* and *Emperor of India* joined the fleet in December, but it took time for them to work up to real efficiency. The annihilation of Spee's squadron at the Falkland Islands on 8 December meant that the battle cruiser shortage was soon to be alleviated, and the two battle cruisers were ordered back from the Mediterranean (but needed refits). On the other hand, the *Conqueror* and *Monarch* collided entering Scapa Flow in bad weather on the 26th, and the *Conqueror* in particular was badly damaged. The problem with destroyers had not improved either. On 4 December Jellicoe wrote the Admiralty that his present weakness in destroyers would handicap him in obtaining the crushing victory over the High Sea

Fleet that was expected of him. I have related these incidents to show how the apparent British superiority could be dissipated. Jellicoe's correspondence for the period is full of very real concern. It was only after February 1915 that the ratio of strength slowly but steadily improved for the British as the superdreadnoughts (armed with 15-inch guns) of the *Queen Elizabeth* and *Royal Sovereign* classes began to enter service.[38]

As a result of these circumstances the High Sea Fleet probably had at this time the best chance of victory in a major naval encounter that it would ever have. The Germans soon learned of the loss of the *Audacious*, but they probably did not know of the other British problems. The Germans also added new ships. By the end of January 1915, they had completed the dreadnoughts *Grosser Kurfürst, König,* and *Markgraf,* as well as the battle cruiser *Derfflinger,* but the latter three had been only recently commissioned and were still working up to full efficiency.

Tirpitz remained a persistent voice for offensive use of the German fleet. He wrote the chief of the Admiralstab on 16 September that they could not achieve an equalization of forces by guerrilla war, that the aim of all their work for more than twenty years had been battle, but that given their numerical inferiority they must strive to give battle not more than 100 nautical miles from Helgoland. Their best chance for victory had been in the first two or three weeks of the war, for the British became stronger through new building while the spirit of the German crews declined. Moreover, Tirpitz declared, there were domestic political considerations: "If we come to the end of a war so terrible as that of 1914, without the fleet having bled and worked, we shall get nothing more for the fleet, and all the scanty money that there may be will be spent on the army."[39]

Despite Tirpitz's arguments, a meeting aboard the commander in chief's flagship on 3 October between Ingenohl, von Pohl, and the three commanders of the battle squadrons reaffirmed the decision to continue the defensive *Kleinkrieg* strategy and to avoid an offensive with the fleet. This strategy did not, however, preclude offensive minelaying off the British coast or the bombardment of coastal towns by battle cruisers. Ingenohl was anxious for such an operation for reasons of morale and, consequently, Hipper's battle cruisers bombarded Yarmouth on 3 November, while a cruiser slipped close inshore to lay mines. Two of the German battle squadrons came out to the edge of the Bight but did not enter the North Sea. Although British forces in the Yarmouth area were weak—an ancient minesweeper and some old destroyers—they were not sunk, and the bombardment did little damage. A British submarine, *D.5,* was sunk coming out of Yarmouth by a floating mine, but the Germans suffered a much severer loss when the armored cruiser *Yorck* blundered into a German minefield returning to port and was sunk.[40] The raid did result in the transfer of the Third Battle Squadron—the latest predreadnoughts of the *King Edward VII* class—from Scapa Flow to Rosyth, where it would be better placed to counter raids or a possible invasion. The War Office in November was apprehensive about a German invasion, although there was little basis in reality for these fears. Unfortunately for Jellicoe, the detachment of the Third Battle Squadron and the cruisers and destroyers necessary to support it came at time when, as we have seen, the British margin of superiority was dangerously low.[41]

Hipper believed he had a better use for battle cruisers than raiding coastal towns or vainly trying to entice the British fleet into a trap. In November he developed a plan, originally submitted by one of his captains, that would have sent the four newest battle cruisers to the West Indies or South Atlantic to conduct commerce warfare and over-whelm any enemy cruisers assigned to protect trade. Hipper maintained this was the one way the big German ships could damage the enemy and thereby justify their existence. His plan was vague on the inevitable question of coaling. The battle cruisers would be blistered to increase their bunkerage, and it was believed that "it would not be difficult to surprise them and coal by force of arms in English bases at least once." Hipper's plan was not approved. Ingenohl preferred giving U-boat warfare a chance to succeed before detaching surface forces for commerce war and depriving the High Sea Fleet of its battle cruisers. He did see the advantages of isolating Great Britain and even considered the possibility of the battle cruisers linking up with Spee's newly victorious squadron. Von Pohl, however, preferred the U-boat strategy and maintaining the fleet intact, whereas Tirpitz still favored a fleet action, but not cruiser warfare.[42]

Ingenohl was anxious to make another raid on the east coast of England, this time choosing Scarborough and Hartlepool. The raid once again included both bombardments and minelaying. The strategic purpose was to lure the Grand Fleet or a portion of it over a freshly laid minefield or within range of U-boats. The kaiser, encouraged by the news of Spee's victory at Coronel, gave his consent, but the necessity of using every available battle cruiser delayed the operation until December because of problems with the *Von der Tann*'s machinery. The British, it seems, were not the only ones with technical problems. Then came news of the destruction of Spee's squadron at the Battle of the Falkland Islands on 8 December. For psychological reasons Ingenohl was anxious for a quick success to counteract the morale effects of the British victory, and he now knew with certainty that at least two British battle cruisers were away in the South Atlantic. He would therefore strike before they could return. The High Sea Fleet came out in support as far as the Dogger Bank—the sand banks approximately halfway across the North Sea. Ingenohl did not inform the kaiser of this deployment because it would have risked a major fleet action.

Ingenohl was ignorant of one factor that nearly brought about disaster for Hipper's battle cruisers. Room 40, which had not been able to give warning of the Yarmouth raid, was now able to intercept and decode enough information to predict a raid. The Admiralty ordered Jellicoe to send Beatty's battle cruisers and Goodenough's light cruiser squadron, supported by a dreadnought squadron, to a position where they could intercept the Germans on their return. Jellicoe wanted to go with the whole Grand Fleet, but the Admiralty insisted only one battle squadron was necessary. Jellicoe sent Vice Admiral Sir George Warrender's Second Battle Squadron, six of the best dreadnoughts (the *King George V* [flag], *Ajax, Centurion, Orion, Monarch,* and *Conqueror*) accompanied by eight destroyers. He chose an almost perfect rendezvous for Warrender (proceeding from Cromarty) to meet with Beatty's battle cruisers, screened by Goodenough's light cruisers, roughly off the southeast corner of the Dogger Bank. Tyrwhitt's Harwich Force completed the trap from the south, and Keyes with his two destroyers and eight submarines was ordered to the vicinity of Terschelling. Unfortunately there was a gap in British intelligence. Room 40 had not established the fact that the High Sea Fleet itself would be at sea, and Ingenohl actually planned to be in a position about 30 miles from the British rendezvous at dawn. This put fourteen German dreadnoughts and eight predreadnoughts in dangerous proximity to Warrender's six dreadnoughts. The Germans, as a result of the Admiralty's decision to refuse Jellicoe permission to take the whole fleet to sea, might have been able to do what they had always hoped to do—destroy or severely maul an isolated portion of the Grand Fleet, thereby whittling down British strength. Both sides came very close to disaster on the 16th of December.

Poor visibility and squally weather had much to do with saving both the British and Germans that day. Before dawn on the morning of the 16th, Warrender's destroyers clashed with the destroyers and light cruisers of the High Sea Fleet. However, it was Ingenohl who turned away, when he was only some 10 miles from Warrender and Beatty, perhaps ending once and for all his chance for fame in naval history. He was convinced the destroyers he had engaged were the advanced screen of the Grand Fleet and that a general engagement for which he did not have the kaiser's permission might be at hand. Ingenohl also left Hipper in the lurch, for the High Sea Fleet was supposed to hold its position until Hipper's bombardment was finished.

The bombardments of Scarborough, Whitby, and Hartlepool were accomplished without undue difficulty. The Germans brushed aside the weak opposition of local forces and inflicted heavy civilian casualties and considerable damage, while the light cruiser *Kolberg* laid one hundred mines. Would the British be able to intercept the Germans on their return? The answer was no, for a number of reasons. Jellicoe was finally ordered to sea with the Grand Fleet to block any German strike at the north, but the Germans did not come anywhere near him. Bad weather forced Tyrwhitt's destroyers coming from the south to turn back and drastically reduced the speed of his light cruisers, which continued. Goodenough in the *Southampton*, screening the advance of Beatty, made contact with and engaged the light cruiser *Stralsund* and accompanying destroyers. He was soon joined by the light cruiser *Birmingham*, but he unfortunately failed to inform Beatty that there were other German cruisers in the distance. This would have indicated that Hipper's group was probably advancing behind them. Beatty, in turn, anxious to spread the search for Hipper and believing the *Southampton* and *Birmingham* were sufficient to handle a single German cruiser, ordered Goodenough's other cruisers, the *Falmouth* and *Nottingham*, now on the scene, to resume their position for lookout duties and to take station 5 miles ahead. The signal made by Beatty's flag lieutenant, Ralph Seymour, was badly worded—the first of a series of similar mistakes Seymour would make at critical moments—and could be interpreted as addressed to the light cruiser squadron as a whole rather than the two individual ships. Goodenough, not realizing that Beatty had a mistaken view of the situation because he had only reported one German cruiser, turned away and lost contact with the Germans in the deteriorating visibility.

The *Stralsund* group next passed Warrender's squadron. Rear Admiral Arbuthnot of the Second Division reported that the enemy was in sight but chose to await orders rather than open fire himself. Warrender did not fire but contented himself with ordering three armored cruisers in pursuit and reporting the sighting. The signal, in turn, diverted Beatty from a course that might well have brought him in contact with Hipper. The result was that the Germans got away, and when Room 40 did intercept a signal from Ingenohl's flagship indicating the High Sea Fleet was at sea, the Admiralty ordered Warrender not to go too far to the east.

The Admiralty's last chance was Keyes and his submarines on the Terschelling line. Keyes had been cruising about in the destroyer *Lurcher*, trying to gather the submarines after he had received word the Germans were off Scarborough. He had collected four when the signal arrived advising him the High Sea Fleet might return at dawn the next day and ordering him to proceed to Helgoland to intercept it. Keyes sent the four submarines on and continued to try to find the others. The Admiralty, though, had misjudged the movements of the High Sea Fleet, which was home before midnight. Keyes might have been able to catch Hipper's forces with his two destroyers—it seems like a suicide mission—but the message failed to reach him in time, due to a mistaken attempt (that wasted hours) at trying to reach him on the short-range "D," or destroyer, wavelength instead of the long-range "S," or ship, wavelength. A British submarine did get a shot at the dreadnought *Posen* proceeding from the Elbe to the Jade the next day, but the torpedo ran deep and missed, perhaps symbolic of the whole frustrating affair.[43]

Shortly afterward Beatty summed up his feelings to Jellicoe: "There never was a more disappointing day . . . We were within an ace of bringing about the complete destruction of the enemy cruiser force—and failed."[44] Beatty also remarked on the initial destroyer action and that there was no doubt they had run into a screen in front of the whole High Sea Fleet. The British must have realized very quickly that Hipper was not the only one who had a close shave. The 16th of December 1914 deserves to be better known. It demonstrates that even a great advantage such as Room 40 and well-chosen initial deployments could not offset the combination of human errors and the uncontrollable nature of the weather. To make matters even worse, the British had come close to disaster. Surely no event illustrates more clearly the old adage that nothing is certain in war.

Could the Royal Navy retaliate in any manner for this affront to the English coast? Certainly in the fall and winter of 1914–15 there were a number of schemes directed either at the islands off the German North Sea coast or at some operation in the Baltic. They were not very practical and ultimately came to nothing (see chapter 5). There was one ingenious way to get at the German ships if the Germans would not come out, and that was by air. In fact the first air raids were primarily directed against German airships rather than warships. The large zeppelins of the German Naval Air Service were a potentially valuable tool for reconnaissance. In the autumn of 1914, the zeppelins had not yet played an effective role in the naval encounters, but they had the range and disturbing potential to bomb the British Isles. Although the first zeppelin raid on England did not take place until the night of 19–20 January 1915, the zeppelin hangars at Cuxhaven were already an attractive target for the British.

The Royal Naval Air Service carried out the Cuxhaven raids with seaplanes carried in the converted cross-Channel steamers *Engadine* and *Riviera*. Those who regard the naval and military leaders of the First World War as hidebound, unimaginative, and unwilling to adopt new technology may be surprised to learn how comparatively early in the war aircraft were employed on imaginative endeavors such as this. One might say that imagination outran the technical ability to achieve results. Because of the limited range of the aircraft, the raids required an offensive sortie into the Bight by Tyrwhitt's flotillas and Keyes's submarines. The first attempt on 25 October was a failure, largely due to heavy rain, and four aircraft did not even get off the water. On 21 November the Royal Naval Air Service attacked the zeppelin works at Friedrichshafen with land-based aircraft. Three planes took off from Belfort in eastern France, one was shot down, and, contrary to what the British thought, the zeppelin under construction at the target was not damaged. The attacks with seaplanes were the most promising, but remained frustrating. The next attempt, on 23 November, was recalled after Room 40 intercepted signals indicating German cruisers might be out in the Bight in the area where the attack would be launched.

The Admiralty made a major attempt on Christmas Day 1914. This time three seaplane carriers were involved, the *Engadine, Riviera,* and *Empress.* The Germans were expecting an attack that day; they believed an attempt would be made to block the German ports with merchant ships. They also feared a repetition of 28 August, when the battle cruisers had overwhelmed their scouting forces, and therefore kept only submarines and their two available zeppelins out in the Bight. The result was the first significant encounters between aircraft and warships, a preview of the great air-sea battles of future wars. The zeppelin *L.6* attacked the *Empress,* which had fallen behind because of condenser trouble. A pair of seaplanes from Borkum also made a second attack. The British launched their nine seaplanes a half hour before dawn, but two failed to get off the water. None of the remaining aircraft did any damage to the zeppelin sheds; in fact, only one plane even reached them, and then it failed to recognize the target because the pilots had been given the wrong location. The other aircraft dropped their bombs on different targets with little effect. One plane did fly over the German fleet in Schillig Roads, obtaining intelligence and creating considerable excitement, but accomplishing little else. This should not detract from the courage of these early pilots, who pressed on in their primitive aircraft in the face of quite often heavy fire.

The British ships were attacked by the zeppelin *L.5* and seaplanes as they searched for their aircraft that had failed to reach the designated recovery positions. Only three of the crews were rescued by surface craft. Keyes's submarines rescued another three and were attacked by the zeppelin *Z.5* in the process. The seventh crew was picked up by a Dutch trawler, treated as "shipwrecked mariners," and subsequently returned without being interned. None of the ships suffered serious damage from zeppelins or aircraft—a German submarine on the scene also failed to get into a firing position. The British, in fact, seem to have come to the conclusion that ships had little to fear from the air as long as they had sufficient room to maneuver. The Christmas Day air raid of 1914 should probably be treated as a learning experience that pointed the way to the future when technology and experience would make aircraft much more effective.[45]

The boost to British morale provided by the Cuxhaven raid on Christmas Day was soon offset by another startling German submarine success. Early on the morning of New Year's Day, the submarine *U.24* torpedoed and sank the predreadnought *Formidable* of the Channel Fleet. Vice Admiral Sir Lewis Bayly, commander of the Channel Fleet, had been conducting tactical exercises, and the ships, in apparent disregard of the submarine danger, were steaming slowly without zigzagging. Although a predreadnought, this was the first battleship to be sunk by a submarine during the war, and the loss of life was high, only 233 out of 780 officers and men surviving in the rough seas. Bayly, who claimed the Admiralty had failed to warn him submarines might be found so far west in the Channel, was relieved of his command. He eventually redeemed himself with his successful command at Queenstown later in the war (see chapter 11).[46]

The Germans had been encouraged by the results of 16 December but were puzzled as to how the British seemed to have an uncanny ability to know when they were at sea. There was the usual suspicion of spies and a feverish hunt for subversives. Other Germans, including Hipper, suspected that the numerous fishing trawlers in the North Sea, usually under neutral Dutch colors, probably included some equipped with wireless, serving as British scouts and reporting German movements. Many of these vessels often were centered around the Dogger Bank, because these shallow patches were some of the best fishing areas in the North Sea. The Dogger Bank was also located athwart the direct route from the German bases to the east coast of England. Additionally, Hipper had intelligence that unsupported British light forces might also be found on the Dogger Bank. It thus became a tempting target for another raid by the German battle cruisers.

Hipper had wanted the High Sea Fleet to come out into the eastern part of the North Sea in support, but the kaiser remained firmly against risking the fleet outside of German waters. Ingenohl therefore accepted the calculated risk of sending the First and Second scouting groups (the battle cruisers, four light cruisers, and two flotillas of torpedo boats) in an operation he believed would be over within twenty-four hours. Hipper, flying his flag in the *Seydlitz*, was short a battle cruiser. He had only the *Moltke* and *Derfflinger* because the *Von der Tann* was under refit. He also took the armored cruiser *Blücher*, and this decision has been the subject of much criticism, for this hybrid had only 20.5-cm guns compared to the 30.5- and 28-cm guns of the other German battle cruisers. The *Blücher* was also slower, and this supposedly imperiled the entire squadron and eventually led to the ship's loss. A recent biographer of Hipper has, however, pointed out that the *Blücher*'s guns, although lighter, actually had the longest range of any of the German battle cruisers and that she had been well able to maintain the squadron's speed until damaged by a hit in the engine room.

Ingenohl left an important factor out of his calculations. He did not realize that the British intercepted his wireless order to Hipper on 23 January to reconnoiter the Dogger Bank—and that Room 40 was able to read it. The British were able to set what they hoped would be a trap. Beatty with five battle cruisers and Goodenough's light cruiser squadron sailed from Rosyth to rendezvous with Tyrwhitt's Harwich Force (three light cruisers and thirty-five destroyers) near the Dogger Bank at dawn the following morning. Keyes with the *Lurcher* and *Firedrake* and the British submarines were sent in the direction of Borkum Riff and instructed to remain in wireless contact. The Third Battle Squadron (seven predreadnought "King Edward VIIs") and the Third Cruiser Squadron (three armored cruisers) sailed from Rosyth for a position where they could cut off the Germans if they tried to escape to the north. Farther to the north, Jellicoe sailed from Scapa Flow with the Grand Fleet on a sweep of the North Sea, ready to intervene if the High Sea Fleet came out.

The action began at dawn on the 24th, when the light cruiser *Aurora* of the Harwich Force clashed with the cruiser *Kolberg*. Both Beatty and Hipper steamed toward the far-distant gun flashes, Beatty on a southeasterly and Hipper on a northwesterly course. The various reports from German cruisers and intercepted wireless traffic convinced Hipper the British were probably out in force and that he might be heading into a trap. He altered course to the southeast, that is, in the general direction of home. Beatty in the *Lion*, his ships working up to full speed, could actually see the German battle cruisers by 7:50 A.M., and a chase developed. Beatty repeatedly signaled for increases in speed, beyond what any expected the older battle cruisers could do. The British stokers made extraordinary efforts, but as the distance between the Germans and the British battle cruisers *Lion*, *Tiger*, and *Princess Royal* decreased, the older battle cruisers *New Zealand* and *Indomitable* gradually fell behind.

The range had fallen sufficiently by 9:05 for the British to open fire. It was some time before the *New Zealand* was in effective range to join, and longer still for the *Indomitable*. The Germans returned fire at 9:11, hampered by the dense smoke. Hipper's heavy ships were now arranged with the *Seydlitz* in front, followed by the *Moltke* and *Derfflinger*, with the *Blücher*, the weakest ship, in the rear, where throughout the action she would tend to attract the brunt of the British fire.

The British did not achieve the decisive victory they should have, largely due to faulty signaling combined with damage to the *Lion*, which included flooding of the capstan compartment from which salt water reached the secondary condenser, eventually leading to salt contamination of the boilers, which stopped the ship. Things began to go awry after Beatty's 9:35 signal "Engage the corresponding ship in the enemy's line" was misinterpreted by the *Tiger*, leaving the *Moltke* undisturbed and free to concentrate on the leading British ships. There was another serious error when Beatty, observing that the *Blücher* was in a bad way, ordered the *Indomitable* to deal with her. He then signaled the other battle cruisers to "close the enemy as rapidly as possible consistent with keeping all guns bearing." In the poor visibility, these signals were either not, or only partially, received. While the *Lion*'s speed steadily diminished, other hits led to the port engine being stopped and additional flooding, which increased her list and knocked out the remaining dynamo. Furthermore, only two signal halyards remained; the others had been shot away. It had been difficult enough to read the signals in the poor visibility, and Beatty's control of the battle was slipping away as the *Lion* fell behind.

At 10:54 Beatty, in the erroneous belief he had sighted a submarine periscope, ordered a turn 90 degrees to port. The signal was made without the submarine warning signal, and this caused further confusion as to Beatty's intentions. It also allowed the Germans to pull farther ahead, as if Beatty was giving up the chase. Then, as the battle cruisers raced ahead of the *Lion*, the flagship gave what turned out to be the most damaging signal of all. Beatty wanted to signal to "engage the enemy main body," but there was no signal in the signal book for this, and Lieutenant Commander Seymour chose the signal he considered to be most similar in meaning: "Attack the rear of the enemy." However, because the signal for "course northeast" was still flying, the signal seemed to be "Attack the rear of the enemy bearing northeast." In the *New Zealand*, Rear Admiral Sir Archibald Moore, who was now senior officer, interpreted this to mean the already doomed *Blücher*. Beatty and his staff were appalled as they saw the battle cruisers apparently concentrating on the doomed German ship, and they thought of Nelson's old signal to "engage the enemy more closely," only to discover it was no longer in the book. The nearest signal was, "Keep nearer the enemy," but this had no effect.

The *Blücher* fought bravely until she capsized and sank a little after 11:45. Beatty shifted his flag to the destroyer *Attack* at 11:20, but by the time Beatty caught up to and boarded the *Princess Royal* at 12:27 it was too late. The Germans had gotten away. Keyes, who had hoped the Germans might have been delayed by crippled ships, also was too late to find any targets.[47] The Battle of Dogger Bank was a victory to cheer the British public; the picture of the capsized *Blücher* with her crew scrambling like ants over the hull is one of the best known of the war and frequently reproduced to this day. It was, however, an incomplete victory, and Beatty recognized this. He wrote his friend Keyes: "The disappointment of that day is more than I can bear to think of, everybody thinks it was a great success, when in reality it was a terrible failure. I had made up my mind that we were going to get four, the lot, and *four* we ought to have got."[48]

The battle cruiser squadrons were reorganized into three squadrons and designated the Battle Cruiser Fleet, with its primary base at Rosyth. The relative weakness in battle cruisers compared to the Germans in the North Sea eased for the British as ships returned from distant waters. Moore, however, paid the penalty for his misjudgments and was quietly given command of a squadron of old cruisers working off the Canary Islands, where he was not likely to see much action.

The battle had greater repercussions on the German side. The Germans assumed at first that at least one British battle cruiser had been sunk and that Dogger Bank had been a partially successful encounter. They were probably confused by a spectacular and highly visible but nonfatal fire in the *Tiger*. When the truth became apparent after a few days, Admiral von Müller, chief of the kaiser's Naval Cabinet, came to the conclusion that a change in command of the High Sea Fleet was necessary. This view was widely shared; some of the more political officers in the High Sea Fleet intrigued viciously against the commander in chief. Ingenohl was replaced by von Pohl who, in turn, was replaced at the Admiralstab by Vice Admiral Gustav Bachmann. Kaiser Wilhelm approved, according to Müller: "The matter was settled smoothly. No trace of human sympathy displayed." Von Pohl had an outstanding record as a squadron commander and was well known for his exploits in China during the Boxer Rebellion. On the other hand, he was not popular with the officer corps, largely because of a certain arrogance. Bachmann was described as "a calm, experienced man," not suited to be commander in chief, definitely not a "strong man," but someone who would probably get on better with Tirpitz, to whom he was acceptable. There was a certain lack of enthusiasm about the new appointments, but, Müller lamented, "At the time there were no better alternatives."[49]

The strategy of *Kleinkrieg* was not working. There were alternatives proposed. Tirpitz, in a surprising move for the creator of the powerful big ships of the High Sea Fleet, concluded that British building would alter the situation still more to Germany's disadvantage in the future. He now advocated airship attacks on London; a submarine blockade, using Zeebrugge and Ostend as bases for submarine and destroyer raids, with minelaying in the Thames; and the immediate launching of cruiser war in the Atlantic. Tirpitz claimed: "In view of the extraordinary importance of trade disruption, namely in supplying the west of England with food, I can promise an unqualified success from a cruiser war."[50]

The losses of Dogger Bank only made the kaiser more determined than ever not to risk the big ships, which had to be preserved "as a political instrument." The High Sea Fleet might make occasional sorties, but von Pohl would not seek battle outside of the Bight. Here he could enjoy a great advantage in light craft and extensive minefields. As Jellicoe was unwilling to put his head in the German noose, a major encounter was unlikely. The long-term results of this on the morale of the High Sea Fleet were not healthy. If the capital ships would not be used, what could the German navy do? The answer was submarine warfare against British trade. It was becoming more and more apparent that the defeat of Great Britain was the key to German victory. On 4 February 1915 the Germans declared the waters around Great Britain and Ireland, including the entire English Channel, to be a military area in which every hostile merchant vessel would be destroyed, even if it was not possible to provide for the safety of passengers and crew. Neutral ships would also be in danger in those areas, and because of the alleged British misuse of neutral flags and the accidents of war, the Germans warned that attacks might involve neutrals. Shipping north of the Shetland Islands, in the eastern part of the North Sea, and in a strip at least 30 nautical miles along the Dutch coast would not be threatened.[51] This policy incurred serious diplomatic consequences that ultimately had much to do with determining the outcome of the war (see chapter 10).

The character and ordinary routine of the war changed for the British in 1915. Commander Stephen King-Hall, who had been in the light cruiser *Southampton*, observed that the policy of large ships such as battleships and battle cruisers cruising about in hope of seeing something was the first thing abandoned, and patrols and sweeps were increasingly left to light cruisers. By the spring of 1915 this too had fallen into disfavor, and ships would go to sea for three reasons: (1) to intercept blockade runners or bring to action enemy ships whose presence was known, (2) to carry out an offensive operation as far as the strategic situation offered scope for such an operation, and (3) for exercises. The rationale for this was that the Germans would not come into the North Sea without a definite operation in mind, and the presence of mines and submarines made it an unhealthy place merely to cruise for the sake of cruising. The operations in 1915 were three- to five-day "stunts," which King-Hall defined as operations "trying to get at the inaccessible Hun." Stunts were usually preceded by "flaps" or "panics"—the frantic efforts necessary to accomplish the myriad tasks necessary to get ships at four hours' notice ready to sail. Stunts might include air raids directed at zeppelin sheds, minelaying expeditions to the Bight, or sweeps up the Norwegian coast. The area between the Shetlands, Iceland, and the Norwegian coast was termed the Grand Fleet's "front garden," and here tactical exercises—known as "P.Z.s"—would be performed.[52]

The submarine danger had indeed contributed the most toward making the North Sea for capital ships somewhat similar to the no-man's-land between the opposing trench systems on land. They would be risked there, but only for specific purposes. Sea power came to be exercised more and more by smaller craft, often not even originally built as warships. They included trawlers and drifters from the fishing fleets, and freighters or liners taken from the merchant service. This was particularly true of the blockade, that relentless, grinding daily exercise of sea power. The work was hardly glamorous and largely unknown to the public, who tended to think of sea power solely in terms of "real" warships.

The Tenth Cruiser Squadron was a prime example of this aspect of the naval war in northern waters. Its initial patrol area went from the Shetlands to Norway in the east and from the Shetlands to the coast of Scotland in the south. The first commander was Rear Admiral Dudley de Chair, who had eight *Edgar*-class cruisers, among the oldest in the Royal Navy. The duties included intercepting German merchantmen, and when these had disappeared from the high seas, intercepting neutrals carrying contraband to Germany.

The old *Edgar*-class cruisers were not up to the strain of working in heavy weather in these waters and the Admiralty concluded that all the cruisers would have to be replaced with armed merchant cruisers, and on 22 November ordered them back to port to pay off. De Chair hoisted his flag in the former Allan liner *Alsatian* (18,000 tons), a ship large enough to cope with the arduous conditions of the patrol. The theoretical strength of the squadron was to be twenty-four ships, although this many were not always available. The ships themselves were diverse, including a number of banana boats from the Caribbean trade. The Admiralty armed them at first with 4.7-inch guns taken from obsolete cruisers that had been broken up, but they soon realized that these would be inadequate against the potential armament of German raiders, or even submarines, and they were replaced with 6-inch guns as quickly as possible.

The captains of the armed merchant cruisers were usually regular naval officers; the other officers were temporary or permanent Royal Naval Reserve officers, and often their peacetime employment had been in the same ship. There was usually a party of

Royal Marines, but most of the ships' companies were reservists or former merchant marine ratings. Each ship also carried members of the Newfoundland Naval Reserve, and these former fishermen became famous for their expert small-boat handling in carrying officers and boarding parties to inspect intercepted ships in the rough waters. The weather was usually bad, and frequently too rough to lower boats. The boarding crews had an adventurous life, and the same could be said for prize crews in ships sent in to Kirkwall in the Orkneys. They were generally under a young midshipman, with only five or six armed bluejackets or marines who found themselves in a strange ship with a frequently none-too-friendly crew or an uncooperative master. As the number of interceptions went up, it often took several weeks before the prize crews could get back to their respective ships, and an armed merchant cruiser might have as many as sixteen crews away at the same time. These men were on the sharp end of the blockade; they were the ones who endured the almost inevitable friction with neutrals. Certain captains of the Norwegian American line seemed particularly hardheaded, and ostensibly neutral liners such as the *Bergensfjord* (10,666 tons) became notorious for playing a cat-and-mouse game and testing the blockader's skill. There were often other dangers for the prize crews, particularly if a submarine stopped or attacked the ship being taken in for examination.

On 5 November 1914, the Admiralty declared the entire North Sea a war area, and all ships passing through the line from northwest of the Hebrides to the Faeroes to Iceland would do so at their own peril. The Admiralty wanted all traffic, even that bound for Scandinavia, to pass through the English Channel, where it would be given sailing directions. These measures obviously caused great inconvenience for the northern neutrals, and eventually eight of the leading Scandinavian shipping companies received permission for their ships to go north about the British Isles provided they called at Kirkwall for inspection. The actual patrol areas changed in the course of the year, reflecting the submarine danger, the tightening of the blockade, and of course the seasons. In the summer months they even included the north of Iceland.

The work of the northern patrols was also to a large extent bound up with diplomacy. There was something of an adversarial relationship between the Foreign Office and the Admiralty over the enforcement of the blockade. The men often felt as if they were being let down by the authorities in Whitehall. In this the men of the Tenth Cruiser Squadron were in a similar situation to the German submariners and German diplomats. But there was a major difference. British blockade measures caused inconvenience and loss of property; German measures generally led to loss of life. In Britain the civilian arm of government had the final say and was firmly in control. Diplomatic considerations at times had to take precedence over purely military ones. There is no space here to give an account of the changing definitions of contraband or the legal measures enforcing the blockade, but their complexity often resulted in a ship that had been brought into Kirkwall being allowed to proceed.[53]

The work of these northern patrols can be sketched in this volume only in very broad terms.[54] The Tenth Squadron, after being steadily reduced, was finally abolished at the end of November 1917, for by then the United States, the source of much of the contraband, was safely in the war on the Allied side, and there was relatively little work for the squadron. By then 12,979 vessels had been intercepted, 1,816 sent in under armed guard, and an additional 2,039 reported voluntarily at British examination ports. The squadron failed to intercept 642 vessels. Seven of the armed merchant cruisers were lost to submarines, one was sunk in action with a raider (the *Alcantara* and the raider *Grief*, which also was sunk), and two foundered in heavy weather.[55] Rear Admiral Reginald Tupper, who succeeded de Chair as commander of the squadron in March 1916, proudly quoted the words of the First Lord Sir Eric Geddes shortly after the close of the war. Geddes remarked that in every case where an armistice was signed with their enemies, and even before, the one cry that went up was to release the blockade. Geddes declared: "If anything more strikingly demonstrating the value of sea power can be given, I do not know of it."[56]

Neither Tupper nor his predecessor de Chair ever forgot that the many facets of sea power were linked. The armed merchant cruisers were extremely vulnerable, and de Chair noted that if at dawn they had ever spotted a German battle cruiser in proximity, they would have been quickly sunk. Their only solution would have been to steam full speed straight at the enemy in the hope of getting within range before their guns were knocked out. A single battle cruiser could have sunk the entire blockading squadron. De Chair concluded, "Providentially, the Germans were afraid to risk a first class ship on such a venture although it would have paid them well to do so." Tupper also recognized that one properly built and commissioned German cruiser could have wiped out within twenty-four hours the whole squadron enforcing the strangling blockade of Germany. Tupper knew the reason why they never did. The German cruiser could not pass Scapa Flow: "the battleships at Scapa Flow prevented hostile cruisers from getting out to the Atlantic; thus they permitted the Tenth Cruiser Squadron to exist and carry on its work."[57]

Tupper may have been oversimplifying, but he made the essential point. The many facets of British sea power were linked; the armed merchant cruisers did the actual work, but it was the menacing presence of those great dreadnoughts, always ready to intervene if challenged, which enabled them to work undisturbed. The British also went to sea often, accepting the inevitable risks. In 1918 Geddes remarked at an Allied conference that the Grand Fleet had probably steamed more miles in a month than the Italian fleet had since the beginning of the war. By that steady, relentless work, innumerable sweeps and exercises, the British gained an intangible advantage in confidence and expertise, manifest in the morale of their officers and men, which would distinguish the Royal Navy in the course of the war. Ships were made to be risked within reason, not hoarded in port as a "fleet-in-being" or as bargaining chips for a future peace conference. There was something different about the Royal Navy—a mixture of tradition, confidence, and seamanship—hard to quantify, but definitely there.

3

THE MEDITERRANEAN: 1914–1915

The opening of the war in the North Sea had proved to be anticlimactic. The long-awaited battle for command of the sea that many had expected did not take place. Given the respective strategies of the British and the Germans, the ratio of forces, and the realities of modern warfare, this is less surprising in retrospect than it might have appeared at the time. But what of the Mediterranean? The Triple Alliance Naval Convention had originated in hopes that a combination of the rival but allied Austro-Hungarian and Italian fleets with the Mittelmeerdivision just might be enough to wrest control of the sea from the French fleet and whatever British forces were left in the Mediterranean after the British had concentrated their strength in the north. This hope may have been unrealistic, but at least on paper it was a possibility. The contingency of joint action by the Triple Alliance forces was a very real one for all parties concerned in the opening hours of the war.

The Italian Ministry of Marine, not fully cognizant of the exact terms of the Triple Alliance and its strictly defensive character, issued warning orders, and sealed orders went out on 29 July to various naval authorities outlining the circumstances under which Italian participation in the war on the side of Germany and Austria would take place.[1] The Germans, after the kaiser on 5 and 6 July had warned the armed forces to be prepared for all eventualities, sent the battle cruiser *Goeben* into dry dock at Pola, and experts sent down from Germany worked feverishly to replace defective boiler tubes. Rear Admiral Wilhelm Souchon, commanding the Mittelmeerdivision (consisting of the *Goeben* and new light cruiser *Breslau*), was determined to strike at French lines of communication regardless of any eventual combination with his allies. The primary interest of the Germans was to cut off the repatriation of French troops from North Africa.[2] Cooperation with Germany's allies could then follow.

The opening shots of the war were fired by the monitors of the Austro-Hungarian Danube flotilla on 28 July, when the Dual Monarchy declared war on Serbia (see chapter 9). The fact that aggressive action came from the Austrian side and without prior consultation about altering the status quo in the Balkans provided the Italian government with the justification to remain neutral. It was in every respect a most sensible move. The Italian naval staff was highly aware of Italy's long, vulnerable coastline, and the capo di stato maggiore, Vice Admiral Paolo Thaon di Revel, had a healthy respect for the improvements made by the French fleet in recent years. On 1 August he warned the Italian prime minister, Antonio Salandra, that if Great Britain should intervene on the side of the French, the Triple Alliance naval forces had scant possibility of victory and the Italian navy could not protect the exposed and vulnerable Italian coastal cities or keep open communications with the Italian colonies.[3] There were a variety of reasons for Italy's decision to remain neutral, but surely naval considerations must have had an important place among them. On 2 August the Italian government formally declared its neutrality, and with the Austrian fleet now hopelessly inferior to the French, the prospect of a great naval encounter in the Mediterranean disappeared and the Triple Alliance Naval Convention proved to be an illusion. The Italians had rendered one of their biggest services to the British and French during the war.

Souchon was at Messina when he learned of the Italian declaration of neutrality. He was now in a vulnerable position. Anticipating the outbreak of war with France, he was at sea steaming for the Algerian coast when news of the formal declaration of war came by wireless on the evening of 3 August. Souchon fired the opening shots of the war in the Mediterranean at 6:08 A.M. on the 3d when the *Goeben* bombarded Philippeville for ten minutes while the *Breslau* fired at Bône. French coastal batteries returned the fire. The physical damage on shore was minor; the psychological damage far greater. That afternoon Souchon received orders by wireless to break through to Constantinople, for the Germans and Turks had just concluded an alliance. He could not reach the Dardanelles without replenishing his bunkers, and he therefore headed back to Messina to coal. There was a tense moment when the Germans encountered the British battle cruisers *Indefatigable* and *Indomitable* steaming in the opposite direction. Great Britain and Germany were not yet in a state of war, and the British in this more-innocent age observed the traditional proprieties. The customary salutes were not exchanged, but the British could only turn and try to follow. Through the heroic efforts of the German engineers and stokers, the *Goeben* was able to take advantage of her speed and eventually outdistance them. Souchon was back at Messina on the 5th, but the Italian authorities gave him only twenty-four hours to remain in port. This was not sufficient time to refill his bunkers, and he had to arrange for a collier to meet him in the Aegean. Actually the Italian action may have been a blessing in disguise, for Messina was likely to become a magnet for British and French warships. Souchon also was alarmed to learn that a hitch had developed in obtaining Turkish permission to pass the Dardanelles, but, on learning the Austrian fleet would not be coming south to support him, he elected to gamble Turkish approval would be granted in time, and late on the afternoon of the 6th he left port for the dash to the east.

The threat of the Austrian fleet was very much on the minds of the British, for it had the potential to overwhelm their forces closing in on the *Goeben*. At 3:00 A.M. on the morning of 5 August the Austrian naval command received a somewhat garbled cable from Messina requesting the Austrian fleet to come at once, reporting British but no French ships off Messina, and asking the estimated time of arrival. The Germans had a clear assignment for the Austrians: proceed to Messina to the assistance of the Mittelmeerdivision. The Austrian naval commander did not consider this to be either wise or practical.

Admiral Anton Haus had been Marinekommandant and chief of the Marinesektion of the Ministry of War since February 1913. The sixty-three-year-old Haus was certainly the best known man in the k.u.k. Kriegsmarine and had been designated in the Triple Alliance Naval Convention to command the combined Austrian, Italian, and German naval forces in the Mediterranean. He was acknowledged as brilliant but with little patience for fools and was noted for his biting sarcasm.[4] Largely forgotten by all but specialists in Austrian or naval history, he easily could have had a significant place in history as winner or loser of a classic naval encounter in the Mediterranean had Italy not elected to remain neutral. On the outbreak of war with Serbia, Haus was concerned initially with the defense of Austria's southernmost Dalmatian coast and the blockade of the rather restricted coastline of Montenegro, Serbia's potential ally. The southern Austrian naval base in the Gulf of Cattaro was dominated by Montenegrin artillery on Mount Lovčen. The expansion of the war from a local to a general struggle, coupled with the defection of Italy, radically changed the situation. Haus was now faced with the need to counter suggestions by the chief of the Austrian general staff, Conrad von Hötzendorf, that the fleet move to the Dardanelles and operate with good effect against the Russians in the Black Sea before the overwhelmingly superior British and French could destroy it in the Adriatic. These suggestions were apparently instigated by the naval representative at Armeeoberkommando (AOK). Count Berchtold, the Austrian foreign minister, found the idea attractive, and for the next few days the Austrian Foreign Office pushed the proposal, hoping to delay a declaration of war with France and, possibly, to completely avoid a state of war with Great Britain. The Germans supported the proposal. This uncertainty over when and with whom Austria-Hungary would be at war added greatly to the concerns and influenced the actions of all the naval leaders in the Mediterranean.

The proposal to send the k.u.k. Kriegsmarine or a substantial portion of it to Constantinople was totally unrealistic. There would have been no adequate base available for it at Constantinople or elsewhere in the Black Sea, the fleet would have lacked sufficient stocks of coal, the fleet train was only partially mobilized, and, finally, there was a great danger of being overwhelmed by the superior French and British forces on the way. Furthermore—and this alone would have been decisive—such a move would have left Austria's coastline and security in the Adriatic at the mercy of the Italians. The Black Sea proposal was rejected out of hand.[5]

The request to assist the *Goeben* at Messina was more difficult to refuse. Austrian mobilization on 5 August was not complete, but Haus could count on three dreadnoughts, three *Radetzky*-class semidreadnoughts, two armored cruisers, and at least twelve destroyers and high-seas torpedo boats. He knew the British were concentrating on Messina and his fleet would have been superior to them. But he did not know the location of the much larger French fleet (potentially two to four dreadnoughts, six semidreadnoughts, and five or more predreadnoughts), which he knew had sailed from Toulon early on the morning of the 4th. Haus estimated that the French could arrive off Messina twenty to twenty-four hours earlier than the Austrians, and French ships from Bizerte even sooner, for Bizerte is 350 miles closer to Messina than Pola is. He also had somewhat conflicting orders from the Austrian Foreign Ministry, anxious to escape war with Great Britain, to be very careful to avoid conflict with British warships and to support the *Goeben* and *Breslau* only when they were actually under the protection of the Austrian fleet in Austrian territorial waters.

When Souchon broke out of Messina, he was reported to be heading for the Adriatic, and the Admiralstab asked the Austrian fleet to come at least as far south as the parallel of Brindisi. This put the situation in a different light, and Haus sailed on the morning of 7 August. Morale was high in the Austrian fleet, but there was also considerable tension, because the position of the superior French fleet was still unknown. Were they too heading for the Adriatic?

Souchon's move toward the Adriatic had been only a feint, and when Haus was informed the Germans were actually headed east, he was off Cape Planka. He promptly returned to Pola. The major encounter between the Austrian, French, and British forces would never take place. The reluctance of the Austrians to rush out of the Adriatic to Souchon's rescue at Messina or to send their fleet to Constantinople left a certain chill in Austro-German relations, with sarcasm or bitterness on the part of some German naval officers and a certain defensiveness in Austrian literature.[6] Given the realities of the situation in August 1914, however, one cannot really fault the Austrians.

The French fleet that had worried the Austrians so much was actually nowhere near Messina, for the commander in chief of the 1ère armée navale—the major French force in the Mediterranean—was preoccupied with the protection of the troop transport between Algeria and metropolitan France, and, from the information at his disposal, convinced the Germans would operate in the western rather than the central or eastern Mediterranean. Like Haus, Vice Admiral Augustin Boué de Lapeyrère would miss his place in naval history because of Italy's decision to remain neutral. Lapeyrère would have commanded the French and British forces in a major naval encounter. There was nothing the sixty-two-year-old Gascon would have liked better, for he was offensively minded and as minister of marine from 1909 to 1911 and commander in chief of the 1ère armée navale since 1911 had played a major role in the renaissance of the French fleet and in training it for what he had assumed would be a classic naval battle against the forces of the Triple Alliance.[7]

Unfortunately Lapeyrère's intense desire to close with the enemy battle fleet conflicted with the primary objective of the French Ministry of War, the repatriation of the XIXème corps from North Africa. The problem was not new; the Ministries of War and Marine had been arguing over it for more than forty years.[8] Lapeyrère objected to relegating his fleet to the role of convoy escort with the movements of transports determined by the fixed mobilization plans of the army. He naturally wanted to be free to assume the offensive at the beginning of the war. The Ministry of War, on the other hand, agreed to transports sailing independently instead of in convoy but insisted on the fixed timetable. Lapeyrère countered with the argument that only the naval commander in chief could determine when it would be safe for ships to sail. The question had supposedly been settled in May 1913 by the Conseil Supérieur de la Défense Nationale, which, not surprisingly, ruled that it was more important to get the troops needed for the anticipated decisive frontier battles to France as soon as possible. The transports would sail independently according to the fixed schedule, covered indirectly by the anticipated offensive of the French fleet, and more closely by a special division consisting of an old battleship and seven elderly protected or armored cruisers that would concentrate east of the line Toulon-Algiers, roughly halfway between the French and Algerian coasts. The effectiveness of this protection was questionable, especially by 1914, when it was obvious the *Goeben* and *Breslau* would remain in the Mediterranean. Their speed was a source of great concern to Lapeyrère, as was the powerful armament of the *Goeben*. There was nothing in the French fleet to match her.

On 28 July, the day Austria-Hungary declared war on Serbia, Lapeyrère proposed increasing the special division covering the transport to six old battleships that would escort two successive convoys sailing from Oran and Algiers, while he would pursue the enemy with the major portion of the French battle fleet. The Ministry of Marine, now thoroughly irate, replied that the agreed plan could not be changed at the last moment and that the transports would have to sail independently at the fixed dates. Lapeyrère, however, took advantage of a clause in his orders authorizing the formation of convoys if no significant delay resulted. This authorization was abrogated by the signal from the ministry announcing the outbreak of hostilities with Germany, which reached the fleet at 1:15 in the morning on 4 August. By then Lapeyrère was at sea, having sailed with the major portion of his fleet at 4 A.M. on the 3d. There was a series of signals exchanged between the ministry and Lapeyrère in which the commander in chief resisted demands to sail the transports independently. The transport was, however, very much on his mind in his subsequent actions.

Lapeyrère, once he was reasonably sure Italy would remain neutral and Britain would be an ally—despite the ministry's inexcusable delay later in informing him of the official declaration of Italian neutrality—divided his fleet into three groups headed toward the coast of Algeria. Lapeyrère interpreted the bits of intelligence that reached him through the fog of war as pointing to the western basin of the Mediterranean becoming the decisive area. There were, for example, reports the Germans had colliers in the Balearic Islands and that the latter would serve as bases for attacking the French convoys. The French fleet therefore missed Souchon after the *Goeben* and *Breslau* had raided the Algerian coast, and by the time the presence of the Germans at Messina was signaled on the 6th, some of Lapeyrère's ships needed to coal, and he remained convinced the ultimate objective of the Germans was either the Austrian base at Pola or a breakout into the Atlantic.[9] French forces were therefore far from the scene when Souchon came out of Messina and headed for the Dardanelles. Would their presence have made a difference? The fact France and Austria-Hungary were not yet at war might have inhibited French action in any pursuit into the Adriatic, while respect for Italian neutrality would have prevented a really close blockade. Perhaps even more important, once the *Goeben* got to sea the French had nothing large enough to damage her that could catch her.

All of this meant that the primary task of destroying the *Goeben* after she broke out fell on the British. French and British coordination at the very beginning of the war was difficult because the Entente Cordiale had not been a binding alliance, and the British had been careful to limit their prewar contacts in the Mediterranean.[10] Moreover, the orders to Vice Admiral Sir Archibald Milne, the British commander in chief in the Mediterranean, had the effect of drawing his attention to the French transport. On 30 July the Admiralty informed him that his first task would be to assist the French transport by covering and, if possible, engaging individual fast German ships such as the *Goeben*, but to avoid being brought to action against superior forces except in combination with the French as part of a general battle. He was also to avoid becoming seriously engaged with Austrian forces before Italy's attitude was clarified, and when it was, Milne was subsequently ordered to respect Italian neutrality and not allow any of his ships to come within 6 miles of the Italian coast. This meant British warships could not enter the 2-mile-wide Strait of Messina.[11]

When Souchon broke out of Messina, he feinted toward the Adriatic and then turned eastward. Captain Howard Kelly in the light cruiser *Gloucester* followed and exchanged fire with the *Breslau*, but had to break off pursuit on the afternoon of the 7th when his bunkers were nearly empty. This left Rear Admiral E. C. T. Troubridge patrolling south of Corfu off Cephalonia. Troubridge commanded the First Cruiser Squadron, consisting of the armored cruisers *Defence, Black Prince, Duke of Edinburgh,* and *Warrior.* Troubridge could have intercepted the *Goeben.* He began a move toward this objective, but, finally, influenced by his flag captain Fawcett Wray, turned away after deciding that to engage would be a violation of orders not to engage a superior force. His cruisers had only 9.2-inch and 7.5-inch guns and might have been destroyed by the faster *Goeben*'s 11-inch guns before they could get within range. Souchon therefore had a clear run to the Aegean, for Milne with the three battle cruisers wasted twenty-four hours by diverting northward to combine with Troubridge at the entrance to the Adriatic after receiving an erroneous signal on 8 August to commence hostilities with Austria.[12] Souchon coaled unmolested in the Aegean at the island of Denusa, near Naxos, and was eventually allowed by the Turkish government to enter the Dardanelles on the evening of the 10th. Thanks to the fumbling of their enemies, the *Goeben* and *Breslau* had escaped to exercise an important role for the remainder of the war.[13]

The escape of the *Goeben* and *Breslau* opened the war on a sour note for the British and French, far overshadowing any Austro-German coolness over the reluctance of Haus to rush to the aid of Souchon at Messina. Actually Haus's action was a blessing in disguise, for the *Goeben* might then have been bottled up in the Adriatic. It is interesting to see how the differing dates for the respective declarations of war managed to upset everyone. Troubridge's decision not to engage was probably the most controversial, because he had interpreted his orders to avoid action with superior forces as meaning to avoid the *Goeben* rather than the Austrian fleet, which the Admiralty had intended. Troubridge was later tried before a court martial for failing to engage the *Goeben* but was "fully and honourably" acquitted. He was not, however, employed at sea again, although he was later given command of the British mission to Serbia, where he would have an adventurous time (see chapter 9). Milne's conduct was approved by the Admiralty, at least on the surface, but he too was never employed again.[14]

The escape of the *Goeben* had its effect in France too, and Lapeyrère was the subject of fierce criticism, particularly after he relinquished his command in October 1915. A retired naval officer and nationalist deputy, Vice Admiral Bienaimé, led the attack, which culminated in hearings before the Chamber of Deputies Commission de la Marine de Guerre in 1917. The hearings, in which the minister of marine in the first year of the war, Victor Augagneur, strongly backed Lapeyrère, provided an insight into the personal animosities and rivalries within the French navy among the minister, the commander in chief, and the naval staff. Charles Chaumet, former president of the commission, himself became minister in August 1917 and conducted his own enquiry. These enquiries resulted in at least a partial exoneration for Lapeyrère. The general conclusions were that although he had used the fleet to convoy transports despite orders not to, the minister had declared that he approved and covered the dispositions taken, and in view of the speed of the *Goeben*, it was impossible to affirm that if offensive measures against her had been taken from the first day of operations the enemy cruisers would have been destroyed.[15]

The Ottoman government evaded any British and French protests over sheltering the *Goeben* and *Breslau* by announcing it had "purchased" the ships, and in a formal ceremony on 16 August, both hoisted the Turkish flag. The Turks were able to justify their action by claiming the ships were substitutes for the two dreadnoughts, the *Sultan Osman* and *Reshadieh*, which they had been building in Great Britain and which had been seized by the British on the outbreak of war although Turkish crews had already arrived to bring them out. Churchill had been well advised to seize the ships, which became the *Agincourt* and *Erin* in British service, for after the signature of the Turkish-German alliance on 2 August, the Ottoman government had offered to send the *Sultan Osman* to a German port. Turkish public opinion was incensed because the two ships had been the object of public subscription and had been symbolic of Turkish aspirations to avenge the losses of the Balkan Wars. The Turks were not mollified by an Admiralty offer of a fixed payment per day for their use for the duration of the war. The *Goeben* now became the *Jawus Sultan Selim* and the *Breslau* became the *Midilli*, and Souchon later became chief of the Turkish fleet (*Befehlshaber der schwimmenden Türkischen Streitkräfte*). The sale was a fiction, and it was also not until 23 September that the Turks offered Souchon command of the Turkish fleet and general supervision over a naval reform program to be undertaken by a German naval mission. Souchon was appointed a vice admiral in the Ottoman navy while remaining a rear admiral on active service in the German navy.[16] The wearing of Turkish uniforms and fezzes was another pretext, used only for ceremonial purposes, and few Turkish personnel initially joined the ships. On the other hand, the Germans became trapped in their fiction, for after a short time it was very difficult to take the ships back without alienating the Turks. Souchon and the Admiralstab were also far from happy over the prospect of having to fight under the Turkish rather than their own flag.[17]

There were other disadvantages as well, as the *Goeben* and *Breslau* were now removed from the Mediterranean scene with little likelihood of ever joining the Austrian fleet and more easily bottled up in the Dardanelles than they would have been in the Adriatic. The French troop transport was virtually undisturbed, and for the next several months the British and French enjoyed the free use of the Mediterranean. They made good use of it, and large convoys and a steady stream of shipping brought men and supplies to the western front with the Germans powerless to impede it. Yet the Germans had gained a significant diplomatic advantage, because the *Goeben*, as one historian expressed it, greatly facilitated, although not necessarily caused, Turkish entry into the war on the side of Germany.[18]

While the fate of the *Goeben* was still undecided on 6 August, the First Sea Lord of the Admiralty, Prince Louis of Battenberg, and Captaine de vaisseau Schwerer, subchief of the French naval staff, concluded a convention in London that gave the French the general direction of naval operations in the Mediterranean. The British naval forces in the Mediterranean would cooperate with the French fleet until the *Goeben* was destroyed, but once this was accomplished, the three battle cruisers and two or three armored cruisers would regain their liberty of action unless the Italians broke their neutrality. The British forces remaining in the Mediterranean, namely, one or two armored cruisers, four light cruisers, sixteen destroyers, and the mobile defenses of Malta and Gibraltar, would be placed under the orders of the French commander in chief, and Malta and Gibraltar would serve as bases for the French. The French navy would assure the protection of British as well as French commerce throughout the Mediterranean and also would watch the exits of the Suez Canal, as well as the Straits of Gibraltar, to prevent enemy cruisers or auxiliary cruisers from entering the Mediterranean. If war was declared between Austria and France, the French would act against Austrian naval forces and assure a vigorous surveillance of the entrance to the Adriatic.[19] The Anglo-French Convention of 6 August 1914 reveals to what a startling extent the British were ready at the beginning of the war to turn over their historic role in the Mediterranean to the French in order to concentrate against the Germans in the North Sea, where they anticipated the decisive encounters would take place. The British discovered, as the war became a protracted one, that their interests in the Mediterranean were simply too great to entrust everything to the French, and they were forced to devote more and more resources to this theater.

Actually, the ink was hardly dry on the convention when the British realized that they could not abandon as much in the Mediterranean to the French as they might have desired. The *Goeben* had escaped, and this now meant that the battle cruisers *Indomitable* and *Indefatigable*, supported by the *Gloucester*, had to keep close watch off the Dardanelles. The news that German crews were to remain in the *Goeben* and *Breslau* despite their alleged sale to Turkey led the Admiralty on 15 August to order the armored cruiser *Defence*, all available British destroyers, and the destroyer tender *Blenheim* to the Dardanelles. Although Lapeyrère retained theoretical command over these British forces, in practice the eastern Aegean was to become what amounted to a British zone outside of direct French control.[20]

Lapeyrère was not terribly concerned with the Dardanelles and apparently happy to leave watching them to the British. The *transport spéciale* was his first major concern, and once that was successfully accomplished, he was preoccupied with the Austrian fleet in the Adriatic. In the beginning the French government was as reluctant to declare war on the Austrians as the Austrians were to declare war on the French. The French had, however, to take their Russian allies into account, for the Russians were and would remain apprehensive that the Austrian fleet might go to the Dardanelles for operations in the Black Sea. There was, as we have seen, little basis in reality for this concern.

By 13 August the French had finally declared war on the Austrians, and the minister of marine ordered Lapeyrère to undertake immediate action against the Austrians with a view to influencing the Italians. He left the choice of an objective up to Lapeyrère. The French actually had no plan for war against Austria alone, but the naval staff hoped the demonstration might lead to the Austrian fleet coming out for a decisive battle and cause the Austrians to lift their blockade of the Montenegrin coast. The naval staff did not consider an attack on the major Austrian naval base at Pola possible, and penetration into the Gulf of Cattaro would be equally difficult. Lapeyrère's solution was a sweep into the Adriatic to surprise the Austrian ships blockading the Montenegrin coast. Joined on 16 August by Troubridge's cruisers and destroyers, the French fleet managed to cut off the small Austrian cruiser *Zenta* off Antivari and overwhelm it. An Austrian destroyer managed to get away.[21] The operation used the proverbial hammer to swat a flea, and naturally the Austrian fleet was sensible enough to refrain from coming out to certain defeat. A curious feature of many prewar plans was the near total absence of what to do next if the enemy fleet did not come out to do battle.[22] Lapeyrère was now faced with the problem of what action to take while his fleet consumed about five thousand tons of coal and one thousand tons of fuel oil per day. He needed a base in the Adriatic or near its entrance, but the search for one was complicated by the necessity to respect Italian and Greek neutrality. The French navy also possessed little in the way of colliers or oilers. As Admiral Docteur later put it, the naval authorities seemed to think that a battle would take place off the piers of Toulon in the first days of a war. In good weather the French were able to improvise limited replenishment at sea, but Lapeyrère was eventually forced to establish a system of rotation between the Adriatic and distant Malta for replenishment and essential chores such as boiler cleaning.[23]

The French had difficulty bringing their superior force to bear on the Austrians. Haus would do little to oblige them, especially after the loss of the *Zenta*. Moreover, he kept a wary eye on his former ally Italy. As long as the possibility existed that Italy might attack Austria, he considered it his first duty to keep the Austrian fleet intact as much as possible "for the decisive struggle" against the Austrians' "most dangerous foe." He would therefore risk little against the British and French, for even a glorious victory that resulted in heavy losses would be much more harmful than useful. He had the full support of Kaiser Franz Joseph in this policy.[24]

The lack of a major fleet action or serious landing attempt in the Adriatic did not preclude minor operations with limited risks on both sides. The Austrians operated against the Montenegrin coast, which was restricted in length and where the Montenegrin port of Antivari was only 35 miles from Cattaro. The French made periodic sweeps into the Adriatic, frequently to cover ships carrying supplies to Montenegro. The French operations hardly troubled the Austrians. A serious operation against Cattaro certainly would have, and the Austrian naval base in the gulf—commonly referred to in the Austrian navy as the *Bocche*—was vulnerable, relatively isolated, and dominated by Montenegrin guns on Mount Lovčen. The navy studied the project, but any serious expedition was vetoed by the French army's general staff.[25] General Joffre, chief of the general staff, opposed any expedition against the Austrians anywhere in the Balkans. The army could not spare troops from the western front, and it was necessary to defeat the Germans, not the Austrians. At the beginning of 1915, he ordered the Operations Bureau of the general staff to prepare a paper to "kill the project in the egg."[26] The expedition against Cattaro as far as the French were concerned would never occur. The Italians, the British, and the Americans all considered projects against the Dalmatian coast during the war, but for various reasons the plans came to nothing. The common thread was that there always seemed to be better places to employ troops. Cattaro remained in Austrian hands and was eventually used as a valuable submarine base until the end of the war.

The French eventually and with great difficulty established artillery on Mount Lovčen, but the Austrians took effective measures in their own defense. When the French 15-cm guns on Mount Lovčen were finally in a position to open fire on 15 October, they found themselves faced with strong counterbattery fire from the 24-cm guns of the small, old *Monarch*-class battleships in the Bocche. On 21 October Haus sent the semidreadnought *Radetzky* to Cattaro, and her 30.5-cm (12-inch) guns were decisive. The French artillerymen on Mount Lovčen were forced to evacuate their positions.[27]

Haus continued his refusal to be drawn into a risky and what some Austrian officers termed a *hurrah* action against the French despite pressure from some Austrian and German quarters. It was the old embarrassing question, at a time when the army was fighting so hard with such heavy losses: What is the navy doing? This pressure became particularly strong after the beginning of the Dardanelles campaign (see chapter 5). The Austrians could provide strong technical reasons for it being impracticable to send desperately needed ammunition to the Turks by means of an Austrian light cruiser or to use any of their handful of submarines to attack Allied warships off the Straits.[28] The inability of the Austrians to do this would be the major reason why the Germans eventually established their own submarine force in the Mediterranean (see chapter 12).

In March 1915 it was more difficult for the Austrians to reject a German request for a diversionary attack on the French at the mouth of the Adriatic for the purpose of drawing Allied ships away from the Dardanelles. Haus had the courage of his convictions and defended what was to many an inglorious and certainly an unpopular position with a classic statement of defensive strategy. He argued that despite their great superiority, the French had not really achieved anything in the Adriatic, and their blockade line had been forced farther to the south. If the Austrian fleet could not get out of the Adriatic—and where would it go or what would it want to do?—the French had not been able to seriously disturb Austrian shipping along the Dalmatian coast. The strategy of patient waiting, the fleet-in-being, was the only rational one for the Austrians because Lapeyrère had nothing to do with the Dardanelles landings and none of the French ships reported at the Dardanelles had come from the Adriatic. Even an Austrian success at the mouth of the Adriatic would not alter the situation at the Dardanelles. Haus argued that it was difficult to make many men understand that in certain cases not to do anything was the only correct thing.[29]

The great limitation on the exercise of French naval superiority was of course the submarine. The k.u.k. Kriegsmarine had a mere seven in service in the autumn of 1914, with the two oldest suitable only for local defense or training. The French continued to provide large targets for Austrian submarines with their periodic sweeps into the Adriatic to cover supplies sent to Montenegro. Finally, on 21 December *U.12* torpedoed Lapeyrère's flagship *Jean Bart*. The torpedo struck the bow, and the dreadnought's watertight compartmentation prevented her from sinking. Lapeyrère drew the inevitable conclusion—sweeps into the Adriatic were not worth the risk—and the French blockade became a distant one of the Strait of Otranto.[30] The French armored cruisers patrolled a line along the parallel of Paxos (north of Corfu), accompanied by destroyers when winter weather permitted. The French made a brave effort with their own submarines, and on 8 December the *Curie* was sunk in a daring attempt to penetrate Pola. She was salvaged and put into service as the Austrian *U.14*.

Political and diplomatic pressure forced the French to continue sending at least some supplies to Montenegro, and Lapeyrère eventually tried to use small neutral Italian steamers to run up to the little Albanian port of San Giovanni di Medua. Antivari, farther to the north, was too dangerous, and the French lost their first ship in the Adriatic, the destroyer *Dague*, to a mine off Antivari on 24 February. The port became very hazardous because of Austrian naval raids and bombing by Austrian aircraft. It grew much safer, although it took longer and was more difficult, to send supplies to Montenegro by means of Salonika, then by rail north to Ipek in Serbia, and then overland to Montenegro.

The French also remained vulnerable. Anticipating Austrian naval activity as a result of Allied negotiations with Italy in April 1915, Lapeyrère moved his patrol line farther to the north. On the night of 26–27 April the Austrian submarine *U.5*, commanded by Linienschiffsleutnant Georg Ritter von Trapp (later well known in the United States as the father of the Trapp family singers of *The Sound of Music*), torpedoed and sank the French armored cruiser *Léon Gambetta*, which went down with the loss of 684 lives. The French cruiser patrol was moved back south of the parallel of Georghambo on Cephalonia, except for indispensable sweeps made at high speed to the mouth of the Adriatic. The heavy use of Malta at this time for the needs of the Dardanelles expedition meant the French cruisers would have to go all the way to Bizerte to coal, reducing still more the effectiveness of the French blockade of the Strait of Otranto.[31] The situation in the Adriatic was a stalemate. The larger French warships could not operate without considerable risk, and lacking a convenient base, the French submarines could not operate effectively either. The Austrians could not get out, assuming they wanted to. The major question by the end of April 1915 was whether the entry of Italy into the war on the side of the Allies would change the situation (see chapter 6).

The other major event of significance for the Mediterranean in 1914 was the entry of Turkey into the war on the side of Germany and Austria-Hungary. This had serious repercussions for the British and French. It would cut off easy access to Russia through the Black Sea and probably reduce Russia's effectiveness as an ally. It would also require substantial forces to protect the Suez Canal and Mesopotamian oil fields (see chapter 5). The maintenance of those forces would also require significant maritime commitments that were felt when the submarine campaign developed later. On the other hand, the fact that the Ottoman Empire was now an enemy provided the British, French, and Russians with new opportunities for imperial gains at Turkey's expense. The common wisdom had been that the escape of the *Goeben* and *Breslau* brought about Turkey's entry into the war with Constantinople held under the threat of the big German guns. This is an overstatement; the situation was far more complex than that, and as previously stated, the *Goeben* probably facilitated but did not necessarily cause the Turkish action.[32]

Initially Souchon felt frustrated by Turkish neutrality, longing to get at the Russians with his ships. Command of the Turkish fleet was a dubious honor. The major units were the two old former German battleships *Hairredin Barbarossa* and *Torgud Reis*, launched in 1891 and purchased from Germany in 1910. There were two protected cruisers, both launched in 1903 and rather slow for working with the *Goeben* and *Breslau*, and eight relatively modern French- or German-built destroyers. German officers and men from the Mittelmeerdivision, and later sent out from Germany, were seconded to the Turkish ships. The destroyer flotilla received a German officer as commodore and would probably offer the Germans their best opportunities. Two German liners, the *General* and *Corcovado*, served as depot or accommodation ships. Somewhat awkwardly, the British naval mission to the Turkish fleet under Admiral Sir Arthur Limpus remained in Constantinople after the outbreak of war. The members were relegated to shore duties until finally expelled in mid-September.[33]

The defense of the Dardanelles was an obvious and major concern, and Souchon asked for experts from home. By early September approximately four hundred naval artillerymen and mine specialists were formed into a Sonderkommando under Admiral Guido von Usedom, who later received the title "inspector-general of coastal fortifications and minefields." Souchon considered the Strait secure by 20 September.[34]

The Ottoman government and the Allies were on a collision course. The British never really accepted the fiction of the "sale" of the *Goeben* and *Breslau*, and on 27 August the Admiralty ordered Troubridge, then commanding the British forces off the Dardanelles, to attack the ships if they came out, regardless of what flag they wore. Because of the known presence of Germans in other Turkish warships, the cabinet later ordered the sinking of any that tried to get out of the Dardanelles. After Limpus had been expelled by the Turks, Churchill and Battenberg wanted to take advantage of his local knowledge and give him command of the forces off the Dardanelles. This was vetoed by the Foreign Office, which still hoped to preserve Turkish neutrality and thought the action would be unnecessarily provocative. Limpus therefore replaced Vice Admiral Carden as admiral superintendent at Malta, and Carden took command off the Dardanelles.[35] It is an intriguing question whether Limpus's expertise would have made any difference to the subsequent Dardanelles campaign or what his qualities of leadership would have been. He proved to be an excellent and generally praised administrator at Malta.

The French, at British request, sent two predreadnoughts to the Dardanelles in order to match the two battleships in the Ottoman fleet, and on 25 September the British tightened the blockade further by informing the Turks that, knowing German methods, any Turkish warships coming out of the Dardanelles under present conditions were to be regarded as having the intention of attacking some British interest. The British sent back a Turkish destroyer trying to enter the Aegean on the night of 26 September because Germans were found on board. The Turkish and German reply was predictable: they closed the last narrow channel through the Dardanelles minefields, and the route to Russia via the Black Sea was thereby completely cut off by the 29th.[36]

The pro-German factions within the Young Turk government, whose best-known leader was the minister of war Enver Pasha, succeeded in maneuvering Turkey into the war during the month of October with the enthusiastic connivance of Souchon. On 22 October Enver provided Souchon with sealed orders to attack the Russian fleet wherever it was found. Souchon went beyond this, deciding to attack the Russian coast in advance of any encounter at sea.[37] Souchon decided to leave the two slow old battleships in port but used all other Turkish warships fit for sea. On the evening of the 27th, the Ottoman fleet left the Bosphorus "for exercises," steamed eastward to deceive a Russian postal steamer stationed off the Strait, and then separated into four parts. The *Goeben*, two destroyers, and a minelayer were to attack Sebastopol; the *Breslau* and a Turkish cruiser were to attack the strait at Kertsch and then Novorossisk; another Turkish cruiser was to attack Feodosia; and two destroyers and a minelayer were to attack Odessa. The attacks took place on the morning of the 29th. A Russian gunboat, the *Donetz*, was sunk at Odessa; the old minelayer *Prut* was sunk off Sebastopol; a few Russian warships were damaged; and approximately six merchant ships were sunk or captured (see chapter 8). The Turkish-German force returned unscathed.[38] Souchon, the man who had initiated hostilities in the Mediterranean, also initiated them in the Black Sea and boasted to his wife: "I have thrown the Turks into the powder-keg and kindled war between Russia and Turkey."[39]

The Turkish-German aggression had failed to inflict any significant damage on the Russian Black Sea Fleet, but it had the diplomatic effect the Germans wanted. The Russians did not accept the Turkish alibi that the Russians had attacked first and on 31 October declared war on the Turks. The British and French delivered an ultimatum, and on 1 November the British destroyers *Wolverine* and *Scorpion* were ordered to cut out a large armed yacht in the Gulf of Smyrna that was supposedly laying mines. The yacht was set afire by her own crew and blew up. The Admiralty ordered Carden to make a demonstration by bombardment against the forts at the entrance to the Dardanelles without, however, risking ships and retiring before counterfire became effective. On 3 November the battle cruisers *Indefatigable* and *Indomitable*, joined by the French battleships *Suffren* and *Vérité* under Rear Admiral Guépratte, began the bombardment. The Suddel Bahr fort suffered considerable damage, and a magazine exploded. On 5 November the British declared war on Turkey.[40]

One might argue that the opening shots of the Dardanelles campaign had been fired. This bombardment in early November was not followed up and has often been criticized as serving only to alert the Turks to the danger at the Strait. The argument is not really valid, however. The Germans were perfectly well aware of the danger and, as we have seen, had been working at making this obviously vital point secure.[41]

The naval war in the Mediterranean had begun with mixed results for the British and French. They enjoyed unchallenged control of the sea as a result of Italy's defection from the Triple Alliance, and that control would not be disturbed until the arrival of German submarines later in 1915. The Austrian fleet was bottled up in the Adriatic where, however, due to changed conditions of warfare the French were not able to effectively exert their superior strength. The chain of errors allowing the *Goeben* and *Breslau* to escape also led, at least indirectly, to Turkish entry into the war with the closure of the Black Sea route to Russia and potential threats to the Suez Canal. It remained to be seen in 1915 if the damage could be undone by the British and French expedition to the Dardanelles and if Italian entry into the war would alter the situation in the Adriatic.

4

SWEEPING THE SEAS

THE DEFENSE OF ALLIED TRADE

On the first of July 1914, 8,587 steamers and 653 sailing vessels representing approximately nineteen million gross tons flew the red duster—the British mercantile ensign. If one included the overseas dominions, the tonnage rose to twenty-one million, or approximately 43 percent of the world's shipping. The Germans were a distant second with 2,090 steamers and 298 sailing vessels, approximately 5.5 million tons, or nearly 12 percent of the world's tonnage.[1] The United States, Norway, France, and Japan jockeyed for third place, but were far behind and at barely more than a third of the German total.

The huge volume of British shipping, however, implied a certain vulnerability. The Germans did not have to look far to harm British interests; wherever they went on most shipping lanes, they were bound to find attractive targets flying the British flag. Furthermore, it was a well-known fact that Great Britain as an island nation had to import food to survive. In the five years before the war, nearly two-thirds of British foodstuffs came from abroad, and the proportion was particularly high in terms of cereals. The British also had to import sizable quantities of other essential commodities, iron ore, manganese, colonial products such as tin and rubber, and, of course, petroleum products.

British interests were also worldwide. Not only was there much to protect, but it had to be protected all over the globe. Could the Germans hurt the British by striking at this trade? The answer was yes, they could and did inflict considerable damage. But the very volume of British shipping made it extremely difficult for the Germans to do enough damage in comparison to the vast amount of that trade to really hurt. The British successfully met the challenge of German surface attack on their trade in the first six months of the war. This resulted in a certain complacency still evident in British writing on the subject. The complacency vanished, however, once the Germans turned their submarines primarily against commerce.

What was the extent of the threat the Germans could pose to British trade at the beginning of the war? The British and French blockade naturally sought to prevent German forces from breaking out of the confines of European waters. But what of German forces abroad when the war began? These were certainly a potential threat. The Germans had the third largest empire in the world in 1914, although the European population was small and the colonies were run at a deficit.

Tsingtau was probably the most important of the German possessions from a naval point of view, for it was the base of the East Asiatic Cruiser Squadron under the command of Vice Admiral Maximilian Graf von Spee. Spee's flagship *Scharnhorst* and her sister ship *Gneisenau* were the newest of the armored cruisers, armed with eight 8.2-inch and six 5.9-inch guns, well protected and capable of 20 knots. They were also crack ships, winners of prizes for their gunnery. Spee's squadron also included the light cruisers *Emden, Nürnberg,* and *Leipzig.*

The Germans also had the light cruiser *Königsberg* on the east coast of Africa and the light cruisers *Dresden* and *Karlsruhe* in the Caribbean, where the turmoil in Mexico had attracted warships from other nations to protect their nationals. The Germans, like other colonial powers, also had the usual assortment of gunboats, surveying vessels, river gunboats, and other minor craft not fit for a real naval encounter. On the outbreak of war, those in the Far East either scrambled for the temporary security of Tsingtau—where the old torpedo boat *S.90* gave a good account of herself—or, in the case of some river gunboats, were laid up in Chinese ports. Other German naval vessels led a fugitive existence but were eventually captured, sunk, or interned. They were not a serious naval factor.

In addition to regular warships, the potential threat of German auxiliary cruisers was taken very seriously by the British. The Germans, with the second largest merchant marine in the world, possessed a number of fast liners that could have been converted into auxiliary cruisers and set loose on the trade routes. Before the war the naval powers provided subsidies for certain vessels to have their decks strengthened so that guns could be mounted after the outbreak of hostilities, and the prewar naval literature discussed the subject at length. Naval annuals such as *Jane's Fighting Ships* regularly included silhouettes and particulars of liners capable of being employed as auxiliary cruisers. Aside from those that might be fitted out in German ports and then sent to break out into the high seas, the beginning of the war caught considerable numbers of German merchant ships far from home. The ships sought shelter in neutral ports, and the British and French feared they might secretly be converted, evade neutrality regulations, and put to sea. This meant that throughout the world, in places as scattered as Manila, Lisbon, Genoa, Buenos Aires, or New York, the British had to watch these liners as well as other interned merchantmen that might be used as storeships or colliers for raiders or for Spee's squadron. This was primarily a British responsibility; the French helped wherever they could, but outside of the Mediterranean and English Channel, they had relatively few resources. The Russians also provided a little assistance in the Far East, but the realities of geography kept the great bulk of

Russian naval forces in the Baltic or the Black Sea. The threat from auxiliary cruisers turned out to be exaggerated, but there were some and they did do damage, and had the Allies been less vigilant they might have accomplished much more.

In conducting cruiser warfare, the Germans suffered from an almost insoluble problem—their lack of overseas bases. Unlike the great corsairs of the seventeenth or eighteenth century, which could keep to the sea for long periods of time and need touch land only to replenish water and food, modern warships needed coal at regular intervals. The Hague Convention of 1907 restricted the amount of coal a warship could obtain in a neutral port to that necessary to reach the nearest port of her own country—which in practical terms usually meant full bunkers for German warships overseas—but the warship could not coal again in the same neutral territory for a full three months. The Germans could evade this by coaling at sea from supply ships. Coaling, though, was a laborious process, notorious in all navies, and the British had begun the strategic gamble of shifting to fuel oil in order to escape its limitations. Coaling was hard enough in port; the Germans would be forced at times to attempt it on the open sea. They would have preferred to use isolated anchorages in neutral waters, but these were not always available.[2]

The Germans attempted to solve the potential difficulty before the war through the establishment of the *Etappe* system. Areas where cruiser operations were likely to take place were divided into zones. The *Etappenoffizier* in charge of each Etappe coordinated the activities in each zone directed at supplying cruisers or auxiliary cruisers with coal and provisions. German commercial representatives, particularly those involved with shipping concerns, also played an important role. Coal, fuel oil, drinking water, provisions, and other supplies were also dispatched to predetermined points, known to the captains of the German cruisers.[3]

The Etappe system was an interesting attempt to circumvent the lack of overseas bases. It was only partially successful. The German officials constantly skirmished with the various neutral authorities over neutrality regulations, and after the war broke out, there was a cat-and-mouse game between the Germans and the diplomatic and mercantile representatives of the Allies in numerous neutral harbors who constantly sought to uncover their activities and protest them to the authorities. Neutral powers curtailed the export of coal in some places. Moreover, some of the German supply ships and colliers were caught by Allied warships. German commanders often had to coal from prizes, and coal in fact became their constant preoccupation, limiting the amount of time they could spend on the sea lanes.

The Germans had a substantial number of ships sheltering in neutral harbors. By mid-September 1914, there were more than one hundred, and approximately thirty more were actually in use as supply ships. There were also, perhaps inevitably, certain neutrals willing to take the risk of supplying the Germans for profit. They, like the potential auxiliary cruisers, had to be watched. The number of suitable anchorages in many areas also was limited, and once uncovered they would be visited regularly by Allied patrols. The Etappe system tended to be a diminishing asset: strict enforcement of neutrality regulations by the Dutch in the Netherlands East Indies or by the United States in North American and Caribbean waters—although the British complained of American laxness at Manila—curtailed German endeavors. The activities of the Etappen remain one of the lesser-known stories of the war; indeed, an American historian was recently informed by the current Bundesarchiv-Militärarchiv that the records of the service were burned for security reasons in 1919—a statement one hopes some historian will accept as a challenge.[4]

The Germans naturally established an intelligence service to complement the Etappe system. Modern technology in one sense had made the conduct of cruiser warfare much more difficult. The presence of a raider could be quickly signaled by wireless or cable. This often happened; it resulted, for example, in the destruction of the *Emden*. But wireless could be used two ways. The Germans became very adept at interpreting wireless messages to estimate the positions of Allied cruisers. Powerful wireless signals could indicate an enemy was close, even if the Germans could not establish the direction. Allied wireless operators, especially in India, were almost incredibly lax in divulging call signs and other vital information. Wireless was new technology, and in the early stages of the war the British had much to learn. The Germans also derived a considerable amount of intelligence from ordinary newspapers, which contained shipping mails giving the time and date of departures and arrivals of steamers. The captain of the *Emden* could assume an omnipotent air with captured officers, hinting at vast knowledge and an immense intelligence network, when the information actually had been gathered through close reading of the press.[5]

The objective of cruiser warfare, in addition to actually sinking merchant ships, would have been to drive marine insurance rates to prohibitive heights, thereby paralyzing trade. The British were prepared for the threat, and before the war the British government undertook a very farsighted move to reduce the potential danger of panic and paralysis of trade. In May 1913 the prime minister appointed a subcommittee of the Committee of Imperial Defence to study the question of war risks insurance. The committee, under the chairmanship of the Rt. Hon. Huth Jackson, director of the Bank of England, issued its report on 30 April 1914, and when the crisis came shortly afterwards, the Government accepted the recommended scheme, with modifications, which was published on 4 August. In general terms, the government would reinsure 80 percent of all war risks, and would in turn receive 80 percent of the premiums. Insurance clubs, such as the Liverpool and London War Risks Association, would assume the remaining 20 percent of the risks and would receive 20 percent of the premiums. The scheme was, in effect, a partnership between the state and the shipowners for running risks and sharing losses, and the participation of the insurance associations in setting values was supposed to be a safeguard against fraud or negligence. The standard forms of insurance policy adopted were also a convenient form of control because they contained a clause stating that ships sailing under the policy had to obey all Admiralty directions regarding routes and ports of call. The French, Russian, and German governments adopted similar schemes.[6]

British plans for the defense of trade were based on the principle that it could best be achieved by a concentration of force in the main theater of war, which would reduce to a minimum the chances for enemy cruisers getting out on the trade routes. The Admiralty recognized that German ships would be at sea when the war began and that mercantile losses during the period they were being hunted down would occur. The Royal Navy could not hope to adequately patrol all the trade routes, and the Admiralty therefore concentrated its attention on those focal points where the routes converged. British shipping was ordered to disperse from its usual routes, and the Admiralty trusted that the vast extent of the ocean would provide a certain measure of protection. Losses might occur, but they would be kept in acceptable proportions. Concentration of patrols on the focal points, however, conflicted with the necessity of watching those ports where there were German liners capable of being turned into auxiliary cruisers.[7]

The decision to disperse British merchantmen meant there was no attempt at convoy. The Admiralty opposed the idea, for it would have tied down cruisers they considered better employed hunting for German warships. The idea of convoy, the traditional and time-honored way of protecting merchant shipping in the age of sail, was in disfavor in the early part of the twentieth century. The authorities believed the use of steam made it easier for a merchant ship to escape from hostile cruisers by enabling it to choose its route without regard to the wind, and thereby pass through danger areas at times of its own choosing and as rapidly as possible. The introduction of the telegraph also made it much more difficult to keep the assembly of a convoy secret, and the enemy would have ample opportunity to prepare an attack. The mass of smoke would also attract enemy cruisers. Moreover, modern commercial pressures worked against the convoy: valuable time was lost waiting for escorts, and the speed of the convoy was reduced to that of the slowest vessel. Delays associated with convoys did not occur only as they started out. The sudden arrival of a large convoy caused serious congestion in ports, leading to still further delay. The fear of inordinate delays was a very real consideration for profit-conscious shipowners, and for a long time masters and ship-owners were probably even more opposed to the idea of convoys than was orthodox naval opinion at the Admiralty.[8]

There was one major exception to the neglect of convoys. Troopships were almost always escorted or gathered in convoys, and in the first few months of the war, there were the great "imperial convoys" from Canada, India, Australia, and New Zealand. They absorbed considerable naval forces to escort them, if only because regardless of what the Admiralty might have preferred, the dominion governments did not stand for letting the troops sail unprotected. Furthermore, very soon after the opening of the war, the Admiralty found itself forced to support a number of overseas expeditions against German colonies, launched perhaps prematurely through the pressure of the dominions. These expeditions, joined with the need to escort the troop convoys, drained forces that might have been used for the protection of trade or for hunting German cruisers. This stretching of British resources resulted in two major weak spots in the system of defending focal points. They were the focal points off

Colombo in the Indian Ocean and between Pernambuco and the island of Fernando Noronha off the northeast coast of Brazil in the South Atlantic. These points were where the *Emden* and *Karlsruhe*, respectively, enjoyed some of their greatest success.[9]

GERMAN FORCES OVERSEAS: COLONIES AND CRUISERS

In 1912 and 1913, the British and French commanders in chief in the Far East, Rear Admiral Alfred Winsloe and Contre-amiral H. de Kerillis, had engaged in similar informal nonbinding discussions to those held at home on the subject of cooperation in case Britain and France should find themselves allies in the event of war. With little likelihood that French Indo-China would be attacked, French naval forces (armored cruisers *Montcalm* and *Dupleix*, torpedo gunboat *D'Iberville*, and three destroyers) would join the British. However, Winsloe's successor, Vice Admiral Martyn Jerram, who became commander in chief of the China Station in March 1913, considered the French ships "very broken reeds to rely on" because of their age and lack of speed.[10]

British naval forces on the China Station included: the battleship *Triumph* with nucleus crew at Hong Kong; armored cruisers *Minotaur* and *Hampshire;* light cruisers *Newcastle* and *Yarmouth;* eight destroyers; three submarines; and smaller craft such as torpedo boats and gunboats. Without the demobilized battleship *Triumph*, Jerram's superiority over his potential German foes was questionable. The armored cruiser *Minotaur*, armed with four 9.2-inch and ten 7.5-inch guns, was certainly equal to the *Scharnhorst*, but the *Hampshire*, with only four 7.5-inch and six 6-inch guns, was weaker than the *Gneisenau*. The British concentration in home waters and other pressing problems, such as the Mediterranean, prevented Jerram from being reinforced. Moreover, when the war broke out, his French counterpart, Contre-amiral Huguet, was off on a cruise to the South Pacific in his flagship *Montcalm* (two 7.6-inch and eight 6.5-inch guns), his exact location unknown beyond the fact that he had left Tahiti for Samoa, where he was due on 7 August. He could not be contacted by wireless, and there was some apprehension that in his ignorance of the fact that war had broken out, he conceivably could have blundered into Spee's squadron and annihilation. On the other hand, the French armored cruiser *Dupleix* (eight 6.5-inch and four 3.9-inch guns) promptly joined the British at Hong Kong early on the morning of 5 August. The ancient *D'Iberville* and three small French destroyers proceeded according to the prewar plans to assist in guarding the Strait of Malacca.[11]

The British also began fitting out the Canadian Pacific liners *Empress of Asia*, *Empress of Japan*, and *Empress of Russia* and the P. & O. liner *Himalaya* as armed merchant cruisers, and the majority of the river gunboats in China were laid up so that their crews could join the *Triumph*. Neither the crews from the gunboats nor the mobilized reservists at Hong Kong were enough to man the battleship, and the navy turned to the local commanding general for assistance. There was a flood of enthusiastic volunteers; two officers, one hundred rank and file, and six signalers of the Duke of Cornwall's Light Infantry joined the ship, which was able to sail the afternoon of 6 August. There were also difficulties manning the armed merchant cruisers, and the *Empress of Asia's* crew was complemented by an officer and twenty men of the Royal Garrison Artillery and twenty-five men of the Fortieth Pathans when she left on 9 August. The *Empress of Russia*, the last of the armed merchant vessels to be ready, did not sail until the 28th, and by this time there were few naval ratings left. Consequently, her crew included Chinese from her mercantile crew, volunteers from shore, the island guard of marines from Weihaiwei, and crews from French gunboats in China that also had been laid up. The Admiralty study intriguingly described it as a "miscellaneous and possibly unique crew, who throughout worked together in perfect—though occasionally vociferous—harmony."[12]

Admiral Spee was actually far from Chinese waters when the war began, and his squadron was scattered. The *Scharnhorst* and *Gneisenau* had sailed from Tsingtau at the end of June for a long cruise through the German possessions in the Pacific and were not scheduled to return until September. The *Leipzig* was even farther away, looking after German interests on the troubled Pacific coast of Mexico, and the *Nürnberg* was en route to relieve her. The *Emden* was the sole cruiser at Tsingtau, and her captain, Karl von Müller, was senior officer on the station. He was joined during the period of tension preceding the war by the lonely representative of the k.u.k. Kriegsmarine in the Far East, the old protected cruiser *Kaiserin Elisabeth*. The Austrian cruiser—in which Archduke Franz Ferdinand had once cruised around the world—was too slow, consumed too much coal, and was too weakly armed (six 5.9-inch guns) for the Germans to use with their squadron, and some of her guns and their crews were landed to help in the defense of Tsingtau. Of the other German ships in the Far East, the gunboats *Jaguar* and *Luchs* and the torpedo boat *S.90* managed to get back to Tsingtau before the war broke out; another gunboat and three river gunboats had to be laid up in Chinese ports.

The *Scharnhorst, Gneisenau*, the supply ship *Titania*, and the chartered Japanese collier *Fukoku Maru* were at Ponape in the eastern Carolines, where Spee learned of the different declarations of war. He was joined by the hastily recalled *Nürnberg* on the 6th. She replenished her coal from the Japanese collier, which was then released according to the peacetime plan. To avoid her betrayal of the anchorage, however, Spee sailed at night for Pagan in the Marianas. This location had the advantage of being roughly equidistant from northern Japan, Tsingtau, Shanghai, and Manila—all points from which he expected supplies—and here Spee awaited the colliers, supply ships, and auxiliary cruisers that had been ordered to join him.[13]

What were Spee's plans? The major German operations plan was for commerce warfare in East Asia, and later, if the occasion arose and if coal supplies could be secured, in Australian and Indian waters. The squadron would be supplied at first from Tsingtau, would avoid being shut in, and only under especially favorable circumstances would it promptly attack enemy naval forces for the purpose of winning sea supremacy. Unfortunately the entire situation would change if Japan entered the war. Cruiser warfare in East Asian waters would be impossible, and the cruiser squadron would have to move to another area. Spee ruled out the Indian Ocean, and coal supplies from the Dutch East Indies would be too insecure. He decided to take the squadron to the west coast of America, where the supply of coal would be most secure and where he could maintain the squadron for the longest time.[14]

Fregattenkapitän Karl von Müller of the *Emden*, an exceptionally able officer, promptly sailed on 31 July in accordance with his orders to avoid being trapped. He proceeded to the shipping lanes between Nagasaki and Vladivostok, where he captured the Russian steamer *Rjasan* (3,500 tons) on 4 August and brought the prize back to Tsingtau. The ship was renamed the *Cormoran* and armed with guns taken from the old gunboat *Cormoran*, then under refit at Tsingtau and useless for serious work at sea. Müller did not linger long at Tsingtau, sailing on the 6th for the rendezvous with Spee at Pagan along with the *Prinz Eitel Friedrich* (8,797 tons), a North German Lloyd liner converted into an auxiliary cruiser with crews of laid-up gunboats, and the Hamburg-Amerika line steamer *Markomannia* (4,505 tons), used as a collier and supply ship. Spee himself was reluctant to be drawn back to Tsingtau with the *Scharnhorst* and *Gneisenau*, because of the uncertain attitude of Japan. The *Cormoran* sailed on 10 August. She was the last German warship to leave Tsingtau, where the German garrison and torpedo boat *S.90*, gunboat *Jaguar*, and Austrian cruiser *Kaiserin Elisabeth* faced an uncertain future.

By the time the *Emden*, *Prinz Eitel Friedrich*, and *Markomannia* reached Pagan on the 12th, Spee had a small fleet of colliers and storeships—eight including the *Titania*. Nevertheless, four others sent out from Tsingtau had been captured by the British and French, underscoring how precarious the coal situation was likely to be. The Japanese decided Spee's future course for him when he learned of their threatening attitude on 12 August. He had been ready to forgo operations in East Asian waters to try to preserve their neutrality; now operations in these waters were out of the question. He held a meeting of his captains in his flagship on the 13th. Here he explained why it would not be feasible for the squadron to act in East Asian, Australian, or Indian waters: lack of bases and coal was the overriding consideration, and the coal consumption of the *Scharnhorst* and *Gneisenau* was too high. The Germans decided to send a single cruiser to the Indian Ocean to disrupt trade and possibly acquire coal from her prizes. The logical choice was the *Emden*, newest and fastest. The *Prinz Eitel Friedrich* and *Cormoran* were sent to Australian waters, but Spee did not expect much from them. Their speed was too low and their coal consumption too high.

Spee and his small armada sailed eastward from Pagan and away from the Japanese on the evening of 13 August, and the *Emden*, together with the supply ship *Markomannia* carrying 5,400 tons of Shantung coal, 45 tons of lubricating oil, and provisions, parted company shortly afterward. Spee disappeared into the vast emptiness of the Pacific Ocean. Müller fulfilled his mission brilliantly; he had, as we shall see, one of the most famous cruises of the war.[15]

The *Emden* might not have gotten away if Admiral Jerram had been allowed to follow his original war orders, which had been approved by the Admiralty. His plan had been to concentrate his forces north of the Saddle Islands at the mouth of the Yangtze and to keep his squadron generally to the north of a line from there to the south of Japan. The objective would have been to keep the *Scharnhorst* and *Gneisenau* from returning to Tsingtau from the south. This deployment would also have cut off the Italian protected cruiser *Marco Polo*, then at Kobe, from seeking refuge at Tsingtau. Italy, which also had a river gunboat at Shanghai, was still considered an ally of Germany and Austria, although the *Marco Polo* was very old and not well armed (six 6-inch guns). The Italian declaration of neutrality on 2 August solved the problem. Most of Jerram's squadron was conveniently located at the British station at Weihaiwei on the Shantung Peninsula, and the cruisers *Minotaur*, *Hampshire*, and *Yarmouth* and four destroyers could have been at the rendezvous on 31 July. Then, "to my horror"—as Jerram later wrote his wife—just before leaving Weihaiwei he received an order from the Admiralty to concentrate at Hong Kong. He wrote in his report: "I must confess that I was reluctant to do so, as it placed me almost 900 miles from what I conceived to be my correct strategical position. I assumed, however, that their Lordships had good reason for sending me there, and proceeded accordingly, at a speed of 10 knots, in order to economize coal." Jerram told his wife, "I was so upset I very nearly disobeyed the order entirely. I wish now that I had done so." He reported his action, deliberately giving the Admiralty a chance to cancel their order. They did not. He complained, "Here was a definite plan of action formed in peacetime after mature consideration thrown to the winds by one peremptory telegram."[16]

By the time war between Britain and Germany had been declared, and British forces, now reinforced by the French cruiser *Dupleix*, were back on Jerram's intended deployment, the *Emden*, the auxiliary cruisers, and the colliers had sailed. Jerram knew she was out and assumed she was heading for Yap in the Carolines. He tried to cut her off and was unsuccessful. The *Minotaur* and *Newcastle* were detached to destroy the powerful German wireless station on Yap by gunfire, which they successfully accomplished on the 12th. Although the German surveying ship *Planet* managed to partially repair the wireless and resume transmitting on the 22d, the new transmissions were much shorter in range. Spee was therefore cut off from another means of direct communication with Germany since Yap was linked by cable to Tsingtau and Shanghai. The *Emden*, however, had gotten away, and the arrival of the British and French forces off Tsingtau was akin to locking the barn door after the horse had been stolen. The responsibility for altering Jerram's plans lay directly with the Admiralty and their unfortunate tendency to try and control distant operations. Churchill undoubtedly played a major role. The first lord apparently was concerned at the narrow margin of British superiority over Spee in Asiatic waters and wanted to make sure Jerram had the battleship *Triumph* with him.[17]

The question of naval supremacy in Asiatic waters was decided on 15 August when the Japanese delivered an ultimatum to Germany, followed by a declaration of war on the 23d. Jerram was now free to leave Chinese waters in pursuit of either Spee or the *Emden*. The fate of Tsingtau was quickly settled. The kaiser ordered that Tsingtau be defended to the bitter end, but the German government could do nothing to help beyond the kaiser's personal message "God be with you in the difficult struggle. I think of you, Wilhelm." The Japanese had their own ambitions in China, and on 30 August a Japanese expedition landed on the Shantung Peninsula. The British battleship *Triumph* and destroyer *Usk* joined the Japanese Second Fleet, the naval force attacking Tsingtau. It included three old battleships, two coast-defense ships, three armored cruisers, and a destroyer flotilla with a cruiser leader. A single British battalion, later supplemented by an Indian battalion stationed in China, joined the siege. It was a purely symbolic participation. The Japanese were definitely in control of these waters. The Japanese First Fleet, consisting of a dreadnought, two semidreadnoughts, four light cruisers, and a destroyer flotilla, patrolled the southern portion of the Yellow Sea to block any potential intervention on the part of Admiral Spee, and then escorted the expeditionary force. To the south the Japanese Third Squadron—a light cruiser and two first-class and four second-class gunboats—patrolled the Formosa Strait and northern approaches to Hong Kong. Jerram therefore did not have to worry about waters to the north of Hong Kong.

The Germans put up a stout defense. On the night of 17 October, *S.90* sortied and torpedoed and sank the old Japanese cruiser *Takaschio* (employed as a minelayer), evaded the blockade, and scuttled herself along the Chinese coast. The outcome of the siege, however, was never in doubt, and on 30 October—the emperor's birthday—the Japanese began a massive artillery assault and a week later broke through the German defenses. The collection of German warships trapped in the port, as well as the *Kaiserin Elisabeth*, were scuttled before Tsingtau surrendered on 7 November.[18]

There is no guarantee Jerram would have stopped the *Emden* if he had been able to follow his original plan. There are too many uncertainties in war at sea, and he was going to institute a line of patrols, not a close blockade of Tsingtau. But the damage was done, and Müller was now on the loose. The *Emden* was the most modern of Spee's cruisers, completed in 1909, with a contract speed of 24 knots and armed with ten 4.1-inch (10.5 cm) guns and two torpedo tubes. Müller also tried to alter the *Emden*'s profile by constructing a dummy fourth funnel, two dimensional, but from a distance a successful simulation of the four-funneled British cruisers on station.

Müller intended to avoid the usual steamer routes and proceeded southward to enter the Indian Ocean by means of the Molucca and Buru straits and the Banda Sea through the maze of islands of the Netherlands East Indies. The Germans may have been unpleasantly surprised by the fact that the Dutch intended to rigorously enforce their neutrality. They had the strength to do so: their squadron in the East Indies included the coast-defense ships *De Zeven Provinciën, Tromp, Koningin Regentes,* and *Hertog Hendrik* and six destroyers.[19] The major concern of the Dutch was probably to avoiding giving the Japanese any pretext to intervene in their colonies, but they definitely served as a brake on German freedom of action. The *Tromp* (two 9.4-inch and four 5.9-inch guns) which the *Emden* met at Tanahjampea on 27 August, was clearly superior to the German cruiser— and what was even worse, had just sent the collier Müller was expecting to find there away for lingering too long in territorial waters. Müller found that the prewar German plan to send supply ships to neutral ports to await further orders was impractical because of the Dutch attitude. He did make use of the island of Simaloer south of Sumatra, but after another polite but firm encounter with Dutch officials, he was careful to anchor just outside of territorial waters when he returned to those waters in the future.

The British assumed the *Emden* was with Spee's squadron, and Müller achieved complete tactical surprise when he appeared in the Bay of Bengal on the Colombo-Calcutta track. Traffic here had resumed the normal peacetime routine, the presence or likelihood of a raider unsuspected. Between the 10th and 14th of September Müller sank six steamers, captured and retained another two as colliers, and released a third to carry the crews of his prizes. These sinkings were technically in the East Indies station, but the commander in chief East Indies, Rear Admiral R. H. Peirse, had his hands full with the Indian convoys and the threat of the German light cruiser *Königsberg* in the western portion of the Indian Ocean. The hunt for the *Emden* was therefore taken up by the ships of Jerram's China Squadron, with the *Minotaur, Hampshire,* and *Yarmouth* joined by the second-class battle cruiser *Ibuki* (four 12-inch, eight 8-inch, and fourteen 4.7-inch guns, but only 20.9 knots speed) and light cruiser *Chikuma* of the Japanese navy. The Russian cruisers *Zhemchug* and *Askold,* the old French cruiser *D'Iberville,* auxiliary cruisers *Empress of Asia* and *Empress of Russia,* and the Japanese light cruiser *Yahagi* were all ships eventually involved in operations against the *Emden,* and at the moment she was finally destroyed Vice Admiral Tochinai was at Singapore with the armored cruisers *Tokiwa* and *Yakumo* to form a Japanese squadron to work in the eastern half of the Bay of Bengal.

Müller, despite the forces gathering against him, kept the initiative, and after cruising off Rangoon, recrossed the Bay of Bengal and on the night of 22 September bombarded the oil-storage tanks at the port of Madras, destroying two, thoroughly upsetting trade in the Bay of Bengal for the second time, and, needless to say, doing immense damage to British prestige. Müller then steamed to the Minikoi focal point—a coral island 400 miles west of Colombo—and between the 25th and 27th of September sank another four ships, captured and retained a fifth as a collier, and released another captured ship with the crews from his prizes. The *Emden* disappeared to the south to coal in the Maldives and then proceeded farther south to remote Diego Garcia, where she rested and executed repairs, assisted by the fact that the islanders had not yet heard of the outbreak of the war. The British missed the *Emden,* but the *Yarmouth* captured and sank the faithful collier *Markomannia,* caught coaling from Müller's Greek prize the *Pontoporos* off Simaloer on 12 October. The latter was rescued from German control.

Müller returned to the Minikoi area and between 16 and 19 October sank another five steamers, retained another as a collier, and released another with the crews from his prizes. Müller, after eluding his pursuers once again, embarked on what was probably his boldest stroke. He steamed eastward and raided Penang at the entrance to the Malacca Strait. Using the dummy funnel, *Emden* surprised and sank by gunfire and torpedo the Russian light cruiser *Zhemtchug* and was on the verge of capturing a British steamer loaded with explosives when interrupted by the returning small French destroyer *Mousquet,* which was promptly sunk.

Müller had therefore added two Allied warships to his score, caused renewed consternation, and delayed the sailing of the large convoys from Australia and New Zealand, which now had to be given strong escorts. However, he had exhausted his share of luck. The forces hunting him in the Indian Ocean were increasing, and Müller decided to steam southward again to raid the remote Cocos Islands and destroy the cable and wireless station on Direction Island. The *Emden* appeared off the island on 9 November, and a landing party promptly set about the work of destruction. However, the island had managed to send off a warning that was picked up by the escorts of the Australian convoy only 52 miles away. Müller had no idea of the existence of the convoy, whose sailing his activities had delayed. The convoy commander detached the Australian light cruiser *Sydney*, commanded by Captain John Glossop, who reached the scene around 9:00 A.M. The *Emden* had to leave her landing party and give battle, but the *Sydney*, with eight 6-inch guns, was superior in armament, and the battered *Emden* was eventually run ashore on nearby Keeling Island and burnt out.[20] The odyssey was not quite over. Kapitänleutnant von Mücke, the *Emden*'s first officer in charge of the landing party, escaped with his men in the small schooner *Ayesha*, sailed to Padang in the Dutch East Indies, transferred to the German steamer *Choising*, and eventually reached Yemen, where after surviving bedouin attacks, they managed to reach the railhead and arrive in Constantinople to a hero's welcome in June of 1915.[21]

Müller and the *Emden* sank the warships *Zhemchug* (whose captain and first officer were later court-martialed and sentenced to prison for their lack of preparedness) and *Mousquet*, captured the *Rjasan* and converted her into the auxiliary cruiser *Cormoran*, and sank sixteen British steamers, representing 70,825 gross tons. He appears to have behaved with scrupulous correctness toward his captures, invariably making careful provision for the safety of the passengers and crew of his prizes, and has on the whole received a very good press. The British, at least until the submarine war turned bitter, seemed to have had some of that same high regard for him that they would later show toward Rommel in the Second World War.[22] The official histories written shortly after the war, however, are inclined to take the line that the *Emden*'s career was helped by laxness and luck, that some captures would never have taken place had elementary precautions been observed, and that she was very lucky, narrowly missing capture on at least three occasions. They also point out that the losses represented a very small portion of the vast amount of British trade and had little bearing on the war, and imply that the destruction of the *Emden* was inevitable.[23] The Admiralty statements early in the war had the same tone. They had always considered there would inevitably be some losses and apparently did not respond when the thoroughly alarmed Bengal Chamber of Commerce in October had urged the establishment of a system of convoys. The Admiralty, busy with escorting troop convoys, expected the situation to improve when the convoys were accomplished and more cruisers could be released for hunting purposes. They considered it undesirable to impose on trade the delays and restrictions associated with convoys.[24] The destruction of the *Emden* and the neutralization of most of the other German surface raiders by the end of the year seemed to justify this attitude. However, when the Admiralty looked at the question in the midst of the Second World War, the results were less inspiring:

The naval measures taken to deal with the *Emden*'s attack on trade consisted in employing numerous cruisers in searching anchorages and areas in which she had been reported or was suspected of operating. . . . Some of these cruisers were slower than the *Emden* so that even if they had located her, she would probably have escaped like the *Karlsruhe* did. In any case frequent changes in the theatre of operations usually rendered the intelligence, on which they acted, misleading or out-of-date.

The system did not effectually protect the trade or succeed in bringing the *Emden* to action. Her eventual destruction was due to a lucky chance that the *Sydney*, escorting troop transports from Australia, happened to be in the vicinity when she raided the Cocos Islands. If the attack had been timed a few hours earlier or later she might have escaped.

The Admiralty calculated that out of the ten times the *Emden* had coaled during her raid, five had been from her prizes. The most effective method of protection from surface raiders was the same as that from submarines. The Admiralty concluded:

There can be little doubt that convoy on the principal trade routes in the Indian Ocean would have greatly reduced the losses and deprived the *Emden* of coal from captured colliers on which she largely depended. It is true that convoy would have slowed up the normal flow of trade but not to the extent that actually happened. Uncertainty as to the *Emden*'s movements led to shipping being held up for long periods in Bombay, Calcutta, Aden and Singapore, so that trade was seriously dislocated throughout the Middle and Far East.[25]

The situation in the Indian Ocean was complicated by the presence of the light cruiser *Königsberg* (completed in 1907, ten 4.1-inch [10.5-cm] guns, 24 knots) on the East Africa station. Fregattenkapitän Looff's orders in the event of war were to attack traffic at the entrance to the Red Sea.[26] He sailed from Dar es Salaam on the evening of 31 July and eluded the *Hyacinth, Astraea,* and *Pegasus,* which were patrolling off the port. Rear Admiral King-Hall, commander in chief of the Cape Squadron, had been ordered to watch the *Königsberg* in the period preceding hostilities, but as was the case with the *Goeben* and *Breslau* in the Mediterranean, the elderly cruisers of the Cape Squadron were not fast enough to keep up with their potential German foe.

The *Königsberg* never lived up to her potential. Her operations were crippled by a lack of coal. The British prevented her collier *Koenig* from leaving Dar es Salaam, and through preemptive purchasing, blocked the Germans from obtaining coal in Portuguese East Africa. The *Königsberg* captured and sank only a single merchant ship in the Gulf of Aden. The monsoon season further hampered her activities, and a sortie to the vicinity of Madagascar proved fruitless. The *Königsberg* lived a fugitive existence, hiding on the African coast and scrounging for coal from any small German colliers that were available. She was a potential danger, however, and proved it on 20 September when she surprised and sank the old light cruiser *Pegasus,* which had been repairing defects in her machinery at Zanzibar. The psychological effects, especially when coupled with the activities of the *Emden* on the other side of the Indian Ocean, were probably more far-reaching than the actual damage.

The New Zealand government delayed the sailing of its portion of the great troop convoy, which was in the process of gathering in Australian waters. The light cruisers *Dartmouth*, *Chatham*, and *Weymouth*, the latter specially detached from the Mediterranean, spent more than a month looking for her. The effect on trade did not appear to last long, however, due to the *Königsberg*'s inactivity, and even before she was located her presence had ceased to have any appreciable effect. The eventual discovery of the *Königsberg* was due more to a lucky accident than any of the British measures. On 19 October the *Chatham* discovered the small supply ship *Präsident* (1,849 tons) of the Deutsche Ost-Afrika line in the Lindi River, and papers found on board indicated that the preceding month she had carried coal to the *Königsberg*, which was in a branch of the swampy delta of the Rufigi River. This area had previously been searched but was considered too shallow for the German cruiser. The new lead was enough. On 30 October the *Dartmouth* discovered the *Königsberg* 6 miles up the Rufigi. The British instituted a close watch, and on 10 November sank a collier to block the channel. The ship's artillery could not reach the German cruiser and the British discovered there were other channels by which the ship might escape. The result was a small expedition, complete with monitors and aircraft, before the final destruction of the *Königsberg* was achieved in July 1915.[27] It was another of those troublesome sideshows, absorbing men and ships that might have been employed elsewhere. The *Königsberg*'s crew, and some of her guns, which were landed, continued to fight with the German forces in East Africa. But that was almost irrelevant. She had ceased to be a factor in the naval war from the moment she was blocked in early November.[28]

Of the other German cruisers abroad when the war began, the *Karlsruhe* gave the British and French as much trouble as the *Emden*, although her career, lacking a dramatic episode such as the raid on Penang, has not attracted the same amount of attention. The *Karlsruhe* was a new ship and had just completed her trials when she arrived in the Caribbean to relieve the *Dresden* as station ship on the East Coast of America station. She was armed with twelve 4.1-inch (10.5-cm) guns and capable of better than 27.5 knots, which gave her an advantage in speed over any of the British or French ships in these waters. Fregattenkapitän Erich Köhler, her commander, needed every bit of it on a number of occasions.

Köhler began the war hiding in an isolated anchorage at Cay Sal Bank in the Florida Strait to the north of Cuba, where he had gone to hide once the warning messages that war was imminent had been received. After the hostilities began, the *Karlsruhe* met the North German Lloyd liner *Kronprinz Wilhelm* (14,908 tons) at a rendezvous in the open sea approximately 120 miles northeast of Watling Island in the Bahamas. The *Kronprinz Wilhelm* had slipped out of New York the evening of 3 August for the meeting with the *Karlsruhe* on the 6th. The *Karlsruhe* transferred two 3.4-inch (8.8-cm) guns, ammunition, a machine gun, and some ratings. Kapitänleutnant Paul Thierfelder, the *Karlsruhe*'s navigating officer, assumed command of the auxiliary cruiser. The Germans had just finished transferring the guns and were in the process of shifting ammunition when Rear Admiral Cradock arrived on the scene in the armored cruiser *Suffolk*. The British had been guided to the area by intercepting the *Karlsruhe*'s wireless messages to the *Kronprinz Wilhelm*. Both German ships made off in different directions. The *Suffolk*'s stokers made heroic efforts, but the *Karlsruhe* was out of sight by sunset. Köhler intended to make for Newport News in order to coal, but the light cruiser *Bristol* steaming down from the north was in a position to cut him off, and the two met that evening. There was an exchange of fire in the moonlight, but once again the *Karlsruhe*'s superior speed enabled her to get away. The *Bristol* had not been able to develop her full speed, possibly due to unsuitable coal. Once more, as with the *Goeben* and *Königsberg*, the British had failed to catch a German cruiser at the beginning of hostilities. And once again they would experience much trouble as a result.

Köhler managed to elude his pursuers in the Caribbean, but usually with only the barest margin of coal, and he shifted his field of operations to the less-patrolled Pernambuco area off the northeast coast of Brazil. Here for just under two months he successfully preyed on the rich South American trade route, frequently cruising in company with one or two supply ships (often prizes), spread far apart in line abreast to widen the search. He had no trouble obtaining enough coal from either German-owned or chartered colliers or from prizes. He usually anchored off the Laveira Reef on the Brazilian coast to coal. Köhler eventually decided it would be too dangerous to remain in the area, especially after one of his prizes loaded with passengers and crews from sunken ships that he had sent across the ocean to Teneriffe in the Canary Islands reached port. He therefore decided to head northward to the West Indies and raid Barbados and Fort-de-France, Martinique, and attack the trade route between Trinidad and Barbados. He never arrived. On the evening of 4 November, about 300 miles from Barbados, the fore part of the *Karlsruhe* was destroyed by an internal explosion—the exact cause was never determined—and the ship sank. Köhler did not survive. The survivors were taken aboard the supply ship *Rio Negro*, which managed to evade the blockade and return to Germany a month later. The Germans kept the loss of the *Karlsruhe* a strict secret, and it was March 1915 before the British could confirm that the raider was gone. In the interim they expended considerable effort searching for the phantom ship. The *Karlsruhe* accounted for sixteen ships (fifteen British, one Dutch) for a total of 72,805 gross tons. The official history *Seaborne Trade* is once again complacent; the *Karlsruhe* had damaged only a small portion of total Allied trade, and she had not interrupted trade the way the *Emden* had done. This may be true, but there were no grounds for complacency. The British and French measures against her, such as searching suspected anchorages in the West Indies, the coast of South America, or as far away as the Canary Islands, the Azores, and even the west coast of Africa, were singularly ineffective. The Allies were spared further loss not from their own efforts but by what was—from their point of view—a lucky accident.[29]

The other German warships abroad when the war began accomplished relatively little as far as cruiser warfare was concerned. The *Dresden* was on her way home from the east coast of Mexico when war came, and she was ordered to work her way down the coast of South America and attack trade off the Plate. The *Dresden* had sunk only two ships when the Admiralstab on 8 September ordered her into the Pacific to work in company with the *Leipzig*. The *Dresden* was working her way up the Chilean coast, with little success, when she learned that Spee's squadron was heading eastward across the Pacific, and she joined it at remote Easter Island on 12 October. The *Dresden's* fate was now linked to that of Spee's squadron, although working as a part of it she sank another two British steamers, making a total of four steamers and 12,927 tons.[30]

Fregattenkapitän Haun of the *Leipzig* also might have accomplished more. He was on the western coast of Mexico when the war broke out. His first inclination was to rejoin Spee, but he quickly realized this was impossible and decided to operate against British trade on the Pacific Coast of North America. There was little to oppose him, only the very old Canadian cruiser *Rainbow* operating out of Esquimalt and, on the coast of Mexico, the old and weak sloops *Algerine* (launched in 1895, six 4-inch guns) and *Shearwater* (launched in 1900, six 4-inch guns). The sloops, suitable for the colonial or policing duties they were engaged in, were too weak to fight a modern adversary and too slow (13 knots) to run away. They might have provided the *Leipzig* (completed in 1906, ten 4.1-inch [10.5-cm] guns, 22.4 knots) with a cheap victory if they had encountered her. There was considerable anxiety at the Admiralty over their fate, particularly as it was at first erroneously believed that the *Nürnberg* was operating in company with the *Leipzig*. The two would also have been more than a match for the old *Rainbow* (completed in 1893, two 6-inch, six 4.7-inch guns, 20 knots). The two little sloops were out of contact, making very slow progress northward, but because nothing was heard of them, the Admiralty, concerned they might have been lost, ordered the *Newcastle* from Asian waters to North America.

The effects on shipping were serious; according to the official history of seaborne trade, rumors of the two German cruisers "paralysed shipping from Vancouver to Panama," and when the *Leipzig* appeared off San Francisco on 11 August, cruising just out of sight of shore, she was able to "establish a virtual blockade of the port," detaining twenty-five British steamers, and, "somewhat illogically," even holding up traffic at Yokohama and Asian ports. The *Leipzig* demonstrated the ability of a single cruiser at a focal point to dislocate traffic. The crisis was short lived. The second German cruiser *Nürnberg* was actually on her way to rejoin Spee. The impending entry of Japan into the war meant that the Japanese armored cruiser *Idzumo*—protecting Japanese interests on the coast of Mexico—was free to act against the Germans, for whom even a successful encounter with the *Rainbow* might involve damage far from a friendly base. Haun left San Francisco on the 18th, after a day in port to coal, and steamed south. British trade on the west coast quickly revived. The *Leipzig* hid in the bays and inlets of Lower California before receiving orders to go south to join Spee at Easter Island, where she arrived on 14 October. During this time the *Leipzig* sank only two ships, as well as another two after joining Spee. The total for her career in cruiser warfare was therefore four ships and 15,299 tons.[31]

The remaining German warships abroad accomplished little. The gunboat *Geier* made a long voyage from the east coast of Africa across the Indian Ocean and Pacific, eluding capture, but capturing and disabling only one British steamer in the eastern

Carolines—whose crew later repaired their engine and escaped—before she reached Honolulu and was interned. The *Emden's* prize converted into an auxiliary cruiser, the *Cormoran*, spent much of her career seeking coal and supplies, made no captures, and was finally interned by the Americans at Guam. The little gunboat *Eber* steamed from the West African coast across the Atlantic to the isolated island of Trinidada, where she transferred her guns to the new Hamburg Sud-Amerika line's *Cap Trafalgar* (18,710 tons), which had been requisitioned by the German naval attaché in Buenos Aires. The *Eber's* commander, Korvettenkapitän Julius Wirth, assumed command of the new auxiliary cruiser, but her career was brief. Before *Cap Trafalgar* could make any captures, the armed merchant cruiser *Carmania* (19,524 tons) found her coaling at Trinidada on 14 September, and after a hotly contested action in which the *Carmania* herself was badly damaged, the *Cap Trafalgar* was sunk. By this time the *Eber* had taken refuge in Bahia, where she was interned by the Brazilians.[32]

The only German auxiliary cruiser to fulfill the classic expectations of a raider and successfully put to sea from a home port in Germany after the war began—besides the *Berlin*, whose mines had accounted for the *Audacious*—was the North German Lloyd liner *Kaiser Wilhelm der Grosse* (14,349 tons), which had won the Blue Riband for fastest crossing of the North Atlantic on her maiden voyage in 1897. She sailed on 4 August before the blockade was fully in place and passed around to the north of Iceland before heading for the area off the Canary Islands. Her career at sea seemed dominated by an insatiable demand for coal; she captured and sank only two ships and a small trawler—two other steamers were stopped and released—for a total of 10,683 tons before she was caught coaling on the African coast in neutral Spanish waters at Rio de Oro by the cruiser *Highflyer* on 26 August. The cruiser's commander, Captain Henry T. Buller, undoubtedly violated Spanish neutrality in attacking and inflicting sufficient damage to cause her crew to scuttle the *Kaiser Wilhelm der Grosse* while she was in Spanish waters. Once the raider had been safely eliminated, the British government in its note of apology to Spain argued that the German raider had used the anchorage as a base for nine days and had been met there by supply ships and colliers. The Spanish had been unable to enforce their neutrality, and to have left the German ship untouched would have been to invite similar violations of neutrality by German raiders in isolated anchorages and bays throughout the world.[33]

The *Kronprinz Wilhelm* (14,908 tons) and the *Prinz Eitel Friedrich* (8,797 tons) were the most successful and long lived of these early auxiliary cruisers. The *Kronprinz Wilhelm*, after being surprised while being armed by the *Karlsruhe* at the beginning of the war, escaped and proceeded to the vicinity of the Azores, where she coaled from a German collier and then went south to operate in an area roughly 500 by 750 miles in the vicinity of the isolated Brazilian island of Fernando Noronha. Her commander, Kapitänleutnant Thierfelder, former navigating officer of the *Karlsruhe*, managed to keep his ship under way for over eight months without anchoring. He satisfied most of the former liner's considerable demands for coal by coaling from eight of his prizes. The coaling was also accomplished at sea while steaming slowly ahead, accepting the risks and damage this entailed as liner and collier came together in the swell. By the time the cruise had ended, this method of coaling had resulted in appreciable damage, with the ship leaking badly and the boilers and engines in a poor state. Thierfelder, his crew suffering from lack of fresh food, finally had to bring his ship into Hampton Roads on 11 April 1915 and was interned on the 26th. The *Kronprinz Wilhelm* had accounted for fifteen ships (including one ship released with the crews of the prizes), or a total of 60,522 tons.

The *Prinz Eitel Friedrich* (Korvettenkapitän Max Thierichens), which began her cruise at Tsingtau, captured and sank eleven ships, representing 33,423 tons, before she limped into Newport News and eventual internment on 11 March 1915. As with the *Kronprinz Wilhelm*, it was essentially a lack of coal and supplies that ended her career, rather than any countermeasures on the part of the Allies.[34] The large liners had not fulfilled their expectations as far as cruiser warfare was concerned, primarily because of their excessive coal consumption. They were also a diminishing asset; the Germans were running out of suitable liners with sufficient speed to employ. The same was true with the supply of colliers that could service them. Neutrality regulations coupled with steady diplomatic pressure on the part of the British and French made the work of the Etappen officers increasingly difficult. When the Germans tried raiding with surface ships again, they used a different type of vessel.

The British problem of hunting German warships abroad was exacerbated by the conflicting obligations of the Royal Navy to support two other major endeavors in the opening months of the war. Surprisingly, early in the war there were the expeditions against the German colonies. There were also the great imperial convoys, in which sizable numbers of troops were moved about the British Empire. The Royal Navy supported the expeditions when necessary, protected the convoys, and of course hunted for the German warships on the loose, which, in addition to single raiders, included Spee's powerful squadron. The margin of superiority and the watch on the German fleet in home waters also had to be maintained. The British received some French naval assistance—a small portion of the troop movements were also French—and after the Japanese entered the war, there was significant Japanese naval assistance in the Pacific and Indian oceans; but inevitably, the major part of the burden fell on the Royal Navy, which had to do the job without drawing more than was absolutely necessary on modern warships from the Grand Fleet.

The question of the German colonies was examined by a special subcommittee of the Committee of Imperial Defence under the presidency of Admiral Sir Henry Jackson. The committee worked under the general guidelines that all operations were to be for the defense of maritime communications rather than territorial conquest and should use local troops rather than dissipate forces from the main theater. Bounded by these limitations, the committee in its report of 5 August recommended as suitable objectives Togoland, with its powerful wireless station at Kamina; the port of Duala in the Cameroons, where there were a number of German steamers that might be converted into raiders; Rabaul, the major port for German New Guinea and the Bismarck Archipelago, to be seized by Australian forces; and Apia, in German Samoa, to be seized by New Zealand forces.[35]

These initial and comparatively limited objectives were soon surpassed and, perhaps inevitably, the question of territorial conquest and of seizing prizes to be used for future compensations to balance German gains in Europe overrode the idea of merely protecting maritime communications. When the cabinet discussed the project, Prime Minister Asquith was quoted as describing them as appearing "more like a gang of Elizabethan buccaneers than a meek collection of black-coated Liberal Ministers."[36] Moreover, in the Pacific the expeditions were undertaken before command of the sea was assured, while Spee and his powerful squadron were still loose—indeed, when their exact location was unknown. There were many reasons for this; many might be summed up under the term *war fever*. There was certainly the enthusiasm of the Australians, New Zealanders, and South Africans for gains and the desire to eliminate the German threat from the vicinity of their territory, and of course the fact that no one realized how long the war would last and that prizes had best be seized while opportunity permitted.[37]

Togoland, the smallest of the German colonies in Africa, was the easiest to conquer. The port of Lomé was captured on 7 August, and the entire colony surrendered before the end of August. The Cameroons were a much larger colony and a much tougher one to conquer. The British, later joined by the French, began naval operations on the coast in early September and took Duala on the 27th. They then went beyond the initial objective of destroying a German base and entered into a long and difficult campaign in the interior that involved tying down British naval forces (old cruisers and gunboats) near the coast for some months. The last German garrison did not surrender until February of 1916. There was little naval activity in the campaign for German South West Africa, which was not completed until July of 1915.[38]

On the other side of Africa, the campaign against German East Africa began badly with the repulse of a landing by Indian troops at Tanga in November 1914, and the commander of the German forces, Lieutenant-Colonel Paul von Lettow-Vorbeck, proved to be a master of guerrilla warfare, evading attempts by South African, Belgian, and Portuguese forces to trap him. He had still not surrendered when the war in Europe ended, and a special clause in the Armistice referred specifically to him.[39] The campaigns, though, have little naval interest except for the ingenious and successful effort by the British in 1915 to bring two armed launches overland by way of the Belgian Congo to wrest control of Lake Tanganyika from the German flotilla that had enjoyed uncontested superiority on the more than six-hundred-mile-long lake since the beginning of the war. The expedition, only twenty-eight men commanded by Lieutenant-Commander G. Spicer-Simson, overcame formidable natural obstacles to get their launches, whimsically named *Mimi* and *Tou-Tou*, in place and succeeded in capturing the German gunboat *Kingani* on 26 December. The damaged vessel quickly sank but was raised and renamed *Fifi* in British service. On 9 February 1916, the British flotilla captured the German steamer *Hedwig von Wissmann*. The two remaining German steamers were eventually run ashore or scuttled in port. The Lake Tanganyika expedition was one of the few bright spots for the British in a generally frustrating and dismal campaign.[40]

The capture of the German islands in the Pacific had more significance for the naval war and certainly greater potential for disaster because of the presence of Spee. Rear Admiral Sir George Patey, commander in chief of the Australian Squadron, had the battle cruiser *Australia,* which with her eight 12-inch guns and 25 knots speed was superior to anything in Spee's squadron. The Australian Squadron searched the waters around New Britain for the German Squadron on 11 and 12 August, but Patey had to suspend the hunt in order to cover both the New Zealand expedition to Samoa and, afterward, the Australian expedition to New Britain. Patey was reluctant to see these expeditions take place before Spee had been located.

The New Zealanders were first off the mark, and an expedition of approximately 1,400 troops captured Apia, the main port on the island of Upolu (German Samoa), on the 30th. The New Zealand garrison was landed, covered by three old light cruisers and the *Australia, Melbourne,* and *Montcalm,* but Patey decided that with Spee's squadron at large, it would be safer to leave no warship in Samoa where it might be overwhelmed. This turned out to be a wise precaution.[41]

Patey now faced conflicting demands for his squadron. The large convoy containing the expeditionary force of approximately twenty thousand men which the Australian government had offered to the British for service in the war was in the process of formation and had to be covered on its voyage through the Indian Ocean to Aden. The whereabouts of Spee's squadron, or isolated German warships such as the gunboat *Geier,* and the activities of German cruisers such as the *Emden* and *Königsberg* posed threats to its safety. However, Patey first had to cover the Australian expedition to Rabaul. The "Australian Naval and Military Expeditionary Force," approximately five hundred naval reservists and a battalion of infantry, roughly fifteen hundred troops, began landing on the island of Neu-Pommern (New Britain) on 11 September. There was some scattered but sharp resistance from the German garrison, roughly 61 Europeans and 240 native troops, but the issue was not in doubt and the British flag was formally raised at Rabaul on the 13th.[42] These expeditions were minor footnotes to the war, and one might legitimately ask if it would not have been better for the German islands in the Pacific to have been left "to wither on the vine" until they could be seized at a later date after other, more pressing problems had been resolved.

THE IMPERIAL CONVOYS

The most urgent problem for Patey was the Australian and New Zealand convoys. The combined convoy, sometimes referred to as the Australasian Convoy, was one of largest of the great imperial convoys. The New Zealand contingent, approximately 8,300 men and 3,800 horses in ten transports, was due to leave Wellington for Fremantle on 25 September. Somewhere on the route it would join the Australian Expeditionary Force, some twenty thousand men in twenty-six transports, which was concentrating at King

George Sound on the southwestern tip of Australia. Patey would meet the convoy with the *Australia, Melbourne,* and *Sydney,* reinforced by the *Hampshire* from the China Squadron, and escort it across the Indian Ocean to Aden. The China Squadron, on the east and north of the route, would act as a distant screen.

The situation changed drastically when the *Scharnhorst* and *Gneisenau* appeared off Apia on 17 September and then made off in a northwesterly direction, that is, apparently heading back toward Asian waters. At the same time, the *Emden* had appeared in the Bay of Bengal. The Admiralty felt obliged to order the *Australia, Sydney,* and *Montcalm* back to Simonshafen to protect the New Britain expedition. The armored cruiser *Minotaur* and the Japanese battle cruiser *Ibuki* would cover the convoy across the Indian Ocean. The New Zealand government, however, was very concerned that its contingent would have only the three old P-class cruisers as an escort on its 3,000-mile voyage to western Australia. What if Spee turned to the south? The Admiralty took the position that the Germans would not know of the convoy arrangements and that it was not likely they would steam over 2,000 miles southward to an area where they were not apt to find coal. The Admiralty considered Spee's goal much more likely to be New Guinea and New Britain, and they would not abandon that expedition by withdrawing the *Australia.*

These questions reflected a potentially serious disagreement between Great Britain and Australia and New Zealand. The phenomenon of public opinion played a large role. The Royal Navy had not appeared to be very successful in the Pacific. Almost two months after the war had begun, the German Squadron was still on the loose, while in the Indian Ocean the *Emden* seemed to be making fools of the British. The destruction of the large Australian–New Zealand convoy seemed an obvious goal to the public, whether or not it would have been practical for the Germans to have attempted it, or if they even had sufficient intelligence of the date of departure or route. It seemed monstrous that Australia's own battle cruiser, *Australia,* and the other ships of the Australian Squadron were not used for the direct protection of their own men. The New Zealanders had equally strong feelings, and *their* battle cruiser, *New Zealand,* was on the other side of the world with the Grand Fleet.

To satisfy New Zealand public opinion, the Admiralty had to send the *Minotaur* and *Ibuki* to Wellington to join the old P-class cruisers in escorting the New Zealand contingent to Australia. The convoy could not sail until 16 October despite the fact that on 30 September the *Scharnhorst* and *Gneisenau* bombarded Papeete, the capital of the French island of Tahiti. This was more than 2,000 miles east-northeast of New Zealand, and in both the Admiralty's and Admiral Jerram's opinion, confirmed the fact that Spee was heading eastward toward South America rather than back toward New Guinea or Asia. The New Zealand government, however, regarded the bombardment as another failure of the navy to counter the German menace and refused to agree to the Admiralty's new request for the transports to sail without waiting for their powerful, and probably unnecessary, escort. The combined Australian–New Zealand convoy left King George Sound on 1 November. After two ships joined at sea, it numbered thirty-eight transports escorted by the *Minotaur, Ibuki, Melbourne,* and *Sydney.* A fifth cruiser, the *Pioneer,* broke down with condenser defects and had to leave the convoy, but the remaining escort was more than enough to handle any possible threat. After intelligence that Spee seemed headed eastward toward Easter Island, the only danger came from the *Emden* and *Königsberg.* On the morning of the 8th, the *Minotaur* received the order to leave the convoy and proceed to South West Africa in case Spee should round Cape Horn and head for South Africa. The next morning the convoy commander, Captain Silver in the *Melbourne,* intercepted the wireless message that a strange warship was approaching Direction Island in the Cocos group, 55 miles to the south. Captain Silver detached the *Sydney,* leading to the destruction of the *Emden* later in the day. By this time the *Königsberg* had been located in the Rufigi and placed under a close watch. This ended any real danger to the convoy, which proceeded without incident to Colombo, and then on to Aden and Suez, where the main body arrived on 1 December. The troops did not go on to England, however. Turkey had entered the war on the side of the Central Powers, and the British government decided to land the men in Egypt to complete their training and assist in the defense. The decision was taken as much for lack of suitable training sites in England as for reasons of military necessity.[43] They were supposed to move on to the front in France, but in fact were diverted to the Dardanelles campaign in the spring of 1915.

There was substantial shifting of troops within the British Empire, which required a number of convoys. The cabinet decided to bring home the majority of British regular troops from abroad and replace them with territorial battalions from home. Two convoys were devoted to repatriating regular troops from South Africa. The regiments in India were replaced by British troops from North China, Hong Kong, and Singapore. Those Indian battalions that could be spared were sent to Egypt, and some were even sent to the front in France. Other Indian battalions went to East Africa and, after Turkey entered the war, the Persian Gulf. There were seven major Indian convoys from Bombay and Karachi beginning in the second half of August, with the last one arriving at Suez on 2 December. The entry of Turkey into the war created new dangers in the Red Sea area, and from the 9th to the 11th of November, the *Duke of Edinburgh* and three fast transports of the sixth Indian convoy were detached on a successful minor operation to destroy the Turkish artillery positions in the Bay of Sheikh Syed, opposite Perim just outside the northern limits of the Aden protectorate. The *Duke of Edinburgh* bombarded the forts, and under the cover of her fire, troops landed to demolish the Turkish fortifications.[44]

The Canadian convoys, the last but certainly not the least in this brief survey, had certain similarities to the Australia–New Zealand convoy in the strong objection raised by the Canadian government to the proposed scale of escort. The initial escort was to have been Rear Admiral Wemyss's four light cruisers from the Western Patrol, and the initial size of the convoy was to have been fourteen ships. The Admiralty relied on the distant protection offered by the Grand Fleet, which was located between the German North Sea bases and the convoy route and the cruisers of Rear Admiral Phipps Hornby's North American Squadron, which were watching the German liners sheltering in New York and other North American ports. The latter were potential auxiliary cruisers.

Wemyss wondered why the Germans did not all try to break out together, for it would have been "an absolute impossibility to prevent some of them from escaping our two ships which were lying off New York watching them." The Germans, if boldly handled, might have gotten among the convoy at night and caused "much mischief." Wemyss regarded the large convoy as taking too many risks. Had one of the German cruisers still on the loose attacked, he later wrote, "None of my old tubs had sufficient speed to chase off such an enemy."[45] Wemyss could not know that these fears had little basis in reality. The nearest German cruiser actually at sea was the *Karlsruhe*, thousands of miles to the south off Pernambuco.

The convoy swelled to thirty-three ships before sailing, and the planned escort seemed utterly inadequate to the Canadians. The Admiralty therefore agreed to allay Canadian concern by ordering the old battleship *Glory*, then in the Halifax area, to meet the convoy off Cape Race after it left the Saint Lawrence River on 3 October. Admiral Hornby in the armored cruiser *Lancaster* joined the convoy on its southern flank as far as the limits of his station, leaving the cruiser *Suffolk*, armed merchant cruiser *Caronia*, and Canadian cruiser *Niobe* in the New York area. The old battleship *Majestic* was sent from the Seventh Battle Squadron of the Channel Fleet to meet the convoy in the mid-Atlantic on the 9th, a day after the *Glory* and *Lancaster* turned back. The *Majestic* was accompanied by a surprise from the Admiralty—the powerful battle cruiser *Princess Royal*. The Admiralty had kept her departure secret even from Wemyss because of security lapses in the Canadian press concerning the convoy's composition. This scale of protection was more than enough to handle any single raider that might have slipped through; the only thing likely to have challenged it would have been Hipper's plan to send all the battle cruisers to sea (see chapter 2). But the ability of Hipper to reach the Atlantic undetected at this particular moment was problematical thanks to Jellicoe's dispositions. The real protection of the convoy came from the occupation by close to three cruiser squadrons of the cruiser areas in the North Sea. These zones between Peterhead and Norway had been established in September. The light cruisers and battle squadrons of the Grand Fleet were out in support, and there was a second line of protection with the two battle cruiser squadrons to sight any ship that might have passed through the main line at night. Jellicoe kept his screening operation at full force from the 2d to the 10th, and the official history describes the cover as "stronger than it had been at any time during the war."[46]

The story of the imperial convoys does not make very exciting reading, for it is really a story of what did not happen. It is also an example of the exercise of sea power. The British and French had been able to move hundreds of ships and thousands of troops throughout the world, and the Germans, as well as their Austrian allies in the Mediterranean, had been powerless to stop them. This was also a period when the Germans had the greatest number of warships at large during the entire war. The worldwide operations had certainly strained the resources of the Royal Navy, which also had to support the overseas expeditions and hunt for raiders. But neither ship nor man in the convoys had been lost due to enemy action.

CORONEL AND THE FALKLANDS

The most powerful and dangerous of the German forces at large in the opening months of the war was Spee's squadron, and it is time to take up his story once again. The British and French could not rest easily until he had been accounted for. After detaching the *Emden*, Spee had proceeded eastward through the Marshall Islands. On 22 August he sent the *Nürnberg* to Honolulu with mails and dispatches and orders for German agents in South America to prepare coal and provisions in anticipation of his arrival. The German Squadron continued eastward at a leisurely pace, conserving as much fuel as possible. Spee learned of the Japanese declaration of war on the 26th. There could be no thought of return to Tsingtau, and great danger now lay to the north and west. The *Nürnberg* rejoined Spee at sea on 6 September, and he detached the cruiser along with the tender *Titania* to cut the cable between Fiji and Honolulu at Fanning Island. The *Nürnberg*, wearing a French ensign when she approached the island, accomplished this on the 7th and rejoined the squadron the following day at Christmas Island, where they coaled.

Spee, who had now learned of the New Zealand occupation of Apia, decided to take the calculated risk of revealing his whereabouts and running into the one ship in the southern Pacific he was really concerned about, the *Australia*. He turned back to the southwest with the *Scharnhorst* and *Gneisenau* for a raid on Apia that he hoped might catch vulnerable British ships at anchor. The *Nürnberg* escorted his supply ships to a prearranged rendezvous. The *Scharnhorst* and *Gneisenau* appeared off Apia on 14 September and found only a three-masted American schooner in the harbor. The Germans had demonstrated the wisdom of the British decision not to leave any small naval force likely to be overwhelmed with the garrison. The Germans refrained from firing on the town, as they did not want to cause casualties among the civilian (and German) population or damage German property. The first officer of the *Gneisenau* reported that German colonists at the extreme west of the island of Upolu gave valuable intelligence on the situation and offered to serve as guides for an attack on the New Zealand garrison, but this was beyond the scope of the ships' mission and might have entailed losses that would diminish their fighting efficiency.[47] Moreover, the garrison was probably much too strong to be overcome by a landing party from the two cruisers.

Spee had ostentatiously steamed off to the northwest, and this deception had its effect, for we have seen how fears for the safety of the Australian expedition to New Britain and New Guinea had forced the Admiralty to alter Patey's plans and divert the *Australia* away from the large Australia—New Zealand convoy to the waters around New Britain to cover the expedition. An Australian force, escorted by the *Australia*, *Montcalm*, and *Encounter*, occupied Friedrich-Wilhemshafen on the mainland of New Guinea on 24 September.

Spee was actually heading in the opposite direction again. There was too much of a swell for him to coal at isolated Suvurov Island, so he proceeded to Bora Bora in the

French-owned Society Islands to try and obtain provisions. There was no resistance when the Germans reached Bora Bora on the 21st. They supposedly were careful to have only French- and English-speaking officers deal with the islanders and implied they were English to a gendarme who boarded. The Germans politely paid cash for the provisions they obtained from the islanders, but there was not enough to satisfy their needs, and Spee, who had learned there were stocks of coal at the administrative capital of Papeete, decided to proceed to Tahiti.

The *Scharnhorst* and *Gneisenau* were off Papeete on the 22d, but there was a small French garrison of colonial infantry here as well as a French gunboat, the *Zélée*. There were also five thousand tons of Cardiff coal on shore, and more in a German steamer, the *Walküre*, which had been captured by the *Zélée* the preceding month. The *Zélée* (700 tons, with two 100-mm and four 65-mm guns) was another classic example of a colonial ship serving in an isolated location that had no chance against a modern warship. Although the island had learned of the outbreak of war from a British steamer on 6 August, the official notification from France only arrived on the 29th. Lieutenant Destremau, commanding officer of the *Zélée*, anticipating attack by a gunboat such as the *Geier*, had already landed his ship's stern 100-mm gun and 65-mm secondary armament to add to the ancient artillery of the local fortifications on the hill overlooking the town. The French fired warning shots at the German cruisers on their arrival, set fire to the stock of coal, and scuttled the *Zélée* at her moorings. The guns of the German cruisers completed the job of sinking the gunboat and bombarded the town, but Spee could not disregard the possibility that there were mines at the harbor entrance and, far from any base, he could not run the risk of damage. The Germans steamed off without coal or provisions, having wasted ammunition and once again disclosed their presence.[48]

The news of the attack on Papeete indicated that Spee had moved eastward again, but the Admiralty feared he might undertake similar attacks on Fiji, Samoa, or even New Zealand, and ordered Patey to make Suva (Fiji) his base and search for the Germans in those waters. Patey received the order to proceed to Suva on 3 October and immediately sailed with the *Australia, Montcalm,* and *Sydney,* followed the next day by the light cruiser *Encounter,* two destroyers, a submarine, and four supply ships. He concluded that New Guinea was not in danger and the German objective was South America and was therefore happy to be heading in what he considered the right direction.

The role of the Japanese fleet in the first few months of the war is sometimes overlooked, possibly because it engaged in no major action with the Germans at sea. Nevertheless it was the steady pressure exerted by Japanese sea power that had much to do with forcing Spee toward South America. Vice Admiral Yamaya with the force designated as the First South Sea Squadron—the second-class battle cruisers *Kurama* and *Tsukuba,* the armored cruiser *Asama,* and a flotilla of destroyers—had sailed from Japan on 14 September to search the Caroline and Marshall islands and to destroy the German facilities at Jaluit in the Marshall group. This squadron reached Truk on 11 October.

On 1 October another Japanese force, Rear Admiral Tsuchiyama's Second South

Sea Squadron—the battleship *Satsuma* (four 12-inch and eight 10-inch guns) and light cruisers *Yahagi* and *Hirado*—sailed from Japan for Rabaul. This squadron, according to an agreement reached between the British and Japanese admiralties, would cruise in the area north of 20° south and west of 140° east—an area stretching from Japan to Australia and including Yap, Anguar, and the Philippines. The First South Sea Squadron would cruise north of the equator and east of 140° east, while the Australian Squadron would cruise south of the equator and west of 140° west, to include the French islands. The three squadrons were to communicate whenever possible with each other and their respective admiralties and "by their movements assist each other's operations."[49] This meant the Japanese Second South Sea Squadron would assist the British Borneo Squadron (sloops *Clio* and *Cadmus*, destroyers, and armed merchant cruisers), based at Sandakan and, later, Darvel Bay, in watching Philippine waters to guard against the possibility German ships sheltering in neutral U.S.-controlled territory might put to sea. The Japanese also sent a battleship to North American waters where the *Hizen* (the former Russian battleship *Retvizan*, captured in the Russo-Japanese War) reinforced the Allied force (the *Newcastle, Rainbow,* and *Idzumo*) protecting trade.

The Japanese were equally ready to intervene in the Indian Ocean where, as we have seen, the armored cruisers *Tokiwa* and *Yakumo* were sent to Singapore to serve as a nucleus for a squadron. The battle cruiser *Ibuki* had been an important part of the Australian–New Zealand convoy's protection, and for a short time after the destruction of the *Emden*, she had been the convoy's sole protection, a situation not without irony because of strong anti-Japanese racial feeling in Australia before the war where the Japanese Empire was seen as the potential enemy. The important Japanese role was recognized by the official historian of the naval war, Sir Julian Corbett. Commenting on the many demands put on the Royal Navy in eastern waters during the first months of the war, he wrote, "Indeed it is not easy to see how the thing could have been done effectively but for the assistance which Japan so opportunely provided."[50]

In reality, the Japanese intervention on a large scale was not always welcome and posed certain delicate problems. Those relating to diplomatic matters, such as Japanese demands in China or ambitions for the German islands in the Pacific north of the equator, are beyond the scope of this book.[51] On strictly naval matters, the British were not happy to see a Japanese vice admiral senior in rank to the British commander in chief East Indies, and to get around the difficulty, the Admiralty suggested separate spheres of action with the Japanese working east of the meridian of 90° east, which bisected the Bay of Bengal. The Japanese Squadron guarded the focal points of Cape Negrais, Acheh Head, and Sunda Strait and had the use of Singapore, Penang, and Rangoon as bases. Racial feeling also played a role in causing the Admiralty to alter the original Japanese proposal for division of the Pacific that would have had the First Japanese South Sea Squadron and the Australian Squadron operating east of 140° east and both Australians and Japanese ships reinforcing the French Islands east of 160° east as necessary. This would have entailed placing the Australian Squadron under a Japanese vice admiral and was rejected.[52] Too much should not be made of this. There had been a tradition of pro-Japanese feeling in the Royal Navy—quite evident during the Russo-Japanese War. Moreover, jockeying for position between Allies as to who would have command was probably the norm rather than the exception. The situation vis-à-vis the British and Japanese was no different than that between the British and French or the French and Italians at other times and places during the war.

Spee in the meantime had gone to Nukuhiva in the French Marquesas Islands where he spent a week, 26 September to 3 October, coaling and replenishing his provisions. He also sent two of his supply ships, the *Ahlers* and *Holsatia*, now empty, to Honolulu with dispatches and more precise instructions for colliers to meet him at Easter Island and Mas a Fuera in the Juan Fernandez group, extremely remote islands under Chilean sovereignty, where he could hope to coal in peace. Spee's wireless operators were also able to intercept wireless transmissions from the *Dresden* to the *Leipzig*, so that he learned for the first time that both German cruisers were on the west coast of South America. On the night of 6–7 October, the *Scharnhorst* managed to reach the *Dresden* with her wireless, enabling Spee to coordinate a concentration of the German warships. When Spee arrived off Easter Island on 12 October, the *Dresden* was waiting with her tender, the *Baden*. The *Leipzig* joined on the 14th, with three steamers of the Kosmos line. The German concentration—two armored cruisers and three light cruisers—was complete.

What was the Admiralty doing as Spee headed inexorably away from the South Seas to South American waters? On 5 October they were able to read a German signal intercepted by the wireless station at Suva that the *Scharnhorst* was on her way between the Marquesas and Easter Island. Two days later there was another wireless message, this time *en clair*, warning that the *Australia* and other large ships had left Rabaul going eastward and that "the Japanese squadron was all over the place." This could only confirm Patey's and Jerram's belief that the Germans were on their way to South America.

The closest British force to the southern portion of the west coast of South America was the squadron of Rear Admiral Christopher Cradock, who had begun the war in Caribbean waters and who had been working his way down the eastern coast of South America, searching for raiders and attacking German trade. On 14 September the Admiralty had informed Cradock that there was a good chance Spee might arrive on the west coast of South America or pass through the Strait of Magellan and that Cradock was to concentrate a squadron strong enough to meet the *Scharnhorst* and *Gneisenau*. Until the arrival of the armored cruiser *Defence*, ordered from the Mediterranean as a reinforcement, Cradock was to keep the old battleship *Canopus* and at least one County-class cruiser with his squadron. As soon as he had superior force, he was to search the Strait of Magellan, ready according to information either to return to the Plate area or search the Chilean coast as far north as Valparaiso. In the light of the tragedy that followed, the Admiralty cables to Cradock and what he assumed them to mean became controversial. The Admiralty was probably more concerned with protection of trade and the Australia–New Zealand troop transport in the Indian Ocean than with the situation on the west coast of South America. The destruction of Spee's squadron apparently was not, considering the navy's many responsibilities of the time, given a high priority. The Admiralty were also deceived, at least temporarily, by Spee's departure in a northeasterly direction after his appearance at Apia. There could have been little doubt in their minds, however, of his intentions after the bombardment of Papeete, and even less after interception and decoding of a wireless message indicating the Germans were on their way to Easter Island.

Cradock's force was inferior to the German Squadron. The *Good Hope* and *Monmouth* were weaker than the *Scharnhorst* and *Gneisenau* to begin with. The *Monmouth* was described as having been practically condemned as unfit for further service when she was "hauled off the dockyard wall" and commissioned with a scratch crew of coastguardsmen and boys, arriving in South American waters only half-equipped and kept going only by "superhuman efforts." The German squadron was markedly superior in gun power, with a far heavier weight of broadside, and the German superiority was increased still more by the fact that neither the *Good Hope* nor the *Monmouth* could have used effectively the guns in their lower casements in a heavy sea, whereas the casement guns of the *Scharnhorst* and *Gneisenau* were mounted farther above the waterline and were less affected by the state of the sea. The old battleship *Canopus* might have helped to even the odds, although there is some doubt she would have given Cradock superiority. She too was manned by a scratch crew from the training schools, coast guard, and Naval Reserve. Her 12-inch guns were characterized as antiques, with a maximum range that was actually three hundred yards less than the 8.2-inch guns of the German cruisers. The *Canopus*'s guns were also difficult to load and lay in heavy seas.[53]

The major problem with the *Canopus* in Cradock's mind was probably her speed. Would he have been able to bring the German Squadron to action if his force was tied to her? Moreover, it is now apparent that Cradock was deceived as to the real speed the *Canopus* was capable of by erroneous and exaggerated reports of her defects issued by her engineer commander, who had broken down under the strain of war.[54] Cradock therefore believed he could not bring the Germans to action if he remained in company with the *Canopus* and that in the Admiralty's eyes this was his primary objective. The Admiralty did nothing to discourage him, although Churchill, who consistently denied any responsibility for the disaster, and Battenberg did have serious doubts about the situation and thought Cradock should concentrate his main force at the Falklands and send only the light cruiser *Glasgow* around to search the west coast of South America. They did not make this clear to Cradock, who was not the man to flinch, especially when the Admiralty's orders implied they considered his force adequate. The Admiralty finally did signal Cradock to concentrate his squadron with the *Canopus* and wait for the arrival of the *Defence*—whose voyage they had delayed—but the signal was only issued on 3 November, and by then the battle had already been fought.[55]

Spee left Mas a Fuera on the night of 26 October, steaming eastward, and on the 31st he learned of the presence of the *Glasgow* at the little Chilean port of Coronel. He proceeded to intercept, and in the late afternoon of 1 November encountered not only the

Glasgow but Cradock in the *Good Hope* with the *Monmouth* and the armed merchant cruiser *Otranto*. Cradock was searching for the *Leipzig*, whose wireless transmissions had indicated she was in the area. Spee had been clever in using only the *Leipzig*'s transmitter to conceal the presence of the other German cruisers. The *Canopus* was then 300 miles astern, convoying Cradock's colliers.

The *Glasgow* was first to spot the German Squadron and fell back on the *Good Hope* at around 5:00 P.M. Cradock formed his line of battle with the *Good Hope, Monmouth, Glasgow*, and *Otranto* against the *Scharnhorst, Gneisenau, Leipzig,* and *Dresden*—the *Nürnberg* joined only later in the battle. Cradock altered course toward the Germans and tried to force the action immediately, when the Germans would have had the setting sun directly in their eyes. Spee declined and kept his distance. The armed merchant cruiser *Otranto* really could have accomplished little in this type of encounter, and Cradock sent her away. The *Otranto* survived and took no further part in the action.

The conditions altered to the great disadvantage of the British once the setting sun dropped below the horizon just before 7:00 P.M. Now it was the British who were silhouetted against the afterglow, whereas the German ships were lost in the gathering dusk. This was the moment for the Germans to begin the action in earnest, and their superior gunnery quickly began to tell. By the time the battle ended in the darkness, the *Good Hope* and *Monmouth* had been sunk with no survivors. The *Glasgow* reluctantly had to abandon the *Monmouth* after 8:20—there was nothing she could do, and someone had to warn the *Canopus* steaming toward the scene lest she be surprised and overwhelmed: German jamming blocked wireless transmissions until the *Glasgow* was well out of range. An officer in the *Glasgow* remarked on the "heartbreaking hours of depression that followed, the compulsory abandonment of our 'chummy ship' weighed more on us than the bitterness of the general defeat."[56]

The Battle of Coronel was the first defeat suffered by the Royal Navy in a naval action in more than one hundred years. German losses in men and matériel were trifling, although they had expended 42 percent of their 8.2-inch ammunition, which could not be replaced away from home. The British loss of life—more than 1,600—was tragic, but the matériel loss—two elderly cruisers—was insignificant as far as the naval balance was concerned. The psychological effects were much greater. It was a nasty shock, but the effects did not last long. Spee is reported to have had a premonition of this. On 3 November the *Scharnhorst, Gneisenau,* and *Nürnberg* entered Valparaiso for the twenty-four hours allotted under international law to coal and reprovision—only three ships were allowed under the law; the other two cruisers had to return to Mas a Fuera to coal. As Spee was about to depart, an admiring lady presented him with a bouquet of flowers. "Thank you, they will do very nicely for my grave," he is reported to have said.[57]

The British reaction was swift. Fisher had become First Sea Lord on 31 October. On 4 November the Admiralty received word of the Coronel disaster. Fisher, whatever his faults, now appeared at his best. He ordered not one but two battle cruisers—the *Invincible* and *Inflexible*—to the South Atlantic, and when the dockyards pleaded for more time to make them ready he implied they would sail with dockyard workers aboard if necessary. The work that had to be accomplished at Devonport in only three days was, according to an officer in the *Invincible*, "colossal," but the two ships sailed on the 11th.[58] The command was given to Vice Admiral Sturdee, the chief of staff. Fisher detested Sturdee and was anxious to get rid of him, but Churchill did not want it to appear as if he was being dismissed because of the Coronel disaster.

The detachment of the battle cruisers was a calculated risk, for as we have seen, Jellicoe's margin of superiority in this type over the High Sea Fleet was virtually nonexistent. Jellicoe did not relax until they returned. Fisher had in this respect considerable nerve and moral courage, for he correctly foresaw the need for overwhelming force at the decisive place, even if he could not foresee how long the ships would be gone. Furthermore, the Admiralty sent yet a third battle cruiser—*Princess Royal*—to North American waters.

This deployment demonstrated the far-reaching effects a single powerful naval force could have. The Admiralty had to guard against the prospect that Spee would proceed north and then pass through the Panama Canal into the Caribbean. He might then defeat the relatively weak Allied forces in the West Indies (two British armored cruisers and two old French cruisers) and steam north to "liberate" the sizable number of German liners sheltering in New York. Here Admiral Hornby had only the old battleship *Glory*, three equally old armored cruisers, and an armed merchant cruiser to oppose him. United States regulations placed a limit of three belligerent warships in transit through the Panama Canal at any one time, with another three allowed at either terminal, for a maximum of six in United States territorial waters at one time.[59] Spee's five cruisers would therefore have been able to transit from the Pacific to the Caribbean in less than a day's time. There were also rumors that a German battle cruiser might slip out to attack the North Atlantic sea lanes in a move coordinated with operations off the Plate should Spee proceed around Cape Horn. The prospect seems far-fetched now, but at the time it was considered real enough for the very great risk of sending the third battle cruiser to be taken. The *Princess Royal* sailed for Halifax on 12 November in a move so secret that Admiral Hornby, commander in chief North America, did not even know she was coming. Hornby concentrated the armored cruisers *Essex, Lancaster,* and *Berwick* and the French *Condé* in the West Indies to guard against Spee's breaking through the Panama Canal. The Admiralty rejected his proposal to send the *Princess Royal* to the West Indies until a false report on 29 November that the Germans were off the north Chilean port of Iquique indicating a move toward Panama gave Hornby sufficient justification for ordering the battle cruiser to Jamaica.

The other British forces in South American waters under Admiral Stoddart, the armored cruisers *Carnarvon, Cornwall,* and *Defence,* together with the *Canopus* and Coronel survivors the *Glasgow* and *Otranto* to be reinforced by the *Kent* from the Cape Verdes Station, would concentrate at Montevideo (later altered to Abrolhos Rocks) to await Sturdee's arrival.

Like a powerful magnet exerting lines of force, the influence of Spee's powerful squadron was felt throughout a considerable portion of the world. The mobility of sea power meant that each of the widely scattered British squadrons had to be powerful enough to deal with a sudden appearance of the German Squadron. What if Spee passed around Cape Horn and made for South Africa? Here the Germans might encourage an anti-British revolt, particularly if Spee convoyed transports with German reservists from South America.

The Admiralty had considered this possibility even before the Coronel disaster, and ordered the old battleship *Albion* to the Cape Station to cover the expedition against German South West Africa. After Coronel the Admiralty ordered the armored cruiser *Minotaur* to leave the Australia–New Zealand convoy in the Indian Ocean and join the *Albion*. In the light of what had happened to Cradock, deprived of the support of the *Canopus*, the Admiralty warned the commander in chief at the Cape, Admiral King-Hall, that the *Albion* and *Minotaur* "must always act in concert to avoid defeat in detail." The armored cruiser *Defence*, a sister ship of the *Minotaur*, was ordered to proceed to the Cape from Brazilian waters. The situation on the east coast of Africa and in the Indian Ocean also had been eased by the discovery and immobilization of the *Königsberg* and the destruction of the *Emden*. The light cruiser *Weymouth* could therefore be ordered to South African waters to give King-Hall (who already had the small cruisers *Hyacinth* and *Astraea*) a force capable of handling Spee's squadron. The seaborne South African expedition to Walvis Bay was postponed until the *Defence* joined.[60]

A new squadron was formed farther to the north on the West African coast to guard against the possibility that Spee might seek to interfere with the Cameroons expedition or attack the British and French West African colonies. The powerful armored cruisers *Warrior* and *Black Prince* were detached from the Mediterranean to join the cruisers *Donegal* and *Highflyer*, with the *Cumberland* also available from Duala if needed. The old battleship *Vengeance* came south from the Channel Fleet. The command was given to Admiral de Robeck of the Ninth Cruiser Squadron, who flew his flag in the *Warrior*. The squadron did not last very long. By 19 November the Admiralty decided it was no longer necessary, and de Robeck was ordered to resume command of the Ninth Cruiser Squadron, and the *Warrior*, *Black Prince*, and *Donegal* were to join the Grand Fleet, where the addition of the first pair of armored cruisers would be particularly welcome after the three battle cruisers had been detached for distant service.

The British and Japanese ordered similar measures to block Spee in the Pacific. The *Newcastle* and *Idzumo* would move south from Canadian waters to San Clemente Island off California, where they would be joined by the Japanese battleship *Hizen* and Admiral Patey in the *Australia*. The *Hizen* and the armored cruiser *Asama* had been off Honolulu, where the German gunboat *Geier* finally turned up on 15 October. Once the American authorities agreed to intern the warship on 8 November, the two Japanese warships were free to proceed to the American coast. The combined British and Japanese force then would sweep southward toward the presumed position of Spee in Chilean waters. The Japanese also agreed to move their First South Sea Squadron (battle cruisers *Kurama* and *Tsukuba*, armored cruiser *Iwate*) to the area between Fiji and the Marquesas, reinforcing it with another battle cruiser (the *Ikoma*) to ensure superiority over Spee.

After the *Emden* had been accounted for, the light cruisers *Chikuma* and *Yahagi* from the Indian Ocean also would join the squadron. The battle cruiser *Ibuki* and armored cruiser *Nisshin* would join the Second South Sea Squadron, with headquarters at Truk in the Caroline Islands. These powerful Japanese squadrons would guard against the possibility of Spee attempting to double back into the Pacific and toward the Indian Ocean. The destruction of Spee's squadron ultimately made the deployment of the First South Sea Squadron to Fiji unnecessary.[61]

The role of Patey and the *Australia* is usually overlooked. The admiral, convinced that the Germans were heading for South America, had been anxious to follow since before the middle of October, but the Admiralty held the Australian Squadron in the waters around Fiji. There was a period of nearly four weeks in which, as described by the Australian official history, the *Australia*, "like a dog tethered to his kennel, made darts into neighboring waters and was pulled back before any results could be obtained."[62] The *Australia* finally was allowed to sail from Suva on 8 November with a collier in company. She coaled at Fanning Island and joined the *Newcastle* and the Japanese warships at Chamela Bay, just south of Manzanillo on the Mexican coast on the 26th. Patey assumed command of the squadron, and Captain Moriyama of the *Idzumo* was promoted to rear admiral by his government to work the Japanese warships under Patey's general direction. The combined force steamed south to search the Galapagos Islands and were just off the Gulf of Panama for a search of the waters between the Gulf of Panama and the Gulf of Guayaquil in Ecuador when they received word of the Falklands battle, to the chagrin of the ship's company of *Australia*, who felt they and their powerful ship had been wasted.[63] Would the timely dispatch of the *Australia* to the west coast of South America, coupled with a clear order to Cradock to join her at some prearranged rendezvous, have avoided the disaster of Coronel? This is another "what might have been" of history that can never be answered.

Although everywhere Spee turned there were powerful squadrons gathered against him, the oceans were vast and he might elude his pursuers and turn up in an unexpected place, if only he could solve his coal difficulty. What were the German plans? The Admiralstab, before they knew of Coronel, had warned Spee in a message he received when he called at Valparaiso that the rendezvous positions with colliers in the Atlantic were compromised and that the trade lanes were strongly patrolled. Cruiser warfare could only be carried on by ships operating in groups, and the Admiralstab intended to concentrate ships operating abroad and order them to break for home. The lack of a base in which to refit or replenish ammunition, and the knowledge that news of the Battle of Coronel would hasten an Allied combination against him, meant Spee had no interest in staying long on the west coast of South America.

Spee returned to Mas a Fuera, where he found both the *Leipzig* and *Titania* had made prizes full of valuable coal. He finally made his decision to proceed around Cape Horn into the Atlantic, and sailed on 15 November. The faithful tender *Titania*, old, slow, and not up to the dangers of the trip around Cape Horn, was likely to have only delayed them and was scuttled. The German Squadron proceeded to the Chilean coast, and in the sheltered Saint Quentin Bay (Gulf of Peñas) met colliers that had slipped out of Chilean ports. The German cruisers crammed all possible coal and supplies into their ships for the voyage to the Atlantic. When they sailed on the 26th into the rough seas, some of the small cruisers had to heave to and throw some of the coal overboard for stability.

Spee had three supply ships with him, but the last letter he received from Berlin amplified the difficulties of coaling in the Atlantic: the Germans could anticipate that British pressure on neutral governments to restrict the supply of coal would intensify. The Admiralstab recommended carrying on a vigorous cruiser warfare but left it to his discretion when to break off, collect all the ships he could, and then break for home. The auxiliary cruiser *Kronprinz Wilhelm*, with her huge fuel consumption and scant military value, could be disposed of. The Admiralstab did not believe the breakthrough to Germany, with luck, would be impossible if sufficiently prepared. Allied forces operating separately for trade protection must not be given the time to concentrate, and Spee was advised to communicate his intentions in advance so the High Sea Fleet could assist. The Admiralstab did not, however, accept the recommendation of Korvettenkapitän von Knorr, the Etappen officer in San Francisco, that the battle cruisers of the High Sea Fleet make a raid into the Atlantic to support Spee's squadron. The difficulties of providing sufficient coal and maintaining these big ships at sea ruled this out.[64]

These recommendations had a vague, uncertain quality to them. Would they have produced the encounter in the North Sea that the Grand Fleet desired if the High Sea Fleet had made a significant sortie to cover Spee's return? Again, we have a question that can never be answered, another "what might have been" to be played out by today's wargamers. Tirpitz apparently favored authorizing Spee to refrain from undertaking cruiser warfare on the east coast of South America, where strong British forces were known to be gathering. He preferred that Spee should move out into the center of the Atlantic and break for home. Pohl, however, did not want to impinge on Spee's freedom of action.[65]

Spee had been proceeding in a surprisingly leisurely fashion since Coronel. Ultimately it proved disastrous. He captured a British bark loaded with coal and spent 3-6 December anchored off Picton Island in the Beagle Channel transferring coal while the sportsmen among the officers hunted on shore. On 6 December he called a conference of his captains and announced his fatal decision to attack the Falkland Islands. According to his intelligence, there were no British warships there, and other British warships had been drawn from the South American coast to South Africa because of the Boer revolt. Spee hoped to destroy the British wireless station and stocks of coal known to be there, and perhaps to capture the governor in retaliation for the imprisonment of the German governor of Samoa. The *Gneisenau* and *Nürnberg* would carry out the operation, screened by the remainder of the squadron. While Spee's chief of staff and the captain of the *Nürnberg* supported the plan, the captains of the *Gneisenau, Dresden,* and *Leipzig* were opposed and recommended avoiding the Falklands in order to appear off the Plate without advance warning. Unfortunately for Spee, he was out of wireless contact with German intelligence sources and could not receive the warnings about the approach of

Sturdee's battle cruisers.[66] Certain wireless operators had been guilty of indiscreet chatter about the big ships, but the intelligence never reached Spee.

Admiral Sturdee was also steaming for the same destination as the Germans and also proceeding in a surprisingly leisurely fashion, stopping to examine merchant ships and spending forty-eight hours coaling and transferring stores at the Abrolhos Rocks. These islets, about 300 miles south of Bahia and 30 miles off the Brazilian coast, were uninhabited except for a Brazilian lighthouse keeper. There were treacherous reefs and navigation was tricky, but it was possible for ships to anchor in shoal waters outside the limits of territorial waters. The British therefore had a base where they could coal, although it was exposed to an unpleasant swell. In the absence of any base on the neutral coast of South America, the place sufficed. The English Bank, outside of Argentine and Uruguayan territorial waters in the Plate, served a similar function farther to the south.

Stoddart's squadron waited at Abrolhos for Sturdee, who intended to proceed to the Falklands, coal, and then go on to the west coast of South America where Spee had last been reported. Sturdee sailed on the 28th, still at a leisurely pace to conserve fuel, conducted battle practice, and wasted still more time when a towing wire used for a target fouled one of the *Invincible*'s screws, necessitating the use of divers to clear the problem.

The Falklands, contrary to Spee's intelligence, were not devoid of British warships. The Admiralty decided that if operations against the German Squadron on the west coast of South America were necessary, the Falklands would be valuable as a coaling base, and the wireless and coal stocks therefore must be defended. The *Canopus* had been en route to join Stoddard's concentration when the Admiralty ordered her on 9 November to return to Port Stanley and anchor (beached if necessary for a good berth), so that her guns could command the entrance to the harbor, with an extemporized minefield laid outside, observation stations on shore, and the governor of the Falkland Islands to assist in organizing a local defense force to cover possible landing sites.

Sturdee finally arrived at the Falklands on the morning of 7 December and began coaling, an operation that was expected to take forty-eight hours. The British were therefore in the midst of coaling and only the *Kent* had steam at less than two hours' notice when the arrival of German warships was signaled by British lookouts just before 8:00 A.M. the following morning, 8 December.

Spee neglected the opportunity to inflict serious damage while the British were still unprepared. The *Gneisenau* reported the presence of British warships but initially believed them to be only cruisers, or possibly a slow old battleship like the *Canopus*. The *Kent*, first to leave the harbor, might have been overwhelmed, but the *Canopus* fired a salvo at her maximum elevation overland toward the Germans. The large columns of water from the shell splashes surprised the Germans and indicated the island was defended. Spee may have concluded a battleship was present but that it could not catch his squadron. The Germans did not approach closely and Spee's squadron turned away, thereby failing to take advantage of the British lack of readiness.

Sturdee, however dilatory he had been in reaching the Falklands, was calm in the crisis and is quoted as saying the Germans came at a most convenient hour, for he was able to give the order to raise steam and then go down for a good breakfast.[67] He was also assisted by good luck. Most of the day was fine and clear, unusual weather for that area, and the Germans could not take advantage of the frequent mist to escape. By 11:00 A.M. the *Bristol*, having had an engine open for repair, had sailed, the last of Sturdee's ships to leave harbor. She was, however, diverted from the main action. Spee had ordered his three colliers to remain off Port Pleasant, roughly 30 miles south of Port Stanley. They were observed and reported by a Mrs. Felton, one of the few residents.[68] Sturdee ordered the *Bristol* and the armed merchant cruiser *Macedonia* to find and destroy the German transports. There was always the possibility they might contain German reservists from South America who had been detailed to invade the colony.

The main British force, Sturdee in the *Invincible* with the *Inflexible, Glasgow, Kent, Carnarvon,* and *Cornwall,* followed the fleeing Germans in a southeasterly direction, the British working up to full speed with the battle cruisers belching great clouds of black smoke that all participants remarked on and that would later hamper gunnery. The battle cruisers pulled steadily ahead of the British armored cruisers, and at 10:50 A.M. Sturdee successively reduced speed to give them time to catch up. At 11:30 Sturdee signaled for the crews to take their midday meal and for those still in the coal rig to use the opportunity to clean up. The *Inflexible* was close enough to fire the first shot at the *Leipzig* at 12:50 P.M., and the *Invincible* followed shortly afterward. Spee decided that he might yet save something from the situation, and at about 1:20 he signaled the three light cruisers to break off and scatter in a southerly direction. They might escape to resume cruiser warfare. The *Scharnhorst* and *Gneisenau* would sacrifice themselves to cover their withdrawal. Sturdee's battle instructions had provided for this contingency, and without any further signal, the British light cruisers turned away in pursuit of their German counterparts. The German light cruisers were not in the best of condition after hard steaming and a long time without docking, and in the end only the *Dresden*, the fastest, was able to escape.

As the German forces diverged, there were three separate actions. The *Glasgow,* joined by the *Cornwall* when she was able to catch up, sank the *Leipzig*. The *Nürnberg* was eventually caught and sunk by the *Kent*. In the main action, Sturdee skillfully kept the range at about 12,500 yards, just beyond the maximum range of Spee's 5.9-inch secondary armament, which the Germans repeatedly tried to employ. The dense smoke of the battle cruisers hampered gunnery on both sides, but the weight of metal on the British side slowly began to tell, and by 4:17 the *Scharnhorst* had sunk with no survivors. The *Invincible* and *Inflexible,* joined by the *Carnarvon,* which had finally managed to catch up, finished off the *Gneisenau,* which sank a little after 5:45. The day ended in rain and mist, and in the cold, choppy waters there were few German survivors; many died of exposure after they had been picked up. There were 215 survivors from the four cruisers whose officers and men had numbered about 2,200. Neither Spee nor two of his sons in the squadron were among them. None of the British ships suffered serious damage; ten men were killed or died of wounds. Far to the north, the *Bristol* and *Macedonia* found two of the German colliers, the *Baden* and *Santa Isabel*, and sank them. A third ship, the *Seydlitz*, managed to get away without being seen and eventually made port in Argentina, where she was interned.[69]

The Germans had fought hard and well; their gunnery was excellent as usual, but in the end, as at Coronel, superior matériel had been decisive. The general law of the sea that big fish eat smaller fish and are in turn eaten by bigger fish appeared to have been demonstrated once again. The effects of Coronel were undone. Except for a few raiders soon to be interned, there was no organized German force at sea. Fisher was furious with Sturdee for having let the *Dresden* escape, and he behaved ungenerously toward the admiral. He was the exception: Sturdee received a baronetcy for his victory, and for most Coronel had been avenged. The battle cruisers were ordered home long before the *Dresden* was found—to the immense relief of Jellicoe. The *Dresden*, hiding in the numerous bays and inlets of Tierra del Fuego and the wild coast of southern Chile, accomplished little in terms of cruiser warfare. She was finally caught almost out of coal in Cumberland Bay at the remote island of Mas a Tierra on 14 March 1915 by the *Glasgow*, *Kent*, and the armed merchant cruiser *Orama*. Captain Luce of the *Glasgow* disregarded Chilean neutrality—which the *Dresden* also had violated by staying since the 9th instead of the customary twenty-four hours—and opened fire. The Germans hoisted a white flag, sent an officer in a boat to parley, and scuttled the ship.[70]

The destruction of Spee's squadron was an immense relief to the Admiralty, for, coupled with the virtual elimination of the other surface raiders, it freed a considerable number of ships for other purposes. For Great Britain and Germany, the two major naval antagonists, the war became much more concentrated in the North Sea and the Mediterranean. German surface raiders appeared again later in the war, but the losses they inflicted, although not negligible, paled in comparison to those inflicted by submarines, which came to be Germany's major hope in the war at sea. Even Spee, however dangerous his squadron, had accomplished little in terms of cruiser warfare. The ships attached to his squadron had accounted for very few merchantmen. His disappearance in the vast emptiness of the Pacific Ocean had not seriously harmed the British or French. There were few important trade routes in this area, and the destruction of an old gunboat like the *Zélée* was not much for a powerful squadron of cruisers in three months of war. There are some historians, such as Captain Bennett, who argue he would have accomplished far more had he operated in the Indian Ocean, despite the difficulties of coaling.[71]

The large number of cruisers and armed merchant cruisers released by the elimination of German surface forces on the world's oceans also gave the British the wherewithal to try the traditional maritime strategy of overseas expeditions, which will form the subject of the next chapter.

5

THE OVERSEAS CAMPAIGNS

ABORTIVE NORTH SEA
AND BALTIC PROJECTS

A common and traditional view in Great Britain was that the British army was a "projectile" to be fired by the British navy. How could the British make use of their naval superiority to strike the Germans at a strategic point where relatively small land forces could have a disproportionate effect the way they were perceived to have had in the Napoleonic Wars? Well before the outbreak of the war, the fertile mind of Winston Churchill had been seeking to use the navy in an offensive fashion and had ordered studies of possible landings on the Dutch, German, Danish, or Scandinavian coasts. The objective was to establish bases close to the major German ports. Rear Admiral Sir Lewis Bayly; Rear Admiral Arthur Leveson, the director of operations; and Major-General Sir George Aston (Royal Marines) prepared reports on the North Sea Islands of Borkum, Sylt, Helgoland, and Esbjerg (on the Danish Peninsula) as well as a scheme for seizing the western end of the Kiel Canal and a raid by destroyers on the Elbe. On 31 July, shortly before Britain entered the war, Churchill sent these reports to the prime minister and asked the War Office to study the plans. He then asked the War Office to study plans for (in order of priority) landings at Ameland or Born Deep (Holland), Ekersund (Norway), Laesø Channel (Denmark), and Kungsbacka Fjord (Sweden). Significantly, these all involved neutral rather than German territory, and, because he knew the requisite troops were not likely to be available, he assigned a lower priority to other studies he desired concerning Esbjerg, Sylt, Borkum, and Helgoland.

Churchill's proposals aroused little enthusiasm among the naval or military authorities, and one can imagine the horrified reaction of the Foreign Office to the idea of turning neutrals into enemies. The rationale behind the seizure of these points on neutral coasts or North Sea islands was to establish a secure base for destroyer and submarine flotillas as well as for aircraft to be used in a close blockade of the Helgoland

Bight. This would, it was hoped, create an intolerable situation for the Germans and force their fleet to sortie.

The naval staff managed to deflect Churchill from his scheme to capture Ameland with three thousand Royal Marines. The island could be taken easily and shelter a flotilla much closer to the Helgoland Bight than British bases, but the protection of this new base would tie up a strong force exposed to attack from both the Dutch and German bases close by. The Dutch would almost inevitably declare war and had torpedo craft and a few submarines that could be troublesome, while adequate defenses against cruiser attack at the new base would take considerable time to prepare.[1]

Helgoland was another potential objective. The little island was strategically placed at about 20 miles off the entrances to the Elbe, Weser, and Jade rivers and consequently would have been an ideal place from which aircraft could subject German naval movements to close observation. The island could also serve as a base for destroyers and submarines and provide early warning of sorties by German warships for British submarines. The seizure of Helgoland was a pet project of the former First Sea Lord Admiral Sir Arthur K. Wilson, despite the results of the 1913 study by Bayly that regarded the cost of its seizure as prohibitive. The island, not surprisingly, was heavily fortified. Wilson submitted plans for Helgoland's capture shortly after the outbreak of the war and continued working on them after he returned to the Admiralty in an unofficial capacity in October. Wilson was convinced improvements in range-finding gave ships an advantage over the land-based forts and that Helgoland could be seized without excessive cost by a landing party of marines covered by a fleet of predreadnoughts. The island could be defended, according to Wilson, by a small garrison equipped with a dozen machine guns to cover possible landing places and by a handful of 4-inch or 6-inch guns to ward off destroyers or light cruisers. The real defense would come from mining the mouths of the rivers the German fleet would have to use and then closely watching those exits with submarines.

Helgoland was discussed at the Loch Ewe Conference in Jellicoe's flagship *Iron Duke* on 17 September and dismissed. Contrary to Wilson's assertions, ships would have been no match for the heavy fortifications of Helgoland, where the high velocity and low trajectory of naval guns would be ineffective against the well-concealed and well-placed land guns. Even if they succeeded, the British could not hold the island so close to the German coast, and if the British could take it with fortifications intact, the Germans would surely have an easier time retaking it once the fortifications were demolished. Jellicoe reported: "Naval opinion was unanimous that the reduction of Heligoland would involve far more serious losses in capital ships than would compensate for any advantage gained, and that the difficulties in the way of a successful bombardment would be very great." Bayly brought up the subject of the Baltic, favoring an attack on Kiel by light cruisers and destroyers. This also was ruled out, largely because of the danger from minefields, although the possibility of a pair of submarines making the attempt was left open. Even Tyrwhitt, the bold and aggressive commander of the Harwich Force, was strongly opposed to the proposals, describing them later as "the equivalent of the death-warrant of a very large number of officers and men, besides being impossible and displaying considerable ignorance of the defences of Germany!"[2]

Borkum was probably Churchill's favorite among the North Sea projects, and with the continuing deadlock on the western front, he began pushing for it at the end of the year. The little island, 4 miles long by 3 miles wide, was located off the entrance to the Ems River, far enough (120 miles) from Wilhelmshaven that it could be seized before heavy reinforcements could arrive. It had figured prominently in the Admiralty prewar studies, and in December 1914 Churchill was convinced, as he wrote Fisher, that it was "the key to all Northern possibilities." He pointed out to Jellicoe that the possession of an overseas base here would quadruple their submarines by enabling the older B- and C-class boats to operate in German waters and would facilitate an invasion of Schleswig or possibly Oldenburg.[3]

Borkum was really the first stage in the policy of taking pressure off Russia by an attack on Germany in the Baltic. The plans have been generally associated with Fisher, who certainly spoke of the Baltic often enough, although there may be some doubt concerning the depth or seriousness of his intentions by this time. The general scheme was to seize Borkum, which could then be used as a base for the invasion of Schleswig-Holstein, which would lead to the occupation of the Kiel Canal. Intensive mining, supported from Borkum, would keep the German fleet out of the North Sea. Denmark would be won over to the Allied side, and the British army might land on Fyn to secure the passage through the Great Belt. The navy could then move through the Danish belts and the Kiel Canal into the Baltic, gain control of that sea, and then use Russian troops for a landing on the Pomeranian coast less than 100 miles from Berlin. May 1915 would be the target date for securing control of the Baltic.[4] The Danes apparently had an inkling of these views, and naturally regarded the consequences for Denmark as extremely dangerous. There were reportedly sighs of relief in the Danish government when Fisher and Churchill left office in 1915.[5]

Churchill and Fisher managed to persuade Prime Minister Asquith and the War Council on 7 January 1915 to approve in principle the proposed attack on Borkum, with detailed planning to commence for the operation to take place in three months' time. Lord Kitchener, the secretary of state for war, agreed somewhat surprisingly to spare a division.[6]

The Borkum operation never took place, largely because it was overshadowed by the Dardanelles campaign and a wide spectrum of naval opinion was resolutely opposed to it. The reaction to Churchill's paper by Captain Herbert Richmond, then assistant director of operations, was typical: "It is *quite mad*. The reasons for capturing it are NIL, the possibilities about the same. I have never read such an idiotic, amateur piece of work as this outline in my life." Richmond considered it "pure foolery" to risk troops in waters full of submarines. There were also strong technical reasons to recommend against the landing. The prevailing conditions of haze made it extremely difficult to range guns on the flat, featureless island with no marks on which to fix the ship. Navigation of deep-draft ships in the vicinity of the island with its sandbanks and minefields and without navigation marks would be very difficult. The batteries it would be necessary to destroy were not visible from the sea even under the clearest weather conditions—not likely to last very long—and one could not land troops until the area over which the transports would have to pass had been swept for mines, which, in turn, would not be possible until the batteries had been silenced.[7]

Churchill later felt that Fisher, although speaking favorably of Borkum in principle, "did not give that strong professional impulsion to the staffs necessary to secure the thorough exploration of the plan" and seemed ready to enter the Baltic without securing Borkum first. When questioned on how he would prevent the German fleet from falling on the British lines of communication in the North Sea or the Danish belts, Fisher spoke in general terms of sowing the North Sea extensively with mines and bottling up the Germans in this fashion. Aside from the fact that the British did not have at this stage the requisite number of mines, nor were the ones they had reliable, there was another obvious problem with this line of reasoning. Sir Julian Corbett, the noted naval historian and friend of Fisher whom the First Sea Lord had charged with preparing a paper arguing in favor of the Baltic operation, pointed it out: If they were to paralyze the movements of the German fleet in the North Sea through the extensive use of mines, what was to prevent the Germans from doing the same thing to the British in the Baltic? Fisher never really replied, and one of his more recent biographers argues that he was by this stage of the war not really serious about a Baltic operation. Certainly Fisher spoke of the Baltic; his vast building program was supposedly shaped by it. The most noted examples were the three "freak" battle cruisers, the *Glorious*, *Courageous*, and *Furious*, with large-caliber armaments, high speed, and drafts deliberately kept below twenty-two to twenty-three feet for Baltic operations.[8] The battle cruisers, however, may have owed their characteristics as much to Fisher's obsession with speed and gun power at the expense of protection as to planned operations in the Baltic. Other portions of Fisher's program, submarines and destroyers, were as much for the North Sea as the Baltic, and even the large numbers of armored landing craft and monitors could have been used for operations on the Belgian coast. Fisher, whatever the characteristic violence of his language, knew the reality of modern war and was cautious in his actions. He frequently stressed the necessity of maintaining the margin over the German fleet and avoiding useless losses in subsidiary operations. Fisher, contrary to his later assertions before the Dardanelles Commission in 1916, which were shaped by his need to justify opposition to the Dardanelles expedition, may actually have regarded the Baltic project as a useful talking point, which could be used to deflect Churchill's wilder and more dubious projects.[9]

Oliver, chief of the Admiralty war staff, also was skeptical about the Baltic and wondered how Fisher would answer the problem of the British fleet passing the Great Belt in single line ahead with the German battle fleet deployed and "crossing the T" in front of it or how the British would be supplied in the Baltic. Oliver summed it up neatly: "I hated all these projects but had to be careful what I said. The saving clause was that two of the three [Churchill, Fisher, A.K. Wilson] were always violently opposed to the plan of the third under discussion. I was glad when the Dardanelles project came along as it took the old battleships out of the North Sea picture."[10]

The last of the abortive North Sea projects to be discussed before turning to the Dardanelles are the plans concerning the Belgian port of Zeebrugge. Jellicoe and Bayly discussed a plan for blocking the port by sinking ships across the channel, and Jellicoe suggested it to the Admiralty only to be told it was not considered practicable at the time. The potential for a German submarine base at Zeebrugge did alarm the Admiralty, and in mid-November they took up a suggestion from the commander in chief of the British Expeditionary Force (BEF) in France, General Sir John French, for a large-scale flanking operation directed against Zeebrugge. The Admiralty wanted a landing on the coast to take place at the time of the army's advance. Kitchener, initially favorable, backed away when he realized the amount of guns and ammunition required, and the army tried to turn it into a purely naval operation. Fisher opposed this and did not regard coastal bombardments by themselves as effective. He believed an advance by the army in conjunction with a naval attack was necessary and that ten thousand troops landed at Zeebrugge would turn the German flank. The plan presupposed the British army would occupy the coastal sector—now held by the Belgians—so that it could advance with the support of naval artillery, but General Joffre, the French commander in chief on the western front, refused to shift the BEF. On 28 January the War Council abandoned the idea of an attack.[11]

Zeebrugge remained a magnet for the British throughout the war, and its strategic importance increased as the submarine threat developed. The Germans made effective use of both Zeebrugge and Ostend for their Flanders Submarine Flotilla. Both ports were linked by canal with the inland city of Bruges, where the Germans eventually constructed vast bombproof submarine pens. In 1915 Zeebrugge and Ostend became the target of long-range bombardments by monitors screened by an elaborate force of destroyers, paddle minesweepers, and drifters of the Dover Patrol. The Germans transformed the Belgian coast into some of the most heavily fortified real estate in the world, with, for example, the powerful "Tirpitz" battery (four 11-inch guns) in the suburbs of Ostend and the "Kaiser Wilhelm II" battery (four 12-inch guns) at Knocke to the eastward of the Bruges Canal. The bombardments were unsuccessful in knocking out the batteries or destroying the submarine bases.[12] In 1916 and 1917 there were different schemes for either landing on the Belgian coast from an enormous pontoon pushed by monitors or blocking Zeebrugge by various means. The plans are generally associated with either Commodore Tyrwhitt of the Harwich Force or Admiral Sir Reginald Bacon, commander in chief Dover Patrol. They were never implemented.[13] In the spring of 1918, Zeebrugge and Ostend were the targets of a raid in an attempt to block the entrances of the canal (see chapter 13).

The schemes for overseas expeditions in the northern theater of the war remained abortive. They had various points in common in that they were generally plans to seize locations close to the German coast that could be used as bases for the implementation of a close blockade. Even if successful, they would also have put the

British in positions difficult to hold, usually in range of artillery located on the mainland, and one can generalize that the costs and disadvantages of the operations outweighed the possible advantages. As Admiral Oliver said of Helgoland, "Every time supplies were required would involve a major operation for the Grand Fleet in the minefields."[14] As for the Baltic, any operation, regardless of the maritime hazards, obviously would have depended on major Russian military assistance to have had any chance of success. Would the Russians, reeling from heavy military defeats at the beginning of the war, have been able to play the desired role?

THE DEFENSE OF EGYPT AND THE SUEZ CANAL

The entry of Turkey into the war on the side of the Central Powers brought about three of the four major overseas campaigns conducted beyond the western front by the British during the First World War—Egypt and Palestine, the Dardanelles, and Mesopotamia. The three were conducted predominantly by British or British Empire forces, and naval forces at certain moments played important, if not critical, roles. The fourth campaign—Macedonia—was one in which the French tended to have the leading role, and in which naval forces played a minor role, limited to transporting troops and supplies and supporting the flank of the British army with monitors at Stavros. The enmity of Turkey posed a particular threat to the British, for it threatened two areas vital to British security, the Suez Canal in Egypt and the oil supplies in the Persian Gulf. The British and French, and later the Italians to a lesser degree, faced another danger from Turkey. The Turkish sultan in his capacity as caliph, or successor to Mohammed, proclaimed a *Jihad*, or "holy war," against the enemies of Turkey. This was potentially a major threat to the British and French, whose empires contained huge numbers of Muslims. Would they remain loyal? The psychological impact of defeat or apparent defeat on their own subjects was never absent from British or French reasoning. Neither was colonial rivalry, and this complicated reaching agreement on what should have been purely naval and military operations.

The British reacted quickly to Turkish hostility with a bombardment of the Dardanelles, the landing to neutralize the Turkish fort at Sheikh Syed (see chapter 4), the diversion of troops to the Persian Gulf, and the retention in Egypt of Indian troops en route to France. Turkish seapower was negligible and unable to influence events outside of the Black Sea. Turkish military power was not negligible, however, and the Turkish Fourth Army in Syria—approximately sixty thousand men—posed an obvious threat to the Suez Canal. The bulk of this Turkish force was not likely to reach Egypt, because the Sinai Desert, which lay between the canal and the Turkish army, was a formidable natural obstacle, devoid of regular roads and with little water to support a large army. But if only a portion of the Turkish army could reach the canal and hold it just long enough to block it, they could do immense damage to the Anglo-French cause.

The best defense of the Suez Canal would have been for the British and French to make use of their seapower—as yet unchallenged by submarines in the Mediterranean—to strike at the Turkish army's lines of communication, paralyzing any advance toward Egypt. Lord Kitchener believed the best place to strike would be Alexandretta, where a branch line of the Constantinople–Baghdad Railway ran down to the Gulf of Iskanderun. The main Constantinople to Baghdad line was not yet complete: there were two major gaps, one of approximately 20 miles in the Taurus mountains and the other of approximately 5 miles in the Amanus mountains. The mountain road through the Amanus gap was not suitable for wheeled traffic until 1916, and it was actually easier and faster to proceed via the branch line to Alexandretta and then by road to rejoin the railway just west of Aleppo. Therefore, to cut the Alexandretta route, particularly in the winter months, would be a devastating blow at Turkish communications.

Diplomatic considerations overruled sound military ones. The French had a long-standing interest in Syria, and the Foreign Office was afraid British operations at Alexandretta would be misinterpreted by the French and therefore harmful to Allied unity. The French were indeed, and not without reason, suspicious of British designs in this area. The Alexandretta scheme was shelved and the decision taken to defend Egypt along the line of the Suez Canal.[15] Nevertheless, plans centering on the region of Alexandretta would continue to appear.

The naval defense of Egypt was under Vice Admiral R. H. Peirse, commander in chief East Indies. The destruction of the *Emden* and the immobilization of the *Königsberg* drastically altered the situation on the East Indies Station, which was now free of any major threat, and Peirse proceeded to Suez where he hoisted his flag in the battleship *Swiftsure*. The Admiralty authorized him to use his ships to watch the Syrian ports, and the result was the remarkably successful raid by Captain Frank Larken in the cruiser *Doris*, which cut the railway line between Adana and Alexandretta where it ran close to the coast to the north of Alexandretta. The activity of the *Doris*, as well as the French cruisers *D'Entrecasteaux* and *Amiral Charner* and the Russian cruiser *Askold*, demonstrated the vulnerability of Turkish communications to naval artillery and undoubtedly contributed to the Turks' decision to cross the Sinai by the more difficult central route rather than by the traditional path along the coast. The Turkish advance also profited from unusually heavy rains, which permitted a far larger body of troops to be supported on the desert route than the British had anticipated. A prewar study by the War Office in 1906 had concluded that five thousand men would be the most that could be brought across the desert. However, the Turkish invasion force numbered approximately twenty-five thousand, with nine batteries of field artillery and one of 15-cm howitzers. The Turks also had pontoons of galvanized iron, each capable of holding twenty men, as well as rafts for the canal crossing. Colonel Freiherr Kress von Kressenstein and a staff of six German officers attached to the VIII Turkish Corps played a leading role in organizing the advance. The commander of the Fourth Turkish Army in Syria, Djemal Pasha (who was also minister of marine) hoped the Turkish invasion would set off a nationalist uprising in Egypt to take the British from the rear.[16]

The Turks had only a small chance of succeeding. The bulk of the troops defending the western bank of the canal were from the Indian army, and the British left only a few bridgeheads on the east bank. The canal was patrolled by six torpedo boats and a flotilla of armed tugs and launches, provided by the Suez Canal Company and fitted with 12-pounders or 3-pounders, Maxim guns, and with some armor protection for the wheel and boilers. Canal hoppers served as parent ships in each sector of the defense, and they were fitted with searchlights mounted on a platform high enough to clear the canal banks. British and French warships served as mobile floating batteries, with the battleships *Swiftsure* at Port Said and *Ocean* at Suez; and the cruisers *Minerva* and *D'Entrecasteaux*, the sloop *Clio*, the armed merchant cruiser *Himalaya*, and the *Hardinge* of the Royal Indian Marine scattered along the one-hundred-mile length of the canal. A special berth was dredged for the French coast-defense ship *Requin* in Lake Temshah, and aiming stakes were set out on land before the Turkish attack. French Nieuport seaplanes based at Port Said provided intelligence of the Turkish advance.[17]

The main Turkish attack came at night in the early hours of 3 February in the Tussum sector just to the south of Lake Timsah. Only three boatloads of Turkish troops managed to get across the canal; they were all quickly killed, wounded, or captured. Turkish artillery fire during the day found the range of the *Hardinge*, which suffered some damage and had to move up to Lake Timsah to avoid the danger of being sunk in the fairway. The Turkish artillery then turned on the *Requin*, which located the battery and managed to silence it. The Turkish attack was a failure, and the Turks soon began their retreat. The British did not seek to exploit it; they did not have an overabundance of trained troops, and Kitchener had warned Maxwell not to risk a reverse. They were also ignorant of Turkish strength and movements, as the French seaplanes, after hard use, had suffered mechanical breakdowns. The pursuit was limited to 10 miles from the canal. By 11 February the canal was reopened for night traffic. It had only been closed for daytime traffic on the 3d. The vital lines of communications were never seriously interfered with.[18]

The naval aspect of the defense of the Suez Canal became purely secondary with the development of the Dardanelles campaign. In fact the Dardanelles campaign was probably the most effective defense of Egypt, for the best Turkish troops and most experienced officers were withdrawn from Palestine. For the remainder of the year, Turkish efforts against the canal were more in the nature of pinpricks. The Turks did make attempts to mine the canal; the defenders found tracks in the desert and, on one occasion, an abandoned mine. The launches regularly searched for mines, but on 30 June the Holt liner *Teiresias* struck a mine in Little Bitter Lake and swung about, blocking the channel. The Suez Canal Company managed to clear it that night. This was the only Turkish success. The threat remained, however, and with the end of the Dardanelles campaign at the close of the year, the decision was taken to establish the line of defense roughly eleven thousand yards to the east of the canal, beyond artillery range.[19] Egypt and the canal were not seriously threatened again, and the British reverted to the offensive in which the navy played its usual role supporting the seaward flank of the army.

A NAVAL HISTORY OF WORLD WAR I

In late 1915 a threat to Egypt developed from the opposite direction, the west. The problem concerned the Senussi, a religious sect that had been waging war against Britain's ally Italy in Cyrenaica. Italy's hold on her Libyan colony, wrested from the Turks in the Italo-Turkish War of 1911–12, was tenuous, and after the outbreak of the world war in Europe, the Italian army pulled back to a few coastal points, leaving the vast interior to the desert tribes. In the absence of real roads, the British and Egyptian frontier garrisons were dependent on the sea for their communications. There was little that could be spared for the Egyptian coast with the Dardanelles campaign in progress and the Macedonian campaign just beginning. Unfortunately, at this moment the Entente's control of the sea in the Mediterranean was seriously challenged for the first time by the appearance of German submarines. On 5 November *U.35* sank the armed boarding steamer *Tara*, an 1,800-ton former London and Northwestern Railway Company steamer, off the Egyptian coast. The survivors were subsequently towed by the U-boat to the Cyrenaican coast and handed over to the Senussi. *U.35* then returned to Sollum and attacked a pair of Egyptian Coast Guard gunboats at their moorings, sinking the *Abbas* and damaging the *Nuhr-el-Bahr*. The British decided to evacuate Sollum, which had already been unsuccessfully attacked by the Senussi, and concentrate at Marsa Matruh, roughly halfway between Alexandria and the frontier. Sollum was evacuated on 23 November, but the hard-pressed naval commander at the Dardanelles, Admiral de Robeck, had to lend Peirse the sloop *Clematis* and six trawlers to cover the evacuation and concentration of approximately forty-five hundred troops, laboriously transported at night in the trawlers. By 11 December the British were ready to begin their counteroffensive. These operations were successful; Sollum was reoccupied on 14 March, the survivors of the *Tara* and the torpedoed transport *Moorina* were rescued by armored cars led by the Duke of Westminster in a daring raid on an oasis approximately 120 miles west of Sollum on the 17th, and the threat to Egypt from the west was ended.[20]

THE DARDANELLES CAMPAIGN

The Dardanelles campaign was probably the most famous of the overseas campaigns of the First World War. It is considered *the* "what might have been" of the war and has been a subject of fascination and controversy ever since. It is also inextricably linked with one of the major figures of the twentieth century, Winston Churchill. At first, however, the Dardanelles was only one of the first lord's schemes, competing with projects such as Borkum, in which for a time he was far more interested. The project became increasingly attractive after the turn of the year. It seemed to offer a way to use Britain's maritime strength in a traditional manner, exercising leverage at a critical point and avoiding the deadlocked struggle in France, where some British leaders resented the constant demands of the French for more and more men. The French, with their larger army, also had the decisive say on the western front. The Dardanelles was certainly a critical point: if the Strait could be seized, the road to Constantinople would be open and the Ottoman capital would be at the mercy of the guns of the Allied fleet. It was confidently assumed Turkey would be forced out of the war, thereby removing the threat to Egypt and the Persian Gulf oil fields. Furthermore, the route through the Black Sea to Russia would be opened. Success at the Dardanelles would have its effect on the Balkan situation, where the Serbians had been fighting desperately, but so far successfully, to resist the Austrians. The attitude of neutrals such as Italy, Bulgaria, and Romania would be affected. The Russians, who had been badly battered by the Germans in the autumn of 1914, also appealed for assistance in January. Grand Duke Nicholas, commander in chief of the Russian armies, asked for some diversion to counter a Turkish offensive in the Caucasus mountains. An offensive at the Dardanelles also would have the immediate advantage of deflecting the anticipated attack by the Turks on the Suez Canal.

Churchill, who was renowned for his persuasive powers, managed on 13 January 1915 to secure the provisional consent of the War Council for preparing a naval attack on the Dardanelles. The fact that success seemed possible without the commitment of substantial bodies of troops made the project seem attractive, although it is now apparent Churchill did not have the wholehearted support of the naval and military experts that he assumed he had. Moreover, that support was often based on the assumption that the naval attack could be easily broken off if the prospects for success did not appear promising.[21] Fisher's support was particularly equivocal; he considered the Dardanelles a diversion from what he assumed to be Churchill's wilder and more dangerous schemes, such as Borkum. Fisher, however, became steadily opposed to the idea on strategical grounds; the ships and men were needed in the North Sea. After the failure of the naval attack in March, Fisher's opposition grew to the point where he would resign over the issue.[22]

The French agreed to their naval forces cooperating with the British in the Dardanelles attack. This was a squadron of old battleships under Rear Admiral Emile-Paul Guépratte, which had been working with Rear Admiral Sir Sackville Carden, British naval commander at the Dardanelles, since the autumn. The real reason for French participation was admitted by Victor Augagneur, the French minister of marine, later during the war: the French did not want to see the British fleet appear off Constantinople alone in an area where they had considerable interests. The military commitment was made to draw the diplomatic benefits from a success. The chief of the French naval staff was, in fact, rather skeptical of the British plan, largely because of the lack of troops to seize the Turkish fortifications once they had been reduced by the fleet.[23]

On 28 January the War Council approved the commencement of the naval attack. The British, at least initially, had no need for French naval reinforcements. They had the new superdreadnought *Queen Elizabeth* with long-range 15-inch guns—whose absence from the Grand Fleet made Fisher particularly nervous—the battle cruiser *Inflexible,* ten predreadnoughts, later joined by the semidreadnoughts *Agamemnon* and *Lord Nelson,* four cruisers, sixteen destroyers, twenty-one minesweeping trawlers, six submarines, the seaplane carrier *Ark Royal,* and two destroyer depot ships. The French contribution was four predreadnoughts, a cruiser, six torpedo boats, and four submarines. The Allied fleets planned to work methodically but cautiously to avoid excessive risk or losses, silencing the fire of concealed guns, keeping down the fire of machine guns and trenches so the minesweepers could work. They calculated that they might advance only a mile a day, but the steady advance would shake the morale of the defenders and the Turkish capital. Two battalions of Royal Marines also were sent out for temporary landings, along with a squadron of "dummy" warships, that is, merchantmen whose upper works had been altered to resemble dreadnoughts for the purpose of deception.[24]

However imposing this Allied naval force might have been, the hopes for its success rested on faulty tactical assumptions. The effects of flat-trajectory naval guns on land targets were overestimated, whereas the difficulties of spotting and fire control were underestimated. Ships were also at a disadvantage when facing shore batteries; they were inherently more vulnerable. There was an equally questionable strategic assumption that the Turks would throw in the sponge once the fleet had blasted its way past the fortifications and appeared off Constantinople. In other words, warships alone would do the job. There is no way of knowing what really would have happened, but Admiral Souchon, chief of the Mittelmeerdivision, did not think the Allied ships in the Marmara would be able to accomplish anything without strong landing detachments. They might fire off their ammunition at Constantinople or the Turkish fleet, perhaps setting fires, but if the Turkish fleet did not oblige them by giving battle and retired into the Bosphorus, the British and French eventually would have to withdraw back through the Dardanelles when they ran short of coal.[25]

The doubts that a purely naval attack would succeed were strong enough to cause the British government to hedge. Colonel Maurice Hankey, secretary to the War Council, wrote on 10 February: "From Lord Fisher downwards, every naval officer in the Admiralty who is in on the secret believes that the Navy cannot take the Dardanelles position without troops. The First Lord [Churchill] still professes to believe that they can do it with ships, but I have warned the Prime Minister that we cannot trust to this."[26] A partial meeting of the War Council on 16 February agreed to send the 29th Division to Lemnos, a Greek island roughly 50 miles to the west of the Dardanelles, which the British were using as a base. The Australian and New Zealand troops from Egypt also would proceed to Lemnos. Lord Kitchener blocked the move of the division at a full meeting of the War Council on the 19th; in his opinion the Australian and New Zealand troops would suffice. He would not finally agree to send the 29th Division until 10 March, by which date there was no possibility of it being employed in the impending naval attack. The French cabinet also decided on 18 February to send a division to Lemnos once they heard the British were doing so. They reached the decision before consulting the army chief of staff, General Joffre, and for the same reason they had committed their naval forces. The British should not be allowed to establish themselves alone in the Levant. The French did suggest postponing the naval operations until the arrival of the troops, but Churchill, with Kitchener's approval, was opposed. Churchill argued that every delay would add to the danger that German or Austrian submarines would arrive and prejudice the moral effect in the Turkish capital.[27]

The British and French bombardment of the Turkish forts at the entrance to the Dardanelles began on 19 February, and then was delayed by bad weather until the 25th. The naval guns outranged the guns of the forts, and the latter proved relatively easy to silence. By 1 March the Allies were ready to proceed to the next phase of the operations, the destruction of the intermediate defenses and the clearing of the minefields below Kephez Point. The plan now began to go awry, for the ships were operating in the restricted waters of the Strait, where minefields kept the battleships at a distance while mobile Turkish batteries including howitzers kept the battleships on the move, reducing the accuracy of their fire against the forts and hampering sweeping. Carden reported that it was impossible to locate and silence the concealed Turkish guns and howitzers solely by ship's fire. It was necessary for the ships to anchor for accurate and deliberate long-range fire, but this was very difficult when they were within range of those concealed guns. Minesweeping with slow trawlers, manned by volunteer fishermen rather than by regular naval personnel, was also much more difficult than expected, particularly when they had to move against the swift Dardanelles current. Commodore Keyes, now chief of staff at the Dardanelles, concluded, "We are going to get through—but it is a much bigger thing than the Admiralty or anyone out here realized."[28]

The idea that military assistance might be necessary began to grow, but the military arrangements for the Mediterranean Expeditionary Force slowly gathering at Mudros, the base on the island of Lemnos, left much to be desired. The loading of stores and equipment destined for the troops at Mudros had been chaotic, and the facilities at the advanced base to correct the mistakes were inadequate. The commander of the Mediterranean Expeditionary Force, General Sir Ian Hamilton, was forced to send some of the transports back to Alexandria and to reroute others. The mess associated with the logistical side of the campaign required a month to straighten out. Rear Admiral Rosslyn Wemyss, who was now senior naval officer at Mudros, complained on 4 March: "The General has been up here from Alexandria and he seems as much in the dark as everybody else—doesn't know where he is to disembark his army, or what the objective is when they are disembarked." Wemyss was critical of the government: "The fact of the matter is that I am afraid they are trying to rush matters at home without giving the people who are to carry the job sufficient time or opportunity to organise the matter properly." Rear Admiral Hugh Miller, who had been Wemyss's assistant at Mudros, would later write, "In those early days the whole campaign seemed to me to have been very sketchily thought out" and "the naval command was most unfortunate in its appreciation of the situation and . . . the strength of the Dardanelles defences was underestimated long after their strength was being made obvious to the most inexperienced layman."[29] All of this meant that significant numbers of troops would not be ready before the naval attack.

Ironically, in the light of traditional nineteenth-century rivalries, the British and the French were fighting at the Dardanelles for territorial prizes that would have gone to the Russians. On 10 March the War Council accepted Russian demands for Constantinople, the western shores of the Bosphorus, the Sea of Marmara, the Dardanelles, southern Thrace up to the Enos-Midia line, and Imbros and Tenedos. They were motivated by a desire to avoid a breach with Russia, and the possibility of a separate Russian peace with Germany.[30] But as for the business at hand—forcing the Strait—could the Russians have made any military or naval contribution? Churchill back in January had asked the Russians to be prepared to act at the Bosphorus at the proper moment. The Russian reply had not been encouraging: until the completion of their Black Sea dreadnoughts, they did not consider they had any great advantage over the Turkish fleet and were dubious about the effectiveness of naval artillery on the Bosphorus fortifications. After the Dardanelles bombardments began, Grand Duke Nicholas did promise on 28 February that the Russian Black Sea Fleet would attack Constantinople and that an army of forty-seven thousand men would be used. However, the Russians would do this only *after* the Allied fleet had entered the Sea of Marmara and appeared off the Princess Islands. They considered forcing the Bosphorus without the assistance of the Allied fleets from the other side to be "impossible." The Russian naval demonstration took place on 28 March—after the Allied naval failure—and was limited to a long-range bombardment of the Turkish forts at the Bosphorus. No significant results were achieved, and as far as the Dardanelles campaign was concerned, the Russians were only a distant and very indirect factor.[31]

If the Dardanelles were proving a tough nut to crack, and if Russian or Greek assistance was not available, what of some move to try to divert Turkish attention and strength from the Strait? Kitchener had his choice, already mentioned—an attack on Alexandretta. In January Churchill had replied to Kitchener that an operation at Alexandretta ought to be carried out simultaneously with the attack on the Dardanelles so that if the Allies were checked at the Dardanelles, they could claim it was a mere feint to cover the seizure of Alexandretta. Kitchener returned to the proposal at the War Council on 10 March, adding that Alexandretta would compensate for recognizing Russia's control at Constantinople. The Admiralty supported the Alexandretta proposal because of the access it would provide to Mesopotamian oil. Alexandretta was, however, subject to French objections, and once again the project was deferred.[32]

There was another diversion, an attack on Smyrna, although this should really be seen as an attempt to forestall the establishment of a German submarine base at what was Turkey's largest port on the Mediterranean. The attack was coupled with a curious diplomatic maneuver. There were reports that the Turkish ruler of the district, the Vali of Smyrna, was pro-Allied and would be amenable to a British proposal to surrender his small craft, permit the British to sweep the minefields, and in effect neutralize the port and surrounding vilayet. There was no mention of how the Turkish commanders in the Smyrna fortifications might have been neutralized, whatever the Vali's sentiments.

Diplomacy at Smyrna was backed by force. Admiral Peirse arrived from Egypt in the cruiser *Euryalus* to command the operation, and the battleships *Triumph* and *Swiftsure* were detached from the Dardanelles to join him. Peirse also had minesweepers, a seaplane carrier, and eventually the Russian cruiser *Askold*. He was ordered to destroy the forts protecting the harbor to facilitate a blockade and leave the harbor open to attack.

Operations began on 5 March, developing much like operations at the Dardanelles, although on a smaller scale. The ships could not close to effectively silence the forts until the minefields were swept, and the concealed mobile guns prevented the sweeping.[33] The negotiations with the Vali came to nothing, and on 15 March the Admiralty ordered the *Triumph* and *Swiftsure* back to the Dardanelles for the impending attack, while Peirse returned to Egypt. In the end the Turks themselves accomplished a large part of the British objective. They sank five steamers in the channels to the port as a defensive measure, blocking the port and making it unsuitable as a submarine base.

The attempt to bluff the Vali of Smyrna out of the war was accompanied by an even more bizarre and daring attempt to get Turkey herself out of the war, open the Dardanelles to the Allied fleet, and surrender the *Goeben*. "Blinker" Hall, the director of naval intelligence, opened negotiations with a member of the Turkish government at Dedeagatch, which was then Bulgaria's port on the Aegean. The sum of £4 million was supposed to have been advanced to the Turks. Hall acted through the intermediary of a British businessman and a civil engineer who had long been resident in Turkey, but apparently pledged the money without informing his superiors, the Foreign Office, or the cabinet. Fisher was taken aback when he learned of it, and acting on his own intelligence that the Turks were short of ammunition, he ordered the talks broken off on 17 March. It is difficult to believe the affair had any real chance of success or that the Turkish negotiators had the power to circumvent Enver Pasha and his German advisers and really take Turkey out of the war. It would have been even more difficult to reconcile Hall's negotiations with the agreement promising Constantinople to the Russians.[34]

The intelligence concerning the Turkish shortage of ammunition that had led Fisher to order the talks at Dedeagatch broken off also caused Churchill and the Admiralty on 11 March to order Carden to shift from his methodical bombardment and advance and press for a decision, accepting losses if success could not be gained without them. The attempts to sweep the Kephez minefields at night were not going well, for the warships were unable to knock out the searchlights exposing the fragile trawler minesweepers to deadly fire from the Turkish batteries. The arrangements for minesweeping were probably the Achilles heel of the expedition. Carden and his staff decided the only chance for success would be a daylight attack to silence the forts at the Narrows as well as the batteries protecting the Kephez minefields. The trawlers could then clear a channel by night, which would permit the fleet to destroy the Narrows forts at short range the following day. The trawlers would then be able to sweep the Narrows minefields, which would open the way for the fleet to move into the Marmara. Carden's health gave way just before the attack, and he was forced to relinquish command to his second-in-command, Rear Admiral de Robeck. Wemyss at Lemnos was actually senior to de Robeck, but courteously stepped aside for his colleague, who had been in on the planning from the beginning of operations.[35]

The Allied naval attack came on 18 March. The British and French warships succeeded in silencing the Turkish intermediate batteries, and later the forts at the Narrows. They could not, however, silence the hidden Turkish artillery and the mobile batteries, and these kept the trawlers from sweeping the Kephez minefields. The Allied warships also ran into an undetected row of twenty mines that had been moored *parallel* to the shore in Eren Keui Bay by the little Turkish minelayer *Nousret*—another ship with a claim to have altered history. The British battleships *Irresistible* and *Ocean* and the French battleship *Bouvet* were sunk, and the battle cruiser *Inflexible* was badly damaged. The French battleships *Suffren* and *Gaulois* were badly damaged by gunfire, and the latter had to be beached on Rabbit Island outside the Strait. It was the Turkish minefields, however, rather than gunfire that had proven decisive, and the Allies with their fragile trawlers had not been able to clear them.[36]

What should the Allies do? De Robeck was buoyed by his ever-confident chief of staff, Roger Keyes, and ready to resume the attack. Guépratte, the French admiral, was by reputation a gallant old fire-eater ready to follow. Replacements for the losses were on their way. The battleships *Queen* and *Implacable* were already steaming toward the Dardanelles, and the Admiralty ordered the battleships *London* and *Prince of Wales* to follow. The French sent the coast-defense ship *Henri IV*. Keyes now set to work furiously reorganizing the sweeper force, fitting destroyers with sweeper gear. Destroyers would be able to work better under fire and in the strong currents. One can only speculate what would have happened had this been done *before* the attack of 18 March. The results might well have been different. Keyes was and would always remain confident that once the sweeper force was reorganized—accomplished by 4 April—they would break through the Narrows, enter the Sea of Marmara, destroy the Turkish fleet, and cut the communications of the Turkish army on the peninsula. His chief de Robeck, however, changed his mind and concluded he could not get through without a combined operation with troops to take the peninsula. A conference of naval and military leaders took place in the *Queen Elizabeth*, and de Robeck, on Wemyss's advice, decided to defer a further attack until a joint operation could take place later in April. De Robeck, once he had made up his mind, could not be moved, and as a result the Dardanelles campaign became primarily a military rather than naval operation. Was he correct? The matter has been endlessly debated, and even during the war there was an exhaustive examination by the Dardanelles Commission. Keyes, on one side, was always convinced they would have gotten through after the sweepers had been reorganized.[37] Souchon, on the Turkish-German side, was confident the Turkish forts would hold and hoped the Allies would try again and suffer further losses.[38] Nevertheless the weak point of the Turks was their ammunition supply.[39] Direct rail communications between Germany and Constantinople were blocked by the Serbian resistance to the Austrian offensive, and neutral Romania hampered transit of munitions through Romanian territory. The Germans had been conscious of the acute dilemma, and in January they and their Austrian allies had examined proposals to use either a merchant ship or one of the Austrian fast light cruisers to run precious munitions to the Turks. The proposals came to nothing, largely for technical reasons, and were out of the question once the Dardanelles campaign began in earnest.[40]

German concern over Turkish powers of resistance led to the decision to send

German submarines to the Mediterranean. The results were actually even more damaging for the Anglo-French cause than the failure of the Dardanelles campaign. In early March, as the British and French warships pounded away at the Dardanelles, Enver Pasha and the Turkish leaders pleaded for submarines to attack the Allied fleet. The Germans tried to induce their Austrian allies to send a submarine out from the Adriatic to the Dardanelles. The Austrians declined, largely for technical reasons. They had only seven submarines, and most of them lacked the range. Moreover, with their former Triple Alliance ally Italy drifting into a position of open hostility, they were obviously loath to lose the services of any of their handful of underseas craft, which had so far proved so effective in restricting the operations of the overwhelmingly superior French fleet. The Germans eventually despaired of getting anything from the Austrians and resolved to do the job themselves. On 13 March they decided to send one large boat with extra fuel oil directly to the Mediterranean, while a pair of small *UB.I*-class boats would be sent in sections by rail to Pola, where they would be assembled by German engineers. They anticipated the UB boats would arrive in Turkish waters about the end of April.[41]

A major problem for the British and French was therefore on the way, but it would have no effect on their landings on the peninsula, which took place on 25 April. The British 29th Division landed at the tip of Cape Helles, and the Australian and New Zealand Army Corps—the ANZACs—landed farther to the north on the Gallipoli Peninsula and at great cost established a beachhead. The French landed on the Asiatic shore as a diversion, and later shifted their forces to the European side. The Turkish counterattacks failed to push the Allies into the sea, but the Allies in turn could not progress far beyond the beachhead nor capture the commanding height of Achi Baba. Barbed wire and machine guns proved as difficult to overcome at Gallipoli as they were on the western front. The result, despite the landing of new British divisions, was a stalemate, and the Royal Navy had the major obligation of supplying the army over open beaches from island bases 50 to 60 miles away, providing artillery support, and the added worry that intelligence indicated German submarines were on their way.[42] The logistical aspect should not be underestimated. In September Wemyss wrote that at Mudros harbor there were always between 150 and 170 ships, not counting innumerable small craft.[43]

The supplies of the Turkish army on the peninsula were to a large extent waterborne, and on 10 May de Robeck cabled the Admiralty about the possibility of a renewed naval attack to force the Dardanelles and cut off the supply line. De Robeck himself, apparently, did not believe the presence of the Allied fleet in the Marmara would be decisive and was prodded into sending the cable by his chief of staff, Keyes. According to Keyes, de Robeck realized the importance of a successful attack to the army struggling on shore, but feared for the army's fate should the attack fail, and declined to take responsibility for running the risk of failure. Keyes told him to place the responsibility for ordering the attack on the government but to make it clear that if ordered, he would be prepared to attempt to force the Strait. Guépratte, although not present at the conference, would have been more than ready to participate.

The cable arrived at a bad time in London, where Churchill was in the midst of the negotiations for the naval convention that would accompany Italy's entry into the war and knew that German submarines were on their way to the Mediterranean and that the Italians would have to be supported by British ships. He therefore favored a "limited operation" to attempt to sweep the Kephez minefield under the cover of the fleet, compelling the forts to exhaust their ammunition. Fisher, however, was against any attempt to rush the Narrows before the army had occupied the adjacent shores and found even the limited operation excessive. Churchill had to compromise with a very weak telegram to de Robeck on the 13th, instructing him to inform the Admiralty and obtain its approval before taking any decisive step. Fisher, supported by the other sea lords, dispatched an additional cable that effectively killed any idea of a renewed naval offensive. They informed de Robeck, always lukewarm about the whole idea, that the Admiralty thought the moment for an independent naval attempt had passed and would not rise again, and that his role was to support the army.[44] After all these years, the bitterness and disappointment of Keyes can still be felt: "So the great opportunities which had been open to the Fleet since 4th April [when the destroyer minesweepers were ready] were allowed to slip away, and the Allied Army, having suffered 26,000 casualties in its effort to secure the Gallipoli shore, was to continue the struggle, in order that the Fleet might steam by without any undue loss."[45]

The British suffered a severe loss even before the submarines arrived. The old battleship *Goliath* had anchored in Morto Bay, an exposed position, where her artillery support to the army had provoked the Germans and Turks. On the night of 12–13 May, Kapitänleutnant Rudolph Firle, a German officer commanding the Turkish destroyer *Muavenet*, succeeded in torpedoing and sinking the *Goliath* with heavy loss of life.[46] The loss eventually had important political repercussions in England. Fisher, knowing submarines were on the way, had been very nervous over the superdreadnought *Queen Elizabeth* at the Dardanelles and anxious to bring her back to the Grand Fleet. He now renewed these demands more vigorously than ever, and he and Churchill decided to replace the *Queen Elizabeth* with the old battleships *Exmouth* and *Venerable* and two monitors with 14-inch guns. Kitchener, however, objected to the effect the *Queen Elizabeth*'s withdrawal would have on the army's morale. The next few days brought the Fisher-Churchill disagreement over the Dardanelles to the boiling point when Churchill prepared to send additional reinforcements to the Dardanelles, and on 15 May Fisher resigned. Fisher's resignation came shortly after a scandal over the shortage of artillery shells in France. The government was in danger of being overturned, and Prime Minister Asquith was forced to form a coalition government with the Conservative opposition on 25 May. Their price for joining the government included the demand that Churchill leave the Admiralty, and he was banished to the meaningless sinecure, the Duchy of Lancaster, from which he would shortly resign in disgust for service with the army in France. Arthur J. Balfour, a former prime minister, became first lord, and Admiral Sir Henry Jackson became First Sea Lord.[47]

Churchill's departure from office coincided with the arrival of German submarines at the Dardanelles. The small *UB.7* and *UB.8* were assembled at Pola in the first half of May and towed through the Strait of Otranto at night by Austrian warships in order to conserve fuel. They then slipped the tow and headed for the coast of Asia Minor. The larger U-boat, *U.21* under Kapitänleutnant Otto Hersing, sailed for the Mediterranean from German waters on 25 April. Hersing met a chartered Spanish supply ship in the Gulf of Corcubion in northwest Spain on the night of 2 May and took on oil. He discovered, however, that the fuel oil was unsuitable for his diesel engines. Hersing made careful calculations and decided to proceed to Cattaro directly, where by economical use of his engines he arrived on 13 May with only 1.8 tons of his original 56.5 tons of fuel remaining. Hersing proved it was possible for U-boats to make the voyage to the Mediterranean directly from Germany, and in the future newer U-boats would be able to omit the potentially troublesome clandestine call in neutral Spain.[48]

The wireless messages to *U.21* at Cattaro were intercepted and read by Room 40, which passed on the warning to de Robeck. De Robeck decided to meet the danger by ordering troop transports to go no farther than Mudros, where troops would be ferried to the Gallipoli Peninsula at night by fleet sweepers. Vital ammunition ships would also discharge their cargoes into trawlers and sweepers at Mudros. Regular supply ships would still go, if necessary, to Cape Helles or Kephalo (Imbros), where advance bases would be created by means of net and boom defenses. Ships required by the army as "covering ships" would be the only ones at sea, they would sail only at night, if possible, and as ships had to anchor for accurate fire, they would be protected by nets, if they had them, during daylight hours. It is not surprising that de Robeck wrote on 16 May: "Now my *most important* requirement are nets & lighters on which to hang the nets and place them round these ships."[49]

Hersing and *U.21* demonstrated that the antitorpedo nets, which had been such a prominent feature of the prewar battleships, were unable to stop a U-boat's torpedo. On 25 May he sank the battleship *Triumph*, and on the 27th the battleship *Majestic*. The smaller UB boats were less successful; they made Smyrna safely, but only *UB.8* sank anything before they reached Constantinople, and that turned out to be a dummy ship, the former transport *Merion* disguised to resemble the battle cruiser *Tiger*. Hersing also had less luck when he passed through the Dardanelles on his second mission early in July. He sank the French steamer *Carthage* (5,601) on 4 July, but the ship had been risked unnecessarily, and *U.21* was hindered by the strong Allied countermeasures from achieving further success. The cruise came to a premature end when *U.21*'s hull was damaged by an underwater explosion, probably a mine. The submarine limped back to Constantinople and was out of action for at least six weeks.

German submarine successes against the Dardanelles expedition in the summer of 1915 did not live up to their promising beginning. *UB.14* after completion at Pola was towed by the Austrians through the Strait of Otranto, called at the island of Orak off Bodrum on the Turkish coast, and then operated against the transport route between Alexandria and the Dardanelles, where on 13 August her commander, Oberleutnant zur See von Heimburg, sank the transport *Royal Edward* (11,117 tons), with a loss of more than nine hundred lives, and damaged another transport before reaching Constantinople. But von Heimburg also found his work hampered by the large number of small craft in the vicinity of the Dardanelles and the weak battery capacity of the UB boats. The UB boats could only carry a very limited number of torpedoes and could only spend a few days on station. The serious submarine campaign against Allied shipping in the Mediterranean did not begin until September and October when the new large boats arrived. It caused great damage, but most of the German successes took place far from the Dardanelles and on the lines of communication.[50]

The arrival of German submarines consequently did not and could not end the Dardanelles expedition. Except for ships foolishly risked, such as the *Carthage,* the British measures at the Strait were reasonably effective. German submarines found operations off the Strait unprofitable because of wiser British tactics, the hoard of small craft, extensive and heavy net and boom defenses, and eventually shallow-draft monitors for artillery support.

The British and French conducted their own submarine offensive against the Turks. This began even before the commencement of the Dardanelles expedition, when on 13 December 1914 Lieutenant Norman Holbrook in the old *B.11* sank the ancient Turkish battleship *Messudiyeh* near the entrance to the Dardanelles and received the Victoria Cross. The passage through the Dardanelles and the Narrows was extremely difficult, and also tricky because of the current and differences in density between layers of the water that made the craft difficult to control. The British boats were more successful than the less-handy French craft, none of which returned. There is no space in a general history of this sort to tell the story in any detail, but British submarines operated in the Sea of Marmara from April to the end of the campaign. Two of the commanders, Lieutenant-Commander Edward C. Boyle (*E.14*) and Lieutenant-Commander Martin Nasmith (*E.11*), won Victoria Crosses. Nasmith sank a steamer anchored alongside the arsenal in the Golden Horn at Constantinople in May, and on another cruise on 8 August sank the Turkish battleship *Barbarossa,* which had steamed down to support the Turkish defenses at the Strait. *E.11* and *E.14* made a deliberate attempt to cut the road to Gallipoli where it ran near the water, shelling troops attempting to pass. The Germans and Turks constantly worked at improving their defenses, particularly the Nagara net, and the game grew more and more difficult. The submarines by themselves, however, no matter how spectacular their exploits, could not alter the outcome of the campaign. The British and French each lost four submarines either trying to pass the Dardanelles or in the Marmara. The British claimed 1 battleship, 1 old coast-defense ship, 1 destroyer, 5 gunboats, 11 transports, 44 steamers, and 148 other vessels. There are discrepancies with German figures, possibly because some of the Turkish craft were beached and later salved. The German official history credits British submarines with twenty-five steamers (about 26,000 tons) totally destroyed and ten steamers (about 27,000 tons) badly damaged and out of action for the Dardanelles campaign, as well as the destruction of about 3,000 tons of small craft, for a total of 56,000 tons. The exploits of their submarines were for the British the proudest and most successful aspect of the Dardanelles campaign.[51]

The army, reinforced by five new divisions, made a final major attempt to break the deadlock with a renewed offensive combined with a landing on 8 August by fresh troops at Suvla to the north of the original beachheads. The naval part of the landing went well and included use of the special armored landing barges—nicknamed "beetles"—which Fisher had ordered, ostensibly for his Baltic projects. Unfortunately the army commanders at Suvla failed to exploit their initial surprise and push on to seize the high ground commanding the bay when they might have done so. The Turks were given time to recover, and after a short time the same stalemate prevailed, and the army was unable to advance.[52]

The French had their own plan to break the deadlock with a landing of four new divisions from France and their two divisions from Gàllipoli at Yukyeri on the Asiatic shore. This would have opened what amounted to a second front at the Dardanelles and was prompted by repeated complaints from the French naval and military commanders at the Dardanelles about the deadly effects of Turkish harassing fire from the Asiatic shore. The scheme was immersed in the intricacies of French domestic politics, for the command would have gone to General Sarrail, an able but controversial soldier who had strong ties to the political left. Joffre had removed Sarrail from his command on the western front, but his powerful political friends insisted on this new command that also required tearing troops from the reluctant Joffre. The landing at Yukyeri never took place, for in September the Entente lost the contest for the allegiance of Bulgaria, which began to mobilize to enter the war on the side of the Central Powers. Sarrail and his army, joined by British forces, were diverted to Salonika in a futile attempt to march northward to save Serbia. They ended up having to fall back to the vicinity of Salonika, and the Allies were committed to yet another new campaign.[53]

The failure at Suvla, the entry of Bulgaria into the war, and the opening of a new front in Macedonia meant the end of the Dardanelles campaign. The British army in the peninsula in the autumn of 1915 may have been secure in their positions, but they could not advance. The troops also suffered greatly from sickness, especially dysentery. The British were now faced with the prospect of a winter campaign and the difficulty of supplying the army over open beaches during the season when fierce local storms could be expected. Furthermore, Bulgaria's entry into the war led to a combined Austro-German-Bulgarian offensive that overran Serbia. This, in turn, led to the prospect of direct rail communications between Germany and Constantinople and the danger that the Germans and Turks would have an unlimited supply of heavy ammunition to overwhelm the Allied positions on the peninsula. On 16 October Ian Hamilton and his chief of staff were replaced. General Sir Charles Monro, the new commander, had commanded the Third Army in France and believed in the primacy of the western front. Shortly after his arrival he recommended evacuation.

The idea of evacuation was abhorrent to a man like Keyes. Ever since the failure at Suvla, he had been trying to persuade de Robeck to propose another naval attack. Keyes was convinced there were new factors that had been lacking on 18 March that would make such an attack successful. The British now had long-range monitors, cruisers that were specially bulged to withstand mines and torpedoes, capable aircraft for spotting, and, most important of all, an efficient minesweeping flotilla. Once past the minefields, the British fleet might be able to subject the Turkish positions to enfilading fire and shake the hold of the Turkish army on the peninsula by cutting off its supplies. The army might join in a combined attack with the fleet. The Turks might be knocked out of the war once Constantinople came under the guns of the Allied fleet. Keyes in September and October prepared plans for forcing the Strait. He was assisted by Captain William W. Godfrey, a Royal Marines officer on de Robeck's staff. The ships involved, it should be added, were mostly old, certainly not suited for service with the Grand Fleet in a major encounter with the High Sea Fleet. Any losses, therefore, would not have affected the strategic balance in the North Sea. The loss of trained men, however, would have been a different story.[54]

De Robeck was not convinced by Keyes. He did not think they had ever tackled the real minefield in March, and he doubted they were capable of clearing it under fire. Nevertheless, de Robeck was remarkably tolerant and was willing to let Keyes return home to plead his case. He gave Keyes private letters to Balfour and Jackson explaining his own argument, which ran as follows: The British might get four or five ships into the Sea of Marmara, although de Robeck doubted it, and might bombard Constantinople. The Turks on the peninsula, however, would not lay down their arms, for they had several months' supplies. Moreover, the British could not carry on an effective campaign in the Marmara until they could pass unarmored colliers and supply ships through the Dardanelles, and they would not be able to do this until they captured and destroyed all the Turkish forts in the Strait. This could only be accomplished in a combined operation with the army. Should the attack fail, the losses in personnel and ships would be large, which would have a heavy effect on the morale of the army while encouraging the Turks. The position of the British army on the peninsula would then become critical.[55]

Keyes arrived in London at a time of great indecision, because of the situation in Macedonia and the collapse of Serbia. Jackson later told de Robeck that Keyes had not made much of an impression, except perhaps on Kitchener, but that owing to the indecision of the government, things changed daily. Nevertheless, and despite the handicap of de Robeck's negative opinion, Keyes had more effect on Balfour than many might have thought. Some of this was probably due to very real fears of what an evacuation of Gallipoli under fire would entail. The landings in April had been very expensive in terms of casualties, an evacuation might be even more so. Would not an evacuation be more costly than a renewed naval attack? Kitchener rejected General Monro's recommendation for an evacuation and decided to go out to the Dardanelles for a personal tour of inspection. The indefatigable Keyes on his way back to the Dardanelles stopped in Paris where Admiral Lacaze, an old friend from their days as naval attachés in Rome before the war, had just become minister of marine. Lacaze agreed to support a renewed naval attack and ask his government to supply six French battleships. He too feared the enormous losses an evacuation might entail.[56]

The relative success that Keyes had alarmed de Robeck, who wrote Limpus on 7 November:

The Admiralty, probably on the advice of Roger Keyes, are evidently anxious that we should again attack the Dardanelles with the Fleet. I am perfectly determined to do nothing of the sort, as it would probably lead to a colossal disaster & then Rumania & Greece would come in against us & we should lose our army on the Peninsula & Salonika. Unless we can clear the mines away & destroy the torpedo tubes it is madness, fancy bringing these old battleships into the Narrows to be torpedoed. It is like sending an unfortunate horse into the bull ring blindfolded!

Limpus, former head of the naval mission in Turkey, agreed. They might get some armored ships into the Marmara, but they could not accomplish anything without colliers and supply ships. He believed that "an attempt by the Fleet to rush the Dardanelles would provide us with the biggest disaster of the whole war. Imagine my thankfulness — this time — we have a man who is strong enough to say *no*." But Limpus too feared the losses inherent in an evacuation.[57]

Kitchener's visit to the Dardanelles muddied the waters still more. No doubt he was heavily influenced by Monro, and he recommended evacuation. De Robeck warned him it would take six weeks, and unless they had "the most wonderful luck," they would lose at least 30 percent in men and matériel. Kitchener then proceeded to return to an old alternative scheme of his—Alexandretta. This time he proposed landing two of the divisions withdrawn from Gallipoli combined with two drawn from Egypt at Ayas Bay in the Gulf of Alexandretta. Their objective would be to move inland far enough to sever Turkish communications with Syria, which would forestall a new Turkish attack on the Suez Canal. The success would also offset the political effects of the evacuation of Gallipoli in the Muslim world. Once again Alexandretta, a perennial "what might have been" of the war, had surfaced.

The Ayas Bay proposal ran into the same heavy opposition Alexandretta had encountered at the beginning of the year. Both de Robeck and Keyes were opposed. The former thought the defense of Egypt would be best on the Suez Canal, where the Allies had mobility and seapower, while Keyes declared: "As if Gallipoli wasn't the place to fight for Egypt in—the maddest thing!" The Admiralty and the general staff turned their guns on the project. They would eventually have to pour in large numbers of troops—at least sixty thousand—who would have to push inland about 25 miles and hold a perimeter of 50 miles. The general staff considered that those troops would be better employed if concentrated for a great offensive on the western front, the decisive theater of the war. Operations outside the main theater should be limited to holding in check dangerous political and military developments that might threaten the security of British or French possessions and interests. The Admiralty also insisted on a sizable perimeter, for after their Dardanelles experience they were opposed to trying to supply an army over an open beach or through a port open to submarine attack or shelled by the enemy from surrounding heights. The expedition would add 400 miles to the already insufficiently protected transport routes that had to be guarded, and the small craft and lighters required for the evacuation of Gallipoli would not be available for Ayas Bay. The Admiralty concluded that they could undertake the Ayas Bay expedition if it were not for the large drain on resources caused by the Dardanelles and Salonika expeditions and the protection of transport routes in the Mediterranean, North Atlantic, and across the Channel, as well as the detachments sent to the Adriatic and North Russia.

The Ayas Bay scheme aroused such opposition that one historian of the Dardanelles campaign has even advanced the suggestion that it was never meant as a serious proposition and had been concocted by a member of Monro's staff as a diversion to allow time for the principle of an evacuation to gain acceptance. On the other hand, Alexandretta has its supporters. At the time the debate over the evacuation was taking place, the British Expeditionary Force in Mesopotamia was advancing up the Tigris, and the landing at Ayas Bay would have threatened Turkish communications with Mesopotamia. A historian of the Mesopotamian campaign has speculated that Alexandretta might well have been a preferable alternative to both the Mesopotamian and Dardanelles, and even Egyptian, campaigns in bringing about the collapse of Turkey. The debate will go on.[58]

On 22 November Kitchener made his final recommendation for the evacuation of Suvla and Anzac but the retention of Cape Helles. The War Committee decided all three beaches would have to be evacuated.[59] De Robeck was at this critical moment, and with the major decision to evacuate taken, forced to leave his command for a brief period of rest. His health was breaking down from the strain of command and chronic insomnia. He left Wemyss in charge, and this gave Keyes an opportunity to forestall the evacuation. Wemyss came to the conclusion something must be done to stop the evacuation, and the renewed naval attack seemed the only thing left. He wrote Jackson: "I believe attack is the only Policy left to us—beaten in Servia, outmanoeuvred by Greece, evacuation of the Peninsula would be disastrous politically and when I contemplate the operation and think of what it means I positively shudder."[60]

The last-minute campaign by Keyes and Wemyss was to no avail. In London de Robeck was called to the War Council meeting on 2 December and made a strong impression with his opposition to a new naval attack, and in France an Allied military conference at French headquarters from 6 to 8 December unanimously agreed to a request for an immediate and complete evacuation. On 7 December the cabinet decided on an evacuation of Anzac and Suvla. Wemyss and Keyes recognized that once this evacuation had been ordered, Cape Helles by itself could not be held during the winter months because the warships supporting the army and the supply ships would be exposed to the gales, and the submarines. Moreover, now that direct rail communications between Germany and Constantinople were about to be opened, they could anticipate an unimpeded flow of heavy munitions to the Turks and a storm of high explosives to rain down on the army clinging to Cape Helles. It was, as Keyes expressed it, a question of "get on or get out."

The evacuation of Anzac and Suvla on the night of 19–20 December proved a pleasant surprise, or as pleasant as any evacuation marking the failure of a campaign could be. The British organized the operation very carefully and enjoyed good luck. The anticipated heavy losses did not occur. De Robeck returned just as the first evacuation was completed, and on 27 December the cabinet decided to order the evacuation of Cape Helles. Once again, through careful organization and good luck—and one would have thought the Germans and Turks would have been forewarned by the first evacuation— the British successfully accomplished the operation on the night of 8–9 January. One sometimes suspects that if the campaign had been launched nearly a year before with the same care as the evacuations were organized, the outcome might have been a different story.[61]

THE MESOPOTAMIAN CAMPAIGN

The Mesopotamian campaign actually began a few months before the Dardanelles campaign and continued to the end of the war. It began with deceptive ease and success and reflected commendably prompt action on the part of the British government to protect British interests in the Persian Gulf as relations with Turkey deteriorated. The major cause for concern was the pipeline of the Anglo–Persian Oil Company, which had its terminal and refinery at Abadan island in the Shatt-al-Arab, the channel by which the Tigris and Euphrates rivers reach the sea after coming together at Kurnah. The British, in the light of German propaganda among the Arab sheiks and worsening relations with Turkey, decided to secretly assemble a force in the Persian Gulf. The Royal Navy's Gulf Division was old and weak, the lightly armed sloops *Espiègle* and *Odin* and the Royal Indian Marine armed transport *Dalhousie*. Traditional colonial vessels for carrying out "gunboat diplomacy," they were adequate for defeating whatever Turkish naval forces were likely to be found in the area, of which the largest was the 500-ton gunboat *Marmariss*, but would not have been a match for either of the German cruisers in the Indian Ocean, the *Emden* or *Königsberg*. The Admiralty therefore detached the old battleship *Ocean*, under Captain Hayes-Sadler, to provide naval cover for the expedition. Transports carrying a brigade of the 6th Indian Division separated from one of the convoys from India to Egypt and headed for the island of Bahrain in the Persian Gulf, where the Sheik, although nominally independent, had allowed a British political agent to function and substantially gave control of his foreign relations to the British.

The Government of India initially had control of the operations in the Persian Gulf and Mesopotamia. The expedition, commanded by Brigadier W. S. Delamain and escorted by the *Ocean* and the Royal Indian Marine armed transport *Dufferin*, reached Bahrain on 23 October. The Government of India therefore had a striking force well up the Persian Gulf when the Turkish navy attacked the Russians in the Black Sea. They ordered the expedition to the Shatt-al-Arab and prepared a second brigade for the Persian Gulf Expeditionary Force—otherwise known as "Force D." The *Ocean* herself drew too much water to cross the outer bar, but Hayes-Sadler armed launches and tugs, fitted minesweepers, and on 5 November—the day war with Turkey was formally declared—crossed the outer bar. The *Espiègle* was in position protecting the oil refinery at Abadan. The following day the Turkish guns at Fao at the entrance to the Shatt-al-Arab were silenced and by the 10th Delamain's brigade, except for a small garrison left at Fao, was in position at Saniyeh on the Turkish side of the river about 2½ miles upstream from the refinery, awaiting the arrival of additional troops from India under the command of Lieutenant General Sir A. A. Barrett.

The port of Basra, about 70 miles up the Shatt-al-Arab and the furthest point oceangoing ships could reach, was considered the key to the area, and General Barrett, once he and his troops had arrived, was ordered to take it if he could. The advance would be the best means of securing the oil refinery, supporting the pro-British Sheik of Muhammerah, and offsetting the effects of the Jihad, the holy war proclaimed by the Sultan of Turkey. Barrett decided to advance on 19 November, and by the 22d the British and Indian troops, supported by the *Espiègle*, *Odin*, and *Lawrence* (a paddle steamer of the Royal Indian Marine) had broken through the Turkish positions along the banks and the obstructions in the river and captured Basra. The war with Turkey was barely three weeks old, and so far the campaign had been the classic type of colonial action: great political and diplomatic gains at small matériel loss.

The temptation to push on was irresistible. Sir Percy Cox, the newly installed British agent and political resident at Basra, strongly recommended taking advantage of their momentum and apparent Turkish weakness and pushing on toward Baghdad. The Government of India found this suggestion premature. The difficulties of communication were too great and the number of troops available too few. They compromised and agreed to advance as far as Kurnah, some 45 miles up the Shatt-al-Arab where the Tigris and Euphrates joined. This would provide a good defensive position for the entire Shatt-al-Arab. The advance began on 3 December, and navigational difficulties in the shoal water proved as hard to overcome as Turkish resistance. The *Espiègle* and *Odin* accompanied the advance, but the *Odin* disabled her rudder, and armed launches of a much shallower draft along with river steamers played an increasingly important role. By 9 December the British had taken Kurnah, capturing the Vali of Basra, the Turkish commandant, and approximately one thousand prisoners. The fighting at times had been stiff, and not without loss, but still very much in the colonial mold.[62]

The psychological dimension of the campaigns against Turkey was always very strong, coupled with the threat that the proclamation of a Jihad might bring about a second mutiny among Great Britain's Indian subjects. This made it hard for the Mesopotamian expedition to stand still in early 1915. To quote the historian David French, "The fear that Mesopotamia might be the domino which could bring down the Eastern empire underlay the whole policy of the government of India in 1915."[63] The British therefore could not limit themselves to minor expeditions to punish hostile and troublesome Arabs in the marshes of the Euphrates near Kurnah. They had to respond to two Turkish threats: one a concentration at Nasiriya on the Euphrates, followed by a move south of the marshes and along the new channel of the Euphrates toward the west of Basra; and the other a thrust across the frontier into Persia by a Turkish column directed at Ahwaz on the Karun River, with its oil fields and the pipeline that ran down to Abadan. Kurnah itself, during the winter inundations, was virtually an island and largely secure from attack.

In March 1915 the navy was engaged in an interesting and unusual form of naval guerrilla war in the attempt to stop Turkish supplies, mostly carried in *mahailas*—a shallow-draft dhow native to the area—moving down the new channel of the Euphrates. The British created a special flotilla including two armed stern-wheel river steamers, a barge armed with a 4-inch gun, tugs, and motorboats. Operating in a vast, uncharted swampy waste, usually no more than three feet deep, grounding constantly, they pursued *mahailas* that hid in the high reeds and on the whole succeeded in blocking the Turkish Euphrates supply route. They also gained the dividend of weakening the allegiance of the local Arabs to the Turkish cause. The expedition up the Karun, assisted by the Sheik of Muhammerah and supported by armed launches, suffered an initial setback and had to be reinforced. The pipeline was cut in a number of places, and Persian Arabistan was still threatened.[64]

The psychological element again played its role with the failure of the naval attack on the Dardanelles. Turkish strength in Mesopotamia was growing, they were obviously preparing for an attack, and the British realized they would have to increase their force. The government of India felt unable to do so, the garrison of India had been stripped to the bone, and in the end the troops—an Indian brigade—were taken from Egypt. The Mesopotamia Expeditionary Force was now roughly an army corps, with two divisions of infantry and a cavalry brigade but without a full complement of artillery. The Admiralty provided another sloop, the *Clio*. On 9 April 1915, General Sir John Nixon assumed command of the force with orders to retain complete control of lower Mesopotamia. This included the vilayet of Basra and all outlets to the sea, as well as all portions of neighboring territories that might affect his operations. He was also, as far as practical and without prejudicing his main operations, to secure the safety of the oil fields, pipelines, and refineries in Persia. Moreover, in anticipation of possible contingencies, he was to study a plan for an advance on Baghdad.

The Turkish attacks began on 11 April, notably against Shaiba to the west of Basra. The Turkish attacks did not succeed, and the British promptly counterattacked. On 14 April the British broke the Turkish resistance, and the Euphrates flotilla helped to turn the retreat into a rout. The threat to Basra from the southwestern flank was ended. Nixon was now free to turn his attention to the Karun River, sending a division as reinforcements, and by 4 May the British had entered Bisaitin near the frontier. Persian Arabistan and the oil fields had been secured.

The inevitable question now was how to exploit the victory and where to move next. The Allied forces were hung up at the Dardanelles; an advance in Mesopotamia was thus all the more attractive. Nixon realized that the Turkish attacks had developed from two centers, Nasiriya on the Euphrates and Amara on the Tigris. He concluded that their occupation was necessary to secure the position in lower Mesopotamia. The attack up the Tigris toward Amara took priority, for there was a chance to cut off the Turks retreating from Ahwaz. The attack posed considerable tactical difficulties, however, because of the inundations that had made Kurnah virtually an island and the area around it a vast, reedy waste of water, only about two feet deep but crisscrossed by numerous canals and ditches so as to make wading impossible. A few low sand hills provided the only dry emplacements for Turkish artillery and infantry. The British made their infantry amphibious by collecting a large number of *bellums*—rough paddle canoes used by natives. As many as possible were given some armor protection, with steel plates to deflect rifle and machine-gun fire, and the troops were trained in their use. There were ten men to a *bellum*, but the attempts at armor plate proved a mistake, because it made them more difficult to pole through the reeds. Under these conditions the naval flotilla took the place of cavalry, and after the attack had advanced beyond range of the Kurnah emplacements, provided the only artillery. The flotilla, commanded by Captain Wilfrid Nunn, included the sloops *Espiègle, Odin,* and *Clio* and the paddle steamer *Lawrence* as the heavier units, but also consisted of two armed launches fitted for minesweeping, two naval horse boats with 4.7-inch naval guns, two gun barges with 5-inch and 4-inch guns, and a large flotilla of small craft for supplies and field ambulances, rafts for machine guns, and about sixty *bellums* per battalion.

The 6th Indian Division under the command of Major General Charles Townshend began its attack on 31 May, the troops during the preparatory bombardment "making their way like rats through the jungle of reeds" and largely unseen. The British took the Turkish outposts on the first day, and as the attack developed against the main position the following day, the Turks began to retreat. Townshend pursued, using his flotilla as cavalry in lieu of aircraft, which were hampered by a lack of dry ground on which they could land and deliver their reconnaissance reports. The infantry, loaded in river steamers, followed. Townshend was in the *Espiègle,* well ahead of his army, and the three oceangoing sloops steamed on against the current, approximately 150 miles from the sea, under conditions their builders could scarcely have imagined. The river grew narrower, the channel more and more tortuous, and the ships repeatedly scraped against the banks as they rounded the bends. The pursuit halted briefly during the hours of darkness and continued the next day. When the sloops could proceed no farther due to their draft, Nunn kept up the pursuit with the armed tug *Comet* and three launches, each towing a horse boat armed with a 4.7-inch naval gun. The Turkish river flotilla abandoned the gunboat *Marmariss,* the steamer *Mosul* surrendered, and the British flotilla also captured seven *mahailas* and two steel lighters. On the following day, Nunn continued the pursuit, and on the afternoon of the 3d the British captured the objective, Amara. It was only the following day that enough troops arrived by riverboat to really secure the town. The offensive had been a spectacular success, and the flotilla with improvised means had done wonders against a defeated and disorganized enemy, perhaps breeding a certain overconfidence about what river craft could and could not accomplish and, in the army as a whole, what the Turkish powers of resistance were likely to be.[65]

Nixon's next objective was to secure the western flank of the Basra vilayet by capturing Nasiriya on the Euphrates, approximately 70 miles west of Kurnah. The advance again posed considerable navigational difficulties as the hottest time of the year was approaching, and while much of the district was still inundated, the water level was falling. The Lake of Hammar, into which the Euphrates flowed some 40 miles west of Kurnah, could be navigated by only the shallowest-draft river craft, which meant that the sloops could not pass beyond the approaches to the lake. Once again the flotilla relied on the stern-wheelers, launches, and horse boats. The advance began on 27 June, but due to stout Turkish resistance, Turkish obstructions in the channel, and the steady toll of heat and sickness on the British force, the British had to commit additional forces. Nasiriya was finally taken on 25 July after the Turks evacuated the town. The campaign has been described as very much of an endurance contest for the British and Indian troops.[66]

During the summer months of 1915, the British had to divert some troops and naval forces to Bushire in the Persian Gulf, where in March the British had established a garrison to protect the cable station that was an important link in the line of communications between Basra and India. The German consul, Wassmuss—often characterized as a would-be German Lawrence of Arabia—was successful in stirring up the Tangistani tribesmen to attack the British lines in July, and in August and September a minor expedition involving the cruisers *Juno* and *Pyramus,* the paddle steamer *Lawrence,* and a landing detachment of bluejackets, Royal Marines, and Indian troops defeated the threat. Bushire was nominally Persian, and Persia was a neutral state. However, the Persian government obviously could not control the situation at Bushire, and so this classic example of old-fashioned "gunboat diplomacy" took place in the midst of a great world war.[67]

The British objectives in Mesopotamia had so far been essentially defensive. Nixon, however, had grander prospects—the capture of Baghdad. The first stage would be an advance to Kut, some 90 miles northwest of Amara, but twice as far by the tortuous river. Kut was just beyond the boundaries of the Basra vilayet, but Nixon justified its occupation as necessary to "perfect" the occupation of the Basra vilayet. The advance to Kut began on 12 September with the naval component of the army reduced to the armed tug *Comet,* armed launches, horse boats, and barges. The British broke through successive Turkish defenses and obstructions and reached the town on 29 September. The Turkish forces, however, were not routed and fell back to positions they had prepared long in advance at Ctesiphon, about 30 miles below Baghdad on the Tigris. The British lines of communications had grown much longer—nearly 400 miles by winding river to the base at Basra—and the force they could bring to face the Turks proportionately weaker.

In late October the War Committee made the fatal decision to try for Baghdad. There is no space here to go into the decision in detail, but that old consideration of "prestige" in the east played a major role. The Mesopotamian campaign, so far, had been one of the few bright spots for the British in the Muslim world in 1915 in which the attack on Constantinople through the Dardanelles had been a failure, Egypt was threatened from the west by the Senussi, and German and Turkish intrigue seemed to threaten revolt among Britain's Muslim subjects in India. The capture of Baghdad would cut German communications with Persia and Afghanistan and offset the effects of the failure at the Dardanelles. Nixon, although warned that he could not expect further reinforcements, thought he had enough forces to take the city and decided to press on.[68]

It took nearly a month after the authorization to advance was received from London before the column under General Townshend was able to begin its advance on Baghdad. The low state of the river delayed the preparations. Townshend had with him HMS *Firefly*, the first of twelve so-called small China gunboats ordered by Fisher and shipped out to the Persian Gulf in sections to be assembled at Abadan. The Fly-class were armed with a 4-inch gun, a 12-pounder, a 6-pounder, a 2-pounder pom-pom, and four Maxim guns. They could steam at best at 9.5 knots. Their most ingenious feature was a screw that worked through a tunnel in the hull, giving them a very shallow draft of between two and three feet. They were fitted with wireless but, designed primarily for police work, they lacked any real protection. The Insect-class, the first of which only reached the Tigris front in March 1916, after having been towed out from England, were the "large China" gunboats. The term "China" was actually a cover; they were intended for operations on the Danube. The Insect-class were larger and more powerful, with two 6-inch guns and twin screws in tunnels. Captain Nunn described the Fly-class as "useful little craft" that would have been more useful had they more powerful engines and twin screws as well as more than one boiler. If a boiler was put out of action by a shell, there was no reserve and they became helpless. Nunn considered the Insects a little large and of too great a draft for the Tigris and Euphrates. He thought the ideal craft for Mesopotamian conditions would have been a cross between the two.[69]

In the fighting before the Ctesiphon position 22–25 November, Townshend was unable to break through the Turkish position and decided he would have to retreat. The naval flotilla had been able to do little to help; the banks were too high in the reach below the Turkish position for direct fire, and the frail gunboats proved vulnerable to artillery fire from the opposite side of the river where there were no British troops to harass the Turkish batteries. The flotilla helped to cover the retreat of Townshend's army, losing a launch that grounded. On the first of December there were more losses. The gunboat *Firefly* was disabled by Turkish artillery, which managed to secure a position from which it could open enfilading fire into the reach where the river craft were anchored. Unfortunately the tug *Comet* ran aground trying to tow the *Firefly*. Both had to be abandoned.[70]

Townshend was besieged in Kut on 9 December. From January to April successive British commanders made unsuccessful attempts to break through Turkish defenses along the Tigris and relieve the town. The flotilla was strengthened by the arrival of more of the Fly-class and the *Mantis*, the first of the larger gunboats. The flotilla, though, had little scope for action in these operations to relieve Kut. To succeed, the British would probably have had to employ a far greater mass of troops and artillery than they had available or than could have been supported by the transport then available on the Tigris. There were attempts to drop supplies into Kut by air, but the amount of matériel that could be delivered by this means in 1916 was very small.

In April a desperate attempt was made by means of river steamer to get more supplies into Kut. The steamer *Julnar* was stripped of all surplus woodwork, covered with plating, and crammed with 270 tons of supplies. There was no lack of volunteers from the river flotilla for the venture, which was generally reckoned as having little chance of success. On the night of 24 April, the *Julnar,* with three officers and twelve ratings, made the attempt. The Turks had been expecting some effort, and the steamer was detected, brought under fire, and forced aground after running into a cable the Turks had stretched across the river. The commanding officer, Lieutenant H. O. B. Firman, Royal Navy, was killed by a Turkish shell, and second in command Lieutenant-Commander C. H. Cowley, Royal Naval Volunteer Reserve, a former Tigris river steamer captain, was murdered by the Turks as a renegade after capture. Both received the Victoria Cross. With all hope gone, Townshend and more than thirteen thousand officers and men surrendered on 29 April.[71]

The attempt to retrieve the prestige lost through the failure of the Dardanelles had therefore ended in the most appalling disaster. The British learned from their mistake. The first step came during the siege itself, when in February 1916 the War Office assumed control of the Mesopotamian expedition from the government of India, which had proven unequal to the task. The next essential step in the months following the fall of Kut was to put the expedition on a much sounder basis from the logistical point of view. The question of river transport was particularly crucial. Wemyss, after visiting Mesopotamia, was particularly critical of the Royal Indian Marine, which was not capable of handling the needs of an expedition greatly exceeding its normal responsibility. Moreover, it was not an independent service, but rather an adjunct of the Indian Army and subject to the Indian Army Council. The director of the Royal Indian Marine, although a naval officer, was located at Bombay, far removed from the Army Council at Delhi or Simla, and therefore handicapped in providing adequate advice or making his influence felt. The results were pernicious. The craft sent for river use in Mesopotamia often proved unsuitable or arrived in poor condition, if they did not sink on the way. For example, when the authorities in Mesopotamia asked for iron barges, they were sent wooden ones not strong enough to withstand constant bumping against the river banks. Basra was inadequate through want of organization and horribly congested. In April 1916 twenty ships waited at anchor for six weeks to unload. This waste of tonnage became even more intolerable once the U-boat war developed in earnest. Wemyss was unable to persuade General Lake, Nixon's successor as commander in chief in Mesopotamia, to accept naval control of the transport. Nevertheless there was a thoroughgoing administrative reorganization. Sir George Buchanan, the experienced head of port administration at Rangoon, who had been out in Mesopotamia in an advisory capacity since early 1916, was given increased responsibilities for port administration and river conservancy. In April Brigadier General G. F. MacMunn was appointed inspector-general of communications and worked diligently and successfully at setting the logistical groundwork for future success. Lake arranged for the delivery from England and India of large numbers of river steamers, tugs, barges, and lighters, including a number specially adopted for medical use. The medical arrangements for the expedition had been scandalously inadequate. These improved when the P-50-class of steamers began to arrive toward the end of the year. These were modifications of the paddle steamers employed on the Tigris and Euphrates, could carry four hundred tons of cargo, and drew only four feet of water. To relieve congestion at certain restricted portions of the Tigris, the British also constructed railways, notably between Kurnah and Amara.[72]

In July 1916 Lieutenant General Sir Stanley Maude was appointed to command the Tigris corps and in August became commander in chief of the Mesopotamia Expeditionary Force. The government at first warned Maude in September that he could expect no reinforcements and that a renewed advance on Baghdad was not immediately contemplated. He was to maintain British control of the Basra vilayet.[73] Maude's initial objectives were limited: he intended to secure a position on the Hai River at Kut. On 12 December he began his offensive. The British logistical buildup included quantities of ammunition and howitzers and medium-caliber guns that gave the British artillery a preponderance effective against the Turkish trenches. The British advance was slow but steady, and by 24 February 1917 they had broken through the Turkish positions and the gunboats were able to anchor off the deserted and ruined Kut. The Russians had also undertaken an offensive in the Caucasus, and to allay any danger the Russian army might reach Baghdad, the government was now anxious for Maude to take the city.

The advance gave the river flotilla another opportunity. During the long lull following the fall of Kut the preceding April, the vessels had been distributed up and down the Tigris and Euphrates, guarding the lines of communications against raids. Nunn now had the three 6-inch gun gunboats, the *Mantis, Tarantula,* and *Moth,* as well as three of the smaller Fly-class. He asked for and received Maude's permission to cooperate in the pursuit, and once again the flotilla had the opportunity to act like cavalry. On the afternoon of the 26th, brushing past Turkish stragglers, the gunboats caught sight of the retreating Turkish river flotilla after passing Bughaila. Nunn ran into the Turkish rear guard at the Nahr al Kalek bend, and steaming full ahead through the hairpin turn the river made here, the *Tarantula* (SNO), *Mantis,* and *Moth* ran the gauntlet of heavy fire from Turkish artillery, machine guns, and rifles coming from three sides at ranges of only four to five hundred yards. They suffered heavy casualties but kept going, and in fact really could not retreat. The *Moth* was hit eight times by artillery fire and had four out of five officers and half her ship's company killed or wounded. Nunn wisely sent a message by wireless for the smaller, less-protected and much slower *Gadfly* not to follow them around the bend. Once clear of the Turkish rear guard, the gunboats were able to spread confusion among the main body of the retreating Turkish army and overhaul the Turkish river flotilla. The Turks abandoned the steamer *Basra,* the tug *Pioneer,* and the gunboat *Firefly,* which to the great satisfaction of Nunn and the men of the flotilla came back under the white ensign after fifteen months in Turkish hands. The official history praised the proceedings of the gunboats: "This action of the Navy had the effect of turning the orderly retreat of the rear of the Turkish army into a panic-stricken flight."[74]

On 11 March the British occupied Baghdad. The major work of the river flotilla was done. Although the gunboats moved with the army north of Baghdad and cooperated in operations during the following months, the Tigris above Baghdad was not really suitable for their operations. In March 1918 the Admiralty decided they needed the crews for the antisubmarine war, and the eight Fly-class gunboats were transferred to the army. Four had their guns removed and were used as ordinary steamers; the remaining four were manned by officers and machine gunners from the Inland Water Transport Service with gun crews drawn from the Royal Artillery. The four larger Insect-class gunboats remained under naval control down river.

The Mesopotamian campaign, unlike the Dardanelles, ended in victory. When the armistice with Turkey was concluded, the British were far north of Baghdad marching on Mosul. The campaign required a degree of effort few might have imagined when the first brigade was landed in November 1914 to secure the oil refineries. The ration strength of the Mesopotamia Expeditionary Force on 19 October 1918 was more than 410,000, of which about 217,000 were actually in the army, and, in the usual story of the ratio of "teeth to tail" only about 112,000 of them were fighting troops. There were more than 71,000 men, mostly Indians, in the Labor Corps and 42,000 in the Inland Water Transport. It will be a matter of perennial debate whether the imperial gains that the advance to Baghdad and beyond were assumed to bring justified this considerable effort.[75]

THE EASTERN MEDITERRANEAN AFTER THE DARDANELLES

The end of the Dardanelles campaign brought a gradual decrease in British and French forces in the eastern Mediterranean. The submarine war became the dominant theme in this part of the world. There were various schemes for overseas expeditions. The French, who patrolled the coast of Syria and Lebanon with a heterogeneous collection of old ships, occupied the tiny island of Ruad off the coast of Lebanon on 1 September 1915 and the little island of Castelorizo off the Turkish coast on 28 December. Both islands served as outposts or intelligence centers for the operations off the Turkish coast, which were little more than pinpricks. The Turks were apparently annoyed enough at Castelorizo to secretly bring up artillery on the mainland opposite the island, and on 9 January 1917 they opened fire, sinking the British seaplane carrier *Ben-my-Chree*, which had anchored in the port. On 20 January the French easily repulsed a Turkish landing attempt. Late in the year, on 4 November, the Turks also bombarded Ruad, sinking a French trawler whose engines were under repair. At the height of the submarine war, the little islands were probably more trouble to supply than they were worth as intelligence centers.[76]

After the evacuation of the Dardanelles, the British attempted to keep at least some maritime pressure on the Turks. This took the form of the Anatolian cattle raids of 1916. De Robeck, who was forced to witness the inevitable rundown of his command, proposed minor raids on the coast of Anatolia for the purpose of seizing livestock the British believed were being commandeered by the Ottoman government for shipment to Germany. De Robeck hoped to pin Turkish troops down through the threat of landings. He wanted to use regular troops, but none were available, and so he had to employ Greek irregulars, carried in a heterogeneous collection of British ships, which were used in the blockade of the Anatolian coast. Many of the irregulars had been expelled from their homes on the mainland, and de Robeck believed there was a certain amount of rough justice involved, as much of the livestock was supposedly confiscated from these people by the Turks. The proceeds of the raids were to be divided among the irregulars and the Royal Navy on return to port. The Admiralty agreed, provided the raids remained small in scope and did not require any special transport.

The raids began in March 1916 and were continued by Vice Admiral Thursby, de Robeck's successor in the Aegean, until the latter part of October. At the time the term *cattle* actually meant all types of livestock, and a considerable amount was seized, especially sheep. The role of cattle rustler was a strange one for the Royal Navy. Professor Myres, an Oxford classics professor commissioned in the Royal Naval Volunteer Reserve, proved particularly talented and knowledgeable in carrying out this type of warfare. It is doubtful if it really hurt the Turks very much; these areas of the Anatolian coast were not heavily populated or well served by roads to the main centers of population, and inevitably the coastal districts were denuded of suitable targets. The irregulars were hard to control, and there were some diplomatic repercussions. The Greek government protested because of the danger of reprisals against other Greeks living on the mainland, and the Ottoman government protested through the United States that the use of irregular bands instead of regular forces was contrary to international law. Thursby considered the cattle raids had served their purpose and ended them at the end of October.[77]

At the end of December 1917, the new commander of the British Aegean squadron, Rear Admiral Sydney Fremantle, proposed a resumption of the raids on a somewhat larger scale, involving five to six hundred men. The proposal was rejected on the familiar grounds. The Admiralty could see no really important objectives or anticipate any significant results for raids on the Anatolian coast.[78]

A similar fate befell proposals for amphibious operations on the Syrian coast. This type of operation had always appealed to people such as Captain Richmond, and in May 1917 after he had returned to the Grand Fleet he produced a plan that attracted Beatty, who forwarded it to the War Staff for further consideration. Richmond envisaged operations against the Turkish line of communications from Mersina to Gaza, conducted by monitors, seaplane carriers, destroyers, drifters with mines, self-propelled lighters, and fast motorboats. A military force would be embarked for raids inland. The problem with this and similar schemes in the eyes of the Admiralty was directly connected with the submarine war, which taxed all their resources. In the Admiralty's final judgment, minor operations such as Richmond proposed were apt to develop and tend toward a further dispersion of forces. Wemyss, when First Sea Lord in October 1917, took a similar position when the War Office approached him about possible operations. Aside from direct naval assistance to the British army advancing in Palestine, Wemyss did not think any demonstration by the forces at their disposal would have any appreciable effect in drawing Turkish troops toward the threatened coastline.[79] For various reasons, and because Macedonia, Egypt, and Palestine were essentially land campaigns, the Dardanelles campaign of 1915 would remain from the naval point of view *the* major overseas campaign in the Mediterranean.

NORTH RUSSIA

German domination of the Baltic and Turkish control of the entrance to the Black Sea meant that the only feasible way to transport large quantities of supplies to Russia during the First World War was by means of the north Russian ports. Archangel, the traditional port in the north, was located in the southeast corner of the White Sea and was generally considered closed by ice from November to May. The Russian government therefore developed Murmansk-Romanov in the Kola inlet on the northern coast, which although further north than Archangel, was warmed by ocean currents and relatively ice free. Once it became apparent that the war would not be over within a few weeks, Russian needs for war matériel from abroad became large and were destined to grow. This would eventually place serious demands on British shipping, and relations between the Allies would not always be harmonious.[80] The quantities involved were considerable. During the 1915 season, 700,000 tons of coal and 500,000 tons of general cargo, mostly munitions and supplies, were carried to the White Sea from Great Britain and France. In the 1916 season the tonnage from Great Britain, France, and the United States rose to 2.5 million tons, which represented approximately twenty-five times the normal peacetime trade of the White Sea.[81]

For the greater part of the first year of the war in Arctic waters, the Russians and their allies faced greater problems from the weather than from the Germans, and the Admiralty assisted by sending the old battleship *Jupiter* (launched 1895) to the White Sea to work as an icebreaker. The *Jupiter* reportedly set a record as the first ship to ever reach Archangel in February and remained on station until May 1915. The Russians were worried, however, that their immunity from German action would not last. They were particularly concerned about potential minelaying and asked the British for assistance. The Admiralty recognized the potential danger and, despite the many demands on their resources, managed to scrape together in June a flotilla of six trawlers fitted with minesweeping gear. Even before they sailed, the Germans demonstrated that the

Russian fears had some justification. The German auxiliary cruiser *Meteor*, actually the former British cargo liner *Vienna* (1,912 tons), which had been caught in Hamburg by the outbreak of the war, laid 285 mines in the northern approaches to the White Sea, cleverly scattered in the channels between the headlands that vessels were likely to follow on route to Archangel. Between June and September the *Meteor*'s mines had sunk or damaged nine Allied freighters.[82]

The British trawlers began sweeping on their arrival—one was mined within a week—and merchant ships were formed into convoys preceded by a pair of minesweepers on routes in and out of the White Sea. The British naval presence grew slowly with more trawlers, the obsolescent cruisers *Intrepid* and *Iphigenia* and the old battleship *Albemarle*, sent out to serve as an icebreaker and keep the channel to Archangel open as long as possible during the winter of 1915–6. The Russians also provided what they could, notably fishing vessels converted into auxiliary minesweepers and a minelayer and pair of small destroyers transferred from Vladivostok.[83]

The White Sea traffic enjoyed relative immunity for much of the 1916 shipping season. The Germans did not repeat their attempt to send surface raiders but tried to disrupt operations with their large minelaying submarines. In addition, in five weeks between late September and early November, five submarines from the High Sea Fleet worked off the Murman coast between North Cape and Kola Inlet. By the time the onset of the Arctic winter forced the Germans to stop operations they had sunk thirty-four ships, nineteen of them Norwegian.[84] The losses, considering the volume of cargo carried, were small, barely exceeding 3 percent.[85] When compared to other areas, notably the Mediterranean, it is apparent the Germans devoted relatively little attention to Arctic waters.

The Allies in a conference at Petrograd in January–February 1917 committed themselves to the delivery of 3.5 million tons of supplies, munitions, and coal to Archangel and Murmansk during the 1917 shipping season. By the winter of 1917, British forces in the White Sea under Commodore (later Rear Admiral) Thomas Kemp had grown to include the old battleship *Glory*, which served as a depot ship at Murmansk, 3 old cruisers, 4 armed boarding steamers, 2 yachts, 23 trawlers, and 4 drifters. Russian forces had also grown to include 6 destroyers and torpedo boats, 17 dispatch vessels and auxiliary cruisers, and at least 36 minesweepers. During the winter the Russians also received the welcome reinforcement of 3 to 4 new icebreakers that had been built in England.[86]

The German switch to unrestricted submarine warfare in February 1917 did not immediately affect Arctic waters. There was, on the whole, relatively less submarine activity than the preceding year. The British maintained patrols off Kola Inlet to meet and protect incoming traffic, and when the White Sea opened, ships proceeded independently to Yukanski, where they were assembled into convoys that sailed for Archangel every forty-eight hours preceded by trawler sweepers. In September and October shipping from the United Kingdom was ordered to proceed independently via the Norwegian Inner Leads, that is, to take advantage of Norwegian territorial waters.

Trawlers met them in Arctic waters off Vardo or Kirkenes and every forty-eight hours escorted them to Archangel. The losses in Arctic waters during 1917 were not severe given the volume of traffic. The real losses on the route to north Russia appear to have taken place further to the south, outside of Arctic waters. They were much heavier than the preceding year, about 13 percent on the total number of round voyages, and the total volume of cargo delivered to north Russian ports was about 16 percent less than the preceding year. About three-quarters had been carried by the British, one-fifth by the Russians.[87]

The Allied activity in north Russia during 1917 took place amid growing disorganization following the March revolution, which culminated with the Bolshevik seizure of power in November and the commencement of negotiations for peace with the Central Powers. Russia was effectively out of the war. The Treaty of Brest-Litovsk was signed on 3 March 1918. The relevant provisions of the treaty for northern Russia included the stipulations: the German submarine blockade in the Arctic Sea would continue until the conclusion of a general peace; Russian warships were to be brought into Russian ports until the conclusion of peace; and Allied warships "within Russian sovereignty" were to be treated as Russian warships.[88] This meant that technically the Russians might have to insist on the internment of Allied warships caught in their waters.

The British could take comfort from at least one aspect of Russia's defection. The Allies would no longer have to fulfill a 1918 program of shipping to the White Sea for they had been strained almost to the breaking point to meet their commitments at the height of the submarine war in 1917. Ships released from service to and from the White Sea would be employed in the French and Italian coal trade or to carry cereals and other essential imports to Great Britain. Furthermore, the British were to requisition approximately fifty Russian steamers representing an aggregate tonnage of about 150,000 gross tons.[89]

The British and their allies were worried about the vast backlog of supplies at Archangel and suspected that the Germans might attempt to seize them. The Royal Navy was also afraid that the German use of Murmansk and Archangel as bases for submarines or raiders would to a large extent render the planned northern Barrage (see chapter 13) useless.[90] The British were correct in worrying about German designs on northern Russia. A major German offensive was anticipated on the western front before significant American forces could arrive, and the German High Command considered a drive on Murmansk as another aspect of their war against the Entente. Admiral von Holtzendorff, chief of the Admiralstab, certainly found the idea of a base on the Barents Sea very attractive.[91] The situation and events in northern Russia in 1918 were very complex, and one cannot do justice to them here. The motives of all concerned, British and Allied, German, Red and White Russian, Red and White Finn, were mixed.[92] The initial Allied intervention gradually changed from protecting supplies and northern Russia from Finnish or German incursions to hostilities against the Bolshevik government in a murky and shifting political situation.

In July British, French, Serbian, Italian, and, eventually, American troops were established at Murmansk and extended their activity southward along the railway to Kandalaksha, Kem, and Soroka on the White Sea. By the beginning of August the Allies had taken Archangel. The majority of naval forces were British, including the light cruiser *Attentive* and seaplane carrier *Nairana*, although the Americans were represented by the cruiser *Olympia*—Admiral Dewey's flagship at the Battle of Manila Bay—and the French by the old armored cruiser *Amiral Aube*. The Allies then began an advance southward up the Dvina River in an attempt to make contact with the anti-Bolshevik Czech Legion, reportedly anti-German and anxious to continue the war but stranded deep in Russia along the Trans-Siberian railway. Captain Altham of the *Attentive* was named senior naval officer Dvina. The British were forced to improvise, converting two paddle steamers to fragile gunboats, joined by Russian naval motor launches and other river craft. The motley flotilla was later joined by the monitors *M.25* and *M.23*. The Dvina Flotilla even improvised its own seaplane carrier with the *Attentive's* fore derrick fitted to a barge to hoist in and out single-seater seaplanes from the *Nairana*. The riverine warfare was somewhat reminiscent of Mesopotamia, but with far greater extremes of climate. In June, according to Captain Altham, the ice in the White Sea made it scarcely navigable, while a month later the weather was almost semitropical and they were glad to have mosquito nets.

The Dvina Flotilla, acting in concert with Allied forces on shore, clashed repeatedly with Bolshevik forces, both river craft and batteries on land. By the end of September they had cleared the river channel as far as Pushega, roughly 250 miles up the Dvina. By that time, however, the gunboats had to be withdrawn to prevent them from being trapped by ice, which could form up to a foot thick within a single night, and army outposts eventually had to be pulled back.[93] On 11 November the Armistice on the western front went into effect, marking what is generally considered the end of the First World War. On this date in north Russia, Allied troops under General Maynard held Murmansk and the Murman railway as far south as Soroka, while further east General Poole's forces held Archangel and the Archangel-Vologda railway as far south as Obozerskaya and the Dvina upstream to the fortified base at Bereznik with outposts at Kurgomin-Tulgas. The Czech Legion, one of the ostensible causes for intervention in the first place, remained far out of reach and never would join the forces in north Russia. Although the gunboats *Glowworm*, *Cockschafter*, *Cicala*, and *Cricket*, originally built for operations in China, reached Archangel just before ice closed the port, the Allies had a period of enforced inactivity due to the winter to decide what to do. The 1919 campaign of intervention in north Russia in which the Allies sought to assist the anti-Bolshevik White Russian forces that were in the process of forming that winter is well beyond the scope of this study.[94] The operations in the north were complemented by operations in the Black Sea, the Caspian, and a lively campaign in the Baltic.[95] A Russian campaign, given the natural difficulties and distances involved, was likely to be an open-ended commitment, and it is not surprising that after the tremendous strain of four years of war, the Allied governments and public finally chose to limit their operations and, ultimately, to cut their losses and withdraw.

6

THE ADRIATIC

ITALY ENTERS THE WAR

The geography of the Adriatic played a major part in determining the nature of the naval war fought there. The Adriatic forms a long, relatively narrow rectangle between 60 and 100 miles wide. Consequently, there was not the scope for the large sweeps characteristic of the North Sea. The enemy was only a few hours' steaming distance away. This proximity put a premium on quick reaction and allowed small craft to be used to a far greater extent than in the North Sea. With the development of mines, torpedoes, submarines, and, later, high-speed motor torpedo boats, the campaign in the Adriatic took on the features of naval guerrilla war. The ambush, rather than the classic encounter between rival squadrons, characterized the war. Nevertheless, both sides had powerful dreadnoughts and battleships. The numbers were far smaller than in the North Sea: four Austrian dreadnoughts against six Italian dreadnoughts when all had entered service. These ships *might* be used at any time, and the possibility always had to be provided for. The core of the Austrian fleet, four dreadnoughts and three modern semidreadnoughts of the *Radetzky* class, was the classic example of the fleet-in-being, and the potential menace of their big guns eventually tied up more than twice their number watching them.

Politics also played an important role. The Italians might later have the theoretical support of up to seven French dreadnoughts, but the two fleets were not combined and the efficacy of their cooperation was questionable, even if the problem of command had not proved insolvable. The Italians had one constant demand on which they would not compromise: command in the Adriatic must be Italian. The Italian naval leaders also had one burning desire—to avenge the defeat at Lissa in 1866. One would have to study the history of the *Risorgimento*—the movement by which Italy achieved unification in the nineteenth century—to understand the intensity of Italian feelings on the subject of the

Austrian enemy, the Adriatic, and command in that sea.

As far as the Italians were concerned, the Austrians possessed all of the geographical advantages. The coast on the eastern, or Austrian, side of the Adriatic was irregular, indented with bays, and for the most part screened by a chain of offshore islands with navigable channels between them, behind which ships could move and emerge suddenly for attack. The Italian coast, on the other hand, was open to attack and relatively unprotected. The Austrians had excellent naval bases at both ends of the Adriatic, the strongly fortified Pola—their main base—in the north, and the Bay of Cattaro in the south, with secure anchorages in between. The Italians had few secure anchorages on their side of the Adriatic, except for Venice and Brindisi, and the capacity of the latter was limited. The Italians later found that even the character of the water favored the Austrians; the Italian side was muddier and aided concealment of submarines, whereas the Austrian side was often clear, enabling submarines to be seen even when submerged. As the air war developed, the Italians found conditions also favored the Austrians. Italian airmen making dawn attacks found the sun in their eyes and the coast obscured in shadow; Austrian airmen attacked the Italian coast from out of the sun. Virtually all Italian naval literature and planning of the period stress these geographical factors.[1]

The leaders of the Austrian and Italian navies, Admiral Anton Haus and Vice Admiral Paolo Count Thaon di Revel, respectively, were in a unique position. Before the war they were allies in the Triple Alliance and in 1913 had even met secretly in Zurich to discuss possible joint operations. Both men realized they were just as likely to be at war with each other, and the possibility they would be allies disappeared when the Italians proclaimed their neutrality at the outbreak of the war. The major question became, Would the Italians remain neutral (and gain more by doing so) or join the ranks of the Entente? The matter was hotly debated within Italy and was by no means a foregone conclusion. However, the Entente had a fundamental advantage. They could offer the Italians territory torn from their Austrian enemy. The Germans could only offer territory they could pressure their Austrian ally to give up. The Entente could invariably offer more for Italian participation than the Central Powers could offer for continued Italian neutrality. Italy's "defection" from the Triple Alliance, or "treachery" in Austrian eyes, meant that Haus pursued an even more cautious policy in the face of the superior French fleet in order to preserve his own forces to counter an eventual Italian move (see chapter 3).

Thaon di Revel was the dominant figure in the Italian navy for much of the First World War. He was capo di stato maggiore from March 1913 until his resignation in October 1915, and commander in chief at Venice from October 1915 to February 1917. Revel had resigned because of chronic divergence of views with the ministers of marine and disputes over the power and functions of the chief of the naval staff. In his mind there could not be two heads of the navy. The minister, Vice Admiral Camillo Corsi, attempted to combine the political office of minister of marine with the position of chief of the naval staff. The experiment was not a success, and Revel returned in February 1917 as capo di stato maggiore and commander in chief of the mobilized naval forces. This not only gave him increased powers but also implied he could assume command of the fleet in a major action. This was another dubious assumption, that Revel would always arrive from Rome before the fleet had to sail in an emergency. Nevertheless, this energetic, autocratic, and forceful Piedmontese, whose family had a long tradition of service to the kings of Piedmont in the days before unification, made his mark not only on the Italian navy but eventually on the Allies. By 1918 Thaon di Revel was notorious for his rigid insistence on due regard for Italian concerns and needs, which he felt the other Allies did not always adequately appreciate. The Allies often viewed this as selfish egoism, and the British, Americans, and French regarded him as a major obstacle to Allied unity, the man most to blame for the fact that the Allies would never achieve the same degree of unity in the war in the Mediterranean as they would achieve on the western front under the leadership of Marshal Foch.[2]

Revel was also thoroughly realistic, and quite conscious of the changes in naval technology that made it suicidal to try to carry on the traditional close blockade. He also had the example of the war in the north. The Italians assumed, correctly, that the Austrian strategy would be a continuation of the methods they had used against the French. They would maintain the fleet-in-being, keeping their big ships secure in their well-fortified bases, while whittling away the Italian superiority in numbers through mines and torpedoes and waiting for the opportune moment to strike. How could the Italians induce the Austrians to sortie from Pola for a naval battle under conditions favorable to them? The possible courses of action included a blockade of the Strait of Otranto, bombardments of Fiume or Trieste, the temporary occupation of Adriatic islands such as Lagosta and Curzola, attacks on Austrian signal and semaphore stations, and mining the channels between the islands. The bombardments of Fiume and Trieste could be ruled out, the former was too dangerous and difficult to approach up the gulf known as the Quarnero, while the latter contained a large Italian population and was close to the main Austrian base, which would expose the bombarding vessels to torpedo attack at night. An attack on Cattaro, the southernmost Austrian base, might cause the Austrian fleet to sortie, but the Italians did not think they had the means for such an attack. Revel's emphasis, however, was clear. Whatever the Italians did to further their objectives, they should never run the risk of putting their battleships in danger from mines and torpedoes, nor should they subordinate the conduct of their forces to opposing fleeting raids by the enemy on the Italian coast. Their objective in all operations, Revel wrote in January 1915, was to cause major damage to the enemy while receiving the minimum, and this was to be achieved by aggressive action on the part of light craft and torpedo boats. The big ships were to be preserved for combat against their enemy counterparts.[3]

The commander in chief of the Italian fleet was initially inclined to be more aggressive. The Italian battle fleet at the beginning of the war was led by Vice Admiral Luigi Amadeo di Savoia, Duke of the Abruzzi. Abruzzi, a cousin of King Victor Emmanuel III, was the third son of Amadeo di Savoia, Duke of Aosta, who had been briefly King of Spain (1871–73). Well born, and with the manners and charm of a *grand seigneur*, Abruzzi was probably one of the best-known Italians of his time, owing to a series of well-publicized expeditions before the war to the Arctic, the Himalayas, and the Ruwenzori Mountains of central Africa. He presented the image of a dashing chief, but somehow, because of the changed conditions of warfare, never lived up to the high expectations people had of him.[4] Abruzzi was loath to expose the Italian fleet to the attrition of a distant blockade of the Strait of Otranto and wanted through a series of aggressive measures to *force* the Austrians to sortie by means, for example, of a bombardment of Fiume or a landing in force at Trieste, or by appearing off Pola and decimating the Austrian fleet as they came out and before they could develop their battle formation.[5]

Revel's strategy, the one the Italians followed, was more Fabian. The most aggressive action at the beginning of hostilities would be to seize a secure anchorage in the Sabbioncello Channel between the Sabbioncello Peninsula and the island of Curzola. This was close enough to Cattaro (72 miles) for the Italians to destroy any light Austrian forces coming out of the base, but far enough from the main Austrian base at Pola (195 miles) to avoid being surprised by the Austrian fleet. Revel envisaged two principal phases for maritime operations in the Adriatic. During the first phase, the Italian fleet would be based at Brindisi and Taranto, and operations would take place in the lower and central Adriatic. They would include all actions permitted by circumstances that might induce the Austrian fleet to come southward and give battle. The Italian fleet would only move into the upper Adriatic in the second phase of operations, which would be after the Italian army had succeeded in pushing the Austrians out of Monfalcone and back toward Trieste. The Italian fleet would then help to speed the occupation of Trieste and the Istrian Peninsula and cut Austrian communications along the coast.

Abruzzi was anxious to include Cattaro in the plans. He proposed sending howitzers to Mount Lovčen, where they would be in a position overlooking the gulf. This would have been roughly on the same scale as the unsuccessful French operations the preceding autumn. Revel also liked the idea of operations against Cattaro, but with a much more serious military force, perhaps in the second phase of operations. He was thinking of a real siege. This might be the means to force the Austrian fleet to come out for battle in waters favorable to the Italians, and in any case causing Austrian morale to suffer. The capture of Cattaro by an Italian force also would support Italian claims on the eastern shore of the Adriatic at any future peace conference. Serious operations against Cattaro involved the Italian army, however, and General Luigi Cadorna, the chief of the army general staff, was strongly opposed. Cadorna envisaged making his major effort with all available troops on the northeastern frontier in the direction of Trieste and was loath to disperse men and matériel on what were for him merely secondary objectives. Cadorna was also very niggardly in the men and matériel he agreed to provide for the seizure of the anchorage at Sabbioncello—a regiment of second-line reserve troops and some artillerymen for four 76-mm landing guns to be furnished by the navy. Only four 280-mm howitzers would be sent to Mount Lovčen. The howitzers never reached Montenegro; they were used instead for the defense of Brindisi harbor, and the plans to seize the anchorage at Sabbioncello were deferred. Revel concluded that the anchorage might become a considerable burden, as even the reduced number of troops would have to be maintained over a none-too-secure line of communications while the enemy fleet was in being, and this would tie down naval forces that could be employed more efficiently elsewhere. The navy was obligated to support the seaward flank of the army's advance in the north, and if this forced the Austrian fleet out to give battle in the early days of the war, the base would be superfluous. If, on the other hand, the Italian fleet had to move north to support the army on the 15th to 20th day of the war, the base would have to be abandoned.[6]

The Italians would not be making war in isolation, they would be part of an Allied coalition. How did the Italian plans and intentions square with those of the British and French? The Treaty of London was signed on 26 April, obligating the Italians to enter the war within a month.[7] The bargaining had been difficult, particularly because of Russian opposition to Italian claims in the Adriatic. Article three of the treaty stipulated: "The Fleets of France and Great Britain will give their active and permanent assistance to Italy until the destruction of the Austro-Hungarian Fleet or until the conclusion of peace."[8]

A naval convention, signed in Paris on 10 May, established the details of this naval cooperation. The bargaining was equally difficult, foreshadowing Italy's turbulent relations with the Allies for the remainder of the war. Revel did not get his requirements, and there were even fears the disputes would call into question the entire Treaty of London before a compromise was reached.

The convention provided for a "First Allied Fleet" to be established under the commander in chief of the Italian fleet. The "First Allied Fleet" would consist of most of the Italian fleet; twelve French destroyers, to be joined by as many torpedo boats, submarines, and minesweepers as the French commander in chief could detach; if possible, a squadron of aircraft and a French seaplane carrier; four British light cruisers, to arrive as soon as they were replaced by French cruisers at the Dardanelles; and a division of four British battleships. The commander in chief of the Italian fleet would have the initiative and complete direction of operations executed in the Adriatic by the "First Allied Fleet."

If this "First Allied Fleet" had to move to the northern part of the Adriatic for any operation requiring *all* of the Allied forces, a "Second Allied Fleet" would be formed. This would be under the commander in chief of the French fleet and would consist of French battleships and cruisers and those Italian and British ships not already allotted to the Italian commander in chief. The "Second Allied Fleet," with its flotilla craft, would be ready to reply to the appeal of the commander in chief of the Italian fleet. The Allies promised that as long as enemy naval forces were in the Adriatic, they would support the Italian fleet so as to maintain, as much as possible, a force clearly superior to the enemy.

There was a codicil to the convention that spelled out the specific details. These included the stipulation that six of the twelve French destroyers would be oil-burning, and, as far as possible, of more than 600 tons displacement; six French submarines would be at the disposal of the Italians; the number of French cruisers at the Dardanelles would increase to four as soon as possible, and each French arrival would release a British cruiser for the Adriatic; and, likewise, four British battleships with 12-inch guns currently at the Dardanelles would leave for Taranto as soon as they were replaced by French ships. The major ambiguity remained unanswered by either the convention or its codicil. Who would command if the "Second Allied Fleet," essentially the French battle squadrons, was ever called to operate inside the Adriatic? The convention of August 1914 stipulated that the French commander in chief was also the Mediterranean commander in chief, and the French were hardly likely to consent to his being placed under Italian orders, just as the Italians would never consent to anyone but an Italian commanding in the Adriatic. The circle could not be squared and the problem surfaced whenever there was any possibility the French battle fleet would actually have to help the Italians.[9]

It is hardly surprising that Revel was not satisfied with the treaty. He suspected Italy's position in the Mediterranean naval balance would suffer to the advantage of the French should a major battle, even if victorious, leave the Italian fleet weakened by the inevitable losses. He was also concerned that the British and French might have suffered greater losses than they had admitted at the Dardanelles. Why else could the British, the world's leading naval power, not send a meager four battleships to the Italians from the Dardanelles until they had been replaced by the French? Would the British and French really be able to live up to their obligations to provide active and permanent support to the Italians until the destruction of the Austrian fleet or the conclusion of peace? Revel suspected that if the Allies could not offer the very little that Italy was asking, it would be proof that they were reduced to a bad way in the war at sea and had, as he put it to Sonnino's secretary, "more need of us than we of them."[10] Revel and the Italians were also strengthened in their determination not to risk their major assets, the dreadnoughts and battleships, unnecessarily. The mutual suspicions among the Allies over Adriatic operations never disappeared.

The actual entry of Italy into the war was by no means a foregone conclusion for there was substantial opposition to it. The former prime minister, Giovanni Giolitti a firm believer in neutrality, returned to Rome and gained widespread support in parliament. The government resigned, but the opposition to intervention melted away under the pressure of mass demonstrations led by fiery nationalists such as Gabriele D'Annunzio and the more covert influence of the king. The majority of Italians probably preferred neutrality.[11]

The events in Italy also provided plenty of warning to the Austrians about what was coming, and Haus decided to strike the first blow as soon as possible after the outbreak of war. He hoped the effect on morale would be great. Haus was ready on 23 May to sail with the fleet as soon as it was dark. There was spontaneous and spirited cheering aboard the Austrian warships when news of the Italian declaration of war reached Pola about 4:00 P.M., and around 8:00 P.M. the fleet sailed. The majority of the heavy ships bombarded Ancona early on the morning of the 24th, while other force attacked Corsini harbor (near Ravenna), Rimini, Senigallia, and the mouth of the Potenza. There were also air raids on Venice and the airship hangars at Chiaravalle. In the northern Adriatic, the Italian destroyer *Zeffiro* attacked Porto Buso, destroying the pier and taking some prisoners. The Austrians, however, with the largest number of warships they would employ in a single operation during the entire war, inflicted the most damage that day with their bombardments. The cruiser *Helgoland* and two destroyers also sank the Italian destroyer *Turbine* in the south off Pelagosa. The operation was in many ways a gesture of spite and contempt by the Austrians, a thunderous opening to the war. There was never any chance of a real naval battle, the bulk of the Italian fleet was far away, and the French even farther.[12]

THE ADRIATIC STALEMATE

Abruzzi planned for a campaign in three phases in order to obtain command of the Adriatic. In the first phase, torpedo boats and light craft would undertake a relentless sweep of the lower and mid-Adriatic in order to seek and destroy enemy torpedo boats and submarines. Once the lower Adriatic was relatively clear, the Italians and their allies would proceed with the second phase, which would be the destruction of the bases for the enemy's light craft at Ragusa, Gravosa, and possibly Spalato. They also would dismantle lookout stations in the lower Dalmatian archipelago, cut submarine cables, and occupy some of the smaller islands as observation posts. The older and smaller cruisers as well as auxiliary cruisers might be used in this phase. The third phase, aimed especially at provoking the Austrian fleet and attracting it to the south, would be the occupation of some island, such as Lagosta or Lissa, in the lower Dalmatian archipelago. This might be followed by other major occupations, such as Curzola or Meleda, again with the idea of tempting the Austrian fleet to battle. The occupations would, however, be transitory. The advance of the fleet to the north, which the Italians had anticipated in the later stages of the war, would be dependent on the outcome and speed of the first three phases.[13] Unfortunately for Abruzzi and the Italians, their entry into the war coincided with the arrival of German submarines at Pola. Moreover, the Austrian fleet refused to be tempted into a move to the south. The Italians would not get very far in implementing their plans.

The reinforcements the Italians received from the British also must have been something of a disappointment. The four battleships under Rear Admiral Cecil F. Thursby that joined the Duke of the Abruzzi's fleet at Taranto were all predreadnoughts, had seen service at the Dardanelles, and needed refitting—two had especially severe defects. They were a far cry from the dreadnoughts or *Lord Nelson*-class semidreadnoughts Revel had wanted. Given the nature of the war in the Adriatic, Revel was more concerned about the four British cruisers that were to be based at Brindisi. Three of the four were little better than the battleships: the *Dartmouth* had two boilers out of action and her speed reduced, and the older *Amethyst* and *Sapphire* could not make more than 20 knots—

nowhere near the speed of the new Austrian light cruisers. The *Dublin*, which was in the best condition, was torpedoed on one of the early operations. Balfour, the first lord, admitted: "We cut a very poor figure with our Allies in the Adriatic." The British, with many calls on their resources, did not believe they had anything better to spare.[14]

The French did better. Lapeyrère, the Mediterranean commander in chief, designated the twelve "best units" of his destroyer flotillas, as well as six submarines, to join the Italians at Brindisi. There was a price for this. Lapeyrère warned the British that with his restricted means he could not guarantee the extensive lines of communication in the Mediterranean, and this, with the impending arrival of German submarines, was ominous. The French suffered from an acute shortage of destroyers. Lapeyrère estimated that, counting patrols and the immediate protection of his battle fleet, the French needed a minimum of 56 destroyers and torpedo boats, but had only 47, and 5 of these had been detached for service at the Dardanelles, leaving a deficit of 15. The 12 destroyers Lapeyrère counted on for the immediate protection of his fleet were notoriously unreliable, and he considered he would need at least 20 in order to be sure of always having 10 ready to sail at any moment.[15]

However, these problems were counterbalanced by the fact that with the entry of Italy into the war the naval superiority of the Allies in capital ships was overwhelming. The big battleships and cruisers of the French navy became in fact something of a reserve force, almost searching for a role. The French battle fleet later shifted from overcrowded Malta to Argostoli (Cephalonia) and later to Corfu. This put them in a better position to intercept the Austrian fleet should it attempt to break out of the Adriatic, for it was not absolutely certain the Italian fleet could get around from Taranto in time. It was a hypothetical question; the Austrian fleet had no intention of, or any reason for, trying to break out of the Adriatic. The French destroyer problem worsened. With the development of the submarine war, no one ever had enough destroyers, and later in the war the French battle fleet at Corfu, unlike the Grand Fleet in the North Sea, had virtually no destroyers attached to it. They had to be recalled from other duties in the event it put to sea.

The French destroyers at Brindisi were a welcome addition to the Allied forces and did good work, but the French were compelled to withdraw them for other duties at various emergencies, such as the heavy troop movements to Salonika later that year. This added to the friction between the French flotilla leader and local Italian commanders.[16]

Abruzzi began his operations with a series of raids and bombardments of Austrian coastal installations in the lower and mid-Adriatic on 1, 5, and 9 June. In the northern Adriatic, Italian warships, usually destroyers operating from Venice, bombarded Austrian positions around Monfalcone. The Austrian light craft proved elusive; none were obliging enough to be caught at sea. Abruzzi thought high speed would preserve his ships from torpedo attack, but this proved a false assumption. On 9 June, despite high speed and a strong destroyer escort, the British cruiser *Dublin* was torpedoed by the Austrian submarine *U.4*. The *Dublin* made it back to port but required extensive repairs.

The Austrians soon resumed their raids against the Italian coast in the north and central Adriatic. These pinpricks contributed to a disastrous decision on the part of the Italian naval staff. The division of old *Sardegna*-class battleships at Venice was far too slow to catch the Austrians. The Italians decided they should be supported by powerful but fast warships and sent the Fourth Division of four large *Pisa*-class armored cruisers and a *squadriglia* of *Indomito*-class destroyers to Venice. The cruisers were commanded by Rear Admiral Umberto Cagni, a well-known personality—he had been with Abruzzi on the Arctic expedition—but, perhaps, excessively bold officer. Revel thought the *Pisas* were fast enough to avoid an unequal encounter with the Austrian battleships and that their presence at Venice would curtail the activity of Austrian light craft or force the Austrians to expose large warships to support their flotillas. The move was also to partially answer the demand by the Italian army for support on their seaward flank. Abruzzi was reportedly "furious" about being deprived of the ships, and foreign observers with the Italians were equally critical. Captain Richmond, now liaison officer with the Italian fleet, regarded the *Pisas* as too slow to catch the *Novaras*—the newest and best of the Austrian light cruisers—as unnecessarily large for fighting them, and as a big target that would now be cut off from the rest of the Italian fleet. They really were, as we shall see, a disaster waiting to happen.[17]

Abruzzi, disappointed at the apparent lack of results from the pinprick raids, decided on 8 June that more tangible results would follow from the occupation of the island of Lagosta. The island, which Abruzzi thought could be taken by surprise with two hundred volunteers, could be part of a chain of lookout stations running eastward from Monte Gargano on the Italian mainland. It also could serve as a submarine base as well as an intelligence center to gather information for an advance to Sabbioncello. Revel and the staff initially had no objections to Lagosta, but questioned the advance to Sabbioncello, which, unlike Lagosta, was part of the mainland and could not be held without powerful forces. He suggested Abruzzi consider occupying and installing a signal station on the little island of Pelagosa in the middle of the Adriatic as a preliminary move toward landing on Lagosta. Pelagosa for Abruzzi had little value by itself to justify the risks involved, except as a complement to Lagosta. They could use Pelagosa as the optical connection between Lagosta and the Italian mainland and thereby reduce wireless transmissions except when urgent necessity or atmospheric conditions prevented visual signals. Nevertheless, Abruzzi ordered the Italian admiral at Brindisi to prepare for the occupation and informed Revel on 6 July that the landing would take place within a few days and that he also was preparing for the occupation of Lagosta.

Revel, however, was becoming increasingly concerned about taking Lagosta. The Italian army's advance in the north had not yet achieved the desired breakthrough into Austrian territory, which meant that the Austrians might be able to spare sufficient troops without excessive risk to recapture Lagosta. Revel considered Montenegrin policy ambiguous, the Serbian army at the moment relatively inactive, and relations with Greece strained—leading to the danger that the Greeks would fall into the camp of the Central Powers. The increasing activity of submarines added to the danger to larger ships participating in the occupation of an island like Lagosta, which was close to the

Dalmatian mainland. On 7 July the capo di stato maggiore advised waiting for the situation to clarify before reaching any definite decision. There was no objection to the occupation of Pelagosa.[18]

The same day the disaster many feared occurred in the northern Adriatic. That morning Cagni sent the large armored cruiser *Amalfi*, escorted by only two torpedo boats, to support a sweep by Italian destroyers. The *Amalfi* was torpedoed and sunk by the submarine *UB.14*, the first naval disaster of the war for the Italians. The small submarine had only just been assembled at Pola, and a week after sinking the *Amalfi* it left for Aegean waters. Her commander, Oberleutnant zur See von Heimburg, and all the officers and men, save for a single Austrian officer embarked as a pilot, were German. Germany and Italy were not yet officially at war, however, and would not be for another year, and the submarine had the Austrian designation *U.26*. The practice of giving German U-boats in the Mediterranean an Austrian number as well as their own created a certain amount of confusion, which was no doubt deliberate on the part of the Germans. They also paid little attention to the technicality of not being at war with Italy. Heimburg had already surprised and sunk the Italian submarine *Medusa* on 1 June while command-ing *UB.15* (Austrian *U.11*), which was on trials before being turned over to the Austrian navy and also had, except for an Austrian second in command, an all German crew.[19]

The loss of the *Amalfi* did not stop the first stage of Abruzzi's plans. On 11 July the Italians occupied Pelagosa without opposition. The island had been undefended; the Italian garrison—just ninety men—found only a few lighthouse keepers hiding in a grotto the morning after they landed. The lighthouse was the principal feature of this barren little island, hardly more than a kilometer in length and 330 meters wide. What now? Was Pelagosa a preliminary to Lagosta? The Italians had not been able to make up their minds. The issue had been debated back and forth between the duke of the Abruzzi, the naval staff in Rome, and the ministry for over a month, to the exasperation of the British and French liaison officers with the Italian fleet. Both Thursby and Richmond urged taking Lagosta at the same time as Pelagosa. Richmond wrote in his diary: "Why the deuce don't the Admiral go on & take Lagosta? If he waits, he will find they've defended it, & instead of walking in he'll have to fight his way in. It is madness to delay." Capitaine de vaisseau Daveluy, the French liaison officer, agreed, but doubted the island's value: "The most certain benefit one would draw from its possession would be the preoccupation with keeping it." A reconnaissance party that had landed from French destroyers gave weight to his words; the island had numerous points suitable for a landing and would therefore require many troops to be held securely.[20]

The landing on Lagosta was finally canceled on 27 July, although a force of almost three hundred sailors, *guardia di finanza*, and *carabinieri* had been assembled at Brindisi for the operation. The deciding factor was apparently the loss of the armored cruiser *Garibaldi* on the morning of 18 July. Abruzzi had shelled Ragusa the preceding month, putting the railway between Ragusa and Cattaro out of action. When Abruzzi learned the line had been restored, he sent the Fifth Division (*Garibaldi*-class cruisers) on another mission to cut the line. The cruisers were apparently spotted by an Austrian aircraft shortly after leaving Brindisi the evening before. Revel blamed the commander of the cruiser division for not informing the commander in chief he had been observed, thereby giving the latter the opportunity to cancel the operation because the essential element of surprise had been lost. The Austrian submarine *U.4* torpedoed and sank the *Garibaldi* off the Dalmatian coast. Revel decided the second major loss in a week made the moment for landing on Lagosta "inopportune" and that it had to be deferred until the impression created by the losses had been "somewhat dissipated."[21]

The decision left the fate of Pelagosa, which Abruzzi had regarded as merely a complement to the occupation of Lagosta, in doubt. The Italian garrison had a few pieces of light artillery for defense, and a submarine, either French or Italian, was stationed at the island. The initial Austrian reaction to the occupation was slow. A seaplane flew over the island on the afternoon of 13 July and returned with the destroyer *Tátra*, which shelled the wireless station, only to move off when the seaplane reported the presence of the French submarine *Fresnel*. The *Fresnel* was unable to get into a firing position and was bombed by the seaplane. The Austrians, now that they knew of the Italian occupation, improved their defenses at Lagosta and Lissa, thereby confirming Richmond's warning that if delayed, future landings would be more costly.

The Austrians counterattacked in the central Adriatic on 23 July. Cruisers, destroyers, and torpedo boats raided the Tremiti Islands and the Italian coast from Grottamare to Termoli. They repeated the attacks, joined by aircraft, somewhat farther to the north between Fano and Ancona on the 28th. The same day they made an unsuccessful attempt to recapture Pelagosa. The expedition consisted of two cruisers, six destroyers, and a number of torpedo boats, with the submarine *UB.14* scouting in advance. The Austrian force subjected the island to heavy bombardment, but they had underestimated the Italian garrison as numbering only thirty, and the landing party of four officers and 104 men had to be recalled after meeting stiff resistance. The Italians did not enjoy the victory for long. Linienschiffsleutnant von Trapp in *U.5* torpedoed the defending submarine, the Italian *Nereide*, under the cliffs of the island on the morning of 5 August.

Abruzzi, who had always regarded Pelagosa as merely the complement of the occupation of Lagosta, continued to argue in favor of the new landing. Lagosta would then be an important part of a line of observation posts running from the Gargano headlands on the Italian mainland through Pelagosa in the center of the Adriatic. Abruzzi warned that if they were going to take Lagosta, they ought to do so at once, and if they were not, they should then consider the possibility of being obliged to withdraw from Pelagosa as well. Revel did not agree that the occupations of Pelagosa and Lagosta were strictly linked. He believed that the uncertain military situation, in which the Italian army was held up on the Isonzo River, precluded a new landing. It would also be much more difficult to supply Lagosta than Pelagosa, for whereas the latter was halfway between the Austrian and Italian ports, Lagosta was much closer to the enemy coast and would require a larger garrison. The disagreement between the capo di stato maggiore and the commander in chief of the fleet was fundamental.

While their chiefs debated, the Italian garrison worked hard to fortify Pelagosa, bringing in another four 76-mm cannons, two more machine guns, and another thirty sailors. Abruzzi wanted to keep the garrison to a minimum because fresh water had to be brought to the barren island in tank ships. The Italians also suffered severely from the summer heat. The Austrians decided the issue by convincing Revel that the inhospitable little island was more trouble to hold than it was worth. On 17 August the Austrian First Torpedo Flotilla and Twelfth Torpedo Division deployed around Pelagosa while the light cruiser *Helgoland*, two destroyers, and a torpedo boat closed the island to shell the Italian positions. They were later joined by the light cruiser *Saida*, another two destroyers, and seaplanes. The Austrians subjected Pelagosa to a thorough bombardment, destroying installations, including the freshwater cistern. Later that day Revel ordered an immediate evacuation, destroying all matériel that could not be quickly embarked. He and the naval staff justified the evacuation in the official account by stressing the lack of resources on the island and the steep slopes that made it difficult to enlarge the Italian positions. A strong cruiser and destroyer force from Brindisi covered the withdrawal, which took place without incident the following day.[22] Richmond's reaction to the evacuation was scathing: "They have by this admitted that the Austrians have command of the sea in the Adriatic in spite of inferior naval force & without fighting an action! They have surrendered to them. They had better sell their Fleet & take up their organs & monkeys again, for, by Heaven, that seems more their profession than sea-fighting."[23]

It would be misleading to think that the Austrians were completely unscathed during the period of the Pelagosa occupation. They lost their first submarine, *U.12*, on 12 August when the boat struck a mine off Venice and sank with all hands. On the 13th *U.3* was sunk by the French destroyer *Bisson* northeast of Brindisi, and on 9 September a torpedo from the French submarine *Papin* blew the bows off the Austrian torpedo boat *T.51*, which had been conducting a reconnaissance of Pelagosa. The craft was towed to safety.

The power of the submarine in the Adriatic greatly reduced the likelihood of a classic encounter between the capital ships of the opposing forces. The Italian deployment split the Italian fleet in three portions and thereby to a certain degree invited attack. The dreadnoughts, better predreadnoughts, and British battleships were at Taranto; the four *Regina Elenas*—fast light battleships (with two 12-inch guns each)—were at Brindisi to compensate for the *Pisas*, along with the French and Italian destroyers and submarines; and the old *Sardegna*-class battleships, *Pisa*-class armored cruisers, as well as Italian destroyers, torpedo boats, and submarines were at Venice. Abruzzi had some intelligence the Austrians might seek to profit from this by attacking with their entire fleet— perhaps on 20 July, the anniversary of Lissa—or possibly bombard Brindisi with the objective of drawing the Italian battle fleet out of Taranto and into submarine-infested waters around Cape Santa Maria di Leuca. He planned to meet the danger by essentially defending Brindisi with submarines; the Italian warships in port would not exit but would cooperate with the defense with their artillery from inside the port. Abruzzi's dreadnoughts certainly would sail to meet the Austrians if they came out of the Adriatic heading for Taranto, and they would engage them, but if the Austrians chose to avoid contact, the Italian dreadnoughts *would not follow them into the Adriatic* because of the danger of a submarine ambush. Admiral Haus could therefore have steamed southward and bombarded Brindisi at leisure without having to worry about meeting the superior forces of the Italian battle fleet. He would, however, have exposed his precious assets, the handful of dreadnoughts and modern battleships, to the same danger of submarines that Abruzzi was so anxious to avoid, and he never chose to take the risk. Aside from the opening shots of the war on 24 May, the newer and best Austrian capital ships never approached the Italian coast. The submarine threat was one of the major reasons the Italian navy rejected in August a request from the French army general staff and the king of Montenegro for long-range guns and heavy howitzers to be established on Mount Lovčen so as to make the stay of the Austrian navy in Cattaro impossible. If the Italian fleet then attacked from the seaward side, the Austrian base might surrender. Revel did not agree. Aside from the fact that the Italian army was not likely to be forthcoming with the heavy artillery, munitions, and men necessary to force a surrender, the difficulties of transport and supply would only grow. Revel emphasized that those risks were much graver because of enemy submarines, whose numbers, aggressive spirit, and commanders' ability in maneuvers were manifestly superior to what could rationally have been foreseen before the opening of hostilities.[24]

After the evacuation of Pelagosa and toward the end of the summer, the war in the Adriatic seemed to be winding down. Revel warned his admirals to be careful to conserve matériel; the activities and services of light craft, torpedo boats, and submarines were to be kept within proper limits to avoid excessively frequent repairs and long periods out of service for what the Italians had found to be relatively fragile craft. They were not to be risked in bad weather if it was not absolutely necessary. The war was likely to last for a long time, and the necessity for energetic action might only come after many months. The Italians also tried to obtain ships abroad, approaching the Admiralty about purchasing two to four of the latest light cruisers under construction for the Royal Navy. The requests were of course politely denied.[25] In October 1915 the British did send five (later six) old B-class submarines to Venice. They were replaced after approximately a year by three of the more modern H class, which were eventually transferred to Brindisi in August 1917. The British submarine operations in the northern Adriatic were another example of the Royal Navy working under unusual and difficult conditions. They achieved no striking success, although they probably inhibited the movements of Austrian heavy ships.[26]

The setbacks and losses suffered by the Italian navy in 1915 and the stalemate at sea seemed to exacerbate tensions within the Italian navy. There were some admirals who objected to Revel's cautious strategy. There was also the problem of public opinion. Italian cities and ports along the entire Adriatic coast were in effect on the front line of the naval war, and their protests and those of the politicians who represented them could not be ignored. The situation was much different than that in England after the German raids on the east coast. The enemy in the Adriatic was much closer, his raids far more frequent, and more people were affected. Vice Admiral Viale, the minister of marine, Revel, and Abruzzi all differed in the policies they recommended, and the prime minister and cabinet were not satisfied with the performance of the navy in general. Viale, attacked for his lethargy and lack of performance, resigned on 24 September. The situation was not helped when the battleship *Benedetto Brin* mysteriously blew up and sank with heavy loss of life in Brindisi harbor on the 27th. The new minister, Vice Admiral Camillo Corsi, inherited the latent conflict between the minister, the various directorates at the ministry, and the capo di stato maggiore. Revel finally resigned on 11 October to become commander in chief at Venice. Corsi did not replace him but combined the office of chief of naval staff with his own office.[27]

The word *stalemate* is the most accurate description for the naval war in the Adriatic by the end of the summer of 1915. Captain Daveluy, the French liaison officer with the Italian fleet, described it in these terms:

From these facts one can draw the following conclusion: submarines prohibit large warships from keeping to the sea, each party scratched their heads to "do something" but one has not found any other thing to do except small operations which have no real significance [*portée*] and are, above all, intended to give the illusion one is acting. But, as one cannot fire indefinitely on the same bridge, the same station, the same railways, the same lighthouses and the same semaphores, it seems clear that now the Italians and Austrians are at the end of their resources; after having wanted to do "something," one no longer knows "what to do."

During this time commercial navigation remains forbidden to both parties, in a way that none of them can claim mastery of the sea; the latter belongs to submarines of all nationalities.[28]

The entry of Bulgaria into the war leading to the overrunning of Serbia and the evacuation of the Serbian army soon brought considerable action to the Adriatic, although when the movements were over, the essential stalemate remained unchanged.

EVACUATION OF THE SERBIAN ARMY

On 6 September the Bulgarian government concluded an alliance with the Central Powers and on the 21st began the mobilization of its army. The stage was set for the collapse of Serbia, which until now had successfully resisted successive Austrian offensives. On 6 October Field Marshal August von Mackensen, commanding the German Eleventh Army and the Austrian Third Army, began an offensive. The Serbian capital of Belgrade fell on the 9th. Two Bulgarian armies joined the invasion on the 11th, and the British and French attempted to assist the Serbians by landing at Salonika and marching up the Vardar Valley. But it was a classic case of "too little, too late" and ended with the British and French having to fall back to the vicinity of Salonika, committed to a new campaign.

The need to cover the troop movements to Salonika caused the withdrawal of the French destroyers from Brindisi. The French assured the Italians this was only temporary, but it caused a serious shortage of destroyers for Abruzzi, which was not helped by the fact Italian destroyers were slightly built and, according to Thursby, could not stand much rough work, with too large a proportion of them continually under repair. The Italians could only transfer a few destroyers from Venice to the south because of the need to protect the right wing of the Italian army at the head of the Adriatic. The necessity of dividing destroyers and torpedo boats between Venice and the south nullified the numerical advantage the Italian navy enjoyed over the Austrians.

The Adriatic grew in strategic importance once the Bulgarian invasion cut off Serbia's supply route from Salonika. The attempt to assist the Serbians now had to make use of Adriatic ports. These ports lay in the Italian zone of command, and the Italians had already assumed the responsibility for escorting the supplies to Montenegro after they entered the war. The supplies for Montenegro were in relatively small quantities and went through the small port of San Giovanni di Medua in northern Albania and then overland to the Bojana River. Montenegro's only port, Antivari, was an open harbor, partially blocked by sunken ships and too close to Cattaro to be safe. Supplies to Serbia—which lacked direct access to the sea—were to be on a much larger scale, and the French naval commander in the Mediterranean would have preferred to use the better ports of Valona or Santi Quaranta in southern Albania. Unfortunately, Valona then had no communications with the interior and the roads from Santi Quaranta ran inland toward the east and Monastir rather than to the north where the Serbian army was fighting. The situation in Albania approached anarchy after the attempt of the European powers to set up the prince of Wied as ruler of the new state collapsed following the outbreak of the war. The prince departed and the Italians attempted to reinforce their claims by occupying the island of Saseno in September 1914. In November they prepared an expedition to take Valona and fortify the surrounding area. The first troops began to land at Valona on 3 December. The Italian navy after Italy entered the war gave priority to the transport and supply of their expeditionary corps in Albania rather than assistance to Serbia.

The British and French were disgusted with the Italian attitude toward protecting supplies sent to the Serbians. Abruzzi did not think it was possible for large steamers to go directly to San Giovanni; cargo had to be unloaded at Brindisi and transferred to small sailing craft that could get up the Bojana River or be towed to Scutari. The coasters would be protected on the approximately 100-mile journey from Brindisi to the mouth of the Bojana by a submarine patrol between Cattaro and the Bojana. The French considered the amount of supplies that could be carried this way inadequate and the protection illusory. The Allies finally reached an agreement on 13 November after hard bargaining. The bulk of the supplies, whatever the danger, would go to the Serbians by means of the northern Albanian ports of San Giovanni and Durazzo, or in small ships sent up the Bojana to Scutari. The British would provide the supplies sent to Brindisi; the expenses would be shared by Britain, France, and Russia; and the Italians, supported by the Allies, would provide the protection for the transit of the Adriatic. The Serbian Relief

Committee, an inter-Allied commission, was established to supervise the operation.

Would the Austrians attempt to disrupt the supply route to Serbia by sea? Field Marshal Conrad von Hötzendorf, chief of the Austrian general staff, advised Haus at the end of October that Serbia had been cut off from Salonika and could only be supplied through the northern Albanian or Montenegrin ports and that it was important to cut the route. Haus took three weeks to react, but on the night of 22–23 November, Linienschiffskapitän Heinrich Seitz led the light cruisers *Helgoland* and *Saida* with the First Torpedo Division—the most modern destroyers of the *Tátra* class—on a sortie to the Strait of Otranto and a reconnaissance along the Albanian coast. The Austrians intercepted and sank a small Italian steamer and a motor schooner carrying supplies of flour to Serbia. The Austrians initially were reluctant to send surface vessels into the Strait again, because they considered it to be closely watched. The navy changed its mind, however, and on 26 November warned its ally that German submarines should be careful in the southern Adriatic to attack only ships they clearly recognized as being enemy. Furthermore, AOK, the Austrian high command (Armeeoberkommando), explicitly ordered Haus on 29 November to establish a permanent patrol of the Albanian coast and to disrupt enemy troop transport. Haus responded by sending the light cruisers *Helgoland* and *Novara*, six *Tátra*-class destroyers, approximately six *T-74*-class torpedo boats, and an oiler to Cattaro. This meant that the newest and fastest units of the Austrian fleet had been transferred to the southern Adriatic, where they remained until the end of the war.

The Allies soon felt the effects of the Austrian deployments. Austrian aircraft and Austrian and German submarines increased their operations, and on 4 December an Italian transport and destroyer were lost to mines laid by the German submarine *UC.14* in the vicinity of Valona. On 5 December the *Novara*, four destroyers, and three torpedo boats raided the Albanian coast from the Bojana to San Giovanni, sinking three steamers and a number of sailing craft, and on their return caught the French submarine *Fresnel* aground on a sandbank off the mouth of the Bojana. The submarine was destroyed and its crew taken prisoner. The next day the *Helgoland* led six destroyers to Durazzo, where two destroyers entered the port and sank two large and three small steamers.

The first attempt to supply the Serbians via the northern Albanian ports had met with heavy losses, provoking a crisis in Franco-Italian naval relations. Durazzo and San Giovanni were open harbors, devoid of facilities for unloading, and within easy reach of Cattaro. The submarine menace prevented escorts from hanging about after they had escorted supply ships, and the latter were therefore left without protection with disastrous results. The Italians linked the issue to the French destroyers withdrawn to cover the Salonika operation. Until they were returned, the Italians argued, they would have to use Valona, a protected harbor, for the Serbian supplies. But what about the lack of roads running northward from Valona to Serbia? The pressure of events was at least partially solving the difficulty. By the end of November, the relentless advance of the Austrian, Bulgarian, and German armies had caused the first civil and military Serbian refugees, along with thousands of Austrian prisoners taken in earlier fighting, to straggle into the northern Albanian ports. The retreat of the Serbian army through the mountains of Albania was one of the epics of the world war. The survivors in northern Albania suffered severely from cold, hunger, and disease. The situation was critical, for the Italians halted the supply of the Serbian army through the northern Albanian ports and declared they would only resume it when at least one of the two escadrilles of French destroyers was returned to them. The Italians argued that they were not asking for an increase in assistance but merely for fulfillment of the engagement made to them in the naval convention. Sonnino, the Italian foreign minister, bluntly told the French ambassador in Rome that it was not Italian good will that was lacking but rather the means, and that destroyers and submarines could not be created by royal decree. They could not defend the transports with what they had, and supply via San Giovanni di Medua appeared to be impossible. The Italians suggested that the exhausted Serbians make their way overland southward to Valona. The situation was critical, however. The number of Serbs in Albania grew constantly while the supply of flour at San Giovanni and Durazzo was altogether insufficient. The specter of mass starvation was very real.

The Italian pressure worked. The French had always intended to restore the destroyers to Brindisi as soon as possible and had planned to free some by reorganizing the supply services to Salonika. On 10 December Admiral Lacaze, the minister of marine, directly ordered the French commander in chief to send enough destroyers to Brindisi to bring the number up to the requisite six, so that the Italians would resume supplies. Abruzzi promised to recommence sending supplies to Valona, where unloading was easier, but would only promise to "try" to resume landing food and matériel at Durazzo and San Giovanni, where the unprotected harbors lacked facilities for unloading and were now partially blocked by sunken ships.[29]

The situation had deteriorated beyond the point where any infusion of supplies could be of use. The chaotic conditions in northern Albania, the slow advance of the Austrian army, the disorganized condition of the Serbian army harassed by Albanian tribesmen as it retreated, and the flood of civilian refugees all pointed toward evacuation as the only feasible solution. But *could* they evacuate? The Austrian army was for the moment less of a threat as logistical difficulties had slowed its advance. Evacuation from San Giovanni was very difficult, however, because the troops had to be ferried out to ships offshore and progress was painfully slow. Austrian air raids added to the misery. The Allies therefore tried to get as many of the Serbians as possible farther south to Durazzo or Valona. On 5 December the Italian high command ordered a brigade of Italian troops northward from Valona to secure Durazzo. The winter rains turned what passed for roads into quagmires, and the Italian troops did not reach Durazzo until the 19th.

What of the Austrian navy? Would or could it make any attempt to interfere with the evacuations? On 28 December Haus cabled the rear admiral commanding the Austrian naval forces at Cattaro that aerial reconnaissance and other intelligence revealed that two Italian destroyers had brought approximately 300 troops to Durazzo. He ordered the Austrian cruiser flotilla to attack them. As a result, Linienschiffskapitän Seitz was given oral instructions to sail with the *Helgoland* and five *Tátra*-class destroyers to search the waters between Brindisi and Durazzo for the two destroyers. If Seitz did not encounter them, he was to proceed to Durazzo by dawn and sink any destroyers or cargo ships found there. This Austrian attempt to pick off isolated forces led to the action on 29 December, the most significant so far of the war in the Adriatic.

The Austrians failed to encounter any Italian destroyers either at sea or in Durazzo, but they surprised the French submarine *Monge* on their way south, and the submarine was sunk by the destroyer *Balaton*. At daybreak four of the Austrian destroyers entered the harbor of Durazzo and sank a Greek steamer (with Italian crew) and a large and small schooner. Shore batteries opened fire on the Austrian destroyers as they were leaving, and they turned sharply to port, supposedly to avoid masking *Helgoland*'s line of fire. The maneuver brought two of them into a minefield; the *Lika* was sunk and the *Triglav* badly damaged. The situation now became serious for the Austrians. They lost approximately one and three-quarters of an hour picking up survivors of the *Lika* and trying to get the *Triglav* under tow. The first attempt by the destroyer *Csepel* failed when the tow fouled her screw, greatly reducing her speed. The *Tátra* did manage to get the *Triglav* under tow, but the Austrians could not make more than 6 knots.

Would the Allied forces at Brindisi be able to intercept? The Italian commander in chief at Brindisi, Vice Admiral Cutinelli-Rendina, received the alarm shortly after 7:00 A.M. and ordered the British and Italian light cruisers *Dartmouth* and *Quarto* to sail immediately. Five French destroyers were to follow as soon as they had steam up. Rear Admiral Bellini, the commander of the Italian Scouting Division, flying his flag in the *Quarto*, was senior Allied officer afloat during the action. The *Weymouth*, the other British light cruiser at Brindisi, was ordered to raise steam but not sail until Cutinelli had further intelligence of Austrian movements. Her captain, Denis Crampton, chafing at his inaction, pleaded with Cutinelli: "For God's sake let me go out." The *Weymouth* was finally ordered to sail at 9:00 A.M. and left with the Italian light cruiser *Nino Bixio* and four Italian destroyers.

Seitz was now in a dangerous position, for by midmorning there were four British and Italian cruisers (armed with 6-inch and 4.9-inch guns) and nine French and Italian destroyers trying to cut off the *Helgoland* (armed with 3.9-inch guns) and three destroyers (one with damaged screw) towing the crippled *Triglav*. Seitz sent a wireless message for help, and the Austrian commander at Cattaro sent out the armored cruiser *Kaiser Karl VI* and four torpedo boats in support. The armored cruiser, with two 9.2-inch guns, but relatively slow at 20 knots, was actually more powerful than any of the Allied ships, but although she came close enough to see smoke from the Allied ships in the distance, she did not take part in the action. The old battleship *Budapest*, the small cruiser *Aspern*, and the light cruiser *Novara*, raised steam and sailed later in the day but were never near the action. Neither were the three *Regina Elena*-class fast light battleships (two 12-inch guns, 20 knots) at Brindisi. Cutinelli did not order them to sea, again demonstrating the Italian reluctance to risk capital ships in the Adriatic.

With the Allied forces between his force and safety at Cattaro, Seitz had no choice but to abandon the *Triglav*. He hoped that the Austrian submarine *U.15*, on patrol in the vicinity, would attack any Allied ship that came upon the destroyer, which the Austrians attempted to scuttle. *U.15* was not, however, in position to make an attack when the five French destroyers arrived and finished off the wreck. The French commander in chief later criticized them for wasting too much time on the wreck, for they could not catch up with the cruisers and saw no further action that day.

The afternoon of 29 December saw a high-speed chase with most of the gunnery exchanges taking place at extreme range and with the *Helgoland* frequently outranged. The Austrians had the advantage of speed, even though the Allies were between them and safety. Seitz steamed westward and southwestward almost up to the Italian coast, all the while trying to work around his pursuers. Darkness permitted him to make his escape. Thursby thought that half an hour's more daylight "would have done it" and blamed Bellini for poor handling of the Allied forces. There was general dissatisfaction that the Austrians, with a much smaller force, had gotten away. There was also dissatisfaction on the Austrian side. Seitz may have been praised for his cool handling of the Austrian force in a difficult position, and the Austrian ships may have received hearty cheers from the other Austrian warships at Cattaro on their return, but Seitz was raked over the coals by Haus. Instead of the anticipated praise, he was greeted with the words, "Herr Captain, you thus ran away, you ran away very ably." Haus considered the failure of the *Lika* and *Triglav* to follow in the wake of their leader in waters suspected of containing mines an inexcusable error leading to the loss of the two destroyers and bringing the entire flotilla into the greatest danger. Haus also termed the fouling of the *Csepel*'s screw in attempting to tow the *Triglav* "ineptitude" and "carelessness." He faulted Seitz for apparent tardiness in sending wireless reports to Cattaro, which resulted in delay in the sailing of the relief force, and for omitting to adequately inform Cattaro of the location of the destroyers; and he criticized Seitz for his failure to plan or execute a torpedo attack with the three surviving destroyers on the two nearest pursuing cruisers after nightfall. Haus relieved Seitz of his command, a move that some Austrian naval officers believed was unjust. Haus's reaction on close examination is understandable. The Austrians had accounted for a French submarine, a steamer, and two schooners, but had lost two of their best destroyers and only just saved a flotilla with one of their most modern cruisers and three of their best destroyers. For a commander whose policy was based on the fleet-in-being, it was an unacceptable exchange.[30]

The offensive by the Central Powers in the Balkans paid the Austrian navy a major dividend. On 8–10 January 1916, the XIX Austrian Army Corps, effectively supported by naval gunfire from the old battleships and cruisers of the Fifth Division, cleared the Montenegrins from Mount Lovčen. This removed observation posts that could report all Austrian ship movements during daylight hours. The Montenegrins requested an armistice on 12 January and dropped out of the war.

The evacuation of the Serbian army and civilian refugees through San Giovanni came to an end by 22 January, and the center of activity shifted southward to Durazzo. The evacuations here ended by 9 February, but the Italians delayed evacuating the port. This was a mistake if they did not intend to hold on to the place. When the Italian army finally left, during the nights of 25–27 February, they were forced to do so under fire and suffered more than 800 casualties. The remaining evacuations took place through Valona. The French sent two large armored cruisers to help cover them, and the British drifters that had arrived at the Strait of Otranto in the autumn of 1915 also did notable work covering the movement between Valona and Corfu. The majority of the steamers and covering forces were Italian. The Italians lost six, and the French two, steamers during the evacuation. Thursby, the commander of the British Adriatic Squadron, praised the duke of the Abruzzi when he wrote the First Sea Lord on 20 February:

We have moved altogether in the last two months over 200,000 people including Servians [sic], Austrian prisoners & Italian troops with hardly a casualty. I do not think that with the scratch pack we have had to deal with, ships & material being supplied by 3 different nations, anyone but the Duke could have done it. In addition to being able & energetic, his position enables him to do more than any ordinary Admiral could do. From a naval point of view it has been a much more difficult operation than the evacuation of Gallipoli.[31]

The national rivalries among Italians, French, and, later, Yugoslavs colored accounts of the event, and to a certain extent they still do. By April 1916 more than 260,000 Serbian military and civilian refugees and Austrian prisoners of war had been evacuated. The remnants of the Serbian army—roughly 160,000 men—were brought to Corfu, rested, reorganized and reequipped, and eventually brought to Salonika to serve on the Macedonian front. The rescue of the Serbian army from certain destruction, whether by starvation or capture, and their resurrection to fight another day was one of the more notable achievements of sea power in the First World War.[32]

The Austrian navy missed a big opportunity to inflict major damage by failing to seriously interfere with the evacuation. On 27 January, responding to the reports from aerial reconnaissance that there were eight steamers and five destroyers at Durazzo, the light cruiser *Novara* and two *Tátra*-class destroyers sailed to raid the port. The two destroyers were damaged in collision with each other and had to turn back. The *Novara* continued alone, only to meet the Italian cruiser *Puglia* and French destroyer *Bouclier*. There was now no possibility of surprise, and the *Novara* broke off the action and returned home. On 6 February the *Helgoland* and six torpedo boats set out to raid the transport route between Durazzo and Brindisi but encountered the *Weymouth* and *Bouclier*, and in the action that followed, two of the Austrian torpedo boats collided with each other, damaging one badly enough to force it to return to base. Once again the possibility of surprise was lost and the Austrians broke off the action. On the same day, the British light cruiser *Liverpool* and the Italian destroyer *Bronzetti* chased the Austrian destroyer *Wildfang*, which had been on reconnaissance, back to Cattaro. Heavy weather frustrated Austrian operations on the 23d and 24th of February, and on the 26th the *Helgoland* and six destroyers failed to find any enemy craft off Durazzo.

In summary, during the months of January and February 1916, bad weather or action by Allied screening forces, which destroyed the essential element of surprise and put the Austrians in danger of being cut off by superior forces, thwarted action by the light forces of the k.u.k. Kriegsmarine against the evacuation. What of the Austrian heavier units? Did Haus miss the opportunity to inflict serious losses on the Allies? Haus was apparently convinced there were too many large Allied ships in the southern Adriatic capable of intervening and overwhelming his forces. The trend in Austrian historiography has been to become more critical of Haus and his policy of maintaining the fleet-in-being. It would have been wrong to take foolish risks, but there were times when certain risks were justified and, if taken, might have resulted in great achievements. On the other hand, there was a sizable number of Allied submarines in the Adriatic and there were very real dangers. The Allied submarines had not achieved much, partially through lack of suitable targets, although a French submarine had sunk an Austrian transport off Cape Planka on 28 December. The results that might have followed the use of Austrian capital ships against the Serbian evacuation is another of those arguments that can never be settled. AOK and the Austrian army also could be faulted for not trying to push farther south in Albania and capture Valona. With Valona in Austrian hands, the Allies might have had a much more difficult time trying to maintain the blockade of the Strait of Otranto.[33]

After the evacuation of the Serbian army, the war in the Adriatic became even more one in which naval guerrilla war flourished. The Italians developed ingenious new weapons, and the Allies in the Adriatic and the Mediterranean as a whole became more and more concerned with the submarine war. The Germans increased their submarine flotillas at Pola and Cattaro, and they achieved spectacular success in the Mediterranean. The unfortunate friction between the French and Italians remained, and so too did the threat from the Austrian fleet-in-being.

THE DRIFTER PATROL AND THE OTRANTO BARRAGE

The first of the British drifters arrived in September of 1915. The British had offered drifters and trawlers with antisubmarine nets for the Strait of Otranto at the moment Italy entered the war, but initially the Italians were not interested. They changed their minds, and with German submarines regularly passing through the Strait during the summer, the Admiralty was glad to send them. By the end of September, sixty had arrived, at first without organization or stores. Thursby sent two divisions out to lay nets in the Strait as soon as possible. An Italian merchant ship acted as depot at Brindisi. Thursby hoped to establish a pattern of two divisions out and one in port, with thirty-five to forty drifters out at a time. Thursby managed to arm most of his drifters, but he quickly discovered he did not have enough drifters: "It is a big place to watch and we want more depth to our screen." The impending winter weather in the Adriatic meant rough seas in which nets would be lost and boats frequently would have to take shelter from the characteristic short, steep seas. Thursby revised his estimate upward; they would need forty boats out at a time, and with the necessary docking and repairs they would need eighty boats on station. Thursby, after a tour of inspection in a destroyer, realized what a small chance of catching a submarine there was with so few drifters. The Admiralty decided in mid-November to send another forty, which began to arrive the following month.[34]

There is something almost quaint about the idea the little drifters would be able to "catch" a submarine in their nets, that is, cause the boat to foul its screw or betray its presence or force it to the surface so that one of the destroyers on the Otranto patrol might move in to finish it off. Thursby and other British commanders were optimistic that they had accounted for submarines, but owing to the inherent nature of submarine warfare, they could not confirm the "kill." The drifter patrol actually had little success in stopping submarines. In 1916 most submarines ran through the blockade on the surface at night. The experience of submarine commanders varied; some might be forced to submerge by the presence of drifters or a destroyer but they would still get through. It is also somewhat misleading to talk of a "barrage," or even of a "line" of drifters. This would suggest a continuous line of small ships with nets constituting a serious barrier to submarines. The real Otranto barrage was far different. A French officer, one day in July 1916, found on a tour of inspection in a destroyer that only 37 of what should have been a daily average of 50 drifters were out, and that only 10 actually had their nets in the seas and the Adriatic currents had caused the groups to drift far apart. Thursby's successor, Rear Admiral Mark Kerr, reported that the Adriatic currents were not only strong, they were unpredictable. Even if the drifter line had been accurately placed the evening before, on most days they would drift 10 miles apart during the night. Kerr thought they really needed drifters deployed in two or three lines with intervals between them of 10 to 15 miles. They also needed far more drifters—say, 300—to make a truly effective barrage. The drifters actually caught only one submarine, the Austrian *U.6*, on 13 May 1916. Two other submarines, the German *UB.44* in August 1916 and the Austrian *U.30* in April 1917, disappeared without a trace, and one or both might have been lost in the barrage, perhaps to a mine.[35]

By April 1916 the British drifters had extended their patrol area to a distance of 80 miles from Brindisi and 40 miles wide at its narrowest point. The strain of constant work with the number of drifters available began to tell, and in April 1916 Thursby applied for an additional 40 drifters. The Admiralty, after much discussion, could not pry more than 10 out of Jellicoe, for by now the little craft were badly needed for the antisubmarine campaign in home waters. The Admiralty managed to send approximately 20 more in the closing months of 1916.

With the detachment of drifters and destroyers for other duties, such as convoying the reorganized Serbian army from Corfu to Salonika in May 1916, even an early enthusiast such as Thursby had to admit that the Otranto patrol was practically nonexistent. The elusive goal remained, however, with the idea that if one could just get enough drifters and make the patrol cover enough depth, submarines might be compelled to travel submerged long enough to exhaust their batteries. The Otranto barrage was later strengthened through the introduction of a fixed net fitted with mines, and by 1918 the Otranto barrage was more elaborate, with plans to make it even stronger after the Americans entered the war and arrived in the Mediterranean. The system claimed another German submarine in the summer of 1918, largely because its commander did not realize the obstructions had been extended and take the requisite measures to avoid them. But the results of the different Otranto barrages were never in the least commensurate with the efforts expended on them.[36]

The drifters, by their nature weakly armed, and manned by fishermen rather than regular naval personnel, were also a tempting target, particularly when they became troublesome. On the night of 31 May, little more than a fortnight after *U.6* had been caught in the nets, the Austrian destroyers *Balaton* and *Orenjen*, along with three torpedo boats and the cruiser *Helgoland*, raided the drifter line and sank one. Admiral Kerr was alive to the danger and feared a major raid. He wanted four British destroyers to avoid having to rely exclusively on the French or Italians for protection. The destroyers at Brindisi were always liable for diversion to other duties. Unfortunately for Kerr and the drifters, there were no British destroyers available.

The protection given to the drifters was steadily reduced as a result of losses. The Italian auxiliary cruiser *Città di Messina* was torpedoed and sunk by the Austrian *U.15* 20 miles east of Otranto on 23 June. The French destroyer *Fourche*, which had been accompanying *Città di Messina*, depth-charged the submarine, observed an oil slick, and incorrectly assumed it had been sunk. The *Fourche* was then cut in two by a torpedo while rescuing survivors. The Italians ceased to protect the drifter line with a cruiser during daylight hours, employing instead only a section of destroyers. This was not sufficient. On 9 July Linienschiffskapitän Nikolaus Horthy, one of the k.u.k. Kriegsmarine's most enterprising officers and its future commander, raided the drifter line with the light cruiser *Novara*, sinking two, damaging two, and taking nine British sailors prisoner. The next day the Italian destroyer *Impetuoso* was sunk by the Austrian submarine *U.17*, and the Italians decided they could no longer protect the drifters and the line was moved farther south. The drifter patrol was eventually established on a line from Otranto to just south of Cape Linguetta. The drifter base was moved from Brindisi to Taranto. The drifters were also supplemented by a dozen motor launches, based on Gallipoli, with a subbase at Tricase. The motor launches were also of questionable utility, good only in fine weather.

The drifters had a close call the night of 22 December, graphically illustrating the difficulties of command and control of a multinational force, particularly at night. Six Austrian destroyers of the older *Huszár*-class (600 tons) attacked the drifter patrol line, which fought back as best as it could, giving the alarm signal. Fortunately six French destroyers, en route from Brindisi to Taranto to escort transports, were in the vicinity and raced to the rescue. Only one drifter was slightly damaged. Their rescuers fared less well. The destroyer following the *Casque*, the lead French ship with the senior naval officer, failed to see the signal to turn and only one destroyer followed the *Casque* into action, only to be momentarily disabled by a hit in the boiler room. The *Casque* continued the chase alone until a hit reduced her speed to 23 knots. Then disaster struck. Three Italian destroyers, followed by the British light cruiser *Gloucester* escorted by a pair of Italian destroyers, had also sailed from Brindisi with the object of cutting off the Austrians from

Cattaro. In the darkness the French and Italian destroyers literally ran into one another. The lead Italian destroyer *Abba* rammed the *Casque*, and a little later the French destroyer *Boutefeu* rammed the *Abba*. The Austrians got away, although with little to show for the risk they had run, and the damaged French and Italian destroyers were towed back to Brindisi the following morning.[37]

The most damaging attack on the drifters took place on 15 May 1917 and led to the largest action of the war in the Adriatic. The plan for the attack appears to have originated with Captain Horthy of the cruiser *Novara*, who had already established a reputation for dash and enterprise. Horthy had the *Novara*'s mainmast removed and replaced with a short steel mast so that from a distance or at night the cruiser would resemble a large British destroyer. The plan was for the *Novara, Helgoland,* and *Saida,* the three best Austrian light cruisers that bore the brunt of the war in the Adriatic, to "mop up" the drifters, counting on their altered appearance to cause them to be taken as destroyers and thereby gain time before the alarm was given. The three cruisers led by Horthy would sail at nightfall, separate during the night, and attack different portions of the drifter line at dawn. They would then rendezvous 15 nautical miles west of Cape Linguetta no later than 7:15 A.M. for the dash home. There would be a diversionary action led by Fregattenkapitän Prince von und zu Liechtenstein in the destroyer *Csepel* accompanied by the destroyer *Balaton*—a third destroyer had to be dropped because of boiler trouble. The *Csepel* and *Balaton* would cruise off the Albanian coast looking for transports and would confuse Italian reports on the movements of the Austrian force. The Austrians also would deploy three submarines: the *U.4* off Valona and the *U.27* off Brindisi. The most effective submarine, as it turned out, was the German *UC.25,* which was ordered to lay mines off Brindisi at dawn. Austrian aircraft from Durazzo and the base at Kumbor in the Gulf of Cattaro would support the action, and the armored cruiser *Sankt Georg,* two destroyers, and several torpedo boats were to be ready to sortie if necessary. The coast-defense battleship *Budapest* and three torpedo boats were prepared to follow them.

The Italians had a patrol at sea the night of the raid, well to the north of the drifter line. It consisted of the Italian flotilla leader *Mirabello* and French destroyers *Commandant Rivière, Bisson,* and *Cimeterre.* A fourth destroyer, the *Boutefeu,* had been forced back to Brindisi by condenser trouble. The *Mirabello* group was supposed to be in a position to intercept any potential raiders on their return from the drifter line. There was also an Italian submarine south of Cattaro and a French submarine south of Durazzo. That night the small Italian destroyer *Borea* was also escorting a convoy of three ships proceeding to Valona. The *Csepel* and *Balaton* attacked the convoy at approximately 3:24 A.M. The *Borea* and a munitions ship[38] were sunk; another ship was left blazing although later salved.

The three Austrian cruisers when they passed through the line of drifters between Cape Santa Maria di Leuca and Fano were at first assumed in some places to be friendly and no alarm was given. The attack on the drifters began at approximately 3:30 A.M. and continued until after sunrise. The cruisers were armed with 3.9-inch guns and were able to overwhelm the little drifters, armed with 6-pounders or 57-mm guns. The Austrians at times behaved with considerable chivalry, blowing their sirens and giving the drifter crews time to abandon ship before they opened fire. Some of the drifter men chose to put up a fight, and Skipper J. Watt of the *Gowan Lee*, which survived in battered condition, was later awarded the Victoria Cross. There had been 47 drifters on the line that night, 14 were sunk and 4 damaged, 3 badly. Seventy-two of the drifter crews were picked up by the Austrians as prisoners.

The Austrian raiding force was now in a precarious position, for the drifter line was actually 40 miles farther from Cattaro than Brindisi and its sizable Allied forces. The Allies were between the Austrians and safety. Rear Admiral Alfredo Acton, commander of the Italian Scouting Division, was in charge of the pursuit. At approximately 4:35 A.M. he ordered the *Mirabello* group of destroyers, located north of Durazzo, to turn southward. Acton and his staff embarked in the British light cruiser *Dartmouth* and ordered the light forces at Brindisi to sea as soon as they were ready. By approximately 6:45 the British light cruisers *Dartmouth* and *Bristol* and the Italian destroyers *Mosto, Pilo, Schiaffino, Acerbi,* and flotilla leader *Aquila* were racing toward the northeast to cut off the Austrians. Behind them in Brindisi the scout cruiser *Marsala*, flotilla leader *Racchia*, and destroyers *Insidioso, Indomito,* and *Impavido* were either ready to sail or getting up steam. The *Marsala* group was ready at least an hour before Acton sent them a wireless message from the *Dartmouth* to sail at 8:25. Revel later criticized him for this delay.

The *Mirabello* group made contact with the Austrian cruisers at approximately 7:00 A.M. They were, however, outgunned, and instead of closing made a wide detour to avoid *U.4* and turned north to maintain contact with the three cruisers. The three French destroyers could not sustain the *Mirabello*'s speed and gradually fell behind. At approximately 7:45 the *Dartmouth* group made contact with the destroyers *Csepel* and *Balaton*. Acton apparently did not realize at first that they were destroyers and not cruisers, and it was twenty minutes before the faster *Aquila* and four destroyers closed the Austrians. The two groups of destroyers exchanged fire at high speed until a shot from the *Csepel* cut a steam pipe and hit one of the *Aquila*'s boilers at approximately 8:30, disabling the ship. The *Csepel* and *Balaton* were able to escape behind the shelter of the Austrian coastal batteries at Durazzo.

Acton was now between Horthy and Cattaro. The Austrian cruisers were still being followed by the *Mirabello* group as they raced toward the Allied ships. The *Bristol* reported smoke astern at approximately 9:00, and the British and Italians turned to meet the Austrian cruisers. The main part of the day's action now began with the two British cruisers *Dartmouth* (eight 6-inch guns) and *Bristol* (two 6-inch and ten 4-inch guns) engaging the *Novara, Helgoland,* and *Saida* (nine 3.9-inch guns each). Although the Austrians were outgunned, Acton's superiority in numbers was soon dissipated. He detached the destroyers *Schiaffino* and *Pilo* to protect the disabled *Aquila*. Astern of Horthy, *Mirabello* was stopped for a time because of water in her fuel. She was back to her normal speed by 11:00, but at 11:45 the *Commandant Rivière* broke down with condenser trouble and the *Cimeterre* and *Bisson* remained behind to protect her from submarine attack. The *Dartmouth* gradually drew far ahead of the *Bristol*, which had been due for docking and whose bottom was foul. The *Bristol's* 4-inch guns were soon outranged, which left the burden of the action on the *Dartmouth*, accompanied by the destroyers *Acerbi* and *Mosto*. The visibility that day was very good, and the aircraft of both sides were very active. They undertook reconnaissances, signaled by wireless or lamp, and bombed and strafed. One of the Italian seaplanes was shot down, but none of the ships on either side were disabled or seriously damaged by the bombs. Nevertheless Captain Addison of the *Dartmouth* found the attacks "most annoying."

The Allies and the Austrians now had other forces at sea. The *Marsala* group, a scout cruiser, flotilla leader, and three destroyers were racing to the scene. Farther to the south, three French destroyers from Corfu were also on their way. Admiral Gauchet, the French commander in chief, had intercepted wireless reports of the action and without receiving any request for assistance sent the destroyers. The Italian admiral at Valona was less enterprising, but received neither direct information nor orders. The forces there, which included a fast flotilla leader, did not intervene. On the Austrian side, the armored cruiser *Sankt Georg* accompanied by two destroyers and four torpedo boats sortied from Cattaro and headed to Horthy's rescue.

The Austrians were suffering from potentially fatal mechanical difficulties. Their safety depended on speed, but the *Saida* could not make more than 25 knots and held back the other two cruisers, which were capable of 2–3 knots additional speed. After a 6-inch shell from the *Dartmouth* struck the *Novara's* forebridge, killing the first officer, Horthy used a smoke screen to try to close the range to where his 3.9-inch guns would be more effective. The *Dartmouth* was straddled and hit a few times, once with a shell that would have put the port propeller out of action had it not failed to explode. Horthy was wounded at 10:10 A.M. by a shell splinter and lost consciousness for a time after trying to direct the action while lying on the deck. The *Novara's* gunnery officer had to take command. The *Dartmouth* was now taking the brunt of the action, and at 11:00 Acton ordered her to open the range and eased to 20 knots to allow the *Bristol* to catch up. The order may have saved the *Novara*, for the cruiser's main feed pumps and an auxiliary steam pipe to the starboard turbine had been damaged and she was losing speed.

The climax of the action was now at hand. Acton apparently turned away at 11:05 in an unsuccessful effort to cut off the straggling *Saida*. He then spotted smoke on the horizon belonging to the Austrian reinforcements from Cattaro and decided that it would be prudent to turn southward to join the *Marsala* group from Brindisi. The two groups met at 11:30 and turned back toward the *Novara*. The interval had been enough to save the *Novara*, which had been forced to stop while the *Saida* attempted to take the crippled cruiser under tow and the *Helgoland* covered them from the approaching Allies. This was a critical moment for the Austrians, and the commander of the *Saida* was criticized for taking what seemed like an excessive amount of time to complete the maneuver. However, Acton apparently did not realize, at least initially, that the *Novara* had stopped. He saw smoke on the horizon, indicating potentially heavy reinforcements from Cattaro, and the *Sankt Georg*, with her pair of 240-mm guns (9.2-inch), outgunned anything in his force. Behind them, the old coast-defense battleship *Budapest* and three torpedo boats were also at sea. Acton knew the Austrian cruisers apparently had the edge over him in speed, and he did not want to run the risk of being drawn closer to Cattaro and having any of his ships that might be damaged cut off by what he presumed to be superior Austrian forces. Acton turned away. The commander of the *Acerbi* misread the recall signal, obscured by smoke, for the signal to attack and maneuvered to deliver a torpedo attack. He was unsupported and was driven off by the concentrated fire of the Austrians. The *Racchia, Impavido,* and later *Marsala* also approached the Austrians, only to be recalled by Acton. By the time Acton realized the *Novara* was disabled, the *Sankt Georg* was closer, and at 12:05 P.M. he ordered a general retirement. The Austrians could never understand why Acton broke off the action; in their opinion the *Sankt Georg* was still far off and there would have been time to sink the *Novara*. Captain Addison of the *Dartmouth* at the time thought Acton's recall was justified; after the war he admitted he had not realized the Austrian cruisers had stopped, and if he had, he probably would have disobeyed orders.

The Austrians' luck held that day. The French submarine *Bernouilli* fired at the *Balaton* but missed, and the *Balaton* and *Csepel* were able to join the *Sankt Georg* group with the crippled *Novara* in tow. They were in turn met by the *Budapest* and her escorts and were able to return to Cattaro where they were greeted with enthusiastic cheers from the warships stationed there.

The Allies' troubles were not over. They returned to Brindisi with the *Aquila* and *Commandant Rivière* under tow in different groups, screened by the destroyers, which now included the French ships that had joined from Corfu. The escorts were needed, because the route brought the *Dartmouth* group within range of *UC.25*, which had already laid her mines off Brindisi. At 1:30 P.M., *UC.25* torpedoed the *Dartmouth* approximately 36 miles from port. Aggressive depth-charging by French and Italian destroyers kept the submarine from making another attack, but the *Dartmouth* had to be abandoned for a period, and it was only with great difficulty and the assistance of tugs sent out from Brindisi that the cruiser was able to return to port. Furthermore, the French destroyer *Boutefeu* immediately put to sea to assist after learning the *Dartmouth* was torpedoed and struck one of *UC.25*'s mines a few minutes after clearing the boom. The destroyer quickly sank.

The Austrians regarded the action of 15 May 1917 as the high point of the war for the k.u.k. Kriegsmarine. They considered the events of the day as a victory in which they had successfully engaged the superior—and potentially far superior, considering that the *Pisa*-class armored cruisers and another British cruiser had been held in port—forces of three enemy nations and had returned safely after inflicting greater losses than they received. The difficulties of commanding a multinational force once again had been demonstrated, for the Italian signaling had been particularly bad that day, and the Italians had not provided the Allies with the call signs of their ships, thereby reducing the value of intercepted signals. Furthermore, the British realized that until they could provide British destroyers to protect the drifters, the line was likely to be raided again.

The destroyers were not available, and the Admiralty therefore ordered the drifters to be withdrawn from the line at night. The drifters now went into various little ports, laying their nets between 5:00 and 10:00 A.M. and taking them up again at 3:00 P.M. The Italians could not provide any protection for the drifters for several weeks and then only on an irregular basis. The question became yet another matter of sharp disagreement between the British and Italians.

If one took a broader strategical look, the action of 15 May did not change very much. There had never been any serious thought of the big dreadnoughts of either side going into action. The Allied supply lines in the Mediterranean were threatened, as before, by submarines, not the surface ships of the Austrian navy. There had only been 47 drifters out that night, and it was estimated that a drifter could effectively cover only a half-mile. That meant only 23 to 24 miles of the 40-mile-wide Strait was covered. Horthy had risked the cream of the Austrian navy to make a not very effective blockade even less effective. Was it worth it? And would the Austrian luck hold in the future?[39]

ATTEMPTS TO BREAK THE ADRIATIC STALEMATE

The Italians, as they always pointed out, bore the brunt of the war in the Adriatic. They had to maintain a sufficient force of destroyers and torpedo boats at Venice to hinder Austrian activity on the flank of their army. But they could not exclude the possibility the Austrian fleet would come out for a major battle and had to provide an adequate number of destroyers to work with their fleet in the lower Adriatic. After the beginning of 1916, they also had to protect the lines of communication of the Italian expeditionary corps in Albania. These considerations took priority in their plans and account for what the British and French often considered a selfish and egoistic approach toward providing destroyers and torpedo boats for the defense of the drifter line at Otranto. The Italians invariably wanted assistance, particularly fast light cruisers from the Royal Navy capable of catching the *Novara*-class cruisers. The British had none of their latest classes to spare from the Grand Fleet, and the French navy did not have any of the type at all.

The Italians also were not confident of their real superiority in capital ships, especially after losses reduced their strength. The battleship *Benedetto Brin* blew up at Brindisi in September 1915, and on 2 August 1916 one of their best ships, the dreadnought *Leonardo da Vinci*, caught fire, blew up, and capsized in Taranto harbor with heavy loss of life. Sabotage was suspected, and apparently confirmed, by Italian espionage activities, notably the ransacking of a safe at the Austrian consulate in Zurich in 1917.[40] At the close of the year, the Italians lost another battleship, the *Regina Margherita*, to a mine at Valona on 11 December. The Austrian capital ships, secure in their bases, had not yet suffered any equivalent losses. They were not likely, however, to seek a classic battle. Regardless of the ratio of strength between the Austrian and Italian fleets or the outcome of an Austro-Italian encounter, there was always the French fleet at Corfu. The French were capable of handling the Austrian fleet on their own. The Italians, with the addition of some French capital ships—the six semidreadnought *Danton*-class were often mentioned—would have been equally confident of facing the situation on their own. However, assistance to the Italians raised the touchy subject of command. The French commander in chief, Vice Admiral Gauchet, from December 1916 until the end of the war was also titular Mediterranean commander in chief. The French would not consent to his being placed under the orders of an Italian admiral, particularly as they had the larger number of battleships. On the other hand, it was unthinkable for the Italians to accept anyone but an Italian admiral commanding operations in the Adriatic. The French were also loath to break the homogeneity of their squadrons and detach just a few ships to fight under the Italians. What would happen to the remainder of the French battle fleet? Without going into the details, the issue was the subject of sterile discussion between the French and Italians throughout 1916, and was never resolved during the entire war. It led to a substantial waste of resources. There were essentially *two* battle fleets watching the Austrians—the Italians at Taranto and the French at Corfu—when one would have been sufficient. The British managed to end at least some of the waste in January of 1917 when they gained Italian agreement to the withdrawal of the old British battleships at Taranto. Only one remained, reduced to the status of a depot ship. The battleships' crews were desperately needed for new construction or for the antisubmarine campaign, and there was little real chance the battleships at Taranto would ever be used.[41]

Offensive operations by the Italians, notably a landing on the Austrian islands or Dalmatian coast, continued to be ruled out in 1916. Corsi asked Abruzzi to reexamine the Lagosta project early in the year, but Abruzzi was no longer very enthusiastic about a landing only on Lagosta; its capture might be the consequence of a larger and more significant action. Abruzzi prepared a plan to seize the most important places on the Sabbioncello Peninsula and adjoining island of Curzola. Sabbioncello had been the object of Churchill's interest in 1915. The plan called for the area between the southern shore of Sabbioncello and the northern coast of Curzola to be turned into a base for the Italian fleet. The Italians would virtually abandon the more distant Taranto as a major base and use Sabbioncello, Brindisi, and Valona to form a "strategic triangle" to envelop the Austrian forces at Cattaro. The operations required the substantial participation of the Italian army, and the plans floundered on this point. Cadorna would have nothing to do with it, especially as the navy approached him in May when Conrad von Hötzendorf, the Austrian chief of staff, had launched his famous *Strafe* (punishment) offensive in the Trentino. In September, after the Austrian offensive had halted and the military situation had improved for the Italians, the navy approached Cadorna about the possibility of a landing on the Istrian Peninsula between Salvore and Cittanova with the idea of drawing Austrian forces from the main front, taking Trieste from the rear and possibly isolating Pola. Once again Cadorna preferred to use all his forces on the main front. Given this attitude on the part of the Italian high command, any use of sea power for an amphibious landing on the enemy coast was out of the question.[42]

Haus also had ruled out participation by the capital ships of the Austrian navy in Conrad's *Strafe* offensive. AOK wanted the navy to enter upon a "ruthless undertaking" aimed at inflicting serious damage and similar to the bombardment they had executed at the beginning of the war. Haus resisted, arguing that the situation had altered since May of 1915, and that the Italians were fully alert with strong coastal defenses, minefields, armored trains on stretches of the railway line along the coast, and, of course, both Italian and Allied submarines. The naval bombardments, even if they succeeded in destroying coastal fortifications, could not alter the situation in the Tyrol, and if all they wanted the navy to do was to inflict injury on the Italians, they could probably do more with air raids.[43] The Austrian capital ships remained in port, the ultimate fleet-in-being, like the Italian battle squadron to be used only under special circumstances against their peers.

Both the Austrian and Italian naval commands changed early in 1917. In Italy there was a growing malaise about the apparent lack of success of the navy, and a campaign in the press was directed against the Duke of the Abruzzi. The experiment of combining the offices of minister of marine and capo di stato maggiore was also an apparent failure, and on 3 February a royal decree was signed naming Thaon di Revel "chief of the naval staff and commander of the mobilized naval force." The return of Revel and the title he received implied he would replace Abruzzi, and the duke relinquished his command, ostensibly for reasons of health. Abruzzi retained the loyalty and affection of a substantial portion of the fleet, as well as the respect of Italy's allies.

On the Austrian side, Haus died of pneumonia aboard his flagship in Pola on 8 February. He was replaced as Flottenkommandant by Vice Admiral Maximilian Njegovan, who apparently shared the strategic thoughts of his predecessor as to the stalemate in the Adriatic and the folly of risking capital ships. The decisive weapons would be submarines. Njegovan was not the commanding presence Haus had been, nor did he ever enjoy the latter's authority and prestige. He faced increasing difficulties as the strain of war began to tell on the Habsburg monarchy and its navy, which also lost the good luck it had so far enjoyed.[44]

The lack of action by capital ships or use of the term *stalemate* does not mean that no operations of any kind took place in the Adriatic. There were many, and both the Italians and Austrians were far more active than most people, especially their allies, realized. The actions, however, were small in scale, a form of naval guerrilla war, a war of ambush and counterambush. One would have to read the detailed and multi-volumed official histories to realize their scope; by their nature they are difficult to summarize in a general history of this sort. Aircraft also played an increasing role. Again, their actions are difficult to recount in detail, but one could say that the Italians gradually whittled down the initial Austrian advantage. British aircraft, operating out of southern Italian bases, also became very active in 1918, undertaking what was virtually a strategic bombing offensive against Cattaro. On 15 September 1916, Austrian aircraft sank the French submarine *Foucault* 10 miles off Cattaro. They were aided no doubt by the extreme clarity of the water on the Austrian side of the Adriatic, which worked to the disadvantage of the Allies, but the incident also demonstrated the potential importance of

A NAVAL HISTORY OF WORLD WAR I

the airplane as one of the antidotes to submarines all navies were desperately seeking.[45]

The Italians developed a weapon well suited to Adriatic conditions. In April 1915 they ordered the first group of small craft, which subsequently became known as Mas, the initials standing for *motobarca armata silurante*. They were, as the name implies, motor torpedo boats capable of 22–25 knots, fitted with two torpedoes and with a crew of eight. There were later versions dedicated for antisubmarine work, but it was as torpedo boats that they won their fame.[46] The Mas showed what they were capable of on the night of 7 June 1916, when Tenente di vascello Pagano di Melito in *Mas.5* and Tenente di vascello Berardinelli in *Mas.7* were towed by torpedo boats to the Albanian coast, an escadrille of French destroyers serving as an escort. Pagano di Melito and Berardinelli penetrated Durazzo harbor and torpedoed the small steamer *Locrum* (924 tons). They raided Durazzo again on the night of 25 June, after aerial reconnaissance reported the presence of two steamers. The scout *Marsala* and Italian destroyers served as an escort. Once again they were successful, the steamer *Sarajevo* (1,100 tons) was sunk, although later salved. The Mas boats were by no means a weapon that would automatically win the war; they were relatively fragile, and their range was limited. The Austrians also worked to improve their boom-and-net defenses, and not all Mas operations were successful. But they were another factor for naval commanders to worry about, and given the limitations of First World War fire control, under the right conditions they could and would be deadly. They were probably the naval weapon that captured the imagination of the Italian public, a weapon ideally suited for bold and dashing young officers.[47]

The Mas boats' most spectacular achievement yet was in December, but by then the Italians were sorely tested and in need of a success. On 24 October the Austrians, reinforced by seven German divisions, broke through the Italian lines in what is generally known as the Battle of Caporetto. The Austrian and German offensive was only halted on the Piave River, barely 30 miles from Venice, and more than 70 miles deep into Italian territory. The Italians had lost more than a thousand cannon, and more than 320,000 had been killed, wounded, or missing. The British and French doubted that the Italians would be able to hold Venice and feared that Italy would be compelled to leave the war. Five British and six French divisions were rushed to Italy from the western front. The Allies' worst fears proved unfounded. The line on the Piave held, and the Italians underwent something of a national renaissance in the crisis. The Italian navy participated in the defense of Venice, employing ingenious floating batteries in the lagoons north of the city.[48]

The fog of war and the fighting on land had obscured the fact that the situation for the Allies had actually been improving in the Adriatic. The Austrian flotillas at Cattaro, under orders to avoid combat with superior forces close to enemy bases, had been unable to disturb communications with Valona or repeat their success of 15 May. The drifters may have been in a less effective position, but the Austrian sorties against them were frustrated by either bad weather or Allied patrols. Njegovan's leadership was subjected to increasing criticism because of the apparent lack of initiative by the navy in exploiting the Caporetto success on the seaward flanks of the armies. The Italians had indeed been worried about extensive raids or amphibious landings. They did not take place. The old coast-defense battleships *Wien* and *Budapest* were shifted to Trieste to support the army, and on 16 November, escorted by fourteen torpedo boats, they bombarded the coastal batteries at Cortellazo near the mouth of the Piave. Mas boats tried to attack them, without success, although the bombardment was broken off. The old battleships at Trieste were, however, a magnet for the torpedo flotilla at Venice, and on the night of 10 December the Italians scored their most spectacular naval success of the war. *Mas.9* (Tenente di vascello Rizzo) and *Mas.11* (Capotimoniere Ferrarini) were towed by torpedo boats to the vicinity of Trieste and succeeded in breaking through the obstructions and entering the port. Rizzo torpedoed the *Wien,* which sank within a few minutes. The Italians escaped unharmed.[49] It was the worst loss the Austrians had suffered to date, and the success was all the sweeter to the Italians for coming at such a critical moment.

The k.u.k. Kriegsmarine, like the Habsburg monarchy that it represented, was feeling the strain of war as the year 1918 began. There were already signs that it could not remain totally immune from the nationality problems that plagued the monarchy (and would eventually tear it apart). The crew of the small torpedo boat *Tb.11* locked their officers in their cabins and, led by a Slovene and a Czech rating, brought the boat from Sebenico to the Italian coast on 5 October. The boat itself had little military value and the mutiny was an isolated event, but the Austrian authorities did not know exactly what had happened and were therefore even more disturbed.

A serious mutiny broke out in some of the ships stationed at Cattaro on 1 February 1918. The center of the revolt was in the armored cruiser *Sankt Georg,* flagship of the cruiser flotilla. It was strongest in the large ships, notably the armored cruiser *Kaiser Karl VI* and the depot ship *Gäa.* The captains of the cruisers *Helgoland* and *Novara,* which had seen so much action in the past, managed to preserve their authority, but even their ships and all the destroyers and torpedo boats eventually were compelled to raise the red flag. There is a good case for the argument that the events at Cattaro were motivated primarily by social and economic causes rather than the nationality conflicts. The sailors demanded peace without annexations, demobilization, complete independence from other powers, self-determination for all peoples, democratization of the regime, and a loyal answer to the peace proposals of President Wilson of the United States. There were very specific demands related to naval issues, which included better food and an equitable distribution of food between officers and men, a common kitchen for officers and men, regular leave, and improved conditions. The sailors, however, loyally promised to resist any Italian attack on Cattaro.

The mutineers never succeeded in winning over the army garrison at Cattaro, and coastal batteries opened fire the next day when the old guardship *Kronprinz Erzherzog Rudolph* attempted to shift position and move toward the center of the mutiny in the middle of the gulf. The *Novara* and *Helgoland,* which had been under the big guns of the armored cruisers, broke away to the innermost gulf. They were joined by nearly all the torpedo boats and destroyers. They had the support of the German submarines at Cattaro, which were ready to torpedo any of the mutineers' ships that tried to break in. The red flags were lowered. On 3 February the Third Division of three *Erzherzog*-class battleships arrived from Pola, and the army forces on land delivered an ultimatum to the mutineers. Germans and Magyars, for the most part, led a counter-revolt on the armored cruisers, and one of the leaders of the revolt, a young ensign, joined by two petty officers fled to Italy in a seaplane. He left his comrades in the lurch; forty sailors were tried and four were promptly executed. More than eight hundred men were considered of questionable loyalty and were removed from their ships.[50]

The mutiny resulted in significant changes in the leadership of the k.u.k. Kriegsmarine. The slogan seemed to be the need for "rejuvenation." Njegovan was relieved and the young Kaiser Karl I, who had succeeded Franz Joseph on the latter's death in November 1916 and was far more interested in the navy than his aged uncle had been, skipped over a number of senior officers and went down to the list of captains to choose the forty-nine-year-old Horthy, whom he promoted to rear admiral, to be the next Flottenkommandant. The choice surprised most, but Horthy had gained a reputation for aggressive handling of the light cruisers, and the kaiser assumed he would be the "new blood" who would bring an innovative spirit to the navy. There was also a rejuvenation of ships. Even before the mutiny, the three old *Habsburg*-class battleships were taken out of service to obtain crews for the submarine and air services. Now other obsolete ships, such as the two old armored cruisers *Sankt Georg* and *Kaiser Karl VI*, also were laid up. The *Erzherzog*-class battleships, with their primary armament of only four 9.2-inch guns, could no longer be considered first line battleships and remained at Cattaro in place of the old armored cruisers. The battle fleet was reduced to only the most modern: the four *Viribus Unitis*-class dreadnoughts and three *Radetzky*-class semidreadnoughts.[51]

The k.u.k. Kriegsmarine needed this general shake-up in the high command, for its problems and challenges were growing. The Austrians also had new enemies, notably the United States. The 110-foot wooden submarine chasers of the United States Navy arrived at Corfu in June to participate in the Otranto barrage (see below). However, the Americans also had plans for the Adriatic well before they arrived. The Adriatic schemes originated with the Planning Section of the staff of Vice Admiral William Sowden Sims, the commander of United States naval forces in European waters. The general idea was to seize the Sabbioncello Peninsula and establish a base between the peninsula and Curzola Island. Once again, Sabbioncello, the objective of Churchill and later Abruzzi, came under discussion. The naval base would enable the Allies to cut all traffic between the northern Adriatic and Cattaro, and would serve as a point from which troops could raid inland to cut rail communications in Dalmatia. They might seize other islands when more troops became available. The American staff also spoke of laying a mine barrage from Gargano Head on the Italian mainland to Curzola. They also considered a surprise raid on Cattaro itself, forcing their way into the gulf with five *Virginia*- or *Connecticut*-class predreadnoughts and sinking all enemy vessels found in the gulf. The Americans also suggested that U.S. Marines join the Italian troops who would probably make up the landing party. The Americans formally introduced their proposals at a meeting of the Allied Naval Council in Rome in early February. There was considerable discussion, and the Italian position was not surprising. Revel and the naval staff would be forced to limit the Italian contribution, but if the Americans were willing to employ sufficient force, there was no reason why at least part of the project could not be implemented *provided an Italian admiral commanded*. The Navy Department back in Washington was also more cautious about the operation than Sims may have assumed. Would the U.S. Marines have added "Curzola" and "Sabbioncello" to their battle honors? We will never know what the results of the operation might have been, for the question was resolved by General Ludendorff and the German general staff. Ludendorff, profiting from the elimination of Russia from the war, launched his great offensive on the western front on 21 March in a desperate attempt to win the war before the American army could arrive in Europe in force. The Germans at first made unprecedented gains on the western front, and even Sims realized the Adriatic plan could not even be considered until the Germans were checked there.[52] The Americans experienced what others who had proposed schemes for landings in the Adriatic had experienced before: there always seemed to be more urgent uses for the troops.

Regardless of the events on land, the Italian navy stepped up its guerrilla war in the Adriatic. Once again the Mas boats were in the fore. On the night of 10 February, three Mas boats were towed to the vicinity of the Gulf of Buccari near Fiume. This was a very bold move, because the objective, a number of laid-up steamers, was deep in Austrian waters. The Mas boats made their attack but did not sink any of the ships, at least partially because faulty torpedoes failed to explode. The noted poet, novelist, and nationalist Gabriele D'Annunzio immortalized the raid as the "Beffa di Buccari," and the propaganda value was immense. The Austrians replied the night of 4 April with a daring raid on Ancona with the objective of seizing a Mas boat and blowing up the submarines that were reported to be there. Linienschiffsleutnant Joseph Veith, five cadets, and fifty-five men landed north of the town, unfortunately in the wrong location owing to a faulty compass. The raid was a failure, and the entire party was captured, although the Italian authorities were dismayed that the raiding party had gotten so close to its objective.[53]

The Italians developed an ingenious device for another bold attempt to get at the Austrian capital ships in their base. They built four *Grillo*-class *barchini saltatori*, or "jumping boats," a form of naval tank fitted with two lateral caterpillar chains for climbing over barrages protecting a harbor. Each was armed with two torpedoes. The Italians made their first attempt against Pola on the night of 8 April but were frustrated by the arrival of dawn before they could get into the harbor. Their second attempt on the night of 12 April was also frustrated by delays, and they had to scuttle two of the craft, the *Cavalletta* and *Pulce*, on the approach of Austrian aircraft. Mechanical difficulties halted an attempt by the *Grillo* on the night of 6 May. Lieutenant Mario Pellegrini was finally successful on the night of 13 May in maneuvering the *Grillo* past some of the barriers at Pola before the craft was discovered, sunk, and the crew taken prisoner. The Italians had bad luck, for Pola was in a state of heightened readiness as a result of special measures that Horthy had ordered a few weeks before in order to guard against the sort of raid that the *Grillo* had attempted. He was determined to preserve the irreplaceable battleships either for combat or to uphold Austria-Hungary's position as a great power. The Austrians raised the *Grillo* and eventually began to build two similar craft of their own, which were incomplete at the war's end. They also tried to build their own versions of the Mas boats, but these were, for the most part and for various reasons, still incomplete at the end of the war.[54]

The ability of the Austrians to disrupt the Otranto barrage was substantially reduced. By the spring of 1918 there were destroyers available to protect the drifters, including six from Australia, which had arrived at Brindisi in October of 1917. There were still not as many as the Allies desired, but their presence made a difference. On the night of 22–23 April, five *Tátra*-class destroyers made a sweep southward toward the Strait of Otranto. The British destroyers *Jackal* and *Hornet* encountered them about 15 miles west of Valona, and there was a sharp fight in which the *Hornet* was badly damaged. The Austrians might have been able to finish her off, but under orders to avoid being cut off by superior forces, and in the vicinity of Valona with a bright moon, they turned for home. The *Jackal*, which had lost her mainmast, pursued, joined by the other destroyers that had been on patrol that night, the British *Alarm* and *Comet*, the Australian *Torrens*, and the French *Cimeterre*. The Austrian destroyers steadily pulled ahead, and the Allied destroyers turned back west of Cape Pali. Once again the Austrians escaped in a night action without suffering any damage or losses; the British lost seven dead and twenty-five wounded. However, there had been no massacre of the drifters as there had been the preceding year. The Allied patrols were both stronger and more alert.[55]

The Austrians also had to call off another raid on the night of 8–9 May when the raiding forces were discovered prematurely. The plan had been for four destroyers of the *Huszár* class to land a raiding party to cut the coastal railway near Silvi to the north of Pescara. This in itself was not exceptional and needs no further comment. What was interesting, however, was that two of the destroyers suffered mechanical breakdowns of one sort or another on their return, which greatly reduced their speed. The *Huszár*-class destroyers were older and had seen much hard use, but it is significant that the Austrian naval command saw fit to inquire as to the nationality of the crewmen on duty in the engine room at the time. The men in one destroyer turned out to be German; in the other destroyer, a Czech and a Hungarian. No sabotage was proven, but it is significant that the question was asked and that the naval command felt obliged to add a warning that in the future machinists in the fleet should be chosen with care. The k.u.k. Kriegsmarine was proud that like the monarchy it served it was a multinational institution and sailors of different nationalities served together on its ships, unlike the army where whole regiments might be of the same nationality. Nevertheless, there had been the mutiny at Cattaro, a conspiracy led by two Slavic ringleaders uncovered in a torpedo boat at Pola in May, and the example of the Russian revolution—all while the condition of the Austro-Hungarian monarchy itself steadily deteriorated. Some commanders thought the socialistic spirit did more harm than the nationalism of the subject peoples, and the submarine ace von Trapp seemed particularly suspicious of Czechs and reported how all work on his boat had to be personally checked. It is difficult to know how much to make of this. As late as 9 August Horthy assured AOK that although the fleet was a mirror of opinion in the Dual Monarchy itself, circumscribed to a certain degree by discipline, the fleet was in hand and in all probability would continue to remain so during and after a hostile action against the Austrian coast. The fleet did continue to function loyally to the very end of the war, but there can be no denying the fact that officers were now inclined to look over their shoulder and that the atmosphere had changed.[56]

Horthy had been hailed as "new blood" with the mission of rejuvenating the fleet, and it was widely anticipated, once he had the battle fleet in hand to his satisfaction, it would see action. The predictions were correct. Horthy planned a major attack on the Allied forces in the Strait of Otranto to take place at dawn on 11 June. The stated reason for the operation was to relieve the pressure the enhanced Allied mobile barrage had been exerting on the German and Austrian submarines seeking to pass through the Strait. The real reason was possibly Horthy's desire to raise morale by giving the fleet something to do. The plan was similar to that of the 15 May 1917 operation. The light cruisers *Novara* and *Helgoland* with four *Tátra*-class destroyers would attack the line Santa Maria di Leuca–Fano while the light cruisers *Spaun* and *Saida* and four torpedo boats would sweep the waters off Otranto and attack the seaplane station located there. The major difference from the operation of the preceding year would be the use of the four dreadnoughts from Pola and the three *Erzherzog*-class battleships from Cattaro. They would be out in seven separate support groups, each accompanied by destroyers and torpedo boats. Horthy expected the Allies to repeat their actions of 1917 and send light cruisers and perhaps armored cruisers out from Brindisi to intercept the raiders. If they did, they would encounter the big guns of the Austrian battleships and suffer accordingly. In addition, German and Austrian submarines were deployed off Brindisi and Valona and Austrian aircraft would join the action.

The dreadnoughts were scheduled to leave Pola in two echelons, steaming at night and anchoring at different secure anchorages during daylight hours. Horthy left Pola in his flagship *Viribus Unitis* together with the *Prinz Eugen* the evening of 8 June, anchored at Tajer the following day, and then proceeded to Slano by night, arriving on the morning of the 10th. The second echelon, the dreadnoughts *Szent István* and *Tegetthoff*, sailed from Pola on the evening of the 9th, escorted by one of the older destroyers and six torpedo boats. By chance, Rizzo, now promoted to capitano di corvetta, was out in *Mas.15* together with *Mas.21*, searching for mines. At about 3:30 A.M. on the 10th, approximately 9 nautical miles southwest of the island of Premuda, Rizzo encountered the Austrian ships. Rizzo torpedoed the *Szent István*; *Mas.21*'s torpedoes missed the *Tegetthoff*. The Italians escaped. The efforts to save the *Szent István* were not successful, and shortly after 6:00 A.M. she capsized and sank with the loss of four officers and eighty-five men. Horthy immediately called off the operation. He believed that the all essential surprise was lost and that the Austrians might encounter a superior force of dreadnoughts from either the French fleet at Corfu or the Italian fleet at Taranto. Allied submarines would probably be off Brindisi and the Albanian coast and other submarines and Mas boats would converge on the approaches to Cattaro. The unspoken sentiment in the Austrian navy might well have been that when Horthy deviated from Haus's policy of the fleet-in-being, the results were disastrous.

One can never know what would have happened if Rizzo had not had his chance meeting with the Austrians. The Allies were alert to some Austrian move because of an increase in Austrian wireless traffic and air activity. There were ten British, Australian, and French destroyers on patrol north of the drifter line that night, so the Austrian light forces might have had a hot time of it. The Allies realized after the aborted raid that they could not afford to relax, although the Austrians had also found they could not really change the situation at the entrance of the Adriatic. There was one harmful result for the Allies. The Austrian sortie led them to believe, quite erroneously, that if the Austrians had been willing to take such risks to attack the Otranto barrage it must really be effective. For the Italians the affair was, perhaps, the one they most like to remember in the entire war. Rizzo's *Mas.15* is still preserved in the Museo del Vittoriano at the base of the Victor Emmanuel II monument in Rome. The news of the sinking arrived at the perfect psychological moment for the Italians, as it helped to strengthen Revel and the Italian navy—the object of often scathing criticism over the lack of activity by their dreadnoughts—to resist British, French, and American demands they integrate their fleet more closely with those of their allies.[57]

The Austrian navy did not undertake any major sortie for the remainder of the war, although, ironically, the last real offensive by the Central Powers was undertaken by the Austrian army in Albania at the end of August and there was some fear on the Allied side the Italians would not be able to hold Valona. The Italians were rather embarrassed about all the Allied attention in Albania where they had their own ambitions, but the Italian army reinforced its forces in front of Valona and the port was secured.[58]

The waters off Albania were also the scene of the last naval action of any size in the Adriatic during the war. General Franchet d'Esperey, the Allied commander in the Balkans, began his offensive on the Macedonian front on 14 September. The Bulgarian lines were broken, and on 29 September the Bulgarian government was forced to conclude an armistice. Bulgaria was the first of the Central Powers to leave the war, and her collapse set off the chain of events leading to the collapse of the others. Franchet d'Esperey now anticipated that German and Austrian forces in the Balkans would be forced to rely on Durazzo for supplies, and he asked for some action on the part of the Allied navies to neutralize the port as an enemy base. The old problem of command in the Adriatic reared its head. Durazzo was in the Italian sphere of operations, and the Italian navy had indeed considered various plans since July involving the place, but they were never implemented for the familiar reason: the potential gains did not seem worth the potential risks. The French government put the Italians on the spot. If the Italians did not act, the French navy would. The prospect of a sizable intervention by the French navy in the Adriatic was unacceptable to the Italians, and Revel decided to act.

The bombardment of Durazzo on 2 October 1918 can be compared to using a hammer to swat a fly. The bombarding force was truly international. Commanded by Rear Admiral Palladini, the first echelon consisted of the three *Pisa*-class armored cruisers, preceded by four British destroyers fitted as minesweepers, and escorted by four British destroyers and eight Italian torpedo boats. The second echelon consisted of three British light cruisers escorted by four British destroyers. The American submarine chasers acted as a screen to the north and south of the bombarding area. Four to six Mas boats were also on patrol. Farther offshore there were three groups serving as advanced covering forces ready to engage any Austrian vessels that might sortie from Cattaro. The covering forces included three *Nibbio*-class scouts and one Italian and two British light cruisers escorted by four British and Australian destroyers. The third and most powerful group consisted of the dreadnought *Dante Alighieri* escorted by seven Italian destroyers and flotilla leaders. Revel was in the *Dante*, although he did not fly his flag. The group was commanded by Rear Admiral Mola. There were also seven to eight British, French, and Italian submarines on either their normal or additional patrols off the Austrian bases, and Revel ordered the torpedo craft at Venice to be ready to attack any Austrian vessels that might come out of Pola. Furthermore, British and Italian aircraft carried out a series of air raids throughout the day. The bombardment of Durazzo was the only thing approaching a fleet action that U.S. naval forces participated in during the First World War.

Revel reduced the scope of the operation to avoid running unnecessary risks. The original plan had called for destroyers to rush into the port to destroy all floating matériel while the cruisers engaged the shore batteries. Revel canceled the destroyer action; it would be a long-range bombardment only. This failure to press home the attack reduced much of the value of the bombardment, and, as the British pointed out, the risks of mines and torpedoes remained. There were only three Austrian warships in port when the bombardment began, the old destroyers *Dinara* and *Scharfschütze* and the torpedo boat *Tb.87*, along with three steamers and the hospital ship *Baron Call*. The Austrian submarines *U.29* and *U.31* were on patrol in the area. The hospital ship *Baron Call* left port at the beginning of the action, and after being stopped and inspected by British destroyers, was allowed to proceed on her way. One of the Austrian steamers in port was burnt out and sunk, the others received only minor damage. The three Austrian warships dodged about, close to land, evaded an attack by the Mas boats, and escaped with only minor damage. There were a number of houses destroyed on shore, the inevitable casualties, and the morale of the garrison was certainly lowered. However, while the second echelon, the British cruisers, bombarded the town, *U.31* succeeded in torpedoing the *Weymouth*, blowing off the cruiser's stern and killing four men. *U.29*'s attempt to get into a firing position was frustrated by the screening forces, and the submarine was subjected to a heavy depth-charge attack. The Americans for many years cherished the erroneous belief that their submarine chasers had sunk two submarines that day. They had not.[59]

This was the last action of the k.u.k. Kriegsmarine, which was destined to disappear forever in little more than a month. The action also may have been unnecessary, for the military situation in the Balkans compelled the Austrians to evacuate Durazzo on 11 October. The empire was beginning to break into fragments. On the 16th

Kaiser Karl issued a manifesto that offered to turn the Habsburg monarchy into a federal state, but it was too late for an offer of this sort. On 17 October the Austrians ceased to participate in the submarine war outside the Adriatic. The kaiser's manifesto had a serious effect on discipline in the fleet; by 23 October officers were noting widespread demands for a return home and the formation of national committees. On 24 October General Diaz, who had replaced Cadorna as head of the Italian army after Caporetto, began his long-expected offensive on the Italian front. The climactic battle generally known as Vittorio Veneto followed. The Austrians resisted fiercely for a few days but began to give way on the 29th with a general collapse on the 30th and 31st. The Austrians were forced to conclude an armistice at the Villa Giusti near Padua on the evening of 3 November.

The kaiser ordered Horthy to turn over the fleet and naval property to a newly formed South Slav National Council in Agram. Those men who were not of the South Slav nationality were free to go home, although Horthy urged those who did not take service with the new Yugoslav navy to remain at their posts during the period of transfer. Linienschiffskapitän Janko Vukovic de Podkapelski was named the provisional Yugoslav fleet commander. At sunset on 31 October, the red-white-red ensign of the k.u.k. Kriegsmarine was lowered for the last time, and Horthy left the ship with the old ensign under his arm. The new red-white-blue Yugoslav flag was raised to a twenty-one-gun salute.

The Slavic sailors were jubilant, and that night the ships were fully illuminated for the first time since the beginning of the war, and apparently no watch on the entrance to the harbor was maintained. This was a mistake, for technically the war was still on, and during the night two Italian officers, Tenente medico (medical lieutenant) Raffaele Paolucci and Maggiore del Genio navale (major of naval engineers) Raffaele Rossetti, penetrated the harbor with a new and ingenious device. The two men, dressed in rubber suits, guided the *mignatta* (leech), a torpedolike self-propelled mine, and attached explosive charges to the hull of the *Viribus Unitis* and Austrian Lloyd liner *Wien* (7,376 tons), which until shortly before had been used as an accommodation ship by German U-boat crews. The two officers were captured, but the charges exploded and the *Viribus Unitis*—the first Austrian dreadnought, symbolic of Austro-Hungarian efforts to become a real sea power—capsized and sank around dawn. The *Wien* also sank, but was later salved.[60] It remains a matter of controversy how much the Italians knew of the situation in Pola before the attack.[61]

Although the war in the Adriatic was over, there was no real peace. The Allies in Paris had drafted stiff terms concerning what warships the Austrians would have to surrender. These terms became moot when the empire itself ceased to exist. The Allies initially were suspicious about recognizing the new Yugoslav flag. There was some distrust this was a ruse to avoid surrendering the ships. The Yugoslavs in the long run received comparatively few of the former Austro-Hungarian warships, which were divided among the Allies. The big ships and most of the old ones were quickly scrapped, but a few of the light cruisers served in the French and Italian navies until the late 1930s, and torpedo boats could be found in the Romanian navy even after the Second World

War. The Italian navy rapidly sought to occupy points Italy claimed in the Adriatic, and very quickly the rivalry between the French and Italians turned poisonous. The new Yugoslav state, supported by the French, seemed a new rival to replace the old Austro-Hungarian empire. The acrimonious disputes that accompanied Italian, French, and Yugoslav policies in the Adriatic are beyond the scope of this book, but it is perhaps indicative of Italian feelings about the outcome of the peace conference that the final volume in the Ufficio Storico's history of the Italian navy in the war is subtitled "The Mutilated Victory."

7

THE BALTIC

GERMAN AND RUSSIAN NAVAL PLANS

The Baltic differed from other theaters of the war because of its geography and climate, both of which produce certain special features. First of all, it is a closed sea that can only be entered through the narrow passages of the Big and Little Belts through the Danish islands and the Sound between Denmark and Sweden. These confined waters could be blocked easily by mines, and any fleet from the outside trying to operate in the Baltic did not enjoy a secure line of communications unless it had troops on shore to safeguard the channels. The passages were also neutral waters; neither Denmark nor Sweden was ever drawn into the war. Nevertheless the Germans had an immense strategic advantage in the Kaiser Wilhelm Canal—more commonly known as the Kiel Canal—which linked the Baltic with the North Sea. This spared the Germans the necessity of making the passage through the Belts or the Sound and the Kattegat and Skaggerak around the Jutland Peninsula. They could shift naval forces from the North Sea to the Baltic and back again with both security and relative speed. On the other hand, the British and French were cut off from easy access to their Russian ally. Even the passage of submarines, despite their advantage of concealment, proved to be a major undertaking. The Allies were forced to use the northern route around Norway to the north Russian ports. With Norway a benevolent neutral, this was nowhere near as dangerous as it would be in the Second World War, but the north Russian ports were limited in their capacity, and the Russians were even more limited in their ability to move matériel from the ports southward.

The northern climate added another special feature to naval warfare in the Baltic. At these latitudes the summer nights, particularly in June, were very short, while the winter nights were correspondingly long. Ice was a major problem. Large portions of the northern and eastern Baltic froze for a few months during the year, particularly the

Gulfs of Finland, Bothnia, and Riga. The Russian navy was especially affected, as its operations substantially ceased from January to the latter part of April, except for some light craft at the southernmost base at Libau on the Lithuanian coast. This meant large numbers of men crowded together in discomfort and relative idleness, which created a fertile breeding ground for the subversion and politics that eventually paralyzed the fleet.

There was another peculiar feature of the naval war in the Baltic. The Germans and Russians each acted on the assumption that the other's fleet was superior. The Russians had embarked on a substantial naval building program in the years before the world war (see chapter 1), but on paper there was still no comparison between the Russian Baltic Fleet and the German High Sea Fleet. The Russians knew this, and their primary objective was defense of the Gulf of Finland and approaches to their capital, St. Petersburg, renamed Petrograd after the outbreak of the war. The Russians also attempted to supplement their admittedly inferior naval forces with extensive minefields and powerful batteries on shore.

The Germans, however, regarded the North Sea as the main theater of their naval war and concentrated the bulk of their naval forces there. The Baltic was a secondary theater for them, and they allocated only the minimum force to it, frequently obsolescent ships that could not be risked in the North Sea. Therefore, the German navy, despite its great paper strength, usually was inferior to the Russians in the Baltic. This became even more evident in the first year of the war as the new Russian dreadnoughts and large destroyers entered service. Nevertheless, the Germans always had the option of rapidly shifting forces to the Baltic at the expense of their North Sea defense. The Germans periodically exercised that option after it became obvious as the war went on that the British would not oblige them with a costly offensive against the German North Sea coast. The Russian navy, however great its momentary superiority, always had to reckon on meeting a potentially overwhelming German force with little warning.

The Russian assumption of inferiority at sea was exaggerated by the belief Sweden would join Germany in a war against Russia with the idea of recovering Finland. They anticipated a Swedish landing on the south coast of Finland with an advance over land in the direction Viborg–St. Petersburg. The mission of the Russian army and naval forces in the Baltic theater would be to delay the expected enemy advance deep into the Gulf of Finland twelve to fourteen days to give time for Russian forces protecting the capital to be mobilized. The defense would be to the east of the meridian of the Gogland Islands in the gulf and on the banks of the River Kyumen on the Finnish shore. Minefields would be laid to the north and south of the Gogland Islands. This implied Helsingfors would have to be abandoned and Sveaborg would serve as the fleet's advance base, while Kronstadt would be the main base. The distant base at Libau on the Lithuanian coast would, of necessity, be abandoned.[1]

These plans envisaged a very restricted role for the fleet, with a relatively close defense of St. Petersburg. They obviously reflected the very difficult position after the severe losses of the Russo-Japanese War. The scope of operations expanded in the years before the outbreak of the war, coinciding with the period when Admiral Nicholas

Ottovich Essen commanded the naval forces in the Baltic. Essen had emerged from the Russo-Japanese War with credit, and in 1908, as a rear admiral, was appointed to the Baltic command. Essen was probably the outstanding Russian naval commander of the war and received favorable comment in both Soviet and émigré literature as well as in the reports of contemporary naval observers.[2] Essen, according to one officer, "literally regenerated the Fleet," with particular emphasis on training and navigation of the difficult channels of the Finnish skerries, a skill the commanders of Russian torpedo craft later performed with great élan.[3] Essen's premature death at fifty-four in May of 1915 was a heavy blow to the Baltic Fleet.

Essen, although still anticipating that Sweden would be an enemy, did not expect the Germans to use their first-line forces in the Baltic. He therefore favored a more active policy of laying minefields along the German coast and in the path of a German force advancing into the Gulf of Finland rather than passively waiting with the fleet at the Gogland position. The Swedes would be deterred from entering the war by a display of force and the possible use of mines off the Swedish naval base of Karlskrona. The Russian naval staff did not agree to Essen's proposal to lay mines along the German coast, but under his prodding produced in 1910 a new naval plan that envisaged the laying of a second major minefield along the line Nargen-Porkkala-Udd, which was much farther to the west in the Gulf of Finland. Essen might offer his initial resistance here before falling back to the Gogland position.

In the 1912 plan, the Nargen-Porkkala-Udd line was designated the "Central Position." The fleet would deploy here behind an extensive minefield, which would be covered by powerful coastal batteries with artillery ranging up to 14 inches. There would also be additional coastal batteries on the northern flank among the skerries on the Finnish coast between Porkkala-Udd and Gange. The main fleet base would be brought forward to Revel on the Estonian coast, although until that was fully equipped, Helsingfors would be used. Moon Sound, the entrance to the Gulf of Finland from the Gulf of Riga, would also be blocked with mines on the outbreak of war. It should be noted that these plans remained essentially defensive. Except for patrols outside of the Gulf of Finland, the Russians had no thought of fighting in the open sea. At the approach of the enemy's main fleet, the battleships and cruisers of the Baltic Fleet would fall back and fight and maneuver *to the east* of the "Central Position." It would be a form of naval trench warfare, with the ships sheltering behind the minefields and coordinating their fire with the powerful coastal batteries. The coastal fortifications of the "Central Position" and flanking positions in the skerries were far from complete when the war broke out, and part of the minefields could not be covered by defensive fire. The Russians also suffered from the lack of docking facilities for big ships at Revel and Helsingfors. Large ships therefore had to proceed to Kronstadt, which might prove difficult to impossible in the winter months when the eastern part of the gulf was frozen.[4]

The Russians steadily improved these minefields and coastal defenses after the war broke out. The Germans, preoccupied with the British, never attempted to break into the Gulf of Finland with the bulk of their fleet. German submarines did penetrate the gulf, but the only time the Germans tried a major surface operation with a destroyer flotilla, in November 1916, they met with disaster.

German naval planning in the years just before the war was dominated by the idea that the real decision would come in the North Sea and that the Baltic would be treated as a secondary theater (*Nebenkriegsschauplatz*). It would be far more important to face the British with an undamaged fleet than to achieve the destruction of the Russian fleet. A decisive German victory at sea in the Baltic would not compel the Russians to seek peace; that could only be done on land. The Germans did not have sufficient naval strength for a two-front war at sea; the Baltic would have to make do with whatever could be spared or not employed in the North Sea. Nevertheless, the slow growth of Russian naval strength in the Baltic would eventually pose problems for the Germans. Admiral von Pohl recognized that too weak a force in the Baltic could lead to a disaster.[5]

The ratio of strength between the Russians and the Germans in the Baltic was even more unfavorable to the Germans at the very beginning of the war because many of the older ships allotted to the Baltic were laid up and would take several days to mobilize. The Germans realized they might well lose the use of their eastern ports of Pillau and Danzig and have to content themselves with defending the island of Rügen, the western Baltic, and their major base at Kiel. Such German forces as were available at the outbreak of the war would therefore have to conduct a game of bluff. They would undertake bold sorties against whatever Russian forces and bases they could reach, lay mines, attempt to disturb the Russian mobilization, and in general try to conceal from the Russians the extent of German weakness. The Germans expected the Russians to undertake an essentially defensive strategy at first, with only brief sorties against the German coast, but they expected the Russians to become bolder as they realized the extent of German weakness. The Germans anticipated a Russian mining offensive against their coast. These points were contained in the operational orders issued to the Baltic forces on 31 July.[6]

On 30 July, at the very moment war was breaking out, the kaiser altered the original mobilization plans for the Baltic and named his brother Grossadmiral Heinrich, Prince of Prussia, as commander in chief, Baltic naval forces (Oberbefehlshaber der Ostseestreitkräfte, commonly known as the O.d.O.). The appointment raised eyebrows. Admiral von Müller, chief of the kaiser's naval cabinet, advised against it on the grounds that Prince Heinrich, who had been in the largely ceremonial position of general inspector of the navy, was not really qualified.[7] Kaiser Wilhelm apparently agreed, but indicated that he had promised his brother the job, that the Baltic was not essential, and that the prince could be given a competent staff.[8] Although Müller wrote that this was done and that the leadership in the Baltic "was satisfactory in the extreme," the reality might have been somewhat different. Captain Heinrich, the prince's chief of staff, apparently reported that the prince had completely lost his nerve when he embarked at the beginning of the war and was faced with the prospect of meeting the enemy in battle. Heinrich proposed that the chief of the High Sea Fleet should receive overall command when he was in the Baltic, and the decision to do this was reached on 9 October 1914. The effect would have been to keep Prince Heinrich from commanding any really important naval action.[9]

OPENING MOVES

On the outbreak of war, both the Russians and the Germans quickly acted or were prepared to act in a high-handed manner with the Scandinavian neutrals in order to secure their own interests. The Admiralstab's operational orders to Prince Heinrich specified he was to secure Kiel Bay against British or Russian naval forces. This meant that while facing the numerically superior Russians, he would have to cover his rear by securing the entrances to the Baltic against possible British incursions. Early on the morning of 5 August, Rear Admiral Mischke, chief of the Baltic coastal-defense division, directed the laying of 243 mines in the Great Belt, part of the minefield extending into Danish territorial waters. At the same time, other German forces mined the Little Belt. Admiral von Müller was horrified: "A pointless measure since we have every reason to respect Danish neutrality." He favored repudiating the prince and sending a note of apology to the Danish government. The measure did jar the Danes into acting to protect their neutrality; the following day, they announced that to block the passage of large ships they would mine the Danish portion of the Sound and the Great and Little Belts. They would provide pilots to guide merchant vessels through the minefields. The Admiralstab therefore ordered Prince Heinrich on 7 August to avoid Danish territorial waters.[10] The Danish navy after the war claimed to have eventually laid twelve hundred mines, which succeeded in preserving Danish neutrality by forestalling the Germans from acting in Danish territorial waters.[11] Although Admiral Scheer later complained that the Danish minefields eliminated the Skaggerak as a possible escape route after a raid in the North Sea, the barrier to easy entry into the Baltic was on the whole more advantageous to the Germans than to the British.[12] The mines made it extremely difficult if not impossible for British surface forces to assist the Russians in the Baltic and essentially freed Prince Heinrich to concentrate on the Russians.

Admiral Essen also was prepared to neutralize the potential danger from Sweden. He too began the war with extensive minelaying in the "Central Position" as planned. The Russians promptly laid 2,124 mines, with additional minefields along the Finnish skerries in the next few days.[13] It was the beginning of what would develop into a formidable position.

This left the unsettled question of Sweden, which the Russian naval plans had assumed would enter the war on the side of Germany. Sweden had declared neutrality, but the Swedish fleet was apparently concentrated at Gotland. Essen interpreted this, along with reports of anti-Russian demonstrations in Sweden, as a threat. His chief of staff for operations, Commander (future commander in chief in the Black Sea and White Russian leader) Kolchak, prepared a plan in which Essen and the Russian Baltic Fleet would appear by surprise before the Swedish fleet and deliver what amounted to an ultimatum to the Swedish admiral, inviting him to proceed with his fleet to the Swedish naval base of Karlskrona and remain there for the duration of the war. If the Swedes refused, Essen was apparently prepared to destroy their fleet. Essen, a bold admiral whose actions are reminiscent of Nelson and the Danish fleet during the Napoleonic Wars, was greatly hampered in the first part of the war by the fact that the Baltic Fleet was actually under the orders of the commander of the Russian Sixth Army. Essen sailed with his fleet on 9 August, sending a report of his proposed actions and a copy of the ultimatum by cable to the commander of the Sixth Army and leaving one of his staff at Helsingfors to await a reply. The Russian naval staff recalled the admiral—one is tempted to say in the nick of time—with the message that in the present political situation the supreme command prohibited all offensive operations. The primary mission of the fleet was to protect St. Petersburg, and that necessitated its presence in the Gulf of Finland.[14] The tsar's attitude toward naval affairs is perhaps best summarized in the remark he reportedly made to Admiral Essen when general mobilization was ordered. The tsar closed the audience with the comment: "We do not want a second Tsushima."[15]

Given the attitude of the Russian supreme command, and their apparent intention to keep a close watch on what many may have considered an overly bold admiral, it was the Germans who assumed the initiative in the Baltic, despite the numerical superiority of the Russians. The first shots of the war were fired early on the morning of 2 August. The fast light cruiser *Magdeburg*—the most modern of the German ships in the Baltic—shelled Libau, while the cruiser *Augsburg* laid one hundred mines northwest of the harbor. The Germans did not realize that the Russian navy had evacuated the port, sinking five steamers as blockships, and the minefield, whose exact location was poorly marked, hampered the operations of the Germans for a long time.

The Germans continued their aggressive sorties; the *Magdeburg*, for example, shelled the lighthouse at Dagerort on 12 August, and throughout the month German cruisers and destroyers shelled other points along the Russian coast from the entrance to the Gulf of Finland, south to the border with East Prussia. The Germans nearly met serious opposition on the 17th when Rear Admiral Mischke led the *Magdeburg*, *Augsburg*, and three destroyers with the auxiliary minelayer *Deutschland* (a converted Sassnitz-Trelleborg ferry) to the entrance of the Gulf of Finland. They encountered the Russian armored cruisers *Admiral Makarov* and *Gromoboi*, and the Germans were forced to lay their mines 45 miles to the west of their planned position. The two Russian armored cruisers armed with 20.3-cm (8-inch) guns actually outgunned the Germans, but the Russian Rear Admiral thought the German force included the much more powerful armored cruisers *Roon* and *Prinz Heinrich* and did not engage. He subsequently lost his command.[16]

Prince Heinrich had not been pleased with Mischke's handling of the expedition and decided to entrust future offensive operations against the Russian coast to Rear Admiral Behring. However, Behring's first sweep against the Russian patrols at the entrance to the Gulf of Finland led to what would turn out to be one of the most serious German losses during the war. Early on the morning of 26 August, the *Magdeburg* ran aground at Odensholm lighthouse off the Estonian coast. The *Magdeburg*'s escort, the destroyer *V.26*, tried unsuccessfully to free the cruiser and then took off part of the crew. *V.26*'s rescue attempts had to be broken off when the Russian cruiser *Bogatyr* and armored cruiser *Pallada* arrived on the scene and opened fire. The Germans blew up the

A NAVAL HISTORY OF WORLD WAR I

fore part of the *Magdeburg*, but the Russians later recovered those precious German code books, which they subsequently passed to the British.[17]

By the beginning of September it was apparent that the Germans were using only second-line forces in the Baltic. Moreover, Great Britain was in the war as an ally, something that had not been anticipated in the Russian plans. Essen, naturally inclined to be aggressive, began a much more active use of his fleet, whose operational zone was extended up to the meridian of Dagerort. Russian cruisers now sortied against the German patrol lines, which had to be pulled back to the meridian of Windau. The Russians shifted a portion of their fleet farther to the west in the Gulf of Finland. A division of cruisers was kept at Lapvik on the Finnish coast; other light forces moved out to the Åland Islands, and the Russians began to prepare a forward base in Moon Sound.

Essen's activity was annoying enough for Prince Heinrich to make a sweep in the Baltic from 3 to 9 September with the hope of enticing the Russian fleet out to battle. The German force included the Fourth Squadron of Vice Admiral Ehrhard Schmidt, composed of seven old *Braunschweig*- and *Wittelsbach*-class battleships mobilized from the reserve, joined by the powerful armored cruiser *Blücher*, five cruisers, and twenty-four destroyers. Although the *Augsburg* detected the Russian cruisers *Bayan* and *Pallada* on patrol to the north of Dagö Island and tried to draw them close enough for the *Blücher* to destroy them, the Russians escaped into the Gulf of Finland and the Germans did not follow. The *Augsburg* and the destroyer *V.25* sortied into the Gulf of Bothnia on the 7th and sank a Russian steamer off Raumo. Essen did steam out of the Gulf of Finland into the northern Baltic with the Russian battleship squadron on the 8th, but the Germans by then were to the south of Gotland on their way home.[18]

Essen remained anxious for a more aggressive use of the Russian fleet. On the night of 27 August, taking advantage of the stormy and moonless night, he sailed in the British-built armored cruiser *Rurik*, in company with the *Pallada* and without any escort, to raid communications between Germany and Sweden along the line Bornholm-Danzig. Essen returned without meeting any German craft, but the raid bolstered the morale of the Baltic Fleet, not to mention Essen's reputation. Nevertheless he was not successful in his proposal that the Russian fleet be used in the southern Baltic and that at least some of the Russian battleships be used to cover mining expeditions against the German coast, with the understanding they would accept battle outside of their pre-pared positions in the Gulf of Finland only with the prospect of certain victory. The tsar would not approve any active use of the Baltic Fleet without his special permission, and that permission also would be required for the use in battle of the new division of dreadnoughts when they entered service. He did authorize the extension of the zone of operations of the Gulf of Finland up to the meridian of Dagerort, including Moon Sound.[19]

Essen had been using his cruisers in a bold fashion, but the Russians learned the same hard lessons the British had about the danger of submarines. On 10 October *U.26*, one of three German U-boats patrolling off the entrance to the Gulf of Riga, fired a torpedo but missed the *Admiral Makarov*. The submarine commander was luckier on the 11th, torpedoing the armored cruiser *Pallada*, which blew up and sank with no survivors.

The Russians withdrew their large ships from the patrol line.

German submarine activity did not deter Essen from mining, the major and most effective Russian activity for the remainder of the year. He began an offensive against the German lines of communication in the southern Baltic, beginning the night of 31 October, when three Russian destroyers taking advantage of surprise and secrecy laid 105 mines off Memel. The destroyers could carry approximately 33 mines each but then could not train their aft guns or torpedo tubes and were therefore extremely vulnerable should they meet the Germans. On 5 November the destroyers laid another 140 mines approximately 40 miles southwest of Memel, and 50 mines approximately 15 miles off Pillau. Less than a fortnight later the Russians could claim a major success. Early in the morning of 17 November, the old large armored cruiser *Friedrich Carl* exploded two of the Russian mines and after a few hours capsized and sank. The steamer *Elbing.9* proceeding to assist ran into another Russian field and also was sunk.[20]

Admiral Essen was encouraged by the results, especially because the arrival of British submarines in the Baltic during October made the Germans much more cautious about risking larger ships such as cruisers on patrol. The approach of winter, with storms, intense cold, and ice, made it more difficult to use the destroyers for minelaying, but it also provided the long nights of the northern latitudes to conceal movement. Essen decided to fit six cruisers, including the invaluable *Rurik*, as temporary minelayers. In the meantime destroyers and the minelayer *Amur* kept up their work with minefields off the northwest Stolpe bank, Brüsterort, and Scholpin. These fields ultimately claimed eleven German steamers and three mine hunters. The Germans retaliated; on 6 December the auxiliary minelayer *Deutschland* laid mines off Björneborg and Raumo in the Gulf of Bothnia, which soon sank three steamers (as well as two Swedish ships the following month) and stopped traffic between Finland and Sweden for several days. The action caused Swedish protests, and the Germans realized that in the absence of a base nearby, the minefields could be easily swept once discovered.

The Russians lost two minelaying torpedo boats on 12 December when their own mines exploded off Odensholm, frustrating an expedition to lay a field southwest of Libau. Essen's major offensive with the cruisers was, however, successful. Admiral Kerber in the *Rurik* led the *Admiral Makarov* and *Bayan* in one group and the minelayer *Yenisei* covered by the cruisers *Oleg* and *Bogatyr* in a second group to lay fields to the north of Rixhöft and Leba, northern and western entrances to the Gulf of Danzig. Essen had wanted to bring the newly commissioned dreadnought *Sevastopol* out in support, but the request was denied by the Russian high command.

Essen continued the minelaying offensive into the new year, as long as ice conditions permitted. On the evening of 12 January 1915, the cruisers *Rossija*, *Oleg*, and *Bogatyr* sailed with mines, covered by the cruisers *Rurik*, *Bayan*, and *Admiral Makarov*. On the 13th and 14th the *Oleg* and *Bogatyr* laid their mines east of Bornholm and the *Rossija* laid hers north of Cape Arkona on the island of Rügen. These were the farthest penetrations into the western Baltic by the Russians, and on the night of 24–25 January, the German cruiser *Augsburg* was mined in the field east of Bornholm and the old cruiser

A NAVAL HISTORY OF WORLD WAR I

Gazelle was mined north of Cape Arkona. Although both cruisers were towed back to port, the *Gazelle* was not considered worth repairing.

With the hardening ice ending the possibility of operations in the northern part of the Baltic, Essen undertook his last minelaying operation on the evening of 12 February when the *Oleg* and *Bogatyr* with four destroyers, all carrying mines, covered by the *Rurik* and *Admiral Makarov*, sailed for Danzig Bay. The Russians, who had been lucky so far, nearly suffered a disaster when the *Rurik* ran aground in the fog near Farö light on the 13th and had to return with her bottom ripped open, one-third of the boiler room flooded, and 2,400 tons of water in the ship. The Russian cruisers returned with her. The four destroyers continued on to lay their mines the night of the 13th, approximately 30 to 40 miles north of Hela in the Bay of Danzig. They returned unharmed.

The situation in the Baltic, when ice ended active operations by the Russian fleet after seven months of war, is subject to differing interpretations. Certainly the Germans had their setbacks, as, for example, on 24 January when Admiral Behring's cruiser *Prinz Adalbert*, proceeding to bombard Libau while returning from a reconnaissance to the Åland Islands, ran aground off Steinort causing the operation to be broken off. The Germans suffered further loss during the same operation when the *Augsburg* was mined east of Bornholm. However, the German official history could claim that thanks to the bold sorties of German cruisers against the Russian coast, the command of the sea (*Seeherrschaft*) in the Baltic remained in their hands despite the numerical inferiority of their Baltic forces. They may have suffered heavier losses, but this was because they were on the offensive. Russian historians hotly dispute the contention that the Germans were in control of the Baltic, and claim that the Russian minelaying offensive forced the German fleet to shift from offensive to defensive operations and concentrate on sweeping mines in the southern portion of the Baltic. They also claim that the minelaying offensive forced the Germans to detach considerable forces from the North Sea and that this has never been acknowledged by British historians.[21] There is some merit to both viewpoints, but it is important to remember that the Baltic was essentially a *secondary* theater for the Germans and that one of their major strategic interests, the crucial traffic in iron ore from Swedish ports, remained essentially undisturbed. The greatest potential threat to that important traffic could come from submarines. In the early months of the war, the Russians lacked suitable submarines for long-range operations, but that situation had the potential to change when the first British submarines were detached to the Baltic.

BRITISH SUBMARINES

We have already seen how the Baltic held a certain fascination for British naval leaders in the early stages of the war. Unfortunately, the bravest and most skillful sailor cannot change the realities of geography. Fisher's great plans for Baltic operations ultimately came to nothing; the potential losses far exceeded the potential gains for any operation aimed at surface ships breaking into that closed sea. But if it was impracticable to send surface ships, what of submarines? The possibility was raised by the commodore of submarines, Roger Keyes, at the Loch Ewe conference on 17 September. The German submarines had quickly demonstrated their potential, but British submarines operating under difficult conditions in the Helgoland Bight had few and fleeting targets. Their chances for success were not improved by the fact it initially had not been realized that the warheads caused the torpedoes to run deeper than the lighter, practice warheads on torpedoes before the war. The Admiralty authorized Keyes to carry out submarine reconnaissances of the Kattegat, and on 10 October Keyes submitted a plan for a submarine attack on the German patrols at the southern entrance to the Sound. The Admiralty approved the proposal and decided the submarines would remain in the Baltic.[22]

Three boats of the new E class, E.1, E.9, and E.11, departed for the Baltic on 15 October, delayed for a day because of E.11's defects. The submarines attempted to pass the Sound at two-hour intervals during the night. E.1, commanded by Lieutenant Commander Noel F. Laurence, succeeded in reaching the Baltic by 11:30 P.M. on the 17th, but the presence of a submarine in the Skaggerak had been reported to the Germans, and E.1's unsuccessful attack on the old training cruiser Viktoria Luise between Möen and Falsterbo Reef confirmed the fact. The Germans realized that it was not likely to be a Russian submarine this far from the Russian coast and that it was therefore British. They strengthened their patrols. They also withdrew all heavy ships exercising in Kiel Bay (including the Third and Fourth squadrons of the High Sea Fleet and the new battle cruiser Derfflinger on trials) into harbor, thereby depriving the British of very attractive targets. The southwestern Baltic until now had been a relatively secure area for training.

The second submarine, E.9, commanded by Lieutenant Commander Max K. Horton—the future commander of Western Approaches in the Second World War—did not get into the Baltic until the night of the 18th, and Horton had to cut short a planned sweep into Danzig Bay because of a defect in his main motor.

The third submarine, E.11, commanded by Lieutenant Commander Martin E. Nasmith, was prevented by patrols from passing the Sound and eventually had to return to England. On the 19th Nasmith fired two torpedoes at what he assumed to be the German submarine U.3 but fortunately missed: the submarine turned out to be the Danish Havmanden. The diplomatic repercussions were slight; it was an honest mistake, for the Danes had, unknown to the Admiralty and therefore not represented in the recognition books, changed the appearance of the submarine by adding two wireless masts. The Danes also admitted that the numeral 3 was painted on the conning tower; the submarine's ensign was old, dirty, and clinging to the mast; and the incident took place outside of territorial waters.[23] The incident demonstrated the very real dangers to neutral warships when the great powers were at war. E.11 subsequently enjoyed brilliant success, and Nasmith earned a Victoria Cross at the Dardanelles the following year.

The two British submarines in the Baltic had been extremely lucky. They had been ordered to proceed to the Russian base at Libau when their fuel ran low. The Admiralty, incredible as it may seem, apparently did not know that the Russians had evacuated the base and blocked the entrance with sunken ships, or that there was a German minefield off the port through which *E.1* blithely passed. It is even more incredible to learn that Admiral Essen had not been advised British submarines were on their way.[24] As the British naval attaché in Petrograd reported:

The Admiralty, and Admiral von Essen [sic], are greatly pleased by the despatch of these boats to the Baltic, where it is hoped that they can produce considerable effect; if not immediately, on account of the lateness of the season, at any rate next spring. At the same time Admiral von Essen confided to me that he would have been even more pleased had he received timely notice of their coming, or been informed beforehand as to whose orders they were intended to be subordinate, since through ignorance on these points his own plans for a full fortnight were entirely upset. . . .

Essen was forced to cancel a planned minelaying operation off Danzig until he could learn more about their movements.[25]

The Germans in the Baltic now had an attack of "submarine-itis" similar to that which plagued the Grand Fleet that autumn. On 19 October there were positive reports of periscopes and torpedo tracks in Kiel Bay at a time when neither *E.1* nor *E.9* was within 100 miles. They also made what turned out to be an ineffective attempt to net the Fehmarn Belt, using herring nets because nothing else was available, in the hope they might foul a submarine's propeller and force it to the surface. By the end of the month, the nets had drifted into Kiel Bay where they hampered shipping. The Germans also prevailed upon the Swedes to extinguish most lights and remove navigational marks in the Sound, and the Danes increased their patrols so submarines could not use channels in Danish territorial waters.[26] The presence of a mere two submarines complicated—but did not stop—German operations at sea for the remainder of the year.

E.1 and *E.9* proceeded from Libau to Lapvik, which was to be their base on the Finnish coast. The Admiralty placed the submarines under the orders of Admiral Essen to work with Russian submarines in Baltic operations. After their refit, Essen ordered them on 13 November to take offensive action against the German fleet near and to the west of Bornholm. In December they were ordered to cooperate with the Russian fleet on the minelaying operations. There is no space here to recount the story of these submarine operations in detail. Neither the British nor Russian submarines scored any major success that year. The British submarines also were plagued with engine defects and other mechanical difficulties, and their supply line for parts and spares from England was a tenuous one, by way of the northern Russian ports and then by slow journey over Russian rail lines to the submarine bases. Furthermore, in 1914 Essen used the boats exclusively against German warships rather than against the vital German shipping carrying ore from Sweden. Unfortunately, the British submarine cruises usually did not coincide with periods when the German squadrons were at sea. The prevalence of mines throughout the Baltic tended to confine submarine operations to waters west of Bornholm, and beyond antisubmarine patrols hardly any Germans were sighted. The winter conditions caused other problems; spray froze, making the bridge a mass of ice and requiring continuous efforts to keep the conning-tower hatch free of ice.[27] The handful of submarines could not accomplish miracles, and it would have been erroneous to have expected them to radically transform the situation in the Baltic. Nevertheless, they would be reinforced and much more successful after the thaw in 1915.

THE 1915 CAMPAIGN

The essential lines of the German and Russian strategies in the Baltic in 1915 did not change. The situation was complicated, however, by the defeats suffered by the Russian army, which gave the German army control of much of the Courland coast and enhanced the importance of operations in the vast Gulf of Riga and its southern entrance at the Irben Strait. British submarines in the Baltic, later reinforced, caused additional problems for the Germans. Prince Heinrich did not expect Russian battleships to undertake any offensive operations against the German coast except in strategic liaison with some British objective. The Germans would therefore with small forces and minor offensive operations discourage the Russians from an offensive. German light forces were deployed as far forward as possible into the Gulf of Finland in order to give prompt intelligence of any threatening movement by the larger ships of the Russian fleet. The Germans did not have a base available for their own battleships in Danzig until that summer, and then it was only sufficient for ships of the *Deutschland* class. The observation of the Gulf of Finland, therefore, had to be as continuous as possible. Offensive and defensive mining secured the approximately 320 miles of German coast from Memel to Swinemunde. As for submarines, the Germans had only a very few generally old craft available for the Baltic.[28]

The Russian high command remained committed to the defensive for the bulk of the fleet with only slight modifications. The naval situation for the Russians would improve in the course of the year with the entry in service of the remaining three dreadnoughts. How soon they would work up to efficient units was another question. The Russians had also begun the war deficient in destroyers, with only the *Novik* (1,260 tons) up to modern standards. The Russians added two more of the same class during the year, as well as three *Bars*-class submarines. The core of the fleet, however, still had as its major objective the defense of the capital by preventing a German breakthrough into the eastern part of the Gulf of Finland. The dreadnoughts and two most modern predreadnoughts (*Andrei Pervozvanny* and *Imperator Pavel I*) together with the cruisers would fight from behind the central mine-artillery position in conjunction with the coast artillery. The battleships would engage the major German units seeking to break through, the cruisers would engage the German minesweepers, and Russian destroyers, deployed between the rear of the minefields and the heavy ships, would engage German destroyers and submarines. The Russians also planned to deploy submarines along the approaches to the "Central Position."

All of this assumed the Germans would make a major attempt to break into the

Gulf of Finland, which by early 1915 the Russian naval staff doubted. They believed the Germans would be more likely to act in the Gulf of Bothnia or the approaches to the Gulf of Finland. They therefore redeployed their forces and shifted two old battleships (the *Slava* and *Tsarevitch*), two cruisers, two divisions of submarines, two gunboats, two minelayers, and a seaplane transport to the area between Abo on the Finnish coast and the Åland Islands. Four gunboats, a destroyer, and two submarines were stationed among the skerries off the southern Finnish coast. A division of destroyers and torpedo boats was deployed to the Moon Sound region along with a division (approximately six) of submarines, joined later by two gunboats and a minelayer. In early July the Russians also began laying a new "Forward Position" between Hangö and the island of Dagö while they strengthened the "Central Position" by laying antisubmarine nets in front of the minefield.

The Russians carried on their policy of integrating coastal batteries with naval operations, continuing the construction of batteries in the Åland Islands region and Moon Sound. The Russians in fortifying the Åland Islands were in violation of the 1856 treaties ending the Crimean War, which had provided for their demilitarization. The Åland and Moon Sound positions were located on the flank of any force trying to blockade or break into the Gulf of Finland. The importance of the Moon Sound and Gulf of Riga regions grew as the German army advanced along the Courland coast, and in the summer of 1915 the Russians began the construction of a forward naval base in the Rogokul Islands in the Gulf of Riga. On 2 May, when the ice had thawed sufficiently, the Russians commenced mining the Irben Strait, the southern entrance to the Gulf of Riga. These minefields were systematically extended and renewed throughout the year with, according to Russian sources, a total of 2,179 mines. The Russians also dredged Moon Sound to a depth of 28 feet, so that eventually battleships and cruisers could enter from the Gulf of Finland. The Russian high command planned to continue their offensive minelaying operations off the German coast, and they also planned to extend submarine operations against German communications, but they continued to eschew an active role for their main forces on the high seas outside of the Gulf of Finland. The distinctive feature about Russian planning was the close integration of naval forces with minefields and coastal artillery. It was indeed a form of naval trench warfare.[29]

The great offensive by the Central Powers began on 2 May in the Gorlice-Tarnów area of western Galicia, hundreds of miles from the Baltic. As a preliminary move, the army high command ordered Armeegruppe Lauenstein to attack on the extreme left of the German line on 27 April in order to tie down Russian forces. The army requested naval support, and on 27 April the cruisers *Lübeck* and *Thetis* shelled Libau. With the success of the German land offensive, the army announced its intention to take Libau by a surprise assault and again requested naval support. On 7 May a strong German naval force under the command of Rear Admiral Hopman, chief of the Baltic reconnaissance forces, shelled Russian positions around Libau. Two destroyers bombarded Steinort to the north. The old (1890) coast-defense ship *Beowulf* joined the armored cruisers *Prinz Adalbert* (flag), *Roon,* and *Prinz Heinrich;* the small cruisers *Thetis,*

Augsburg, and *Lübeck;* and the inevitable destroyers, torpedo boats, and minesweepers. The Baltic forces were reinforced from the High Sea Fleet. The Fourth Scouting Group under Rear Admiral Scheidt, consisting of the cruisers *Stettin, München, Stuttgart,* and *Danzig* and two destroyer flotillas (twenty-one destroyers), covered the operation from any Russian surface forces that might sortie from the Gulf of Finland or Riga by patrolling for several days along the line Gotskar Sandö (island north of Gotland)–Ösel and in the channel between Gotskar Sandö and the Swedish coast (Hufvudskär).

The Russians replied to the German operations in the characteristic manner. On the night of 6–7 May, the *Novik,* four *Okhotnik*-class (615 tons) and six *Ukraina*-class (580 tons) destroyers were sent to lay mines off Libau in areas the German minesweepers had already worked. Rear Admiral Bakhirev with the armored cruisers *Admiral Makarov* and *Bayan* and cruisers *Oleg* and *Bogatyr* came out to support them. The Russians also sent *E.1* and *E.9* to sea, the former, towed by icebreakers to open waters, went on a wild-goose chase due to faulty intelligence that a German battle cruiser would be passing to the north of Bornholm. The Russian cruisers clashed inconclusively with the *München* of the Fourth Scouting Group, but the Germans, uncertain of Russian strength, did not close. The Russian destroyers, steaming to the east and close to the coast, were undetected and succeeded in laying their mines. One of the officers in the *Novik* was surprised they were not spotted with "their funnels emitting flames like torches."[30]

Prince Heinrich now decided to make use of the Seventh Battleship Division of the Fourth Squadron (four *Wittelsbach* class) under Vice Admiral Ehrhard Schmidt, which had been placed at his disposal and were at Kiel. Schmidt, accompanied by the cruiser *Danzig* but without any destroyer screen against submarines, was to proceed to the west of Gotland and Gotska Sandö to waters off the Gulf of Finland in order to be in a position to intercept the Russian cruisers if they tried another sortie. Schmidt did not have sufficient cruisers for scouting (except for the *Danzig*) and encountered nothing on his cruise from the 8th to the 10th of May.

The German bombardment of the Russian positions around Libau on 7 May was undisturbed by the Russian minelaying operations, and the following night the Russians evacuated the city. When German light forces entered the harbor early on the morning of the 8th, however, the new destroyer *V.107* had her bow blown off by a mine and became a total loss. What of the British submarines? *E.1* (Laurence) fired at the cruiser *Amazone* near the approaches to the Sound, but missed, and on the way back to base spotted the four battleships of Schmidt's squadron early on the morning of the 10th, but they were too far off to attack. On the 7th *E.9* (Horton) fired on the destroyer *S.20* on patrol off Brüsterort, but the destroyer saw the torpedo track and took evasive action. On the 10th Horton also appears to have spotted the smoke of Schmidt's four battleships and spent most of the day maneuvering unsuccessfully to get close enough to attack. The next morning *E.9* attacked the armored cruiser *Roon*, one of three cruisers and several destroyers accompanying three transports on their way back from Libau. They were actually the mother ships for the auxiliary mine-hunting division returning to Neufahrwasser to coal. Horton knew he had missed the *Roon*, but thought from the sound of an explosion that he had sunk one of the transports. This was not the case; the torpedo must have exploded after striking the bottom.[31]

The Germans had taken a considerable risk with the old battleships and cruisers and had been very lucky. The forces detached from the High Sea Fleet were recalled to the North Sea shortly after the capture of Libau. The German navy had been sharply divided on the retention of Libau, both before and after the operation. The initial German objective had been to render the port useless to the Russians. Prince Heinrich, who had repeatedly advocated a landing at Libau, and Admiral Hopman had been in favor of its retention, but the Admiralstab, chief of the High Sea Fleet, and Tirpitz had been opposed. They believed retention of the port would require resources the navy could not spare, especially when coupled with the demands for garrisoning and administering bases on the coast of Flanders. In the end it was probably the military success on land that decided the issue. Once Libau was firmly in German hands, the navy eventually developed it into a useful base, much closer to the decisive waters at the entrance to the Gulfs of Finland and Riga.[32]

On 20 May Admiral Essen died suddenly as the result of a lung infection. He was undoubtedly the outstanding Russian seaman of the war. His successor was Vice Admiral Kanin, who had commanded the minelaying forces. Generally acknowledged as competent, he does not appear to have had the commanding personality of his predecessor. A British officer attached to the tsar's staff noted in his diary: "He wears glasses and looks (as the Emperor said to me) more like a Professor than an Admiral." Essen was supposed to have recommended his chief of staff, Vice Admiral Kerber, as his successor, but the latter was alleged to have been passed over because of his German name.[33] Kanin soon asked for permission to employ the new dreadnoughts outside of the Gulf of Finland. Once again the high command refused the request.

The war of mines went on. The *Deutschland*, escorted by cruisers, laid another field near the Oleg Bank southeast of the island of Utö at the entrance to the Gulf of Finland on 24 May, and *U.26* managed to slip into the Gulf of Finland and on 4 June torpedo and sink the Russian minelayer *Yenisei* between Odensholm and Baltic Port. The minelayer, hugging the shore en route to Moon Sound, sank with heavy loss of life. The Germans were less successful from the 3d to the 5th of June when they tried to penetrate the Irben Strait and use torpedo boats to lay mines at the southern entrance to Moon Sound while seaplanes launched from within the Gulf of Riga by the seaplane carrier *Glyndwr* attacked the Mühlgraben works near Dünamünde. The *Glyndwr* (2,245 tons) was a British freighter interned at Danzig when the war began and subsequently modified to carry four seaplanes. The Russians were alert, and the Germans ran into a hornet's nest of opposition, including two gunboats and sixteen destroyers and torpedo boats. The Russian submarine *Okun* attempted to torpedo one of the German armored cruisers covering the operation, only to be rammed by the destroyer *G.135*. The submarine escaped with a bent periscope. The Germans broke off the attempt to break into the gulf, but the *Glyndwr* struck a mine off Windau while returning to Libau and was badly damaged. Off Lyserort, two destroyers coaling from the collier *Dora Hugo Stinnes* were attacked by *E.9* on the morning of the 5th. The collier was sunk and *S.148* badly damaged.

The Gulf of Riga was steadily becoming a focal point of naval activity as the German army advanced in Courland. The First World War on the eastern front was far different than the picture most people have derived from the more familiar fighting in the west. It was much more fluid, and this was particularly true in Courland, for the major fighting and great battles were taking place far to the south in Poland and Galicia. Courland and the Baltic represented the extreme left flank of the German line. The area consisted to a large extent of barren wastes, and when the German offensive began in April, the front lines were made up of block posts at 10-mile intervals. Roads and communications were poor, and the Germans had few troops to spare for the area. The German forces, the Armeegruppe Lauenstein (the name subsequently changed to Niemen-Armee), represented approximately five and a half infantry and seven and a half cavalry divisions. The Russians retreated steadily under German pressure. The Germans occupied Windau on 18 July, and the advance did not stop until the Russians established a strong line before Riga.[34]

The German navy cooperated with the German army as it advanced on Windau, bombarding Russian positions and clashing with Russian destroyers on 28 June. At the end of the month, the Russians decided to use their cruisers for a raid on Memel, ostensibly to influence German public opinion at a moment when the kaiser was supposed to review the German fleet at Kiel and to offset German propaganda about control in the Baltic. Rear Admiral Bakhirev, flying his flag in the *Admiral Makarov*, sailed shortly after midnight on 1 July in company with the *Bayan*, *Bogatyr*, and *Oleg*. The *Rurik* and the destroyer *Novik* followed. The Russians deployed submarines in advance along the possible route of German warships in case they put to sea. The other Russian destroyers were considered to be too slow and were left behind. The *Rurik* and *Novik* lost contact with the other Russian forces in thick fog, and Bakhirev was forced to postpone the bombardment for a day. The Russians initially intended to proceed down the east coast of Gotland with the bombardment of Memel scheduled for dawn on the 2d.

Fresh intelligence of German movements caused Bakhirev to alter his plans. On the evening of 1 July, the minelayer *Albatross* laid minefields to the northeast and northwest of Bogskär. She was escorted by the cruisers *Roon*, *Augsburg*, and *Lübeck* and seven destroyers. The Germans had apparently passed very near to the Russians on the night of the 1st, but fog had prevented them from sighting each other. The German senior officer, Commodore von Karpf in the *Augsburg*, then reported that he had completed his mission and was returning to base, giving his position, course, and speed. This was intercepted by the Russians, and Bakhirev realized he had the opportunity to intercept the Germans with superior forces. He canceled the planned operation against Riga and steamed to intercept. The ability of the Russian naval staff to read German wireless messages enabled them to advise Bakhirev of changes in the Germans' course and speed. Consequently, there was every chance the superior Russian force (two or three armored cruisers and two light cruisers) would catch the single German armored cruiser, two cruisers, minelayer, and seven destroyers.

Despite their advantage in intelligence, the Russians scored only a partial success. Shortly before they encountered the Russians, the *Albatross* and *Augsburg*, accompanied by three destroyers, separated from the German force to proceed via the south end of Gotland to Rixhöft while the remainder of the force proceeded via Steinort to Libau. Just after 6:30 on the morning of the 2d, the *Augsburg* sighted the Russians. Outnumbered by the four Russian cruisers, Karpf broke toward the west and recalled the *Roon* and *Lübeck* by wireless. Although the *Augsburg* was one of the fastest German cruisers in the Baltic and had an advantage in speed over the Russians, the *Albatross* was slower. Karpf ordered the *Albatross* to make for the safety of Swedish territorial waters at Gotland, while the *Augsburg*, under cover of smoke from the destroyers, escaped to the south. The *Albatross*, badly damaged, ran aground in sinking condition in Swedish waters near Östergarn. The Russian cruisers had, according to the Russian official history, wasted time and ammunition in a poorly coordinated effort to destroy her while the remainder of the Germans escaped. They were therefore low on ammunition when they started back toward the Gulf of Finland and encountered the *Roon*, *Lübeck*, and the four destroyers at approximately 9:00. Bakhirev called on the *Rurik* for assistance, but low on ammunition, broke off the action after the *Bayan* and *Roon* scored hits on each other. Neither was seriously damaged. The Russian admiral also called on the old battleships *Slava* and *Tsarevitch*, then anchored at Örö (northwest of Bengtskär) to support the cruisers. The Germans, fearing an attempt to draw them toward superior forces, also turned away to rejoin the *Augsburg*. The *Rurik*, as yet unengaged and whose four 23.5-cm guns outgunned anything in the German force, encountered the Germans at 9:45. The *Rurik* engaged the *Roon* but suddenly turned away as a result of what turned out to be a false submarine alarm. The Russians lost contact.

The Germans' troubles were not yet over. Admiral Hopman put to sea in the *Prinz Adalbert* together with *Prinz Heinrich* after receiving wireless reports of the engagement. The German armored cruisers ran into thick fog at first, and then in the early afternoon (1:57) encountered Max Horton in *E.9*. Horton succeeded in torpedoing the *Prinz Adalbert*. Destroyers hunted *E.9* without success but prevented Horton from following up his attack, and the Germans managed to get the ship back to port.

The Russians had more reason than the Germans to be dissatisfied with the results of 2 July, for despite their initial advantage, they had succeeded in eliminating only the minelayer *Albatross*, subsequently raised and interned in Sweden for the duration of the war.[35] The events of 2 July remind one of similar incidents in the North Sea, especially the Dogger Bank action. Priceless secret intelligence derived from wireless intercepts is used to obtain an initial advantage that nevertheless fails to yield the desired tactical result. The excessive attention paid to the *Albatross* in this case parallels the example of the *Blücher* in the earlier episode.

The immediate German response to the loss of the *Albatross* and damaging of the *Prinz Adalbert* was to offset the bad impression and retain the morale advantage by detaching Vice Admiral Schmidt's Fourth Squadron (the *Wittelsbach* [flag], *Wettin*, *Mecklenburg*, *Schwaben*, *Zähringen*, *Baunschweig*, and *Elsass*) from the North Sea along with the Eighth Torpedo Boat Flotilla (eleven destroyers). To retain that same morale edge, on the 11th and 19th of July the Germans undertook cruiser reconnaissances toward the entrance to the Gulf of Finland, with the battleships in support. They also hoped to catch the Russians should the latter repeat their sortie of 2 July against the light craft supporting the advance of the German army.

The German army entered Windau on 18 July and soon extended its control along the entire southern shore of the Irben Strait and much of the southern part of the Gulf of Riga. Naval operations on the flanks of the army grew in importance, and the vast Gulf of Riga for more than two years became the focal point of surface operations in the Baltic. The Russians also strengthened their naval forces: there would eventually be 4 gunboats, whose shallow draught facilitated support of the seaward flank of the army; a minelayer; 6 submarines; 25 destroyers and torpedo boats; the seaplane carrier *Orlitsa* (with 4 aircraft); the new forward base at Rogokul; an airfield on the island of Runö; new coastal batteries; and, of course, the inevitable minefields. As the German threat to the Gulf of Riga developed, the Russians added the old battleship *Slava* to the defense. Moon Sound had not yet been dredged to a sufficient depth for the battleship to enter the gulf from the north, and she therefore had to come in through the southern entrance at the Irben Strait. This meant leaving the Gulf of Finland and entering the Baltic. The move was made at night, under heavy destroyer escort and with the new dreadnoughts *Gangut* and *Petropavlovsk* entering the Baltic for the first time to cover the operation.

The inherent mobility of sea power enabled the Germans to establish unchallenged superiority in the Baltic any time they cared to detach sufficient forces from the North Sea to do so. The Germans might have had control of the sea in the Baltic, but the Russian navy could have claimed control of the Gulf of Riga. The Germans found it difficult to bring their superior force to bear here, and the Russians proved to be difficult to dislodge.

Vice Admiral Schmidt had developed plans for the Gulf of Riga that called for the southern and central channels of the Irben Strait to be swept clear of mines, allowing his battleships and cruisers to enter the gulf, defeat Russian naval forces, and permit the *Deutschland* to block the southern entrance to Moon Sound with mines. The Germans also intended to sink blockships in the harbor of Pernau and shell Dünamünde. Schmidt hoped his operations against the Gulf of Riga might also succeed in drawing the Russian fleet out of the Gulf of Finland and into the Baltic. The Germans therefore detached powerful forces from the High Sea Fleet under the command of Vice Admiral Hipper. They included eight dreadnoughts (the *Ostfriesland, Thüringen, Helgoland, Oldenburg, Rheinland, Posen, Nassau,* and *Westfalen*) of the First Squadron; the battle cruisers *Seydlitz, Moltke,* and *Von der Tann* of the First Scouting Group; the Second Scouting Group with four light cruisers; and the cruiser *Kolberg* leading three and a half flotillas of thirty-two destroyers. A mine-hunting division of thirteen boats joined the minesweeping forces of the Baltic.

The Germans estimated their operations in the Gulf of Riga would take two days, and the sweepers began their work at dawn on 8 August. The sweeping took much longer than anticipated; the Russian forces including the *Slava* (four 12-inch, twelve 6-

inch guns) and the gunboats *Khrabri* and *Grozyashchi*, as well as aircraft, resisted stoutly. The battleships *Braunschweig* and *Elsass* kept the *Slava* at bay, but Schmidt decided to break off the action when it was apparent that even if they succeeded in breaking through the minefields, the *Deutschland* would not be able to block Moon Sound during the moonless night and if they waited until the following morning the Germans would be exposed to submarine attacks from boats certain to be sent from Revel and Helsingfors. The number of German torpedo craft available for escort was dwindling, and if Schmidt waited until the next day to break into the gulf his light craft would be running low on coal. The unsuccessful operation cost the Germans two mine hunters, and a destroyer and the cruiser *Thetis* were damaged by mines.

Schmidt was determined to try again. In the meantime, on 10 August the cruisers *Roon* and *Prinz Heinrich* bombarded the Russian positions at Zerel at the tip of the Sworbe Peninsula, the southernmost tip of Osel Island, the northern shore of the Irben Strait. The Russian destroyers at anchor off Zerel were surprised, and one was damaged. The same day Hipper sent one of his battle cruisers, the *Von der Tann*, and the cruiser *Kolberg* to bombard Utö in the skerries to the north of the entrance to the Gulf of Finland. The operation was broken off because of repeated reports of submarines. The Russians were not idle during this period either. The minelayer *Amur* and the destroyers continued to lay mines in the Irben Strait, restoring areas cleared by the Germans on the 8th.

The second German attack on the Irben Strait began at dawn on 16 August. Schmidt altered his plans slightly from those of the 8th. He did not take the Fourth Squadron or old armored cruisers of the Baltic forces with him. Instead, he used the dreadnoughts *Posen* and *Nassau* for the break into the gulf, because they enjoyed much better underwater protection. They were accompanied by the light cruisers *Graudenz*, *Pillau*, *Bremen*, and *Augsburg*; the large destroyers *V.99* and *V.100*; three torpedo-boat flotillas (31 boats); the minelayer *Deutschland*; and the minesweepers and blockships. Hipper remained in the Baltic with the three battle cruisers, the four *Helgoland*-class dreadnoughts, the remaining two *Nassau*-class dreadnoughts, the two *Braunschweig*-class predreadnoughts, five cruisers, and three destroyer flotillas (32 boats). This time Schmidt allowed considerably more time for minesweeping, with the entire operation taking at least five days. All unnecessary ships were sent back to Libau, so those on the scene could be given better protection against submarines. The five old *Wittelsbach*-class battleships therefore remained in Libau.

The Germans lost the minesweeper *T.46* the first day, although the *Posen* and *Nassau* succeeded in keeping the *Slava* at a distance. After the first day's operation, Admiral Schmidt sent the destroyers *V.99* and *V.100* to work their way around the minefields close to the coast and make a night attack against the *Slava*. The destroyers succeeded in getting into the gulf, but the *Slava* had been withdrawn behind net defenses in Arensburg Bay (Ösel). The Germans clashed with Russian destroyers a few times in the darkness, and on their return encountered the *Novik* joined by three more Russian destroyers. *V.99* was hit and set on fire, and on trying to break out ran into a minefield, detonated two mines, and was lost. The minesweeping continued on the 17th, with the

Nassau and *Posen* scoring three hits on the *Slava*, which withdrew from the scene to Moon Sound.

The Germans finally steamed into the gulf on the morning of the 19th. Most of the Russian surface ships had withdrawn to Kuiwast anchorage in Moon Sound, approximately 80 nautical miles from the Irben Strait. The minelayer *Amur* laid a minefield to protect the southern entrance to Moon Sound. Some Russian ships were cut off. That evening the *Augsburg*, returning from a reconnaissance of Pernau, encountered the two gunboats *Sivutch* and *Korietz* attempting to escape to Kuiwast after having laid a minefield off Dünamünde the preceding night. The dreadnought *Posen* joined the duel, and the doomed *Sivutch* was sunk. The *Korietz* escaped in the darkness only to run ashore in Pernau Bay. Her crew blew her up the following day. The same night the Germans lost the destroyer *S.31* to a mine just to the west of Runö. On the 20th, the Germans blocked the entrance to Pernau while the bulk of the German forces advanced to the entrance to Moon Sound, but after receiving reports of enemy submarines, Schmidt decided in the afternoon to forego laying mines and to retire. His ships lacked maneuverability in the constricted waters and difficult channels where mines were suspected and poor visibility made it hard to fix his position. He also realized that the Russians were now forewarned, and after the Germans left the gulf the minefield would not hinder them for more than three days. Poor visibility and the potential threat of the *Slava* in their rear also caused the Germans to abandon their intent to bombard Dünamünde. There were three Russian submarines in the gulf, but they did not achieve any success, and the Germans completed their evacuation without further loss. They nearly suffered a very serious loss outside of the gulf in the Baltic when Laurence in *E.1* torpedoed the battle cruiser *Moltke* west of Dagö on the morning of the 19th. The *Moltke* was hit in the bow but was in no immediate danger and could easily maintain 15 knots. German destroyers prevented Laurence from making a second attack.

Prince Heinrich was satisfied that even though the Germans had not achieved all their operational goals, such as destruction of the *Slava* or laying the minefield off Moon Sound, the operation was nevertheless a success if only from the point of morale. They had forced the powerful Russian position at Irben and had inflicted loss on Russian forces in the gulf. The Admiralstab did not agree, and the forces from the High Sea Fleet were sent back to the North Sea. Hipper was not sorry to leave the Baltic. He wrote of the operations: "To keep valuable ships for a considerable time in a limited area in which enemy submarines were increasingly active, with the corresponding risk of damage and loss, was to indulge in a gamble out of all proportion to the advantage to be derived from the occupation of the Gulf *before* the capture of Riga from the land side."[36] He did not favor repeating the operation until the army was ready to cooperate, a view shared by Schmidt and Tirpitz. The capture of Riga would have to wait for another two years. Colonel Max Hoffman, the brilliant staff officer with the German Eighth Army, noted in his diary on 28 August: "We must do without Riga—unless the Russians abandon it to us. We are too weak up there."[37]

The German official history takes the view that the assaults had their most decisive effect in confirming the Russian naval leadership in an essentially defensive attitude—preoccupied with establishing the "Forward Position" in the Gulf of Finland or fortifying the entrances to the Gulf of Riga—in an area that was for the Germans a secondary theater, to be held with what could be spared from the North Sea.[38] But were the attacks on the Gulf of Riga necessary to accomplish this? One could seriously question whether the destruction of a pair of small gunboats and a few merchantmen in the gulf was worth the loss of two destroyers and a minesweeper and the even greater potential risks to capital ships involved, particularly if the Germans were not going to establish a permanent naval presence in the gulf. To do so would probably entail the capture of one or more of the islands (such as Ösel). The Germans would not make another serious attempt on Irben Strait until they took Ösel in October of 1917. In the meantime Russian naval forces in the gulf soon resumed their activities harassing the flank of the German army and, of course, restoring the mines cleared by the Germans. Russian cruisers also resumed minelaying in the Baltic, and at the end of August the *Oleg* and *Bogatyr* laid a field east of Gotland. The dreadnoughts *Sevastopol* and *Gangut* came out into the Baltic as far south as the 58th parallel to cover the operation, their farthest venture so far.

THE BRITISH AND RUSSIAN SUBMARINE OFFENSIVE

The Soviet official history of the war, in a manner reminiscent of the demands for a "second front now" during the Second World War, claims that despite Russian requests for help during the attack on the Gulf of Riga, the British fleet "remained a passive observer throughout the operation."[39] The Germans certainly did not exclude the possibility the British would intervene, and when their Baltic operations began, von Pohl and his flagship *Friedrich der Grosse* along with the *Kaiser*-class dreadnoughts of the Third Squadron were shifted to the Elbe for quick access to the Baltic if necessary.[40] There is the inevitable question of just what the Grand Fleet could have done to influence Baltic operations short of a probably ill-advised attempt to break into the Baltic, which the Admiralty had rejected in the past. The British, in fact, did send more of what had proved to be a most effective weapon—submarines. The French also seriously considered doing so. Up to then the British submarines in the Baltic had been used essentially against naval targets. What of German trade? With the German flag virtually driven from the high seas, British submarines would have found few targets. However, within the closed waters of the Baltic, the Germans were able to carry on a substantial and vital trade, particularly in regard to iron ore from Sweden. This traffic finally became a major object after the summer of 1915.

On 5 June Commander Grenfell, the naval attaché in Russia, recommended to the British ambassador that if the Admiralty could spare more submarines for the Baltic, they would very likely produce useful results, especially as the Germans came to realize their naval strength could not be employed effectively in the North Sea and would be tempted to employ it against the Russians. Initially the Admiralty were inclined to refuse; they had just sent reinforcements to the Dardanelles, and boats could not be spared from home waters. Moreover, the risks to them in their passage to the Baltic had considerably increased since 1914. However, Commander Laurence in a private letter to Commodore Hall (Commodore [S]) on 30 June, pointed out there was employment for plenty of submarines in the Baltic and that the Russians had only two boats—with another pair soon to join—that could be used for offensive action. The Admiralty, for reasons still not clear, reversed themselves, and *E.8* (Lieutenant Commander F. H. J. Goodhart) and *E.13* (Lieutenant Commander G. Layton) sailed for the Baltic on 15 August. Two more British submarines would follow when conditions were suitable. On 17 August, with the submarines on their way, Grenfell reported the Russian admiralty's request for a diversion as German naval pressure on the Gulf of Riga grew.[41]

Commander Laurence had suggested that a suitable action to facilitate the passage of more submarines into the Baltic would be a destroyer and cruiser raid through the Sound to attack the German forces guarding the southern entrance. The Admiralty examined the possibilities of some action of this sort in the autumn of 1915 but were not impressed with the possibilities. Destroyers lacked sufficient range for the operation and would have to be refueled, probably in sheltered waters in the Skaggerak or Kattegat. The British were certain to be spotted, giving the Germans sufficient time to lay their mines at the southern entrance to the Sound and escape. Light cruisers, if they entered the Baltic, would be more vulnerable to mines and liable to be cut off by German forces from Kiel. The cruisers would be forced to seek the shelter of Russian ports to refuel, their route flanked by the German flotillas, and the British were unlikely to see them again in the North Sea.[42]

E.13 did not make it through the Sound into the Baltic. On the night of 18–19 August, the submarine ran aground due to a defective gyrocompass in the shallows off Saltholm Island. Layton was in Danish territorial waters, and early the next morning the Danish torpedo boat *Narhvalen* arrived to inform Layton that according to international law, he had twenty-four hours to leave Danish territorial waters before he and his submarine would be interned. Layton then sent his first lieutenant in the Danish warship to Copenhagen to report the situation. Shortly afterward the torpedo boat *G.l32* (Oberleutnant zur See Graf von Montgelas) of the German Sound patrol arrived but steamed away when the Danish torpedo boats *Støren* and *Søulven* reached the scene. They were later joined by a third Danish torpedo boat, the *Tumleren*. Montgelas reported the situation by wireless and Rear Admiral Mischke, commanding the Baltic Coast Defense Division, ordered the submarine to be destroyed. Mischke felt he had to act at once as the Riga operation was at the crisis point and the report of the *Moltke*'s torpedoing had just been received. *G.132* therefore returned to the scene with another torpedo boat (not mentioned in German accounts) and opened fire on the submarine, first with a torpedo that hit the bottom and exploded short of the target and then with shell fire. The submarine was hit repeatedly and had to be abandoned. The shelling continued, and the Danish torpedo boat *Søulven* prevented additional loss of life by placing herself between the submarine and the German ships. The Germans claimed the submarine had fired back and hotly denied firing at the men in the water. The Danes protested strongly. E.13 was subsequently refloated and interned along with the surviving officers and men for the duration of the war. Layton refused to give his parole and eventually escaped to Norway—as did his first lieutenant—and then home to resume the war.[43]

The brutal German violation of international law was a clear indication of just how seriously they took the threat of those British submarines. Even worse from the German point of view, E.13's companion E.8 reached Revel safely, although not without incident. Furthermore, two additional submarines, E.18 (Lieutenant Commander R. C. Halahan) and E.19 (Lieutenant Commander F. N. A. Cromie), sailed for the Baltic on 4 September. Both also arrived safely, although E.18 had a particularly harrowing passage through the Sound, and the British were perhaps fortunate the German patrols were not yet equipped with depth charges.[44] The Royal Navy now had five submarines in the Baltic, but it was apparent that further passages through the Sound might become prohibitively expensive.

The Russians also were beginning to commission the Baltic submarines of their 1912 program. Their completion had been greatly delayed because portions of their equipment had originally been ordered from Germany and the Russians had to scramble for substitutes after war broke out. The Bars class was somewhat slower than the British E class but carried a more powerful torpedo armament. The torpedoes were, however, externally mounted, and on the whole the Bars class, although the most numerous Russian submarine class of the war, did not turn out to be very effective, largely because of its unreliable surface propulsion.[45]

French submarines never operated in the Baltic. The French naval attaché in Petrograd first suggested that they be sent in December 1914 and repeated the request, this time more urgently, in June 1915 after the Russian loss of Libau and Windau, the German advance in Courland, and the disasters in Galicia. He argued that a few more submarines in the Baltic would not give the Russians mastery of the sea, but would complicate German operations.[46] Vice Admiral de Jonquières, chief of the naval staff, ordered Vice Admiral Favereau, commanding the Deuxième escadre légère in the north, to study the project. Favereau was dubious. The French would have to use their longest-range submarines in the north, the Brumaire class, and recent experiences with their diesel engines cast doubts on their robustness and endurance. Favereau considered their chances for success very uncertain and also believed their eventual departure would create gaps in his Channel flotilla, which had already been reduced below what was considered necessary. As long as the enemy was only 25 kilometers from Dunkirk and in a position to threaten Calais, Boulogne, and the northern coast of France, the Baltic could only be viewed by the French as a secondary objective.[47] In July Admiral Roussin, chief of the Russian naval staff, formally asked the French naval attaché for French submarines to cooperate in Baltic naval operations. It must have been approximately the same time he made a similar request to the British. The French were forced to refuse. There was a suggestion about sending small submarines via Archangel to be transported by rail to the Baltic, but this would have involved old boats of little value. Moreover, de Jonquières, in his report to the minister of marine, rallied to Favereau's belief that efficient submarines from the north could not be spared while the German threat to the Channel was so strong. The minister, Victor Augagneur, agreed.[48] Once again, just as at the Dardanelles and in the Adriatic, the lack of suitable materiél in sufficient quantity had prevented French submariners from realizing their ambitions. However, when one considers the experiences of the unhandy French submarines at the Dardanelles and the nerve-wracking experiences of the much more capable British *E* class in passing the Sound, one must conclude it is fortunate they did not make the attempt.

In September the Russians shifted from the traditional use of submarines against naval forces and sent the first submarines to sea with specific orders to operate against shipping between Germany and Sweden. The exact reasons are not clear, but were probably linked to the failure of the Germans to renew their offensive operations in the Gulf of Riga, the recall of ships from the High Sea Fleet to the North Sea, and the fact the Baltic was obviously returning to its status as a purely secondary theater for the Germans and a major German naval offensive need not be feared.[49] It was, however, a Russian decision, and because the submarines were under Russian operational control, the Admiralty were not involved. This, as we shall see, had certain disadvantages from the diplomatic point of view.

On 28 September *E.8, E.19,* and the *Bars* sailed on what appears to be the first of these patrols. By the time *E.19* returned to Revel on 13 October, Cromie had sunk one ship in the western Baltic, driven another onto a reef (it was later salved by the Germans), and had a narrow escape from an antisubmarine net southwest of Bornholm. He then sank four more ships south of the Swedish Öland Island, drove another ship aground, and sent a Swedish ship, the *Nike* (1,800 tons) carrying iron ore to Germany, into Revel as a prize. Cromie had sunk all ships while surfaced, had been plagued by faulty torpedoes, and suffered from considerable diplomatic controversy regarding his activities. One ship, the *Germania* (1,900 tons), had tried to escape to Swedish waters, ran aground 2 miles off the Swedish coast, and was abandoned by her crew. Cromie tried unsuccessfully to tow her into deep waters and removed the ship's papers and some fresh food. A controversy ensued over whether *E.19* had continued firing at the ship after she was in Swedish waters and had set off an explosive charge in the engine room, which the British claimed was a boiler explosion. The ship was later salved by tugs and taken to Germany. The Russians, anxious to avoid unnecessary complications with Sweden, also released the *Nike* on the grounds that the 1909 Declaration of London had not listed ores as contraband. Of the other two boats on this first sortie, *E.8* managed to sink only a single small ship off Stilo on the German coast, and the *Akula* had no luck off Libau. The permanent loss to the Germans was small, only six ships representing about 13,000 tons. By later standards in the war, particularly in the Mediterranean, it would be trifling. Nevertheless, in an area that represented their own back yard and where they had always enjoyed relative security, the losses were very disturbing. The operations also created thick dossiers in the foreign offices and admiralties as diplomats and admirals thrashed out the legal and diplomatic repercussions of what had happened.

From 17 to 26 October, Horton in *E.9* was at sea, primarily off the Swedish coast. He sank three ships, representing approximately 7,700 tons, in the vicinity of Norrköping Bay—a fourth ship failed to sink after her sea cocks were opened and drifted ashore where she was eventually salved. Horton sank his third ship in the presence of the Swedish destroyer *Wale*, rejecting the Swedish warship's claim he was in territorial waters. In this same period, the Russian submarines *Alligator* and *Kaiman* each captured a ship in the Gulf of Bothnia. Russian torpedo boats captured another, although according to the German official history, it was later determined in 1918 that the three had been captured in Swedish territorial waters. The Russians supplemented these activities in the Gulf of Bothnia with a sweep by four cruisers and five destroyers on 28 October, which examined several neutral ships but captured only a single German. The Russians believed a substantial number of German ships loaded with iron ore had been kept in harbor by Swedish authorities after neutral captains warned them about the Russian cruisers. German shipping was able to make good use of Swedish territorial waters in the Gulf of Bothnia, usually venturing outside only at night. The Russians had scant success. A final raid by four Russian destroyers on the night of 21 December, shortly before ice ended operations for the year, failed to bag a single ship.

Goodhart in *E.8* scored one of the more spectacular successes of the submarine campaign while operating off Libau on 23 October. He encountered the recently repaired armored cruiser *Prinz Adalbert* escorted by two destroyers and torpedoed her. One of the cruiser's magazines exploded, and there were only three survivors. It was the heaviest loss of the war for the German Baltic forces.

At the end of October, Cromie and *E.19* returned to the western Baltic and found targets scarce, but sank a 1,000-ton merchantman and on 7 November sank the German cruiser *Undine*. On a later cruise in deteriorating weather, he sank a 1,300-ton steamer west of Bornholm, the final success against German shipping for the year.

For most of the war it had been the Germans who attacked Allied shipping. Now that the shoe was on the other foot and they themselves were the target, how did they react? The October submarine offensive in the Baltic caused considerable disruption to German trade. Shipping companies held their vessels in port, and ferries such as the Sassnitz-Trelleborg line ceased operations. Prince Heinrich recommended ships stay within Swedish territorial waters and, when they could not, proceed only by night. He repeated his prior request that the Baltic receive at least another torpedo boat flotilla and more trawlers. Once again he was told they could not be spared from the High Sea Fleet. The losses of October forced the Germans to reconsider, and on 25 October they transferred two small cruisers and two torpedo boat flotillas to the Baltic, thereby causing the High Sea Fleet to break off an operation in the Skaggerak and temporarily forego future sorties for lack of sufficient destroyers.[50]

The Germans replied to the submarine menace much the same way the British and French had. They deployed their available light craft to patrol key routes, such as the coastal waters between Libau-Brüsterort-Jershöft and the sectors Jershöft-Sassnitz and Sassnitz-Trelleborg. They arranged for aircraft to patrol the coastline, and even experimented with *U.66* towed behind and connected by phone to an innocent-looking vessel, ready to be cast off and attack a hostile submarine. The necessity for antisubmarine patrols also caused the Germans to draw back and weaken their forward line of patrols in the Baltic. The submarine alarm also involved the Germans in an incident with the Swedes. On 21 October the auxiliary patrol boat *Meteor* opened fire on an unidentified submarine in stormy weather southwest of Ystad. The submarine turned out to be the Swedish *Hvalen* proceeding in company with the repair ship *Blenda*. A Swedish sailor was mortally wounded before the Germans spotted the Swedish flag. The Swedish ships were apparently in Swedish territorial waters. The Swedes now had occasion to be as incensed with the Germans as they were with the Allies over the *Germania*. The Germans expressed their regrets and the incident, like that of the Danish submarine *Havmanden* less than two months before, demonstrated how very dangerous it was for neutral submarines to operate in the war zone.

Prince Heinrich was as reluctant as many of the British and French admirals to form convoys, although they were proposed by some of the German shipping concerns. He replied that he did not have enough torpedo boats to escort convoys and that convoys presented a better target for submarines than individual ships. Moreover, ships proceeding with warships as escorts were liable to be torpedoed without warning. It was actually the Swedes who appear to have furnished the first convoys for their own shipping. At the beginning of November, Swedish warships escorted a dozen Swedish steamers from Landsort to Bornholm.[51] Prince Heinrich, in contrast, established certain positions to be permanently occupied by torpedo boats. The most northerly was Häfringe-Landsort in Norrköping Bay off the Swedish coast. There was another area off the northern tip of Öland Island. Every twenty hours a pair of torpedo boats left Libau to patrol to Landsort, remained there eighteen hours, and then cruised southward to and along the east coast of Öland to Segerstad and then back across the Baltic to Libau. When possible, the passage across the Baltic was arranged to cover—but not directly convoy—merchant ships. Auxiliary patrol boats, sailing alone for the most part, secured the route along the German coast.[52] The Germans, despite this extensive deployment, did not succeed in sinking a single submarine. Essentially, weather conditions had ended submarine operations for the winter. On the other hand, the Germans could claim that their traffic resumed its normal proportions and that the Allies, despite the sinking of fourteen steamers (approximately 28,000 tons), had not succeeded in stopping the traffic in iron ore.

The Russian mining offensive, which resumed with the long nights of autumn, also did not produce extensive results. On the night of 10–11 November, Rear Admiral Kerber with the dreadnoughts *Petropavlovsk* and *Gangut* and seven destroyers covered a minelaying expedition by four cruisers approximately 35 miles south of Gotland. Five submarines also were to be deployed to support the operation, but two (*Gepard* and *E.8*) collided, and the others reached their positions too late because of bad weather. Russian mines, however, claimed only one ship. The cruiser *Danzig* was badly damaged on the night of the 25th.

The Russians also made use of their apparently excellent radio direction finding and radio intercept methods to establish the positions of the German patrols watching the minefields distributed on the line Östergarn-Lyserort. On the night of 19–20 November, seven Russian destroyers, led by the *Novik*, raided the German patrols near Spon Bank off Windau, sinking the auxiliary patrol boat *Norburg* and escaping before German cruisers and destroyers could arrive to assist. The Germans decided to abandon night patrols in the dangerous position off Windau, relying on strengthening their minefields for protection.

In November the Russians attempted to adapt three of their submarines, the *Akula, Bars,* and *Vepr*, for minelaying. The apparatus was fairly primitive and required the submarine to surface to lay the mines. The Russians hoped to use the boats to mine the entrances to Pillau and Danzig, but on the first mission, a shorter run to the south of Libau that began on 27 November, the *Akula* disappeared. She was probably the victim of a German mine, but the Russians abandoned the attempt to use their submarines for minelaying.

The final Russian mining operations for the year produced mixed results. On the early morning of 6 December, five cruisers, covered by the *Petropavlovsk* and *Gangut*, laid a field halfway between Hela and the southern tip of Gotland. The Russian success at radio interception enabled them to avoid a German minelaying expedition at work off Lyserort the same night. However, only the small cruiser *Lübeck* was damaged by the Russian field on 13 January. The far less ambitious operation in which three destroyers laid mines between Windau and Lyserort on the night of 15 December was more productive. The next morning the German cruiser *Bremen* and destroyer *V.191* were sunk in the field, which also claimed on the 23d the destroyer *S.177* and auxiliary patrol boat *Freya*.

The year 1915 was probably the most active year of the war as far as naval operations in the Baltic were concerned. When ice ended operations until the following spring, the Russian navy could claim to have done fairly well, proportionately much better than the Russian army, although there was no comparison in the scale of the effort. Naturally, claims as to success or failure in the Baltic depended on who was doing the talking. The Germans could also claim that they had achieved their essential goals in what was for them a secondary theater. Nevertheless, it was the Russians who might be more hopeful when the campaigning season resumed with the thaw in 1916. They had the four new dreadnoughts in service, new large destroyers and submarines would also be forthcoming, and the British submarines might be able to repeat their success of October 1915. These hopes were destined to be disappointed.

1916: MINE WARFARE PREDOMINANT

Early in 1916 the War Committee in London examined the question of possible British aid to the Russians. Captain von Schoultz, the Russian observer with the Grand Fleet, had also proposed more effective cooperation between the Allies. Once again, the possibility of sending surface ships to the Baltic was dismissed as not practicable.[53] There was the possibility of sending more submarines, as well as what the Russians termed a "timely, weighty and prolonged" demonstration against the Sound and Belts. The outlook for getting more submarines through the Sound was not good. The German mine and net defenses had made passage through the Belts impossible. As for the Sound, new German minefields had been laid since the British submarines passed through the preceding year and an Admiralty study concluded that with great good luck only half the submarines attempting the passage would get through, and if they were unlucky, the probability was all the submarines might be lost. A demonstration by surface ships posed even more difficulties. A fleet could not maintain itself in the narrow waters south of the Skaw without a base to refuel the vital small escort craft. Any serious attempt to force the Belts would have to be a combined naval and military operation, for the narrow passages would have to be occupied to protect the flanks and lines of communication. A military operation of this sort would probably provoke the German occupation of Jutland and would likely be a much larger operation than the Dardanelles. Unlike the Dardanelles, where the Allies had unquestioned naval supremacy, the operation would have to be carried out across the North Sea. Aside from the inevitable danger from submarines, the High Sea Fleet would be able to dash out to attack transports and ships inside the Skaw whenever the Grand Fleet withdrew to refuel.[54]

In July 1916 the Admiralty finally decided to send more submarines, but not by way of the Sound. The four older C-class submarines (C.26, C.27, C.32, and C.35) would be towed around the North Cape to Archangel and then loaded on barges for the nearly 1,000-mile trip south via the rivers and canals of northern Russia to Petrograd and the Baltic. The British were forced to use the obsolescent C-class boats, for the newer E boats would have been too large to pass through the rivers and canals. The submarines and their tugs sailed on 3 August, and after an epic journey that was often a minor miracle of improvisation, they arrived safely at Petrograd on 9 September. Unfortunately, their batteries, which had been shipped separately, arrived late and with many cells damaged and useless due to poor packing. The British with great difficulty managed to get only C.32 and C.35 operational in time for just one patrol from their base at Rogokul in Moon Sound before winter and ice ended operations for the year.[55]

When the 1916 spring thaw began somewhat earlier than usual at the beginning of April, the Russians set to work renewing their minefields in the "Central Position" and extending the minefields started in the "Forward Position." They also worked to secure their situation in the Gulf of Riga, renewing the fields in the Irben Strait and improving their Moon Sound position. The Russians began construction of the powerful 30.5-cm batteries at Zerel on the Sworbe Peninsula, dominating the Irben minefields, and at Cape Tachkona, on the northern tip of Dagö Island, commanding the southern flank of the advanced position.

The Germans, whose 1916 operations in the Baltic were essentially defensive, also made increasing use of mine warfare. They were, after the experience of 1915, reluctant to risk the modern heavy units of the High Sea Fleet on secondary tasks in the Baltic, and the relentless demands for manpower led them to lay up more and more of the old battleships and armored cruisers they had been using in the Baltic since the beginning of the war. Auxiliary patrol craft, armed minesweepers and trawlers, destroyers, and torpedo boats for the protection of merchant shipping were now the most important assets. The Germans were now weak in battle-worthy surface ships and therefore anxious to hamper the sorties of Russian cruisers into the central and southern Baltic. Consequently, they allotted 3,500 mines for minefields to be laid between the island of Dagö and the skerries off Stockholm on the Swedish coast.

The German navy also deferred any offensive in the Gulf of Riga, which would probably require the capture of Ösel and the other islands, until the German army actually requested one. Prince Heinrich was anxious to take the islands but frustrated by the army's lack of interest and the apparently lukewarm attitude of the Admiralstab, who were pressured by the new chief of the High Sea Fleet, Admiral Scheer, to follow a more aggressive policy in the North Sea. In 1916 the German army was preoccupied with the western front, notably their own offensive against Verdun and, later, defense against the British offensive on the Somme. On the eastern front, they faced the problem of helping their Austrian ally repel the Brusilov offensive—the last serious and partially successful Russian effort of the war—and disposing of Romania, which belatedly entered the war on the side of the Entente.[56]

Prince Heinrich turned the greater part of his attention to securing German shipping by manning and fitting out large numbers of small craft. He was also converted to the idea of convoys as the most effective method of protecting trade. He presented his proposals to a conference of German shipowners assembled in Lübeck and attempted to exert some pressure through the marine insurance companies, in the absence of legal means, to force shipowners to comply. German shipowners proved to be less enthusiastic. They were not happy with the delays involved in waiting for convoys to form, or the fact that ships were tied to the speed of the slowest ship in the convoy, and they worried about collisions. These were all familiar objections to convoys, expressed even more emphatically on the British side, and Prince Heinrich himself had shared some of these beliefs just a few months before.

The German convoy service commenced on 7 April 1916 with a group of armed vessels sailing three times a week at fixed times along the shipping lanes from Gjedser Strait to the Sound, the Swedish east coast and Swinemünde. Another group sailed from Swinemünde to the Sound and Sweden; and another to Danzig—Pillau—Memel—Libau. The Germans at first did not have sufficient escorts, and the convoys could only proceed as far as Swedish territorial waters at Smyge-Huk. The Germans sailed a "Q-ship" at regular intervals along the route from here to Landsort to provide some protection at places where steamers had to leave territorial waters. The heavy demands of German and Austrian industry for Swedish iron ore led the Germans to increase the number of Swinemünde—Landsort convoys from three to six on 23 July.[57]

The convoys began just in time, for with the melting of the ice the Russians sent the *Volk*, *E.19*, and *E.9* to report on German movements and patrols. The British, however, were under orders to attack only cruisers and larger ships and encountered none. The Russian *Volk*, which did not have this restriction, was able to sink three German colliers (a total of 6,000 tons) east of Häfringe on 17 May, representing the greatest success for a Russian submarine in the Baltic. The Germans responded by wasting time and effort on submarine "hunting groups," which like their British and French counterparts had no success, but, with more escorts now in service, they were able to extend their convoys along the Swedish coast to Landsort.

The next sortie by three British and two Russian boats was less successful. *E.18* torpedoed the large new German destroyer *V.100* off Libau, but the Germans were able to get the ship into port. The British submarine, however, never returned and was probably lost on a mine west of Ösel. On 27 May the *Gepard* was rammed by the auxiliary ship *K* (*Kronprinz Wilhelm*, 1,700 tons, armed with four 10.5-cm guns), acting as a Q-ship, while attacking a convoy southeast of Häfringe. The Germans believed they had sunk her, but the damaged submarine was able to return to base. The next day in Hanö Bay, the *Bars* attacked the *K*, missed, and suffered a heavy depth-charging. The Germans believed they had accounted for the submarine, but she, like the ships in the convoy, was unharmed.

The submarines did not repeat their success of 1915. There were few sinkings, and German trade was not seriously disrupted. The submarines themselves were now harassed by German aircraft. Cromie, who became senior British naval officer after Laurence returned to England, reported that the British submariners did not have the same warm relationship with the new Russian commander in chief Admiral Kanin that they had enjoyed with Essen, and that it was difficult to dissuade the commander in chief "from doing useless stunts with the boats." By mid-June he reported they were used principally for reconnaissance, as nothing but aircraft and patrols moved about and the Germans were very active in antisubmarine tactics. Cromie later wrote that in 1916 they "were kept idle for months" waiting for a landing in Riga Gulf that never occurred, and, on the whole, "1916 was a wasted year."[58] The Russian submarines scored the occasional success, but the *Vepr* caused diplomatic complications on 16 July in the Gulf of Bothnia when she torpedoed the German steamer *Syria* (3,600 tons) without warning and apparently within the three-mile limit of Swedish waters. The German crew were rescued by a Swedish torpedo boat. According to one authority, in the period from July to the end of November, four British and twelve Russian submarines (five new and seven old boats) undertook a total of thirty-one patrols resulting in the sinking of only two ships. This was probably due as much to the very effective use German traffic made of Swedish territorial waters as it was to German antisubmarine activities. Moreover, the

Swedes tacitly cooperated with the Germans by instituting convoys of their own to enforce Swedish neutrality and protect ships traveling within their territorial waters. The Germans also used seven to eight submarines in the Baltic and Gulf of Bothnia, for both operations against Russian traffic and minelaying. In 1916 they lost one submarine in the Baltic and laid mines that sank a large new destroyer, a smaller destroyer, two minesweepers, and in November badly damaged the *Rurik*. They also sank with torpedoes or mines four naval supply ships and a surveying ship in naval service, although the number of merchant ships they sank or captured was comparatively small.[59] The shipping losses were modest when compared to other theaters. Baltic conditions did not seem suitable for the conduct of *Handelskrieg* by either side.

The Russians inevitably found the German convoys, defended for the most part by lightly armed small craft, to be attractive targets for their surface forces. The comparative weakness of German strength in the Baltic made them even more attractive. Acting on intelligence received from the British about convoys of ships carrying iron ore from Landsort, the Baltic naval commander ordered an offensive sweep along the Swedish coast. On the night of 13 June, Vice Admiral Trukhachev led the armored cruiser *Rurik*, the cruisers *Oleg* and *Bogatyr*, the large destroyers *Novik*, *Pobeditel*, and *Grom*, and six to eight smaller and older destroyers and torpedo boats on the raid. The three large destroyers under Rear Admiral Kolchak separated from the remainder of the force at Kopparstenarne light and closed Norrköping Bay. They encountered a southbound German convoy of approximately ten steamers escorted by three auxiliary patrol boats, southeast of Häfringe Island. The Russian commander fired a warning shot to make sure the convoy was not Swedish. The German escort, led by the auxiliary cruiser *Hermann* (2,030 tons, armed with four 10.5-cm guns), an armed trawler, and two smaller boats, turned to engage the Russian destroyers while the convoy fled for the safety of the Swedish coast. The *Hermann* was sunk, but Kolchak did not close, believing the convoy escort had heavy guns and was accompanied by torpedo boats. Those large new destroyers, after all, were precious to the Russians, who believed they had sunk three to five freighters. In fact, only the luckless *Hermann* had been sunk. The freighters loaded with iron ore had escaped.[60]

The Russians followed the same pattern in a raid on the night of 29–30 June commanded by Vice Admiral Kurosch. This time they used the old armored cruiser *Gromoboi;* the small cruiser *Diana* accompanied by the large new destroyers *Pobeditel*, *Grom*, and *Orfei;* and five smaller destroyers. The three large Russian destroyers, commanded by Captain Wilken, were hampered by thick fog when they closed the coast in Norrköping Bay. There was no sign of the convoy, delayed by fog, but the Russians ran into three large new and five older German destroyers and torpedo boats. The eight Germans pursued the outnumbered Russians until they encountered the Russian cruisers approximately 30 nautical miles south of Landsort. The Germans fired torpedoes, but none of them found their mark, and neither side suffered casualties before the action was broken off. The Russians had failed, once again, to disturb the German ore traffic. Russian surface forces probably had their greatest success against the German ore traffic on 17 July when torpedo boats captured the German steamers *Lissabon* (2,800 tons) and *Worms* (4,400 tons) off Bjuröklubb in the Gulf of Bothnia. The Swedes claimed it was a violation of their neutrality and protested, especially as one of the steamers had been carrying a Swedish pilot.

Swedish neutrality was a two-edged sword. The Germans undoubtedly profited from the use of Swedish territorial waters and also from Swedish convoy arrangements in the Gulf of Bothnia, which were published on 29 July 1916 and had the effect of protecting German merchant shipping from Russian naval attack in Swedish territorial waters between Lulea and Kalmar Sound. Here ships could join the German convoys. The Swedish escort in the north was light, generally only a single torpedo boat that left Lulea every second day (and in the opposite direction at fixed hours) and proceeded at 8 knots. The Germans found certain disadvantages: the Swedish escorts anchored overnight and thereby lengthened the time necessary for the voyage and the Swedes did not concern themselves about stragglers. Nevertheless, they profited enormously, for, joined to the Swedish prohibition on submarines entering territorial waters, they made attacks on German shipping very difficult, if not impossible, particularly if prize rules were followed.[61] The Swedes also instituted a weekly patrol service from Landsort to the Sound and from there to the Norwegian border, but this was of little interest to the Germans. It either paralleled their own convoys or was in waters where they had no fear of attack. If anything, the British and Allies might profit more from it. Later in 1917 the Germans also failed to induce the Swedes to put their convoy in the Gulf of Bothnia on a daily basis. The Swedish navy had neither sufficient ships nor men.[62]

Sweden's political and diplomatic stance is a complicated subject, beyond the scope of this study. Undoubtedly, there were strong pro-German sentiments in certain sections of the Swedish government and society, as well as traditional anti-Russian feelings. In a well-known work published shortly after the war, the former British naval attaché in Scandinavia, Rear Admiral M. W. W. P. Consett, was particularly bitter over Sweden's conduct.[63] Recent studies indicate Consett may have had too narrow a view, and that Esme Howard, the British minister in Stockholm, was more correct in his assessment of the larger picture—the necessity to avoid throwing the Swedes into the arms of the Central Powers and keeping Sweden open as a route for supplies to reach Russia.[64]

The British were nonetheless able to profit from Swedish neutrality by bringing out a number of ships trapped in the Baltic at the beginning of the war. There were no fewer than ninety-two British ships in Swedish and Russian Baltic ports, and by autumn of 1915 the demands on shipping were so great that they could no longer be ignored. An Anglo-Swedish syndicate was formed, and the ships began to make the perilous passage through the Sound, Kattegat, and Skaggerak by hugging Norwegian and Swedish waters whenever possible. The Germans might not have let those ships escape from under their noses, but the Swedish navy provided protection, and on one occasion the Swedish torpedo boat *Pollux* cleared for action when a German torpedo boat threatened the British ship *Thelma* in Swedish waters in the Sound north of Malmo on 16 November

1915. Two more Swedish torpedo boats and an aircraft soon arrived to reinforce the point. On 23 January the Swedish torpedo boat *Castor*, with Prince William of Sweden reportedly on the bridge, saved the *F. D. Lambert* from two German destroyers off Falsterbö. In June Prince William was also reported as having laid his torpedo boat across the narrow channel off Falsterbö in order to prevent a pair of armed German trawlers from following the British steamer *Dunrobin*. The same month Swedish torpedo boats undoubtedly saved the *Penmount* from capture by a German destroyer off Malmo. One could cite other examples.[65] It was those small, hard-worked torpedo boats, rather than the larger Swedish coast-defense ships and cruisers, that were of the most value in enforcing Swedish neutrality.

A total of twenty-nine ships managed to escape from the Baltic by July 1916 before the Swedish government (under German pressure and as a result of friction with the British over the blockade) announced on 28 July that the Swedish navy had laid a new minefield in the Kogrund Channel at the entrance to the Sound and that only Swedish vessels would be taken by pilots through it. This had the effect of forcing vessels beyond the very shallowest draft out of Swedish waters into German minefields. The Allies protested hotly and the question became a matter of considerable discussion, but it was not until May 1917 that the Allies reached an agreement with the Swedes that permitted a total of 90,000 net tons of British and Allied shipping to leave the Baltic through the Kogrund passage in return for the release of a specific number of Swedish ships and cargoes detained by the British.[66]

In September 1916 Vice Admiral Nepenin became commander in chief of the Baltic Fleet, replacing the somewhat lackluster Kanin, who was relegated to the tsar's Council of the Empire. Nepenin, former chief of reconnaissance, was particularly noted for his organization of the intelligence office earlier in the war. It seemed a genuinely popular appointment, and there were strong hopes the Baltic Fleet would enjoy more dynamic leadership.[67] Unfortunately, these high hopes were never realized; Nepenin met a tragic fate early in the Russian Revolution the following year.

The Germans deviated from their generally defensive stance in November of 1916 and met with what was probably their greatest disaster in the Baltic during the war. Rear Admiral Langemak, commander of the German reconnaissance forces, was anxious to raid the western portion of the Gulf of Finland, hoping to catch Russian transports and their destroyer escorts, which German submarine reconnaissance reported sailed by night behind the Russian "Forward Position." The Germans also planned to shell the anchorage at Baltic Port. The Germans were encouraged by the ability of their submarines to penetrate the gulf, and the news of a successful raid by German destroyers in the English Channel was apparently sufficient to provide the psychological impetus and overcome Prince Heinrich's last doubts about the scheme. On the evening of 10 November, the Tenth Destroyer Flotilla, consisting of eleven modern destroyers under the command of Korvettenkapitän Wietling in *S.56*, sailed on the ill-fated mission. The Germans had completely underestimated the strength of the Russian mine defenses and had hardly reached the meridian of Cape Tachkona when first *V.75* and then *S.57* struck mines. Wietling encountered no Russian traffic behind the "Forward Position" and proceeded to shell Baltic Port, which was empty of shipping. The bombardment caused little damage. The Germans then turned for home, but ran into the minefields on their way out of the gulf, and *V.72, G.90, S.58, S.59,* and *V.76* hit mines and sank. The Germans could only console themselves with the fact that they had achieved complete surprise, that the damage was perhaps greater than the Russians admitted (the sheds shelled were apparently full of army horses), the Russian surface forces had been slow to react, and the German loss of life had been small (sixteen dead, twenty wounded) with most of the crews rescued by the German destroyers. This was really quibbling. The loss of seven out of eleven precious modern destroyers for scant results could only be described as a disaster and a glaring example of what could happen if the mine danger was taken too lightly. Although Prince Heinrich took final responsibility for the disaster, it is not surprising that Langemak was superseded by Admiral Hopman, who had held the command the preceding year.[68]

1917: REVOLUTION AND PARALYSIS

The year 1917 was one of revolution in Russia. The autocracy had been shaken by two and a half years of defeat and the population worn down by war. The March revolution brought about the abdication of the tsar and the end of the autocracy. Russia's allies hoped that the new liberal government would be able to continue the war, perhaps even more effectively, and the end of the autocracy relieved the embarrassment of the allies claiming to fight Prussian militarism while allied to Russian despotism. The Bolshevik seizure of power in November ended these hopes. That is the simplified version of events, a benign revolution subverted later on by the Bolsheviks. The picture does not fit the Baltic Fleet. From the very first, the revolution seriously affected the fleet, which then declined steadily to but a fraction of its former fighting value. There had been scattered disorders and disturbances before the March revolution. The relative inactivity of the big ships created a fertile breeding ground for unrest. Admiral Nepenin was one of the early victims, despite his recognition of the provisional government. He was murdered on 4 March (Russian calendar) in Helsingfors where the fleet was still ice-bound. There were numerous other murders of officers, the formation of revolutionary sailors' committees to share in the command of the ships, and a general collapse of discipline. Traditionally the situation was worst in the battleships, better in the destroyers and submarines. The reports of the British and French naval attachés provide a vivid picture of their growing despair, mingled periodically with their hopes that the situation might be settling down, only to be plunged back into despair by fresh outbreaks of disorder. Knowledgeable observers had written off the Baltic Fleet as an effective fighting force long before the Bolsheviks seized power. There is no space in a survey of this kind to go into these events in detail, but given the historical importance of the Russian Revolution, there is substantial literature on the subject.[69]

The tempo of naval operations reflected the fact that politics had superseded military operations in the Baltic Fleet. The Russians concentrated on strengthening their mine defenses, and offensive operations were generally limited to submarines. The British submarines were sent on patrol against the German bases, such as Libau, or in defense of the Irben Strait, but they had no luck. The Russian submarines went out against German shipping on the Swedish coast. They too met with little success in the face of German countermeasures. The Russians lost the submarines *Bars*, *Lvica*, and *AG.14*. The latter had been commanded by the only son of the late Admiral Essen and was one of five U.S.-designed Holland boats built in sections in Canada, shipped across the Pacific, and assembled at Petrograd—six others went to the Black Sea. German submarines also were active, both in minelaying and attacks on shipping. They achieved a certain amount of success, particularly in the Gulf of Bothnia, sinking sixteen mostly very small ships. The mines claimed an old torpedo boat, an auxiliary minesweeper, and a minesweeping motorboat. German aircraft and airships were also alert, and in August aircraft were decisive in frustrating the Russian attempt to salvage the destroyer *Stroini* (350 tons), which had run aground west of the Sworbe Peninsula while covering Russian minelaying in the Irben Strait. On 24 September the destroyer *Okhotnik* (615 tons) was sunk off Zerel by a mine laid by an airplane, possibly the first success in war attributed to aerial mining.

OPERATION ALBION

In October 1917 the Germans executed the major Baltic naval operation of the war in the Gulf of Riga. With the Russian army disorganized by the revolution, the Germans resumed their advance and captured Riga and Dünamünde in early September. This enlarged the amount of Courland coast under German control but also raised the question of Ösel and the other islands in the Gulf of Riga. Russian naval forces still had control of the gulf, which meant that the left flank of the German army along the water remained exposed to naval gunfire. There was also the danger that the Russians might attempt a landing in the rear of the German forces, although the state of the Russian army made this highly unlikely. Perhaps more important was the fact that the Russian naval threat prevented the Germans from using Dünamünde as a supply port. The Germans had already learned to their cost that the German fleet could not remain in the Gulf of Riga without securing its line of communications through the Irben Strait, and this would mean taking Ösel and the batteries on the Sworbe Peninsula that commanded the minefields. There also appear to be some Germans who believed, unlikely as it may seem, that the British had surveyed the Sworbe Peninsula with the idea of seizing it and taking advantage of the situation to establish a foothold on the shores of the Baltic.[70]

The prospect of action in the Baltic was agreeable to some German naval leaders. The operation—code named "Albion"—would require a heavy contribution from the North Sea. Scheer, now chief of the High Sea Fleet, later wrote: "This offered a welcome diversion from the monotony of the war in the North Sea." Captain Levetzow, chief of operations on Scheer's staff, was also happy to bring the heavy ships into action. The chief of the Admiralstab, mindful no doubt of recent disturbances in the fleet, also was anxious for an action in order to raise morale.[71] The psychological factor was also important to the high command. Ludendorff thought of it in terms of increasing the desire for peace in the Russian army: "The blow was aimed at Petrograd, and, since very many people have no idea of time and space, was bound to make a profound impression there." Hindenburg believed the operation would "intensify our pressure on a nervous Petersburg without employing any large forces."[72]

The naval leaders in the Baltic were less enthusiastic about Albion. It was much easier for the High Sea Fleet to detach dreadnoughts to the Baltic than it was to send large numbers of the absolutely essential minesweepers. The minesweepers were needed in the North Sea to keep the exits open for the U-boats, and all agreed the submarine war had priority. Prince Heinrich had severe reservations about the operation, especially because of the lateness of the season and uncertainty of the weather, the formidable mine defenses, and the presence of British submarines. These doubts were shared by his chief of staff Rear Admiral von Uslar and Rear Admiral Hopman, commander of the Baltic scouting forces. Uslar thought the effort too much for merely providing better security for the flank of the army. Hopman wrote Tirpitz shortly before the operation that its military value was "nonsense" but that "it brings a fresh breath of air into the fleet, whose spirit, as far as the ratings are concerned, is in even more dire straits than Your Excellency suggested some time ago."[73]

The doubts were overcome, and on 18 September the orders for the joint operation to capture Ösel and Moon Island were issued. The question of command was a potentially delicate one; both Scheer—half of whose fleet would be employed—and Prince Heinrich laid claim to it. The problem was eventually solved by entrusting the naval command to a *Sonderverband* (task force) under the ranking subordinate admiral in the High Sea Fleet, Vice Admiral Ehrhard Schmidt. The joint operations were to be directed from Riga by Lieutenant General von Hutier, commander in chief of the Eighth Army, in whose zone the operation would take place. Lieutenant General von Kathen would command the expeditionary corps, consisting of the reinforced 42d Infantry Division and 2d Infantry Cyclist Brigade (approximately 24,600 officers and men), which would be transported in two echelons by nineteen steamers to Tagga Bay on the western shores of Ösel.

The Sonderverband was by far the largest and most powerful German naval force to appear in the Baltic during the war. It included: the *Moltke* (flag); the Third Squadron (the *König, Bayern, Grosser Kurfürst, Kronprinz,* and *Markgraf*); the Fourth Squadron (the *Friedrich der Grosse, König Albert, Kaiserin, Prinzregent Luitpold,* and *Kaiser*); the Second Scouting Group (five cruisers); Hopman's three Baltic cruisers; Commodore Heinrich in the cruiser *Emden,* leading the three half-flotillas of destroyers and torpedo boats from the High Sea Fleet; a minesweeping division from the North Sea; the Baltic minesweepers, mine hunters, mine breakers, submarines, and mother ships; and the

"Rosenberg flotilla" (an antisubmarine flotilla of torpedo boats and trawlers under Fregattenkapitän von Rosenberg). The German armada numbered more than 300 vessels of all sorts plus 6 airships and more than 100 aircraft. Nevertheless, as the former chief of staff of the German Eighth Army noted in a detailed study written after the war, the fleet "was lacking in adequate mine-sweeping equipment. This deficiency later, on several occasions, made itself felt most embarrassingly."[74]

The Russian forces in the Gulf of Riga were under the command of Rear Admiral Bakhirev, flying his flag in the cruiser *Bayan*. They included the old battleships *Grazhdanin* (formerly the *Tsarevitch*) and *Slava*, the cruisers *Admiral Makaroff* and (later) *Diana*, 3 gunboats, 12 new destroyers, 14 older destroyers, 3 British C-class submarines, older torpedo boats, minesweepers, minelayers, mine hunters, and assorted patrol craft. The main Russian anchorage was in Kuiwast Roads, between Moon Island and the mainland, roughly 60 miles from the Irben Strait. The Russians, perhaps due to the chaotic conditions in the army, appear to have done little to strengthen the land defenses, preferring to concentrate on minelaying in the Irben Strait. The Ösel garrison, theoretically almost 14,000 strong, was only at 60 to 70 percent strength. Russian morale and powers of resistance were uncertain. The navy on the whole, with exceptions, fought hard, perhaps harder than many had anticipated.

Bad weather delayed the preliminary German minesweeping but improved sufficiently for the main German landing to take place at Tagga Bay at dawn on 12 October, with the *Moltke* and the Third Squadron engaging the batteries at Tagga Bay. A subsidiary landing, covered by the Rosenberg flotilla, took place near Pamerort farther north on the island. The Fourth Squadron engaged the batteries at Sworbe on the southern tip of Ösel. The German plan was to push their light forces through the shallow waters of Soela Sound between Ösel and Dagö Island, obtain command of Kassar Wick (the inlet between Moon Island and the southeast coast of Dagö), support the army's passage from Ösel to Moon Island, and block the passage from Moon Sound to the Gulf of Finland, thereby trapping the Russian naval forces defending the Gulf of Riga. The navy also had to force the Irben Strait so as to provide naval support to the German army advancing on Arensburg, the main town on Ösel.

The landings took place successfully, but very quickly the danger from Russian mines became apparent. The *Bayern* and *Grosser Kurfürst* were both mined while taking up their bombardment positions. A transport also was mined, and her troops and their equipment had to be rescued by the escorting torpedo boats before the ship was beached. The damage to the *Grosser Kurfürst* was not serious; her bulkhead protection limited flooding to between 260 and 280 tons. On the other hand, the damage to the 15-inch gunned *Bayern*—one of the newest and most powerful of the German dreadnoughts— turned out to be much more serious than first assumed; temporary repairs did not hold, and the ship had to put back into Tagga Bay. It took nineteen days for the Germans to get her back to Kiel.[75]

The Germans also had great difficulties in the narrow waters of Soela Sound and in attempting to gain control of Kassar Wick. The hydrographic conditions were difficult, with tricky currents, narrow channels, uncertain depths, sandbars, and rocks. It is not surprising that a number of German torpedo boats and other craft sustained damage from touching bottom. The Germans also ran into Russian destroyers in Kassar Wick on the morning of the 12th, and the Russians forced the German minesweepers back into Soela Sound. The Germans faced a tactical problem: the farther they pushed into Kassar Wick, the farther they got from the big guns of their supporting ships, whereas the Russians could be supported by their cruisers in Moon Sound. In the afternoon two German torpedo boat and destroyer flotillas engaged four Russian destroyers, supported by a gunboat. The Russians were later joined by another five destroyers and the cruiser *Admiral Makarov*, and the Germans did not succeed in getting through to Moon Sound. The Germans did not remain in Kassar Wick after dark and withdrew through Soela Sound.

Commodore Heinrich, commanding the flotillas, asked for reinforcements, but the Germans did not get any farther on the 13th when Russian destroyers, aided by fog, prevented the light cruiser *Emden* from entering Soela Sound or drawing close enough to deliver effective counterfire. Heinrich was convinced that it would require the big long-range guns of a battleship to drive off the Russian destroyers and gunboats and secure control of Kassar Wick. The Russians, in turn, planned on the night of 13–14 October to block the channel in Soela Sound by sinking a ship and laying a minefield. These plans were frustrated when the blockship ran aground and could not be freed and the ship's committee of the minelayer *Pripyat* refused to carry out the mission on the grounds it was too dangerous—a breach of discipline condemned even by the Soviet account of the operations.

The tide turned decisively on the 14th when the Germans, laboriously sweeping and buoying a channel, managed to bring the dreadnought *Kaiser* from Tagga Bay to the entrance of Soela Sound. The *Kaiser* was in position by 11:30 A.M. for her 12-inch guns to drive the Russian gunboats and destroyers away from the eastern entrance to Soela Sound. Commodore Heinrich's reinforced flotilla then dashed through the Sound to engage the Russian warships in Kassar Wick. In the running fight, the large new Russian destroyer *Grom* was hit in the engine room by a 12-inch shell from the *Kaiser*, knocking out both turbines. The destroyer took on an immediate list. The gunboat *Khrabri* tried to take the *Grom* under tow but was engaged by the German flotilla, and after the tow broke, the *Grom* was abandoned. *B.98* raced to capture the Russian destroyer and take her under tow, but the ship was too badly damaged and sank. The Germans might have been cheated of a prize, but they were able to recover an invaluable chart of the local waters from the sinking ship. By 3:00 P.M. the German flotillas had driven the Russians out of Kassar Wick and remained in control until they withdrew after dark. The Russians were still a threat; the Germans came under fire at the eastern edge of the inlet from the cruiser *Admiral Makarov* in Moon Sound.

During the night of 14–15 October, the *Pripyat* assisted by three motorboats laid a field of mines in Kassar Wick north of Cape Pawasterort. According to one account, the *Pripyat*'s mutinous crew had been replaced by more reliable men drawn from the destroyers and torpedo boats. When the German flotillas returned to the inlet the next day, the destroyer *B.98* had her bow blown off and had to be towed back to Libau. The destroyer *B.112*, in seeking a path around the new minefield, grounded and was put out of action. Nevertheless, the heavy fighting in the waters around the north of Ösel was really over. The Russians moved the battleship *Slava* to Moon Sound to join the *Admiral Makarov* in keeping the German flotillas from coming out of Kassar Wick. The Russians deliberately listed both ships to increase the range of their guns. By the 16th, however, the land fighting on Ösel had reached the point where it was essentially a matter of mopping up for the Germans, and the brunt of the naval action had shifted to the southern tip of the island and the Irben Strait.

The Irben Strait had to be opened before the big German ships could get into the Gulf of Riga and eject the Russian battleships and cruisers. It was really the Russian mines that caused the most trouble, although there was also the powerful 30.5-cm battery at Zerel. On the night of 30 September the battery had been badly shaken by an air raid in which a bomb blew up a magazine, causing heavy casualties. Nevertheless, Zerel was in action when Operation Albion began, and for a number of days was able to keep the vulnerable little minesweepers from effectively sweeping, a situation reminiscent of the Dardanelles.[76]

The sweeping operations at Irben were under the overall command of Admiral Hopman, but the Germans had been making at best slow progress. On the night of the 13th, Schmidt ordered Hopman to break through in order to provide naval support for the German army now closing in on Arensburg. The Germans, harassed by the 30.5-cm battery at Zerel, failed to break through the thick minefields on the 14th. The dreadnoughts *König Albert* and *Kaiserin*, later joined by the *Friedrich der Grosse*, bombarded Zerel at long range (7½ to 12½ miles), but accurate counterfire from the battery forced the ships to alter course frequently and disperse. The Germans, always mindful of the danger from submarines and mines, ended the bombardment after about an hour.

The following morning (15th) Vice Admiral Behncke, commander of the Third Squadron, arrived off the entrance to the Strait with the battleships *König* and *Kronprinz*. The Zerel battery did not reply to German fire, and the Germans assumed it had been silenced and they could make progress with their minesweeping. They suddenly had to break off sweeping in the afternoon when the battleship *Grazhdanin* and three destroyers were seen approaching the Sworbe Peninsula. Actually, the Russians were there for another purpose. It was the advance of the German army rather than naval gunfire that doomed Zerel. The Russians evacuated the battery after most of the gun crews had deserted. The remainder blew up the guns and ammunition stores, but the *Grazhdanin* and her destroyer escorts were not sure how effective the destruction had been and bombarded the now-abandoned position. The remaining garrison, cut off on the Sworbe Peninsula by the German advance, were evacuated by sea.

With the menace from Zerel removed, the Germans were able to make better progress with their sweeping, and on the morning of the 16th, Behncke prepared to break through in the direction of Arensburg. However, Admiral Schmidt, the naval commander in chief, decided that it would be preferable to have the big German ships farther to the north, and that morning sent a wireless message to Behncke to attack the Russian naval forces in the Gulf of Riga and in Moon Sound. This deviated from the original German plan, which had been to merely blockade Moon Sound. Behncke's force included the *König* and *Kronzprinz*, the cruisers *Kolberg* and *Strassburg*, and the minesweeping mother ship *Indianola*, escorted by destroyers and smaller craft. As the Germans steamed across the wide gulf, they ran into a new danger—British submarines. *C.26* sighted the German force but grounded in the shallow waters while attempting to get into a firing position. The submarine was kept down by the escorts and later suffered further damage when her hydroplanes jammed and she fouled her propeller in an antisubmarine net. At approximately 4:30 *C.27* fired two shots at the battleships, which missed, but succeeded in torpedoing the *Indianola*, which had to be towed to Arensburg.

At approximately 8:30 Behncke ordered his squadron to anchor for the night. They were on a latitude roughly north of Arensburg, ready to proceed into Moon Sound to attack the Russian naval forces the next morning. They could not effectively do this, however, until they cleared a path through the minefields blocking the channels through Moon Sound. Once again these posed a formidable obstacle.

The German sweepers did not get very far at first when they began sweeping early on the morning of the 17th. The Russians had the old battleships *Slava* and *Grazhdanin* along with the armored cruiser *Bayan* in Moon Sound. The 12-inch guns of these ships, joined by the battery at Woi on Moon Island, frustrated the attempt to sweep to the west of the minefields, and also held off the cruisers and destroyers supporting the sweepers. The Germans then tried to work around to the east where a pair of Russian torpedo boats (which had reported the German advance) retiring to the north indicated there was a mine-free passage. Individually the old Russian battleships might have been no match for the German dreadnoughts, but this was not a battle in the open sea and German accounts indicate they skillfully kept at the outer limit of the range of the German big guns. The Russians had improved the gun mountings of the *Slava* so that her 30.5 cm could be elevated to 30°, much greater than the maximum elevation of the German 30.5 cm. The Germans were unpleasantly surprised to discover the *Slava*'s 30.5 cm outranged the 30.5 cm of the much newer dreadnoughts which had to haul off for a time.[77]

It was only after 10:00 that the sweepers had made sufficient progress for Behncke to order the *König* and *Kronprinz* to begin their dash to the north. Then it would be a very unequal match. At 10:13 A.M. the *König* was finally in range of the *Slava* and opened fire, soon hitting the old Russian ship. Shortly afterward the *Kronprinz* scored hits on the *Grazhdanin* and *Bayan*. At about 10:30 Admiral Bakhirev ordered the Russian ships to withdraw to the north of Moon Sound, but the *Slava*, hit a number of times by 12-inch shells, was now on fire and listing. The gallant old ship that, despite all uncertainty caused by the events of the revolution, had fought hard against overwhelming forces, was doomed. She now drew too much water to pass through Moon Sound, and Bakhirev ordered her scuttled and her crew taken off in a destroyer. She remained afloat after the charges went off, and a Russian destroyer had to complete the job with a torpedo shortly before noon. The Russians also sank three ships in an attempt to block Moon Sound channel, and destroyers and minelayers scattered a large number of mines in the channel and neighboring waters.

One by one the Russian positions on the islands fell to the Germans. The navy wanted to hinder the Russian evacuations but ran into difficulty. Commodore Heinrich tried on the night of 17–18 October to cut off Moon Island from the mainland with his destroyers and torpedo boats but lost *S.64* to a mine. The *Admiral Makarov* and the Russian destroyers also held off the Germans in Kassar Wick on the 18th, and the large destroyer *B.111* had her bow blown off by a mine.

The naval battle was effectively over, although the Russian net and boom obstruction across the deep channel just off Werder kept the big German ships from making a dash through the Sound. Most batteries on land were silenced, but Russian naval forces obliged the German sweepers working in Moon Sound to withdraw under cover of smoke at one point on the 18th. Admiral Hopman was finally able to get two cruisers and a half-flotilla of torpedo boats as far as Schildau Island in the midst of Moon Sound the afternoon of the 19th, and on the 20th the *König*, towed by mine hunters in the poor visibility, arrived in Kuiwast roadstead. By then the fighting on land was largely over. Ösel, Moon, and Dagö islands were in German hands.

The effective pursuit of the retreating Russians was out of the question. On 19 October the Admiralstab ordered operations against the Russian fleet to be broken off and for the battleships to return to the North Sea as soon as possible. The Russians also left the gulf. On the afternoon of the 19th, Bakhirev led the Russian naval forces through the northern exit of Moon Sound into the Gulf of Finland and behind the "Forward Position," which the Russians now prepared to defend. They left the two British C-class boats behind in the Gulf of Riga, and on the 20th *C.32* attempted to attack the netlayer *Eskimo*, only to be badly damaged by the escorting destroyers. The submarine was run ashore on the 21st near Pernau and blown up.[78] The Russian mines continued to cause losses in the sweeping that followed the operation. Furthermore, on 29 October, the dreadnought *Markgraf* was damaged by a mine, probably torn loose by a storm, while leaving the gulf.

During the struggle for the Baltic Islands, the Russians once again appealed to the British for assistance. The Russians feared this was the beginning of a German offensive directed at Revel and Helsingfors and, with so much of the German fleet apparently in the Baltic, wondered if it might be possible for the British fleet to undertake an offensive. The geographical realities that effectively isolated the Baltic had not changed. Admiral Oliver informed the Russian naval attaché that the British sent several squadrons cruising in the North Sea with a view toward stirring German counteractivity, but that the extensive minefields prevented the British fleet from a close approach to the German coast and bad weather had been preventing aircraft from operating and British minesweepers from working. It did not matter what proportion of the High Sea Fleet was in the Baltic, because the defense of German bases rested on mines and heavy artillery.

Once again the British pointed out that even if they succeeded in getting their fleet into the Baltic, they could not maintain its long lines of communications, and the Russians could not supply it.[79]

Although Operation Albion had ended in a German victory, it had not been free of cost. A destroyer, three torpedo boats, and eight of the minesweeping and mine-hunting force had been sunk, and vessels damaged by mines included three dreadnoughts and two destroyers. Other craft were damaged by gunfire or grounding. The army losses were relatively light, barely 400 men, and the Germans had captured more than 20,000 Russians. The Russians lost the *Slava* and *Grom*, along with the British *C.32*, the *Grazhdanin*, and *Bayan*, and two gunboats and three destroyers suffered damage.[80]

A noted historian described Operation Albion, in which the German navy used no fewer than eleven of its most powerful capital ships, as "a classic case of overkill," intended primarily as a morale booster.[81] The question should be put to the German high command rather than the navy. Was it really necessary to take the islands? Once the decision to do so had been made, the navy had little option but to act as it did. The numbers of troops involved—a reinforced division—were certainly not excessive by World War I standards. Once they were committed to the hazards of an amphibious operation, however, the Germans faced a situation best described by General Tschischwitz, the former chief of staff of the expeditionary corps: "The experience of Moon Sound amply proves that one can not dispense with battleships so long as the enemy uses them. It is impossible to conduct a naval war with torpedo-boats and submarines alone when the enemy can effectively bring to bear the fire from long range guns."[82]

Furthermore, there was always the problem of the fleet-in-being. The Russians had four dreadnoughts and two modernized predreadnoughts at Helsingfors. With hindsight, there was little chance those forlorn ships, unkept and with politicized and undisciplined crews, would ever have put to sea, or have stood much of a chance in battle, given the state of training. But the Germans could not take the chance those six capital ships—or at least some of them—would not eventually intervene. The ratio in capital ships would then be 11 to 6, and with two German battleships damaged by mines at the beginning of operations, the German margin of superiority was reduced to 9 to 6. Of course the German ships were qualitatively far superior to their Russian opponents, but the numbers are given to show how an apparently overwhelming German lead could melt away. The Germans actually had great difficulty bringing their superior strength to bear given the geographical realities, difficult hydrographic conditions, and the Russian tactic of fighting behind mine defenses coordinated with coastal batteries. Under these circumstances minesweepers became as valuable as capital ships, and the Germans admitted they did not have as many as they needed. However, the exercise of naval power in this operation required *both* sweepers and capital ships; one could not do without the other. It was in all respects a combined operation.

There was a tendency for some Germans to compare their success in the Baltic with the Anglo-French failure at the Dardanelles. They stress that the Russian batteries were more modern than the Turkish, and the Russians had more than two and a half years to perfect their mine defenses. But the analogy is misleading. The Russian army at this stage could in no way be compared as far as fighting capacity is concerned with the Turkish forces at Gallipoli, and General Tschischwitz added a cautionary note: Albion could not be used as a model for future operations, for the Russian army and navy were "no longer a full-fledged adversary," and the Germans took chances in their presence they would not have risked with an enemy who was a proper match.[83]

The operations in the Gulf of Riga marked the effective end of the Baltic Fleet's participation in the war. On 7 November the Bolsheviks seized power in Petrograd and quickly began negotiations with the Central Powers to take Russia out of the war. On 15 December an armistice was concluded on the eastern front. The Allies, particularly the British, now had to worry about what would happen to the Russian fleet. Would the ships fall into the hands of the Germans? What of the British submarines in the Baltic? There was a wide spectrum of proposals, generally impracticable, which ranged from having the British submarines attempt to torpedo the big ships in Helsingfors to inducing so-called loyal officers and men to try to at least get the valuable destroyers out of the Baltic.[84] According to the armistice terms, the Russian fleet, in theory, was secured from seizure by the Germans.[85] Would the Germans respect those terms? The problem became acute in the winter of 1918 when the Germans resumed their advance in the east in order to compel the Bolshevik government to sign the peace treaty. The Russians gave in, and the Peace of Brest-Litovsk was concluded on 3 March. The Germans also intervened in the civil war that had broken out in Finland between the White and Red forces. In fact the German navy took the initiative before the political decision to intervene had been reached. There were some in the navy, notably Rear Admiral von Trotha, the chief of staff of the High Sea Fleet, who bluntly recommended seizing the Baltic Fleet as "war booty."

On 28 February 1918, Rear Admiral Hugo Meurer, commanding a special division including the dreadnoughts *Westfalen* and *Rheinland* (later joined by the *Posen*), sailed with approximately 1,000 troops to establish a base in the Åland Islands. The Swedes also had a strong interest in the islands, and there were approximately 700 Swedish troops at Eckerö—preserving law and order against the threat of the Red Guards—along with the Swedish coast-defense ships *Sverige, Oskar II,* and *Thor.* The Swedes had been unpleasantly surprised by the arrival of the Germans, and Meurer had a certain amount of difficulty in reaching an agreement on 6 March with the Swedish commander, Vice Admiral Count Ehrensvärd, about Swedish and German zones of occupation.[86]

Ice had greatly hampered the movements of the Germans, who now turned their attention to the Finnish mainland. On 2 March the kaiser authorized sending the Baltic Division (approximately 9,000 men) under the command of General von der Goltz to join the Finnish White Army. On 5 April the German force, convoyed by Meurer's three dreadnoughts, three cruisers, and numerous escorts, landed at Hangö on the southwest tip of Finland. The Russians did not resist, although they scuttled three *AG*-class submarines, a supply ship, and a patrol boat to prevent them from falling into

German hands. In the next few days the navy also transported a brigade of 3,000 men from Revel to a point on the Finnish coast approximately 100 kilometers east of Helsingfors.

The seizure of the Russian Baltic Fleet was not official German policy, and Meurer negotiated an agreement with the Russians at Hangö on 5 April whereby the Soviets agreed not to destroy the port facilities and ships at Helsingfors and to disarm all Russian ships in the harbor. The Germans, in turn, agreed to permit the Russians to move the ships to Kronstadt if ice conditions permitted. The Admiralstab still placed its priorities on the U-boat war, and on 8 April the kaiser ordered Meurer's special division to be disbanded and its ships returned to the High Sea Fleet. Meurer's ships reached Helsingfors on 12 April where German sailors joined in the heavy fighting between the Red and White forces. The German navy, despite the lack of opposition at sea, paid a certain price for the intervention in Finland. The battleship *Rheinland*, which had remained in the vicinity of the Åland Islands, ran on the rocks in foggy weather on 11 April while returning to Danzig to coal. The Germans managed to get the ship off the rocks and back to Kiel, but she was so badly damaged the Germans could not use her at sea again.

The Russians at Helsingfors must have suspected that possession is nine-tenths of the law and worked feverishly to move the Baltic Fleet to Kronstadt. Although hampered by the ice, they managed to get all but a very few ships of little fighting value away before the Germans arrived. They used icebreakers to tow those ships whose engines would not function. The crossing through the ice was particularly difficult for small ships, and the destroyers took eight to nine days instead of the normal ten to twelve hours. Some of the destroyers were also damaged by the ice.[87]

The British did the only possible thing with their submarines: the surviving boats, four *E* class and three *C* class, were scuttled just before the Germans arrived. Lieutenant Downie, commanding the detachment, overcame the Russian reluctance to supply icebreakers by threatening to blow the boats up in the harbor.[88] Naval operations in the Baltic ended until after the Armistice.

A NAVAL HISTORY OF WORLD WAR I

8

THE BLACK SEA

THE GERMAN AND TURKISH
CHALLENGE: 1914–1916

The World War I operations in the Black Sea are not well known in the English-speaking world. There is sometimes a tendency to assume that because the *Goeben*—one of the kaiser's newest, fastest, and most powerful warships—had played such an important role in the series of events that drew the Turks into the war, the Turco-German forces enjoyed domination of the Black Sea. This view is probably reinforced by the events of 1918 when, after Russia dropped out of the war, German forces penetrated deeply into southern Russia, occupied the Russian naval base at Sebastopol, and succeeded in getting their hands on a portion of the Black Sea Fleet. The Allies were genuinely concerned the Germans and their allies would succeed in putting some of these ships in commission and break out into the Mediterranean. Nevertheless, the view of the Black Sea colored by the events of 1918 is quite erroneous. It was actually the Russians who enjoyed mastery for most of the war. The Black Sea Fleet was both more active and more successful than the Baltic Fleet. This is hardly surprising given the weakness of Turkey at sea, which the *Goeben* episode has tended to obscure. Before the disorders following the Russian Revolution slowed naval activity and the Bolsheviks concluded the disastrous Peace of Brest-Litovsk, the Russian Black Sea Fleet had disturbed Turkish communications at sea, executed ambitious amphibious operations on the seaward flank of the Caucasus front—and were planning others—and made innovative use of naval aviation from seaplane carrier groups roaming the Turkish coast.

The Black Sea had been a backwater for the Russians. Their primary concern once Germany became the most likely and dangerous enemy was obviously the Baltic. Here their capital was vulnerable to an enemy naval force breaking into the Gulf of Finland. Nevertheless, the war plans of 1907 and 1908 had called for an offensive stance by their fleet with the objective of blockading the Bosphorus and preventing an enemy force from breaking into the Black Sea. By 1911 the Russian naval command recognized that its superiority over the Turkish navy was "insignificant." The Black Sea Fleet had only two battleships completed since the Russo-Japanese War and the Turks were likely to have allies. In 1912 the naval staff concluded a permanent blockade of the Bosphorus would be impossible. The likelihood that the Turks would obtain two powerful dreadnoughts by the summer of 1914 initiated a crisis. The Black Sea Fleet would now remain on the defensive. The four dreadnoughts of the Russian naval building program were not due to begin entering service until the end of 1915, and in the operational plan for 1914, Vice Admiral Ebergard, commander in chief of the Black Sea Fleet, anticipated the now-stronger Turkish fleet would attempt to destroy or bottle up the Russians. Consequently, he intended to fight the decisive naval battle from a position relatively close to Sebastopol, where he could make full use of submarines, small torpedo boats, and naval aviation—the weapons of the weaker naval power. The minister of marine did not agree to these plans, which apparently failed to take land operations into account, and by the summer of 1914 the Russian naval authorities had not yet agreed on how a war in the Black Sea would be fought. Once the Turkish dreadnoughts proved to be a mirage after the outbreak of the war, the Russians returned to the idea of a distant blockade of the Bosphorus, with variants as to whether or not an attempt would be made to mine the Strait before the enemy fleet tried to pass into the Black Sea. The Russians now thought of a landing near the Bosphorus to take control of the Strait and capture Constantinople. This, however, could not take place until the Russians were victorious on the main front in the north.[1]

During the period of Turkish neutrality the Black Sea Fleet was placed under severe constraints by the Russian high command, which supported the policy of the Russian foreign ministry that if war with Turkey could not be avoided, the Turks should bear the onus of starting it. Ebergard's suggestion that if the *Goeben* and *Breslau* entered the Black Sea they should be treated, regardless of the flag they flew, as German ships was rejected. The Russian navy was thus forced to let the Turks get in the first blow.[2] Whether or not their surveillance of the Bosphorus could have been more effective, and whether they acted effectively when the attack came, are open questions. At one point during the attack on the morning of 29 October, the *Goeben* and two Turkish destroyers were actually observed off Sebastopol in a minefield that had not been activated because the Russians were expecting the arrival of the minelayer *Prut* (scuttled by her crew under fire from the *Goeben* shortly afterward). It took twenty minutes after the *Goeben* was recognized to execute the orders to activate the minefield, and the Germans escaped. Much of the problem may have been due to military rather than naval control of sea defenses during daylight hours.[3] Ebergard put to sea in pursuit, without success. Nevertheless, the Turco-German blow caused no serious damage to the Black Sea Fleet. A gunboat (later salved) and a minelayer were sunk; another gunboat, a minelayer, and a torpedo boat were damaged. Approximately six, mostly small, merchant ships also were sunk or captured.

The *Goeben* posed definite problems for the Black Sea Fleet in 1914. With her ten

280-mm guns she was more powerful than any of the five Russian battleships in service, generally armed with only four 305-mm guns. The Russians, in order to avoid being overwhelmed in detail, had to keep their battle squadron together. They could then concentrate a superior weight of metal if enough ships got in position to open fire, but the *Goeben* was far superior in speed and could disengage whenever she chose. The *Goeben* and *Breslau* also were faster than the sole pair of armored cruisers available to the Russians. There were four modern light cruisers under construction, but none were finished before the end of the war.

Beyond the *Goeben* and *Breslau*, the remainder of the Turkish fleet was weak. The Turks could not risk their two old former German battleships; they were too slow to venture into the Black Sea, and they did not have all their artillery. The Russians also had a numerical advantage in destroyers and torpedo boats. What is even more important, the large Russian *Bespokoiny*-class destroyers (1,320–1,460 tons) just entering service (4) or under construction (9) had the speed and range to operate against the Turkish coast. The Turks had nothing to match them for the closure of the Dardanelles, and Allied superiority in the Mediterranean cut off recourse to foreign yards. The Turks did have eight French- or German-built high-seas torpedo boats (some might classify them as small destroyers) and at least three older and smaller torpedo boats. German officers and men were seconded to the Turkish craft, and a German officer acted as commodore of the Turkish torpedo boat flotilla.

The Russians had six submarines under construction to supplement the four admittedly not very effective boats in service at the beginning of hostilities. The Turks had none until German U-boats reached the Black Sea in the summer of 1915. There was also the specter of the Russian dreadnoughts in the distant future. They were likely to tip the naval balance irretrievably in favor of the Russians.

Rear Admiral Souchon, commander of the Mittelmeerdivision and now chief of the Turkish fleet with the rank of vice admiral in the Ottoman navy, realized that time was not on his side. He was also aware of the deficiencies in training and lack of technical expertise plaguing the Ottoman navy. Souchon hoped to stiffen the Turkish ships by adding as many Germans as possible, particularly in the engine room and to work gunnery and fire control. He had a less-than-favorable view of his Turkish allies and doubted if it would be possible to make extensive reform or improvements during the war, for the rot was too deep.[4] The Ottoman minister of marine intended to order twenty-four destroyers and twelve submarines from the Krupp yards in Germany. Souchon considered this a wise decision, for he thought it would take years of work before the Turks had the technical personnel to man and employ large ships.[5] But the question was largely academic. The Turks obviously had no hope of getting the ships during the war. Incidentally, the term Mittelmeerdivision, although used by the Germans throughout the war, is something of a misnomer. With one fatal exception in 1918, the *Goeben* and *Breslau* had nothing to do with the Mediterranean and sailed mostly in the Black Sea.

The Russian general staff initially did not take such a sanguine view of the war at sea. They were battered by the series of disastrous defeats at the hands of the Germans in the north and very worried over a possible landing by Turkish troops in the vicinity of Odessa. The Black Sea Fleet therefore remained on the defensive, protecting the Russian coastline in the characteristic Russian manner. They laid 4,190 (4,423 according to some accounts) mines at important points along the Russian coast by the end of 1914.[6]

The Russians, with no dreadnoughts or efficient long-range submarines and as yet only a few long-range destroyers, were not in a position to mount a blockade of the Bosphorus. They were, however, able to begin offensive mining against the Bosphorus and attack Zonguldak on the Turkish coast. These remained the two major objectives of the Black Sea Fleet. Zonguldak was located in the region known as the "coal coast," for the port was an important outlet for coal, which was carried in colliers to the Bosphorus and Constantinople. The Russians intended to cut off that traffic, thereby leading to severe shortages in Constantinople and a disruption of the Turkish war effort.

Ebergard sailed on 4 November with his five old battleships, cruisers, and destroyers on the first Russian offensive operation of the war. Four of the new *Bespokoiny*-class destroyers laid minefields northwest of the entrance to the Bosphorus on the evening of the 5th. The operation was not a success. The location was poorly chosen, 8–12 miles from the Strait and outside the usual channels, and the mines later became as much of a hindrance to Russian as to Turkish movements. Moreover, many of the floating mines sank and were exploded prematurely by water pressure. This was only a first effort; the Russians continued their mining activities, and their performance improved. On the morning of the 6th, the Russian squadron was off Zonguldak and the old battleship *Rostislav* and cruiser *Kagul*, accompanied by six destroyers, moved inshore and shelled the port, sinking a Greek freighter. The Russians also were lucky enough to encounter and sink three Turkish steamers en route to Trebizond with men and supplies. The Turks had sent the steamers to sea without coordinating their movements with Souchon, and the result was disastrous. In retaliation, the *Breslau*, which had been in the eastern Black Sea protecting other Turkish movements, shelled the Russian port of Poti. These early operations set the pattern for the naval war in the Black Sea.

The great distance and poor communications between Constantinople and the Caucasus front made transport by sea more attractive to Enver Pasha, the Turkish minister of war, and his German chief of staff Colonel Bronsart von Schellendorff than the long, slow, and difficult route overland. This gave the Russians their opportunities, and much of Souchon's effort was expended in protecting that vulnerable transport. His primary mission as he saw it, however, was protection of the Bosphorus. Although success against isolated Russian ships was possible, a general fleet action had to be avoided. It took considerable argument, including, reportedly, the personal experience of a voyage in the *Goeben* to Trebizond, to finally convince Enver how hazardous reliance on sea transport could be.[7]

The Russians struck again at Turkish maritime communications to the Caucasus on 17 November, shelling Trebizond in the eastern Black Sea. Souchon sailed with the *Goeben* and *Breslau*, hoping that with luck he might be able to overwhelm a portion of the Russian fleet as it returned to the Crimea. He did not succeed. Shortly after midday on the 18th, the Russians and Germans met off Cape Sarych, about 20 miles from the Crimean coast. The conditions were foggy and the poor visibility and short ranges of the encounter nullified the *Goeben*'s advantages in speed and firepower. On the other hand, all of the Russian battleships were not, at least initially, in a position to open fire. The Russian flagship *Evstafi* hit the *Goeben* with one of her first salvoes, but suffered four hits in the engagement, which lasted only ten to fourteen minutes. The Russians drew the appropriate conclusion from the battle: their squadron would have to remain together to face the *Goeben*, and this, in turn, would restrict their operations along the Turkish coast to operations by the entire squadron. The handful of slow and elderly Russian cruisers would have been easy prey for the *Goeben*. The disadvantages caused by the lack of fast light cruisers were painfully clear, for only the few large destroyers were suitable for independent operations away from the protective guns of the plodding old battleships.[8]

The Germans also had their problems. Souchon had kept the lightly protected *Breslau* out of effective range and congratulated himself that the two old Turkish battleships *Heireddin Barbarossa* and *Torgud Reis* had not been with him, for if they had been, as he confided to his wife, their fate would have been sealed. The former German ships would have been too slow to escape, and they did not have all their artillery and were less protected than the Russians.[9] In many respects the *Goeben* was on her own in a precarious existence.

The fears of the Russian army about a possible landing on the Black Sea coast near Odessa had at least some foundation in fact. General Liman von Sanders, inspector-general of the Turkish army and probably the best known of Enver Pasha's German advisers, proposed landing a Turkish army at Akkerman to the south of Odessa. In his mind, this was a logical extension of German-Austrian operations on the eastern front all the way to the Black Sea. The proposal looked good on a map but was another example of the difficulty soldiers and sailors sometimes had in understanding each other's point of view. Souchon, who had already described Liman as a good field soldier but "childlike, silly and impeding cooperation," had great trouble convincing him it would be impossible to transport large numbers of troops over 300 miles and land them on an unprotected open flat coast within 150 miles of the Russian naval base at Sebastopol. There had been no preparation for an operation of this sort, the shipping was lacking, and the mere two German ships could not hope to protect the operation. The Turks did attempt a rash commando raid. On 6 December twenty-four Russian-speaking Turkish cavalrymen, dressed in Russian uniforms, landed near Akkerman with the objective of moving inland and cutting the Bender-Reni Railway, destroying villages and finally escaping into Romania. The raiders landed successfully but were soon captured without accomplishing their mission. It was a far cry from an extension of the eastern front to the sea.[10]

The Russians undertook a raid of their own on the night of 23–24 December, attempting to block the harbor of Zonguldak by sinking four old ships loaded with stones. The Russian battle squadron was at sea to cover this and another mining operation against the approaches to the Bosphorus, which had taken place the evening of the 21st. The mining, in which four minelayers laid 607 mines in two fields northeast of the Strait in waters considered too deep (150 meters) by the Turks and Germans for mining, was a success. The attempt to block Zonguldak was not. Shortly before the mining operation, the *Goeben* and the old Turkish cruiser *Hamidieh* had sailed from the Bosphorus to escort three transports to Trebizond. On the 23d the *Breslau* sailed to rendezvous with the *Goeben* on her return north of Sinope. In the darkness of the early morning hours of the 24th, the German cruiser met the *Oleg*, one of the Russian blockships heading for Zonguldak. Heavy weather had scattered the Russian force, which had been delayed by an explosion in one of the blockship's boilers requiring the ship to be towed. Additionally, some of the blockships had lost contact with their escorts. The *Breslau* switched on her searchlights and sank the *Oleg* but then broke away after encountering the battleship *Rostislav*. At dawn the *Breslau* met a second blockship, the *Athos*, which also had become separated from the main Russian force, and opened fire, causing the Russian crew to scuttle the ship. The remaining pair of blockships failed to reach the harbor. Coastal batteries, which the Turks had now moved up to protect the vulnerable port, kept the blockships from reaching the harbor entrance, and the two were finally scuttled in deep water. The *Breslau* clashed with Russian destroyers later in the morning, then took up a position ahead of the Russian squadron returning to the Crimea. She eventually broke contact after being fired on by Russian battleships off the Crimean coast.

Luck so far had been with the Germans, but that changed. The *Goeben* and *Breslau* met the afternoon of the 25th, the light cruiser continuing her cruise along the Anatolian coast while the battle cruiser steamed back to the Bosphorus. On the afternoon of the 26th, approximately one nautical mile from the outer buoy of the entrance to the Strait, the *Goeben* hit two of the newly laid mines and took on more than 600 tons of water.[11] The torpedo bulkhead probably saved the ship, but as there was no dock large enough in Constantinople to take the ship, there was some question if she would be fully operational again during the war. The Germans solved the problem with their customary ingenuity and energy. Experts were sent out from Germany, two large metal cofferdams were built, and the leaks were sealed with concrete, which held firmly enough so that permanent repairs could be postponed for a number of years. After much hard work, the last of the repairs was completed by the beginning of May.[12] The Germans also appear to have taken great pains to conceal the extent of the *Goeben*'s damage, which was not very evident to the naked eye. The ship was anchored in plain sight off Constantinople before repair in order to quell rumors, and on 28 January, although apparently not fully operational, she came out of the Bosphorus to cover the arrival of the *Breslau* and *Hamadieh* and to demonstrate her evident capability to the Russians, who were pursuing the cruisers after a sortie to the eastern Black Sea. Souchon sent the ship to sea again on 7 February in order to cover the return of the *Breslau* from a sortie to Batum and Yalta and to show herself once more before the major repairs began.[13]

The pattern of war remained substantially the same in 1915. The new Russian minefield claimed a Turkish auxiliary minesweeper on 28 December, and on 2 January the Turkish torpedo gunboat *Berk* received damage that put her out of action for the remainder of the war. The Russian battle squadron made periodic sorties to the

Anatolian coast to shell ports and operate against Turkish shipping. The extensive use of mines for defensive purposes in 1914, as well as the first fields off the Bosphorus, had exhausted the stock of Russian mines and consequently curtailed mining activity the following year. The German and Turkish cruisers escorted shipping and attacked the Russian coast, shelling ports and searching for Russian shipping. There were occasional clashes, such as on 6 January when the *Hamidieh* and *Breslau* unexpectedly ran into the Russian squadron off Yalta and the *Breslau* scored a hit on one of the *Evstafi's* 305-mm gun turrets before escaping.

The major threat to the Ottoman Empire in 1915 was undoubtedly the British and French expedition to the Dardanelles. The obvious question was, To what extent would or could the Russians assist from the Black Sea side? The Russians, as far as the British were concerned, had not displayed great enthusiasm. At the end of January, before Allied operations at the Dardanelles began, Grand Duke Nicholas, commander in chief of the Russian armies, replied to a request from Churchill for Russian naval cooperation at the mouth of the Bosphorus and preparations to land troops in case of favorable opportunities by stressing that the Russians were determined not to weaken their front against the Austrians and Germans. Grand Duke Nicholas emphasized the difficulties facing the Black Sea Fleet: the Russian dreadnoughts were not finished, and there were no modern submarines and only an insufficient number of fast modern destroyers. The Black Sea Fleet was no more than the equal of the Turkish fleet and that only when all ships were together. Russian ships could only carry coal for four days at sea, coaling at sea was impossible in bad weather, their nearest base was more than twenty-four hours from the entrance to the Bosphorus, and the Turkish batteries compared to the guns of the Russian ships "were such as to give little hope of a successful attack by the latter." The Russians expected matters to improve once the first of the dreadnoughts entered service along with modern submarines and more destroyers, but this was not before May. Moreover, they considered a minimum of two army corps necessary for a successful landing, and these troops could not be withdrawn from the principal theater of the war. Otherwise, the Russians claimed to fully support the Allied expedition.[14]

Despite the grand duke's gloomy—or realistic—outlook, depending on one's point of view, Russian general headquarters issued a directive at the moment the Allied bombardment of the outer forts at the Dardanelles began, ordering the Black Sea Fleet to cooperate by creating a diversion at the Bosphorus that, if the Allied operations were successful, might be extended by landing Russian troops. A few days later general headquarters cabled Ebergard that the operations of the Black Sea Fleet should be significant enough to ensure the Russians a major role at any peace talks and that all available resources should be used to develop operations on a large scale without placing the warships in immediate jeopardy. On 28 February Grand Duke Nicholas promised the British the Black Sea Fleet would attack Constantinople and an expeditionary force would be landed but that this would not take place until the British and French had broken through the Dardanelles and their fleets were before the Princess Islands in the Sea of Marmara.[15]

The Russian force designated for the possible landing at the Bosphorus was the V Caucasian Corps, approximately 37,000 men with 60 guns. Russian general headquarters delayed the movement of troops from the Caucasus region after the failure of the Allied naval attack on 18 March, but on 6 April ordered the transfer of corps headquarters to Odessa and the movement of two brigades by rail to Sebastopol and the remainder of the corps by rail to Odessa. The Russians designated seven steamers to carry a first echelon of approximately 9,200 men. The staff of the transport flotilla conducted embarkation exercises at Odessa, which were apparently intended to be noticed by the Turks and to prevent the latter from shifting troops from the Bosphorus to the Dardanelles. Ebergard would have preferred a base closer to the Bosphorus, notably Bourgos in Bulgaria.[16] However, Bulgaria was still neutral, and Bourgos was therefore out of the question.

There is something of the Potemkin village about the V Caucasian Corps, that is, it appears designed more for show than reality. There was also some question if the force would have been large or powerful enough to succeed at the Bosphorus, and it was probably intended to step in and secure Russia's claims to Constantinople should the Turks be defeated by the British and French at Gallipoli. The British were, in fact, ready to recognize future Russian control of Constantinople, but this would have been best assured by having a force ready to move immediately in fulfillment of the old adage that possession is nine-tenths of the law.[17]

The more tangible Russian naval effort came on 7 March when the Russian squadron bombarded the coal facilities at Eregli and Zonguldak, sinking seven steamers and a large three-masted sailing vessel. From the 5th to the 8th of March, the new submarine *Nerpa* cruised off the Bosphorus. The patrol produced no results, but this was the first time the Russians were able to employ a boat capable of operating off the Strait. The diversion the Russians had promised at the Bosphorus took place on 28 March. The five battleships and two cruisers of the Russian squadron were escorted by ten destroyers, trawlers, and minelayers fitted with minesweeping equipment. The Russian force also included the seaplane carriers *Almaz* and *Imperator Nikolai I*. The former was an armed yacht, fitted with a boom, and capable of carrying four seaplanes; the latter one of two 9,240-ton liners purchased in Great Britain (the second was the *Imperator Alexander I*) before the war and fitted to carry seven to nine seaplanes. The battleships *Rostislav* and *Tri Sviatitelia*, preceded by the minesweepers and destroyers, closed the coast and bombarded the lighthouses at the entrance to the Strait while the seaplanes undertook a reconnaissance and bombed, ineffectually, a Turkish torpedo boat and the coastal batteries. The Russian destroyers forced a Turkish steamer to beach herself, but otherwise the bombardment appears to have had little effect.[18] The Russians planned to repeat the bombardment the following day, but thick fog frustrated them, and after waiting vainly all day for the weather to improve, the squadron moved off in the evening to split into separate groups that bombarded Eregli, Kozlu, and Zonguldak the next day, sinking approximately eleven small sailing craft but otherwise, apparently, not causing much damage.

The Turks and Germans were not really worried about a Russian breakthrough at the Bosphorus. They were concerned about the British and French at the Dardanelles. Nevertheless, for psychological reasons and to demonstrate that the *Goeben* and Turkish fleet were capable of action, Souchon decided to strike at the collection of Russian transports reported at Odessa. The striking force, the cruisers *Medjidieh* and *Hamidieh*, accompanied by a half-flotilla of four torpedo boats fitted with minesweeping gear and commanded by Korvettenkapitän Büchsel of the *Medjidieh*, was to surprise the Russians in Odessa at dawn on the 3d. The *Goeben* and the *Breslau* were to be off Sebastopol to cover the operation. The operation failed when the *Medjidieh* was mined and sank in shallow water off Odessa on the morning of 3 April. The torpedo boats rescued the crew, and one torpedoed the *Medjidieh* in an attempt to completely destroy the wreck. This was not successful; the Russians raised the ship in June and towed the hulk to Nikolaev for repair. In October the captured Turkish cruiser entered Russian service as the *Prut*. The *Goeben* and *Breslau* sank two Russian steamers off the Crimea but found themselves pursued by the Russian squadron, which came out in an attempt to intercept the ships that had raided Odessa. The chase lasted all day, but the Russian battleships could not get within effective range. In the evening Russian destroyers attempted to get into position for a torpedo attack, but only the *Gnevny* managed to come within torpedo range, and the German and Turkish force was able to return to the Bosphorus without further loss.[19]

Although the *Goeben* was able to escape from the Russian fleet, it was the latter that kept the pressure on Turkey's vulnerable maritime communications during April. On the 15th, the *Derzki*, *Gnevny*, and *Pronzitelni*, three of the large new Russian destroyers, attacked Eregli, Kozlu, and Zonguldak, sinking four steamers, and shortly afterward cruised the Anatolian coast in the eastern part of the Black Sea destroying a large number of small sailing craft.

On the day the Allies landed at Gallipoli, 25 April, the Russian fleet appeared off the Bosphorus, and two battleships, proceeding behind a number of sweepers and escorted by three destroyers, bombarded the forts at a range too great for the Turks to reply.[20] They returned on 2 May when the battleships *Panteleimon* and *Tri Sviatitelia* moved in to pound the coast defenses while seaplanes launched from the *Imperator Nikolai I* covered the operation. The following day the *Tri Sviatitelia*, accompanied by the *Rostislav*, repeated the bombardment. The *Goeben* moved up to Beikos within the Bosphorus to try to fire indirectly at the Russians, but she did not sortie, and there is no report of any results. On 4 April the Russians moved north, where the *Rostislav* shelled Igneada near the Bulgarian frontier and seaplanes launched by the *Imperator Nikolai I* and *Almaz* bombed the town. During the same period, the cruisers *Kagul* and *Pamiat Merkuria* worked along the Anatolian coast sinking two steamers, capturing another, and sinking four sailing craft in the vicinity of Kozlu. In the closing stages of the operation, Russian destroyers sank another two steamers and a sailing craft.

Souchon sailed with the *Goeben*, *Breslau*, and *Hamidieh* on 6 May on a sweep to reconnoiter and attack Russian shipping. The Turco-German forces found none. The Russian squadron was back on the Anatolian coast on the 9th with cruisers and destroyers sinking four steamers and a large number of sailing craft in the area between Kozlu and Eregli. The *Goeben* immediately put to sea in an attempt to catch them. However, the Russians also intended to bombard the Bosphorus forts again, and early in the morning of the 10th, the battleships *Panteleimon* and *Tri Sviatitelia* and the seaplane carriers *Almaz* and *Imperator Alexander I*, escorted by minesweepers and destroyers, left the remainder of the Russian squadron to close the coast. They were reported by the Turkish torpedo boat *Numune*, patrolling off the entrance. The *Numune's* German commander engaged the Russian minesweepers only to be driven off by the battleships. Captain Ackermann commanding the *Goeben* now thought he had an opportunity to catch part of a divided Russian squadron and steamed back toward the Bosphorus. He was wrong. The *Goeben* was spotted and reported by the *Pamiat Merkuria*, and the Russians broke off the intended bombardment and ordered a concentration of their forces. The *Goeben* therefore would have to contend with all five Russian battleships, not two. The *Panteleimon* and *Tri Sviatitelia* had still not joined when the two sides opened fire at 7:50 A.M. The *Goeben* concentrated on the leading battleship, the *Evstafi*, but her shooting was not good and she did not hit. The Russians were better, and the *Goeben* was hit twice. The damage was not serious, but by this time all five Russian battleships were in action and Ackermann decided to break off. Firing ceased at 8:12. Ackermann hoped to draw the Russians northward away from the Bosphorus and take advantage of the *Goeben's* speed to double back. He succeeded; the Russians followed for a while, but gave up and turned for home. Ackermann could console himself that he had disrupted the Russian bombardment of the Bosphorus. It was also evident that the combined Russian squadron was too much for the *Goeben*, and it was lucky the Russian hits had not affected the speed on which her safety depended. Ackermann was possibly more fortunate than he realized. The *Goeben* had been spotted by the *Tyulen*, the second of the new Russian submarines, but the boat was not in a position to fire. The action also confirmed to the Russians the potential danger of dividing their battle squadron.[21]

The Russian bombardments of the Bosphorus probably had little effect on the Gallipoli campaign. They had been sporadic and the attacks were not pushed home. On the other hand, the Russian attacks on the Turkish coal traffic in the Black Sea had a very real effect on the Ottoman Empire's ability to continue the war. By the first half of April, the Mittelmeerdivision was feeling the pinch, and Souchon complained he had to avoid "useless" sorties into the Black Sea because of the necessity to economize on fuel. The Turks and their German advisors realized the great importance of the Austrian campaign against Serbia in the Balkans, for the stout Serbian resistance blocked the convenient rail and river route from Germany. There seemed a direct link between the ability of the Austrians to open the Danube route and the ability of the Ottoman Empire to continue the war.[22]

By the end of May, the Russians were able to achieve what amounted to a blockade, albeit imperfect, of the Bosphorus. The Russians still had only two modern submarines available for this patrol, and their action was as yet ineffective. It was those large, fast Russian destroyers that really hurt the Turks. Zonguldak, the main coal port, was roughly 150 miles from the safety of the Bosphorus. The Russian destroyers, in groups of two to four, made periodic sweeps along the Anatolian coast destroying or capturing Turkish shipping. There were four of these sweeps in the second half of May, and with their supply of steamers dwindling—by mid-May they had lost about one-third of their commercial shipping—the Turks were forced to make increasing use of smaller sailing craft, which were not as efficient.[23] Souchon used the occasion of a formal visit to Enver Pasha on 9 May congratulating him on recently receiving the Iron Cross (First Class) to warn about the coal difficulty. Souchon, overestimating the capabilities of Russian submarines, wondered why they had not cut off the coal trade long ago. He warned that the Turkish fleet might run out of coal within six weeks.[24] Souchon confided to his wife that he was powerless against the Russian destroyers and that Turkish headquarters did not fully recognize the seriousness of the situation. Souchon, who repeatedly remarked that the struggle against Turkish negligence was as wearing as the struggle against the enemy, observed that the Turks had not restricted the use of coal by private firms and somewhat naively believed the fleet could protect the colliers. Souchon thought, however, that the *Goeben* would burn as much coal protecting the colliers slowly loading on the open coast as the colliers would load. She would also be exposed to submarines.[25]

The arrival of the first German submarines, *U.21* and *UB.8,* at Constantinople during the first week of June brought some relief to the Turks. The Russians, after another sortie of the fleet against Zonguldak, Kozlu, and Eregli on the 7th, decided they did not have enough destroyers to protect the slow old battleships and cruisers and suspended operations by the battleship squadron until the fast new dreadnoughts entered service later in the year. The destroyers, however, continued their raids, and on the night of 10 June, the *Derzki* and *Gnevny,* after sinking two steamers and a sailing vessel in Zonguldak, were sweeping toward the Bosphorus when they ran into the *Breslau* about 30 miles north of the Strait. The Turks had been using their cruisers and torpedo boats to protect the coal traffic. In the short, sharp encounter in the dark, the *Breslau* got in the first salvo, and the *Gnevny,* hit repeatedly and with her main steam pipe cut, was left helpless in the water. The Germans thought they had sunk her. The *Breslau,* in turn, received three hits from the *Derzki,* before the action was broken off. The *Gnevny* was in a dangerous position when dawn broke, unable to move and close to the enemy coast, but fortunately for the ship's company, who were prepared either for desperate resistance or to scuttle the ship, the *Derzki* was the first to arrive and towed her crippled consort back to Sebastopol.[26]

The Russians probably overreacted to the arrival of German submarines. Obviously, the German primary objective was the Allied fleet off the Dardanelles. *UB.7,* considered too underpowered and weakly armed to face conditions at the Dardanelles, cruised in the Black Sea from 5 to 22 July, but without success. The Turks and Germans decided to establish a system of observation and signal posts along the coast to coordinate their defenses, including the submarines. But the Black Sea was never a priority for German submarines, nor did they experience great luck in it.

The Russians also tried their own form of submarine warfare. They had developed the *Krab*, a submarine minelayer, and on the night of 10–11 July, she laid fifty-eight mines between the two lighthouses at the mouth of the Bosphorus. It was a deliberate attempt to prevent the *Goeben* from sailing to disturb the transfer of the as yet unfinished and unarmed *Imperatritsa Maria*, the first of the Black Sea dreadnoughts, from Nikolaev to Odessa and then Sebastopol. The submarines *Morzh*, *Tyulen*, and *Nerpa*, representing the best the Russians had available, also were deployed off the Bosphorus. In fact, the *Morzh* had to tow the *Krab* after the newly completed submarine's engines malfunctioned. The *Krab*, when launched in 1912, had been the world's first submarine minelayer and had aroused a good deal of interest in naval circles. The long delay in completion meant that by the time she finally entered service, the Germans had evolved what turned out to be a superior design in the UC boats. The *Krab* never really fulfilled the great hopes placed on her, and she remained the only one of her class. The *Krab*'s minefield was quickly discovered and swept, although a Turkish gunboat was damaged in the field on the 11th.[27]

The early Russian minefield laid in December 1914, rather than the *Krab*, was responsible for the damage to the *Breslau*, which struck a mine off the Bosphorus on 18 July while leaving to cover the return of transports. The cruiser took on 642 tons of water, and, although in no danger of sinking, was out of action for several months, given the difficulties of repair in Turkish waters. The Turks now had only one cruiser—the slow and weakly armed *Hamidieh*—besides the precious *Goeben* to assist their handful of hard-worked torpedo boats in protecting transports. The Russian destroyers continued their depredations, and Souchon was forced, most reluctantly, to commit the *Goeben* to escort transports. This was dangerous, for the Russian submarines *Morzh* and *Tyulen* were now operating along the Anatolian coast as well as off the Bosphorus, where they had not accomplished very much. On 10 August the *Tyulen* torpedoed a 1,545-ton collier off Kirpen, the lead ship of a convoy of five escorted by the *Goeben*, *Hamidieh*, and three torpedo boats. The two submarines tried unsuccessfully the following day to get into a firing position against the *Goeben* herself.[28]

Regardless of the danger, the *Goeben* was the only ship the Turks had that could guarantee the safety of the coal convoys. This was clearly demonstrated on 5 September when the destroyers *Bystry* and *Pronzitelni* attacked a convoy of three colliers out of Zonguldak despite the escort of the cruiser *Hamidieh* and torpedo boats *Numune* and *Muavenet*. The colliers were ordered to hug the coast while the escorts engaged. The Russian gunnery was described as excellent, and the destroyers kept beyond the range of the Turkish torpedo boat's armament, so that only the *Hamidieh* could engage with her two 150-mm guns. Both guns broke down, and the *Hamidieh* was forced to call on the *Goeben* for assistance. The battle cruiser had steam up and raced out of the Bosphorus, but in the meantime the Russian destroyers doubled back to the convoy and the Turkish ships, with destruction imminent, ran themselves aground near the mouth of the Sakaria River. The *Goeben* had been too late to save them, and while returning to the Bosphorus the following day, she spotted the submarine *Nerpa* on the surface. The *Goeben* opened fire but did not hit. A disgusted Souchon concluded it was better not to use the *Hamidieh* and the remaining colliers, now down to only eight or nine, had best sail independently to the Bosphorus where they could be met by Turkish torpedo boats.

There were, however, political as well as military reasons for protecting those few colliers. The Turkish torpedo boats could only be effective as protection against submarines, not the big Russian destroyers, and the *Goeben* was soon out again to drive off three Russian destroyers attacking three colliers on 21 September. The *Goeben* periodically escorted coal transports until 14 November when, despite an escort of two torpedo boats, the submarine *Morzh* narrowly missed hitting her with two torpedoes off the northeast entrance to the Bosphorus. Souchon then stopped the procedure; the risks were too great. He decided to restrict the coal traffic to colliers, generally belonging to German companies, which were fast enough to make the Zonguldak to Bosphorus trip in a single night. They would be escorted by Turkish torpedo boats off the Bosphorus during daylight hours.[29]

The fact that the Turks and Germans were forced to employ their major asset escorting slow old colliers could be counted as a major success for the Russians. Kapitänleutnant Rudolph Firle, the aggressive young officer in command of the *Muavenet* (who had sunk the battleship *Goliath* in the Dardanelles the preceding spring), complained: "These Russian destroyers with their artillery and speed are the real masters of the sea and need fear no one."[30]

It would be a mistake, however, to exaggerate the effectiveness of the Russian blockade, particularly of the Bosphorus. A British observer with the Black Sea Fleet reported that the Russian destroyers may have been effective, but they did not keep to the sea long enough. Part of the problem was the necessity of the destroyers retaining what the British considered an excessive portion of their fuel as ballast, thereby reducing their radius of action. The Russian submarine crews were also inexperienced, and at the end of 1915 there was still a shortage of submarines suitable for maintaining the watch off the Bosphorus. Vessels coming from Romania and Bulgaria to the north were able to evade the blockade by hugging the Bulgarian coast. The Russians admitted that the Black Sea Fleet still suffered from the fact that until roughly three years earlier it had been a negligible quantity and the major Russian effort had been concentrated in the Baltic, where Germany represented the most formidable potential enemy.[31]

The operations of German submarines in the Black Sea brought some relief to the Turks. In September *UB.7* and *UB.8* worked off the Russian coast, and the former sank the British steamer *Patagonia* (6,011 tons) off Odessa on the 15th. *UB.14* and *UC.13* also entered the Black Sea a few weeks later. The actual German submarine successes in 1915 were relatively small, but the Russians replied to the new menace by forming "submarine hunting groups" composed of varying numbers of destroyers. The Russians had no more success "hunting" submarines than the British and French had elsewhere, but the effort tied up destroyers that might have been better employed on other duties. These operations also delayed the implementation of the directive of the Russian high command issued on 9 September, giving priority to the attack on Turkish shipping as well as cooperation with the Russian army in the Caucasus. The prospect of a landing at the Bosphorus became more distant. With the failure of the new British landing at Suvla, there was little likelihood the Allies would break out of the Gallipoli Peninsula and, consequently, even less probability the Russians would have an opportunity to land at the Bosphorus.[32]

The two new Russian dreadnoughts did much to checkmate the *Goeben*. The *Imperatritsa Maria* was in service by the end of the summer, and the *Imperatritsa Ekaterina Velikaya* was available for operations in December. The Russians paired each with one of their few cruisers to create a "maneuver" or "battle"—accounts differ—group. A third "maneuver" group, really a reserve, was formed from the three to five old Russian battleships. Destroyers were attached to each group in varying numbers as available. The dreadnoughts were each armed with twelve 30.5-cm guns, and the Russians considered each of these groups, although slower, strong enough to take on the *Goeben* and *Breslau* combined. The Russian fleet therefore returned to the Turkish coast, and on 1 October, the old battleships and cruisers moved in to shell Zonguldak and Eregli while the *Imperatritsa Maria* covered their seaward flank.

A new front opened for the Russians when Bulgaria entered the war on the side of the Central Powers in September 1915. This meant the end of Serbia, the opening of the direct rail route from Germany to Constantinople, the dispatch of another Anglo-French expedition to Salonika, the commencement of a new front and campaign in the Balkans, and, finally, the end of the Dardanelles expedition. It had little effect on the naval situation in the Black Sea. Bulgarian naval power was minimal, an old gunboat and a half dozen coastal torpedo boats, but the Bulgarian ports of Varna and nearby Euxinograd were now available for German submarines, and *UB.7* and *UB.8* were transferred to the Bulgarian coast. The Russian fleet conducted three operations against Varna and Euxinograd in the remaining months of the year. The operations of 20 to 22 and 25 October—the latter including aerial attacks by seaplanes launched from the *Almaz* and *Imperator Nikolai I*—and 24 to 26 December do not appear to have accomplished very much. They exposed the Russian squadron to submarine attack off Varna on 27 October when the two German submarines tried to attack the old battleships shelling the port. The submarines were spotted in the smooth water and attacked, but *UB.7* managed to launch a torpedo at the *Panteleimon*. The Germans heard an explosion and thought they had hit, but the torpedo missed. Nevertheless, the Russians broke off the attack.[33]

Admiral Ebergard was very nervous about risking his fleet against Varna. Ebergard, generally described as a courtly old gentleman, honest and never an intriguer, had little of the aggressiveness or fire associated with Admiral Essen in the Baltic. The younger Russian officers, who seemed to have idolized Essen, regarded Ebergard as slow, cautious, and generally unenterprising. He had been ordered to undertake the operations against Varna against his own judgment as he considered the results to be obtained would probably be small. Ebergard, in fact, urged a visiting British admiral to point out to the tsar that if the operations were repeated, they should be prepared for losses, for they could easily have lost a battleship off Varna.[34] A few months later, on 10

March 1916, the Russians aborted a planned seaplane attack on Varna covered by the *Imperatritsa Ekaterina* and the Second Battle Group when German aircraft attacked the covering destroyers and the torpedo boat *Leitenant Pushchin* was mined and sunk.[35]

The Black Sea was not a happy place for German submarines. *UC.13*, returning from a patrol to the eastern portion of the Black Sea, where she accounted for four sailing craft and a steamer, ran aground in bad weather off the mouth of the Sakaria River near Kirpen Island on 29 November. Souchon sent two small Turkish minesweeping gunboats, the *Tasköprü* and *Yozgat*, to help recover matériel from the wreck. They were caught by the destroyers *Derzki*, *Gnevny*, and *Bespokoiny* off Kirpen Island and sunk on 10 December.

Although the end of the Dardanelles campaign relieved the Turks and Germans of the threat of British submarines in the Sea of Marmara, and the fall of Serbia opened the route for munitions, it had little immediate effect on the shortage of coal at Constantinople. The Russians kept the pressure on the Anatolian coast. It nearly cost them one of their precious dreadnoughts on 5 January when the *Imperatritsa Ekaterina* of the Second Battle Group, covering the operation against the coal traffic, was attacked in error by the destroyer *Bystry*, which fired seven torpedoes that, fortunately, missed. The incident was blamed on gross navigational errors on the part of both ships.[36]

The frequent presence of Russian destroyers off Zonguldak brought out the *Goeben* again. Souchon intended for her to arrive off Zonguldak to cover the entrance of the empty collier *Carmen* (4,400 tons). The collier, however, was caught and sunk by the destroyers *Pronzitelni* and *Leitenant Shestakov* in the early morning hours of 8 January off Kirpen before she could reach Zonguldak. While steaming westward back to the Bosphorus, the *Goeben* sighted the destroyers after daybreak and gave chase, only to run into the *Imperatritsa Ekaterina*. The destroyers had used their wireless to warn of the *Goeben*'s presence, and the Russian dreadnought had increased to full speed to reach the scene. She opened fire at a range of approximately 18,500 meters, and the *Goeben* turned away to the southwest. The *Goeben* fired only five salvoes in the first four minutes of the battle before the Russians were out of range. The *Imperatritsa Ekaterina* fired ninety-six 305-mm rounds, and Russian sources report the artillery duel lasted from 9:45 to 10:13 A.M. Her rate of fire declined, however, due to mechanical problems in the turrets caused by the strain of rapid fire. No hits were scored on either side, although splinters from near misses fell on the *Goeben*'s deck before the German ship drew steadily out of range and the *Imperatritsa Ekaterina* broke off the action and turned to the northwest. The brief encounter clearly demonstrated that the *Goeben* was no longer the most powerful single warship in the Black Sea. The new Russian dreadnoughts may have been slower, but they outgunned her.

The Germans tried to redress the balance by stationing submarines off Zonguldak, but their efforts to attack Russian warships were not successful. On 6 February the First Battle Group attacked Zonguldak again. The seaplane carriers *Imperator Alexander I* and *Imperator Nikolai I* launched a total of fourteen aircraft to bomb the harbor after the destroyer bombardment had ended. The seaplanes bombed and sank the collier *Irmingard*

(4,211 tons), which was subsequently raised and temporarily repaired. *UB.7* managed to evade the two destroyers circling the seaplane carriers and fire a torpedo at one of the carriers. The Germans heard an explosion and thought they had scored a hit. They had not, but the seaplane carriers rapidly steamed away, leaving two of their aircraft to be recovered and towed by destroyers. The submarine missed an opportunity to attack the destroyers owing to a lack of torpedoes, and there was a fairly general belief among the German naval officers that the UB boats were too small, weakly armed, and slow to achieve good results in the Black Sea.[37]

The Russian attacks on Turkish shipping also ran into the law of diminishing returns. They increasingly resulted in the destruction of sailing craft rather than steamers. However, many of those small craft were likely to reappear, for they were reportedly sunk by their captains in shallow waters (by withdrawing large cork plugs) and refloated after the destroyers had departed. The extension of Turkish observation posts along the coast, linked by telephone, enabled the Turks to spread the alarm once Russian ships were sighted, and small craft often had the chance to hide in the mouths of rivers or to be safely beached. Starting in the summer of 1915, the Turks also used small craft to carry coal to the mouth of the Sakaria River and then up the river to Adapazar and then by land to Constantinople. Nevertheless, after the loss of the *Irmingard* in February the number of colliers had fallen to only five, and the German high command had to promise in response to desperate pleas from Enver Pasha that starting at the end of February there would be a daily train loaded with 400 tons of coal from Germany. The Germans would therefore provide roughly 12,000 tons of the estimated 30,000 tons of Turkish monthly coal consumption in order to keep the vital railways and munitions factories in operation.[38]

The Turks also continued, with what has been described as dogged determination, to bring coal from Zonguldak, and took advantage of every diversion of Russian warships to other areas, such as Lazistan, to resume shipments. Some historians believe the only way to have cut off coal from Zonguldak would have been an expedition and landing to destroy the mining installations and pitheads. The Turkish garrison would have been weak and the poor communications between Zonguldak and the interior would have hampered the arrival of reinforcements. The Russian navy shrank from this in 1915 and 1916, and although landings were contemplated in 1917, by then the Russians had other objectives.[39]

AMPHIBIOUS OPERATIONS ON THE CAUCASUS FRONT

In the first half of 1916, the Russian navy directed its major effort in the Black Sea toward supporting the operations of the Russian army on the Caucasus front. The Caucasus operations are surely among the least-known campaigns of the First World War. This was not the major front for the Russians, and the general staff had a tendency to syphon off troops from the Caucasus for the benefit of other, more pressing obligations. The Turks had a numerical advantage when they entered the war, and Enver Pasha was tempted to undertake a rash offensive into Russian territory directed at Georgia where he hoped a Turkish victory would provoke a revolution among the non-Russian peoples. The moment was ill timed, for the heavy snow and fierce winter weather worked against the Turks, and in the heavy fighting around Sarikamis at the end of 1914 and beginning of 1915 they suffered a costly defeat. In 1915 the Turks, after an initial success at Malazgirt, were defeated and pushed back near Karakilisse in the area to the north of Lake Van. The Allied evacuation of the Dardanelles threatened to release large numbers of Turkish troops for other fronts at the beginning of 1916, and General Nikolai Yudenich, Russian commander in the Caucasus, decided it would be prudent to forestall them with a Russian offensive, which surprised the Turks on 17 January, capturing Köprüköy. Yudenich gained his major objective by completing the capture of the city of Erzurum by 16 February.[40]

The Russian navy was called upon to assist these operations along the Black Sea coast on the extreme right flank of the Russian front. The region, known as Lazistan, had poor roads, and the mountains with their steep cliffs and deep ravines extended down to the coast. Under these conditions, sea power could be exploited to furnish significant leverage to the army's operations. The Turkish line of communications, particularly the road from their major port Trebizond eastward to Rize, was vulnerable to naval pressure, which might tie down Turkish reinforcements and prevent them from being shifted to other portions of the front. The Russian army commander in the coastal sector, General Lyakhov, recognized the value of enfilading fire from warships and delayed his portion of the offensive until the ships were available. The Russians did not have a naval base in this part of the Black Sea, but in the course of the preceding year they had operated torpedo boats, generally their smaller and older ones, from the port of Batum. The demands of the army now meant that substantial portions of the Black Sea Fleet would be employed in the eastern portion of the Black Sea. Other operations in the western portion of the Black Sea would certainly not cease but would inevitably suffer.

On the 17th and 20th of January, Russian destroyers swept the coast of Lazistan destroying a large number of mostly small sailing craft assumed to be used by the Turks to supply their army. The weak naval force at Batum was strengthened by two torpedo boats and the gunboats *Donetz* and *Kubanetz*, the former salved after having been sunk at Odessa in the Turkish attack that began the war. They were joined by the old battleship *Rostislav*, escorted by two torpedo boats, for the attack on the strong Turkish position to the west of the Archave River that began on 5 February. The *Rostislav* and *Kubanetz* pounded the Turkish positions for three and a half hours and returned the following day to continue the barrage, which forced the Turks to abandon their position. The Turks fell back to new positions at Vice, which the Russians reached on the 8th. The *Rostislav* with *Donetz* and *Kubanetz*, screened by the torpedo boats, returned to the coast to bombard the Turkish positions on the 15th and 16th. This time the Russians established a mobile wireless station on shore to facilitate artillery spotting. Once again the Turks were shelled out of their positions. The Russians were always aware of the danger that the

Goeben might try to intervene. Consequently, the three battleships of the Third Battle Group (the *Panteleimon, Ioann Zlatoust,* and *Evstafi*) were at sea from the 8th to the 11th, to cover the operation. The Second Battle Group with the *Imperatritsa Ekaterina* patrolled 20 to 30 miles offshore.

The Turks rushed reinforcements from Trebizond along the coastal road to Rize, and the retreating Turkish forces established a very strong defensive position along the Büyük-dere River approximately 10 miles west of Vice. This position was likely to have been very costly for the army to take, as there were vertical cliffs at the sea, a wide valley with good fields of fire for the defenders, steep ravines along the river, and deep water with only one ford. The navy suggested an amphibious operation, a landing at the small port of Atina approximately 4 miles east of the Turkish position.

The Russian navy, with the prospect of a major landing at the Bosphorus, had already devoted a good deal of attention to amphibious warfare. They had in the Black Sea and the Sea of Azov a type of vessel easily adapted to it. The Elpidifors were small craft, generally 1,000 to 1,500 tons, whose engines and superstructures were located aft and cargo holds forward. Consequently, when lightly loaded they drew more water at their sterns than at their bows and were well suited for working close to the shore in shallow waters and at the small undeveloped ports characteristic of the area. The Russians made them into troop landing craft by fitting them with gangplanks overhanging the bow and worked by booms. They were also widely used as minesweepers and minelayers. The Russians were also building substantial numbers of Russud-type landing craft similar to the ones the British had used at Suvla. The 225-ton motor lighters were fitted with a bow ramp lowered by a pair of bow booms and could carry more than 500 men in the hold and 240 on deck. The navy ordered 50 from the Russud yards at Nikolaev at the end of 1915. The yards soon concentrated their efforts on these craft because they were highly profitable, by some accounts, and because shortages and nondelivery of crucial items stalled work on the larger warships. Even so, approximately 30 of them had to be delivered without their diesel engines.[41]

The landing force, two *plastun* battalions (dismounted cossacks), two mountain artillery guns, and two machine-gun platoons—a total of approximately 2,100 men—embarked at Batum and in the early morning of 4 March were landed to the east and west of Atina by three Elpidifors, followed by the specially adapted transports *Kornilov* and *Lazarev* with the guns and horses. The *Rostislav, Kubanetz,* and four torpedo boats provided direct artillery support. The landings had taken place before the Turks realized it and could open fire, and, caught off balance, they abandoned the Büyük-dere position. Lyakhov, anxious to forestall the arrival of Turkish reinforcements and profit from his momentum, continued to leapfrog around the Turkish positions. The next day, 5 March, troops were landed farther along the coast at Mapavri, and on the 6th an infantry battalion was landed to the west of Rize, covered by the *Kubanetz,* while two torpedo boats supported the advance along the coast. Rize fell to the combined attack, and the Russians now had their first small port on the Turkish Black Sea coast. The Russian advance halted for a few weeks, stalled by the spring thaw. The successful amphibious operations had demonstrated how a small number of troops could have a disproportionate effect.[42]

The first Turkish response to the Russian offensive in Lazistan was to create yet a new role for the *Goeben*. They used the battle cruiser on 4 February to rush 429 officers and men, a mountain artillery battery, machine-gun and aviation detachments, 1,000 rifles, and 300 cases of munitions to Trebizond. The *Goeben* had to keep well out at sea to avoid the Russian destroyers along the coast, for, crammed with flammable munitions, she was in no condition for a serious action. On 27 February the *Breslau*, restored to service with two new 15-cm guns, was also used to carry 71 officers and men of a machine-gun company, bombs and munitions, as well as fuel oil and lubricating oil for submarines to Trebizond. She was to bring back, if possible, flour and legumes. The cruiser was authorized, however, to operate in the eastern Black Sea after landing the troops. The *Breslau*'s cargo also would have caused embarrassment in case action was necessary. On 28 February the large Russian destroyers *Pronzitelni* and *Bespokoiny* shelled Kerasun and were reported heading west along the Anatolian coast to a possible encounter with the Germans. The *Breslau* put into Sinope to discharge the oil. She was spotted by the Russian destroyers on leaving harbor, but her commanding officer, Korvettenkapitän von Knorr, considered his primary mission was to reach Trebizond with the troops, and he managed to shake off the destroyers in the darkness. After landing the troops at Trebizond, the *Breslau* cruised northward to the vicinity of Tuapse but encountered nothing and returned to the Bosphorus. She had a brief brush with two Russian destroyers north of Zonguldak on the morning of 2 March, but the Russians managed to outrun her. Von Knorr never had the opportunity to pick up the flour and legumes at Sinope.

Of potentially greater importance, the Admiralstab finally agreed to send a large submarine, *U.33*, to the Black Sea. The submarine was commanded by Kapitänleutnant Gansser, a veteran of Mediterranean operations. Until she arrived, Souchon did not believe he could do anything to seriously assist the Turkish army in Lazistan. On 6 March he refused Enver's request to transport a regiment by sea to Trebizond. They now stood a chance of encountering one of the Russian dreadnoughts, and the 510-mile journey from the Bosphorus at high speed would result in excessive consumption of coal, which they could ill spare. Nevertheless, Enver was insistent on how critical the situation at Trebizond was, and Colonel von Lossow, the German military attaché, argued that along the narrow coastal front a few additional troops brought by sea might serve as a reserve to stop the Russian advance until reinforcements arrived by land. Moreover, the troops could be landed at the less exposed Tireboli, to the west of Trebizond. Souchon let the political and military necessities overcome his doubts based on naval reasons. Moreover, the eagerly awaited *U.33* had arrived at Constantinople on 11 March and would be ready for operations after a fortnight's overhaul. The *Breslau* sailed the afternoon of the 11th with 211 officers and men as well as a dozen barrels of fuel oil and lubricating oil for submarines. The troops were landed without incident on the 13th, and the *Breslau* was able to call at Samsun for 30 tons of flour, one ton of maize, and 30 tons of coal before returning to the Bosphorus.[43]

U.33 sailed on her first Black Sea operation on 25 March with orders to attack Russian warships operating off Lazistan and shipping off the Caucasian coast. The Russian advance directed at Trebizond began the following day. The Russian high command had not changed its opinion that this was only a secondary theater of the war, and General Yudenich's resources remained limited. The renewed advance was primarily to consolidate the existing position before the Turkish troops released from Gallipoli could arrive in force, and Trebizond represented the best of the ports along the eastern Anatolian coast. Moreover, the Russian army and navy had as difficult a time understanding each other's point of view as their German and Turkish opponents. Yudenich could not understand why the navy with its superiority could not prevent all Turkish sea transport along the Anatolian coast, and the army preferred continuous naval support on its flank. Ebergard pointed out that a continuous blockade of the Anatolian coast was not possible given the distance from their base at Sebastopol, and that continuous tactical support on the seaward flank of the army was not desirable because of the danger of submarines and the lack of a base in the eastern Black Sea. The navy preferred large amphibious operations of *limited* duration. They did agree to provide full support for the transport of two *plastun* brigades—18,000 men and 4,300 horses—from Novorossisk to Rize. The Russian offensive began on 26 March, and after six days they had managed to advance about 16 to 17 miles to the Kara-dere River, from which they could make no further progress. Yudenich, fearing a counterattack, was anxious for the transport to take place as quickly as possible.

U.33 proceeding eastward off the Anatolian coast sighted the *Imperatritsa Maria* and the First Battle Group on the 28th, but the dreadnought and her two escorting destroyers were zigzagging, and the submarine could not get into a firing position. On the 30th, U.33 torpedoed and sank the hospital ship *Portugal* (5,358 tons) at Sürmene Bay. The *Portugal* was a French ship, trapped in the Black Sea by the war, and its sinking inevitably caused controversy. The Germans claimed that she was not clearly marked as a hospital ship, she had been towing lighters full of troops, and there was a heavy explosion after she was torpedoed, indicating she was carrying munitions. A Russian destroyer attacked the submarine with depth charges, but she escaped and proceeded north to sink the following day a coastal sailing vessel and to destroy a small steamer that had run itself aground after a warning shot off Suchumi. On 1 April U.33 received orders to rendezvous with the *Breslau* at Trebizond.

The *Breslau* arrived at Trebizond with 107 officers and men, 5,000 rifles, and 794 cases of munitions on 3 April. The cruiser then sailed to shell the Russian positions at Sürmene Bay, followed by U.33, which remained 4 to 6 miles off during the bombardment. The *Breslau*'s gunnery set fire to the Elpidifor-type minesweeper *T.233*, and after she departed, U.33's gun finished her off. The *Breslau* proceeded northward and sank a small sailing vessel off Tuapse. The next morning, however, she ran into the *Imperatritsa Ekaterina* and *Kagul*, well screened by destroyers, which had been ordered to patrol off Novorossisk after the Russians learned of the *Breslau*'s attack on the Russian positions at Sürmene Bay. The *Breslau* came under fire for about fifteen minutes from the big guns of the *Imperatritsa Ekaterina*.[44] She managed to escape without serious damage, but she was well splashed, and the Germans commented on the excellence of the dreadnought's gunnery. This phase of the Turco-German naval response ended the same morning when *U.33* returned to Sürmene Gulf and attempted to attack two transports. She was sighted by the destroyer *Strogi*, which rammed and seriously damaged her periscope, and the submarine had to break off operations and return to base.

The Germans and Turks failed to disrupt a major reinforcement of Rize by sea to strengthen the Russian advance on Trebizond. Preparations began in March. The majority of troops were brought to Novorossisk by rail, the transports escorted from Odessa and well screened by the big ships of the navy, and embarkation commenced on 4 April. The convoy, some 22 transports, sailed on the 5th under the direct protection of the *Imperatritsa Maria*, 3 cruisers, 3 seaplane carriers, and 15 destroyers and torpedo boats. The landing at Rize began the morning of the 7th. The battle groups centered around the *Imperatri*:*sa Maria*, and the *Imperatritsa Ekaterina* remained at sea north of Rize to cover the landing against possible interference. Seaplanes from the three carriers patrolled overhead, and netlayers laid an antisubmarine net around the port. The British observer with the Black Sea Fleet summed up the operation: "It has been very fortunate that all troops and stores were put on shore in one day, although everything was in their favor, good landing places, no opposition and a fine day with an exceptionally calm surface, making it difficult for any submarine to approach without being detected. On the whole, as a first landing, it may be considered creditable."[45]

The troops had been landed safely, but the threat of the Turkish counterattack, which began on the 8th, caused Yudenich to request that at least one brigade be landed closer to the front at Hamurkan. Rear Admiral Khomenko, commander of the transport flotilla, refused to deviate from his orders, and Ebergard, flying his flag in the *Imperatritsa Maria*, was anxious to get the big ships away because of the threat posed by submarines and refused to change his plans. Yudenich insisted, however, and on the night of the 7th, a brigade of approximately 8,200 men was moved along the coast in seven of the Elpidifors, which had remained at Rize after the transports departed.[46] The Turkish counterattacks were stopped, and the now reinforced Russians were able to resume their advance, which was covered by the heavy guns of the battleships *Rostislav* and *Panteleimon*, assisted by four destroyers. The Turkish army evacuated Trebizond on the evening of 18 April.[47]

The Russian high command decided that it would be prudent to reinforce Russian forces in Lazistan, especially as a Turkish counterattack was anticipated. They ordered the transport of two more divisions, the 123d and the 127th, by sea. The approximately 34,400 troops with their horses and equipment were assembled at Mariupol in the Sea of Azov and transported in two convoys on 16–19 May and 28 May–4 June. After the convoys had passed through the Kertch Strait from the Sea of Azov into the Black Sea, the commander in chief in the *Imperatritsa Maria*, with two cruisers, three seaplane carriers, and the usual large number of destroyers and torpedo boats, provided the escort. The troops were landed at Kavata Bay, 5 miles to the east of Trebizond. The Russians built temporary wharves, and on the eve of the arrival of the convoys carefully swept the entrance to the bay and laid a 4-mile-long line of antisubmarine nets. There also were four patrol lines outside of the nets. The newly constructed landing craft and motorized lighters were employed extensively and the landings went well. The Germans and Turks made no direct move to interfere.

The navy temporarily deployed the Second Battleship Squadron (the *Ioann Zlatoust, Evstafi,* and *Panteleimon*) with the cruiser *Pamiat Merkuria,* the seaplane carrier *Almaz,* and four destroyers to join the naval forces at Batum. They remained there through the summer with orders to blockade the Anatolian coast to the east of Sinope, protect the army's seaward flank, and provide artillery support or protect valuable transports if necessary. There were other torpedo boats and gunboats at Rize and Trebizond and a pair of small, old, and not very effective submarines at Batum.

The Turks seemed powerless to disrupt these operations, although the Russians had been somewhat lucky, since German submarines were in the area at least part of the time. *U.33* sailed from Constantinople the day Trebizond fell and spent several days in the Trebizond area. The submarine reportedly spotted one of the Russian dreadnoughts at least twice but was never in a position to fire and moved off to the northeast coast of the Black Sea on 28 April and sank three sailing craft and a steamer before serious oil leaks forced her commander to break off the patrol and return to Constantinople on 4 May. *U.33* required a prolonged period of repair. Souchon pointed out that his UB submarines were not suitable for operations in the distant eastern portion of the Black Sea and asked for another large boat as a temporary replacement until one of the improved UB.II-class could arrive. The Admiralstab agreed and sent *U.38,* commanded by Kapitänleutnant Max Valentiner, one of the crack, though controversial, German submariners in the Mediterranean. In the interim, the small *UB.14* worked off Trebizond between the end of May and first few days of June, but returned to Constantinople without having had any success.

U.38 sailed on her first Black Sea cruise on 31 May, and on 3 June landed three agents on the Georgian coast approximately 45 miles north of Batum with orders to attempt to disturb the Russian army's supply. *U.38* did not sight the Russian convoys, but sank four small steamers and a sailing vessel, generally in the area between Tuapse and Sochi, and on 11 June fired two torpedoes, which missed, at a zigzagging dreadnought (probably the *Imperatritsa Maria*) in the southeastern portion of the Black Sea.

The last amphibious operation of the year took place in June when the long-awaited Turkish counterattack broke through the Russian front lines on the 22d. The Turks advanced approximately 20 kilometers toward the town of Of, located on the coast to the west of Rize. The local corps commander decided to shift three infantry battalions from Trebizond to the threatened sector. The troops embarked at Plantane in the Elpidifors and motorized lighters and moved to Of on the 23d and 24th of June. The Turkish attacks were stopped by 4 July.[48]

The *Goeben* and *Breslau* came out to support these Turkish offensives by attacking Russian shipping and supply lines along the Caucasian and Anatolian coasts, and, if possible, destroying any weaker or isolated warships they could catch. The *Goeben* shelled Tuapse harbor on the afternoon of 4 July, sinking a small steamer and a motor schooner. At roughly the same time, the *Breslau* sank a steamer and sailing craft off Sochi and completed the destruction of another steamer that had been torpedoed two days before by *U.38* on her second cruise in the Black Sea.[49] The Germans had, however, placed their head in the noose, for Sebastopol was much closer to the Bosphorus than the eastern shores of the Black Sea and there was a chance the Russian battle squadrons would be able to cut them off. The Russians tried. The *Imperatritsa Maria* sailed on the 4th and the *Imperatritsa Ekaterina* on the 5th of July, and patrolled to the north of the Kirpen Island–Eregli sector. The Germans had anticipated this, and *UB.14* was waiting off Sebastopol; but the submarine was spotted and attacked by one of the *Imperatritsa Maria*'s destroyer screen before she could fire a torpedo. Both the *Goeben* and *Breslau*, steaming independently, evaded the Russians by taking a northerly route, close to the Crimean coast, and returning to the Bosphorus from the direction of Bulgaria. There was fairly widespread criticism of the Russian commander in chief's handling of his forces and the failure to respond promptly and coordinate the movements of Russian submarines. This may have been instrumental in bringing about the replacement of Ebergard by the young (41) Vice Admiral Kolchak, who had earned an excellent reputation for his handling of the destroyers in the Baltic.[50] The new commander in chief was younger than many of the Black Sea captains, and his arrival was greeted with trepidation by some. He was generally expected to bring about a revolution in command and to bring new vigor to operations, with a renewed emphasis on mining off the Bosphorus.[51]

The Russian amphibious operations on the Lazistan coast in the first half of 1916 are interesting. They were successful. On the other hand, it would be wrong to exaggerate their importance. None of the landings faced serious opposition or strong defenses. There is no comparison between the problems the Russians faced and the fierce resistance the Allies met when they landed on the Gallipoli Peninsula. Nevertheless, the Russians had gained considerable experience in moving large numbers of men and equipment over the sea and landing them on a hostile coast. Their force of different types of specially adapted transports and landing craft was also growing. On a minor scale the Russians employed a system of guerrilla warfare. Bands composed of Turkish-speaking Greeks and Armenians, generally seeking to escape Turkish military service, were armed and paid by the Russians and then landed by a destroyer on dark nights on the Turkish shore. The Russians spoke to the British observer with the Black Sea Fleet about a force of 300 men, which they hoped to increase to 2,000, and there was talk of a landing by a whole Russian army corps. Reality was less spectacular. There were eight landings by reconnaissance parties in the Samson area from 10 July to 25 August, and the total number of men landed was 160.[52]

The Russians also executed a raid on the night of 2 November against the Turkish coastal craft, which they had discovered concealed at the mouth of the Terme River, east of Samsun. The destroyers *Kapitan Saken*, *Leitenant Zatzarenni*, and *Strogi*, accompanied by a transport, landed 40 men, together with 140 (mostly Armenian) volunteers, to seize—some accounts report destroy—20 barges and sailing craft.[53] The inevitable question was: As Russian superiority at sea increased and their confidence grew, would they be able to attempt another landing closer to the heart of the Turkish Empire, perhaps even at the Bosphorus itself?

The Turco-German naval forces had been powerless to do more than annoy the Russian operations in Lazistan. Souchon made another effort with the *Breslau* later in July when the cruiser was ordered to lay mines off Novorossisk and then operate against shipping on the Caucasus coast. The *Breslau* sailed on 21 July with 65 mines, but her departure from the Bosphorus was reported to the Russian commander in chief. The Russians had excellent sources of intelligence, and the Germans and Turks may have unwittingly helped them through injudicious use of wireless. The Russians were the ones who had salvaged the codes from the *Magdeburg* in the Baltic, and it is evident they also exploited this advantage in the Black Sea. The French liaison officer with the Russian commander in chief confirmed this later in 1916 when he noted that the Russians were cognizant of Turkish and Bulgarian codes and that thanks to constant use of wireless by the enemy, the Black Sea Fleet was well informed (*au courant*) of everything that was going on.[54]

Kolchak sailed in the *Imperatritsa Maria* with the cruiser *Kagul* and five destroyers to intercept the *Breslau. UB.7* had been stationed off Sebastopol for this eventuality, but was prevented from making an attack when she was spotted and bombed by seaplanes, thereby demonstrating again the difficulties German submarines had in the Black Sea. They repeatedly sighted Russian warships, but were unable to deliver their attacks. At 1:05 P.M. (1:30 according to Russian sources), approximately 100 miles north of Sinope, the *Breslau* met the destroyer *Schastlivy*, part of the screen preceding the *Imperatritsa Maria*. The *Breslau* altered course to the south at full speed and then altered again to a southwesterly course to avoid being cut off. Korvettenkapitän von Knorr had to jettison nine mines in order to give his aft 15-cm a free field of fire and allow ammunition to be brought up. The *Schastlivy* opened fire shortly before 2:00, but was driven off by the *Breslau*'s 15-cm. In the meantime the other Russian warships arrived, and by 2:15, despite the *Breslau*'s efforts to shake her off (which included making smoke), the *Imperatritsa Maria* opened fire at a range of 22,000 meters. The *Breslau*'s use of smoke caused the dreadnought to cease fire after two salvoes, but when the cruiser altered course to avoid drawing too close to the coast, she was able to resume fire. Von Knorr was making 25 knots but could not seem to shake the *Imperatritsa Maria*, whose shooting was good, and a number of the *Breslau*'s men were wounded by splinters from a near miss. Von Knorr repeatedly used smoke, and eventually the *Breslau* slowly drew ahead and out of range. The Germans were worried the Russian destroyers might attempt a torpedo attack in the dark and jettisoned another eight mines. The destroyers, however, lost contact with the *Breslau*, whose escape was aided by a rain squall. The cruiser reached the safety of the Bosphorus early the next morning. The mission had ended in failure.[55]

RUSSIAN NAVAL SUPERIORITY

The focus of the Black Sea Fleet's attention shifted back to the west in the second half of 1916. This was largely due to the events surrounding Romania's entry into the war as well as to Admiral Kolchak's interest in increased mining, particularly at the Bosphorus. Starting on 31 July, when the submarine *Krab* laid 60 mines in the entrance to the Bosphorus, Russian destroyers during the next few nights laid more than 800 mines in a semicircle to the north of the Strait. On the night of 11 August a pair of destroyers laid a minefield to the east of the Bosphorus entrance in shallow water north of Adajiklar, and on the night of the 20th, another field to the west of the Strait northwest of Hissar Kaiasi.

On 27 August, after hard bargaining, Romania finally entered the war on the side of the Triple Entente. Shortly before the declaration of war, the Russian fleet reappeared in force off the Bulgarian coast on the 25th. The *Imperatritsa Ekaterina* and 7 destroyers were out to cover an air raid launched by the 3 seaplane carriers (the *Almaz, Imperator Alexander I,* and *Imperator Nikolai I*) directed at the German submarines reported at Varna. Only 7 of the 19–20 seaplanes with the Russian force were able to take off in the rough sea and strong winds. The Russians, in turn, were subjected to attacks by German seaplanes, and the destroyer *Pospeshny* was damaged.

The Romanian decision to enter the war turned out to be disastrous. The Romanians launched an early offensive into Transylvania to enforce their historic claims, but their armies were defeated and Romania overrun by the forces of the Central Powers led by Field Marshal August von Mackensen. After a few months fighting, they retained only a small portion of their territory, leaving the Russians with new obligations. A special naval detachment was created, including three gunboats, to work with the Romanians in the defense of the lower Danube (see chapter 9). Other Russian warships, notably the old battleship *Rostislav* and a number of torpedo boats, worked along the seaward flank of the front in the Dobrudja region, or attacked what scant shipping—usually small coastal sailing vessels—as could be found along the Bulgarian coast. The Russian navy also ran convoys bringing men and matériel from the Ukrainian coast to Constanza.

On the night of 8–9 September, three Russian destroyers tried to block the use of Varna by German submarines by laying a minefield northeast of the harbor entrance. The mission ended badly when the *Bespokoiny* was heavily damaged by a Romanian mine on the return to Constanza. The submarine *Krab* laid another field south of Varna on the 15th. The Russians also came under frequent German air attack. The battleship *Rostislav* was slightly damaged in Constanza harbor on 2 September, and the minesweeper *T.238* was damaged in another raid on the 10th that also sank two lighters.

Constanza, the major Romanian port, was doomed by the advance of the Central Powers on land, and the *Rostislav,* which had been busy supporting the Romanian army with her big guns, ended by covering the evacuation of the port on 22

October. The Romanian evacuation was so rapid, however, that the storage tanks filled with large amounts of petroleum remained intact. The Russian high command ordered the navy to destroy them with gunfire from the sea, but this proved more difficult to accomplish than had been anticipated. On 1 November the cruiser *Pamiat Merkuria* had to break off her first attempt after a false submarine alarm. The attack by two destroyers on the 2d had little effect, and it was only on the 4th that the *Pamiat Merkuria*, under air attack and fired on by coastal batteries, was able to destroy 15 of the 37 petroleum tanks. The Russians found themselves subjected to heavy air attack in these waters and shifted to approaching their targets during the night and opening fire at dawn. They also increased their minelaying off the Bulgarian and now-hostile Romanian coasts, so that when the extensive minefields off the Turkish coast on the approaches to the Bosphorus are taken into account, the southwestern portion of the Black Sea was on its way to becoming as unhealthy a place for ships as the Baltic. The Russians to a certain extent recognized this when in the latter part of October they began to use the Elpidifors converted into minelayers for operations off the Bosphorus, rather than the destroyers that had largely been employed since the beginning of the war. The shallow draught Elpidifors stood less danger of running onto Russian mines, which more than compensated for their lack of speed.[56]

The mining offensives and Russian submarines continued to cause loss to the Turks and diminish the number of precious colliers. The *Irmingard*, raised and repaired after having been sunk at Zonguldak by Russian bombs, struck a mine and was beached on 2 October between Alacali and Kara Burnu. Two weeks later the submarine *Narval* completed her destruction and sank another collier on 16 October. The Turks also lost the armed collier *Rodosto* (3,662 tons) on 12 October. The ship was captured after a gun duel east of Kirpen with the submarine *Tyulen* and brought into Sebastopol. The Turkish navy lost ships trying to clear the mines, notably the torpedo boat converted to a minesweeper *Kütahya* and the gunboat *Malatya*, damaged beyond repair. Russian mines also sank one of the torpedo boats of the tiny Bulgarian navy off Varna, another torpedo boat was damaged, and one of the Turk's precious German-built destroyers, the *Gairet-i-Watanije*, was also wrecked on an uncharted rock off Varna at the end of October. The Germans and Turks could claim few successes for the mines they laid in different parts of the Black Sea, either with the *Breslau* or by the UC-type submarines. The coal crisis grew toward the end of the year, and Turkey became increasingly dependent on insufficient shipments from Germany. Souchon was forced to curtail the activities of the *Goeben* and *Breslau*, whose movements along with those of the German submarines were also hampered by the extensive minefields. In what amounted to a vicious circle, the Turkish shortage of coal forced them to curtail the efforts at minesweeping, which in turn added to the coal shortage.[57]

The Germans, thanks to their conquest of Romania, had sufficient oil for their submarines in the Black Sea. The Germans eventually managed to get three of the UB.II-class submarines—*UB.42, UB.45,* and *UB.46*—through the Dardanelles to Constantinople in the second half of 1916. A fourth boat sailed from Cattaro for the Dardanelles and was never heard from again; its fate remains unknown. The smaller new boats replaced the large *U.33* and *U.38*, which had better prospects in the Mediterranean. The arrival of the submarines had been delayed by Allied mining off the Dardanelles, which for a time during the summer made them too dangerous for a submarine to pass. German submarines in the Black Sea continued to accomplish little; from the beginning of August to the end of the year they only claimed four steamers and two sailing craft. Their losses almost equalled their success: *UB.7* disappeared after sailing from Varna at the end of September, *UB.45* was mined off Varna on 6 November, *UC.15* was never heard from after sailing from Constantinople later that month, and *UB.46* was mined 30 miles off the Bosphorus on 7 December.[58]

It was an accident, rather than mines, torpedoes, or gunfire, that caused the Russians' worst loss of the war. On 20 October a fire broke out in the forward 12-inch gun magazine in the flagship *Imperatritsa Maria* while she was anchored off Sebastopol. The ship blew up and capsized with a loss of approximately two hundred dead and seven hundred injured. Inevitably there were strong suspicions of sabotage, but the cause was likely an accident or negligence involving powder that had become unstable.[59] The incident was probably similar to the disasters the Royal Navy suffered during the war when the dreadnought *Vanguard*, battleship *Bulwark*, and armored cruiser *Natal* were lost to explosions. The Russians hoped to replace the lost dreadnought with the third of the class, the *Imperator Alexander III*, which with enormous difficulty they were working to complete sometime in 1917. The ship's British-made turbines had been brought to Archangel and then laboriously carried south over the internal system of waterways to Tsaritsyn and then by rail to Yersk on the Sea of Azov. The transports carrying the turbines to Nikolaiev, from 20 to 22 October, received very heavy protection after passing through the Kertch Strait: an inner line of four minelayers, an outer line of four destroyers, and the *Imperatritsa Ekaterina* and an escort of destroyers providing distant cover.[60]

The same pattern of events continued throughout the first half of 1917. Turkish and German naval operations were at a low ebb. The Germans could have had little enthusiasm for sending more submarines to the Black Sea after the experience of 1916, and when the Germans turned to unrestricted submarine warfare, the Mediterranean offered far more attractive possibilities. Here they also had much more opportunity to inflict damage on their greatest enemy at sea—the British. The Black Sea therefore received a very low priority in German naval planning.

For much of 1917 the Russians planned a major amphibious operation in the region of the Bosphorus.[61] They increased their naval aviation striking force when they acquired from Romania in 1916 four small passenger liners that they converted into seaplane carriers. The *Regele Carol I* (2,368 tons), *Dakia, Imperator Trajan*, and *Rumyniya* (all 4,500 tons) could carry four to seven seaplanes, and when joined to the carriers already in service, gave the Russians a carrier force of six. They used them in March and early April to reconnoiter the Romanian coast and the possible landing sites in the vicinity of the Bosphorus. The *Imperator Alexander I, Imperator Nikolai I*, and *Rumyniya*, escorted by destroyers, conducted aerial reconnaissances of Constanza and the coast north of it on 11 March and Lake Terko on the coast of Rumelia on 26 March. In the latter operation, the Russians launched twelve seaplanes divided into three groups, one to take aerial photographs, one to bomb a water works on the lake, and a third to provide cover for the carriers and their escorts. One of the Russian seaplanes suffered a damaged fuel tank and was forced to land at sea. The two-man crew captured a Turkish schooner, removed the compass and a machine gun from the plane, and towed it to their carrier's last anchorage. After finding the ships gone, they towed the seaplane to Russian waters where they were finally picked up by a Russian destroyer and taken to Sebastopol. On 4 April there was a similar reconnaissance of the Bosphorus, in which the seaplanes bombed a coastal battery and the seaplane carriers were, in turn, attacked by seven German aircraft.[62]

DECLINE AND COLLAPSE OF THE BLACK SEA FLEET

The Russian navy was clearly on top in the naval war in the Black Sea when plans were disrupted by political events and the turmoil following the March revolution. At first the Black Sea Fleet seems to have avoided the worst excesses that accompanied the revolution in the Baltic Fleet. The fact that the fleet was winning and that the big ships were not ice bound for several months probably helped. There were no massacres of officers, and discipline seems to have remained better, at least for awhile. There was wholesale changing of ships' names: the *Imperatritsa Ekaterina Velikaya* became *Svobodnaya Rossiya*, the *Imperator Alexander III* became *Volya*, the carrier *Imperator Alexander I* became *Respublikanets*, the *Imperator Nikolai I* became *Aviator*, and the *Panteleimon* reverted to the name under which it had gained fame with the 1905 mutiny, *Potemkin* (shortly afterward altered to *Boretz Za Svobodu*).

However, the fundamental problems remained. A British observer reported as others had:

Here [Sebastopol] I myself have noticed that there is no sympathy between officers and men, that, out of routine, the officers take no interest in the welfare of the men, no attempt to institute games to occupy their spare time and many such small items which all tend to make life on board ship like a large club with a mutual feeling of interest and respect between all ranks and ratings. When I first arrived, I suggested that I should start football, etc., but it was intimated to me that such barbaric and brutal pastimes could not be encouraged.

I have seen divisional officers inspecting divisions on Sunday mornings with broken boots, caps on the backs of their heads and hands deep in their trouser pockets, I have even remarked on it to personal friends amongst the officers, but naturally cannot interfere in any other way. Officers, as soon as they are free, at once proceed on shore, and there, their chief occupation is wine and the courting of women, the moral side of life and society at Sebastopol is remarked by the men, who are not unobservant, and this cannot fail to have a deteriorating effect on the respect of the men towards their superiors.[63]

There is no space here to discuss the progress of the Russian Revolution. The Russian naval officer corps now paid the penalty for its past neglect. The formation of councils or soviets within each ship and the breakdown of authority followed a similar pattern to that in the Baltic Fleet, although with far less violence. The Black Sea Fleet also remained far more active than the Baltic Fleet, although the tempo of operations began to decline as the inner turmoil of Russia was reflected in the yards, where ships were immobilized far longer than they had been in the past awaiting repairs. This was particularly true for destroyers and submarines, which had been hard worked in the preceding year. The Russians also lost one of their best submarines in May when the *Morzh* did not return from a patrol on the Anatolian coast. The boat may have been sunk by German seaplanes off Eregli, or possibly lost on a Russian mine.[64]

In early April the Turkish minesweeping forces at the Bosphorus were reinforced by the arrival of six minesweeping boats from Constanza and were eventually able to clear a channel through the Russian fields.[65] Admiral Kolchak was determined, however, to maintain the pressure of the Russian blockade and to block the movements of the small, shallow-draft craft the Turks had been using. This led to one of the more daring Russian operations of the war. The Russians decided to use the small *Rybka*, or "Little Fishes," mines that would prove so troublesome to the Germans in the Gulf of Riga. They were laid in the Bosphorus by specially adapted motor launches, drawn from the Russian battleships. The cruiser *Pamiat Merkuria* was fitted to carry the launches on her deck. The plan was for the cruiser, accompanied by two destroyers carrying 120 mines each, to bring the four launches to a point 30 miles from the entrance to the Bosphorus. The launches would then be lowered, each draw 30 mines from the destroyers, and then, accompanied by a fast motorboat, proceed into the Bosphorus to lay the mines. The motor launches and their mother ship would then withdraw at daybreak and return to repeat the operation the following evening.

The first attempt, 25–28 April, was aborted because of bad weather. The second attempt took place on the night of 17 May. The *Svobodnaya Rossiya* and three seaplane carriers were at sea off the Romanian coast to cover the operation. The launches successfully laid their mines undetected and with their mother ship withdrew after daylight. Unfortunately, the attempt to repeat the operation the following night was not a success. The launches moved in before dark but were spotted and bombed by two German aircraft. With secrecy compromised, the Russian force withdrew.

The Russians repeated the operation on the night of 24 May. The *Svobodnaya Rossiya* and five destroyers were also at sea to cover the operation and a reconnaissance of Sinope by the seaplane carrier *Aviator*. The Russians varied their original plan slightly. The *Pamiat Merkuria* now brought the launches to within 12 miles of the Bosphorus in order to spare them the long haul to the minelaying area, and they were then towed by the destroyer *Pronzitelni* to the edge of the old minefield, roughly 7 miles from the entrance. The operation was successful, the mines were laid undetected. Unfortunately for the Russians, when the force returned the following night, a mine exploded in one of the launches, killing an officer and four seamen, sinking the launch, and badly damaging two of the launches following close astern. One of the latter subsequently sank while under tow by the fast motorboat. While recovering the surviving craft, the *Pamiat Merkuria* was attacked by a German aircraft. During the night the Turks had heard the sound of the explosion and the Russian motorboats, but could discover nothing with their searchlights. They recovered four bodies and wreckage, and later discovered a new field of 72 mines, which they set about clearing.[66]

While the mining operations were taking place against the Bosphorus, the former Romanian liners employed as seaplane carriers had been active from late April along the Turkish coast farther to the east. The *Regele Carol* and *Dakia* working in company with a pair of destroyers and an armed motor launch attacked factories, coastal installations, sailing craft, and a variety of other targets at Sinope, Samsun, Unye, and Ordu. It would be a bit misleading, however, to regard these operations in the same light as those of the carrier groups of World War II. A closer examination of the details reveals that although aircraft were used, bad weather frequently frustrated their operations, and most of the damage was inflicted by the guns of the destroyers and the seaplane carriers, which had been fitted with four 152-mm cannon. In this sense they operated more as traditional auxiliary cruisers than aircraft carriers. Still one might claim these operations, primitive as they might have been, were a distant—very distant—precursor of what was to come.

The Russians also did not give up on mining by small craft. They shifted, however, from the motor launches to fast motorboats, each of which carried ten of the small mines. This was only one-third what the ship's launches had been able to carry, but the motorboats were much faster. The destroyers *Pylki* and *Schastlivy* towed four of the motorboats to Zonguldak, and on the night of 17 June they successfully laid their mines and repeated the operation the following night at the Bosphorus.

These operations demonstrate that the Black Sea Fleet remained aggressive and very active well after the Russian Revolution. Unfortunately, politics continued to intrude. There was growing friction between Vice Admiral Kolchak and the Central Committee at Sebastopol, culminating on 26 May with the commander in chief's request to the minister of marine that he be relieved of his command.[67] The disciplinary situation deteriorated rapidly, particularly when the Central Committee decided to appropriate all officers' sidearms, swords, and dirks. Kolchak reportedly threw his sword overboard rather than surrender it; other officers broke their swords, and there was some violence against them. Kolchak was replaced, temporarily, by Vice Admiral Lukin. On 23 June the British liaison officer reported that at the Black Sea staff there was much evidence of great disorganization, many officers desired to resign, discipline was quite nonexistent, and the behavior of the men was completely out of control. When he visited the flagship, the sentries were sitting down, the quartermaster and the officer of the watch were not present, and sailors were lying about the quarterdeck.[68]

The Turks and Germans were anxious to demonstrate to the Russians that they were still capable of operations at sea. The first German submarine to operate in the Black

A NAVAL HISTORY OF WORLD WAR I

Sea in 1917, *UB.14*, sailed at the end of May. German submarine success, however, remained as limited as it had been the preceding year. Souchon realized that the coal shortage ruled out operations in the eastern part of the Black Sea, and he looked for an objective closer to the Bosphorus. The *Breslau* was therefore ordered to lay a field of mines off the mouth of the Danube and destroy the wireless station on Fidonisi Island (Schlangen Island in German documents), roughly 23 miles from the mouth of the Danube. The *Breslau* laid 70 mines off the coast in the early morning hours of 25 June; laid another 10 off Fidonisi Island; destroyed the wireless station and lighthouse with gunfire; and put a landing party on shore, which returned with 11 prisoners. One of the German mines later sank the Russian destroyer *Leitenant Zatzarenni* on 30 June.

The *Breslau*'s raid coincided with another Russian operation against the Bosphorus planned for the night of the 26th. Three Russian groups were at sea, the seaplane carrier *Regele Carol* with two destroyers, three minelayers towing four Elpidifor-type minesweepers, and the cruiser *Pamiat Merkuria* with two destroyers. The dreadnought *Svobodnaya Rossiya* and the destroyers *Gnevny* and *Schastlivy* covered the operation. The *Svobodnaya Rossiya* sighted the *Breslau*'s smoke shortly after noon and ordered the *Gnevny* to investigate. The dreadnought altered course in an attempt to cut off the *Breslau* from the Bosphorus. The *Breslau*'s commander raced for the Bosphorus at full speed, the Russians in pursuit. The *Svobodnaya Rossiya* attempted a salvo with her forward turret at 2:15 P.M., but it fell short. The dreadnought fired nine salvoes during the chase but failed to hit. The *Gnevny* overhauled the *Breslau* but was driven off by the cruiser's fire. In the course of the pursuit, the *Breslau* periodically used smoke and there were repeated exchanges of fire. The Russians pursued right up to the edge of the minefield, but the *Breslau* was able to return safely. The French-built destroyer *Basra* was sent out to assist, but as she could not steam faster than 18 knots, she was more of a hindrance. The submarine *UC.23* had also just left the Bosphorus but was not in a position to get off a shot. Neither was the Russian submarine *Nerpa*, also waiting off the Bosphorus. The Russian mining proceeded without incident that night. This brush between the *Breslau* and *Svobodnaya Rossiya* and *Gnevny* was the last encounter between Russian and Turco-German warships in the Black Sea.[69]

The last major Russian mining operation against the Bosphorus took place on the night of 19 July. The *Regele Carol* and the minelayer *Kseniya* (2,700 tons) towed two Elpidifors and destroyers towed four *SK*-type submarine-hunting motor launches (14-ton craft built in the United States and assembled at Odessa) to approximately 30 miles north of the Bosphorus. The Elpidifors and motor launches were then cut loose; the motor launches laid their mines in the Bosphorus entrance, the Elpidifors laid theirs along the coastal route to the east. The *Svobodnaya Rossiya* and *Pamiat Merkuria* escorted by four destroyers covered the operation.

The tempo of operations along the Anatolian coast also began to slacken during the summer months. They continued, but they were more sporadic. On 24 August, 328 sailors and soldiers were landed at Ordu to destroy harbor installations, but through lack of discipline failed to accomplish the major objective, the destruction of a hangar.

Turkish gunfire repulsed a landing attempt at Vona on the 27th. The provisional government in Russia still planned a major landing on the Turkish coast, although the growing chaos and disorganization of all aspects of Russian life made the likelihood of its execution less and less likely. The collapse of the railway transportation system was particularly evident. The Russians considered a landing in the Dobrudja region, on the flank of their army, but at the end of August the prospects for this faded when the high command was forced to order the removal of landing equipment from the remaining transports so that the ships could be used to transport grain. In October the Russians were still contemplating a landing at Sinope. They originally thought of landing a full army corps, which, in a two and a half to three month campaign—designated Operation Nakhimov—would penetrate deeply into the interior of Anatolia to cut the Constantinople to Angora rail line. By October the Russians had scaled down the plan to a surprise raid of eight infantry battalions, eight squadrons of cavalry, and a cyclist battalion aimed at releasing British prisoners held near the coast.[70]

There was still submarine activity by the Germans. *UB.42* was ordered to the eastern Black Sea in early October, where she landed five Georgians with gold and munitions to support a Georgian independence movement. The submarine then operated against shipping, sinking two small sailing craft and a steamer and shelling Tuapse.

The Russians kept up the pressure on the Turkish coal traffic with whatever destroyers they could put to sea until the fall of the provisional government. The German official history concedes that the Russian intelligence service was still excellent, and on 31 October the destroyers *Pylki* and *Bystry* successfully broke up a Turkish minesweeping force at Igneada north of the Bosphorus. The small torpedo boat *Hamidabad* and three minesweeping boats had been clearing the coastal route from Constanza when attacked; the *Hamidabad*, loaded with gasoline for the minesweeping boats, exploded and sank and two Turkish steamers in port were damaged. The three minesweeping boats beached themselves to escape destruction.

The Germans realized, once again, that the remaining Turkish torpedo craft could not protect either transports or minesweepers from the large Russian destroyers and were suitable only for securing against submarines the entry and exit of the *Goeben* and *Breslau* from the Bosphorus. The *Breslau* was ordered out the following day, 1 November, to sweep from Igneada to Midia in search of enemy warships. But the Russians detected the move, and the Russian commander in chief since August, Rear Admiral Nemits, sailed with the *Svobodnaya Rossiya*, two large destroyers, and the old battleships of the Second Squadron (*Evstafi, Ioann Zlatoust*, and *Boretz Za Svobodu*) with a destroyer. They were joined the following day by the new dreadnought *Volya* on her first operation, accompanied by the seaplane carrier *Rumyniya* and a destroyer. It was the swan song of the Black Sea Fleet. The crew of the *Svobodnaya Rossiya* refused to continue the war and forced Nemits to return to Sebastopol. The Second Squadron remained off the Romanian coast for a few days, and the *Volya*'s group cruised off the Bosphorus. None of the Russian ships encountered the *Breslau*, which had slipped back into the Bosphorus on the evening of the 1st.[71]

The Russian navy still controlled the sea and the Turkish and German ships could only make fleeting raids outside of the Bosphorus when the Bolshevik Revolution occurred, and the commander in chief was ordered to obey only the orders of the Central Committee. Operations at sea were broken off, and the Bolsheviks quickly proceeded to arrange an armistice with the Central Powers. The Armistice came just in time for the Turks, for shortly before it was concluded on the night of 15–16 December the bread ration in Constantinople had been cut in half and shortly after the armistice, on 20 December, Ludendorff informed Enver Pasha that the situation in Germany and the anticipated resumption of traffic in the Black Sea meant the Germans would restrict their export of coal to Turkey.[72]

Vice Admiral Souchon was not on hand to witness the final collapse of his Russian opponents in the Black Sea, for the commander of the Mittelmeerdivision had returned to Germany at the beginning of September to assume command of the Fourth Squadron in the High Sea Fleet. His successor was Vice Admiral Rebeur-Paschwitz, who nearly gambled away Turkey's major naval assets through an ill-advised sortie from the Dardanelles. Rebeur-Paschwitz decided that he might provide at least indirect support for the hard-pressed Turkish forces in Palestine by some operation to draw Allied ships from the Palestine coast to the Dardanelles. He also hoped to bolster Turkish morale after the recent fall of Jerusalem, and, perhaps most important of all, demonstrate to the Turks that warships were meant to be used. He was disastrously overconfident about the Allied minefields off the Dardanelles, assuming he knew their location through aerial reconnaissance and that their effectiveness had been diminished by time and tide.

The *Goeben* and *Breslau* came out of the Dardanelles early on the morning of 20 January 1918. They were accompanied by Turkish torpedo boats, which did not venture far from the Strait. The Germans had chosen their moment well and achieved tactical surprise. The British commander, Rear Admiral Hayes-Sadler, who had been guarding the Strait with the semidreadnoughts *Lord Nelson* and *Agamemnon* and an old French battleship at Lemnos, had foolishly divided his force by taking the *Lord Nelson* with him to Salonika at a time when the French battleship was in dock. The *Goeben* and *Breslau* surprised and sank the monitors *Lord Raglan* (14-inch guns) and *M.28* (6-inch guns) at Kusu Bay, Imbros. They then proceeded toward Mudros, where the *Lord Nelson* was raising steam to meet them. The *Lord Nelson*'s captain was none too confident of the results of an encounter with the more modern German ship. It never occurred because the *Breslau* ran into a minefield and subsequently sank; the *Goeben*, in attempting to take her consort under tow, was also mined and broke off the operation. The *Goeben* hit other mines getting back into the Strait, and the damaged battle cruiser then ran aground near Nagara Point as the result of a navigational error.

The *Goeben* was in a very precarious position, but if the Germans had botched the operation so far, it was now the turn of the British to bungle. The British attacked the battle cruiser with aircraft, and although they scored hits, the airplanes could not carry bombs heavy enough to inflict serious damage. The only British submarine on the scene had a fractured propeller shaft and was not employed. The British had to wait a few days for a replacement, *E.14*, to arrive. In the interval the Turks and Germans managed to tow the *Goeben* off the sandbank the day before *E.14* was sent through the Strait, where the defenses were now far stronger than they had been in 1915. The submarine was lost. Shortly afterward Hayes-Sadler was sacked. The Germans and Turks had little cause to celebrate. They had lost their best light cruiser and the *Goeben* was immobilized for the foreseeable future at Constantinople, where complete repair was not possible and where improvised bulkheads had to be set in place and cofferdams once again erected around her damaged hull. The old Mittelmeerdivision had ceased to exist as an effective fighting unit.[73]

The armistice with Russia gave the Mittelmeerdivision a new lease on life and eventually opened dazzling prospects. According to the terms, all Russian warships in the Black Sea were to be gathered in Russian ports and disarmed or detained until the conclusion of a general peace. However, on 9 February 1918, the Central Powers also concluded a treaty recognizing the independence of the Ukraine. The new state was to include Odessa and part of the Black Sea coast. There was some question as to whether or not the Ukrainians might have a claim to all or a portion of the Black Sea Fleet. The fate of the fleet became worrisome to the Allies after the armistice, and the situation turned critical when German and Austrian troops marched into the Ukraine to secure the wheat fields. With Russia prostrate, the question was when and where would the Germans stop? On 13 March the Germans occupied Odessa, and by 17 March they had reached Nikolaiev and its dockyards holding an unfinished dreadnought, three light cruisers, and four destroyers on the stocks. The completion of these ships, given the disorganization in the Russian yards and the scarcity of labor and matériel, was not likely in the foreseeable future.

The Germans continued to the east and then turned southward to the Crimea. They were in front of Sebastopol by 1 May. What would happen to the Black Sea Fleet? The commander in chief was now Vice Admiral N. P. Sablin, but his authority was extremely tenuous and no one could be certain what the sailors would do. The Bolshevik government, now in Moscow, ordered Sablin to sail to Novorossisk on the eastern shores of the Black Sea. Sablin managed to get fourteen destroyers and torpedo boats to sail on the 13th, but the two dreadnoughts and four destroyers remained behind. They finally sailed on the night of the 14th, just as German patrols entered the city. German artillery opened fire on the ships, and the large destroyer *Gnevny* ran aground while an older destroyer was sabotaged in the dockyard. The Germans seized the now thoroughly worn out and decrepit predreadnoughts, the three cruisers, and a substantial number of smaller ships and submarines. They were aided by the fact that demolition parties failed to carry out their orders, but few of the ships at Sebastopol were ready for sea.

The best and most modern core of the Black Sea Fleet, the two dreadnoughts and most of the modern destroyers, were now fugitives at Novorossisk where the situation was very confused. Russia was falling into civil war and a White volunteer army hovered outside of the city, where there was a theoretical Soviet Republic. The Red Army at Novorossisk was reported to be mutinous, and within the fleet there was a wide variety of opinion, and even Sablin's leadership was subject to approval through election.

Ludendorff had plans for the Russian ships. He wanted them to be seized as war booty, and at least some of them put in service to police the Black Sea. The Turks had their own claims, including a substitute for the *Breslau*. The Bulgarians, and possibly the Ukrainians, also had claims, and there was the legal technicality of whether ships seized after the conclusion of the Peace of Brest-Litovsk could be seized as war booty. The Central Powers established the Nautisch-Technische Kommission für Schwarze Meere, commonly known as NATEKO. Vice Admiral Hopman was appointed its head with orders to coordinate the employment of all naval personnel in the Ukraine and in the Crimea in agreement with the local German army authorities and to secure all prizes useful to the navy at Sebastopol and ready them for sea. The *Goeben* proceeded to take advantage of the Sebastopol dry dock for badly needed repairs, and the Turks recovered the cruiser *Medjidieh*, which had been lost to the Russians in 1915. The Germans, however, were very evasive about Turkish claims for other Russian warships, for they doubted their capacity to man them or maintain them.

Ludendorff, who was much more persistent than the navy in coveting the Russian ships, set a deadline for the Russian ships at Novorossisk to return to Sebastopol. If they did not, the German army would resume its advance. Captain Tichmenew, the interim Russian naval commander at Novorossisk in the absence of Sablin, was apparently ready to comply and negotiated an agreement with Admiral Hopman for the Germans to pay, subject to future reimbursement from the Russian government, the Russian officers and men who would remain in the ships after they returned to Sebastopol. All was not as it seemed, however, for apparently the government in Moscow sent secret orders to Novorossisk that the ships were to be scuttled if an order was ever received from Moscow to turn the ships over to the Germans. The state of discipline in what remained of the Black Sea Fleet partially frustrated this order. There was an intense debate in the fleet over what course of action to follow, and a vote was taken. Approximately 450 voted to scuttle the ships, 900 voted to return to Sebastopol to be interned, and 1,000 abstained. On 18 June Tichmenew in the dreadnought *Volya* with three large destroyers, two torpedo boats, and an armed merchant cruiser sailed for Sebastopol. These were all the ships the Germans got their hands on. The other dreadnought, the *Svobodnaya Rossiya*, was torpedoed and sunk by a destroyer off the port. The destroyer then proceeded to Tuapse where she scuttled herself the next day. The remaining destroyers and torpedo boats, including five of the highly desirable large modern destroyers, were scuttled at Novorossisk.[74]

The Entente had only an imperfect idea of what was going on in the Black Sea, but there was a very real fear that the Germans and their Allies would acquire the former Russian Black Sea Fleet and use the warships to break out of the Dardanelles and upset the naval balance in the eastern portion of the Mediterranean. The Allies need not have worried. The Germans, despite the grandiose plans Ludendorff clung to until the very end, were hard put to find the men to man the handful of ships they planned to restore to service (the dreadnought *Volya*, perhaps four or five destroyers, and a few submarines and other craft). With the difficulties the Germans had in getting sufficient men from

Germany, and the necessity to use Russian yards and labor, by the end of July 1918, they were likely to have in service only one of the large destroyers, two small old destroyers, a submarine, and a number of minor craft, particularly shallow-draft vessels for use in the Sea of Azov.

The Germans concluded a supplementary treaty with the Russians on 27 August, which included an article dealing with Russian warships and Russian stores seized by the Germans after ratification of the peace treaty. The Germans recognized Russian ownership of the warships but specified they would remain "under German care until the conclusion of a general peace." A secret letter from the German foreign secretary supplementing the treaty stipulated that the Germans should be given the use of the warships for "peaceful aims," especially for minesweeping and harbor and police service. In case of war necessity, the warships might be used for military aims, but the Germans promised the Russians full indemnity for loss and damage incurred in that service. This precluded, at least technically, the Germans transferring any of the ships to their allies, but the Germans planned to evade the full effect by placing Turkish personnel in some of the ships "for training." They planned to have a nucleus crew bring the best of the Russian predreadnoughts, the *Evstafi* and *Zlatoust*, to Constantinople, where the ships, with largely Turkish crews bolstered by Germans, would be used for the defense of the Dardanelles. They had to abandon this idea; there would not be enough men after the *Volya* was placed in service.

The Germans made secret preparations to quickly seize the ships to preclude sabotage by the Russians remaining aboard once the news of the agreement with the Russian government was made public. On 1 October the Germans seized the *Volya*, four large destroyers, two small old destroyers, and the seaplane carrier *Imperator Trajan*. Only the *Volya* actually entered service under the German naval ensign on 15 October, and the German crew had great difficulty making her battle ready and working the unfamiliar equipment. They had only a fortnight to enjoy their prize, for the Ottoman Empire was tottering, and on 30 October the Turks signed an armistice with the British on the island of Moudros. There was now every prospect the navies of the Entente would be able to appear in the Black Sea in overwhelming strength. Ironically, the *Goeben* really did become a Turkish ship when the Germans formally turned her over to the Ottoman navy on 2 November, to the objections of the Turkish minister of finance, who was not anxious to assume responsibility for a large, costly ship under the drastically altered circumstances. The Germans were equally anxious to return the Russian warships to whatever Russian authorities they could get to accept them, for under the secret supplementary treaty with the Russians, they would have been liable if the Allies had seized them while they were in German hands. The first Allied warships reached Sebastopol in mid-November, but the Russian civil war meant that hostilities would continue in the Black Sea for another two years. Most of the old battleships had their machinery wrecked in 1919 to prevent their falling into the hands of the Bolsheviks; others were scuttled. The Bolsheviks inherited little of the Black Sea Fleet that was usable. With the final victory of the Bolsheviks in 1920, the *Volya* and a small remnant of the former Black Sea Fleet, including the cruiser *Kagul*, the seaplane carrier *Almaz*, seven destroyers, three small old destroyers, and four submarines, steamed to Bizerte where they were interned by the French. They were eventually broken up, although the French retained the 305-mm guns of the *Volya*, which later were captured by the Germans during the Second World War and used for the defense of Guernsey. The most formidable opponent of the Black Sea Fleet, the *Goeben*, survived as the Turkish *Yavuz* until the beginning of the 1970s.[75]

9

THE DANUBE

THE SERBIAN CAMPAIGN

Worldld War I naval operations on the Danube have been largely overlooked in the English-speaking world, although this great river, originating in Germany and flowing through central and eastern Europe all the way to the Black Sea, is navigable for more than 1,700 miles. Oceangoing vessels could proceed up what was known as the "maritime Danube" as far as Galatz in Romania. The importance of this vital waterway to Germany and Austria increased once they were cut off from access to the high seas. It was the German and Austrian equivalent of the North Atlantic seaway used by the British and French, although obviously the volume and importance of the Danube traffic could not compare to what had passed through Hamburg, Bremen, or Trieste before the war. The Danube also was of great strategic importance during the Dardanelles campaign, because it was a potential route for munitions to Turkey. For the first year of the war, it was also a tenuous but viable means for at least small quantities of supplies to reach Russia. The British might have been drawn into a regular campaign on the Danube had the Dardanelles campaign been successful. With these considerations in mind, it is hardly surprising that the first naval shots of the war—indeed the first shots of the World War itself—were fired on the Danube and that naval forces were still in action during the final days of the war.

The most significant naval force on the Danube was the k.u.k. Donauflottille. The flotilla was commanded for most of the war (October 1914–December 1917) by Linienschiffskapitän Karl Lucich. The Austrians had six monitors in service at the beginning of hostilities, and put four more in service during the war. Two monitors were lost to mines during the war, although both were salved after considerable effort. Preliminary work had begun on another pair of monitors when the war ended. The primary armament of the monitors generally consisted of two 12-cm guns mounted in one or two turrets. The secondary armament varied, but usually included a pair of 7-cm, quick-firing cannon, as well as 12-cm howitzers and machine guns. The armor protection was limited by the necessity to maintain light draft and varied from 44–50 mm for the belt, 75–50 mm for the turrets to 19–25 mm for the deck.

The k.u.k. Donauflottille also began the war with six small patrol boats armed with machine guns in lightly armored turrets. The six additional patrol boats entering service during the war grew larger, more powerful, and more extensively protected. The last four in 1916 were 129-ton, 44-meter craft armed with four 7-cm guns and four machine guns. The Austrians also armed and adapted various river craft, ranging from paddle steamers to tugs and barges, for service as command and accommodation ships, minesweepers, and hospital ships. The Austro-Hungarian army had its own craft on the Danube too. The Pioneer Corps employed two armored motorboats that were subsequently transferred to the navy and moved to the Adriatic for work in the lagoons along the Italian front. The common feature for all navies engaged in riverine warfare, whether on the Danube, the Tigris, or the Dvina, appeared to be ingenuity.[1]

Serbia, Austria-Hungary's initial enemy, had no naval forces on the Danube, and the Russians could not bring their trio of fairly powerful gunboats of the *Donetz* class beyond the lower reaches. They did employ a few improvised craft in Serbian waters below the Iron Gates, the famous and most dangerous of the series of rapids that cut through the southern arm of the Carpathian mountains. Romania had a river force on paper, including four monitors built in Trieste in 1907–8 and armed with three 12-cm Skoda cannon. They could have been troublesome opponents for the k.u.k. Donauflottille, but Romania remained neutral until 1916, and when she entered the war the circumstances of the campaign were such that the rival monitors remained far apart. It is therefore somewhat ironical that in the prewar maneuvers the Austro-Hungarian Danube Flotilla, with the example of the American Civil War before them, tended to practice for a classic battle with enemy monitors on the river just the way the major navies prepared for a classic encounter on the high seas, which, as it turned out, occurred only once at Jutland. The real employment of the Austro-Hungarian navy on the Danube during the war was in cooperation with the army in land operations, particularly artillery support, and this aspect of riverine warfare had been neglected in the prewar maneuvers.[2]

The Danube Flotilla was split in three when the war began. The major part of it, including four monitors and three patrol boats, was on the Danube at Zemun, just upstream from the Serbian capital Belgrade. The two oldest monitors, the *Leitha* and *Maros,* and a patrol boat were on the Save, and two patrol boats were at Pancsova, downstream from Belgrade on the Danube. The Save, which formed the boundary between Serbia and Hungary, flowed into the Danube at Belgrade, and the Serbian batteries in the Kalimegdan fortress, on Topcider Hill to the south, and in other positions around the city, were the natural opponents of the monitors. The two rivers and the islands in them near where they joined at Belgrade were the focal point of operations for over a year. Low water, however, prevented the flotilla from operating on certain reaches of the Save for about a month after the end of August.

The Austrians declared war on Serbia on 28 July. On the night of the 28th, the monitors *Temes, Bodrog,* and *Szamos* fired the opening shots of the war against the Serbian fortifications at the Zemun-Belgrade railway bridge over the Save and on Topcider Hill, and after daybreak shelled the wireless station and Serbian positions on the lower portion of the Kalimegdan fortress. The Austrians, however, were caught in a disadvantageous strategic position, for when Russia entered the war, they had to shift forces from their Balkan front to face the far more serious danger in Galicia to the north. The forces left against Serbia were not strong enough to accomplish the mission, and the Austrian offensives against Serbia in 1914 proved to be dismal failures.[3] The Serbians were able to counterattack, and on 9 September the Austrians were forced to evacuate the flotilla base at Zemun. The two small patrol boats at Pancsova were cut off and blown up in the Temes River to prevent them from falling into enemy hands. The Austrians were able to recover Zemun, and on 28 September the monitors *Temes* and *Körös,* a patrol boat, and the minesweeper *Andor* were able to break through the minefields in the Save near Belgrade and then move upstream to support the fighting at Sabac.

The monitors had impressed the Serbians, and they did not know how to deal with them. They outgunned the artillery of the Serbian army and as a moving target were difficult to hit. Their mobility enabled them to rapidly bring artillery support to a threatened sector, whereas artillery on land had to be shifted by horses or oxen or manhandled over poor roads and difficult terrain. The Serbians appealed to their allies for support, and the Russians, French, and, eventually, the British responded. This Allied assistance hampered the work of the Austrian monitors and made their operations much more difficult and dangerous.

The Russians were the first to arrive, but any Russian attempt to assist land-locked Serbia ran into geographical difficulties. Serbia had no seaport of her own or any common border with her allies except tiny impoverished Montenegro, whose meager port and road network were totally inadequate. Although the British and French might make use of Montenegrin facilities, such as they were, Turkey's closure of the Straits ended any prospect of this for the Russians. Neutral Romania denied the use of her railways but agreed to abide by the international character given to the Danube by previous treaties. Russia possessed the port of Reni in the Danube delta, which was linked to the Russian rail net, and this became their major base for shipments to the Serbian river ports of Prahovo and Radujevac. These were located downstream of the Iron Gates, well sheltered from Austrian attack. The Russians formed a special expeditionary force as an independent command under a senior naval captain. The expedition consisted of a naval engineer detachment; mine specialists; a detachment for defense of the Iron Gate region; and another detachment, which was destined to grow, for the transport and protection of supplies.

The first Russian detachment, 106 seamen from the Black Sea Fleet under Senior Lieutenant Volkovitskii, arrived in Serbia at the end of August and set to work installing torpedo tubes and laying mines at various points on the Danube and Save. They also built booms to protect Serbian bridges from floating mines. Another special detachment of seven officers and thirty men with two motor launches and the armed steamer *Tiraspol* was sent to the region just below the Iron Gates, where they laid minefields, booms, and nets to prevent the passage of vessels and protect against floating mines. The Russians also established two batteries of two 75-mm cannons each, equipped with searchlights, near the border villages.[4]

The Black Sea Fleet had no warships that could navigate beyond the lower reaches of the Danube, and the Russians were forced to make use of commandeered river craft, specially adapted for military purposes. The first convoy for Serbia sailed from Reni on 14 October and reached Prahovo on the 23d. The Russians sent a total of five convoys to Serbia in 1914 and found that, under favorable conditions and including unloading at Prahovo, the trip upstream required ten days. The convoys were preceded by two armed vessels equipped with minesweeping gear and then, 3 to 4 miles astern, another pair of armed steamers followed by the transports. The Russians appeared more worried by the prospect of air attack than the unlikely appearance of Austrian warships. By the end of March 1915, the Russian Danube forces had grown to 14 steamers, 40 tugboats, and 40 barges with 28 pontoons and docks. Unfortunately, by the summer of 1915, the volume of supplies to be transported far exceeded the capacity of either the Russian or Serbian ports to handle them. The Russians made an effort to improve Reni by reclaiming some of the foreshore and building additional docks with more loading equipment and new approach roads, as well as a railway marshalling yard. The capacity of the little Serbian river ports, however, was minimal, and supplies had to be transhipped twice. A standard-gauge railway line ran from the river ports through the Timok Valley to Zajecar, from which a narrow-gauge line ran through hilly country to connect with the main Nish-Belgrade line at Paracin. There was a potentially important standard-gauge line under construction from Zajecar to Nish that would have linked the Danube ports directly to the main line from Salonika. The Serbians were using Austrian prisoners as labor and hoped to finish the line by the end of the year.[5]

The lack of transport and unloading facilities frustrated a project by the Russian high command to send troops to Serbia. In February 1915 they investigated the possibility of sending the 53d Caucasian Regiment, to be followed by a militia brigade. This would have involved more than 2,000 men and 1,500 horses; the commander of the special expeditionary force in Serbia had to decline on the grounds that he had neither ships nor barges for the operation. All available shipping had already been mobilized, and the additional ships would have had to come from beyond the Danube.

The Russians also tried to profit from the system by using the return voyage downstream to transport vital war matériel from Britain and France through the Serbian ports to Reni. Between March and May 1915, the Russians reported 10,339 *poods* (the Russian *pood* equalled 36.1 pounds) of war matériel, including eight aircraft, had been brought by rail from Salonika up through Greece and Serbia and then down the Danube. This was not very much.[6]

The Danube route was probably the most difficult of the routes to Russia, although certainly far shorter than shipping matériel all the way to the Far East and then back over the Trans-Siberian Railway, and facilities for moving matériel from the north Russian ports at this stage of the war were not much better. The quantities moved were minuscule by the standards of the First World War, and it is hardly surprising that this route has been forgotten by historians. It was possible only while the Greeks were compliant, Bulgaria remained neutral, and Serbia remained free and in the struggle. That situation was destined not to last.

The Russians and Serbians achieved their major success early in the morning of 23 October near Grabovici on the Save when the monitor *Temes*, flagship of the flotilla, struck a mine and sank with the loss of thirty-one lives, nearly half her complement. The *Temes* was raised in 1916 after the Serbian campaign, and eventually returned to service. The Austrians attempted to counter the mine danger by fitting their river craft with *minenrechens*, literally "mine rakes." These devices were located at the bow and resembled their name, somewhat like the "cow catchers" on mid-nineteenth century American locomotives. They could be lowered in dangerous waters and were fairly effective. Only one other monitor was sunk by a mine during the war. This happened on the Danube, months *after* the conclusion of the Romanian campaign, and was probably due to a mine that had sunk and been missed by sweepers.[7]

The French naval mission to Serbia, designated Mission D, consisted of 4 officers and 97 men, three 14-cm cannons, searchlights, and an electrical generator under the command of Lieutenant de vaisseau Edouard Picot. The guns had been taken from the secondary armament of the coast-defense battleship *Henri IV*, then underemployed as a guardship at Bizerte. The mission came by way of the railway from Salonika, traveling in mufti to avoid offending Greek susceptibilities. The French reached Belgrade the first week in November, but it was not until the 21st that the concrete platforms were finished and the battery ready to open fire. Picot disagreed with the Serbian army's choice of position, but had to conform. The French employed only two of the guns, and kept the third as a reserve. This subsequently proved to be a fortunate decision.

The French guns fired on the monitor's anchorage at their extreme range of 10,800 meters. After approximately eleven minutes a British officer observed a hit, apparently at the base of a monitor's after turret. The monitors raised steam and slipped their moorings. The French guns were an unpleasant development for the Austrian flotilla, for the monitors found themselves outranged. The newly commissioned *Enns* was the only monitor with larger-caliber guns that could reply, and the French guns were well protected by earthworks. The Austrian flotilla was forced to shift its anchorage 2 kilometers upstream. However, at the end of November the Austrians began another offensive, and the Serbians decided to abandon Belgrade to avoid destruction of their capital. The French naval cannon were immobile, and on the 30th Picot, after rapidly firing off his remaining ammunition, removed the gunsights and breeches from the guns and evacuated his men.[8]

The *Bodrog, Szamos*, and *Enns* covered the entry of Austrian troops into Belgrade on 2 December, but this new Austrian offensive proved to be no more successful than the earlier ones, and on the 14th the Austrians were compelled to evacuate the city. The French moved up the naval gun that had been kept in reserve, and the French navy sent another pair to replace the two that had been abandoned. By mid-February Picot had two guns on Topcider Hill to the south of the city in what he considered a far better position than the earlier one.

The Russians also increased their aid and sent two 15-cm guns, which were emplaced in the Kalimegdan fortress. The guns, however, were very old and one was soon put out of action when a shell exploded in the barrel. Russian assistance in mining was potentially more effective. The Russians and Serbians set about replacing the minefields that had been cleared by the Austrians. The Serbians also completed the demolition of virtually all of the already partially demolished Zemun-Belgrade railway bridge over the Save. The debris made the river impassable under normal conditions and assured that the Austrian vessels west of the bridge in the Save, including the monitors *Szamos* and *Leitha*, could not rejoin the remainder of the flotilla. The Austrians found that with the new guns, observation posts, and minefields, the situation around Belgrade was much less favorable in 1915 than it had been in 1914. The French cannon appeared too well protected to be silenced by gunfire from the monitors, and the Austrians realized the best chances for success were in working with the heavy artillery of the army. The activity of the flotilla was greatly reduced during the winter months, and the majority of the vessels went up to Budapest for repair and docking. The headquarters of the flotilla was shifted upstream to Petrovaradin.[9]

The British had been slower than their allies in sending a naval mission. The Admiralty's first step in reply to the Serbian request for assistance in dealing with the Austrian monitors was to send Commander Hubert S. Cardale, a member of the British naval mission to Greece, to Belgrade to advise them. Cardale arrived in Belgrade on 30 October. The Admiralty eventually sent a mining and torpedo detachment, a mixed body of approximately twenty-six Royal Marines and seamen under the command of Captain B. N. Elliott, Royal Marine Light Infantry, which reached Belgrade on 7 January 1915. They were followed by a heavy gun detachment of twenty-four seamen and Royal Marines under the command of Lieutenant Commander Charles L. Kerr with eight 4.7-inch naval guns on traveling mountings. The Admiralty blundered, however, as the guns arrived without telescopes for their sights. Moreover, because of the small size of the mission, only three British ratings could be attached to each gun; the remainder of the crew had to be drawn from the Serbian army. The guns were divided into four batteries of two guns each, commanded by a Serbian artillery officer. They were dragged by bullocks to three positions on the Danube and one on the Save, which varied between 2 and 30 miles from Belgrade.[10]

The Admiralty gave Rear Admiral E. C. T. Troubridge command of the mission. Troubridge, who arrived in Belgrade on 22 February, had commanded the First Cruiser Squadron in the Mediterranean at the outbreak of the war and had been tried by court-martial for failure to engage the *Goeben*. Troubridge was acquitted, but the Admiralty never employed him afloat again, and the naval mission to Serbia appeared to have been a means of shunting him aside.[11] Ironically, it would prove much more adventurous than service in the great majority of naval commands. To avoid duplication of effort or working at cross purposes, the French agreed to serve under Troubridge's command. The Russians remained somewhat aloof, although they agreed to inform him in advance of their actions.

It was and remains difficult to think of Belgrade and the Danube as more than a secondary front in a largely forgotten campaign of the Great War. But it had the potential to be far more important. The Allied blockade of the Dardanelles and the enforcement of Romanian neutrality in preventing the shipment of munitions and supplies for Turkey by rail through Romania meant that the Danube, whose international status had been recognized, would have been an important route. That route was blocked by the Serbians as long as they controlled Belgrade and the right bank of the river up to their frontier with Bulgaria. In December 1914 the German army high command regarded the reinforcement of Turkey as important enough to send Lieutenant Colonel Hentsch of the general staff to the Danube front to attempt to arrange a munitions transport.

The first attempt to run the gauntlet was on 24 December when the steamer *Trinitas* and two tugs sailed from Zemun, escorted by the monitor *Bodrog*, patrol boat *b*, and armed steamer *Almos*. The convoy had gotten as far downstream as Semendria when the *Bodrog* received intelligence warning them of the Russian minefield and log barricade below the Iron Gates. With little possibility of the munitions steamer getting through, the convoy turned back. They were heavily shelled off Semendria but reached Pancsova without serious damage. The *Bodrog* reported back to Petrovardin, and the Austrians and Germans decided to abandon the attempt. The monitor *Inn* was sent to guard the munitions at Pancsova, and on the night of the 30th, with the *Almos* lashed to the transport to increase its speed against the current, the convoy ran the gauntlet of Serbian batteries and searchlights upstream to safety at Petrovaradin.[12] It was a clear demonstration of what a difficult problem supply of Turkey was while the Serbians controlled the approximately 330 kilometers on the right bank of the river between Belgrade and the Bulgarian border. An ordinary steamer would have required roughly $13\frac{1}{2}$ hours to clear Serbian territory, and still would have faced the Russian warships and barricades just below the Iron Gates.

The opening of the Dardanelles campaign and the Anglo-French naval attack on the Strait brought home how desperate the Turkish ammunition situation was, particularly after the Romanians continued to hold back shipments of ammunition by rail. The situation was serious enough for the Austrians to make another attempt to pass munitions by the Danube, although they were not very confident of success. They hoped to take advantage of a rainy and stormy night to run the gauntlet past Belgrade. The steamer *Belgrade* was loaded with munitions and, under the command of Linienschiffsleutnant Viktor Böszl, left Zemun on the night of 30 March, escorted by the monitors *Enns* and *Bodrog*. The little convoy was not detected by the Serbian searchlights around Belgrade, and the monitors returned to their anchorage, according to plan. Unfortunately for the Austrians, several miles downstream the *Belgrade* apparently hit a Russian mine near Vinca, damaging her rudder and alerting Serbian artillery. The steamer came under heavy fire, was set ablaze, and blew up off Ritopek, killing the captain and the majority of the crew. There were no further attempts to run munitions to the Turks until the Danube was cleared.[13]

The idea of operations on the Danube was considered in London at the beginning of 1915. It was, like the Dardanelles campaign, attractive to those who favored overseas operations as a means of sidestepping the seemingly endless bloodletting on the western front. At the meeting of the War Council on 13 January 1915, which agreed to Admiral Carden's plans for reducing the forts at the entrance to the Dardanelles, Lloyd George suggested a major attack on Austria, building rolling stock for the Salonika railway, and perhaps barges for the Danube. Churchill agreed: "At the worst they would be a good feint."[14]

Danube operations would have been even more viable after the Dardanelles campaign had been launched, for if the British and French had succeeded in opening the Straits, they would have opened the seaward route to the Black Sea and the Danube. Nevertheless, the War Council of 28 January tacitly accepted Churchill's opinion that naval force alone would suffice to open the Straits. Any troops available ought to be sent to assist the Serbians via Salonika. The War Council concluded that the Admiralty should order twelve monitors to be built in sections capable of being shipped to Salonika and then sent on to Serbia by rail where they would be assembled for service on the Danube. Lord Fisher promised that next day he would hold a meeting at the Admiralty to begin work on the design for Danube gunboats.[15]

This was the genesis of the twelve Insect-class gunboats that received the cover name "large China gunboats." The design called for a 645-ton vessel with propellers running through tunnels to achieve shallow draft. They would have outnumbered and outgunned their potential Austrian rivals with two 6-inch (15.2-cm) guns as opposed to the Austrian's two 12-cm guns, but unlike the Austrians they had no armor protection and their guns had only open shields rather than being fully enclosed. One historian regards the Austrian craft as much more suited for riverine warfare. The twelve Insect class never served on the Danube during the war, but did excellent work in Mesopotamia.[16]

Churchill was anxious to have troops on hand to exploit success at the Strait, and at the War Council meeting of 24 February advocated sending the 29th Division to the Near East as soon as possible. When Kitchener objected that the Dardanelles was supposed to be a purely naval venture, Churchill replied that the troops could be sent through the Dardanelles or up to the Bulgarian frontier or possibly to Salonika. If Bulgaria joined the Allies, the troops might go through Bulgaria to Nish or up the Danube. He repeated this proposal on the 26th, but could not win over Kitchener or Lord Balfour, the former prime minister and unofficial representative of the Conservative party in the War Council. Danube operations did gain influential support from Colonel Hankey, secretary of the War Council. Hankey circulated a memorandum, "After the Dardanelles. The Next Steps," to the council on 2 March. Hankey examined what he considered to be the best means of exploiting a victory at the Dardanelles. He advocated a British advance up the Danube to protect Serbia and as part of an offensive against Austria-Hungary. In this grand scheme, a British force supported by a powerful flotilla would constitute the center of an Allied army. The Serbians and Greeks on the left would move into Bosnia and Herzegovina while the Romanians on the right would form a connecting link with the Russian armies fighting in the Carpathians. The British force would turn the flank of the forces opposing the Romanians, which would enable the latter to threaten the flank of the Austro-Hungarian forces fighting in the Carpathians. The French and British armies on the western front would continue to exert pressure while the hard-pressed Russians on the eastern front, even if forced back, would at least contain enemy forces.[17] Hankey's plan assumed not only a naval victory at the Dardanelles but that neutral Greece and Romania would enter the war.

The failure of the purely naval attack at the Dardanelles on 18 March did not stop consideration of the Danube project. Admiral Henry Jackson produced a memorandum, "Notes on the Transport of Military Forces to Serbia," dated 25 March, and a memorandum by the hydrographer of the navy, "Report on the River Danube from Budapest to Braila," was printed at the beginning of April.[18] The Admiralty also asked Troubridge for details of tugs, lighters, and suitable and trustworthy agents for hiring them. They wanted information on facilities for disembarking troops at Radujevac and Prahovo—to avoid the difficulties of the rapids at the Iron Gates—as well as the carrying capacity of the railways connecting those towns with the rest of Serbia.[19] The War Office cooperated by providing the services of an intelligence officer, Captain L. S. Amery, a member of Parliament and subsequently one of the most influential men in the Conservative party (who would be first lord of the Admiralty, 1922–24). Amery visited likely sites in Serbia and Romania and prepared a detailed report.[20]

Troubridge was not very encouraging about operations on the Danube. There were no tugs or lighters available in Serbian waters or under Serbian control for the purpose of transport as the Austrians, except for one or two small craft, had destroyed all of the Serbian river craft. Unfortunately the facilities for disembarkation at Prahovo and Radujevac were very primitive and very limited, and it was only with great difficulty that matériel from Russia was disembarked there. The facilities for transporting men and supplies from Radujevac and Prahovo to Parachin on the main rail line were equally limited, and Troubridge doubted they could deal with the requirements of an army. The main Salonika-Nish-Belgrade line was also in poor repair with the whole of the Serbian army living "from hand to mouth" on supplies transported along the railway, and it was not possible to put any further strain on it.

This left the alternative of moving the British forces up the Danube through the Iron Gates and other rapids, but Troubridge did not believe this could be done—even with monitors escorting the troops—until the whole of the left bank, that is, the Hungarian side, was in the hands of the Allies. To proceed beyond Belgrade and up the Save to the western frontier of Serbia, they would have to control the Frushka Gora mountains and the quadrilateral between the Danube and Save. The British would need monitors, small torpedo boats to deal with the Austrian flotilla, and a mining and antimining force able to make raft and net bridges. Troubridge concluded that if they could not occupy the necessary enemy territory and if the railways were insufficient, it would be preferable to march at least as far as Belgrade on foot rather than attempt the river passage with its known disadvantages and dangers. He also warned that if the British sent an expedition to Serbia, they would have to rely entirely on themselves, for the resources of the country were barely sufficient for the population and Serbian army.[21]

The Admiralty could hardly have been enthusiastic about the Danube project after Troubridge's negative report even though Amery had been much more optimistic about the potential of the Serbian railways and the possibility of moving matériel by lighters and tugs up the Danube.[22] Nevertheless there still remained the problem of securing control of the Hungarian bank of the Danube so river craft might move unhampered by enemy batteries. The prospect of actually assembling twelve monitors in Serbia where facilities were lacking seemed equally doubtful, quite apart from the diplomatic difficulties of moving the sections through neutral Greece. The dockyard at Belgrade was within easy range of Austrian batteries, and before they could think of assembling monitors there, the Serbians would have had to capture Zemun and the territory beyond it. The promise of monitors soon faded; on 8 July Troubridge received word that owing to Greek troubles, the monitor sections could not be sent by way of Salonika.[23] This left only the Danube route open, and that of course was dependent on success at the Dardanelles. There is no doubt that the entire Danube project was linked to the Dardanelles venture and to a certain extent to the political differences within the British government.[24]

It is hard to avoid the conclusion that the Danube project had great potential for disaster. The British, unless fully supported by the Balkan neutrals, would have been pushing into an area where it was far easier for the Austrians and Germans to concentrate their military forces against them than for the British to reinforce theirs. Troubridge, however, reached a different conclusion when his mission collapsed. He had poured cold water on the Danube proposal in his official report and was consistently critical of the Serbians in his private diary. Nevertheless, when Belgrade fell and Serbia began to go under in October, he wrote: "We are done by reason of striking at the enemy's foot at the Dardanelles instead of through Serbia at his heart."[25] Unfortunately the logistical, diplomatic, and geographical difficulties of doing this in 1915 were considerable.

The British naval mission was destined never to fulfill any of its grander designs, but there was still the prospect of a form of naval guerrilla war in the waters around Belgrade. Artillery, torpedo tubes, and mines sufficed for defensive measures, although the fluctuating water levels made it difficult to rely on contact mines. The Allies placed much more faith in observation mines, which could remain on the bottom and be fired when an enemy craft was observed to pass over them. The British also were anxious for offensive measures. The means in Serbia were limited, but the Serbians did cover a barge with iron plating as a protection against rifle fire and on 5 January used the barge to cover with rifle and machine-gun fire a flotilla of small boats retaking Little Tsiganlia Island.[26] Both Cardale and Troubridge wanted something more potent and requested a picket boat, which could be fitted with torpedo-dropping gear and used against the monitors. The British naval mission finally received their picket boat from Malta on 21 March. It had been shipped by rail from Salonika, and there was considerable difficulty getting it past Greek customs and then through the tunnels and under the low bridges along the railway. There were even more difficulties in launching what the British, somewhat tongue-in-cheek no doubt, dubbed the "Terror of the Danube." Assuming the

Austrians knew of the picket boat's arrival, Troubridge decided to lull their suspicions and waited a month before using it in a night attack against the monitors in their anchorage above Zemun. The first attempt failed to find the monitors, but on the night of 22 April Lieutenant Commander Kerr managed to reach the Austrian anchorage before he was detected, fire his two torpedoes, and escape unscathed. The British heard two explosions, and ten minutes later a very heavy explosion. They knew the second torpedo had hit the river bank but believed the first had struck the leading monitor. This belief seemed confirmed after daylight when one of the monitors observed the day before was missing.[27] The Austrian sources, however, insist strongly that none of the monitors were lost. The Austrians had constructed a dummy monitor with wood and canvas in order to draw the fire of the Serbian and French batteries and thereby cause them to reveal their location. The Serbians, with good intelligence, do not appear to have been fooled, but the dummy monitor may well have been Kerr's target on the night of the 22d.[28]

The "Terror of the Danube" never had another chance at an Austrian monitor. The Austrians increased their precautionary measures, and the picket boat, already damaged by shell fire in May, struck a wreck on the night of 25 July and was holed and sunk in midstream. She was quickly raised and repaired, but Troubridge did not find the outlook encouraging. He was confident they could stop any attempt to send munitions to Turkey via the Danube, but the Serbians could not resist a full-scale Austrian and German invasion and intended, if that ever occurred, to evacuate Belgrade immediately. Troubridge realized the evacuation of Belgrade would give the Austrians and Germans "command of the key to the whole Serbian waters of the Danube," opening it at once for transport of matériel to the Bulgarian frontier. In distant London the Admiralty sadly realized a regular invasion could not be stopped by sending more boats or men. The First Sea Lord curtly rejected the suggestion that Troubridge should be asked if any reinforcements that could be sent to him would be of any use with the words, "No. He would expect his demands to be acceded to and we can't send him anything."[29]

Serbia was doomed once Bulgaria joined the Central Powers in September. A convention was signed at Pless on 6 September by which six Austrian and six German divisions were to be ready for operations on the Serbian frontier within thirty days, whereas Bulgaria would be ready with at least four divisions within thirty-five days. Field Marshal Mackensen was given supreme command of the allied forces. The primary German interest was to open communications with Turkey. The Germans subsequently increased their obligation by another four divisions when it appeared the Austrians could not meet their commitment because of Russian pressure. The basic plan for the opening moves of the campaign was for the main body of General von Kövess's Third Austro-Hungarian Army, four Austrian divisions reinforced by a German army corps of three divisions, to cross the Danube and Save at Belgrade, while the remainder crossed the Save about 20 miles upstream at Kupinovo. The seven German divisions of General von Gallwitz's Eleventh Army would cross the Danube downstream from Belgrade at Ram and Semendria with a feint crossing at Orsova. The four divisions of the Bulgarian army would invade from the east with the majority aimed at cutting the Salonika railway at Nish and preventing reinforcements from reaching Serbia via the Vardar Valley.[30]

The Germans made careful preparations for the river crossings which were such an important feature of the opening stages of the campaign. These resulted in the first appearance by German river craft on the Danube to support military operations. Fourteen motorboats of the Kaiserliches Motorbootkorps were to support the crossings of von Gallwitz's Eleventh German Army. Technically these were not naval craft, but belonged to the train of the army. The organization was formed by the Prussian Ministry of War to support army operations along lakes, rivers, and the coast. It consisted of a variety of requisitioned small craft, some seaworthy, some purely river vessels, and was initially the "Volunteer Motorboat Corps" with many owners apparently handling their own craft, which were usually armed with a machine gun. The largest, the 24-meter *Weichsel,* which had formerly belonged to the Imperial Motor Yacht Club of Berlin, was fitted with some plating, a 7.5-cm howitzer, two machine guns, and designated an "armored river gunboat." There were a few naval officers in command, but the boats themselves generally wore the red-white-black government service flag (*Reichsdienst flagge*) rather than the naval ensign. The boats supporting the Eleventh Army had been drawn from the Vistula Flotilla and shipped by rail to the Danube. The German motorboats, although the formal titles of their formations would change, stayed on the Danube for the remainder of the war. It is doubtful if any returned to their home ports, and the *Weichsel* fired some of the last shots of the war on the Danube.[31]

The operations of the Third Austro-Hungarian Army along the Danube and Save began with a massive bombardment at daylight on 6 October. The Austrian naval forces on the Save (the monitor *Szamos* and armed steamer *Una*) supported the passage across the Save by two Austrian divisions, and the *Szamos* was hit by shell fire and damaged, but able to make temporary repairs herself and continue in action. The majority of the Danube Flotilla, not surprisingly, was devoted to the difficult crossing of the Danube and Save near the Kalimegdan fortress and Grosser Tsiganlia Island. The river crossings began on the 7th. The defenses of the Allied missions were overwhelmed by the scale of the assault. The Serbians had decided to evacuate Belgrade, but there was heavy fighting. The three divisions of the German XXII Reserve Corps crossed the Save by way of Great Tsiganlia Island. They met heavy resistance, and the first attempt to take neighboring Little Tsiganlia Island was repulsed before the Germans succeeded in taking it later in the day. The two divisions of the Austrian VIII Corps that assaulted Belgrade had an even more difficult time. They embarked in pontoons using Grosser Krieg Island as cover by passing around its northern shore before rowing across the final lap to Belgrade. The Austrians had established a bridgehead before daylight, but could not be reinforced during daylight hours, and their proximity to the Serbians and the lack of any means for transmitting spotting information made it impossible for their own artillery to give them proper support. The monitors *Bodrog* and *Maros* moved downstream to provide that support, and were soon joined by the *Sava, Körös,* and *Leitha.* Austrian and German counterfire occupied the Serbian batteries, and the monitors were able to take up a position under the lee of the Kalimegdan to provide close support. Save for the *Körös*, whose stack was holed, they received little damage at this stage. In the afternoon they were relieved in the role of close support by the monitors *Temes (II)*, *Enns*, and *Inn*. The combat was broken off after dark.

The monitors were less fortunate the following day, when poor visibility hampered assistance from Austrian artillery, and once again the monitors were the only source of close artillery support for the Austrian bridgehead. The *Maros* took a direct hit in the superstructure, and, ablaze, had to haul out of the battle. Shortly afterwards, the *Enns* and *Temes (II)* proceeded downstream to join the *Körös* and *Leitha*, which were firing from their previous position in the lee of the Kalimegdan. The *Enns*, when off Grosser Krieg Island, took a direct hit forward below the water line, which flooded the 12-cm magazine. The *Enns*, ablaze and assisted by the *Leitha* and *Körös*, moved out of range and grounded herself on the river bank to bring the leak under control. The *Temes (II)* turned to engage the batteries in order to draw fire from the wounded *Enns*, but before her guns came into action received a direct hit in the crew's quarters aft and was forced to move out of range before running ashore to put out fires and stop the leaks. The flotilla commander then sent the *Sava* and *Inn* downstream to take up the fight while the armed steamers *Samson* and *Almos* towed the *Temes (II)* and *Enns*, respectively, out of the battle. Both later had to spend time in dock in Budapest under repair.

Although two monitors had been put out of action, the tide of battle was turning. The French battery on Topcider, which had been so effective against the monitors, was finally silenced by a direct hit from a 30.5-cm mortar. The *Körös* and *Leitha* were effective in providing close support for the Austrian bridgehead, and in the southwestern suburbs the Germans were able to consolidate their bridgehead opposite Great Tsiganlia Island. The picket boat on which so many hopes had been expended was destroyed in the shelling, sparing the British the necessity of scuttling it. The British naval mission was able to evacuate the majority of their guns, although they would have to be abandoned in the ensuing weeks during the long retreat. The Austrians and Germans succeeded in consolidating their positions, and downstream to the east the German Eleventh Army, with the assistance of the Kaiserliches Motorbootkorps, successfully completed their crossing of the Danube in the vicinity of Semendria on the 9th. The Danube Flotilla minesweepers were already hard at work clearing the river of mines by the time the last heights to the south, southwest, and southeast of Belgrade were captured by the Austrians and Germans on the 11th. The Austrians were now free to use the Danube past Belgrade.[32]

From the point of view of naval operations, the Serbian campaign was now over and the Danube open to the Bulgarian frontier. The Russian naval mission made a desperate effort to prevent this before leaving Serbia. Captain Illin of the Russian navy led an attempt to blow up the canal in the Danube at Orsova by excavating under the narrow canal and blowing up the bottom to create an overfall that would make navigation by barges impossible. Troubridge was asked to cooperate, and on 19 October supplied two thousand pounds of gun cotton along with a gunner and two petty officers. He did not believe there was much chance of success, for the project had not been well thought out and no preparations had been made for it. His fears proved correct two days later when the demolition party reached their destination and began work. They immediately came under the fire of Austrian guns on the opposite bank of the river and were forced to abandon the operation. The party narrowly avoided capture by the Bulgarians on their return to Serbian headquarters.[33]

The land campaign lasted until the end of November with the Bulgarians cutting off the route from Salonika and preventing an Anglo-French force under General Sarrail from moving up the Vardar Valley to the assistance of the Serbians.[34] The British and French ended by holding the area around Salonika and opening yet another front of the war in Macedonia. The Germans had no immediate interest in taking Salonika and even requested the Bulgarians to refrain, at least for the time being, from crossing the Greek frontier. The Allied naval missions joined the general retreat of the Serbian army. Some were eventually evacuated by way of Salonika, whereas Troubridge and most of the British joined the Serbian army in its epic retreat through the mountains of Albania to the Adriatic coast where they were eventually evacuated to Corfu.[35]

The Austrian Danube Flotilla proceeded downstream to Orsova, on the Hungarian-Romanian frontier, where it waited while sweepers cleared the Danube channels of mines and log booms along the Serbian shore so that the first shipments of munitions to Turkey and Bulgaria could be made. The Danube Flotilla then escorted the first convoy, which arrived at the Bulgarian port of Lom-Palanka on 30 October, where matériel was unloaded for shipment over the Bulgarian railways to Turkey. The shortage of rolling stock at Lom-Palanka soon led the Austrians to move two armed transports and six tugs farther downstream to the Bulgarian ports of Svistov and Rustschuk. By the second half of November, some ten munitions shipments had taken place without incident, and the Austrians no longer felt that it was necessary to directly escort them. The armed Russian steamers on the Danube had either sought shelter in Romanian ports or had moved downstream to Russian territory, but there was always the possibility the Russians would attempt to mount some naval operation from Reni. On 12 November AOK therefore ordered the monitors to concentrate at Rustschuk.[36]

The potential importance of the Danube to the Central Powers, cut off from access to the high seas by the British blockade, was obvious. There were, however, considerable navigational difficulties in moving cargo upstream because of the rapids at the Iron Gates. These rapids in the past had virtually prevented navigation between the upper and lower Danube. Between 1891 and 1896 the Hungarian government had cut a canal roughly 2.5 kilometers in length on the Serbian side of the river. This was later supplemented by the cable tug *Vaskapu*, which used a cable laid in the stream to gain extra traction to assist tugs in hauling loads against the current.[37] The *Vaskapu* was captured by the Serbians at the beginning of the war, and the Germans therefore took the initiative in building a towing railway along the canal that was ready at the end of May 1916. A powerful steam locomotive could now assist tugs in working upstream. Some idea of the increased importance of the Danube can be obtained from the tonnage moved upstream and downstream through the Iron Gates from 1900 to 1922. The tonnage in 1916 and 1917 was more than twice and in 1918 almost twice that of the best year (1909) before the war.[38]

THE ROMANIAN CAMPAIGN

The Austrian navy, joined by the German motorboats, was now faced with the problem of defending traffic on the Danube and the Bulgarian frontier with Romania. The Danube formed the border between Romania and Bulgaria from the Serbian border to about 10 miles west of Tutrakan on the right bank, where the border ran southeastward to the Black Sea. This region between the right bank of the Danube and the Black Sea was known as the Dobrudja and had been lost by the Bulgarians after the Second Balkan War in 1913. The Austrians and Germans patrolled the Danube with a variety of river craft, but Romania, courted by the Entente, could not be trusted and controlled the entire left or north bank of the Danube—more than 300 miles—along the Austrian line of communications. It was, to say the least, a potentially awkward situation.

The Austrians found a way out of the difficulty by establishing a base in the Belene Canal. This arm of the Danube, a few miles upstream from the Bulgarian town of Svistov, was separated from the main part of the Danube by the large island of Persina and provided the Donauflottille with an anchorage sheltered from artillery fire from the Romanian shore. The Bulgarian shore for much of the Danube was higher than the Romanian side, where the shore was frequently swampy, full of lagoons and lakes, and where high ground began some distance from the river. The Austrians improved communications with the Belene base by building a light horse–drawn railway to connect with the nearest Bulgarian railway station. They also ran new telephone and telegraph lines. In time of war the entrance to the Belene arm could be protected by booms and mines as well as artillery batteries on the Bulgarian shore.

The Romanians bargained long and hard with the Entente over their entry into the war, and probably missed the opportune moment when the Austrians had been badly battered by the Brusilov offensive on the eastern front in June of 1916.[39] This was the last great success of the old Imperial Russian army, but by the time the Romanians concluded a treaty with the British and French on 17 August and declared war on the 27th, it had bogged down and the Central Powers had recovered their equilibrium. Furthermore, it gave Germany and Austria-Hungary time in which to make preparations. On 29 July the Germans, Austrians, and Bulgarians reached an agreement, later adhered to by the Turks, on the conduct of the campaign. Field Marshal Mackensen was given command of the southern frontier, that is, the region of the Dobrudja and Danube. AOK decided to retain the majority of the Danube Flotilla in the lower Danube rather than ordering it to make the long trip upstream from Rustschuk. After hostilities began, the flotilla, including the monitors at Rustschuk and the armed steamers spread along the Danube, proceeded to Belene; only the armed steamer *Almos* and patrol boats *Lachs* and *Stör* were upstream at Kladovo, and there were a few German motorboats at Orsova. The Austrians also sent special bridging equipment down to Belene in a few echelons in preparation for a future crossing of the Danube. On 13 August the Danube Flotilla was placed under the orders of Army Group Mackensen.

Mackensen divided the forces along his lengthy front in two, a "Danube army," which would initially remain on the defensive, and a "Dobrudja army," consisting of one German, four Bulgarian, and two Turkish divisions, which would advance into the Dobrudja. Once Mackensen had reached an agreed-upon line in the Dobrudja, he would shift substantial forces back to the region of Svistov, cross the Danube, and drive on Bucharest. The offensive into the Dobrudja was deliberately designed to take the pressure off the Austrians on the Hungarian-Romanian border. The Germans and Austrians correctly anticipated that the Romanians would put their major military effort into an advance into Transylvania, where they had territorial designs, and leave the defense of their southern frontier to smaller and weaker forces. The defense of Hungary was entrusted to the Austro-Hungarian First Army under General Arz von Straussenberg, a comparatively weak force of two battered infantry and one cavalry divisions drawn from the eastern front, and miscellaneous second line units. The Germans promised to reinforce Arz with five infantry divisions and one or two cavalry divisions. The Austrians, who sought desperately to build up their forces in Transylvania, were put under additional pressure by an Italian offensive along the Isonzo in early August that captured Gorizia and forced them to shift additional forces from the eastern front to the Italian front.[40]

Romania's declaration of war on the evening of 27 August might have been overly delayed from the British and French point of view, but it caught the German general staff by surprise, for they had not expected the Romanians to enter the war until after the Romanian harvest in mid-September. The Romanians, on paper, had an army of more than 560,000 men, organized into four armies and twenty-three divisions, although thirteen were either second line or partial formations. The Romanian soldiers were predominantly sturdy peasants, but by most accounts they were poorly led and their army deficient in communications, artillery, supply and technical services, and aviation, although they later received some air support from the Russians and French.[41]

The Romanian navy was small and had never been able to fulfill its ambitions to become a significant force in the Black Sea. Under the naval program of 1899, the Romanians would have had six coastal battleships, four destroyers, and twelve torpedo boats, but none of these ships were ever built. The 1912 program called for six 3,500-ton light cruisers, twelve 1,500-ton destroyers, and a submarine. Four destroyers were actually ordered and laid down in Italy, only to be requisitioned by the Italian navy on the outbreak of the war. The largest Romanian warship in 1916 was the old (1888) protected cruiser *Elisabeta*, whose main armament of four 12-cm guns was landed for use in the fortifications on the left bank of the Danube opposite Tutrakan; she served merely as a guard ship at Sulina. The Romanians also had four old gunboats (110 to 116 tons), which dated from the 1880s and were of doubtful utility, and three old French-built, 56-ton *Naluca*-class torpedo boats. The most useful Romanian contribution in the Black Sea were the four relatively modern liners *Regele Carol I, Dacia, Imparatul Traian,* and *Rumania,* which were converted into auxiliary cruisers and used to good effect by the Russian Black Sea Fleet as seaplane carriers (see chapter 8).

The Romanians in the years just before the war had tended to neglect their seagoing forces in favor of their Danube division, which was somewhat more modern. They had four potentially useful monitors, *Lascar Catargi, Ion C. Brătianu, Alexandru Lahovari,* and *Mihail Kogâlniceanu,* built in Trieste in sections and assembled at Galatz in 1907 and 1908 with a primary armament of three 12-cm cannons and eight British-built (1906–7), *Capitan Bogdan*-class, 50-ton torpedo boats. There were also five to six older gunboats, used for police purposes, and a number of miscellaneous river craft used as transports, supply ships, or minelayers.[42]

The Romanian navy commenced hostilities on the Danube at approximately 9:30 on the night of 27 August. The Romanians sought to whittle down Austrian naval superiority by a surprise torpedo attack on the monitors at anchor off the Bulgarian port of Rustschuk.[43] Three improvised torpedo boats crept out of the Romanian port of Giurgiu across the river and fired five torpedoes and dropped a few mines. The torpedoes missed the Austrian flagship, the monitor *Bosna,* but hit a nearby naval barge loaded with coal and petrol. The barge burned and sank, although Austrian accounts indicate the flotilla had not yet received word of the declaration of war and attributed the explosion at first to spontaneous combustion or the crew's carelessness with open flame near the petrol. The Austrians immediately executed their plan to withdraw to the Belene Canal, with the First Monitor division convoying the noncombatant supply ships while the Second Monitor division (the *Bodrog, Körös, Szamos,* and *Leitha*) with six patrol boats, using lighters to screen against torpedoes, proceeded to an advantageous position to shell the harbor of Giurgiu. Simultaneously, the patrol boats moved in to recover as many Austro-Hungarian lighters from Giurgiu as possible. The monitors then opened fire, setting oil storage tanks, the railway station, and magazines along the shore ablaze and sinking a number of Romanian lighters.

Following the attack the monitors proceeded upstream, destroying two Romanian patrol boats, whose crews had run them ashore behind mines. They reached the safety of Belene in late afternoon of the 28th. On their way they met and promptly sank the Romanian steamer *Rosario,* which had been fitted as a minelayer. The German gunboat *Weichsel,* which had been acting as a guardship east of Rustschuk, also arrived safely under cover of darkness. Far upstream, the armed steamer *Almos* and patrol boats at Kladovo successfully ran the gauntlet of hostile artillery to reach the safety of Orsova on the night of the 28th.

The Danube Flotilla carried out offensive sorties to the east and west of Belene on the 29th, shelling Turnu Magurele and Zimnicea and capturing a number of lighters; the next day, however, Romanian artillery frustrated an attempt to recover more lighters from Giurgiu.

The army high command ordered the Danube Flotilla to remain inactive in September while operations on land took their course. The flotilla was secure in the Belene Canal, although the Romanians brought up heavy batteries to the heights around Zimnicea within range of the eastern portion of the canal and forced the flotilla to shift its anchorage. The Romanians also launched a number of unsuccessful air attacks. The monitors returned to offensive operations on 29 September, when the *Inn* and *Sava* led the patrol boats *Viza, Barsch,* and *Csuka,* the gunboat *Weichsel,* and the armed steamer *Samson* on an offensive sortie to Corabia where they set fire to the railway installations, destroyed many of the Russian ships taking refuge in a swampy arm of the Danube, and towed off nine lighters, two of them fully loaded.[44]

There is little doubt that the Austro-Hungarian Danube Flotilla had command of this portion of the Danube, the areas within easy steaming distance of the Belene Canal. However, one must also remember that this was the back door of the Romanian defenses, and the efforts and attention of the Romanians were focused on other areas, the Dobrudja and Transylvania. Three of the four Romanian armies had been used for the advance into Transylvania; only one was left on the Bulgarian frontier. The flotilla could do nothing to affect the fighting in the Transylvanian mountains, and a strong Romanian mine, boom, and artillery barrier near the frontier east of Rustschuk at Kalimok prevented any movement by the Austrian flotilla to the Dobrudja. These barriers could not be cleared until both banks of the Danube were in the hands of the Central Powers. The Romanian campaign was decided by the fighting on land.

The Romanian invasion of Transylvania made good progress at first against the outnumbered Austrians. The Germans and Austrians, however, enjoyed the advantage of inner lines and a superior rail network, and the Germans were able to rush the reinforcements they had promised the Austrians before the war. General von Falkenhayn, recently relieved as chief of the German general staff, assumed command of the German Ninth Army (three German and two Austrian divisions), which formed to the south of Arz's First Austrian Army (one German and four Austrian divisions). By mid-September the Romanian advance had been brought to a halt.[45]

In the south Mackensen began his attack on the Dobrudja the night of 1 September, and by the 5th and 6th broke through the Romanian defenses and captured the frontier fortress of Tutrakan on the right bank of the Danube. The combined Bulgarian, Turkish, and German forces were soon threatening the important railway line between Bucharest and Constanza, Romania's major port on the Black Sea. The Russians rushed three divisions and a Serbian volunteer division to the Dobrudja, joined by three Romanian divisions shifted from Transylvania. Russian engineers also bridged the Danube in the region of Reni to move troops and supplies.[46] Mackensen's advance was halted, but only for a short time; on 23 October he captured Constanza and the main line from Bucharest. The war turned against the Romanians in Transylvania as well. On 30 September Falkenhayn defeated the Romanians at Hermannstadt, and on 8 October at Kronstadt, driving them back into the mountain passes between Transylvania and Romania where they were now on the defensive trying to stop an Austro-German advance into the Romanian plains.

What of the Romanian navy? The monitors assisted in the defense of Tutrakan and then supported the Danube flank of the Romanian and Russian army in the Dobrudja. On 6 September three Russian gunboats, the *Kubanetz, Donetz,* and *Teretz,* arrived in the Danube as reinforcements. The three 1,280-ton gunboats had been launched in 1887 but modernized before the war. They were armed with two modern 6-

inch guns mounted in sponsons, a 4.7-inch gun aft, and two 11-pounders. The *Donetz* had been sunk at Odessa in the surprise attack that opened the war in the Black Sea but had been salved and repaired. The gunboats had gone up to Silistria at first, and in order to get that far up river they had to be lightened of all ammunition, coal, and boiler water, and then towed. Unfortunately, Tutrakan fell as they arrived, and with the Romanian retreat they had to move back downstream, although a propitious rise in the level of the river spared the Russians from the arduous task of lightening ship once again in order to pass the sandbanks. There were other Russian naval forces on the Danube, according to a British observer, including five to six *Azov* steam "schooners" (grain steamers), four small destroyers, three old torpedo boats, four motor patrol boats, a small submarine at Reni, armed tugs, river steamers, and hospital barges.[47] The Russians also sent mine specialists and sailors, coastal torpedo tubes, and field artillery drawn from the front in the north.

The Russian and Romanian naval forces annoyed Mackensen enough in October for him to order that a mining detachment be sent overland to the Dobrudja army to counter their activities. But the Russians and Romanian naval forces were not sufficient to stop Mackensen.[48] The Russians and Romanians apparently did not work well together. The Russians initially were under the command of a Romanian admiral who attempted to use the gunboats and monitors together despite the fact that the gunboats drew twice as much water and their guns had twice the range of the monitors. The Russians accused the Romanian monitors of going close to the bank, camouflaging themselves with branches, and then refraining from opening fire. The fact that the Romanians reportedly had only 100 rounds per gun when the war began and were down to only 20 to 25 rounds per gun by early November might be at least partially responsible for their attitude. Furthermore, there were seldom accurate maps for artillery spotting. Lack of Romanian cooperation meant that the Russians also landed their own observers and signalmen for spotting. The Romanian army appeared to be equally deficient in its liaison with both the Russian and Romanian river forces, and they were ignorant of troop movements. This was dangerous, for their first knowledge of a rapid Romanian retreat was when they came under fire from light guns mounted on motorcars while still at anchor.[49]

The Romanians made a bold attempt to retrieve the situation in the Dobrudja early in the morning of 1 October when General Alexandru Averescu secretly concentrated a few divisions of the Third Romanian Army and then sent several battalions across the Danube in lighters at Flaminda, approximately 25 kilometers downstream from Giurgiu, near the Bulgarian towns of Rjahovo and Martin. The first wave of troops were rowed across in approximately 120 small boats, which had been brought up in ox-drawn carts. Romanian engineers and sailors hastily began to build a pontoon bridge across the Danube for more troops and supplies to follow. This was well to the rear of Mackensen's army, and with only weak Bulgarian forces to oppose them, the Romanians soon penetrated some 5 miles on a front of 10 miles. The Germans rushed Bulgarian reservists, stiffened by German and Austrian artillery, from Tutrakan and Rustschuk to contain the threat. The Danube Flotilla was sent into action with the obvious mission of destroying the pontoon bridge, although the first serious disruption in its construction, according to two French observers with the Romanians, was accomplished by German aircraft on the afternoon of the 1st. Nevertheless the Romanians managed to finish the bridge around 7:00 in the evening, about half an hour after the last of the German planes departed. Unfortunately for the Romanians, rainy weather and a storm during the night whipped up waves and broke the bridge in three places, delaying further passage of troops for twelve hours.[50]

The Danube Flotilla made its first attempt against the bridge with mines before the monitors could come into action. The officer commanding the field of observation mines protecting the Austrian base was ordered to launch mines from a suitable location on shore, to be carried by the current against the pontoon bridge. The Austrians worked their way behind Romanian lines, but lacking boats, the attempt to launch mines from the shore was probably doomed to failure. The winds carried the mines ashore, and the Austrian mining party narrowly escaped capture.

The Romanians initially were fortunate, for the stormy weather that hampered the crossing also affected the Danube Flotilla. Moreover, the area they had chosen around Rjahovo was very difficult to navigate because of numerous shifting sandbanks. On 2 October the patrol boats *Viza* and *Barsch,* under heavy fire from artillery and machine guns on the shore, managed to approach the bridge and hit several of the pontoons with their light artillery and machine guns, clearing the bridge of troops. The two patrol boats were hit by the shore batteries firing from both sides of the river, and once their ammunition was exhausted by rapid firing they retired. The third monitor group, the *Bodrog* and *Körös* guided through the treacherous sandbanks by the patrol boat *Wels* (which was forced back by enemy fire), took up the fight from a position near Lungu Island, roughly 3 kilometers upstream from the pontoon bridge. For the next few hours the two monitors directed their fire against the bridge, constantly changing their position. Both came under heavy fire from batteries on shore upstream from the bridge, and both were repeatedly hit. At about 2:00 P.M., the *Bodrog,* with her turret and electrical circuits out of action, had to haul off out of range to effect repairs. The *Körös* continued the battle alone until her main steam pipe was cut, and then, with steam pouring out, she drifted rudderless onto the Romanian shore. The *Körös* could not regain the channel until the pipe had been repaired—a difficult job—and after dark both monitors retired to Lelek because of the danger from mines. The pontoon bridge, according to Austrian accounts, had been badly damaged and would require repair before it could be used again. The French officers with the Romanians, however, reported the bridge intact. The Austrian shells had landed either 600 meters over or 200 meters short, with none on target. Nevertheless, the Romanians had begun their retreat. The combined threat of monitors, aircraft, and stormy weather to the operation's lifeline caused Averescu to treat the undertaking as a diversion, and for the moment, to merely hold a bridgehead on the south bank. Storms damaged the bridge once again during the night.[51]

On 2 October the first (*Temes* and *Enns*) and fourth (*Szamos* and *Leitha*) monitor groups were ordered to relieve the battered third monitor group and to bring fresh munitions, coal, and diesel oil to the flotilla craft near Rjahovo. The *Szamos* and *Leitha* left the Belene Canal in late afternoon, towing one lighter loaded with fuel and another loaded with soil. They intended to launch the lighter loaded with soil in the current in the hope it would be swept against and break through the pontoon bridge. The group came under fire by Romanian batteries established on Cinghinarele Island opposite the eastern entrance of the canal, and the monitors and their tows were hit several times, the *Szamos* losing the barrel of one of her 7-cm guns. The Romanian artillery made it too dangerous for the *Enns* to tow her lighter filled with fuel until after dark, and the *Temes* proceeded to Lelek on her own. The Austrians concentrated in Lelek that evening, replenishing their munitions, and the damaged monitors of the third group were ordered back to Belene.

The battle over the pontoon bridge resumed on the 3d, although by now the Romanians were fighting to keep it open as a means to retreat rather than advance. Averescu had lost faith in his enterprise, especially as the news from the Transylvanian front was bad, and, according to the French liaison officer, the Romanians now thought only of holding a small bridgehead on the Bulgarian shore. All heavy and medium artillery was withdrawn back across the river. Romanian artillery made it inadvisable for the *Szamos* and *Leitha* to approach the bridge, and the Austrians resorted to the expedient of loading six mines on the patrol boat *Compo,* and then launching them in the channel so that the current could carry them down against the bridge. They succeeded in destroying about 50 meters of the bridge. German aircraft also returned in the afternoon to inflict additional damage. The Austrians wanted to destroy the bridge once and for all and planned an operation to take place after dark. Covered by the *Temes* and *Enns,* the patrol boat *Viza* and armed steamer *Balaton* were to bring two empty lighters up to the bridge. The lighters would be flooded to the correct depth and along with a dozen mines let loose in the current. The operation was partially successful. The Austrians later found one lighter had grounded but the other had apparently torn away another section of the bridge and drifted all the way downstream to the log boom at Kalimok where it lodged. By this time it did not matter; during the night the remnants of the Romanian force escaped as best they could across the Danube.[52] Averescu's bold attempt to strike at the rear of Mackensen's army had ended in complete failure.[53]

The monitors and patrol boats that had countered the Romanian assault did not linger in the vicinity of the partially destroyed bridge, and on the report, which turned out to be false, that enemy river forces were seen near Tutrakan, pulled back to Lelek, leaving only patrols on watch. The Austrians realized that the combined Russian and Romanian force was potentially superior and could only be opposed from behind their own defensive minefields. Averescu's neglect to call in the Romanian flotilla before the operation is generally considered one of his many faults, but the minefields and barricades laid by each side tended to keep the opposing river flotillas apart.

The Romanians may not have had any warships to oppose the Austrians and Germans upstream from the Kalimok barricade, but while the battle was taking place around Rjahovo, they were able to mine about two-thirds of the channel in the Danube below the eastern entrance to the Belene Canal. The Romanians under cover of their batteries on the Island of Cinghinarele expanded their minefields on the night of 4–5 October, blocking the approach to the Bulgarian shore. The minefields threatened to cut off the Austrian and German force, which had been at Rjahovo from its base, for the fields would have been difficult to sweep when covered by the Romanian batteries on Cinghinarele. The Austrians and Germans were therefore forced to execute a combined operation the night of 7–8 October. The second monitor group, the *Sava* and *Inn*, patrol boat *Compo*, and German gunboat *Weichsel*, along with German artillery brought over to Persina Island, covered the landing. A German Landsturm company and an Austrian Pioneer company were ferried over to Cinghinarele and succeeded in capturing it, while Austrian and German river minesweeping forces proceeded to clear a path through the Romanian minefields.[54]

The Romanian high command was anxious to isolate and destroy the Austrian Danube Flotilla and asked the commander of the Romanian fleet, Rear Admiral Balescu, to report to King Ferdinand on the subject. Balescu concluded that any project would probably fail because sufficient matériel was not available. Capitaine de frégate de Belloy, the French naval attaché and the French naval mission—which consisted of 4 officers and 31 ratings, all specialists—were anxious to at least try something, and the attaché suggested he and a representative of the much larger Russian detachment (47 officers and 1,800 men) operating on the Danube undertake a reconnaissance from the Romanian shore of the Austrian base at Persina. King Ferdinand agreed, and Belloy and Captain Zarine, head of the Russian detachment, made a brief reconnaissance and prepared a joint report. The plan was, roughly, to restrict the Austrian flotilla's freedom of maneuver by establishing "systematic barrages," first to the east and then to the west of the Belene Canal. The "systematic barrage" would consist of an ensemble of lines of mines, defended by artillery and machine guns, illuminated by searchlight projectors, and possibly supplemented by torpedoes and torpedo tubes mounted on shore and sunken lighters. They might eventually try offensive action against the Austrian monitors by bringing up heavy artillery to shell the anchorage, but the guns would have to be very long range, because the marshy ground on the Romanian shore prevented batteries from being established close to the river.

The French and the Russians doubted the ability of Balescu or the Romanians to implement the ambitious project and proposed that Captain Zarine be given command. But before the project could get very far, the Romanian defeats on the Transylvanian front and in the Dobrudja caused the Russian high command to order the Russian detachments on the Danube back to Reni. The Russians feared losing their specialists and matériel and shortly afterward recalled Zarine to take command of the river forces in the Reni-Galatz sector. The French naval mission could do little more than devise an alternate plan dividing the length of the Danube into sectors where naval observation posts, protected by cavalry and infantry, would be established and linked by telephone to central command posts coordinating artillery fire in the sector.[55] These efforts were overtaken by events.

The tempo of river operations declined while the issue of the campaign was decided on land, although on 9 and 13 November the Austrians raided Giurgiu again to carry off more lighters before the Romanians could destroy them. The land campaign also dictated the next important river operation. On 10 November Falkenhayn began his offensive against the Romanian positions in the mountains, anxious to reach a decision before the onset of winter weather brought the campaign to a standstill. Mackensen then shifted forces from the Dobrudja to the Danube front for a crossing of the Danube in order to attack the Romanians from the south. The Danube Flotilla was placed under the command of the Svistov sector commander, Generalmajor von der Goltz, for the operation. The Danube army—consisting of one German and two Bulgarian divisions, a Turkish brigade, a German-Bulgarian cavalry division, German heavy guns and howitzers, and Austro-Hungarian pioneers—crossed the Danube on 23 November in three echelons. The assault companies were rowed in pontoons by Austro-Hungarian pioneers or sailors, or else towed by German motorboats and, in some cases, paddle steamers and ferries. The main crossings were east and west of Svistov, directed against Zimnicea. The western group, the German 217th Infantry Division, set out from the Belene Canal and crossed to the Romanian shore east of Cinghinarele Island. The infantry, cavalry, and artillery followed in lighters, grouped in fours and towed by paddle steamers. The two Bulgarian divisions crossed to the east of Svistov. As a diversion, motorboats carried a German Landsturm battalion across the Danube from Somovit to the Island of Kalnobet and against the Romanian fortifications at Izlazu. Once the initial bridgeheads had been secured, the Austrians brought up the sections of their mobile bridge, which they had quietly positioned in the Belene Canal before the start of hostilities. The monitors and other Austrian and German craft of the Danube Flotilla were deployed to cover the crossing of the three echelons and later to protect the mobile bridge, which was completed on the 24th. The crossings, although hampered by fog, were successful.[56]

The campaign moved to its conclusion, although not without heavy fighting. On the 26th Falkenhayn's forces broke through the Vulkan pass, and by the 5th of December German armies had entered the Romanian capital of Bucharest. The Romanian government moved to Jassy in Moldavia, and eventually Romanian and Russian troops were able to establish a line along the lower Sereth River. The onset of winter and the exhaustion of troops and supplies brought the advance of the Central Powers to a halt. The majority of Romanian territory was in their hands, although British agents had worked feverishly to sabotage many of the oil fields in advance of the German army. The ships of the Danube Flotilla were occupied with the not inconsiderable task of clearing the river of mines, booms, and other obstacles, as well as salvaging lighters and steamers in the Romanian ports after they were captured. Once the channels downstream from Orsova were open, the Germans established a small naval presence with the Imperial German Danube Half-Flotilla. This, as opposed to the motorboat corps, which was army, was a naval force consisting of the former Bayerischen Lloyd paddle steamers *Save* and *Maritza*, each armed with two 5-cm, quick-firing guns and two machine guns. The steamers were used primarily for hydrographic work on the Danube, restoring buoys and lights to mark the channel and later assisting in anti-aircraft defense at Braila. The former motorboat corps was converted into the Deutsche Donauwachtflottille, with launches and motorboats distributed along the reaches of the Danube for police service.[57]

The river front was substantially unaltered for the remainder of the campaign in 1917. The Central Powers held Braila, Isaccea, and Tulcea with the bulk of the Danube Flotilla anchored in Harsova and Braila. The Romanians and Russians clung to Galatz, Reni, Ismaila, and Sulina, along with most of the Danube delta below Tulcea. Galatz and Reni were virtually in the front line, and all floating matériel was evacuated. Tulcea was a key position, for its possession by the Central Powers blocked Russian and Romanian use of the Sulina Channel, the best of the arms of the Danube through the delta. The French naval mission hoped, in vain, for a Russian offensive to retake Tulcea. The Danube itself formed the main line of defense in much of the region; the amount of dry land suitable for troop movements or water suitable for navigation in the delta varied greatly according to the season.

The Romanian and Russian naval forces were deployed in the Kilia and Sulina arm of the Danube and adapted to the local situation. The French naval mission arranged for the Russians to mount 150-mm cannons in six self-propelled barges. The Russians, in addition to the three *Donetz*-class gunboats, had another six lighters with 200-mm or 150-mm cannons, whereas the Romanians, in addition to their four monitors, had two lighters with 120-mm cannons.[58] The lighters were well suited for conditions in this region, and they were similar to the armed lighters used by the Italians in the Adriatic lagoons along the maritime flank of the Italian front. For most of 1917 there was a little known and very singular type of war here among the reeds, canals, lakes, and marshes of the maritime Danube and its delta, marked by extensive mining and small sorties and raids.[59]

There is no space to go into operations in Romania during 1917 in detail, but the Romanian army in Moldavia was reorganized by a French military mission under General Berthelot and emerged as a much smaller but far more efficient force.[60] The Romanians proved strong enough to stop an ill-advised German offensive in August with a successful counterattack in what is known to Romanian historians as the Battle of Marasesti. But any advantage gained by the Entente in Romania was more than nullified by the gradual dissolution of the Russian army following the Russian Revolution. Shortly after the Bolshevik seizure of power, the Romanians were compelled to conclude an armistice with the Central Powers at Foscani on 9 December 1917, followed by the preliminary Peace of Buftea, 5 March 1918, and the formal peace, the Treaty of Bucharest, 7 May 1918.

Romania had effectively dropped out of the war, and this, coupled with the Peace of Brest-Litovsk, in which the Bolsheviks had taken Russia out of the struggle, meant that the Danube route to the Black Sea was open for the Germans and Austrians. The Austrians and Germans had considerable work clearing the numerous mines at the mouth of the Danube and in the Black Sea. They also discovered a curiosity at Reni, a small submarine the Russians had developed for use in the lower Danube but apparently had never had the opportunity to employ.[61] Austrian and German troops had also penetrated far into the Ukraine and southern Russia, and the Austrians found it expedient to form at the beginning of April 1918 the Flottenabteilung Wulff, consisting of the four monitors *Bosna, Bodrog, Körös,* and *Szamos,* patrol boats *Barsch* and *Wels,* and the tug *Odessa,* towing lighters with coal and naphtha. The detachment was named after its commander, Korvettenkapitän Olav Wulff, who had commanded a monitor division for most of the war, and was ordered to support the activities of the Austrian army in Southern Russia in enforcing the peace with Russia and protecting transport of the Russian crop as far up the Bug and Dnieper as they could navigate. The monitors and patrol boats, after certain preparations such as the installation of compasses, were able to cross the open sea to Odessa, and for the next few months were active at Odessa, Cherson, and Nikolaev and in the navigable reaches of the south Russian rivers. The Austrians also manned and employed a number of Russian and Romanian craft. AOK ordered Wulff's detachment back to Romanian waters at the end of August 1918, and by 12 September they were safely anchored at Braila.[62]

The Germans and Austrians on the Danube were in some ways a victim of their own success, for the collapse of the Bulgarian front found them far from home with a hopelessly long front to defend—from the Hungarian border all the way to the Black Sea. The Bulgarians concluded an armistice with the British and French on 29 September which called for the evacuation of all Bulgarian territory by German and Austrian troops within thirty days. There were also signs that the Romanians might reenter the war. On 16 October the 1st Monitor Division was ordered to proceed from Braila to Lom-Palanka to cover the passage of the retreating German army. Mackensen insisted until the 19th that the monitor *Sava* and patrol boat *Barsch* remain at Sulina to keep open the route from the Black Sea. It was almost too late, for the 227th Infantry Regiment of the 76th French Infantry Division, moving rapidly northward through Bulgaria, reached the Danube at Lom-Palanka on the 19th and the Danube Flotilla was in danger of being cut off.[63] The same day French troops fired on the *Wels's* motorboat when it refused a command to surrender after approaching the landing stage to reconnoiter at Lom-Palanka. The Austrians and Germans had assumed that under the Bulgarian armistice they would have until the 26th to leave Bulgaria, but the French obviously had no intention of permitting enemy traffic proceeding up and down the Danube under their noses, particularly as in their opinion it would have meant passively watching the Austrians and Germans cart off "their booty" from Romania. As a French officer bluntly told an Austrian *parlementaire* on the 21st, the French had concluded an armistice with the Bulgarians, not the Austrians or Germans. French artillery had also opened fire the afternoon of the 19th on the steamer *Croatia* towing seven lighters and a pontoon. The steamer cut the tow, and the lighters anchored by the sandbank off Lom. The *Croatia* grounded on the Romanian shore after suffering damage and casualties. The French then used a Bulgarian launch to tow three of the lighters into Lom-Palanka. The following afternoon the *Enns,* supported by the *Temes* and *Viza,* succeeded in bringing off three of the lighters under heavy French fire, but the remainder as well as the steamer had to be abandoned.

The situation continued to deteriorate for the Danube Flotilla, however, as the French and the Serbians were also approaching the Danube in Serbia, both upstream and downstream from the Iron Gates. The flotilla exchanged fire with irregular Serbian bands as it continued the long retreat. The Austrians had been reluctant to reply to the French artillery out of deference to Bulgarian neutrality, but considered themselves freed from this consideration by the actions of the French. Therefore, the last of the flotilla—the *Sava, Barsch,* and the armed steamer *Una*—were authorized to inflict as much damage as possible. The Austrians mined the entrances to the Belene Canal before evacuating, and when French artillery fired on them at Lom-Palanka, they opened fire on the harbor, lighters, and other craft present with their smaller guns while they engaged the French batteries with their main armament. The *Sava*'s group ran the gauntlet at night with only minor damage. The flotilla had more scrapes with the Serbians as it continued its retreat in the following days, and on the night of the 31st the monitor *Bodrog* grounded near Visnica and had to be abandoned. By this time the Dual Monarchy was in dissolution. On 29 October Kaiser Karl had authorized all personnel who were not South Slavs to return home. The South Slavs left the flotilla at Vukovar with what is reported to have been, considering the circumstances, a fairly cordial farewell. The Germans, Hungarians, and Czechs who remained arrived with the flotilla at Budapest on 6 November. The situation at Vukovar was less cordial in regard to the large number of steamers and lighters that had assembled there and were detained by the South Slavs.

The last shots on the Danube were fired by the German boats of the Donauwachtflottille, who had no hope of getting home again. The *Weichsel* exchanged fire with French batteries off Rustschuk on 28 October. The French crossed the Danube near Rustschuk on 10 November using the former Russian/Bulgarian *Varna* along with Bulgarian steam launches to tow lighters and barges. The. *Weichsel*'s 7.5-cm howitzer fired steadily in futile opposition, and the German commander finally gave orders to scuttle all German craft. The *Weichsel* was scuttled off Oltenita the afternoon of the 11th, the day the armistice on the western front went into effect. The Germans scuttled a total of twenty-four boats; six were left afloat at Braila, contrary to orders.[64]

Naval operations on the Danube had lasted from the first to last day of the war. The great sweeping marches and river crossings of the Romanian campaign are as different from the usual First World War memory of trenches and barbed wire on the western front as the plodding monitors or armed paddle steamers on the Danube were different from the great dreadnoughts and battle cruisers that dashed through the North Sea. The monitors were not a decisive superweapon in themselves, contrary to some overenthusiastic accounts. They were able to bring close artillery support at critical moments to troops in exposed positions, but they were vulnerable, a moving but highly visible target out on the river, and often had difficulty spotting fall of shells or locating well-concealed batteries that took them under fire. The riverine forces could not decide a campaign by themselves, but they were certainly a great source of assistance when geography permitted and military commanders faced river barriers or made use of rivers as a line of supply. Riverine operations were another facet of naval power, and the operations on the Danube deserve to be better known.

10

FROM DREADNOUGHTS TO
SUBMARINES: 1915–1916

THE GERMANS SEARCH FOR
A STRATEGY

Kaiser Wilhelm and Admiral Hugo von Pohl, who had replaced Ingenohl as commander of the High Sea Fleet after the Dogger Bank action (see chapter 2), did not deviate from the cautious strategy of not risking the fleet in a major action close to the British coast and in waters that were not of its own choosing. Those waters were considered to be not farther than the distance the High Sea Fleet could steam in a night or a day and where the Germans could bring their maximum strength to bear. They were much closer to German than British bases, and damaged German ships had a much better chance of reaching home safely than their British opponents. Von Pohl, however, considered that there was a fundamental difference between his policy and that of his predecessor. Ingenohl, he claimed, had always sent out only weak forces against the enemy, whereas he, von Pohl, always took out the whole fleet. This might lead to success, but might also lead to heavy losses.[1]

Von Pohl made two sorties in February and March 1915 and four in April and May. They were generally in a westerly or northwesterly direction from Helgoland and extended between 100 and 120 nautical miles.[2] They produced no encounter with the Grand Fleet; nor were they likely to, for the British were no more willing to fight under these terms than they had been at the beginning of the war and were content to maintain the distant blockade that cut off Germany from access to food and raw materials from the rest of the world. The British *did not have to fight* or risk the Grand Fleet to maintain that blockade. The Germans would have to come to them if they wanted to break it.

It was apparent by the end of 1914 that *Kleinkrieg* was not going to wear down the British fleet to the point where the Germans could challenge it with every chance of success. The German submarines had done much better than many might have expected, and certainly they had shown their ability to operate at greater distances than anticipated. They had achieved a few spectacular successes and had for a time made the Grand Fleet a refugee on the west coast of Scotland or Ireland until suitable defenses at Scapa Flow had been prepared. They increased the strain on men and machinery enormously during that period. But it is also true that the warships they sank were for the most part old, and often foolishly handled. They did not succeed, and would not in the course of the war succeed, in hitting a dreadnought-class ship, the accepted standard of naval strength. The only dreadnought lost by the Grand Fleet, the *Audacious,* succumbed to mines laid by the surface minelayer *Berlin.*[3] It was therefore clear that *Kleinkrieg* would not produce the desired results, and in 1915 there was considerable debate in the German navy on the proper course to follow.

Vice Admiral Gustav Bachmann, von Pohl's somewhat reluctant successor as chief of the Admiralstab, hoped in the absence of a decisive naval battle to achieve at least a partial success by drawing portions of the British fleet within striking distance of the High Sea Fleet by means of advances and fleet movements within the Helgoland Bight. Von Pohl, though, never forgot that when he made a sortie with the objective of securing a partial result, he might become involved in a fleet action. He put the matter quite clearly to Bachmann on 7 April 1915:

No one can desire our fleet to achieve such partial results more than I do. But I know of no method by which they can be obtained without at the same time risking the whole Fleet. An advance to the enemy's coast involves the great danger of being forced to fight off the enemy's coast. To assume that the enemy would send inferior portions of his Battle Fleet right into the German Bight, is to credit him with quite exceptional stupidity. In war such underestimation of the enemy always has its revenge.[4]

The inactivity of the fleet was very distasteful to many of the officers, often fervid partisans of Tirpitz. They included Captain Magnus von Levetzow, then commanding the battle cruiser *Moltke,* and Captain Adolf von Trotha of the dreadnought *Kaiser.* Both were destined to hold important positions under von Pohl's successor Scheer. These men regarded the inactivity of the fleet as dishonorable at a time when their comrades in the army were suffering heavy losses. Trotha wrote Tirpitz:

It is my personal and unqualified conviction that a fleet which has helped to secure peace by fighting for it, will rise again even after the heaviest of losses. Such fighting will only serve to make the Navy an intimate part of Germany. I have on the other hand no faith in a fleet which has been brought through the war intact.

... It is always a surprise to me that there are people who regulate their actions by what will be required after peace has been made. We are at present fighting for our existence and the only question is, can the employment of the Navy, the Fleet, be of assistance to us. In this life and death struggle, I cannot understand how anyone can think of allowing any weapon which could be used against the enemy to rust in its sheath. To strike at every opening is the only way to victory.[5]

There was at least some support for the Ingenohl and von Pohl policy within the fleet. Vice Admiral von Lans, commander of the First Squadron—the *Nassau-* and

Helgoland-class dreadnoughts—believed a battle in the open North Sea was an "absurdity" (*Unding*) for the Germans, leading to the annihilation of their fleet. Lans believed that it was only in the Bight that they could fight with any prospect of success. The destruction of the German fleet would also threaten the neutrality of Denmark and permit the British to force their way into the Baltic.[6]

Lans left the First Squadron in February 1915, shortly after he countersigned a memorandum by his admiralty staff officer, Korvettenkapitän Wolfgang Wegener. Lans therefore received the credit—or blame—for "Reflections on Our Maritime Situation," generally known in the fleet as the "First Squadron Memorandum." Wegener is now considered by many the most lucid of the German strategic thinkers of the war, who argued that the political and military point of main effort (*Schwerpunkt*) for the German fleet was in maintaining sea supremacy in the Baltic rather than in the North Sea. The best ships should therefore be shifted to the Baltic, with the older *Deutschland*- and *Wittlesbach*-class ships of the Third and Fourth Squadrons left for simple coast defense in the North Sea. Wegener asserted that sorties in the North Sea were purposeless, for they were undertaken only to "do something" and exposed the German fleet to annihilation without giving it the opportunity to attain a decent goal. Tirpitz termed the memorandum "poison for the fleet."[7]

Between February and August 1915, Wegener wrote his famous trilogy of memoranda: "Thoughts About Our Maritime Situation" (June 1915), "Can We Improve Our Situation?" (12 July 1915), and "Naval Bases Policy and Fleet" (August 1915). He continued to stress the importance of the Baltic, and in the second of the memoranda pointed out that from a geographical point of view the Helgoland Bight was a dead end, because the German bases there were too far from the major trade routes. He argued that it was to Germany's advantage to secure the opening of the Danish Belts. Wegener, in fact, advocated the military occupation of Denmark, so that coaling stations in Danish bays could be established to facilitate employment of the short-ranged German torpedo craft to give the German navy control of the Kattegat and Skaggerak. Wegener was, in fact, fairly brutal in his plans for Denmark, whose neutrality benefitted the British. He wrote: "It must be stated that in the struggle for survival among large nations, a small state simply cannot be accorded the right to neutralize the power of a fleet, schooled over years of hard work, in favor of the [other] side, or to force that fleet to undertake detrimental operations—like an offensive with insufficient means, emanating from the Helgoland Bight."[8]

Wegener looked beyond the Jutland Peninsula and Skaggerak. He wanted to outflank Britain's commanding geographical position by acquiring the Faeroe Islands (possibly by purchase or territorial concessions in Schleswig after the war); foresaw the German fleet might anchor in Norwegian fjords "as protector of Norway"; and looked to the French coast, Cherbourg or possibly even Brest, along with the Portuguese Atlantic islands (Azores and Cape Verdes) as future German bases.[9] Moreover, he did not believe submarines had made battle fleets superfluous in the struggle for global sea control. They might wage war against England with submarines, but a future struggle in the

Atlantic with the United States for global sea control would require capital ships.[10] Wegener was certainly bold and visionary, even if the most ambitious portions of his plans were beyond Germany's grasp. Wegener's arguments, which were widely read in the fleet, were needless to say not popular with Tirpitz and his supporters, and the controversy continued after the war.[11]

Tirpitz displayed a somewhat inconsistent attitude on the question of a fleet action, and on the question of *Grosskrieg* versus *Kleinkrieg* he has been described by a noted historian as attempting "to keep a foot in either camp until events forced him to choose between the two."[12] In September 1914 he wrote von Pohl that from the beginning of the war he held the view that guerrilla war would not bring about an equalization of forces. He declared: "Our whole military and administrative activities for the last 20 years have had the fighting of an action as their object. Consequently our best chance of success lies in an action." Because of their numerical inferiority, the action would have to be fought not more than 100 miles away from Helgoland, but he was confident the fleet would inflict more damage than it suffered at the hands of the British. Moreover, he claimed, in the history of the world it was nearly always a smaller fleet that defeated the larger one, and he failed to see the use of keeping the fleet intact until peace was concluded.[13]

Tirpitz changed his tune after the Dogger Bank action, and in a memorandum to the chief of the Admiralstab on 26 January, he wrote: "After the manner in which our naval war has been handled so far, partial successes do not appear to be very probable in the future." Tirpitz now advocated aircraft attacks against London, a submarine blockade, submarine and destroyer mining operations from the Flanders coast directed against the Thames, and the immediate commencement of cruiser warfare in the Atlantic. He promised: "The interruption of food imports to the west coast of England and of her other commerce would be such a vital danger to her, that I should expect great things from cruiser warfare." Tirpitz thought any losses entailed in this cruiser warfare would be counterbalanced by the derangement of British commerce.[14] Six weeks later, however, the state secretary wrote:

Although I am personally convinced of the necessity of making the enemy, that is Great Britain, feel the pressure of our Navy, I no longer believe that the Fleet will do it. The former Commander-in-Chief . . . and his master (the Kaiser) are of opinion that the fleet can do nothing and the former Chief of the Naval Staff (Admiral von Pohl) always held the same view, whereas I have always considered that it is possible to obtain partial results. I must admit that it is now more difficult to do so, but not as yet impossible.[15]

Tirpitz's inconsistencies alienated the kaiser and probably played a major role in thwarting his efforts and those of his most ardent supporters to have him appointed supreme commander of German naval forces. His violent personal attacks against leading naval figures, not to mention Chancellor Bethmann Hollweg, added to his isolation. His policy on submarine warfare also was described as "difficult to follow as it is shifty and marred by the most odious personal character assassinations."[16] The tone

A NAVAL HISTORY OF WORLD WAR I

and substance of these arguments can be followed in detail, because the postwar official history, *Der Krieg zur See*—which generally followed the Tirpitz line—as well as Tirpitz's own memoirs and papers, plus the partial rebuttal by von Pohl's widow, contains numerous documents.[17] They reveal that the German naval leadership during the First World War was far from a Nelsonic band of brothers.

THE FIRST SUBMARINE CAMPAIGN

It is against this background of dissatisfaction with the situation within the German navy and the search for a viable naval strategy that the Germans seem almost to have stumbled into the submarine war against commerce. The Germans insist that they had made no preparations before the war for a submarine attack on British trade and that the number of serviceable submarines available at the beginning of the war corresponded to an estimate of the numbers necessary for their use as an auxiliary in purely military operations.[18] Nevertheless, before the war a German naval officer, Kapitänleutnant Blum, had studied the question of *cruiser* warfare—that is according to prize rules—against British commerce and in the spring of 1914 estimated that 222 submarines would be necessary to conduct it.[19] The German submarine commanders claimed that at least some of the inspiration came from the British author who had created Sherlock Holmes, Sir Arthur Conan Doyle, who published an article titled "Danger! A Story of England's Peril" in the *Strand Magazine* in the summer of 1914. The article told the story of how a small Continental power with a force of sixteen submarines was able to destroy British commerce and force Great Britain to conclude peace.[20]

On 8 October 1914 the Führer der Unterseeboote (commonly known as F.d.U.), Korvettenkapitän Hermann Bauer, submitted a recommendation to the commander of the High Sea Fleet that the Germans begin commerce raiding with submarines along the British coast. The measure would actually be in retaliation for the British announcement that on 2 October a minefield had been laid in the approaches to the English Channel east of the line Dover-Calais. Bauer claimed the latter was in violation of international law.[21]

The Germans in virtually all measures connected with the submarine war invariably claimed that it was actually the British and the French who had first violated international law with their far-reaching measures against German trade. The British had never formally ratified the 1909 Declaration of London and, indeed, systematically extended their definition of what constituted contraband, liable to seizure. The Germans argued that when this extended to foodstuffs, it constituted an illegal "hunger-blockade" against German women and children. The arguments involving absolute contraband, conditional contraband, free goods, and international law and precedents were frequently complex and legalistic.[22] There is no space to go into them here, but in general one can say that whereas British and French actions involved property and could be contested in prize courts, the German measures in the submarine war frequently involved loss of life. Neutral and other shipowners might on occasion win awards for damages or restoration of their property in prize courts, but a life, once lost, could never be restored. The British and French therefore had a noted advantage in the propaganda war for the sympathy of the richest and most powerful neutral of them all, the United States. The Germans—at least the naval authorities—however well grounded and legalistic their arguments, seemed never to fully comprehend this.

The first of what was to be a long line of British merchant victims of the submarine war was the small steamer *Glitra* (866 tons), which was carrying a cargo of coal, coke, iron plates, and oil to Stavanger. She was intercepted by *U.17*, under the command of Oberleutnant zur See Feldkirchner, on 20 October about 14 miles off Skudesnaes on the Norwegian coast. The crew were given ten minutes to abandon ship before the submarine sank her, but Feldkirchner towed the lifeboats in the direction of land for about fifteen minutes and then pointed them in the proper direction.[23] Nevertheless, although the sinking had been carried out under the general conditions of cruiser warfare, that is the ship had not been sunk without warning and the crew had been given time to abandon ship (and in this case at least a little assistance in reaching land), the submarine had not been able to spare the men for a prize crew and the *Glitra*'s crew had been set adrift in small boats. Had the weather been bad, or the ship far out at sea, they would have been in considerable peril.

The submarine simply did not fit in with the traditional prize law or customs of cruiser warfare or *guerre de course*. The submarine usually could not spare men for a prize crew, there was no room to take crews of a sunken ship aboard the submarine, and, what would become most important of all, a submarine compromised its safety, which lay in invisibility by surfacing and carefully examining ships that were intercepted. The Germans had a striking demonstration of this when they attempted to disrupt British troop movements in the Channel. On 26 October *U.24* torpedoed off Cape Gris-Nez what her commander thought was a troopship laden with troops. The steamer was in fact the Chargeurs Réunis liner *Amiral Ganteaume* (4,590 tons) carrying about 2,500 Belgian refugees. The steamer did not sink and was towed into Boulogne, but thirty to forty lives were lost. The British and French at first assumed she had hit a mine, but later evidence was found of a German torpedo, and the event was described as "the first atrocity of the German submarine war."[24] Giving the Germans the benefit of the doubt that this was an honest mistake, it demonstrates quite vividly that submarine warfare had a political and diplomatic component beyond its purely military effects. The German navy had to wrestle with this problem for much of the war.

There were no further attacks on British merchantmen for more than a month after the sinking of the *Glitra*, but on 23 November the *Malachite* (718 tons), and on the 26th the *Primo* (1,366 tons), were sunk off the Normandy coast by *U.21*. The submarine's commander, Kapitänleutnant Otto Hersing, appeared almost apologetic in his new role as commerce destroyer, explaining he could not accommodate the crews in the submarine, but that war was war.[25]

The sinking of the *Malachite* and *Primo* were not part of a concerted attack by submarines on commerce. The German navy had not yet decided on such a course,

A NAVAL HISTORY OF WORLD WAR I

although Ingenohl had been in favor of giving Bauer's proposal a trial. Von Pohl did not consider that British actions justified, at least for the moment, severe German violations of international law, and the chancellor and German Foreign Office were also opposed. However, pressure for a submarine campaign began to build within the fleet and outside the navy. Albert Ballin, the influential director of the Hamburg-Amerika line, was in favor of such a course, recommending the most brutal blockade. There were other German professors and financial experts who theorized the British had only six to eight weeks' food supply. Tirpitz speculated on the possibility of a submarine campaign to an American correspondent in November, apparently as a trial balloon to ascertain the attitude of the United States. Publication of the interview created a sensation in Germany, and stimulated formation of a "U-Boat party," which demanded unrestricted submarine warfare. Submarine warfare became as much a political as a purely military issue. Von Pohl's attitude also changed after the 2 November proclamation by the British designating the entire North Sea a British military area (see chapter 2).

Bauer submitted a second memorandum at the end of December 1914, arguing that there were enough submarines on hand to justify a commencement of commerce raiding at the end of January. He now had powerful support within the fleet, for on 20 November and 7 December, Vice Admiral Scheer, commanding the Second Battle Squadron, also had submitted private memoranda recommending a commercial blockade by submarines. Scheer, however, tended to look on the submarine blockade as a means of forcing the Royal Navy to give battle. The senior officers of the fleet approved both Bauer's and Scheer's proposals and passed them on to the Admiralstab. They went a step further, for they considered British action had justified using the full potential of the submarine as a weapon, which meant, in effect, sinking ships without warning. They were in fact calling for unrestricted submarine warfare. By January 1915 there was also considerable agitation in the German press for a submarine campaign, and in late January the Admiralstab finally agreed. At a conference at Pless on 1 February, attended by the chancellor, foreign secretary, and chief of the army general staff, the decision was reached to proclaim a submarine blockade on 4 February. Von Pohl—who had just assumed command of the High Sea Fleet—used the opportunity of the kaiser's visit to Wilhelmshaven on 4 February to secure imperial consent. Müller, who claims to have doubted at the time the Germans had sufficient submarines, implies the kaiser was hustled into the agreement.[26]

The German proclamation of 4 February 1915 declared the waters around Great Britain and Ireland, including the whole of the English Channel, to be a war zone in which every merchant ship encountered would be destroyed, without it always being possible to assure the safety of passengers and crew. Because of the British misuse of neutral flags, it might not always be possible to prevent attacks meant for hostile ships from falling on neutrals. There would be no danger for shipping north of the Shetland Islands, in the eastern portion of the North Sea, and in a 30-mile-wide strip along the Dutch coast. The German submarine commanders were ordered to make the safety of their submarines their primary consideration and to avoid rising to the surface to examine a ship. There was no guarantee a steamer flying a neutral flag or carrying the distinguishing marks of a neutral actually was a neutral, and its destruction was therefore justified unless other attendant circumstances indicated its neutrality.[27]

The Germans had only 37 submarines when what is generally called the "first unrestricted submarine campaign" began on 28 February. This figure is deceptively high, for it includes boats used for training, completing trials, or undergoing lengthy repair. Captain Gayer claimed that during the first offensive from February to October the Germans never had more than 25 trained submarines available for blockade duties in the North Sea. Eight were elderly, with unreliable gasoline engines, and not all submarines had deck guns.[28] Normally only about one-third of the available boats were in their operational areas at any given time. These were very slender resources with which to begin a campaign that Kapitänleutnant Blum's prewar study had estimated needed more than 200 submarines and that, most important of all, was virtually guaranteed to embroil Germany in difficulties with neutrals.

The U-boat Inspectorate, established as a separate entity at the end of 1913 to control submarine training, maintenance, and development, had operated on the assumption that it would be a short war. At the beginning of the war, there were approximately 17 boats still in varying stages of construction. The German mobilization plan provided for the immediate award of contracts for 17 additional submarines on the outbreak of war. These contracts were placed between August and October of 1914 and allowed for a building time of 18 months for the first boat of the series, with the 17 submarines to be delivered between December 1915 and December 1916. Few thought the war would last that long, so not surprisingly the U-Boat Inspectorate gave priority to finishing those prewar contracts that could be made ready within three months. The German navy also appropriated a submarine under construction in German yards for Norway and in November took over five submarines under construction for the Austrians.

The conquest of Flanders and its proximity to the British coast led the Germans to order 17 (two were earmarked for the Austrians) UB.I-class coastal submarines and 15 UC.I-class minelayers in October and November. These small, relatively simple submarines were attractive to the Germans because they could be built quickly—four months was the contract time for the UB boats—shipped in sections by rail to Antwerp and Hoboken for final assembly, and then towed through the Scheldt and the Ghent-Bruges canal to their base at Bruges. The UC boats had the disadvantage of having their mine storage tubes under water, so that the crew could not change the depth settings while at sea. The Germans did develop a true oceangoing minelayer with dry storage for the mines, but in January 1915 ordered only four of these UE-class minelayers on the assumption the war would be over by autumn of 1915. In April the Imperial Naval Office also ordered 12 of the improved and larger UB.II coastal submarines. They deliberately limited the order to the number of submarines that could be finished before the end of the year, for they did not anticipate much use for the type in peacetime.[29]

The Germans did not find it easy to rapidly increase the number of submarines in service. By the end of February 1915, they had commissioned only twelve submarines since the beginning of the war. On the other hand, by that date they had only lost seven.[30] However, losses to enemy action were not the real problem; except for a few periods, new construction always surpassed losses. The actual problem was to obtain a surplus sufficient to operate against the trade routes. The German yards encountered the same problems the other belligerents had with rapid wartime expansion. Many of the yards called to work on the new larger submarines were relatively inexperienced, subcontractors who provided engines ran into technical difficulties, and everyone felt the shortage of trained labor, especially as many experienced men had been mobilized. The result was that deliveries on time throughout the war proved to be the exception rather than the rule. Furthermore, the U-boat Inspectorate has been criticized for failure to do everything possible to accelerate construction. They prepared an extensive submarine construction program for no less than 154 newer and better boats, but the program was really designed for the postwar period, and deliveries would have been spread out until 1923–24.[31]

It is not surprising that there was fairly widespread criticism by German writers in the postwar period that the Germans embarked on this first submarine campaign prematurely and without the proper means. Tirpitz is a prime example. He asserted the decision had been made without consulting him, and that it would have been preferable to restrict the submarine blockade to the Thames rather than the grandiose proclamation concerning the entire North Sea.[32]

The sweeping nature of the first German unrestricted submarine campaign ran into stiff diplomatic opposition and was modified even before it began. The United States government delivered a stiff note that declared that if American ships or lives were lost, the German government would be held to "a strict accountability." Bethmann Hollweg and the German Foreign Office tried to reassure the Americans by announcing that submarine commanders would be ordered not to harm neutral shipping provided it was recognized as such. This, however, infuriated the naval leaders, for it would have greatly diminished the effect of the submarine campaign. They had hoped to increase the impact of the small number of submarines available by terrorizing neutrals, who were responsible for about one-quarter of all traffic to the British Isles. Scheer considered the U-boat campaign "ruined," and von Pohl protested that submarines could not determine the nationality of ships without exposing themselves to great danger. The new head of the Admiralstab, Vice Admiral Bachmann, was in fact ready to call off the campaign, but because the announcement had already been made, the Germans were prisoners of their own rhetoric. The result was something of a compromise. On 18 February submarine commanders were ordered to spare ships flying a neutral flag unless they were recognized as enemy by their structure, place of registration, course, and general behavior. Hospital ships also were to be spared unless they were obviously being used to transport troops from Britain to France. Ships belonging to the Belgian Relief Commission were to be spared as well. The submarine commanders were ordered to prosecute the submarine campaign with the utmost vigor, and were assured they would not be held responsible if, despite the exercise of great care, mistakes were made.[33]

The situation was ripe for diplomatic incidents. Comparatively young German officers, naturally aggressive—and if an officer was not aggressive he had no business being a submarine commander—had to make quick judgments under what were frequently difficult conditions. His actions had a certain finality; there was apt to be no chance for second guessing. His British or French counterpart enforcing the blockade had the advantage that his actions could be second guessed by others, for he fulfilled his duty by capturing suspicious vessels and sending them into port. It was up to others, diplomats or admiralty lawyers, to argue over the fine points, and if he had erred, no lives were lost and it is likely the only damages were monetary.

In the first three months of the campaign, March to May 1915, the Germans had an average of six U-boats at sea each day. There were usually four actually in the operational areas and usually two to the west of the British Isles. They did well, and in the North Sea and around the British Isles they sank: in March, 29 ships representing approximately 89,500 gross tons; in April, 33 ships, 38,600 tons; and in May, 53 ships, 126,900 tons. The Germans lost only 5 submarines, establishing what Admiral Hezlet terms an "exchange ratio" of 20, that is 20 steamers sunk for every German submarine lost. The British antisubmarine measures were largely ineffective. The substantial numbers of small craft in the Auxiliary Patrol doggedly put to sea, often in appalling weather, but they were spread thin given the large area to protect. The British began to arm merchant ships, whose masters were ordered to turn toward a hostile submarine and force it to dive. Captain Fryatt, master of the Great Eastern Railway packet *Brussels* (1,380 tons), used this method to escape from *U.33* off the Maas light vessel on 28 March, but in doing so made himself a marked man in German eyes.

Although now largely forgotten, the case of Captain Fryatt aroused considerable attention at the time. On the night of 22–23 June 1916, the *Brussels* was intercepted by German destroyers and taken into Zeebrugge. Fryatt was tried before a military court-martial as a *franc-tireur*, that is, an individual outside the regular armed services who had tried to injure German military forces. He was found guilty and promptly shot. The British regarded it as judicial murder aimed at terrorizing merchant seamen, and once again German harshness backfired on the diplomatic front. Their action was widely condemned in the neutral press; the *New York Times*, for example, termed it "a deliberate murder." For the British, Captain Fryatt became yet another victim of German atrocities.[34]

The British attempted to establish barriers in the Dover Strait and in the North Channel to the Irish Sea. The British minefields were a disappointment, if only because British mines for much of the war were defective. In the Straits of Dover and North Channel there were also lines of drifters towing so-called indicator nets equipped with flares, which, in theory, would fire should a submarine foul the net. Other drifters were equipped with "explosive sweeps"—wires fitted with explosive charges. The British also tried an ambitious steel net, supported by wooden booms, moored to buoys running from Folkestone to Cape Gris-Nez. Weather and strong tides frustrated the attempt, and the British abandoned it in May of 1915. Nevertheless, after a few submarines had experienced difficulties in the Straits of Dover, the F.d.U., Bauer, on 10 April ordered the route to be abandoned. Submarines were forced to proceed to their operational areas around the north of the British Isles, which added approximately 1,400 miles to their passage and cut the time they could remain on station. The large German submarines eventually returned to the Dover route, but not until the end of 1916.[35]

The Germans were able to offset some of the disadvantages by the development of the Flanders Submarine Flotilla once the UB and UC boats began to enter service. The Marinekorps Flandern under Vice Admiral Ludwig von Schröder had been expanded from division to corps strength in November 1914, and was directly responsible to the kaiser. There were four submarines at Zeebrugge by the end of 1914, and one, U.24, had been responsible for sinking the battleship *Formidable* on 31 December (see chapter 2). The objective was to conduct a naval guerrilla war against the British, although in February von Pohl successfully resisted an attempt by the Admiralstab to send a half-flotilla of the High Sea Fleet's destroyers to Flanders.[36] The Germans eventually turned the Belgian coast into one of the most heavily fortified areas in the war, including the 11-inch gun batteries "Tirpitz," "Hindenburg," and "Turkijen" and the 15-inch gun batteries "Deutschland" protecting Ostend; and the 12-inch gun battery "Kaiser Wilhelm II" and 11-inch gun batteries "De Haan" and "Donkerklok" protecting Zeebrugge.

The Flanders U-boat flotilla, commanded by Kapitänleutnant (soon promoted Korvettenkapitän) Bartenbach, used Bruges, which was about 7 miles inland, as its base and reached the open sea by canals that ran to Zeebrugge and Ostend. The first UB boat arrived on 27 March, and the flotilla was formally commissioned on the 29th. The other boats arrived gradually. There were six UB boats operational in the latter part of April, the first UC boat became operational in early June, and by October 1915 the strength of the flotilla had risen to sixteen. The coastal submarines operated at first in the Hoofden, the German name for the area southwest of the line Terschelling–Flamborough Head, against traffic between England and the Netherlands. The UC boats at first concentrated on mining the mouth of the Thames, but by early July the UB boats were passing through the Dover Strait demonstrating that the barriers that had caused the deviation of the larger High Sea Fleet submarines were not insurmountable. The UC boats also passed through the Strait in August, working off Dunkirk, Calais, and Boulogne. On the whole the German submariners were pleasantly surprised by the performance of the coastal submarines of which they had, initially, not expected significant results. The next series, the UB.II and UC.II boats, were even more capable.[37]

The diplomatic implications of the German submarine campaign were as important, if not more so, than its military effects, and from the very beginning there were incidents involving neutral shipping. Shortly after the German war zone went into effect, the Norwegian tanker *Belridge* carrying oil from the United States to the Netherlands was torpedoed without warning by U.8 on 19 February in the approaches to the Dover Strait. The ship, which was not trading with Britain or France, did not sink and was towed into port. The Germans later admitted it was a mistake and agreed to pay compensation. On 13 March the Swedish steamer *Hanna* carrying coal from the Tyne to Las Palmas was torpedoed and sunk without warning off Scarborough with the loss of nine lives. Dutch shipping soon fell victim too. On 25 March the steamer *Medea* (1,235 tons) was stopped by *U.28* off Beachy Head and then, although there was no doubt about her nationality, deliberately sunk. The second week in April, the Dutch steamer *Katwijk*, bound from Rotterdam to Baltimore, was torpedoed and sunk without warning off the North Hinder light vessel in the channel the Germans had declared to be safe. Shortly afterward, the Greek steamer *Ellispontos* bound from Amsterdam to Montevideo was torpedoed and sunk without warning. These were both neutral steamers, trading between neutral ports. The sinking of the *Katwijk* aroused considerable indignation in the Netherlands, and the German government and the German Foreign Office replied to Dutch protests that if the sinking of the *Katwijk* was actually the work of a German submarine, they would pay compensation. The Germans later offered compensation for the *Ellispontos* as well.[38]

The *Katwijk* affair and German friction with the Dutch are now largely forgotten, along with similar incidents with other neutrals. The major question was, of course, what of incidents between Germany and the United States? They too were not long in coming. On 27 March *U.28* stopped the Elder Dempster liner *Falaba* (4,806 tons), outward bound from Liverpool to Sierra Leone. The submarine gave the liner only five minutes to abandon ship, and then, before the process was ended, torpedoed her. There were 104 people who lost their lives, and one of them turned out to be a United States citizen. The United States government eventually chose not to make a major issue over the death, largely due to the pacifist sentiments of the secretary of state, William Jennings Bryan. Other incidents followed. On 28 April the American freighter *Cushing* was bombed by German aircraft in the North Sea, without loss. On 1 May the tanker *Gulflight*, en route to Rouen, was torpedoed without warning off the Scilly Islands. Two men dove overboard and were drowned, and the master died of a heart attack, but the tanker managed to reach port.[39] These incidents are also largely forgotten, but the incident remembered to this day, the sinking of the *Lusitania*, would follow within a few days.

The Germans had a difficult time resolving their somewhat conflicting orders. They lost two submarines in March. *U.12* was rammed by the destroyer *Ariel* off the Forth, and *U.29*, whose commander, Weddigen, had been responsible for sinking the *Aboukir, Cressy,* and *Hogue* the preceding September, was rammed and sunk by the *Dreadnought* while attempting to attack the battleship *Neptune*. The Germans did not learn the full circumstances of Weddigen's loss until after the war, and there were strong rumors he had been lost as a result of a trap laid through the misuse of neutral flags. On 2 April the kaiser ordered submarines to no longer surface in order to establish the identity of neutral vessels, although it was not clear how this could be reconciled with the instructions to spare certain neutrals. Moreover, after the *Katwijk* affair, the German government issued orders on 18 April that no neutral vessels were to be attacked.[40]

The Cunard liner *Lusitania* (30,396 tons) was not a neutral steamer; none of the neutrals, not even the Dutch, had a large four-funneled liner. Moreover, the silhouette of the *Lusitania* and her sister ship *Mauretania* had appeared in the 1914 edition of *Jane's Fighting Ships* as auxiliary cruisers. In an age that looked with awe on great passenger liners, both were among the best-known ships in the world, and the *Mauretania* held the Blue Riband for the fastest Atlantic crossing. The commander of the submarine *U.20*, Kapitänleutnant Walter Schwieger, could have had little doubt what he was firing at when he put a torpedo into the liner in the western approaches off the coast of Ireland on 7 May. The *Lusitania* sank with the loss of 1,201 lives, many of them women and children, and 128 of the dead were United States citizens. The incident set off a major diplomatic controversy between Germany and the United States in which the torpedoing without warning of the homeward-bound American steamer *Nebraskan* off the Irish coast on the 25th seemed to add insult to injury, although the damaged ship was towed back to port.

Schwieger appears to have believed the liner was being used as a troop transport, and ever since there has been considerable ink spilled over how much ammunition the *Lusitania* was carrying, because there had been a second explosion. There have even been suggestions that Churchill manufactured the incident to embroil the Americans as the liner was reported to be foolishly steaming at a slow speed. There is no space to enter into the question in detail, but the Germans, however strong their case from the legal and perhaps even moral point of view given the ruthless nature of the Allied blockade, had committed a particularly brutal act, and in the long run they paid the consequences in the alienation of American public opinion and the circumstances that eventually resulted in American entry into the world war.[41]

The Germans, in what today might be called diplomatic "damage control," managed to avoid an open break with the United States and to ward off President Wilson's demands for a virtual cessation of submarine warfare against commerce. They paid a price, even before any public compromise with the Americans. On 5 June Bethmann Hollweg, despite the fierce opposition of the naval authorities, won the kaiser's agreement to an order that submarines would not attack large passenger liners even if they flew the enemy flag. Bachmann and Tirpitz submitted their resignations, which were not at first accepted. The Germans proposed to the Americans that a special transatlantic service be established for Americans who desired to travel. The ships would be clearly marked and the Germans would be notified in advance of their movements. The Americans indignantly rejected the proposal, but President Wilson seemed to be moving toward acceptance of submarine war as conducted in June and July, that is, with passenger liners spared and no incidents involving American seamen.[42]

How did the U-boats perform under the restrictions? The answer is not badly at all. The tonnage sunk in June and July was only slightly less than it had been in April and May, and the number of ships sunk was actually higher. Both the number of ships sunk and total tonnage was greater in August and September than it had been in April and May. The average number of submarines at sea each day during August and September was also high, 8.6 compared to 5.6 between March and May. The relevant figures concerning sinking were: June, 114 ships and 115,291 tons; July, 86 ships and 98,005 tons; August, 107 ships and 182,772 tons; and September, 58 ships and 136,048 tons. The Germans lost 10 submarines and gave another to the Austrians during these months, but they commissioned 15 new boats, of which 10 were UC coastal minelayers.[43]

There was another reason why the Germans, whatever the laments of the naval leaders, continued to do well despite the restrictions imposed after the sinking of the *Lusitania*. Ships had been torpedoed without warning when they were too large or too fast for the submarine's gun to be effective. Submarine commanders much preferred to use gunfire or explosive charges in order to preserve their precious and limited supply of torpedoes. Therefore, from June to September 1915 the number of ships torpedoed without warning decreased, but the number of those sunk by gunfire and explosives increased. Ironically it seemed more humane. It is a peculiarity of public opinion that the sinking of passenger liners carrying innocent men, women, and children aroused great indignation, but the slaughter of grubby freighters and merchant seamen plying their hard trade was passed over, if not in total silence, at least with far less comment—provided of course they were not American. However, it was upon those rusty and unglamorous freighters, not the passenger liners, that the British depended for the bulk of their vital supplies.

The arrangement was threatened by any spectacular incident, which remained likely because submarines were still authorized to torpedo without warning when they could not establish a ship was neutral. Moreover, while British antisubmarine defenses were relatively ineffective, they were employing one weapon that made it very dangerous for the German submarines to observe the proper restraints. This weapon was the Q-ship, which made it too hazardous for submarines to employ the customary forms of cruiser warfare and made it, perhaps, inevitable that they would be involved in another incident with the United States. The Q-ships were decoys, generally tramp steamers but sometimes sailing vessels, deliberately designed to appear harmless and easy prey. They carried concealed guns and hoped to entice a submarine close enough to where it could be destroyed. On 26 November 1914, Churchill ordered the commander in chief Portsmouth to fit out a small- or medium-sized steamer to trap the German submarine operating off Le Havre. The first vessel chosen proved unsuitable and was soon paid off, but the second, the salvage tug *Lyon*, began operations in February 1915.

The British also concealed guns on fishing trawlers in order to protect the fishing fleets. There was another variant, a trawler working in coordination with a submarine. The trawler would tow the submarine, which was linked to it by telephone, and should a German U-boat approach on the surface the submarine would be warned, the tow would be slipped, and the submarine would attempt to attack the U-boat. The first Q-ship success actually came in this manner when the trawler *Taranaki* working in conjunction with the submarine *C.24* sank *U.40* on 24 June. The trawler *Princess Louis* and *C.27* accounted for a second U-boat, *U.23*, on 20 July. The Germans learned of the ruse, however, took precautions, and the trawler-submarine combinations had no further success and were later ended. On 24 July the *Prince Charles* became the first Q-ship operating alone to destroy a U-boat, *U.36*, and the *Baralong* sank *U.27* on 19 August and *U.41* on 24 September. The successes achieved by the Q-ships in the summer of 1915 were all the more important because so few methods had appeared to work against the submarine. This resulted in Q-ships being employed in sizable numbers for much of the war, and long after they had passed the peak of their effectiveness.[44]

The destruction of *U.27* by the *Baralong* caused another diplomatic incident in which the Germans were able to charge the British with committing an atrocity which they attempted to use to offset charges of German atrocities. This was very convenient, because on the same day Kapitänleutnant Schneider in *U.24* had torpedoed and sunk without warning south of the Irish coast the White Star liner *Arabic* (15,801 tons), which had been en route to America. The destruction of the liner was a violation of German assurances to the United States, and there were two or three Americans among the forty-four dead. The steamer had only one funnel but was large—600 feet long—and should have been easily recognized as a liner. Schneider, who had had a brush with a large steamer a few days before, reported that the unknown steamer had turned toward him and he thought she was attempting to ram.

The *Baralong*, commanded by Lieutenant Commander Godfrey Herbert, was more than 100 miles away and had intercepted the wireless calls from the *Arabic*. Herbert knew the Germans had committed what in his and his ship's company's mind was another atrocity when, later in the day, they steamed to the assistance of the Leyland Line steamer *Nicosian* (6,369 tons), carrying a cargo of mules from America, which had been shelled and then stopped by Kapitänleutnant Wegener and the *U.27*. The *Baralong*, wearing American colors, made the international signal that she was approaching to rescue the crew, but when shielded from the submarine's view by the *Nicosian*, hoisted the white ensign and opened fire. The submarine was repeatedly hit and began to sink, but Herbert noticed about a dozen Germans who had dived overboard swam to the *Nicosian* and were seeking to climb the ropes left hanging when the steamer had lowered her boats. Herbert feared that the Germans would either scuttle or set fire to the ship and opened fire on them. Six Germans succeeded in getting back aboard the *Nicosian*, and Herbert sent a boarding party of Marines to the ship. The Germans in the *Nicosian* were killed, and when some American muleteers who had been accompanying the mules returned to port, they spread stories of a massacre. The stories varied, some were suspect, but when seen in the context of the *Lusitania* and *Arabic* affairs, it is probable that the Marines, searching an unlit and strange ship for a hated enemy they thought had committed atrocities, and in this particular case might have been armed, shot first and asked questions later.[45]

The Germans now had a "British atrocity" charge of their own to counter the charges against them and undoubtedly would have charged Herbert as a war criminal had they won the war. The *Baralong* affair doubtlessly hardened the attitude of U-boat commanders, and the use of Q-ships made it much more dangerous for the Germans to wage the submarine war under prize rules. The *Arabic* and *Baralong* incidents, coming on the same day, also demonstrate how difficult it was to reconcile the submarine war and the methods used to counter it with what had been the traditional rules of warfare. Technically, until 15 September 1915, Q-ships might well have been considered "pirates," for it was only on this date that the Admiralty finally decided they must be commissioned.[46]

The *Arabic* affair caused another crisis between Germany and the United States, which was fueled by the sinking of the Allan liner *Hesperian* (10,920 tons) southwest of Fastnet, Ireland, by Schwieger and the *U.20*—the man who had sunk the *Lusitania*—with the loss of thirty-two lives, none American. There was an equally severe crisis within the German government. Falkenhayn, chief of the general staff, supported the chancellor, for he wanted to avoid further complications with neutrals because of the impending entry of Bulgaria into the war and the prospect of a Balkan campaign. He would have been hard pressed to find sufficient troops to meet the situation in the north had the Dutch been drawn into the war. The crisis ended with another temporary victory by Bethmann Hollweg over the admirals when the kaiser issued the order that henceforth no passenger liners, even small ones, would be sunk without warning and safeguarding the passengers. Shortly afterward the kaiser ordered that for the time being U-boats would not be stationed in the western approaches, which were where passenger liners were most likely to be found and where the worst incidents had occurred. Now the question was would a submarine commander have to stop and search even a small ship that appeared to be a freighter to make sure it was not carrying any passengers? Von Pohl believed this would make further prosecution of the U-boat campaign impossible and asked to be relieved. Müller replied he had submitted von Pohl's protest but not his resignation to the kaiser. Müller did help to arrange for Bachmann, whose opposition had incurred the kaiser's displeasure, to be replaced as head of the Admiralstab by Admiral Henning von Holtzendorff, a known enemy of Tirpitz. Holtzendorff assumed office on 6 September, but the situation in the navy was so acrimonious that Müller, in consultation with the new chief of the Admiralstab, drafted a memorandum for the kaiser's signature warning against insubordination and criticism.[47] Tirpitz had also submitted his resignation for the second time, but he was considered too popular and was retained in office. He was, however, deprived of his advisory status with the Admiralstab and restricted to purely administrative duties at the Imperial Naval Office.

Holtzendorff decided that the U-boat campaign had not achieved its goal, and on 18 September ordered that for the next few weeks there would be no submarine attacks on merchant shipping off the west coast of Great Britain or in the English Channel; in the North Sea submarine warfare would be conducted strictly according to prize law.[48] The effect of this was to end the first submarine campaign against commerce. Submarines shifted back to primarily military tasks while the Germans began to build up their strength in the Mediterranean, where they found favorable opportunities and fewer risks of incidents with the United States (see chapter 12). It is important to remember, however, that by the admission of the Germans themselves, the suspension of activity by the North Sea flotillas "did not work quite so much hardship," because after the detachment of the U-boats to the Mediterranean, only four of the remaining U-boats available for operations on the west coast of Great Britain did not need extensive repairs.[49]

The bitterness among the naval leaders remained, and Tirpitz continued his opposition, constantly seeking outside support until his resignation in March 1916. He went back to what Müller termed his "old refrain" on 3 December, arguing that "the Fleet must be engaged or otherwise the Kaiser's life work would be destroyed," and that he would be ready to take over the fleet himself.[50] One can guess the atmosphere by the derogatory names applied to naval leaders. Müller was known as "Rasputin," Holtzendorff as "the father of the lie," and Capelle (Tirpitz's successor at the Reichsmarineamt) as "Judas Iscariot."[51]

It is interesting to examine what effect the first submarine campaign had on the British and their allies. The first three months, February, March, and April, were not very effective and British and Allied communications were not interrupted. The rate of sinking was actually lower than it had been at the height of the cruiser campaign at the beginning of the war, and thanks to new construction and the capture of enemy shipping, the tonnage available to the British actually rose. The British were able by diplomatic measures to tighten the blockade and exploit neutral shipping. Neutrals were definitely not frightened away. There was, however, an increasing shortage of tonnage for commercial purposes due to requisitioning of ships for naval and military purposes, redistribution of trade, and congestion of ports. The period was perhaps deceptive for the British, as losses were low not because of the effectiveness of antisubmarine operations but because the number of submarines actually operating was still small.[52]

Losses from June to September 1915 rose considerably to the point where they surpassed the old rate of sinking under cruiser warfare and the rate of new construction. The losses, however, were still small in proportion to the total volume of traffic. On 31 July, the end of the first year of war, the total British losses from *all* causes in steamers of 1,600 tons or larger was under 4 percent in numbers and a little more than 3.5 percent in tonnage. August was a shock, for the average monthly loss in numbers or tonnage, which had been under one-third of 1 percent, rose to .92 percent in numbers and .78 percent in tonnage. Losses fell in September to .53 percent in numbers and .47 percent in tonnage, still above the previous average. The monetary value of losses in ships and cargo was so high that but for the spreading of risks through the State Insurance Scheme, the losses would have been so onerous to individual owners and merchants that trade might have been paralyzed. In terms of losses and gains, from August 1914 to September 1915, total losses in tonnage were 1,294,000 tons, whereas 1,233,000 tons were added through new construction and 682,000 tons were added through the capture or detention of enemy ships. However, the total tonnage available was now a diminishing figure, for new merchant tonnage steadily declined. This was probably due to the diversion of men and matériel to purely naval construction as well as the enlistment of many workers. The demands on tonnage for overseas expeditions—the Dardanelles, Mesopotamia, and Salonika—also increased. The heavy losses of August 1915 were also an indicator of the potential of the submarine, and Admiral Hezlet concludes that it was undoubtedly a great relief when the Germans called off the first submarine campaign.[53]

The "Restricted" Submarine Campaign

The German navy now entered into what is sometimes called the "twilight phase" of submarine warfare, which lasted, except for two months (March–April 1916), until September of 1916. It was also a period in which the High Sea Fleet returned to active surface operations, resulting in the Battle of Jutland and the near-battle of 19 August. *Restricted* submarine warfare is also a very loose term, for the Germans tended to go as far as they thought they could get away with, and the term had less meaning for the Mediterranean. The Flanders Flotilla, which was frustrated at having its activities curtailed just as the long nights of autumn and winter were approaching, resorted increasingly to mine warfare with the new UC boats. On 21 November 1915, Holtzendorff ordered the Flanders Flotilla to sink enemy freighters without warning in the zone between Dunkirk and Le Havre, although the measure was not really practical until the new UB.II boats were available in mid-February 1916. On 24 January 1916, the kaiser agreed to the sinking without warning of *armed enemy* freighters, and on 13 March to sinking without warning *all enemy* freighters within the war zone. The rules were therefore constantly changing according to the diplomatic situation.[54]

A German submarine commander complained after the war of the numerous restrictive orders:

> As a matter of fact, so many were issued that it was impossible for a submarine commander to learn them all, and many a time it was necessary for the helmsman or some other trusty support to bring the orders to the conning tower and hastily run through the mass to find out whether or not a certain vessel could be torpedoed. Even then it frequently turned out that "whatever you do is wrong." For a commanding officer to be continually harassed by the thought that he will be held accountable for this or that sinking, when returning from a long and arduous cruise, makes his task especially difficult.[55]

Although originally brought into office to restrain the U-boat zealots, Holtzendorff was converted to the idea of unrestricted submarine warfare by the end of 1915. He apparently was convinced by the report of a group of German shipping experts, which, correctly, took account of the substantial portion of British merchant tonnage now devoted to military purposes combined with the reduction in new tonnage from the shipbuilding yards because of the diversion of men and matériel. They calculated the amount of new tonnage likely to enter service in 1916, then an average monthly loss of so many thousand tons achieved by a force of thirty-five U-boats. They theorized that a force of U-boats doubled in size would inflict twice the losses, and subtracting these forces from new construction, the British would be forced to end the war within six to eight months. The United States could be safely disregarded. Even if the Americans entered the war, they would not be likely to be able to render any significant assistance within this time. Holtzendorff in January 1916 confidently predicted that, based on past performance, they could assume in the future each U-boat would sink at least 4,000 tons daily and that, counting U-boats on station in the North Sea and Mediterranean and adding average losses from mines, they could sink 631,640 tons per month for a six-month total of almost 3.8 million tons. The full argument was, of course, more sophisticated than this crude summary. It also reflected how the submarine had changed the nature of the war at sea for naval staffs. It was now a question of graphs and curves; "tonnage" was the important word rather than individual ships or men.

Holtzendorff won the support of Falkenhayn, who planned to weaken England's foil on the Continent, the French army, through a massive battle of attrition—the battle of Verdun, which began on 21 February—but did not believe he could achieve a final decision against the British on land. The submarine campaign consequently was a powerful auxiliary in discouraging the British from continuing the war. Tirpitz, ever fractious, did not believe any single weapon, even submarines, could defeat England, but believed submarines could so increase Great Britain's difficulties that the British would give way.

There were other factors as well. The commander of the High Sea Fleet, von Pohl, was a sick man and died of cancer in February 1916. He was replaced on 8 January by Vice Admiral Scheer, much more vigorous, far more offensively minded, and an ardent partisan of U-boat warfare. The spread of the practice of arming merchantmen also gave German advocates of unrestricted submarine warfare another lever. Their small submarine force in the Mediterranean had done extremely well, but in mid-January 1916 the Mediterranean U-boat flotilla commander Korvettenkapitän Kophamel warned that too many armed steamers were escaping from submarines. He argued that a steamer armed by its government was really a warship—some even had military gun crews on board—and there were no armed "merchant ships" unless they were pirates. He recommended notifying neutrals that all armed steamers would be treated as warships and sunk on sight. The Germans also were encouraged by the well-meaning proposal of the American secretary of state, Robert Lansing. This so-called modus vivendi proposal sought to recognize the changed conditions of war. German submarines ought to obey international law by stopping and searching vessels and assuring the safety of passengers and crew before they were sunk. In turn, the British and French would have to stop arming merchant vessels, which, if they were armed, would be treated as auxiliary cruisers. This argument, needless to say, was rejected by the British, but the combination of circumstances was sufficient to overcome the objections of Bethmann Hollweg and lead the German government to resume "sharpened," if not totally unrestricted, submarine war.[56]

The Germans followed a somewhat confusing course on the question of unrestricted submarine warfare that must have exasperated submarine commanders. On 3 February Holtzendorff informed Kophamel that as of 20 February armed British and French steamers in the Mediterranean could be attacked without warning. On 11 February the order bearing the kaiser's signature was issued to the fleet that as of 29 February armed enemy merchant vessels could be sunk without warning, but that submarine commanders should bear in mind that mistakes would lead to rupture of diplomatic relations with neutrals and that they should destroy a merchant ship because of its armament only if its armament was clearly recognized. Neutral vessels remained exempt. Holtzendorff issued a supplement to these orders, directing submarines that had attacked while submerged not to surface after firing the torpedo, but to depart while still under water. Submarine commanders could also treat merchant ships as warships when they had been listed by the Admiralstab as armed, even if their armament was not clearly discernible, as long as there was no doubt about their identity.

The kaiser, influenced by Bethmann Hollweg, hesitated at the implications of unrestricted submarine warfare. When he met the new commander in chief of the High Sea Fleet aboard the latter's flagship *Friedrich der Grosse* on 23 February, he counselled sparing passenger liners and remarked, "Were I the Captain of a U-boat I would never torpedo a ship if I knew that women and children were aboard." The Admiralstab therefore issued the order that passenger liners were not to be attacked, even if they were armed. The United States, however, continued to protest the proposed treatment of armed merchant vessels as warships, and the crisis within the German government continued. A crown council met at Charleville on 4 March, but a clear decision regarding unrestricted submarine warfare was not forthcoming. The kaiser concluded unrestricted submarine warfare against Great Britain was unavoidable and would probably begin on 1 April, but until then Bethmann Hollweg was ordered to try and secure American understanding for the German position with the objective of giving Germany a free hand. Until an agreement with the Americans was reached, German submarines would operate under the orders of 1 March, which provided for what might be termed "sharpened," as opposed to "unrestricted," submarine warfare. Enemy merchant ships inside the war zone would be destroyed without warning; enemy merchant ships outside the war zone would be destroyed without warning if they were armed. Passenger liners, either inside or outside the war zone, could not be attacked from under water whether they were armed or not. The orders permitting attacks on troop transport between Le Havre and Dunkirk remained in effect. Tirpitz, who was not invited to the meeting, resigned. This time his resignation was accepted, and he was replaced by Vice Admiral Eduard von Capelle.[57]

What was the German U-boat strength as they prepared to embark on a second submarine campaign? In March 1916 there were 52 operational boats, compared to 29 to 30 at the start of the first campaign. There were 16 U-boats in the North Sea, 20 in the Flanders Flotilla (8 UB.I, 4 UB.II, and 8 UC.I), 4 in the Baltic, 7 in the Adriatic, and 5 at Constantinople. The Germans could reasonably expect 38 of the U-boats under construction to enter service in the period between April and August of 1916. As for the future, at the beginning of the year Tirpitz had inquired how many UC.II minelayers could be finished by the end of the year if all new shipbuilding and torpedo-boat projects that would not be completed until after the start of the new year were deferred. The U-Boat Inspectorate determined the total to be 31, and the boats were promptly ordered on 11 January 1916. This was the largest single order of the war to date, representing the enhanced importance given to minelaying, given the other restrictions on submarine warfare. The smaller UC boats took priority because they could be finished fairly quickly. Nevertheless, in late May the Imperial Naval Office also ordered 12 large, long-range (10,000 miles at 8 knots) "Project 42" submarines (*U.127* to *U.138*), armed with six torpedo tubes and two 10.5-cm guns to act as offensive U-boat cruisers against merchant shipping. At virtually the same time they also ordered 10 large long-range minelayers (*U.117* to *U.126*), capable of carrying 42 mines plus an additional 30 in deck containers. The delivery times on these large and complex boats were necessarily long, and the Imperial Naval Office therefore ordered in early May 24 UB.III-class medium-sized boats suitable for operations around the British Isles and in the Mediterranean. The boats were more powerful than those of the UB.II class, with larger caliber torpedoes and an 8.8-cm gun. The last of the boats was supposed to enter service by April 1917, but once again the yards made overly optimistic delivery promises and the last of the boats was seven months late.[58]

The sharpened U-boat offensive was once again curtailed by diplomatic rather than military factors. The neutral Dutch were hard hit. On 16 March the Royal Holland Lloyd liner *Tubantia* (13,911 tons), outward bound for Buenos Aires, was torpedoed and sunk near the North Hinder light vessel by *UB.13*. The *Tubantia* was the largest neutral ship sunk by submarines during the war. Two days later the Germans sank another Dutch steamer, the Royal Rotterdam Lloyd liner *Palembang* (6,674 tons). The Dutch packets that plied the North Sea between the Netherlands and Great Britain were decimated by German actions. On 1 February the *Princess Juliana* (2,885 tons) was beached near Felixstowe after hitting a mine laid by *UC.5* and became a total loss. Her sister ship the *Mecklenburg* (2,885 tons) was sunk on 27 February by a mine laid by *UC.7*. On 16 May the Rotterdam-London packet *Batavier V* (1,568 tons) was mined and sunk near the Inner Gabbard light vessel. Other Dutch packets were captured by the Germans and taken into Zeebrugge. Some were released, but others, such as the *Zaanstroom* (1,657 tons), captured by a German submarine in March 1915, were retained. The harassment, losses, and damage continued throughout the war. It is hardly surprising that the Dutch press was furious and the Dutch parliament spoke of military preparations. The Dutch subsequently laid up a few of their largest and most valuable liners for the duration of the war. It was not easy to be a small neutral next door to great powers at war.

The Netherlands was a small neutral whose military potential was limited. The United States was a large neutral with great potential; consequently the most serious incidents from the German point of view involved Americans. On 24 March Oberleutnant zur See Pustkuchen in *UB.29* torpedoed without warning the French cross-Channel steamer *Sussex* (1,353 tons) off Dieppe. The steamer managed to reach port, but there were fifty fatalities, including some of the twenty-five U.S. citizens on board. The submarine had not been seen, and the German suggestion that the *Sussex* might have been damaged by a mine was disproved after fragments of a torpedo were found in one of the lifeboats. In his limited view through the periscope, Pustkuchen had assumed the passengers crowding the *Sussex*'s deck were troops. The *Sussex* was actually in an area where submarines had been authorized to attack without warning since the preceding November, but it was only after UB.II-class boats, such as *UB.29*, came into service that they had been able to exploit the order. The young officer had plunged his government into a major diplomatic crisis, for the *Sussex* incident seemed a direct challenge to President Wilson, and on 20 April the United States delivered what amounted to an ultimatum, threatening to sever diplomatic relations if the Germans did not abandon their present methods against passenger and freight carrying vessels.

Holtzendorff yielded on the submarine question in the face of pressure from the civilian members of the German government. Tirpitz's successor Capelle apparently felt submarines could accomplish almost as much under prize rules, and may possibly have been willing to delay an unrestricted campaign until more of the submarines under construction had entered service. On 24 April the Admiralstab issued orders for the High Sea Fleet and Flanders Flotilla submarines to act against merchant ships according to prize regulations. But this was to hold only if they did not offer resistance or attempt to escape. Scheer, nevertheless, was furious, for he believed that war waged by U-boats according to prize law in the waters around Great Britain "could not possibly have any success" and "must expose the boats to the greatest dangers." He recalled all submarines by wireless and announced that the campaign against British commerce had ceased. The Flanders Flotilla UB boats were also recalled; the UC minelayers continued their operations. Schwieger and *U.20* apparently did not hear the signal, and on 8 May torpedoed and sank without warning the White Star liner *Cymric* (13,370 tons), which went down with a loss of five lives.[59]

What was the effect of this "sharpened," though brief, second submarine campaign? The figures given by Admiral Spindler in the German official history indicate that following the cessation of the first submarine campaign from October to December 1915, German submarines in all theaters sank a total of 140 ships representing 361,326 tons. The figures are inflated by the Mediterranean, which accounted for 80 ships and 293,423 tons, a staggering 81 percent of the tonnage lost. In January 1916 German submarines in all theaters sank 25 ships, 49,610 tons; and in February 44 ships, 95,090 tons. The bad winter weather no doubt affected these figures. During the second submarine campaign, German submarines in all theaters sank in March 60 ships, 160,536 tons; and in April 83 ships, 187,307 tons. The sinkings understandably declined after the sharpened submarine campaign was called off. In May the sinkings in all theaters were 63 ships, 119,381 tons (37 ships and 72,092 tons in the Mediterranean); and in June 63 ships, 93,193 tons (43 ships and 67,125 tons in the Mediterranean). What portion of these losses were suffered by what the Germans now referred to as the *Hauptfeind*, the British? Fayle in the official history of seaborne trade lists British losses in March 1916 as 26 ships and 99,089 tons, and in April 43 ships and 141,193 tons.[60] These figures were still far from Holtzendorff's objective of 630,000 tons per month, but worrisome enough to the British because the April losses closely approached those of the record month of August 1915. They were greatly relieved when the campaign was called off, for British losses in May, a little more than 64,000 tons, were less than half the April total, and the June loss of 37,000 tons represented the lowest since August 1915. Nevertheless, Fayle acknowledges that the cumulative effect was serious. In the first half of 1916, the British lost nearly half a million tons of shipping, which represented two and a half times the shipbuilding output for the same period. The monthly entrances to British ports by British shipping showed a heavy decrease on those of 1915, and only relatively steady entrances under non-British flags kept the volume of imports from a sharp decline.[61]

The Germans lost only four U-boats in the waters around the British Isles in March and April. One of those losses, *U.68* in the southwestern approaches on 22 March, was due to the depth charges of the Q-ship *Farnborough*. The *Farnborough* was under the command of Lieutenant Commander Gordon Campbell, considered the most famous of the Q-ship commanders, and the episode was a classic example of Q-ship tactics with the ship blowing off steam and the stokers and spare men pretending to abandon ship in a panic after the submarine had surfaced and fired a shot across the steamer's bow. Once the submarine had closed, Campbell opened fire and finished her off with a depth charge.[62]

Scheer's obstinacy in refusing to conduct U-boat warfare under prize rules has been criticized by former German naval officers. It may not have been devoid of political motivation, that is, a desire to provoke a sufficiently strong outcry to force Bethmann Hollweg—the enemy of unrestricted submarine warfare—from office. It is at least partially based on the experiences of the F.d.U., Bauer, who made a cruise in *U.67* to the British coast and returned strongly opposed to the idea of trying to carry on under prize rules. However, the relatively high rate of sinking in the Mediterranean, where most submarine operations were conducted under prize rules, as well as the subsequent success of the Flanders U-boats in the Channel, seems to indicate Scheer had forfeited an opportunity. Captain Gayer, who was equally critical of the Admiralstab for failing to override Scheer's orders, reported that there were some German submarine officers who estimated that from May to September 1916 the refusal to continue the submarine offensive under prize rules had saved the Allies as much as 1.6 million tons.[63]

The submarine was far and away the major weapon used by the Germans against British commerce. However, surface raiders also reappeared during this period. The first and most successful was the *Möwe* (4,788 tons), converted from the Laeisz Line's fruit carrier *Pungo*. The *Möwe* sailed from the Elbe on 29 December 1915 under the command of Korvettenkapitän Graf zu Dohna-Schlodien with five hundred mines in addition to her armament of four 15-cm guns, one 10.5-cm gun, and two torpedo tubes. Her first mission before turning to commerce destruction was minelaying, and on 1 January she laid 252 mines off the Pentland Firth. The mines sank the predreadnought *King Edward VII* and two merchant vessels on the 6th. The *Möwe* proceeded to lay more mines off the estuary of the Gironde, which claimed three steamers and three to four French fishing craft, before heading out into the Atlantic. By the time she returned safely to Wilhelmshaven on 4 March 1916, she had sunk fourteen ships, all but one British, representing 49,739 tons. Her commander, who appears to have behaved quite humanely toward his prisoners, also sent another captured ship into Norfolk, Virginia, with the crews taken from his prizes.

The other raiders were less successful. On 26 February *Wolf (I)*, the former Hamburg-Amerika line *Belgravia* (6,648 tons), ran aground in the lower Elbe while proceeding to sea and damaged her engines attempting to get free. She had to be taken out of service. The *Greif*, the former German-Australian line's *Guben* (4,962 tons), sailed from the Elbe on 27 February, but British wireless intelligence had been aware of a raider's departure, patrols were deployed off the Norwegian coast, and when the *Greif* broke wireless silence her position was established by direction-finding stations. On the 29th the *Greif* was intercepted by the armed merchant cruisers *Alcantara* (16,034 tons) and *Andes* (15,620 tons). The raider attempted to pass as a Norwegian ship and lured the *Alcantara* close enough before opening fire to inflict mortal damage. The *Greif* was also badly damaged, and the *Andes*, joined by the light cruiser *Comus*, completed her destruction.[64]

The *Möwe*'s average monthly bag on a two-month cruise of more than 24,800 tons of shipping was substantial but small in the context of the submarine war. The German naval leaders obviously regarded the submarine as the most potent weapon against merchant shipping, but in their eyes the diplomatic restrictions hobbled them, and Scheer refused to operate under prize rules in the north. On 30 April he received the kaiser's approval for the cessation of the submarine war on commerce. The submarines of the High Sea Fleet were now employed for military purposes until the political and military situation demanded the resumption of the campaign against trade. Scheer intended to use the submarines in conjunction with operations by the High Sea Fleet, and this set in motion the train of events that led to the Battle of Jutland.[65]

THE BATTLE OF JUTLAND

Shortly after he assumed command of the High Sea Fleet, Vice Admiral Scheer and his staff, notably Captains Adolf von Trotha and Magnus von Levetzow, produced a program in early February that bore the title "Principles Covering the Conduct of the Naval Campaign in the North Sea." The objective was to implement a more aggressive and active strategy for the fleet. The Germans recognized that the existing ratio of strength prohibited them from seeking a decisive battle with the British, and their strategy would have to be such as to prevent this decisive battle being forced on them. Nevertheless, by exercising systematic and constant pressure, the Germans would attempt to force the British to abandon their waiting attitude and send out some of their forces, thereby giving the Germans favorable chances for attacking. This pressure would be exerted by the submarine war against commerce, mining, attacks on trade between the British Isles and Scandinavia, aerial warfare, and intensive sweeps by the High Sea forces. This would include airship raids on England in conjunction with destroyer sweeps. Finally, the Germans would exert still greater pressure by bombarding coastal towns, again with the object of inducing the British to take countermeasures that would give the Germans the opportunity to engage under favorable conditions. At first glance this might sound like more of the same methods employed earlier in the war, but Scheer was quick to point out the earlier sweeps had been undertaken with either inferior forces or under circumstances in which the main fleet could not intervene in time to be of any use.[66]

The first German action came on the night of 10 February when a strong German destroyer flotilla sank the sloop *Arabis*, which, together with the newly formed Tenth Minesweeping Flotilla, had been sweeping one of the war channels kept clear for the fleet east of the Dogger Bank. Jellicoe and Beatty, along with Tyrwhitt and the Harwich Force, were ordered out, but had no chance to engage. Unfortunately on returning to Harwich, Tyrwhitt's flagship, the cruiser *Arethusa*, was mined and sunk in a new field laid by one of the submarines of the Flanders Flotilla.[67]

On 5–6 March, Scheer carried out the first of what he termed the High Sea Fleet's "greater enterprises," bringing the fleet to the latitude 53° 30' (approximately that of Terschelling), the farthest south it would come during the war. The sweep was made in conjunction with a zeppelin raid on Hull and Immingham, while submarines from the Flanders Flotilla were stationed off the British coast. Scheer hoped to intercept British patrols. The Grand Fleet and Harwich Force were out again, but there was never any chance of an encounter. The British were able to recall their patrols in time once Scheer broke wireless silence, thereby indicating he was at sea. The Germans, in turn, apparently intercepted the British recall signal and Scheer turned for home.[68]

The main British strategy remained unchanged. Jellicoe told the first lord: "The Grand Fleet can never have any other objective than the High Sea Fleet, and until the High Sea Fleet emerges from its defenses I regret to say that I do not see that any offensive against it is possible." Minor offensives were possible, notably seaplane attacks against zeppelin bases in Schleswig. The offensive means were feeble, consisting of the seaplane carrier *Vindex*, a former Isle of Man Steam Packet Company vessel that had been converted to carry five seaplanes in a hangar aft, with a launching platform for two aircraft with fixed undercarriages forward.[69] After two abortive attempts the British launched a raid on 25 March directed against the presumed zeppelin station at Hoyer on the Schleswig coast. The Harwich Force escorted the *Vindex* to well inside the Vyl light vessel south of Horn Reefs, while Beatty and the battle cruisers were out in support. Despite constant snow squalls, the *Vindex* managed to launch five seaplanes. Unfortunately, they found no zeppelins at Hoyer. One aircraft did locate zeppelin sheds farther inland at Tondern, but ice jammed her bomb racks and she could not release them. Only two aircraft returned; the other three had been forced by engine trouble to land in German territory. While searching for the missing aircraft, Tyrwhitt's destroyers clashed with two German patrol trawlers, which were sunk, but the British force was now subjected to air raids. Unfortunately, the destroyer *Medusa* was rammed by the destroyer *Laverock*, and despite efforts to tow her home in bad weather, she eventually had to be abandoned. The Admiralty, on intelligence that the High Sea Fleet was putting to sea, ordered Tyrwhitt to withdraw at once. Scheer, however, unsure of British intentions, kept the big ships back and contented himself with sending out strong cruiser and destroyer forces. He lost one destroyer, *S.22*, to a mine. During the stormy night the Harwich Force, steaming in close order and without lights, had another brush with German forces, and the light cruiser *Cleopatra* rammed and sank the German destroyer *G.194*, only to be rammed in turn by the cruiser *Undaunted*. The latter was badly damaged and could not steam faster than 6 knots. The Germans intercepted the wireless message reporting the accident, and Scheer ordered the High Sea Fleet out toward the British position, whereas the Admiralty ordered the Grand Fleet to concentrate east of the Long Forties—the area of the North Sea approximately 100 miles east of Aberdeen. But the German cruisers reported the weather too rough for an engagement, and Scheer returned to port. Once again there was no clash between the major fleets.[70]

It is not surprising that after these experiences Jellicoe concluded that air raids and mining activities could not be used as a means of drawing the High Sea Fleet to sea and must be treated as definitely minor operations. Jellicoe was apparently worried that there was a feeling at the Admiralty that might lead them to push him into a more active policy. The Admiralty, despite the lack of results, still gave air raids heavy support and pressed him to plan another in the belief it would force the German fleet out. Jellicoe disagreed, for to draw the Germans out the raid would have to take place in daylight, so that the British force would be reported as approaching. If the German heavy ships decided to come out, they would not be clear of their minefields and in a position where the British could engage them until 4:00 P.M. As Jellicoe told Beatty, "This is no time to start a fight in these waters." It would mean the British hanging around "in a bad locality" expending fuel, especially from destroyers. The British could not wait for the following day, because by then the destroyers would be out of fuel and the light cruisers running short. Jellicoe opposed engaging the High Sea Fleet close to the German minefields and the German submarine and torpedo-boat bases. He concluded: "Patience is the virtue we must exercise." The British would have to wait until the Germans gave them a chance in a favorable position.[71] Beatty agreed: "Your arguments re the fuel question are unanswerable and measure the situation absolutely. We cannot amble about the North Sea for two or three days and at the end be in a condition in which we can produce our whole force to fight to the finish the most decisive battle of the war: to think it is possible is simply too foolish and tends towards losing the battle before we begin." Beatty believed that "when the Great Day comes it will be when the enemy takes the initiative," and until then they ought to investigate the North Sea with minesweepers to ascertain what waters were safe, so that when the Germans did take the initiative they could judge where they could engage them.[72] The exchange between Jellicoe and Beatty is interesting, for Jellicoe anticipated one of the major British problems at the Battle of Jutland when the main encounter between the fleets did indeed take place late in the day with only limited time before the onset of darkness.

Would the fleets ever meet? It seemed not. On 20 April British cruisers sailed for a raid into the Kattegat to operate against German trade and divert German attention while the Russians relaid minefields that had been displaced by winter ice. The move was altered by intelligence on the 21st that the High Sea Fleet was preparing for sea; the Grand Fleet and Battle Cruiser Fleet were ordered to sea. The next morning the Admiralty found that the High Sea Fleet was returning to port but that there was a chance to intercept the German battle cruisers near Horn Reefs. Beatty, followed by Jellicoe, rushed to the scene, but unfortunately for the British, a dense fog developed during the night and the battle cruisers *Australia* and *New Zealand* collided. Later that night three of Jellicoe's destroyers were also in collision, and a neutral merchantman collided with the dreadnought *Neptune*. Frustrated by the fog, the British canceled the operation and returned to refuel.

Scheer gave the British another chance with a "tip and run" raid by the German battle cruisers, supported by the High Sea Fleet, against Lowestoft on 24–25 April. The operation was to coincide with the Easter Sunday Irish rebellion in Ireland. The Admiralty, as usual, knew the Germans were at sea but did not at first know their objective. The Grand Fleet and Battle Cruiser Fleet were ordered to sea, but their southward journey was slowed by heavy seas. Tyrwhitt's Harwich Force, 3 light cruisers and 18 destroyers, were also approaching from the south, but Tyrwhitt had been weakened by having to detach 12 destroyers to cover the laying of new minefields and a mine and mine-net barrage off the Flanders coast.

The operation began badly for the Germans when the *Seydlitz*, flagship of Rear Admiral Boedicker—commanding the German reconnaissance forces in the temporary absence of the ill Rear Admiral Hipper—struck a mine near Norderney and had to return to port with 1,400 tons of water in the ship. Boedicker transferred his flag to the *Lützow*, and the four remaining German battle cruisers and six light cruisers encountered the much weaker Harwich Force at about 3:50 A.M. on the morning of the 25th. Scheer and the High Sea Fleet remained off Terschelling, roughly 70 miles away. Tyrwhitt turned south and tried to draw the Germans after him. Boedicker refused to be drawn, and the battle cruisers proceeded to bombard first Lowestoft and then Yarmouth. Tyrwhitt consequently returned to the north and engaged the Germans in an action in which his flagship, the light cruiser *Conquest*, was hit by five 12-inch shells and badly damaged. Boedicker apparently lacked the killer instinct and refrained from attempting to cut off and destroy the weaker British force. Instead, the German battle cruisers turned for home, and Scheer also turned for home when Boedicker was about 50 miles from him.

The Grand Fleet without its destroyers, which could not keep up in the rough seas, and the Battle Cruiser Fleet did not even come close to intercepting the Germans. None of the British submarines on defensive patrol—nor another group sent with the destroyer *Melampus* to form a patrol line in the middle of the southern North Sea after the Germans were reported at sea—were ever in a position to attack. The Germans sank two armed trawlers, *E.22* was torpedoed by *UB.18* in the North Sea, and another of Tyrwhitt's cruisers, the *Penelope*, was damaged by a torpedo during the pursuit. The Germans also destroyed about two hundred houses at Lowestoft; they did far less damage at Yarmouth. The Admiralty were worried about the vulnerability of the east coast and the seeming inability of the Grand Fleet based at Scapa Flow or the Battle Cruiser Fleet at Rosyth to prevent the raids or successfully intercept the Germans on their return. They decided to permanently detach the Third Battle Squadron, the *Dreadnought* (currently refitting) and the seven surviving *King Edward VII*-class battleships to the Swin, the northern channel of the Thames estuary. They were joined by the Third Cruiser Squadron (*Devonshire*-class armored cruisers). The great majority of the submarines formerly at Rosyth were shifted to Yarmouth.[73]

The apparent weakening of the Grand Fleet was less serious than it might appear. Although the *King Edwards*—nicknamed the "wobbly eight" for their crabwise movement when steaming at full speed—were among the newest of the predreadnoughts, they were about three knots slower than the remainder of the Grand Fleet and their employment posed considerable tactical problems for Jellicoe. As for the *Devonshire* class, the experience of Jutland soon demonstrated that the armored cruisers were obsolete, their employment in a modern battle almost suicidal.

The move of the Third Battle Squadron was also the preliminary to a major strategic decision. On 12 May the First Sea Lord Admiral Jackson met Jellicoe and Beatty in a conference at Rosyth where the decision was made to shift the Grand Fleet southward from Scapa to the Firth of Forth as soon as an anchorage below the Forth Bridge could be made secure against submarines. Although the project had priority, the defenses were not completed before 1917, and it was not until April 1918 that the Grand Fleet moved to its new base.[74]

The British quickly followed up the Lowestoft raid with another seaplane raid, designed to lure Scheer out of his bases. On 4 May the seaplane carriers *Vindex* and *Engadine*, escorted by the First Light Cruiser Squadron and sixteen destroyers of the First Flotilla, moved to a position off Sylt to launch a raid against the zeppelin sheds at Tondern. The raid was only of secondary importance; the High Sea Fleet was the major objective. The preceding night the British had laid minefields off the outer ends of the German-swept channels, and submarines had been stationed off Terschelling bank and in the Horns Reef area. Jellicoe and Beatty were both at sea with their forces. The air raid was, like the earlier ones, a failure. Only three of the eleven seaplanes launched managed to take off. The remaining eight damaged their propellers in the rough sea and had to be hoisted in again. The three that took off had little luck. One promptly hit the mast of a destroyer and crashed, the second had to turn back with engine trouble, and the third, which bombed Tondern, missed the zeppelin shed. The Germans launched two zeppelins to search for the force; one, *L.7*, found it only to be shot down. Jellicoe waited in position for more than six hours without the High Sea Fleet coming out, and, with some concern over the fuel situation, finally turned for home. The High Sea Fleet did sortie later in the day, but the British were gone. Once again there was no encounter.[75]

It is against this background of raid and counter-raid with both sides baiting traps—Jellicoe to catch the High Sea Fleet away from its coast and Scheer to catch an isolated portion of the Grand Fleet—that the great naval battle of the war occurred almost by accident. At the end of May, Jellicoe decided to send two light cruiser squadrons around the Skaw into the Kattegat on 2 June to sweep as far south as the Great Belt and the Sound. There would be a battle squadron in the Skaggerak in support, and Jellicoe and Beatty would be to the northwest with all their forces ready to intervene if the High Sea Fleet moved north out of the Bight. British submarines would also be off the Dogger Bank and south of the Horns Reef, and the minelayer *Abdiel* would extend the minefields laid on 3–4 May. The seaplane carrier *Engadine*, escorted by a light cruiser squadron and destroyers, would be off Horns Reef to watch for zeppelins.

Scheer had his own plans for a bombardment of Sunderland by cruisers in order to draw out British forces. This time the High Sea Fleet would be to the south of Dogger Bank, and eighteen U-boats (three of them large minelayers) made available by the cessation of the war on commerce would be concentrated off the British naval bases. The submarines would inflict losses on Beatty's forces, which Scheer expected to hurry out in pursuit of Hipper's battle cruisers. Hipper would then lead the surviving British battle cruisers to the High Sea Fleet and destruction. The plan presupposed extensive reconnaissance by zeppelins to ensure that Jellicoe and the Grand Fleet would not be at sea. Scheer was forced to postpone his operation until the end of May because of condenser troubles in the battleships of his Third Squadron—the newest dreadnoughts—and until repairs on the *Seydlitz* were completed. He then found weather conditions unfavorable for zeppelin reconnaissance, and the endurance of the U-boats deployed off the British ports set limits on the time within which the operation could be carried out. Scheer therefore altered his plans and dropped the bombardment of Sunderland in favor of a sweep against British patrols and merchant shipping outside and inside the Skaggerak. The German cruisers were ordered to deliberately show themselves off the Norwegian coast so that they might be reported and draw the British.[76]

Hipper and his battle cruisers sailed from the Jade at 1 A.M. on the 31st, and Scheer and the main portion of the High Sea Fleet sailed from the Jade and the Elbe shortly afterward. The British were already at sea. Room 40 had been able to warn the Admiralty that the Germans were preparing to put to sea, and at 5:40 on the afternoon of 30 May, the Admiralty ordered Jellicoe, who along with Beatty had already been alerted, to concentrate in the Long Forties. By 10:30 the Grand Fleet had sailed from Scapa Flow and the Moray Firth, and Beatty sailed from the Firth of Forth at 11:00. Jellicoe (in the *Iron Duke*) had a total of 24 dreadnoughts, 3 battle cruisers (Rear Admiral Hood's Third Battle Cruiser Squadron), 12 light cruisers, 8 armored cruisers, 5 flotilla leaders, 46 destroyers, and a minelayer. Beatty (in the *Lion*) had a total of 6 battle cruisers (the *Lion, Princess Royal, Queen Mary, Tiger, New Zealand,* and *Indefatigable*), 4 dreadnoughts, 14 light cruisers, 27 destroyers, and the seaplane carrier *Engadine.* Beatty's 4 dreadnoughts (the *Barham, Valiant, Warspite,* and *Malaya*) were the powerful (15-inch guns) and fast *Queen Elizabeth* class of Vice Admiral Evan-Thomas's Fifth Battle Squadron, which had been temporarily attached to Rosyth to compensate for the absence of Hood's Third Battle Cruiser Squadron which was carrying out gunnery exercises at Scapa.

On the German side, Hipper (in the *Lützow*) had the First Scouting Group (5 battle cruisers), the Second Scouting Group (4 light cruisers), and 30 destroyers led by the light cruiser *Regensburg.* Scheer (in the *Friedrich der Grosse*) was approximately 50 miles astern with a total of 16 dreadnoughts, 6 predreadnoughts of the *Deutschland* class, 5 light cruisers, and 31 destroyers led by the light cruiser *Rostock.* Scheer had included the *Deutschland*s of the Second Squadron largely for sentimental reasons: it was his old squadron, and its commander, Rear Admiral Mauve, made an "eloquent intercession" not to be left behind. One senses it was probably against Scheer's better judgment, for they were older, slower, and less well armed or protected than the other German capital ships.

The total of the combined forces showed a clear British predominance: dreadnoughts, 28 to 16 (plus 6 predreadnoughts); battle cruisers, 9 to 5; armored cruisers, 8 to 0; light cruisers, 26 to 11; and destroyers, 78 to 61. The approximately 250 ships involved made this by far the biggest naval battle of the First World War, and as submarines played no role and aircraft only a minimal one, it was essentially a one-dimensional combat between surface ships. Jutland is likely to remain, therefore, the largest encounter between surface ships of modern times.

The work of Room 40 had given the British a priceless advantage in enabling them to get to sea even before what was assumed to be a German raiding force. However, that advantage was diminished by a series of mistakes by the Admiralty in actually interpreting and disseminating the precious information. Part of the problem stemmed from the fact the officers of the Admiralty's Operations Division tended to distrust the civilian "amateurs" of Room 40 and confided in them as little as possible. Admiral Oliver, the chief of staff, ran what has been described as "a one man show" and zealously kept Room 40's information in his own hands. Consequently, Captain Thomas Jackson, director of the Operations Division, entered Room 40 just before noon on the 31st and inquired where the directional finding stations placed the German call sign "DK," which was normally the call sign of the flagship. He did not explain why he wanted this information and was told, correctly, that the location was Wilhelmshaven. On the basis of this information, Oliver sent a signal to Jellicoe at 12:30 P.M. that the German flagship was still in the Jade. A few hours later, Jellicoe encountered the entire High Sea Fleet. What had happened?

The Germans made a practice of transferring the commander in chief's call sign to a wireless station on shore whenever the flagship put to sea. The flagship then took another call sign. The object was obviously to conceal the fact that the fleet was at sea, and before Jutland the Germans had transferred not only Scheer's usual call sign but also his usual wireless operator, so that the British would not detect any difference in the actual method or "touch" with which the signal was sent. The Germans were still not aware their code was compromised and that their messages could be read; the move was presumably to frustrate the British direction-finding stations. The men of Room 40 were aware of the German practice, and if Captain Jackson had only said *why* he wanted the information about call sign "DK," they could have provided a correct evaluation. The mistake had important consequences, for Jellicoe assumed he had plenty of time and steamed at an economical speed in order to conserve fuel. He also wasted time examining neutral ships. Had he arrived at the rendezvous with Beatty with an extra hour or two of daylight, the Germans might have suffered far heavier losses than they escaped with. Moreover, the error made Jellicoe very suspicious of further intelligence from the Admiralty, and this affected his decisions later in the battle.[77] Oliver, who was not certain until later in the day the older German battleships were with Scheer, also held Tyrwhitt's Harwich Force in the south in case the older German ships attempted to raid the Thames or block the French channel ports.[78]

Jellicoe ordered Beatty to reach a position (latitude 56°40′N, longitude 5°E) approximately 69 miles south-southeast of his own estimated position at 2:00 P.M. on the 31st, which was 240 miles from Scapa. If he had no intelligence of the enemy, Beatty was to turn north for the rendezvous with Jellicoe, and their combined forces would steam toward Horns Reef. Beatty, whose forces were converging on the Germans at a right angle, turned north as planned at 2:15, still unaware Hipper was only about 45 miles to the east, with perhaps 16 miles between the nearest cruisers of their respective screens. Beatty's dispositions were considered by some to be faulty in that he stationed the powerful dreadnoughts of the Fifth Battle Squadron 5 miles from his forces where they could not provide close support in the early stages of a battle. He may have done so out of an ardent desire that his battle cruisers, and not the Fifth Battle Squadron from the Grand Fleet, should be the ones to bag Hipper to make up for the lost opportunity at Dogger Bank the year before. The dominant idea was that the Germans must not be allowed to escape again.[79]

The actual contact between the forces was almost accidental, although the British and Germans were on converging courses and contact eventually would have been made, but probably much later and closer to Jellicoe. At approximately 2:00 P.M. the cruiser *Elbing* of Hipper's screen spotted a small Danish steamer, the *N.J. Fjord*, and sent two destroyers to investigate. The steamer had stopped and was blowing off steam when she was spotted by the light cruiser *Galatea* of Beatty's screen. The *Galatea* and *Phaeton* also closed to investigate, spotted and reported the Germans, and at 2:28 opened fire. Two of Beatty's light cruiser squadrons steered toward the *Galatea*, although Beatty himself appears to have waited twelve minutes before altering course to the southeast and increasing speed in order to cut off the enemy from returning to the Bight. Unfortunately, Evan-Thomas missed the flag signal to alter course and did not turn until after it was repeated by searchlight, which should have been used together with the signal flags in the first place. The result was that a 10-mile gap opened between Beatty and the Fifth Battle Squadron, which did not come into action until twenty minutes after Beatty joined battle. The consequences of this were costly.

The *Lion* spotted Hipper's force at 3:30 at a distance of about 14 miles. Beatty immediately altered course to the east to cut them off from the Bight and increased to full speed. He had, of course, no idea the entire High Sea Fleet was at sea. The seaplane carrier *Engadine* managed to launch one of her four aircraft at 3:08, but low clouds kept the aircraft at an altitude where vision was limited, and when sighting reports were sent by the pilot to the *Engadine*, the seaplane carrier failed in her attempt to relay the information by searchlight. The sea became too rough to launch other aircraft, and a burst petrol pipe finally forced the sole plane aloft to land at 3:47. The *Engadine* lacked the speed to keep up with battle cruisers and dropped out of the action, thereby ending the very limited role aircraft played in the battle. Nevertheless it was the first time ship-borne aircraft had participated in a fleet action. Jellicoe might have had the seaplane carrier *Campania* with him, but the converted Cunard liner for some reason had never received the signal to sail from Scapa, and when the error was discovered she was two hours behind the fleet.

Jellicoe, perhaps erroneously, believed she lacked the speed to catch up, and, worried over the submarine danger to the unescorted ship, ordered her back to port.

Hipper on sighting Beatty's force had immediately altered course 16 points to starboard, that is 180°, in order to draw the British to Scheer's High Sea Fleet. This phase of the battle is accordingly usually known as "the run to the south." The British and Germans opened fire almost simultaneously at 3:48, both sides overestimating the range, which was probably approximately 16,000 yards. At this moment Evan-Thomas was about 7½ miles from the *Lion*, too far to play any role in the action. Jellicoe in the *Iron Duke* was about 53 miles from the *Lion*, and the van of the High Sea Fleet was about 46 miles from Hipper's flagship *Lützow*.

The Germans corrected their initial error in estimating the range more quickly than the British, and they were assisted by an error in fire distribution on the British side. There were six British ships to five German, and Beatty had intended for each of the British to engage their opposite number with the two lead ships, the *Lion* and *Princess Royal*, concentrating on the *Lützow*, the leading German ship. Unfortunately, the *Queen Mary*, the third British ship, fired on the *Seydlitz*, the third German ship, leaving the second German ship *Derfflinger* undisturbed for approximately ten minutes. The *Tiger* (which also had missed the distribution signal) and *New Zealand* concentrated on the *Moltke* while the two rearmost ships, the *Indefatigable* and *Von der Tann*, engaged each other. In the controversy following Jutland, much was often made of this error in fire distribution. However, a recent close analysis of the battle by John Campbell points out that it has probably been overrated, for the first German ships to hit were the *Lützow* and *Moltke*, the two ships that were receiving concentrated fire, and the *Derfflinger*'s initial shooting was not effective. This may have been due in part to the fact that in concentration of fire it was difficult to distinguish between the splashes of each ship's shot, and the results were correspondingly less effective than imagined.[80]

All accounts agree that in this first phase of the battle German gunnery was both faster and more accurate. The conditions of light and visibility favored the Germans, although it has also been pointed out they were not always bad for the British. The British ships, darker in color, tended to be silhouetted against the western sky, while the German ships, lighter gray in color, were less visible against the overcast sky to the east. Moreover, the wind was from the west, carrying smoke between the British and the Germans and hampering gunnery. At 4:00 the *Lion*'s "Q" turret (midships) was hit by the *Lützow* and put out of action. Everyone in the gunhouse was killed, and it was fortunate that the order to flood the "Q" magazine was given, because less than a half-hour later, possibly when the *Lion* had altered course sufficiently to create a strong draft, a smoldering fire in the gunhouse spread to the working chamber below the turret and ignited the charges there. There was a tremendous explosion with flames shooting as high as the mastheads, and had the magazine not already been flooded, the entire ship might have been destroyed.[81]

The *Indefatigable* was not so lucky. At 4:02 she was hit by at least four 11-inch shells in two salvoes fired by the *Von der Tann* and blew up and sank after a magazine explosion with a loss of 1,017 officers and men. A German destroyer picked up only two survivors a few hours later. The loss was partially offset by the fact that Evan-Thomas's squadron had by now been able to draw close enough for his flagship *Barham* to open fire on the *Von der Tann* at 4:08, and within a few minutes all four of his battleships were firing. The gunnery of the Fifth Battle Squadron was more effective than that of the battle cruisers, owing to, among other factors, their being fitted with much better range finders. Nevertheless the British suffered their most serious loss at 4:26 when the *Queen Mary*, after being hit within a few minutes by two or three 12-inch shells from the *Derfflinger*, blew up and sank with a loss of 1,266 officers and men. There were twenty survivors. Beatty coolly remarked to his flag captain: "There is something wrong with our bloody ships today." With the Fifth Battle Squadron in action, it was actually Hipper who was feeling the pressure. Both commanders ordered flotilla attacks, and at about 4:30 a fierce destroyer action took place for 10–15 minutes. The Germans and British each lost two destroyers, the *Nestor* and *Nomad* on the British side, *V.27* and *V.29* on the German. The British fired 19 to 20 torpedoes of which only two hit. The *Petard* hit *V.29*, and either the *Petard* or *Turbulent* hit the *Seydlitz*. The *Seydlitz* was not seriously damaged; her torpedo bulkhead held and she took on only a slight list and was able to maintain full speed. None of the British ships were hit by German torpedoes.

The situation was radically transformed by the arrival of Scheer and the High Sea Fleet, which Commodore Goodenough commanding the Second Light Cruiser Squadron reported to both Jellicoe and Beatty by wireless from his flagship *Southampton* at 4:38. Beatty, after closing Goodenough and sighting the High Sea Fleet himself, turned 16 points to starboard (180°) and began to draw the Germans after him and toward Jellicoe. Once again there was faulty signaling. Evan-Thomas failed to see the signal made by flags to turn, and when it was repeated at 4:48 as the Fifth Battle Squadron drew abreast of the *Lion*, it called for a turn in succession rather than together, and to starboard rather than to port. The result was to open a gap of 3 miles between Evan-Thomas and Beatty and to bring the Fifth Battle Squadron into considerable danger from the Third Squadron of the High Sea Fleet (the *König, Grosser Kurfürst, Markgraf, Kronprinz, Kaiser, Prinzregent Luitpold,* and *Kaiserin*) as Scheer had ordered his fleet to turn by divisions toward the British. Evan-Thomas engaged the van of the High Sea Fleet but escaped without serious damage, and "the run to the South" was over.

The situation was now reversed, with Beatty drawing Scheer and Hipper toward Jellicoe in the second phase of the battle, not surprisingly known as "the run to the north." The British at first continued to be plagued by poor visibility, but after about 5:40, the light tended to favor them and dazzle the German gunners. Visibility, though, was really a complicated factor, changing frequently for different ships, and, as Campbell points out, for the British "it was seldom good and frequently poor." On the German side, the conditions often might have been difficult, but on the few occasions they could see their targets clearly, "their shooting was as dangerous as ever."[82] The British achieved far better results in "the run to the north" between 4:54 and 6:15. Hipper's First Scouting Group was badly battered, particularly the *Lützow, Derfflinger,* and *Seydlitz,* and lost a good deal of its fighting value. All of the *Von der Tann*'s heavy guns were at least temporarily disabled. German ships, though, were well protected, and German ammunition more stable than that of the British. The ships did not blow up and were exceedingly difficult to sink.

The Germans ran into more trouble. At 4:05 Jellicoe had ordered Rear Admiral Hood with the Third Battle Cruiser Squadron—the *Invincible, Inflexible, Indomitable,* two light cruisers, and four destroyers—to reinforce Beatty. The estimates of Beatty's position were incorrect, and Hood was too far to the east. The light cruiser *Chester* on Hood's starboard beam turned to investigate gun flashes to the southwest and at 5:36 ran into Rear Admiral Boedicker's Second Scouting Group (light cruisers *Frankfurt, Pillau, Elbing,* and *Wiesbaden*), which had been screening Hipper. The *Chester* had a harrowing time and was hit seventeen times before she could fall back on Hood. Boedicker's cruisers, in pursuit, met Hood's battle cruisers, and the *Wiesbaden* was disabled before they could get away. The appearance of Hood's battle cruisers convinced Hipper, still hotly engaged with Beatty, that he had encountered the British battle fleet, and he fell back on Scheer, reforming in front of the German battleships. Hipper had been preparing to launch a destroyer attack against Beatty. The attack was diverted to Hood but was not effective, although the British destroyer *Shark* was disabled and later sank.

The major and probably most important effect of the intervention by Hood's Third Battle Cruiser Squadron was to screen the approach of Jellicoe from the Germans. It also had the effect of moving the lead German squadron, the Third Squadron of Rear Admiral Behncke, more toward the east. There were some Germans who thought this decisive, for if Behncke had carried on to the north he might have surprised Jellicoe while the latter was deploying, and might have even "crossed the T" of the British.[83]

Jellicoe and his three battle squadrons (two divisions each) were rapidly approaching the scene. The Grand Fleet was in its cruising formation of divisions in line abreast, that is, six parallel columns, each column composed of four dreadnoughts in line ahead. There were approximately 5 miles between the far right and left columns. Jellicoe could not effectively fight in this formation, for he would only be able to use a fraction of his heavy guns because of ships masking one another. The Grand Fleet would have to deploy for battle, on either its port or starboard column, depending on the estimated direction from which the enemy would appear. The deployment of the 24 dreadnoughts into a single line ahead was no easy matter and would require a full 15 to 20 minutes. The problem for Jellicoe was that from 4:45 to 6:00 he had received no reports from Beatty on the location of the enemy. Beatty has been greatly criticized for this. Moreover, thanks to errors in dead reckoning and estimating position in the reports Jellicoe did receive, Beatty was actually much farther to the west—on Jellicoe's starboard bow rather than ahead—and the Germans about to appear much sooner than he had anticipated. By 6:00 Jellicoe could see the *Lion,* and at 6:15 he ordered a deployment on the port division, that is, to the east. This had the disadvantage of deploying the British battle fleet farther from the advancing Germans but placed Jellicoe in the tactically advantageous position of "crossing the T" of the advancing Germans. This meant he could employ the great majority of his heavy guns whereas the Germans could only employ a fraction of their own. There have been voluminous discussions of this decision, and the great majority of opinion—but certainly not all—has concluded Jellicoe made the correct decision.[84]

Beatty, once in contact, steamed across the British fleet to take his prescribed position at the head of the line. This had the unfortunate effect of hampering British gunnery as well as obscuring vision with the battle cruisers' smoke. It also caused Jellicoe to reduce speed to let him get clear, thereby delaying the deployment. Evan-Thomas realized he did not have enough speed to follow with the Fifth Battle Squadron and therefore took position at the rear of the British line. In doing so the *Warspite*'s helm jammed, and she made two complete circles in the face of the advancing Germans. She came under the concentrated fire of the German dreadnoughts and was hit thirteen times by heavy shells, but suffered no vital damage. The *Warspite* regained control for a time, but the helm later jammed again, and Evan-Thomas subsequently ordered her to return to port.

While the *Warspite* was having her narrow escape, Rear Admiral Robert Arbuthnot led the old armored cruisers *Defence* and *Warrior* of the First Cruiser Squadron across Beatty's bows to engage the light cruisers of the Second Scouting Group. Arbuthnot, a stern disciplinarian and physical-fitness fanatic, had been one of the characters of the Royal Navy, and there were some who were not really surprised at his brave action and subsequent fate. The two obsolete armored cruisers suddenly came in close contact with the advancing German battle cruisers and dreadnoughts and were smothered by the fire from large-caliber guns. Arbuthnot's flagship *Defence* blew up and sank with all hands at 6:20. The diversion caused by the *Warspite*'s mishap probably permitted the badly damaged *Warrior* to limp away. She was later taken in tow by the *Engadine*, but sank the following morning.

At approximately 6:20 Hood's Third Battle Cruiser Squadron opened fire on Hipper's advancing battle cruisers. Hood turned to a parallel course and the British ships made excellent shooting. Hood's flagship *Invincible* was particularly effective. The *Lützow* was hit repeatedly and suffered the damage that eventually proved lethal. Nevertheless the fatal flaw in British battle cruisers revealed itself for a third time that day. At 6:32 a heavy shell hit the *Invincible*'s "Q" turret and blew the turret roof off. The flash that followed shot down to the magazines, and the ship blew up, splitting in two parts. The bow and stern remained visible above the water for a long time, and a photograph of them is one of the most frequently reproduced images of the battle. There were only six survivors; 1,026 officers and men, including Hood, were lost. Hood was a particularly able and respected officer, and his role in the battle had been effective. Had he lived, he probably would have attained the highest rank.

The Grand Fleet's deployment was not completed until about 6:40, but the *Marlborough*, flagship of the rear division, opened fire at 6:17. Firing did not become general until 6:30, and visibility was not good, with targets appearing and disappearing in the haze. Campbell estimates that of Jellicoe's 24 dreadnoughts only 12 (perhaps only 10) fired on German battleships at this time, and the four dreadnoughts of Vice Admiral Jerram's First Division at the head of the British line did not fire a single shot.[85] Still, Hipper's battle cruisers and the dreadnoughts of the Third Squadron, particularly the *König*, which took 8 hits, were undergoing a heavy pounding, and the doomed *Wiesbaden* lay helpless between the lines, a target for many of the British ships. The irony is that there were so many ships firing at her that spotting was inaccurate and she did not suffer any fatal damage.

Scheer was in a desperate situation and escaped from it by the maneuver known as the *Gefechtskehrtwendung*, which can be translated as the "battle-about-turn." At 6:33 Scheer made the signal "Turn together 16 points to starboard and form single line ahead in the opposite direction." The German Third Destroyer Flotilla delivered a torpedo attack—which was not pressed home—and made a smoke screen to cover the maneuver. The move, aided by mist and a wind from the southwest that blew smoke toward the British line, was successful and competed by 6:45. The Germans disappeared to the southwest. At 6:57 the *Marlborough* was hit by a torpedo, probably fired by the *Wiesbaden*, but although listing was able to steam at 16 knots for the remainder of daylight.

Jellicoe did not at first realize that the Germans had turned away, and those Grand Fleet captains who might have observed the maneuver did not, with that distressing lack of initiative that plagued the British in the battle, report it to him. When he discovered the Germans were gone, he did not pursue closely, but instead, steaming at 17 knots, 4 knots below maximum speed, ordered the fleet with its divisions in echelon on to a course that would cut across the line of retreat to the German bases, and then altered to a more southerly course when he assumed he had steamed far enough to the east to achieve this purpose. Jellicoe's failure to pursue the Germans closely is another of the more controversial aspects of the Battle of Jutland that was and remains hotly debated. He was, of course, aware of his immense responsibility and the frequently quoted remark that he was the one man who could lose the war in an afternoon. Jellicoe's actions reflect the policy embodied in the Grand Fleet Battle Orders, in which there was no signal for a "general chase," and Jellicoe did what he had always said he was going to do. By not, however, ordering his divisional commanders to pursue independently, he may well have lost a great opportunity.[86]

Scheer gave Jellicoe another chance when he blundered back into the arms of the British. At 6:55 he signaled for another 180° turn. He tended to be vague about his reasons for doing so, implying it was too early to assume night cruising order, that the British could still have compelled him to fight before dark or cut off his retreat, that he wanted to surprise and shock his opponents, and that he wanted to render assistance to the *Wiesbaden*. None of this is terribly convincing. Professor Marder suggests, although he admits it cannot be proven, that Scheer was attempting to slip astern and to the north of the British fleet in order to escape home via the Skaggerak. He misjudged Jellicoe's position.[87] Perhaps Scheer betrayed the truth to Holtzendorff in an unguarded moment after the battle. According to one of his staff officers, the admiral in a mellow frame of mind after dinner admitted, "My idea? I had no idea. . . . The thing just happened—as the virgin said when she got a baby."[88]

At about 7:10 the two rearmost British divisions sighted and opened fire on the Germans, and by 7:15 the firing extended all along the British line at ranges varying between 11,000 and 14,000 yards. Once again the Germans ships in the van, notably the battle cruisers of the First Scouting Group and the *Königs* of the Fifth Division, Third Squadron, received heavy punishment during the few minutes the British were able to see them. The Germans, for their part, could see little of the British ships save gun flashes. Scheer was in a desperate position, and at 7:13 signaled the battle cruisers to make what in effect was a suicidal charge. His signal *Schlachtkreuzer ran an den Feind, voll einsetzen* has been translated as "Battle cruisers at the enemy, give them everything." The battle cruisers at that moment were actually commanded by Captain Hartog of the *Derfflinger*, for Hipper and his staff had been compelled to abandon the badly damaged *Lützow* shortly before 7:00 and were trapped for two hours in the destroyer *G.39* before they could transfer to the *Moltke*. Hipper later described how he could never forget those hours in the little ship amidst the tremendous shell splashes of the battle while he tried to keep up with the big ships.[89] At 7:14 Scheer ordered the battle cruisers to engage the British van, thereby altering the orders for the "death ride" to a turn to the south. At 7:15 Scheer ordered his destroyer flotillas to attack and make smoke, and at about 7:17 or 7:18 signaled another "about-turn to starboard." The ships of the Third Squadron were close together and under heavy fire, and the maneuver was carried out under difficult conditions.

Jellicoe countered the German destroyer attack with his own destroyers and Fourth Light Cruiser Squadron and, most important of all, turned away with the battle fleet. This once again was in accordance with his stated intentions and the Grand Fleet Battle Orders. The turnaway permitted Scheer to escape for the second time that day. The Germans had been badly pounded, for in this phase of the battle, from 7:00 to 7:45, the British had scored 37 hits with large-caliber guns, including 14 on the *Derfflinger* and 5 each on the *Grosser Kurfürst* and the doomed *Lützow*. The Germans had managed only two hits on the *Colossus*.

There was still an estimated hour and a half of daylight remaining, and the turnaway at this moment when the British were beginning to pay back the Germans for the losses earlier in the day horrified many. It is perhaps *the* most controversial aspect of the battle, the crux of the division between Jellicoe and Beatty supporters after the war. Jellicoe's justification was that by turning away, the German torpedoes reached the British line running at a much slower speed and were easier to avoid. A turn toward the torpedo attack meant encountering torpedoes when they were running at their maximum speed. None of the German torpedoes hit. There was also the danger that the British, had they turned toward the torpedoes, might have encountered successive torpedo attacks from another quarter, and these would have been difficult if not impossible to avoid. Jellicoe after the loss of the *Audacious* in 1914 was conscious of the vulnerability of British capital ships to underwater damage. The counterargument to this was that however valid the reasons for turning away, Jellicoe forfeited the chance of a decisive victory in order to avoid losses. Would not some British loss have been justified if it meant sinking a substantial portion of the High Sea Fleet? The argument will no doubt continue as long as historians write about the battle of Jutland.[90]

There was no further contact between the main battle fleets, although just before darkness Beatty clashed with the First Scouting Group and part of the High Sea Fleet. The British scored 8 large-caliber hits, 5 on the battered *Seydlitz*, compared to one German 11-inch shell that hit the *Princess Royal*. The British might have been able to achieve more had Beatty been closely supported by at least some of the battle squadrons—Jerram's Second Battle Squadron had been closest—yet another controversy over lost opportunity.[91]

Jellicoe was still positioned between Scheer and the German bases, and he hoped to resume the battle at daylight. He was and always had been determined to avoid a night engagement. As he wrote shortly after the battle, "Nothing would make me fight a night action with heavy ships in these days of T.B.D.'s [destroyers] and long range torpedoes. I might well lose the fleet. It would be far too fluky an affair."[92] The problem was not merely torpedoes, however. The Grand Fleet was not trained in night fighting, and German equipment and technique were clearly superior. German searchlights were larger and had iris shutters so the light could be kept ready and burning behind the shutters. The Germans had made their searchlights an integral part of their gunnery control system with searchlights following the lookout's binoculars. Admiral Hezlet writes: "There is little doubt that had the two battle fleets engaged at night at Jutland the Germans would have invariably hit with their first salvo before the British had fired a shot. At point-blank ranges at which the ships would have sighted each other the effect would have been devastating."[93]

Jellicoe set course to cover the so-called Ems route between the minefields and the Frisian Islands by which he assumed Scheer would attempt to return to his base. Scheer elected to return via the Horns Reef and Amrun Channel close to the Jutland and Schleswig coast, which Jellicoe had left uncovered. The Second German Destroyer Flotilla returned via the Skaw, which, had there been a resumption of the battle, would have deprived Scheer of 10 of his best destroyers and 57 remaining torpedoes. The two fleets actually steered converging courses, but Scheer was able to pass astern of the British. There were a series of short, sharp night encounters—Marder describes seven phases—between the British flotillas and the High Sea Fleet as it passed astern in which, for the most part, the superiority of German night-fighting techniques was demonstrated. The British lost: the armored cruiser *Black Prince*; the flotilla leader *Tipperary*; and the destroyers *Sparrowhawk* (rammed by the cruiser *Contest* and destroyer *Broke* and subsequently scuttled), *Fortune*, *Turbulent*, and *Ardent*. The British destroyer *Spitfire* collided with the German dreadnought *Nassau* and suffered the blast of two 11-inch guns fired at maximum depression, which wrecked her bridge. Miraculously, she survived to reach the Tyne.

The Germans did not escape unscathed, losing the predreadnought *Pommern*, which blew up and sank with all hands after being torpedoed by British destroyers; the light cruisers *Frauenlob*, *Elbing* (rammed by the dreadnought *Posen* and subsequently scuttled), and *Rostock* (disabled by a torpedo hit and scuttled while under tow the next morning on the approach of the cruiser *Dublin*); and the destroyer *V.4* (possibly due to a drifting mine). The effort to tow the crippled and sinking *Lützow* was abandoned during the night, her crew was taken off, and at 1:45 A.M. she was torpedoed by a German destroyer. The *Lützow* was the most powerful ship lost during the battle.

The night encounters produced a series of gun flashes in an easterly direction astern of the British fleet but, with that curious lack of initiative that continued to plague the British, the fact that heavy ships were apparently crossing to the east was never reported to Jellicoe. He would still not have sought a night engagement, but he would have had a positive indication that Scheer was making for Horns Reef and acted accordingly. Captain Roskill suggests that fatigue and the cumulative effect of the day's strain and concussion from the blast of heavy guns and enemy shell fire may also have played a role in numbing and dulling the reactions of the senior officers of the Grand Fleet.[94] He also finds the lack of initiative of senior officers understandable because of the whole system of training junior officers, which persisted up until the Second World War. It was: "based on unquestioning discipline and absolute subordination to authority. More gold braid, we were taught, necessarily meant more wisdom; and any signs of originality were frowned on if not actively suppressed."[95]

The most tragic blunder, however, was once again due to the Admiralty. Room 40 had intercepted a signal from a German destroyer giving the position and course of the rearmost battleship of the German fleet. This was passed on to Jellicoe and received by him at 10:23. The position was obviously wrong, possibly due to an error in navigation on the part of the Germans, but it may well have induced Jellicoe, who had been told the High Sea Fleet was still in the Jade earlier in the day, to dismiss subsequent reports from the Admiralty. He therefore seems to have paid no attention to a later signal sent at 10:41 that reported the German fleet had been ordered home and gave a course and speed clearly indicating Scheer was heading for the Horns Reef channel. Room 40 reported incontrovertible evidence of this a few minutes later when they discovered Scheer had asked for a zeppelin reconnaissance of Horns Reef. Unfortunately, the Operations Division of the Admiralty *did not* pass on this information to Jellicoe, who did not learn of its existence until years after the war. Had Jellicoe received the information, it would have been possible for him to have taken up a position to resume the battle at daybreak against a very battered Scheer and possibly achieve another "Glorious First of June."[96] The following morning, once it became apparent Scheer had passed Horns Reef and was in the swept channel, Jellicoe could do nothing more and returned to port. The next night, at 9:45 on 2 June, he reported that the Grand Fleet was refueled and ready for sea at four hours' notice.

The first Admiralty communique concerning the battle was sparse, and after listing losses created the impression of a distinct defeat leading to a great public outcry. The later reports after more was learned of German losses did much to offset this impression and erred in the opposite direction by overestimating German losses. The actual losses were as follows:

	British	**German**
Battle cruisers	*Queen Mary*	*Lützow*
	Indefatigable	
	Invincible	

	British	**German**
Predreadnoughts		*Pommern*
Armored cruisers	*Defence, Warrior,*	
	Black Prince	
Light cruisers		*Wiesbaden, Frauenlob*
		Elbing, Rostock
Flotilla leaders	*Tipperary*	
Destroyers	*Ardent, Nestor,*	*V.27, V.29, V.48,*
	Turbulent, Shark,	*S.35, V.4*
	Nomad, Fortune,	
	Sparrowhawk	

In terms of casualties this translated into:

	British	**German**
Killed	6,094	2,551
Wounded	674	507
Prisoner	177	NA
Totals	6,945	3,058[97]

On the basis of these matériel losses the Germans very quickly claimed a victory. The kaiser visited Wilhelmshaven on 5 June and addressed the crew of the *Friedrich der Grosse* with what Admiral Müller considered "exaggerated epithets," declaring: "The spell of Trafalgar has been broken," and Scheer was promoted to the equivalent rank of Hindenburg. The kaiser wanted the battle to be called the "North Sea Battle of June First" in imitation of the "Glorious First of June"—Admiral Howe's victory over the French in 1794. The navy had a difficult time getting him to accept what he considered the "unhistorical" name "Battle of the Skaggerak," but henceforth the battle was known by this name and celebrated as a victory. This view is reflected together with the idea that the battle represented a vindication of Tirpitz's shipbuilding policy in the German official history.[98]

The battle left a feeling of disappointment on the British side. It was not another Trafalgar. There was and would remain a sense of missed opportunity. The division between Jellicoe and Beatty supporters would be a very real one, although both men, at least publicly, tried to tone down the controversy. Nevertheless, as late as the Second World War, Churchill canceled plans to name two new battleships *Jellicoe* and *Beatty* in favor of the less controversial *Anson* and *Howe*.[99] The battle would be refought repeatedly in the interwar period and eventually the detailed studies and track charts—corrected and uncorrected—can in themselves become misleading. Shortly after the battle, Jellicoe admitted to Beatty, "I never felt so `out of it' as at the meeting [between their respective forces]. I could not make out the situation a bit."[100] It is well to remember the commonsense caution of John Campbell: "Endless speculation is possible as to what might have happened at Jutland if Jellicoe and Scheer, or their subordinate commanders, had acted differently, but for much of the battle lack of visibility had a more dominant influence than any of the Admirals."[101]

There was certainly not the same controversy on the German side regarding Scheer's *tactical* handling of the fleet. The German controversies seemed centered more on the strategic employment of the fleet or submarines, not the battle itself. The senior German officers seemed to close ranks around Scheer, although his chief of staff Trotha privately admitted, somewhat jokingly, that if an admiral had gotten himself in such a situation at maneuvers or in a war game as Scheer did at Jutland, he never would have been entrusted with another command again.[102]

There is no doubt the Germans inflicted the heavier matériel losses. Their own ships were exceedingly tough. The *Seydlitz* was drawing so much water forward that she grounded off Horns Reef and later in the Amrun Channel, and it was only with great difficulty that salvage ships managed to get her into port on 2 June. Her repairs were not completed until 16 September. The *König* was also drawing too much water to get over Amrun bank until 9:30 A.M. on 1 June. She remained in dockyard hands until 21 July. The repairs on the *Derfflinger* were not completed until 15 October. The Germans suffered another casualty before reaching port when the *Ostfriesland* was mined in a field laid by the *Abdiel* on 4 May. These factors mitigate the higher matériel losses suffered by the British, for the eight damaged ships of the Grand Fleet represented a much smaller proportion of its strength than the ten damaged capital ships of the High Sea Fleet. Immediately after the battle, the British could still send 24 capital ships against the 10 of the Germans. The damaged British ships were also repaired more quickly. For example, the *Warspite* rejoined the fleet on 22 July, and the *Lion* underwent successive short periods of repair, although it was not until 23 September that "Q" turret was replaced.

The British undertook a thorough investigation into the battle, and although there is no space to enter into details, the Grand Fleet that emerged was a much more formidable instrument. There have been voluminous discussions on the deficiencies of British ships, particularly the battle cruisers. There was little that could be done aside from some strengthening of armor plating at vulnerable points, but the true problem resided more in British powder than in inadequate protection. John Campbell states flatly: "The real cause of the disasters was that the precautions for preventing flash of ignited propellant reaching a magazine were not matched to the behavior of British charges, though if the British ships had German charges it is very unlikely that they would have blown up. This was not, however, clear at the time."[103]

The problem was compounded by the unsafe nature of the British cordite quarter charges—the four bags of propellant that made a full charge—which had a gunpowder igniter at each end. The igniters were unprotected and twice as many as needed, presumably to spare the crew concern over which way to load the charges. The German system, in contrast, used only two charges, the front one protected in a light metal container consumed in the blast and the rear charge in a brass container ejected after firing. There is also evidence that the British in the understandable desire to increase the rate of fire had departed from safe handling practices by stacking charges at the bottom of hoists, keeping magazine doors open in action and even removing flash-tight scuttles that had originally been fitted.

There has also been considerable discussion on the inadequate performance of British shells, which broke up on striking armor at an oblique angle and which detonated from a concussion explosion in the lyddite burster before penetrating very far into the plate.[104] British armor also was inferior to German armor, and like the shells suffered from inadequate inspection and testing with too much discretion apparently left to armaments firms. Even after the war, the British found rust-coated armor salvaged from scuttled German ships at Scapa Flow remarkably resistant to new 14-inch shells.[105]

A brief word should be added about fire control. The British undoubtedly paid a severe penalty for the failure to adopt before the war the system devised by Arthur Hungerford Pollen. The alternate system the Admiralty adopted, the Dreyer Table, was not able to cope with the high change of range rates experienced in the battle. Ironically, the ill-fated *Queen Mary* had Pollen's Argo Clock Mark IV and before her destruction her shooting had been the best of the battle cruisers. The Pollen system would undoubtedly have enabled the British battle cruisers to hit before they were hit in return, thus offsetting their deficiencies in armor protection and unstable propellant.[106]

The Battle of Jutland was fought and refought in the war games of navies throughout the world in the period between the two world wars. One can become lost in the fascinating tactical and technical details. But what of strategy? One can state unequivocally that Jutland was a strategic defeat for the Germans. It changed nothing, and the pithy comment attributed to a journalist that the German fleet had assaulted its jailer and was back in jail was essentially true. Scheer had been lucky to escape, and British superiority in capital ships—with the exception of battle cruisers—was larger than ever. Certainly a great British tactical victory involving the destruction of a substantial portion of the High Sea Fleet would have freed many British resources, particularly the large number of destroyers that had to remain tied to the Grand Fleet and might have received alternate employment in the protection of trade and the antisubmarine campaign. But as to the strategic picture, the route to the open seas remained as closed to the Germans as ever. The blockade was still in force.

Scheer, perhaps unwittingly, delivered the true verdict on the strategic results of Jutland. In a report to the kaiser on 4 July 1916, he spoke of the success due to eagerness in attack, efficient leadership through subordinates, and admirable deeds of crews. He claimed that the battle had proven that the enlargement of the fleet and the development of the different types of ships had been guided by the right strategical and tactical ideas. He then went on to the main point of his argument:

> With a favourable succession of operations the enemy may be made to suffer severely, although there can be no doubt that even the most successful result from a high sea battle will not compel England to make peace. The disadvantages of our geographical situation as compared with that of the Island Empire and the enemy's vast matériel superiority cannot be coped with to such a degree as to make us masters of the blockade inflicted on us, or even of the Island Empire itself, not even

were all the U-boats to be available for military purposes. A victorious end to the war at not too distant a date can only be looked for by the crushing of English economic life through U-boat action against English commerce.

Scheer went on to propose the resumption of unrestricted submarine warfare.[107] Even before Scheer's memorandum, the chief of the Admiralstab, Holtzendorff, had asserted in a naval audience at the palace on 10 June that U-boat warfare with few restrictions should be increased starting 1 July to compensate for the reduced activities of the High Sea Fleet as a result of battle damage received at Jutland.[108] This pressure for unrestricted submarine warfare grew.

RESUMPTION OF THE SUBMARINE CAMPAIGN

The assertion is sometimes made that the German fleet never came out again after Jutland. This is false. The Germans did sortie, because Scheer, however anxious to avoid a major encounter, still hoped to whittle down the British advantage with submarines. The German submarine traps so carefully prepared before the battle had proven to be a major disappointment. There were numerous reports of submarine sightings and attacks in the Grand Fleet during the battle, but they were all false. The Germans did have an unexpected dividend: one of the new long-range minelayers, *U.75*, laid a field off the northwest Orkneys—ironically in the wrong place—which sank the cruiser *Hampshire* after she had sailed from Scapa on 5 June carrying Lord Kitchener on a mission to Russia. The loss of Kitchener was a major disaster for the British public, but the circumstances that produced it were purely accidental.[109]

Scheer decided that a concentration of U-boats directly off the British bases was counterproductive, for the submarines would tend to get in each other's way. He decided to try a variation, deploying the submarines in a movable base line across the probable line of approach of the British heavy forces. The German fleet would put to sea at night and advance toward the British coast. If there was no contact with British ships, and if reconnaissance indicated the British fleet was not out and attempting to cut off the German line of retreat, the First Scouting Group would push on to the British coast and bombard the town of Sunderland at sunset. They would then return to the Bight under cover of darkness while the U-boats shifted to secondary positions across the probable line of approach should the British come out as a result of the bombardment. Scheer had no intention of being surprised by Jellicoe the way he had been at Jutland, and his new plan placed great emphasis on zeppelin reconnaissance. There would be four zeppelins deployed on patrol lines across the North Sea from Scotland to Norway and another four between the Firth of Forth and the North Hinder light vessel, patrolling to the north and in front of the advancing Germans. No fewer than twenty-four submarines were employed in the operation. The High Sea Fleet submarines were deployed in lines of five boats each off Blyth, Flamborough Head, and the Dogger Bank, and nine U-boats from the Flanders Flotilla were deployed in two lines in the southern part of the North Sea.

Scheer sailed on the night of 18 August. The *Moltke* and *Von der Tann* were the only two battle cruisers then available for the First Scouting Group, and Scheer had to reinforce them with the dreadnoughts *Grosser Kurfürst, Markgraf,* and *Bayern,* the latter newly commissioned and the first German dreadnought with 38-cm guns. The First and Second scouting groups were 20 miles ahead of the High Sea Fleet, which numbered 18 dreadnoughts. The surviving predreadnoughts of the Second Squadron, which had been such a hindrance at Jutland, were left behind.[110]

Room 40 was as alert as ever, and starting on the 15th had indications the Germans were preparing for sea by intercepting orders for minesweeping, instructions to light vessels, and information the Third Squadron would pass the outer Jade the night of the 18th. The result was that both Jellicoe and Beatty were at sea a few hours before Scheer. Tyrwhitt's Harwich Force—5 light cruisers, a flotilla leader, and 19 destroyers—also was ordered to sail and be at a position approximately 50 miles east of Yarmouth at dawn. The author of the relevant volume of the German official history published in 1937 complained: "Unfortunately it has not been possible to clear up entirely what the intelligence was which made the Admiralty feel sure that the German fleet was about to leave harbour."[111]

Despite this precious intelligence, there would be no fleet encounter on 19 August, a day Professor Marder terms "Blind Man's Bluff." At 5:05 A.M. *E.23,* one of the British patrol submarines, torpedoed the German battleship *Westfalen* approximately 60 miles north of Terschelling. The battleship was not seriously damaged but had to return to port, and the wireless message intercepted by British direction-finding stations provided the first firm intelligence the High Sea Fleet was at sea and gave its position as well. The information was immediately transmitted to Jellicoe, but he did not receive it until 7:00 A.M. By then Jellicoe had already been delayed. At 5:57 A.M. the light cruiser *Nottingham* of the Second Light Cruiser Squadron, part of Beatty's screen, was torpedoed and sunk by *U.52,* one of the U-boats on Scheer's northern submarine line. The battle cruisers were approximately 30 miles in advance of the Grand Fleet. There was no clear evidence as to whether the *Nottingham* had been torpedoed or mined, but Jellicoe, fearful he was being drawn into a minefield trap, turned north at 7:03 until the situation could be clarified. He thereby lost four hours.

Jellicoe resumed his course to the south-southeast after it had been clearly established the *Nottingham* had been torpedoed. He might still have intercepted Scheer with the battleships in supporting distance of the battle cruisers; the weather was clear and there was plenty of daylight left. A German error deprived the British of their chance. At 12:03 the zeppelin *L.13,* which had been shadowing the Harwich Force, reported that a strong British force including heavy ships was approaching Scheer from the south. Scheer believed he might have the long-sought opportunity to catch a portion of the Grand Fleet with his superior forces and turned away from Sunderland to the south. The zeppelin commander, Kapitänleutnant Prölss, was a reserve officer who was not a mariner by profession, but rather chief of the Magdeburg Fire Department.[112] He has been understandably criticized in German publications for mistaking Tyrwhitt's light cruisers for heavy ships but unwittingly may have saved the High Sea Fleet from a major defeat. After learning of *E.23*'s signal concerning the *Westfalen*, Tyrwhitt had steamed north looking for the Germans, but seeing nothing he turned—unknowingly away from Scheer—and proceeded southward to his station.

Scheer abandoned his southward movement at 2:35 P.M. and set course for home. By then he had received the report from one of the submarines of the northern line that the Grand Fleet was approaching him from the north, whereas the British force to the south was apparently out of reach and it was too late to bombard Sunderland. Jellicoe, once he had been advised of Scheer's change of course, realized a meeting was impossible and also turned for home. The British now had to run the gauntlet of submarines, and the light cruiser *Falmouth* of Beatty's screen was torpedoed by *U.66* at 4:52 and finally sunk by *U.63* the next day while under tow to the Humber.

Tyrwhitt also had turned in pursuit of the Germans and actually had Scheer in sight by 6:00. He considered the possibility of a night attack but finally realized he would not be able to get into a favorable position ahead of the Germans before the moon rose, after which such an attack would have been suicidal. Tyrwhitt later apologized to Jellicoe: "I hope I was right in not making a night attack. I could have made one but I don't think I should have succeeded in doing any harm and should most certainly have been badly cut up as the night was not very dark." He concluded, "I was groping in the dark all day!"[113] On this note we might conclude our discussion of this frustrating day, which was indeed "Blind Man's Bluff."

The 19th of August had important strategic results, or as the naval staff study remarked: "It is typical of the vagaries of naval war that while the Battle of Jutland, whose name is a household word, had no immediate effect on fleet strategy, August 19, a day when not a shot was fired on either side marks a definite turning point in the war at sea."[114] On the British side, Jellicoe complained to the Admiralty on 24 August that the number of destroyers available was inadequate for full screening, and it was extremely probable there would be further serious losses should the fleet move south on operations similar to 19 August. The Admiralty replied on 9 September that they could not supply vessels not yet available, were making great efforts to hasten completion of destroyers, would continue allocating new destroyers to the Grand Fleet until the number reached 100, but could not neglect their responsibilities in other areas.[115]

These factors contributed to a change in strategy in which Jellicoe and Beatty were in full agreement. Beatty wrote Jellicoe on 6 September that the old proverb "When you are winning, risk nothing" might well be applied now, and that the North Sea south of latitude 55° 30' N was a very unhealthy place for capital ships and should be left entirely to submarines. Jellicoe more than agreed, and on 13 September an important conference took place in his flagship *Iron Duke* with Vice Admiral Oliver, chief of the Admiralty war staff. Jellicoe argued that the main fleet should not go south of 55° 30' N in longitudes east of 4° E unless under exceptional circumstances. The waters so far to the east could not be watched by their cruisers or submarines, and therefore offered the Germans the opportunity to prepare a mine or submarine trap on a large scale. In waters to the west, British submarines could probably report such traps, but because of the submarine danger the fleet should not go south of the Dogger Bank unless the number of destroyers was sufficient to provide a thoroughly efficient screen—which was not the case at the moment. Oliver revealed that the Admiralty had informed the cabinet the Grand Fleet could not be depended on to interfere with German raids on the east coast until twenty-eight hours after the arrival of the raiding forces. Oliver then proceeded to visit Beatty, and on the question of the fleet coming south found him "if anything more emphatic on this point than the C.-in-C.."

The Admiralty decided on 25 September that they agreed with the conclusions reached at the conference in the *Iron Duke* and promised to press on with work at Rosyth to enable the main portion of the fleet to be based farther to the south. The fleet would not be ordered south of the concentration point to the east of the Long Forties in rough weather when destroyers could not keep up, and, unless there was a German invasion attempt or a good opportunity to bring the German fleet to action in daylight in appropriate waters, capital ships were to keep to the north of the parallel of Horns Reef and avoid the vicinity of mined waters.[116]

There were strategic changes after 19 August on the German side as well. Scheer was ready to try a similar operation in September with three rows of U-boats instead of a single line, with the boats in the second and third lines deployed opposite the gaps in the front line. Scheer reported that poor weather made scouting impossible and prevented implementation of the plan. He was ready to try again in October, but by then found that the Supreme Command had decided to withdraw the U-boats from the High Sea Fleet and use them for the resumption of the war against commerce under prize rules. Scheer opposed this; in his mind it must be unrestricted submarine warfare or nothing. However, the commander of the Flanders Flotilla, Korvettenkapitän Bartenbach, after a trial mission by *UB.18* at the end of July in which only ships clearly established as transports would be attacked without warning, had come to the conclusion that submarine warfare against commerce, even under prize rules, could still produce useful results in the western portion of the English Channel.[117]

The German high command's decision in early October to resume restricted submarine warfare against commerce was in direct opposition to Scheer's opinion. The campaign was not totally restricted; the Germans reserved the right to sink armed merchantmen without warning. Scheer therefore had to relinquish the High Sea Fleet's U-boats and alter his plans for a new sortie. On 10 October he sent out a screen of destroyers to examine merchantmen and capture prizes in the North Sea. The High Sea Fleet came out in support, but Scheer was careful as to his choice of favorable waters, light and wind conditions, and the amount of time between a possible encounter and the onset of darkness.[118] The fleet came out to the center of the North Sea east of the Dogger Bank with a wide destroyer screen and preceded by zeppelins, but bad weather restricted the ability of the destroyers to go as far as planned, and the German wireless interception station at Neumünster warned Scheer they had intercepted British signals diverting merchant ships and recalling light forces, thereby indicating the British knew he was out.

Scheer returned to port without accomplishing anything. The light cruiser *München* was torpedoed off Terschelling by *E.38* but was towed home by the cruiser *Berlin*.

The British once again knew from wireless interceptions that the Germans were planning to come out. The local defenses on the east coast were alerted, but the Grand Fleet was only brought to short notice. It did not leave harbor while the German intentions were unknown. This reflected the new strategy and indicated that in the North Sea a stalemate was in effect as far as the major surface fleets were concerned. The situation was basically imposed by submarines. The major British offensive patrolling also was now carried out by submarines, although the Admiralty did not seem to realize their value and held back submarines in east coast harbors to defend against German raids. The Germans were never able to come out again without being detected by British submarine patrols.[119]

Scheer, deprived of submarines to provide advance warning that Jellicoe was at sea, had to abandon his strategy of trying to catch a portion of the Grand Fleet. The High Sea Fleet did not undertake another offensive sortie in the North Sea until April 1918. The role of the great ships was now to support the activities of the submarines. On the night of 23–24 October the Third and Ninth Flotillas, representing twenty-four precious destroyers, were transferred from the High Sea Fleet to Zeebrugge and placed temporarily under the orders of the Marinekorps Flanders. Their objective was to combat the light forces of the Harwich Force and Dover Patrol and to facilitate the passage of submarines through the Strait. The transfer indicated the Germans recognized that the center of gravity of the naval war had shifted to the submarine campaign against commerce.[120]

There was also an incident early in November, small in the context of the war, but which clearly demonstrated how the role of capital ships and submarines had been reversed. On 2 November *U.30*'s diesel engines broke down while the submarine was operating off the Norwegian coast approximately 25 miles west of Bergen. The submarine sent a wireless message for help, and *U.20*, returning from the southwest of Ireland and approximately 40 miles away, heard the message and came to assist. The British also intercepted the message and destroyers were sent to sweep up the Norwegian coast. They were too late, for the two submarines had proceeded in company toward Bovsbjerg on the Jutland Peninsula where *U.30* was to be met by tugs. They reached the vicinity of Bovsbjerg on the evening of 4 November when a fog came up and both boats ran aground. *U.30* managed to free herself but could no longer submerge freely and remained in the vicinity of the stranded *U.20*. The Germans feared that British patrols would catch the submarines or that the Danes would intern *U.20* if they did not get her off quickly enough. Scheer sent powerful reinforcements—the destroyers of the Fourth Half-Flotilla, covered by the battle cruiser *Moltke* and the Third Battle Squadron. The British were able to intercept the German wireless messages and alert the British submarine *J.1*, which was on patrol in the vicinity. Commander N. F. Laurence of *J.1* managed to get in an attacking position and fire four torpedoes, one of which hit the *Grosser Kurfürst* and another the *Kronprinz*. The dreadnoughts were not sunk, however, and were able to return to port on their own power. The destroyers could not dislodge *U.20*, which was blown up and her crew brought home.

The Kaiser subsequently criticized Scheer over the affair, pointing out that to risk the *Moltke* and an entire battle squadron and have two battleships put temporarily out of commission for the sake of a single U-boat showed a lack of proportion and must not happen again. Scheer disagreed and felt that the kaiser's policy would impose too great a restraint on the fleet. He was summoned to Pless on 22 November and defended himself with the argument that the dangers that submarines normally faced were so great that the fullest possible support from the fleet was justified. The submarine crews could not be allowed to feel that they would be left to their fate if they ran into difficulties. The whole German naval strategy would sooner or later have to be concentrated on the U-boat campaign, and the fleet would have to devote itself to a single task, getting U-boats safely to sea and bringing them safely home again.[121] There can be no more striking demonstration as to how the nature of the war at sea had changed by autumn of 1916. An entire squadron of precious capital ships—the prewar standard of naval strength—had been risked to salvage a single submarine. The next step was for the Germans to make the fateful decision to resume unrestricted submarine warfare regardless of the diplomatic consequences. The naval war was about to reach its crisis.

11

THE SUBMARINE CRISIS: 1917

THE DECISION FOR
UNRESTRICTED WARFARE

In October 1916 Holtzendorff launched the restricted submarine campaign according to prize rules, which has been overshadowed by later events but was not devoid of results. Sinkings had already risen sharply in September to 172 ships, representing 231,573 tons. This was largely due to the entry into service of the larger and more potent UB.II boats of the Flanders Flotilla, which could now operate well beyond the Channel into the western approaches or as far south as the Gironde. The Allied losses grew higher: in October 185 ships, 341,363 tons; in November 180 ships, 326,689 tons; in December 197 ships, 307,847 tons; and in January 1917, 195 ships, 328,391 tons. The Germans lost during this period only 10 boats (3 in the unhealthy Black Sea), giving an exchange ratio of 65 ships sunk for every U-boat lost.[1]

The German submarines continued to extend their operations on a significant scale, reinforcing the Mediterranean Flotilla (see chapter 12), working briefly off the coast of North America, and making a successful raid into the Arctic. There were sinkings involving American citizens, of which the most noteworthy were probably the *Marina* and the *Arabia*. There were six Americans among the eighteen lost when the Donaldson line's *Marina* (5,204 tons) was torpedoed without warning by *U.55* off Fastnet on 28 October. The *Marina* had, however, carried defensive armament, which in German eyes made her fair game. On 6 November the P&O liner *Arabia* (7,933 tons) was torpedoed by *UB.43* off Cape Matapan in the Mediterranean. The loss of life was restricted to eleven of the engine room staff killed in the first explosion, but the liner had been torpedoed without warning by a submerged submarine, and it was thanks only to good seamanship, luck, and the prompt arrival of rescuing ships that the 439 passengers (169 of them women and children) survived. The *Arabia* incident demonstrated that the Germans had broken their promise about not sinking passenger liners without warning, but they were prone to take liberties in the Mediterranean where American citizens were less likely to be encountered.[2] The United States government protested these and other sinkings; the Germans replied with justifications and excuses.

The Americans were equally if not more affected by the appearance of German submarines in American waters. The Germans developed the large submarine *Deutschland*, ostensibly under the merchant flag, to serve as a blockade runner with admittedly small but vital cargoes. The *Deutschland* made two round voyages in the summer and fall of 1916. Her sister ship the *Bremen* disappeared without a trace after sailing at the end of August. The *Deutschland* was undoubtedly a great curiosity for Americans. The U.S. government managed to skirt potentially awkward diplomatic repercussions and the Germans garnered an extensive amount of publicity, even if in the final analysis the tangible results were small.[3] The visit of Kapitänleutnant Hans Rose and *U.53* to Newport, Rhode Island, on 7 October was much less benign. The submarine remained in port only a few hours, and Rose invited American naval officers for a tour of inspection. A number of officers from the Destroyer Force, Atlantic Fleet accepted. He then proceeded to sink five ships off the American coast. None were American, three were British and the others Norwegian and Dutch. The sinkings took place in international waters off the Nantucket light vessel under prize rules, and, in fact, were observed by American destroyers who rescued the survivors. At one point the submarine had actually been forced to reverse engines to avoid a collision with a destroyer. At another moment Rose even asked an American destroyer lying near the Dutch ship to move a little farther away so the freighter could be torpedoed. The voyage of *U.53* was an obvious demonstration of what German submarines were capable of and a not very subtle reminder to the United States that American waters were not immune.[4]

The results of this final "restricted" submarine campaign may have been impressive, a reflection of the much larger number of submarines the Germans had available for the campaign. This grew from 87 out of 119 operational boats in October to 103 out of 148 operational boats in January. Nevertheless, only 20 percent of the Allied ships sunk during this period had been torpedoed without warning, while about 75 percent had been sunk by gunfire. Scheer and his chief of staff, Trotha, were convinced the campaign could not be decisive. Trotha believed that the American attitude prevented them from wielding the U-boat weapon as a sword certain to bring them victory, that they had used it instead "as a soporific for the feelings of the nation, and presented the blunt edge to the enemy." A modern analyst is inclined to agree. Admiral Hezlet points out that at the end of the two-year period 1915–16, the British merchant marine was still 94 percent of the size it had been at the beginning of the war, and even if the Germans had been able to employ twice the number of submarines and the British had not taken any new countermeasures, it would still have taken the Germans another two years to defeat them by this method alone.[5]

By the close of 1916, the balance of strength in the lengthy debate within Germany over unrestricted submarine warfare shifted inexorably in favor of those who favored its resumption. The failure of German peace proposals to arouse an acceptable response from the Allies and the successful conclusion of the Romanian campaign, which freed troops the high command considered necessary to deploy in case unrestricted submarine warfare brought Denmark and Holland into the war, had much to do with helping to create the favorable atmosphere.[6] Holtzendorff, the chief of the Admiralstab, had played a role described by Professor Herwig as "tortuous." His policy pleased no one and made him a target for the intrigues of partisans of unrestricted submarine warfare in the High Sea Fleet, notably Scheer, Trotha, and Levetzow. Holtzendorff was finally converted in December and submitted the widely quoted memorandum on the subject to Field Marshal von Hindenburg, now chief of the general staff. The memorandum, which Holtzendorff described as an extension of an earlier one of 27 August, was subsequently printed and apparently widely distributed. The German naval attaché in Vienna, for example, handed a copy to the Marinesektion on 17 January. Obviously it had not been created in a vacuum. There had been a series of earlier and lengthy memoranda sponsored by the Admiralstab officers Captain Grasshoff and Commander Ernst Vanselow. They included two by economic experts, the banker Dr. Richard Fuss and Professor Hermann Levy. The latter emphasized Great Britain's vulnerability to a stoppage of vital imports, particularly wheat. The memoranda provided a scientific veneer for what would become Germany's fateful gamble. Significantly, Admiral von Müller, chief of the kaiser's naval cabinet and generally regarded as a moderate on the U-boat question, disregarded Chancellor Bethmann Hollweg's request to keep the memoranda secret and circulated close to five hundred copies to naval and military leaders.[7]

The Holtzendorff memorandum of 22 December 1916 is well known, for most of it was published by Scheer in his memoirs immediately after the war.[8] A rough summary of Holtzendorff's argument is as follows. A decision in the war would have to be reached by the autumn of 1917 lest it end in the exhaustion of all parties and, consequently, disastrously for Germany. Italy and France were really sustained only by Great Britain's energy and activity, and if they could break Britain's back the war would at once be decided in Germany's favor. Britain's backbone (*Rückgrat*) was tonnage (*Schiffsraum*), which at the moment amounted to 20 million gross tons. At least 8.6 million tons of this were requisitioned for military purposes, half a million tons were occupied in coast traffic, about a million tons were under repair or temporarily unfit for use, and about 2 million tons were necessary to supply the needs of Great Britain's allies. This left at most 8 million tons available for Great Britain's own supplies. The statistics concerning traffic in British ports gave even smaller results. From July to September 1916, only 6.75 million gross tons of British shipping was engaged in traffic to Great Britain. There was also an estimated 900,000 gross tons of seized German and Austrian shipping and about 3 million gross tons of neutral shipping proceeding to England. This gave a rough total of only 10.75 million gross tons of shipping supplying the British.

The poor harvest in wheat and produce throughout the world gave the Germans another opportunity. North America and Canada would probably be unable to send additional grain to Great Britain after February, and the British would be forced to import grain from distant Argentina. However, the Argentines had also experienced a bad harvest and could spare little, which in turn would force the British to import from India and, above all, from Australia. The greater distances involved would force the British to use an additional 720,000 tons for grain shipments. This meant that until August 1917 the British would have to use three-quarters of a million tons of the 10.75 million tons at their disposal for purposes that had not previously been necessary. Holtzendorff repeated earlier statements that it was absolutely unjustifiable not to make use of the U-boat and made the flat assertion that as matters now stood, the Germans could force England to make peace in five months through unrestricted submarine warfare. He emphasized, however, it would have to be real unrestricted warfare, and not merely cruiser warfare in which the submarines were only allowed to attack all armed steamers.

Holtzendorff calculated that based on the former results of 600,000 tons of shipping per month sunk by unrestricted submarine warfare and the expectation that at least two-fifths of the neutral traffic would instantly be terrorized into ceasing voyages to Britain, the Germans after five months could count on reducing traffic to and from Britain by about 39 percent. The British could not bear this, for reasons Holtzendorff described (which are too lengthy to reproduce here). Cruiser warfare waged by U-boats would only result in about half the estimated sinkings of unrestricted warfare and would therefore not have the desired results.

Holtzendorff minimized the potential consequences of war with the United States. Certainly it would be a serious matter and everything ought to be done to avoid it, but "fear of a break must not hinder us from using this weapon which promises success." The effect on tonnage "can only be very small," and it was not probable more than a small fraction of the tonnage belonging to the Central Powers lying in American and neutral ports would be quickly available for voyages to England. The Germans had made preparations to sabotage the greater part of it to such an extent that it would be useless during the first months, which would be the decisive period. Moreover, the crews would not be available to man them, nor could American troops be brought over in considerable numbers owing to the shortage of shipping. Holtzendorff added that American money could not make up for the shortage of supplies and tonnage. He emphasized that the unrestricted submarine campaign must begin no later than 1 February, so as to ensure peace before the next harvest, that is, 1 August.

Holtzendorff's argument contained, as we shall see, a number of false assumptions, but the constellation of forces favoring unrestricted submarine warfare was able to overwhelm the objections or hesitations of their opponents, and at the Schloss Pless conference of 9 January 1917, the Germans reached the fateful decision to commence unrestricted submarine warfare on 1 February. Bethmann Hollweg felt he could no longer oppose, given the opinion of the general staff and naval leaders. For the chancellor, it was not so much approval as an acceptance of the facts.[9]

The Germans had 105 U-boats available on 1 February. They were deployed as follows: High Sea Fleet, 46; Flanders, 23; Mediterranean, 23; Kurland (Baltic), 10; and

A NAVAL HISTORY OF WORLD WAR I

Constantinople, 3. Thanks to new construction, and despite losses, U-boat strength rose steadily to a peak of 129 on 1 June; for the remainder of the year it did not fall below 120, ending the year at 125.[10] The U-boat construction program itself remained plagued by difficulties, exacerbated by the severe winter of 1916–17, which brought shortages of coal, difficulties in transport, and poor morale among workers. The situation was serious enough for Hindenburg to send a special emissary to the U-Boat Inspectorate at Kiel on 15 January to examine the problems. The high command agreed to give priority to the transport of certain raw materials and components necessary for submarine construction and furnish the names of soldiers skilled in U-boat construction who might then be released from the army. Capelle and the Reichsmarineamt were anxious to get as many boats into action within the shortest possible time and therefore did not intend to order boats that could not be delivered by the beginning of 1918. This in practice meant most orders were for the medium-sized UB.III class, which had a relatively short building time and were handy and well suited for operations around the British Isles or in the Mediterranean.

In February contracts were signed for 45 UB.III boats (*UB.88* to *UB.132*) as well as for 6 of the larger Ms boats. The orders, given attrition, were not likely to result in a noteworthy addition to total U-boat strength, and the U-Boat Inspectorate, worried about gaps in production in 1918, complained to the army high command at the end of May that the Reichsmarineamt was reluctant to place new orders with the end of the war presumably in sight, fearing the financial effect of the large orders on peacetime estimates and the fleet plan. Shortages in labor, material, critical components, and submarine engines also continued to plague the work on submarines already under construction.[11]

This optimism about a quick end to the war did not last long, for on 2 June a conference between the various authorities concerned with the submarine war concluded that in the light of war experience and operational losses, everything that could be built in any possible way by 1 January 1919 ought to be put in hand right away "as the general outlook of the war gave no justification for any reduction in the most committed work on, improvements to, and increase in numbers of U-boats."[12] The immediate result at the end of June was an order for an additional 95 U-boats. These included 39 UC.III boats (*UC.80* to *UC.118*), an improved version of the successful UC.II minelayers, 37 additional UB.III boats (*UB.133* to *UB.169*), 9 800-ton Ms boats (*U.164* to *U.172*), and 10 large U-cruisers (*U.173* to *U.182*). The boats were all to be ready between the summer of 1918 and early 1919.

There was some doubt about fulfillment of the program, for what were termed "crippling" shortages of material and skilled labor continued. On 23 July Capelle asked the War Office that submarine construction be given priority over all other forms of production. The War Office would not go quite that far, designating submarine deliveries only "as of the utmost importance." In August the Reichsmarineamt decreed that in private yards submarine and torpedo-boat construction should take preference over new capital ship construction, and new U-boat construction, with a few exceptions, should even take preference over new torpedo-boat construction.[13] This meant that the two powerful battleships *Sachsen* and *Württemberg*, armed with eight 38-cm guns and already launched, would never enter service. The same was true of the recently launched 35-cm-gun battle cruiser *Mackensen* and three of her sister ships, already laid down. The Germans also had laid down the even more powerful battle cruiser *Ersatz Yorck*, armed with 38-cm guns, and planned another two of the same type.[14] These, given the experience of Jutland, would have been formidable opponents, and their potential certainly worried the British. They were all sacrificed for submarine construction—yet another striking example of how the nature of the war at sea had changed.

THE PEAK OF GERMAN SUCCESS

The German blockade of the British Isles, the so-called *Sperrgebiet,* or "prohibited area," might be described as a rectangle with cut corners. It ran from 20 miles from the Dutch coast to the Terschelling light vessel, then north to Utsire off the Norwegian coast, and then northwest to 62° N at its most northerly point, dipping to 3 miles south of the Danish-owned Faeroe Islands. It reached its most westerly point at 20° W before angling back to the Continent 20 miles off Cape Finisterre and then extending 20 miles off the neutral Spanish coast to the French frontier. There was also a prohibited zone in the Arctic Ocean, notably the approaches to Archangel and the Kola Peninsula. The Germans declared the waters in the *Sperrgebiet* closed to traffic, and that all neutral ships entering them would do so at their own risk. The Germans offered to permit one American steamer per week to proceed to Falmouth, provided its hull was marked with prominent red and white vertical stripes and it flew red-and-white-checked flags at each masthead. A daily Dutch paddle steamer with the same markings could also sail between Flushing and Harwich.[15]

The entire Mediterranean was also a *Sperrgebiet,* except for the area west of a line running southeast from near the mouth of the Rhône to a point approximately 60 miles off the French North African coast. There was also a 20-mile-wide corridor running through the Mediterranean to Cape Matapan and Greek territorial waters. Unarmed neutral vessels were allowed in these waters, although subject to prize rules. The exceptions catered to the maritime needs of neutral Spain and then-neutral Greece. The Germans eliminated the corridor in November 1917.[16]

The Germans soon paid the diplomatic price for their 1 February resumption of unrestricted submarine warfare. President Wilson of the United States felt mere diplomatic protests would no longer suffice, and on 3 February the United States severed relations with Germany. The president was still not convinced war was a foregone conclusion, but German action served to make it inevitable. At the end of February, the president learned of the Zimmermann telegram. This proposal by the German foreign secretary for a German-Mexican and possibly German-Japanese alliance in the event of war with the United States seemed to furnish further proof of Germany's aggressive intentions. Its interception and disclosure were handled in a masterful fashion by British Intelligence. The inevitable sinkings by submarines also occurred. The Cunard liner *Laconia* (18,099 tons) was torpedoed and sunk by *U.50* 160 miles northwest of Fastnet on 25 February. The loss of life was relatively small among the 292 aboard, but there were three to four Americans among the twelve dead. There were also at least five American steamers sunk, including the *Algonquin* torpedoed without warning on 12 March. The German provocations were sufficient to bring the United States into the war.[17] On 2 April Wilson asked Congress for a declaration of war. On 6 April the United States declared war on Germany—but not Austria-Hungary—and the same day seized German ships interned in American ports.[18] The primary question now was whether the German naval and military leaders were correct in their assumption that it would not really matter and that the war would be over before American power could have any significant effect on events.

The priority given by the Germans to submarine construction in 1917 reflects the results of the unrestricted submarine campaign. At first it seemed all the Germans might have hoped for, even if by late spring it was evident the British might not succumb as fast as the Admiralstab's U-boat enthusiasts had predicted. The losses inflicted by submarines rose from 328,391 tons in January to 520,412 tons in February, 564,497 tons in March, and a staggering 860,334 tons in April. April 1917 represented the peak of German success in the submarine campaign, for Allied losses fell to 616,316 tons in May. They went up somewhat to 696,725 tons in June, but would never again reach the April total.[19] The "exchange rate" went from 53 in February to 74 in March to an astonishing 167 in April. In February, March, and April the Germans lost only nine submarines; two of them succumbed to their own mines rather than British countermeasures. Three months of unrestricted submarine warfare had reduced the world's tonnage by more than two million tons, nearly 1.25 million tons British. The annual wastage of oceangoing tonnage was nearly 23 percent per year, rising to more than 50 percent per year in the last fortnight of April. The chance of a vessel safely completing a round voyage from the British Isles to a port beyond Gibraltar was now only one in four. The tonnage added through new construction or by transfer from foreign flags was simply insignificant in the face of these losses, and if they had continued at that rate, the British would have been compelled to make peace by November.[20] As Henry Newbolt admitted in the official history, "Everything, indeed, combined to show that the Allies were really in sight of disaster."[21]

The Germans also succeeded at first in their goal of terrorizing neutral shipping. British, Allied, and neutral ports were filled with neutral ships whose owners ordered them not to sail, and for a few weeks there was a general paralysis of neutral shipping. The British countered the crisis with ruthless measures of their own. They detained all neutral vessels in British ports and permitted them to sail for another Allied port only if they had received assurances they would not be laid up or diverted to a neutral port. Vessels trading with a neutral port were released only if they arranged to return with an approved cargo to a British or Allied port. Finally, in dealing with Dutch or

Scandinavian ships, the British followed the so-called ship-for-ship policy in which vessels were allowed to sail only on the arrival in a British port of a similar vessel of the same flag.[22]

The intense British pressure on neutral ships to continue trading with British or Allied ports was of little use if the ships were sunk. The German onslaught was now overwhelming the British system for the defense of trade, which was exposed as totally inadequate. Troopships had been specially escorted or convoyed since the beginning of the war. Commencing in early March 1917, ships carrying cargo termed "of national importance" were given special routes through one of three triangles that had their apexes at Falmouth, Queenstown, and Buncrana. The ships were ordered to enter the base line of the triangle at a designated degree of longitude and relied for protection within the triangle on patrolling destroyers, sloops, and trawlers. The method was far from perfect; there were only about 20 ships to patrol the approximately 10,000 square miles of each triangle. The loss rate was high; from March to June 1917, 63, or 7 percent, of the 890 ships routed in this manner were sunk, and in June the loss rate was a disturbing 11 percent.[23] For the great majority of their ordinary shipping the British relied on a system of dispersion and patrolled lanes along coastal routes, which they considered "had sufficed" in 1915 and 1916. Steamers left ports at dusk and made port at dawn, followed dispersed routes far from the main trade routes, and crossed dangerous points in the hours of darkness. Every steamer received its orders from a specially appointed naval officer, and when the number of patrol craft in service had increased to a sufficient point, were directed to follow certain well-defined and closely patrolled routes that, whenever possible, were close to the shore. The Admiralty would act on intelligence of U-boat activity, anticipate the U-boat's future movements, and divert trade to alternate routes. When all routes appeared to be threatened, the Admiralty suspended all traffic until the submarine had been destroyed or changed its area of operations.

There were flaws in the system; for example, owing to the requirements of secrecy, local commands did not always have the latest intelligence available from intercepts. Ships could be diverted only as they left port, and there was no method of controlling them while they were at sea. Inbound ships on the approach routes would be acting on even older intelligence. Furthermore, while the suspension of traffic might have saved ships from being sunk, it also had the effect of enforcing the German blockade.[24] The very detailed technical history produced by the Admiralty after the war made a significant point: "It is important to realize that the Routing System was not an alternative to direct protection, whether by patrols or convoy, but an auxiliary to such methods; when such methods were not available, owing to lack of ships, the Routing System could only hope to act as a palliative, and could never be a substitute for proper defensive methods."[25] Finally, there was another fatal flaw in any system of dispersion. However effective dispersion might have been, there were invariably certain focal points where approach and departure routes converged, and here submarines could count on finding attractive targets.

One of Jellicoe's first actions after he became First Sea Lord at the beginning of December 1916 was to form the Anti-Submarine Division at the Admiralty. While still commander in chief of the Grand Fleet he had advocated that "a Flag Officer of authority" should preside at the Admiralty over a committee or department charged with the exclusive purpose of developing antisubmarine measures and empowered "to follow through suggestions with all speed and press their execution."[26] Rear Admiral Sir Alexander Duff was its first head, succeeded when he became assistant chief of the naval staff in May 1917 by Captain William W. Fisher.

The question of what *should* be done to counter the submarines became the major issue of the naval war by the spring of 1917. For a long time the majority of naval officers, and certainly the prevailing opinion at the Admiralty, was in favor of the system of hunting patrols as opposed to escort or convoy work. The latter was considered "defensive," as opposed to "offensive" hunting patrols in areas where submarines were known to be operating. Hunting patrols were generally considered the proper role for men-of-war and naval officers. The traffic lanes close inshore were patrolled by the auxiliary patrol, converted vessels that entered service in large numbers during the war. Farther out, the approach routes were patrolled by sloops or Q-ships. The general idea was that no merchant vessel attacked by gunfire ought to have far to steam before a patrol vessel arrived to assist. The fitting of merchantmen with defensive armament had also offered hope earlier in the war when statistics indicated they had less chance of being sunk and a greater chance of escape if attacked. The German switch to ruthless underwater attack without warning canceled that advantage. The initial effectiveness of Q-ships also declined once the surprise factor had been lost and the Germans routinely attacked without warning. There is some evidence the Germans made a deliberate effort to destroy Q-ships in 1917, sinking those that were recognized before they had the slightest chance of defending themselves. U-boat commanders became much more proficient at recognizing through periscopes characteristics such as seams for collapsible plates, which betrayed the nature of the ship. No fewer than sixteen Q-ships were lost to submarine attack in 1917.[27]

The idea of hunting patrols with destroyers or sloops patrolling areas where submarines were known to be operating was also attractive, but the results were disappointing. Naval officers who rode to the hounds ashore sometimes even used the metaphors of fox hunting to describe their goals. But they lacked the "hounds" or tools to pick up the "scent." Science and technology raised some hopes for defeating the submarine when hydrophones of various sorts were introduced. The hydrophones were first developed by Commander C. P. Ryan, who founded the Admiralty Experimental Station at Hawkcraig, which remained the most important hydrophone research center throughout the war. It was not the only one; there were ultimately no fewer than twenty-nine antisubmarine research centers of various sorts in the British Isles and another two run by the British in the Mediterranean. The British established hydrophone stations on shore and eventually fitted with various types of listening devices all sorts of craft, ranging from motor launches to P-boats,[28] trawlers, and destroyers. Special hydrophone hunting units were formed to try to trap a submarine by triangulation. The listening devices generally failed to fulfill the great hopes placed in them. Without entering into the technical details, they were on the whole too primitive to be a serious menace to the submarine. The hydrophone hunting groups might also necessitate all vessels in the area stopping their engines so as to avoid masking the sound of the submarine. Stopping a ship in waters where submarines were known to be operating was hardly an attractive activity for most skippers. After they entered the war, the Americans also lavished a great deal of effort on hydrophones. The results were equally disappointing.[29] Success in the effort to render the oceans transparent was as elusive then as it remains today. The real counter to the submarine offensive was the system of convoys to which the British belatedly turned. Before discussing this, however, it would be well to examine methods on which the British lavished considerable effort with only limited success.

British Minelaying

The policy of minelaying to prevent German submarines from leaving or returning to their North Sea bases was an attractive one, because the minefields laid deep in enemy waters could be seen as "offensive." British policy on minelaying had changed course since the beginning of the war when the Admiralty had been reluctant to lay mines that might hamper the movements of British warships. The first minefield off Amrun was not laid until 8 January 1915. In May 1915 large fields were laid in the Helgoland Bight, but the British proceeded in spurts followed by periods of inactivity. By the end of 1915, they had laid a total of 4,538 mines in the Bight, followed by 17 fields and a mere 1,782 mines in 1916. The Royal Navy was hampered at first by a shortage of suitable mines and then by defects in the British Elia mine, and "an enormous amount of time and ingenuity was wasted in trying to improve what was later recognized as an unsuitable design."[30] In 1916 minelayers and mines also were fully occupied on the Belgian coast. The 13 September conference between Jellicoe and Oliver in the *Iron Duke* (see chapter 10) had among its strategic decisions an extensive policy of mining in the Bight for 1917. The lack of mines crippled the policy, although the British managed to lay 712 mines in January.

Beatty, who had succeeded Jellicoe as commander in chief of the Grand Fleet when the latter became First Sea Lord in December 1916, favored mining. On 10 January he urged the Admiralty to form a special mining organization capable of carrying out an extensive program. Beatty considered 80,000 mines necessary to close the Bight and bar the passage to German submarines. The barrage would be watched by destroyer and light cruiser sweeps at varying intervals as well as submarine patrols. The major problem was a shortage of mines. Although Beatty scaled down his mine requirements to 54,000 moored mines and 5,700 ground mines laid in a 155-mile barrage roughly 50 miles from the Jade, the navy actually expected to have only 34,000 mines available in the near future, and a mere 300 of them would be ready for service at the end of January.[31] Jellicoe was far less enthusiastic about mining and disagreed with Beatty's proposal to lay mines close in. He favored laying them farther out, where German minesweepers would face greater risk. The First Sea Lord also thought Beatty had an exaggerated view of their effectiveness against submarines, citing the ease with which German submarines were apparently passing the Dover barrage. Moreover, he considered Beatty's ideas in regard to the facility with which mines or anything else could presently be produced in Britain "far too optimistic."[32]

Regardless of the quantities available, British mines were still notoriously unreliable. In April 1917 only 1,500 of the 20,000 mines supposedly on hand were considered fit for laying. In the spring of 1917, the Admiralty finally adopted the desperate expedient of copying the well-proven German contact E mine. The First Sea Lord (H. B. Jackson) had actually ordered this done in the spring of 1916, but the Admiralty departments wasted almost a year trying to improve on the design. Consequently it was not until late 1917 that the reliable Mark H-2 mine was available in quantity.[33]

Beatty still complained in April that British minefields were being laid "in driblets," although 2,560 mines had been laid in seven fields in March and 2,997 mines in twelve fields in April. In the first half of 1917, British mines in the Bight accounted for a few small minesweeping craft but only one U-boat in April (UC.30), and the Germans lost U.59 to their own mines. Minelaying tapered off in the summer months, owing to the short nights, and submarines were used for a portion of the mining. It is somewhat misleading to talk merely of quantities of mines and numbers of fields. Intelligence, that is the knowledge of where and when to lay mines to the most effect, was as important as mere quantities, and here the British improved throughout the year. The Germans made use of a limited number of swept channels for U-boats, which were given color code names; notably, *Weg Gelb, Weg Grün,* and the coastal *Weg Schwarz* near the Frisian Islands in the south; *Weg Blau* and *Weg Rot,* the northerly routes west of Horns Reef; and the centrally located *Weg Braun.* The British, who gave the routes the names of streets, such as "Kingsway" and "Mall," developed very good intelligence about the extent of German sweeping and the location of the swept channels. They relied on reports from their own submarines on patrols, and, perhaps most important of all, on intercepted and deciphered German wireless messages. British minelaying in 1917 therefore achieved a certain measure of success, compared to the loss of only two destroyers to German mines off Horns Reef at the beginning of August.

British submarines sank six U-boats between 31 August and 13 December.[34] However, mines were more effective, and the Germans lost another seven U-boats to mines in British waters and four to mines off the Flanders coast. These statistics led two leading authorities to point out that the much-derided British mines were actually the most effective single antisubmarine weapon in 1917.[35] This may be true, but it in no way alters the fact that if some additional means had not been found of countering the U-boat in the spring of 1917, Great Britain would not have been able to remain in the war.

THE DOVER BARRAGES

The Straits of Dover and the minefields off the German submarine bases in Flanders were other focal points in the antisubmarine struggle, particularly after U-boats resumed their passage through the Strait. The periodic transfers of German destroyer flotillas from the High Sea Fleet to the Flanders bases made British and French antisubmarine activities much more dangerous. The vital lines of communication of the British armies in France also ran through these waters, and their protection was of paramount importance. In April 1916 Vice Admiral Bacon, commanding the Dover Patrol, had laid a barrage of deep mines and moored mine nets off the Belgian coast, the whole being known as the "Belgian coast barrage." In September the Admiralty began to lay a similar barrage of mine nets—called the cross-Channel barrage—from the southern end of the Goodwin Sands to the southwestern end of the Outer Ruytingen Shoals, the whole lying just to the east of the line Dover-Calais. The mine nets were supplemented by a line of deep mines laid a half mile to the west, which unfortunately dragged into the nets and threatened the drifters patrolling the barrage. The barrage was not finished until December and was unsuccessful in stopping the passage of submarines.

The German flotillas in Flanders struck even before the barrage was completed. Captain Andreas Michelsen, commodore of flotillas in the High Sea Fleet, brought the Third and Ninth Flotillas (twenty-four destroyers) from the Bight to Zeebrugge under cover of darkness. The two flotillas were placed under the command of Admiral von Schröder, commander of the Marinekorps Flandern, who up to now had been frustrated in his desire to achieve anything substantial against the Belgian coast barrage because of the handful of weak surface craft under his command. The Germans had resumed the restricted U-boat campaign against commerce, and their immediate objective was to attack the guardships on the Dover barrage in order to obtain a freer passage for U-boats leaving Zeebrugge and Ostend or passing through the Strait. Even though the barrage had not prevented German submarines from passing, it had been a considerable inconvenience.[36]

On the night of 26 October, Michelsen's two flotillas reinforced by the half-flotilla of Flanders destroyers attacked the British lines of communication. The Germans, aided by an extremely dark night with overcast sky, succeeded in sinking the destroyer *Flirt*, six drifters, and the empty transport *Queen*. They also torpedoed the destroyer *Nubian*, which, however, remained afloat. The Germans escaped without loss, but there had been no fewer than fifty-seven steamers at sea in the Strait that night that escaped harm, shielded by the same darkness that aided the German raiders.[37] The raid shocked British public opinion and led to attacks on the Admiralty. There was also no assurance it would not happen again. Bacon described the situation: "It is as easy to stop a raid of express engines with all lights out at night, at Clapham Junction, as to stop a raid of 33-knot destroyers on a night as black as Erebus, in waters as wide as the Channel."[38]

The operations during the German raid had also demonstrated to the Admiralty

A NAVAL HISTORY OF WORLD WAR I

that the cross-Channel barrage was less effective than they imagined, for fourteen British destroyers had crossed over it without suffering damage. The Admiralty agreed that Bacon needed more destroyers, but faced the problem of where to obtain them. The destroyer under the changed conditions of warfare was rapidly becoming even more important than the dreadnought. Bacon was finally reinforced from Tyrwhitt's Harwich Force and the Humber. But this forced the Admiralty to detach a division of destroyers from the Grand Fleet to bolster the Humber, which meant there might not be enough destroyers to screen the Grand Fleet when it put to sea, and a portion of the Fourth Battle Squadron would have to be left behind.[39] Once again the demands of *Kleinkrieg* were impinging on the requirements of what had been the premier instrument at the beginning of the war.

The Germans found certain disadvantages in keeping a large number of destroyers in Flanders. They could not lie alongside the mole at Zeebrugge because of the danger of air attack and had to be sent up the canal to Bruges. This meant a time-consuming trip through the canal locks, and Scheer claimed it took two and a half hours for four destroyers to make the passage. Furthermore, they were usually spotted by the Allies after leaving Bruges. British aerial reconnaissance of Zeebrugge increased after the October raid, and the Germans were forced to cancel a raid planned for the night of 1 November because they feared the British had been forewarned. The Third Flotilla was ordered back to Wilhemshaven. The ten destroyers of the Ninth Flotilla that remained in Flanders were joined on the night of 23–24 November by three destroyers of the Flanders Half-Flotilla in a raid on the northern entrance of the Downs. The Germans clashed with the British patrols, escaped unscathed, but accomplished little beyond damaging a drifter and lobbing a few shells into Margate. They had been dangerously close to the shipping in the Downs, and the German escape contributed to the agitation against the Admiralty.[40]

The pattern of temporary reinforcement of the Flanders flotillas by destroyers from the High Sea Fleet continued in 1917 when on the night of 22–23 January the Sixth Flotilla (destroyer leader *V.69* and ten destroyers) proceeded from the Bight to Zeebrugge. Room 40 provided advanced intelligence of the move to Tyrwhitt's Harwich Force. Tyrwhitt was reinforced by six destroyers from Bacon's Dover Patrol and attempted to intercept the German destroyers between the Schouwen Bank and the Maas. He was able to deploy no fewer than six light cruisers, two destroyer leaders, and sixteen destroyers, but in the confusion of the night action the Germans were able to reach Zeebrugge. *V.69* was damaged, her helm jammed, and she was rammed by another German destroyer, *G.41*. Both Germans survived. The British destroyer *Simoom* was torpedoed and sunk by *S.50*, a German straggler that blundered unexpectedly into the British patrols. *V.69* was later discovered and pounded by the cruisers *Penelope*, *Cleopatra*, and *Undaunted*, but the British switched off their lights prematurely on the assumption she was sinking and the destroyer was able to limp into Ymuiden. The Dutch did not intern her as the British could not actually prove she had run into port to escape pursuit. Given the British had advance intelligence of the move and were in superior strength, it was a thoroughly unsatisfactory affair. Part of the problem probably lay in the recent reinforcement of Tyrwhitt's force from the Grand Fleet. The new captains had been used to less independence than Tyrwhitt was accustomed to granting and were less likely to exercise their own initiative. The Harwich Force was therefore far from homogeneous, and this had been cruelly exposed. Tyrwhitt was criticized for not providing proper guidance as to when an officer should remain on station and await further orders or act independently.[41] The Germans had been lucky, but the problems of command and control were inherent in fast night action typical of these destroyer clashes in the Dover Strait, North Sea, or Adriatic. The episode demonstrated Jellicoe's wisdom in seeking to avoid a night action at Jutland the preceding year.

The Sixth Flotilla and the two Zeebrugge half-flotillas made a three-pronged but widely dispersed attack on the night of 25–26 February, another dark night when the moon was hidden by clouds. The Second Zeebrugge Half-Flotilla raided the route between England and the Hook of Holland near the Maas light vessel, while the First Zeebrugge Half-Flotilla (5 destroyers) attacked the Downs and the Sixth Flotilla (6 destroyers) attacked the barrage patrols. Room 40 did not detect the movements in advance, but the Germans failed to inflict any damage, and the Sixth Flotilla turned back after clashing with the *Laverock*, one of the destroyers patrolling the barrage. The *Laverock* was lucky and suffered little damage, although later she was found to have been hit by a torpedo that did not explode. The attack on the Downs was equally ineffective, beyond killing a few civilians when the Germans shelled the North Foreland wireless station. There was no Dutch traffic at sea that night, and the Second Zeebrugge Half-Flotilla's operation off the Maas—the third prong of the German attack—was also futile.[42]

The Germans made a much more concentrated attack on the night of 17–18 March when the Sixth Flotilla (7 destroyers) and First Zeebrugge Half-Flotilla (5 destroyers) raided the barrage and the Second Zeebrugge Half-Flotilla (4 destroyers) attacked shipping in the Downs. The German commander, Korvettenkapitän Tillessen of the Sixth Flotilla, was very careful in his preliminary dispositions to give each group a distinct line of approach and zone of operations. They would then be able to assume anything they met was hostile and could open fire without challenging. Room 40 provided at least some advance warning that something was up, but once again the Germans were able to inflict loss and escape unscathed. Two of the destroyers patrolling the barrage were torpedoed, the *Paragon* blew up and sank, and the *Llewellyn* was hit in her fore part but was able to steam stern first. The Germans also sank a steamer forced by engine trouble to anchor just outside of the Downs and shelled Ramsgate and Broadstairs. Bacon complained anew of the advantage the Germans had in being able to choose their moment and then fire a torpedo at anything they saw before escaping.[43]

There was apparently a certain tension on the German side between the requirements of Scheer for destroyers to support operations in the Bight and the demands of Flanders for destroyers to support the guerrilla war against the cross-Channel barrage. The dual control of the flotillas also produced problems. The Third Flotilla arrived at Zeebrugge on 23 March, and the Sixth Flotilla returned to the

Helgoland Bight at the end of the month. Scheer considered the Sixth Flotilla as necessary to support the High Sea Fleet's operations in the Helgoland Bight, which at that moment consisted largely of supporting the operations of the *Sperrbrechers* ("mine bumpers" or "barrier breakers") and minesweepers in keeping the *Wege* open for the U-boats passing in and out of the North Sea bases. The Third Flotilla was now stationed permanently in Flanders with its commander, Fregattenkapitän Kahle, serving as F.d.T. (*Führer der Torpedoboote*) Flandern, and Korvettenkapitän Albrecht's Flanders destroyers were raised to full flotilla status and Korvettenkapitän Assmann's Flanders Torpedo Boat Flotilla was similarly reinforced. Assmann's smaller torpedo boats, although less prominent in the raids, had been able to claim success in largely clearing the old Belgian coast barrage by the beginning of 1917.[44]

The German forces in Flanders now numbered 24 to 25 destroyers supported by 14 to 15 torpedo boats. They were in a position to wage a troublesome, but not likely to be decisive, guerrilla war against the British in the Straits of Dover. The Germans launched a raid on the night of 20–21 April and came up short. They attempted a novel form of direction to solve the problem of command and control on a dark night. Kahle, the F.d.T. Flandern, directed the operation from German headquarters at Bruges where he could gather German and whatever British wireless intercepts that could be deciphered, collate them, and issue the appropriate orders. The 12 German destroyers, launched 1915–16, were new, 34-knot, 824- to 960-ton craft armed with 3.4- or 4.1-inch guns. They were divided into two distinct groups, one to operate on the Dover and the other the Calais side. The German orders called for an attack on the barrage patrol and, failing this, a vigorous bombardment of Dover and Calais. Room 40 and other intelligence sources apparently failed to provide any advance warning of the German move, and that night there was only the normal night patrol of the destroyer leaders *Broke* (1,794 tons) and *Swift* (2,207 tons) on the Dover side and four destroyers on the Calais side. The Germans bombarded first Calais and then Dover. The *Swift* and *Broke* engaged the Germans, who had bombarded the latter. In the ensuing mélée the *Swift* torpedoed *G.85* and the *Broke* rammed *G.42* and, with the two ships temporarily locked, fought to repel German boarders in a hand-to-hand action reminiscent of an earlier age. The two British leaders were badly damaged, the *Broke* had to be towed back to port, but the two German destroyers were sunk. The *Broke*'s captain, Commander E. R. G. R. Evans, caught the imagination of the British public and was henceforth known as "Evans of the *Broke*." The run of German success in the Strait was ended and they refrained from raiding the cross-Channel barrage for ten months.[45]

The German destroyer raids in the Straits of Dover had a dual objective: to damage the barrage and facilitate the passage of U-boats, and to disturb communications between England and France. The raids were hazardous and the Germans depended on surprise, darkness, and speed to escape potentially overwhelming forces. The Germans failed to seriously disturb communications, and in waging a war of attrition against the patrols guarding the cross-Channel barrage they were really attacking, and the British defending, an obstruction that at the time had little real value. The barrage had been extended to the Snouw Bank off Dunkirk in February, but the great tidal pressure restricted the nets to only 40 to 60 feet in depth. There were also three lines of moored mines a half-mile to the west of the nets, with secret gaps for patrols, which were changed periodically. Unfortunately the mine nets (with two electro-contact mines in each net) proved to be difficult to maintain in Channel conditions, whereas the moored mines dragged their moorings and fouled the nets. They became so hazardous for the patrols that from May to June the entire western portion of the barrage had to be lifted, swept, and relaid with stronger moorings southwest of their original position. The U-boats may have been bothered less than the patrols. They were normally able to cross the net barrage during the hours of darkness by drifting over the nets at high tide. If they were unlucky enough to foul a net, they were usually able to break through without exploding a mine. It is estimated that from January to November of 1917 only one U-boat out of the six sunk in the Dover Strait area was actually sunk by a mine during the 253 passages through the barrage.[46]

In the latter part of April it was obvious the British would have to find some method of stopping their huge shipping losses. There was always the possibility of another "offensive" action—a direct assault on the Flanders submarine bases themselves. The Dover Patrol had conducted periodic bombardments with big-gun monitors of the German-held coast since the beginning of the war. The Germans had expended considerable effort in fortifying this area, making it one of the most heavily defended zones in the world, and the coastal bombardments had become dangerous for the navy. Bacon's bombardments of Zeebrugge in the spring of 1917 were an attempt to destroy or damage the lock gates of the canal to Bruges, thus bottling up the U-boats. The Zeebrugge bombardment was followed by a bombardment of one of the dockyards and workshops at Ostend. The attempts were not successful.[47]

Jellicoe's pessimism over the submarine war helped make the capture of the Flanders submarine bases one of the most important initial objectives of the British army's offensive in the summer of 1917. Jellicoe was convinced that "a naval bombardment alone will never turn the Hun out of Zeebrugge and Ostend." Even if the bombardment succeeded in destroying the workshops at both ports, the Germans would only have been driven up to Bruges where the navy could not get at them.[48] Jellicoe's insistence on Haig's offensive, which ended in the horrendous losses and futility of the Third Ypres (or Passchendaele) battles, undoubtedly earned him the ill will of the prime minister. Lloyd George was much more attracted to the idea of the bombardment than to a costly land offensive. Admiral Bacon also had developed a scheme for a landing near Westende on the Belgian coast by means of huge pontoons pushed by monitors. The objective was to turn the German flank from the sea, but the plan was stillborn when the army failed to advance far enough.[49] Perhaps this was fortunate. The slow-moving monitors and huge pontoons would have made easy targets, and the Germans were confident they could defeat a landing from the sea.[50] However, these problematical operations were in the future and would do nothing immediately to stop the hemorrhaging from submarine losses at sea. Furthermore, even if the Allies were successful, the

Flanders U-boats accounted for only a portion of the Allied sinkings, and their bases could have been shifted back to the German coast.[51]

Zeebrugge and Ostend remained attractive targets, but the dramatic attack on them did not take place until the following year (see chapter 13). By then the Admiralty had stumbled on the most effective counter to the submarine, the general convoy system. It was not a new idea, convoy was actually a very old and traditional idea, but the Admiralty for a variety of reasons resisted its widespread introduction for a long time.[52]

THE CONVOY SYSTEM

The Admiralty were finally driven in desperation to the introduction of convoys at the end of April. There were actually a series of preliminary experimental and small convoy systems instituted before the oceanic convoys that eventually frustrated the submarine campaign. These were the Dutch, the French coal trade, and the Scandinavian convoys. The little-known Dutch convoys on the Hook of Holland route were the first. They were more in response to the threat from German surface flotillas than the submarine danger. The Dutch route was vulnerable to sudden dashes from either the Bight or Zeebrugge on its flank, such as the one resulting in the capture of the *Brussels* and Captain Fryatt in June 1916 (see chapter 10). The first Dutch convoy sailed on 26 July 1916, and for the remainder of the war British vessels going to and from Holland proceeded simultaneously in convoys of four to nine ships at intervals of two to three days. Tyrwhitt's Harwich Force was responsible for the convoy's protection and referred to them as the "Beef Trip" after an agreement with the Dutch that supposedly diverted Dutch foodstuffs from Germany to England. They became, according to Tyrwhitt's biographer, "a principal—and often blasphemously execrated—activity of the Harwich Force."[53] The details of protection changed, but the convoys were extremely successful, despite the fact the route had German submarine and destroyer bases on both flanks. The British lost only one escorted ship—a straggler, which was captured—in the interval between the introduction of the convoys and unrestricted submarine warfare.[54] Afterwards there were only 6 losses in convoy out of a total of 1,861 sailings, or a loss of .32 percent. Moreover, the losses were all prior to the introduction of a close formation in June 1917, in place of the long straggling columns that had been the rule up to then.[55]

A skeptic might argue that the Beef Trips represented too small a portion of the volume of British and Allied trade and the conditions too restricted for these convoys to be a true test of the system. The French coal trade convoys represented a truer precedent for the general system of convoy. The French coal trade convoys were a response to the heavy losses inflicted on the colliers carrying British coal to France during the last quarter of 1916. Roughly half the colliers were neutral ships, largely Norwegian, which could not be detained if they wished to sail and had not received the special warnings or routings provided to British and Allied vessels. The French were heavily dependent on the British for coal, and the detention of British and Allied colliers when submarines threatened the route was tantamount to a successful German blockade. A special representative sent by the chief of the French naval staff to London pointed out on 2 January that these detentions represented an effective blockade for 30 to 40 percent of the last two months of 1916. The French presented a detailed plan for convoys based on an apparently meticulous study by the French naval staff of statistical data pertaining to the coal trade. The Admiralty balked at the term *convoy*, which they considered might embarrass neutrals, and proposed substituting the term *controlled sailing*. They apparently feared the word *convoy* might represent protection and that the Germans might respond by sinking all neutral shipping on sight, a threat that might paralyze sailings to Scandinavia. Nevertheless, the First Sea Lord approved the arrangements on 22 January, and the first convoy sailed from Mount's Bay to Brest on 10 February. There were three routes: Mount's Bay to Brest, Weymouth to Cherbourg, and Weymouth to Le Havre. There was also a fourth very short route from Southend to Boulogne and Calais. The crossings were made every twenty-four hours, and the slow colliers proceeded either in groups steaming in rough formations without direct escort but following special routes assigned by the Admiralty or under direct escort by armed trawlers of the auxiliary patrol. The escorts were weak; in the first quarter of 1917 fewer than 30 trawlers protected more than 4,000 crossings. The results were startlingly successful: from March to May 1917 only 9 of the 4,016 ships convoyed were lost. The entire loss in convoys on the four French coal trade routes during the war was only 53 out of 39,352 sailings, or .13 percent.[56]

The heavy losses suffered in 1916 by Norwegian shipping trading on behalf of the Allies on the Scandinavian routes led the *Norges Rederforbund*—the Norwegian shipowners association—to ask the Admiralty in September for some form of relief. They had been prompted by their insurers and were supported by the British Board of Trade. The Admiralty balked at the idea of convoys or any special forms of protection, and by mid-November Norwegian crews were threatening to refuse to sail without more effective protection. There was seemingly endless discussion between the Admiralty, the Foreign Office, and the Board of Trade, and the Admiralty answered criticism by pointing out that routing and patrol was complicated by the dictates of Norwegian neutrality and British men-of-war could not enter Norwegian ports. Admiral Oliver, the chief of staff, peevishly remarked: "It had never been contemplated that we should have a big enough Navy to protect the whole of the world's commerce." After apparently interminable discussion, and under the threat of the resumption of unrestricted submarine warfare, the British finally adopted a scheme whereby vessels on the Bergen-Lerwick (Shetland Islands) route covered as much as possible of the journey during the hours of darkness and armed trawlers escorted them on the so-called daylight stretch from a rendezvous approximately 50 miles from Lerwick.

The absolute and ruthless nature of the German declaration of blockade may have helped to resolve the problem, for it removed from the Norwegians the last vestiges of protection their neutrality might have given them, and they gave up their scruples against accepting British orders in regard to routes. The British government also agreed to take over the reinsurance of all Norwegian steamers carrying contraband for the Allies in the war zone. The first British steamer to be escorted left Lerwick on 29 January, and the first Norwegian left on 10 February. The first convoy to be escorted through the 50-mile "daylight stretch" consisted of one British and eight Norwegian steamers and sailed on 24 February, but convoys remained a temporary measure in February and March when vessels were escorted singly or in pairs.[57]

Norwegian shipping in the North Sea was hard hit by unrestricted submarine warfare in March when twenty-seven Norwegian ships were lost. The Norwegians lost confidence in the Shetlands-Norway route; they complained they never saw a British warship except near the naval ports. Moreover, German submarines were active off the east coast of Scotland, and the Norwegians considered the stretch from Lerwick to Peterhead as even more dangerous. The British also had intercepted German wireless messages from Bruges to U-boats reporting the departure of Norwegian shipping from Bergen. Once again driven by the crisis, Vice Admiral Sir Frederick Brock, Admiral Orkneys and Shetlands, called a conference at Longhope in Scapa Flow. The first meeting on 30 March considered local measures for protection of traffic between the Shetlands and Norway. Certain specific rendezvous were established and would be changed at intervals of three to ten days. Eastbound traffic from Lerwick would be escorted to the rendezvous, then dispersed so as to arrive on the Norwegian coast at daylight. Westbound traffic would leave the Norwegian coast daily so as to arrive at the rendezvous at 6:00 A.M. where they would be met by an escort to bring them into Lerwick. On 4 April a second conference at Longhope unanimously recommended a system of convoy from Lerwick to the south along the east coast of Scotland. Beatty, now commander in chief of the Grand Fleet, approved with the observation that as it was impossible to provide an escort for each individual vessel, the only alternative would be a system of convoys.[58]

Something had to be done, for the Bergen-Lerwick route was suffering heavy losses. Between the 10th and 15th of April, *U.30* sank nine ships between the Norwegian coast and the rendezvous, or in the vicinity of the rendezvous for the "daylight stretch" escort into Lerwick. The Admiralty approved the proposals of the Longhope conference on 24 April, although Oliver still doubted they would be successful, as in his opinion convoys invited torpedo attack and the available escorts were too few. The convoys sailed south from Lerwick and north from Immingham on three days out of four. The first southbound convoy left Lerwick on 29 April.[59] By the time the Scandinavian and east-coast convoys went into effect, the issue of local convoys, which the Admiralty regarded as experimental, had merged into the larger question of a general system of oceanic convoys to protect the great majority of trade coming into the British Isles from the rest of the world. At this point it would help to examine exactly why it was so difficult to institute a system of defense of trade, which had worked so well in preceding centuries.

The First Sea Lord in November 1916, Admiral Sir Henry Jackson, and the chief of the war staff, Admiral Oliver, had rejected the idea of convoy when it was mentioned in the War Committee on the grounds that convoys had only been successful when it had been possible to allocate a separate escort for each vessel. Convoys also presented too big a target and it would not be possible to keep merchant ships together. In the opinion of

Jackson and Oliver, the fitting of merchant ships with defensive armament offered the most effective means of protection. Oliver also was inclined to believe, as he has already been quoted in regard to Norwegian shipping, that however necessary and effective escorts might have been for troopships and special cargoes or under certain circumstances, it was simply impracticable to attempt to use them for the maritime trade of the entire world. Many naval officers were loath to employ warships merely to convoy trade when, in their opinion, their proper function was offensive, that is, attacking and combating enemy warships. The popularity of so-called hunting flotillas was the result.[60]

One would have thought that the experience of the war might have changed this view, but at the beginning of 1917 it had not. In January 1917 the War Staff issued a paper entitled "Remarks on Submarine Warfare," which concluded that the system of sailing ships in company as a convoy was not recommended in any area where submarine attack was a possibility. The larger the number of ships forming a convoy, the greater the chance that a submarine would be able to deliver a successful attack and the harder the task of an escort in preventing that attack. It was also preferable for a defensively armed merchant ship to sail singly rather than be placed in a convoy with other ships. A submarine also might be able to remain at a distance and fire a torpedo into the middle of a convoy with a good chance of success. The War Staff at the end of January delineated specific reasons for rejecting the idea of convoy: it would be impracticable to supply the numbers of escorts convoys would require; it would be difficult for convoys to meet at a rendezvous; there was danger of attack while convoys were assembling; numbers in a convoy would have to be limited or they would have to sacrifice the protection of zigzagging; it was difficult to form convoys of equal speed; it would be disadvantageous to sail faster ships with slower ones; congestion at ports would result when numbers of ships arrived at the same time, which would result in a decrease of available tonnage; there would be increased risk from mines; and masters would not be able to maintain station in convoy. In the words of the study made by Lieutenant Commander Waters of the Naval Historical Section after the Second World War, "Not one of these objections was valid."[61]

The objection to convoy was not confined to naval circles. The merchant marine held similar views. A special meeting of ten masters of merchant ships was convened at the Admiralty on 23 February. These presumably highly experienced mariners were firmly of the opinion that they would prefer to sail alone rather than in company or under convoy. They also expressed doubts about the ability of merchant ships to keep station, for they considered the officers left in the merchant marine as not sufficiently reliable, and the poor quality of coal some complained of receiving caused additional difficulties in keeping a regular speed.[62] The ten masters also doubted that more than two ships could usefully sail in company and support each other, a conclusion the postwar staff study rightfully pointed out ignored the large imperial convoys at the beginning of the war.[63] Nevertheless, naval and mercantile officers seemed united, or as Admiral Duff wrote: "The more experienced the Officer the more damning was the opinion expressed against mercantile convoy."[64]

A NAVAL HISTORY OF WORLD WAR I

The belief that there would be insufficient escorts available was a very real obstacle to the introduction of a general convoy system. In the early part of 1917, Jellicoe claimed they "had nothing approaching a sufficient number of cruisers, or vessels of any other type" to bring convoys from Canadian waters to the edge of the submarine zone, and they could not provide the necessary escort of fast vessels to bring the convoy through the submarine zone. Moreover, before the United States entered the war, they could not use American ports as points of assembly for convoys, although it is not clear why Canadian or West Indian ports, or even Bermuda, could not have been substituted. Jellicoe summed up his own attitude: "We could not possibly produce the necessary escort vessels; and, that until this difficulty was overcome we should have to postpone the introduction of a convoy system."[65]

This attitude was due to what turned out to be a gross overestimation of the number of escorts required. It was partially based on the false assumption that escorts would have to equal the number of ships escorted, and an exaggerated idea of the number of ships that would have to be protected. The latter was caused by returns supplied by the customs authorities on the number of arrivals and departures from British ports each week. The figures were published in conjunction with the weekly shipping losses, and the higher the number of movements the more encouraging to morale, because it could then be demonstrated that submarine losses were only a small percentage of total movements. Unfortunately the statistics included the same ship as a separate arrival and departure, even when it was engaged in coastal traffic or cross-Channel voyages. The results were misleading, for the statistics tended to give equal weight to small coasters on short hauls and large freighters engaged in ocean voyages. The number of oceanic voyages that had to be protected was much smaller and therefore a much more manageable problem than the Admiralty had anticipated.

The situation was supposedly discovered by Commander R. G. H. Henderson, who organized the French coal trade controlled sailings in the Anti-Submarine Division at the Admiralty, and who contacted the Ministry of Shipping for figures the Admiralty had been unable to provide. The misleading statistics seemed to indicate more than 2,400 arrivals per week and more than 300 ships requiring convoy per day. The actual number of oceangoing ships arriving from the North and South Atlantic per week was only about 120 to 140 and approximately 20 per day. This meant that the organization of convoys for this traffic was a much more practical proposition than the Admiralty had believed. The Admiralty actually had more realistic figures on hand. In December of 1916, Jellicoe had considered convoys for the North Atlantic when the German raider *Möwe* was at large. The Trade Division of the Admiralty had then prepared a study of the daily number of British ships en route in the North Atlantic.[66]

This left the question of escorts as the major obstacle to introducing a general system of convoys. There were really two types of escorts needed. Ocean escorts were needed to accompany the convoy on the high seas; smaller escorts were necessary to bring the convoys through the submarine danger zone around the British Isles. The ocean escorts were probably easier to find than the destroyers or sloops. Old cruisers, battleships, and even armed merchant cruisers were well suited for the work. Destroyers were the critical issue. The numbers cited by different authorities naturally vary. According to the naval staff study, on 31 March the British in ports around the United Kingdom had 311 destroyers of all classes completing or in service, of which 62 (20 percent) were refitting or under repair. About one-third of these destroyers—107— belonged to the Grand Fleet. However, 13 were under refit or repair and 15 had been detached to other ports, notably Devonport (4), Queenstown (4), Harwich (6), and Portsmouth (1). Beatty therefore had only 79 destroyers actually available for work with the fleet. The dreadnoughts could not sail without their indispensable destroyer screen, and if any more destroyers were taken from the Grand Fleet, it might have to sail without some of its forces in the event the High Sea Fleet sought battle. The Germans were apparently placing all their hopes on the submarine campaign, but there was, of course, no guarantee the Germans would not come out. The weight of the High Sea Fleet as a fleet-in-being was evident in this passive contribution to the submarine campaign.

Of the remaining destroyers, 36 were used for local defense only and were considered too old for convoy work. The 36 destroyers assigned to Harwich and the 40 assigned to Dover could not safely be reduced because of their many and varied duties, the threat of German destroyer raids, and the necessity of securing the lines of communication with the armies in France. There were 12 to 20 destroyers at Portsmouth already engaged, for the most part, in escorting cross-Channel traffic. After 24 April the 27 destroyers at the Humber and Forth were assigned to the Scandinavian convoy. This brought the number of available destroyers down to about 42, of which 4 were completing and 8 assigned to the submarine flotillas.

Numbers are always tricky to interpret, and some destroyers, such as the 29 in the two flotillas at Devonport, were already engaged in quasi-convoy work. It might be better to turn the problem around and ask how many destroyers the Admiralty considered necessary for a convoy system. In a memorandum of 26 April advocating the establishment of a convoy system for traffic coming from the North and South Atlantic, Admiral Duff determined a total of 45 destroyers were needed. He quickly revised this figure to 72, and this seems to have been the total generally considered as necessary. The destroyers were to be divided between Lough Swilly, Queenstown, and Brest or Devonport. There were 11 destroyers (including 7 lent by the Grand Fleet) of the 72 required presently at these ports, leaving 61 to be provided. However, the 29 destroyers of the Second and Fourth Flotillas at Devonport were already engaged on quasi-convoy work and could easily be switched to the new system. This reduced the number of additional destroyers to be found to a seemingly intractable 32.[67]

The most likely potential source was the U.S. Navy. Would the Americans cooperate? The United States had declared war on Germany on 6 April. The Germans, in Machiavellian fashion, tried to maintain the fiction that they were not at war with the United States, and U-boat commanders were ordered not to attack American warships for the time being. The somewhat questionable rationale was to avoid inflaming American opinion and to give pro-German or isolationist forces, presumably strong in the Midwest, time to assert themselves. There was no immediate German intention to carry the war to the American coast. The kaiser himself rejected suggestions along this line, and it was only on 22 May that the Admiralstab authorized attacks on American shipping in the blockade zone around the British Isles.[68]

The Americans, of course, could not know this. At the time diplomatic relations with Germany were broken off, the U.S. Navy had no real plan for war against Germany when the United States was on the side of the Entente. The Americans had only the old "Plan Black," drawn up at the Naval War College for the contingency the United States was at war with Germany alone (with Britain neutral) and the Germans attacked the Panama Canal and sought to grab territory in Latin America.[69] Plan Black had little relation to the reality of 1917. The question of coast defense was also very much on the minds of the Americans, and it was only natural that they should be concerned with the defense of the Americas. Moreover, it should not be forgotten that the battle squadrons of the United States fleet would be as hampered as the Grand Fleet by the lack of an adequate destroyer screen. Would the Americans really weaken the potential ability of their battle fleet by sending the precious destroyers across the Atlantic to the waters around Great Britain?

As the United States moved inexorably toward the declaration of war on Germany, President Wilson authorized the navy to establish contact with the Admiralty in order to discuss potential cooperation. The navy chose Rear Admiral William Sowden Sims, then president of the Naval War College. The choice was an excellent one, for the Canadian-born Sims had the reputation of being an Anglophile,[70] knew Jellicoe from prewar days, had been naval attaché in Paris and St. Petersburg at the end of the nineteenth century, was well suited by temperament to cooperate with officers of different nationalities, and lacked that certain prickliness toward the British that could then be found in the American navy. The potential for friction was always there, given the history of the U.S. Navy, which began its life fighting the British and which was still regarded as somewhat junior to the larger and more experienced Royal Navy with a consequent need to assert itself. There was a tendency for American civilians and naval officers, including President Wilson and Admiral William Shepherd Benson, chief of naval operations, to believe the British had wasted their large naval superiority against Germany, had not employed their forces correctly, and were too "defensive" and not imaginative enough in their tactics. Wilson on more than one occasion spoke of wiping out the "hornets' nests" rather than chasing individual hornets, implying that the German submarine bases themselves should be attacked.[71] His British ally Prime Minister Lloyd George shared at least some of these sentiments, but the American leaders were far from the scene and had less opportunity for their optimistic illusions to be shattered by the realities of modern war.

Sims proved to be the right man in the right place at the right time, but he always had to guard against the impression that he was too much under the thumb of the British. There was perhaps a natural tension between Benson and Sims, which has been compared to the differing outlook of the field commander and the chief of staff (who must take the bigger picture into account). Benson certainly had no inherent love of the British and reportedly told Sims before he sailed, "Don't let the British pull the wool over your eyes. It is none of our business pulling their chestnuts out of the fire. We would as soon fight the British as the Germans."[72] Benson was concerned with what he considered the big picture, and was apparently worried over a situation in which the British and French would be compelled to make peace, leaving the United States to fight a triumphant Germany, perhaps joined by Japan, alone. These considerations influenced his policy on questions involving keeping the U.S. Fleet intact and maintaining the building program of large ships rather than shifting construction priorities to antisubmarine craft. The United States would always need to have a balanced fleet to face all future eventualities, not just the immediate threat of German submarines.[73] Anglo-American cooperation was not something that would happen automatically, British and American interests could easily diverge, but in the long run it was as successful as the most optimistic might have imagined in those dark days of April 1917.

On the evening of 31 March, Sims, accompanied only by his aide, Commander J. V. Babcock, sailed under a false name (wearing civilian clothes) in the American line's *New York* (10,508 tons). The *New York* reached Liverpool on 9 April, and as she neared the harbor she ran onto a mine laid by *UC.65*. The liner was not seriously damaged, but the passengers were transferred to lifeboats as a precautionary measure and then brought into Liverpool by the packet arriving from the Isle of Man. It was a vivid introduction for Sims to the dangers of submarine warfare. The Admiralty had arranged for a special train to carry Sims to London, where he conferred with Jellicoe on the 10th.[74] In the meantime the Allied governments also had arranged for Vice Admiral Sir Montague Browning, commander in chief North America and West Indies, and his French counterpart, Contre-Amiral Grasset, to visit Hampton Roads and Washington on 10 and 11 April to confer with the Americans.[75]

When Sims reached the Admiralty he quickly discovered the difference between the published version of the war and the real situation. Like most American naval officers he had followed the war from the press and what official information was available in the United States, and confidently assumed the Admiralty had matters well in hand. He now discovered:

Yet a few days spent in London clearly showed that all this confidence in the defeat of the Germans rested upon a misapprehension. The Germans, it now appeared, were not losing the war—they were winning it. The British Admiralty now placed before the American representative facts and figures which it had not given to the British press. These documents disclosed the astounding fact that, unless the appalling destruction of merchant tonnage which was then taking place could be materially checked, the unconditional surrender of the British Empire would inevitably take place within a few months.[76]

Jellicoe had been candid with Sims about the gravity of the situation, and Sims did not mince words in his first cable to Washington on the 14th. He recommended that the maximum number of American destroyers be sent, accompanied by small antisubmarine craft, repair ships, and staff for a base. The destroyers were to be based at Queenstown and patrol to the west of Ireland. He urged the maximum increase of merchant tonnage and a continuous augmentation of the advanced force of antisubmarine craft. Sims pointed out that under present circumstances the American battleships could serve little purpose and minimized the dangers of German submarine activity in the Western Hemisphere as anything more than raids to cause diversion of antisubmarine forces and influence public opinion. Sims followed his first cable with a series of similar messages and was fully supported by the American ambassador Walter Hines Page, who on 27 April asked for the immediate dispatch of thirty or more destroyers and concluded his cable to the State Department with the statement there was no time to be lost.[77]

On 13 April Commander Joseph K. Taussig, commander of the Eighth Division, Destroyer Force, Atlantic Fleet, was ordered to prepare his six destroyers for "special service." Taussig's flagship, the *Wadsworth*, and the other destroyers of the division sailed from Boston on the 24th with the mission "to assist naval operations of Entente Powers in every way possible." The 1,100-ton destroyers were among the newest in the navy. The first tangible American naval assistance to the Allies arrived at Queenstown on 4 May and received a warm reception. The historic moment was immortalized in the painting by Bernard Gribble, evocatively titled *The Return of the "Mayflower."* The American destroyers were placed under the command of Vice Admiral Sir Lewis Bayly, commander in chief, coast of Ireland. "Luigi" Bayly had the reputation of being somewhat crusty, and in 1914 had been relieved of his command under a cloud after the loss of the battleship *Formidable* (see chapter 2). He had a chance to redeem himself, and, perhaps somewhat to the surprise of many, worked well with the Americans. It was another case of the right man in the right place at the right time.[78] Commander Taussig undoubtedly helped matters with his first impression. Destroyers were then a notoriously cantankerous type, requiring a great deal of tinkering. The six American destroyers had taken a pounding crossing the Atlantic and had a long list of defects. Nevertheless, when Bayly asked when they would be ready for sea, Taussig made the reply in which destroyermen have taken pride ever since: "We are ready now, sir, that is as soon as we finish refueling. Of course you know how destroyers are—always wanting something done to them. But this is war, and we are ready to make the best of things and go to sea immediately." Bayly gave them four days.[79]

The arrival of the destroyers might have been a happy moment, but they were only 6 and a small portion of the estimated 51 available to the United States. Sims was alarmed when he failed to hear more were on the way, and on 28 April cabled that "we can not send too soon or too many." He was relieved to learn on 3 May that the United States intended to eventually send 36 destroyers. The first six American destroyers sailed on their first patrol on the afternoon of 8 May. In the course of May, another two divisions of destroyers arrived, followed ten days later by a division of six 750-ton destroyers. The tenders *Dixie* and *Melville* also arrived to support the destroyers, and by the end of June there were 28 American destroyers at Queenstown—35 at the end of August. At first they were employed on patrols rather than on convoy duty, perhaps escorting a single merchant ship through their assigned sector and hoping that at the least they were succeeding in keeping submarines down and preventing them from getting into an advantageous position to launch their torpedoes.[80]

By the time the first contingent of American destroyers arrived at Queenstown, Jellicoe and the Admiralty had been driven by the pressure of events to make the important decision to adopt a general system of convoys. The idea had been steadily gaining strength and converts. On 11 February Sir Maurice Hankey, the influential secretary of the War Cabinet, prepared a memorandum, "Some Suggestions for Anti-Submarine Warfare," for Lloyd George on the advantages of the convoy system. It is quite likely that Hankey acted on information supplied by Commander Henderson, possibly in conjunction with Norman Leslie of the Ministry of Shipping, who acted as liaison with the Admiralty. The two had discovered the fallacy of the Admiralty statistics that had been used to argue against convoys. Henderson may well have acted outside of regular channels and behind the backs of his superiors at the Admiralty in order to get something done.[81]

The prime minister; Hankey; Sir Edward Carson, the first lord; Jellicoe; and Duff discussed these ideas at breakfast on the 13th, but there were no immediate results. Lloyd George was probably preoccupied with the press of other business and perhaps not yet ready for a serious dispute with the Admiralty. The horrendous losses of April changed the situation. On 25 April the War Cabinet concluded that the prime minister should investigate all the means used at present in antisubmarine warfare on the grounds there was not sufficient coordination in present efforts. The Admiralty moved in a similar direction, and on 26 April Admiral Duff, head of the Anti-Submarine Division, submitted a minute in favor of convoying all vessels bound from the North and South Atlantic to the United Kingdom. Jellicoe approved the following day and also recommended to the first lord that the British expeditionary force at Salonika be withdrawn. This would reduce the need for escorts in the Mediterranean and would be an important means of providing sufficient escorts for convoys. The crucial decision concerning convoys had therefore been made before Lloyd George made his celebrated visit to the Admiralty on 30 April, and was not, as is sometimes stated, something he forced on a reluctant Admiralty that day.[82]

The first trial convoy sailed from Gibraltar the evening of 10 May. It consisted of 16 ships arranged in three columns escorted by the Q-ships *Mavis* and *Rule*. Three armed yachts escorted the convoy through the danger zone to 11° W. The station keeping about which the Admiralty had such anxiety was reported as "on the whole satisfactory." There were some problems; the convoy turned up 20 miles west of its rendezvous with the destroyers sent from Devonport and their meeting was delayed eight hours. There were, however, no submarine attacks. The five ships bound for the west coast were detached off the Scillies with an escort of two destroyers. The remainder of the convoy proceeded to Plymouth on the 20th and then proceeded up the Channel in three divisions, escorted by twenty-four drifters that met them off Poole. The convoy reached the Downs safely on the 22d. The naval staff study declared: "The trial had been an entire success, and from that moment it may be said that the submarine menace was conquered."[83]

This may have been true in the long run, but the convoy system took time to establish, and things were not always so clear to those involved. Sims became a hearty supporter of the concept, but Admiral Benson and the U.S. Navy Department remained skeptical, and the Americans denied an Admiralty request to form a convoy of 16 to 20 ships sailing from Hampton Roads to be escorted by one of the groups of American destroyers on their way to Queenstown. The Navy Department did not consider such a large number of ships in convoy to be practicable and recommended groups of no more than four. The destroyers sailed separately. Almost a month later, Sims received a cable from the Navy Department stating that they considered American vessels having armed guards were safer when sailing independently than when in convoy.[84]

The U.S. Navy Department was slow to learn. The first trial convoy of twelve ships sailed from Hampton Roads on 24 May escorted by the British armored cruiser *Roxburgh*. On the evening of 6 June on the other side of the ocean it was met at 50° N, 16° W by eight destroyers from Devonport. The convoy separated into west and east coast sections south of Ireland, and by the 10th all ships had arrived safely at their destinations. Unfortunately two ships had been compelled to drop out because they were unable to maintain the required speed, and one of them was torpedoed and sunk.[85] As for the convoy as a whole, the *Roxburgh*'s captain reported the merchant captains had been attentive to signals, kept good station, and zigzagged in a satisfactory fashion, and he would be prepared to escort as many as thirty ships instead of twelve.[86]

The convoy system grew out of the deliberations of a convoy committee nominated on 15 May to devise a program. The committee's report of 6 June resulted in the formation of a separate Convoy Section at the Admiralty with Fleet Paymaster H. W. E. Manisty appointed as "organising manager of convoys." The Convoy Section would work in close liaison with the Ministry of Shipping and with the Intelligence Division. The latter was particularly important, and there was now some loosening of the great secrecy that had surrounded the work of Room 40 and that may have cost the British a decisive victory the morning after Jutland the year before. Previously, information derived from Room 40's intercepts could not even be plotted on the charts of the enemy submarine section of the Intelligence Division. Now, however, a pneumatic tube connected the enemy submarine section and direction-finding sections with the convoy section, and the information derived from intercepts and directionals could be plotted on the convoy chart so that the latest intelligence on the location of submarines could be compared to the convoy track and, if necessary, the convoy could be diverted by means of a wireless message to the convoy commodore's ship. All convoy commodores were now in ships equipped with wireless.

The use of wireless for diversions was a great improvement over the routing systems used in the past. In the judgment of the naval staff study, "Part of the undoubted efficacy of convoy lay in the simplicity of 'Carrington's Chart.'" The latter referred to Commander John Carrington, who kept the 7-foot-high convoy chart hung on the west wall of the drawing room of Admiralty House. Three navigating lieutenants kept a constant watch on it, using red flags to indicate today's positions, blue flags yesterday's, and grey flags the day before yesterday's. A thread of red silk represented the position of each convoy.[87]

The system quickly showed results. There were five HH convoys from Hampton Roads in June, each with a single armored cruiser or armed merchant cruiser as ocean escort until the rendezvous with the Devonport destroyers. A total of 71 ships representing 363,170 tons arrived safely. Only one ship was torpedoed in the Channel, and she was salved. No ships were lost.[88] The Admiralty had been forced to institute the HH convoys from Hampton Roads and run successive convoys in June because the stocks of oil fuel for the Grand Fleet had fallen below requirements. There was as a result a pressing need to protect oilers from North America and include as many oilers as possible in these convoys.[89]

Admiral Sims by mid-June had become an eloquent partisan of the convoy system, but the U.S. Navy Department remained hesitant and still regarded arming merchantmen with adequate guns and trained crews a suitable answer to the submarine. Sims countered that this would merely force the U-boats to use torpedoes to sink ships.[90] There would always be a distinct difference between the British and Americans: the British were primarily concerned with protecting the flow of supplies to the United Kingdom; the American emphasis would be on protecting the transport of American troops to France. Josephus Daniels, secretary of the navy, informed Sims at the beginning of July that the "paramount duty" of American destroyers in European waters was the protection of American troop transports and that "everything is secondary" to having a sufficient number of escorts to protect those troops.[91] This position had the potential to become a major controversy in 1918 when American troops were brought across the Atlantic in large numbers. The issue was still minor in July 1917. The Allies had yet to survive the submarine onslaught.

The success of these experimental convoys led the Admiralty on 15 June to institute a regular system of HH convoys sailing from Hampton Roads every four days, bound alternately for the west or east coast of England. The east-coast convoys were met by escorts from Devonport and proceeded around the south coast, whereas the west-coast convoys were met by escorts from Buncrana and proceeded around the north of Ireland. The need for fuel oil was so pressing that whatever their original destination all oilers, if ready when a convoy departed, were included in that convoy. On 22 June and 6 July, respectively, the Admiralty ordered the system extended to vessels sailing from Canadian ports and North American ports, with New York as the point of assembly. The HS convoys sailed from Sydney at intervals of eight days, except from November 1917 to July 1918 when, with the closure of the St. Lawrence in the winter months, the port of assembly was altered to Halifax. The New York convoys were designated HN. Both HS and HN convoys alternated between west and east coasts, although eventually the HN convoys sailed only to the east coast. The U.S. Navy provided cruisers as ocean escorts for the HN convoys, and the American destroyers at Queenstown were switched from their sterile patrols to meet and escort HS and HN convoys bound for the east coast. The other North Atlantic convoys had as ocean escorts either British cruisers or armed merchant cruisers drawn from the Tenth Cruiser Squadron. They were supplemented by commissioned escort ships, which were merchantmen carrying cargo but fitted with three or four 6-inch guns. There was a retired flag officer in each commissioned escort ship, and when in the company of a convoy they wore the white ensign—that is, naval flag—and had the status of a warship.

On 26 July Gibraltar was brought into the system when the first HG convoy sailed, to be followed by regular convoys alternating between the west and east coast at four-day intervals. The escorts that met the HG convoys came from either Falmouth, for the east coast, or Milford Haven for the west coast and were usually trawlers rather than destroyers. The ocean escorts of the Gibraltar convoys were also a mixed bag. They were Q-ships at first, and later small American light cruisers, U.S. Coast Guard revenue cutters, old American gunboats, and, in 1918, a pair of small British light cruisers. The last of the initial system, the South Atlantic convoys, were ordered on 31 July. The HL, or fast, convoys (10 knots or more) assembled at Sierra Leone, whereas the HD, or slow, convoys would assemble at Dakar. The ocean escorts were armed merchant cruisers from the Ninth Cruiser Squadron (West Coast of Africa Station) supplemented by the Tenth Cruiser Squadron.

The system was modified and refined as the war went on. In August 1917 the HX convoys—fast (12½ knots or more) combined troopship and merchant ship convoys for Canadian troops—were introduced using Halifax as the port of assembly. In October and November, the HE and OE "through Mediterranean" convoys were introduced (see chapter 12). The need to transport large numbers of American troops caused further changes in 1918. The minimum speed for ships in the HX convoys was raised to 13 knots (with the ability to steam 13½ knots through the danger zone), and their port of assembly was shifted from Halifax to New York. In return a series of intermediate speed (11½ knot) convoys—designated HC—were instituted from Halifax. Troop convoys such as the HX and HC had either an armored cruiser or old predreadnought battleship as ocean escort. The Americans also reinforced them with a U.S. predreadnought and destroyer. The need to supply American troops in France also led in April 1918 to the introduction of HB convoys between New York and French ports in the Bay of Biscay. French armored cruisers contributed to the ocean escort of these convoys.

It should be noted, however, that with all convoys it was invariably much easier to find ocean escorts than it was to provide the destroyers and other small craft to bring them through the submarine danger zone as they approached the British Isles. Destroyers were the limiting factor, and it is hardly surprising the naval staffs came to consider them as worth their weight in gold. When the needs of the Grand Fleet were added to these considerations, it is little wonder Jellicoe informed the war cabinet in November 1917, "It is not too much to say that the whole of our naval policy is necessarily governed by the adequacy of our destroyer forces."[92]

The size of convoys steadily increased as fears associated with station keeping and the "too many eggs in one basket" argument diminished and confidence in the system grew. The first HH convoy from Hampton Roads had been limited to 12 ships. The limit was increased to 20 by the end of June 1917. In September the Admiralty required special permission for convoys larger than 26 ships, but the limits expanded and soon the Admiralty insisted on special permission only for convoys larger than 36. They tried to keep this as a maximum for convoys to the west coast, which went north around Ireland and into the Irish Channel. The largest Atlantic convoy, HN.73 in June 1918, had 47 ships and was reported to be completely successful.[93]

The convoy system was extended gradually, and the initial emphasis was on homeward-bound vessels. These were the ships carrying vital supplies; the U-boats also had concentrated their attention on them. In the disastrous month of April 1917, 18 percent of homeward-bound ships had been sunk, compared to only 7 percent of those outward bound. This changed after the introduction of convoys. The U-boat command- ers now found convoys hard to find and difficult to attack. The presence of escorts worked against attack on the surface by gunfire, and with the convoy zigzagging it proved difficult to get into a favorable firing position, particularly as those same escorts made maneuvering on the surface dangerous.[94] The outward-bound ships remained, however, much easier targets, and before long losses of outward-bound ships rose steadily. It was obvious that a ship sunk outward bound was as much of a reduction in available tonnage as the loss of a ship bringing cargo to the United Kingdom. On 11 August 1917, the Admiralty arranged for convoys to take outward-bound ships through the submarine danger zone. There were eventually a series of outward convoys that matched the homeward convoys.

But where would the escorts for these outward convoys come from? The Admiralty tried to solve the problem by making the escorts do double duty. That is, the escorts took the outward convoy through the submarine danger zone and at the dispersal point parted company with the convoy, generally at dusk or after dark. They then steamed during the night to a rendezvous with a homeward convoy. Each H convoy therefore had a corresponding O convoy. These arrangements called for precise sched- ules and certainly put a heavy load on the escorts, which instead of merely steaming to meet the homeward convoy now had to spend about two days zigzagging with the outward convoy before the rendezvous. The senior naval officers of the destroyer escort were instructed that in case of delay with the outward convoy, the governing factor must always be meeting the homeward convoy at the correct time and place. It should also be noted that the outward convoys were only convoys through the submarine danger zone. The ships were then dispersed. This was modified in October 1917 when the Falmouth (OF) and Milford (OM) convoys, the east and west coast branches of the Gibraltar convoys, were to be kept together all the way to Gibraltar with any ships bound for the North or South Atlantic being detached en route. The OE/HE "through Mediterranean" convoys were also, as their name implies, kept together after their introduction in the fall of 1917.[95]

The statistics compiled by the Technical History Section at the Admiralty after the war demonstrated that the system worked. The percentage of loss of ships in the homeward Atlantic convoys had been reduced to 1.43 in the weekly return of 8 September 1917, and the loss in the outward convoys had fallen to .88 percent. By the end of the war, there had been 9,250 ships convoyed safely in homeward Atlantic convoys and 104 sunk, giving a loss of 1.11 percent. There had been 7,289 ships convoyed safely in outward convoys and only 50 sunk, for a loss of .68 percent. The combined homeward and outward Atlantic convoy loss was .92 percent, and the preceding figures include 16 ships sunk by marine peril and 36 ships sunk when not actually in contact with the convoy.[96]

These figures refer to convoys, but convoys did not operate everywhere, nor were all ships in convoys. There were also areas where losses were heavier than average, particularly, as we shall see in the following chapter, in the Mediterranean. The German bid for victory was based on the destruction of tonnage, that is, cargo-carrying capacity. Individual ships did not really matter, the tonnage they represented did. How then did the introduction of the convoy system show up in the worldwide shipping losses and in the losses among U-boats themselves? The amount of tonnage sunk throughout the world by submarines had fallen from a peak of 860,334 in April to a still-high 696,725 in June. With convoys in operation, worldwide sinkings fell to 555,514 tons in July, 472,372 tons in August, and 353,602 tons in September. Losses rose to 466,542 tons in October, only to fall to 302,599 tons in November, ending with 411,766 tons in December.[97] The monthly success of U-boats in the last five months of 1917 was therefore well below their success in the first five months after the introduction of unrestricted submarine warfare.

As for U-boat losses, there were 6 in all theaters in July, 5 in August, 10 or 11 (it is not clear whether one of the U-boats was sunk in September or October) in September, 5 or 6 in October, 8 in November, and 8 in December. Mines were or probably were responsible for about 21 to 22 of the 43 U-boat losses. Five of the U-boats had been sunk by escorts.[98] The exchange ratio, the numbers of ships sunk for every U-boat loss, had been as high as 167 in April, and the average was as high as 73 in May, June, and July when the first convoys were being introduced. It fell to only 16 in the six-month period from August 1917 to January 1918. Nevertheless, submarines continued to cause substantial losses, and at the end of the second six months of unrestricted submarine warfare, the total shipping available was still declining. World shipping losses had been roughly 2.25 million tons, of which only somewhat more than 1.5 million tons had been replaced by new building and about a half-million tons of interned German and Austrian shipping, which was seized and brought into Allied service. Admiral Hezlet points out that imports were down 20 percent by the end of 1917 from the preceding year, and that it was only by rigid controls, the exclusion of nonessentials, and strict rationing that the situation was "just kept in hand."[99]

There were other factors that played important roles in frustrating the U-boat campaign. These fall under what Admiral Hezlet termed the "immense skill" with which the Allies eventually organized their shipping and the flexibility of world shipping itself. These considerations included shorter turnarounds and alleviation of congestion in Allied ports, the reduction of imports to essentials, the concentration of ships on the relatively shorter North Atlantic routes as opposed to the longer voyages to South

America and the Far East, and a whole range of measures that cannot be described here but that had the cumulative effect of greatly increasing the efficiency of the declining amount of tonnage available. The measures were supplemented by generally skillful diplomacy, which kept neutral shipping working for the Allies.[100]

It would be an oversimplification of what really happened to assume that when the crisis of April 1917 forced the adoption of the convoy system, the Admiralty staff recognized its error, put every effort into making convoys work, and steadily checked the submarine menace. Unfortunately matters were not so clear to those in authority at the time. The Admiralty appears to have given only reluctant and grudging acceptance to the convoy system in the summer of 1917, even while it was proving itself. A staff officer later reported deletions of favorable remarks about the convoy system from weekly appreciations and a reluctance to start the outward-bound convoys, in the mistaken belief that outward-bound ships were being sunk because escorts had been detached to meet the homeward convoys.[101]

The idea that "offensive" operations ought to be continued along with the merely "defensive" convoys also appears to have died hard. Considerable resources were still devoted to operations aimed at hunting submarines. At the very moment the first homeward convoys were being instituted in June, the Grand Fleet was ordered to mount a grandiose submarine-hunting operation with destroyers and submarines, designated Operation BB. The operation covered a vast area around the north of Scotland divided into five destroyer areas and four submarine areas. The areas were along known routes taken by U-boats, and the timing of the operation was based on Admiralty intelligence that a number of German submarines would be passing through between 15 and 24 June. The objective was to force the U-boats to dive through the areas occupied by destroyers, so they might then be on the surface when passing through the adjacent areas occupied by submarines. Operation BB employed no fewer than 4 flotilla leaders, 49 destroyers—about 34 on patrol each day—and 17 submarines. The operation had priority over all other operations. Admiral Bayly's requests for destroyer reinforcements to meet the incoming convoys from North America were denied. The destroyers represented about 56 percent of the Grand Fleet's destroyers. Beatty wrote his wife that he had denuded himself of all destroyers, submarines, patrol vessels, seaplanes, and airships and that the fleet "is immobilised for the time being." However, he justified it: "It's no use pecking at it and have taken the largest steps I can."[102]

The results of this colossal effort were disappointing. During the eleven days of Operation BB, 12 homeward-bound and 7 outward-bound U-boats proceeded in and out of the North Sea while another 5 were working on the Bergen-Lerwick route. There were probably 15 submarines that passed through the hunting area east of the Shetlands, but after 26 sighting reports and 8 attacks by destroyers and 3 by submarines, the only tangible contact took place in the area east of Fair Island when a torpedo fired by the submarine *K.1* hit the homeward-bound *U.95* but failed to explode. The postwar naval staff study admitted that there was no evidence on the German side to indicate the passage of U-boats had been seriously interrupted.

The British seemed slow to realize the futility of Operation BB. Beatty was optimistic and reported that the operation as regards the actual destruction of submarines was unsuccessful, but indirectly it may have harried the enemy and it undoubtedly prevented heavy losses in shipping on the Lerwick-Bergen route. Beatty recommended that in future operations of this sort a larger number of destroyers should be concentrated in fewer areas. The director of the Anti-Submarine Division at the Admiralty, Captain W. W. Fisher, believed that if the entire force had been concentrated in one area there would have been a definite success and recommended a similar operation when ships and fuel were available. Jellicoe agreed the operation should be repeated when the dispositions of the fleet would permit.[103]

The great problem with an operation like BB in the eyes of the Admiralty staff was that the destroyers had to operate too far away from the fleet. A similar operation was not mounted until October. In the meantime the Grand Fleet executed a much more modest, but interesting, operation. Operation CC took place on 5–9 July when six of the Grand Fleet's destroyers patrolled a suspected German submarine route approximately 60 miles north of Muckle Flugga in the Shetlands. Five of the destroyers were equipped with kite balloons, and with excellent weather and visibility the observers in the balloons sighted a submarine. Unfortunately, despite their best efforts, when the destroyers attempted to hunt the submarine, they could not locate it, and with their fuel running low the force returned to Scapa with nothing but valuable experience in balloon work.[104]

Beatty's frustration at hunting submarines was expressed in a letter to his wife on 7 July:

Our luck has been very bad. Every day we are within an ace of success, sometimes in two & even three places, but they can't quite pull it off. . . .

. . . It is a prodigious job, as it is like looking for a needle in a bundle of hay, and, when you have found it, trying to strike it with another needle. But we must stick to it, and I am sure the answer to the conundrum will be found, and also found quite a simple one. In the meantime it is very disheartening for everyone, who are as keen as mustard, and all do their best.[105]

The major antisubmarine action by the Grand Fleet was designated Operation HS and took place on Admiralty orders when intelligence indicated that an exceptionally large number of German submarines were operating in the Atlantic and that three or four would be returning through the North Sea to their bases about 1–8 October. The general plan was to focus activity in four areas along the assumed homeward track, which extended approximately 300 miles between 59° 30' N and 54° N and 0° 30' E and 4° E. The southernmost area, roughly 150 miles from Harwich, was to be patrolled by destroyers from the Harwich Force. A mine-net barrage was laid in the northern end of the next area to the north, between the latitudes of the Firth of Forth and Flamborough Head. The barrage was patrolled by 16 armed trawlers, equipped with hydrophones, and the senior officer in the armed yacht *Gossia*. The trawlers hoped to edge submarines into the net. There also were 4 destroyers on patrol in the area. The next area to the north, between the latitudes of the Moray Firth and the Firth of Forth, was patrolled by 2 leaders and 14 destroyers from the Grand Fleet along with the armed yacht *Shemara*. The northernmost area was watched by submarines from the Grand Fleet flotillas, 4 on patrol at a time. Operation HS required sizable forces: 42 net drifters, 24 armed trawlers, 21 destroyers, a flotilla leader, and 4 submarines. Moreover, in order to maintain the destroyers and leaders at the required strength, Beatty had to detach 15 to 29 destroyers and leaders, and Harwich contributed 18.

Approximately 22 miles of nets were laid in a somewhat irregular fashion on 1 October. The destroyers and submarines were on patrol, with gaps, from 27 September to 10 October. The destroyers did not see any submarines, and the weather was so bad that at one point the high seas made it dangerous for them to put their helm over. They were forced to shelter at various intervals, and a patrol was only maintained about 10 days out of 15, or 60 percent of the time. The storm-battered trawlers occasionally heard suspicious noises. And there were a number of explosions—some probably mines that had fouled the nets, but some fairly positive contacts that led to depth-charge attacks. The operation ended when the weather damaged the mines and nets to the point where they were no longer a menace to submarines. The DNI later reported three U-boats had been accounted for, citing *U.50, U.66,* and *U.106*. He was only partially correct. These boats had been sunk, but subsequent research has revealed they were sunk farther to the south in other minefields. The Admiralty were encouraged and prepared to effect a similar operation in the spring.[106] Their evaluation was, of course, wrong. Operation HS, like Operation BB a few months before, and despite the persistent efforts of the men in the small ships during the appalling weather, had not been worth the considerable efforts devoted to it.

On the German side, the confidence of the high command began to wane as the date the Admiralstab had confidently predicted would see the collapse of Britain approached. They now began to qualify their former extravagant claims on behalf of unrestricted submarine warfare. In early July Ludendorff declared, in agreement with Holtzendorff, that he was confident of the effect of the submarine campaign but that it was impossible to specify an exact date on which Britain would collapse. When the British would submit was not solely dependent on the U-boat war but to a large degree on the will of the German people to hold out, and the realization this will was unbroken and unshakable. Hindenburg on 19 June advised Chancellor Bethmann Hollweg that he was certain submarines would eventually force the Entente to seek peace, but he could not say exactly when. The common belief the war would be over by the autumn was dangerous, and it was time to enlighten the public of the true situation.[107] The German high command was in danger of becoming a victim of its own propaganda.

The Germans missed the opportunity for a tactical innovation that might have partially offset the advantage the British gained with the convoy system. At the beginning of April the F.d.U. of the High Sea Fleet, Fregattenkapitän Bauer, proposed converting *U.155*, the former merchant submarine *Deutschland*, into a radio command boat in which the F.d.U. or his representative would proceed to the western portion of the blockade zone and by means of experienced wireless personnel analyze intercepted wireless traffic to gain intelligence on the approach of convoys, alterations in their routes, and the movements of antisubmarine escorts. *U.155* would then use its wireless to direct U-boats to advantageous positions. The Admiralstab, however, ordered *U.155* to the Azores.[108] These large submarines proved clumsy to handle, and notwithstanding their great endurance, a disappointment. They could and did carry the war to the coast of North America, the Azores, and the African coast off Dakar, where they encountered less danger from escorts. However, this had to be balanced by the longer passages to and from their station and the smaller amount of traffic they encountered. The restricted number of U-cruisers available was also too small to really spread terror off the American coast. Captain Michelsen, the former commander of submarines, estimated that when the time required by refits was included in their calculations, one would have been able to obtain twice the results in British waters with smaller boats, fewer men, and less expenditure of effort.[109]

The success of the convoy system led the Germans in early October to begin shifting U-boat operations from the Western Approaches to inshore waters in the Irish Sea, English Channel, Bristol Channel, and other coastal waters. Ships continued to sail independently in these waters when bound for either convoy-assembly ports for outward convoys or their home ports after homeward convoys had been dispersed. In the last three months of 1917, 33 percent of the ships lost to U-boats were ships proceeding independently from their port of embarkation to outward-convoy assembly ports, and 40 percent of losses were ships proceeding independently from convoy-dispersal points to their ports of disembarkation. The loss rate for ships sailing independently in coastal waters was estimated to be ten times that of ships in convoys.[110]

The losses forced the British to abandon the outward convoy from Queenstown because of the danger to ships proceeding there through the Irish Sea. They hastened completion of the defenses of Lamlash, which became a port of assembly for ships from Liverpool and the Clyde. However, in 1918, persistent losses to ships proceeding from Liverpool to Lamlash led to convoys being assembled at Liverpool and sailing directly from Liverpool. Lamlash remained merely for Clyde traffic except when the absence of submarine activity in the Irish Sea permitted its use, which would economize on escorts. A system of daylight sailings with "ports of refuge" was also established in 1918 along the south coast for traffic between Folkestone gate and the outward-convoy assembly points at Devonport and Falmouth. As for the east coast, after 20 January 1918, the Scandinavian convoys assembled off Methil in the Firth of Forth and were escorted directly to Norwegian waters.[111] Unfortunately, from January to May only a proportion of shipping on the east coast was in convoy, and the losses were high. From June until the end of the war, the proportion of shipping in convoy was increased until by the end of the war almost all traffic had been included in convoys.[112]

On 22 November 1917, the Germans expanded their prohibited zone, where shipping could be torpedoed without warning, to 30° W in the Atlantic and established a new zone around the Azores. The latter was extended eastward on 11 January 1918, when the Germans also proclaimed a prohibited zone off most of the east coast of North

America and from west of the Cape Verde Islands to Dakar and the west coast of Africa. They wanted to take advantage of the longer range of the U-cruisers to attack shipping off the Azores, which had become an important staging point for traffic to the Mediterranean, where the neutral channel to Greece was also closed. The Germans hoped their extension of the Atlantic zone to 30° W would provide more opportunities for submarines to attack and thin out the protection that could be given by the available escorts.[113]

Would the Germans have enough submarines to make their expanded blockade effective? The realization the war would not end quickly had resulted in orders for an additional 95 U-boats in June 1917, but shortages of labor and material and other production difficulties as well as the recalcitrance of the War Office to give submarine construction the priority the navy demanded made fulfillment of the program slower than desirable. In November Scheer began pressing for the creation of a central authority under the Admiralstab empowered to surmount the difficulties. The normal channels of organization within the past few months had proved insufficient. He argued that the U-boat war had entered a critical stage and the convoy system had restricted German opportunities. Experienced commanders were being lost, new ones could not initially replace them adequately, and the reduction in U-boat effectiveness could only be offset by increasing the numbers of U-boats available for the submarine campaign. The problem was compounded by Ludendorff's refusal on the question of providing labor to go any further than he had promised in the past. The army was finding it difficult to reduce losses in its own labor force, and its armaments program would not be reduced.

To attack some of these problems the U-boat Office was established on 5 December 1917 under Vice Admiral Ritter von Mann, who was directly responsible to the state secretary of the Reichsmarineamt and charged with accelerating production and delivery of submarines. The 1919 program was decided a few days later and represented a sharp increase over the original proposals for 78 boats of all types. There would now be no fewer than 120 U-boats: 36 UB.III class (*UB.170* to *UB.205*), 34 UC.III class (*UC.119* to *UC.152*), 12 Ms class (*U.201* to *U.212*), 18 U-cruisers (*U.183* to *U.200*), and 20 UF class (*UF.1* to *UF.20*). The latter were a new class suggested by the commander of the Flanders U-boat Flotilla and designed to operate in the English Channel and North Sea. Although the Germans did not realize it at the time, it was really too late. None of the boats in the 1919 program were ever finished; the handful that had been started before the end of the war were scrapped on the stocks.[114]

German Surface Raiders

The huge losses caused by the unrestricted submarine offensive far overshadowed the losses caused by German surface raiders. However, the threat from raiders had never really ceased and caused appreciable losses to the dwindling Allied tonnage and forced them to devote considerable resources to counter it.[115] Two months before the start of unrestricted submarine warfare the *Möwe* sailed on her second cruise from Kiel on 23 November 1916 under the command of Korvettenkapitän Graf zu Dohna-Schlodien. The raider disguised herself as a Swedish steamer before passing through the Little Belt into the North Sea, and on 26 November intercepted and partially deciphered wireless messages arranging a rendezvous between the auxiliary cruisers *Artois* and *Moldavia* of the Tenth Cruiser Squadron in the Iceland–Faeroe gap. The *Möwe* had been heading right toward them and was now able to avoid the patrols and pass into the Atlantic to operate against the North American trade routes.

The *Möwe* sank her first ship on the 30th, but on 4 December encountered the Belgian relief ship *Samland*, which had a safe conduct from the German embassy. Dohna was obligated to let the ship proceed unharmed, but ordered her wireless to be smashed. He gained only a slight respite, for three days later the *Samland* arrived at Falmouth and the Admiralty had definite news a raider was at large. The Admiralty responded by ordering troop transports at Dakar, the Cape, and Sierra Leone to remain in harbor until further notice while cruisers and auxiliary cruisers patrolled the trade routes in the North and South Atlantic. The numbers involved were substantial, approximately 24 British cruisers and auxiliary cruisers and an undetermined number of French cruisers. The efforts did not stop the *Möwe*, and the raider eventually proceeded to the south after transferring 400 prisoners to the captured British steamer *Yarrowdale* (4,652 tons) on 12 December. The German prize crew eventually managed to reach Germany.

Dohna repeated the practice of earlier German raiders by coaling from the 7,000 tons available in the *St. Theodore* (4,992 tons) and subsequently arming her, installing a wireless set and turning the prize into the auxiliary cruiser *Geier* with orders to operate against the sailing ship route between Cape Horn and Europe. The *Geier's* primary mission, however, remained to serve as a collier for the *Möwe*, and various rendezvous were arranged before the *Geier*, with engines and boilers in need of repair, was finally scuttled on 14 February. Her month and a half career as a raider was not spectacular; she sank only two sailing ships representing about 1,442 tons.

The *Möwe's* career in the Fernando-Noronha-Rocas zone was successful, although the British missed a chance to catch her on 9 January when the *Minieh* (2,890 tons), serving as collier for the cruiser *Amethyst*, failed to report the approach of a suspicious vessel until it was too late to get off a warning message by wireless. A later study made by the Admiralty was inclined to believe the German account that the *Minieh's* master had been found in a semi-intoxicated state. On the other hand, the *Amethyst's* wireless operators did not recognize the importance of the jammed signal from the *Minieh*, although the cruiser was very close. The failure to realize a jammed signal might be evidence of a ship under attack undoubtedly permitted the *Möwe* to escape. The raider also survived an encounter on 10 March with the steamer *Otaki* (9,575 tons), which put up a plucky fight with her single 4.7-inch gun. Merchantmen were not equipped with range finders, which put them at a great disadvantage when faced by the more heavily armed raiders, but this action took place at very short range because of the rough seas and the *Otaki* hit three times before being sunk, starting a fire in the *Möwe's* bunkers that took two days to extinguish and was dangerously close to the ammunition supply.

On 22 March the *Möwe* returned safely to Kiel after a four-month cruise, having sunk or captured 22 steamers (20 British) and 3 sailing ships, a total of 123,265 tons. This was the most successful cruise of any of the German raiders. Most of the Allied loss was probably unnecessary. An Admiralty study on cruiser operations made during the Second World War with the obvious intent of countering similar German operations was quite harsh in its conclusions. The *Möwe* had continued to sink ship after ship on the principal trade routes despite the expenditure of an enormous amount of fuel and energy by the British and French navies to stop her. The reason, of course, was "the fundamental difficulty of locating ships on the wide expanse of the ocean." The conclusion: "There can now be little doubt that if the Atlantic trade had been organised into convoys and escorted by the numerous cruisers that were scouring the sea, these heavy losses would have been prevented."[116]

The raider *Wolf(II)* sailed on 30 November 1916, little more than a week after the *Möwe*. The raider was formerly the Hansa Line's *Wachtenfels* (5,809 tons), now armed with seven 15-cm guns, three smaller guns for arming auxiliaries, four torpedo tubes, 465 mines, and a Friedrichshafen seaplane, dubbed *Wölfchen*. Her commander, Korvettenkapitän Karl-August Nerger, had by far the longest cruise—close to fifteen months—of any raider during the war, for the *Wolf* did not return to German waters until the latter part of February 1918. The Admiralstab ordered Nerger to mine the approaches to major ports in South Africa and British India and to continue the war against commerce only after he had expended his mines. His major objective was then to be the grain trade between Australia and Europe.

The *Wolf* was escorted through the North Sea by U-boats, passed through an ice field in the Denmark Strait, and then made the long journey to South African waters without attacking any ships. She laid her first minefield off the Cape on the night of 16 January. Nerger laid minefields off Capetown, Cape Agulhas, Colombo, and Bombay during the months of January and February. On 28 February he captured the British steamer *Turritella* (5,528 tons), which he commissioned as the auxiliary cruiser *Iltis*, and, after arming her and transferring 25 mines, ordered her to operate in the Straits of Perim and mine the main channel between the Red Sea and the Gulf of Aden. The captured Chinese crew agreed to work under the Germans.

British, French, and Japanese warships on the Cape, East Indies, and China stations had been placed on guard against raiders in January, but this had been based on news the *Möwe* was out. There was no definite intelligence of the *Wolf* until 5 March. In February, March, and April of 1917 there were approximately 31 cruisers (including 10 Japanese and 3 French), 14 destroyers (British, Australian, and Japanese), and 9 sloops searching for the raider. By the end of March, there was even the old battleship *Exmouth* working the transport route between Colombo and Bombay, and in April the light cruisers *Gloucester* and *Brisbane* were detached from the Adriatic and Australia, and a seaplane carrier, the *Raven II*, arrived at Colombo. The significant Japanese contribution has largely been forgotten, although Newbolt admitted in the official history that the

Japanese did rather more than was asked of them and really became the predominant partner in the Indian Ocean.[117] There was eventually a Japanese vice admiral at Singapore with four cruisers and four destroyers, and another Japanese rear admiral with two cruisers protected commerce on the east coast of Australia. Two Japanese cruisers patrolled in the region of Mauritius and then escorted traffic between Mauritius and the Cape, and another detached squadron of two Japanese cruisers escorted traffic between Australia and Colombo.

The *Iltis* was not particularly successful. Shortly after laying her minefield, which subsequently damaged but did not sink two ships, she was challenged by the sloop *Odin* in the Gulf of Aden on 4 March and scuttled herself to avoid capture. The Admiralty responded to the news by first halting all transports in the Indian Ocean and then escorting one or two transports with cruisers while other patrols searched fruitlessly for the raider. The *Wolf* continued to coal from prizes, and after six months at sea overhauled her engines and boilers at remote Sunday Island in the Kermadecs northeast of New Zealand. Nerger then proceeded to lay mines off the northwest corner of New Zealand and then near the Cook Strait and in the Bass Strait. The *Wolf*'s final minefield was laid off the Anamba Islands near Singapore. The Admiralty, having had no news of the *Wolf* for some time, had canceled the Indian Ocean escorts on 2 June, and when the raider reentered the Indian Ocean in September, shipping was unprotected.

Nerger, thanks to coaling from prizes, was able to prolong his voyage beyond original expectations. He was always far ahead of Admiralty intelligence in the vast oceans. For example, the report of the *Wolf*'s visit to the Maldive Islands in September did not become known to the Admiralty until December. They promptly resumed escorts of transports in the Indian Ocean. By this time Nerger was far away in the Atlantic, on his way home in company with the captured Spanish steamer *Igotz Mendi* (4,468 tons), which had been serving as a collier since her capture on 10 November. The *Wolf*, by now leaking badly, finally reached German waters on 17 February 1918, although the *Igotz Mendi* ran aground in fog off Skagen and was interned by the Danes. The *Wolf*'s mines had sunk a total of 13 steamers (11 British) representing 75,888 tons. Three ships had been damaged by mines but brought safely into port. The *Wolf* also captured or sank another 7 steamers (5 British) and 7 sailing ships (one British), representing 38,391 tons for a combined total of 114,279 tons.[118] This is of course impressive, but it represented a cruise of almost 15 months and would only average out to about 7,700 tons of shipping destroyed per month. It appears minuscule compared to what the U-boats were accomplishing.

The last of the German raiders that proved so troublesome in 1917 was the *Seeadler* (1,571 tons), which sailed on 21 December 1916. She was by far the most romantic, for she was a full-rigged sailing ship equipped with an auxiliary motor. Originally the American *Pass of Balmaha*, she had been captured by the *U.36* and then fitted with two 10.5-cm guns hidden under a cargo of timber. Her commander, Kapitänleutnant Felix Graf von Luckner, thanks to his own memoirs and the admiring work of the American correspondent Lowell Thomas, became one of the best-known and certainly most popular German naval officers in the interwar period.[119] The *Seeadler* had been meticulously disguised as a Norwegian ship, and the Germans had taken pains to obtain some Norwegian-speaking sailors for the crew. They were equipped with carefully prepared Norwegian cover stories and ephemera such as letters and photographs. The *Seeadler* was therefore able to pass inspection when stopped by a cruiser of the Tenth Cruiser Squadron. She was able to proceed to her first operating area in the South Atlantic northwest of St. Paul Rocks and begin taking prizes. This was the same area where the *Karlsruhe* had been so successful in 1914 (see chapter 4). By the time the Admiralty received definite intelligence she was at work when a barque carrying her prisoners arrived at Rio de Janeiro on 30 March, Luckner had left the area to round Cape Horn well to the south and proceed to the sailing ship route in the Pacific.

The *Seeadler*'s career came to a premature end when she called at the uninhabited island of Mopihaa (Mopeha) in the Society Islands to obtain fresh food to counter the scurvy that had appeared among the crew. On 2 August a sudden wind and heavy sea developed with little warning, the ship's anchor dragged, and the *Seeadler* was wrecked. Two of the *Seeadler*'s boats survived, and three weeks later Luckner and five officers and seamen set out in one to attempt to capture a schooner. They did not succeed, and in late September the Germans were captured at Wakaya in the Fiji Island group. Luckner was transferred to New Zealand and succeeded in escaping from rather lenient imprisonment to the Kermadec Islands before he was recaptured. The Germans left by Luckner at Mopeha set out in the other boat and managed to capture a small French schooner, which they renamed *Fortuna* (126 tons), and sailed to Easter Island. A Chilean cruiser picked them up and brought them to the mainland where they were interned. The *Seeadler*'s career, eight and a half months long, may have been colorful and romantic, but it was the least productive of the 1917 raiders. She captured or sank only 3 freighters and 13 sailing ships, a total of 30,099 tons. Only six of the ships were British.[120]

The *Leopard*, the last of the German raiders during the war, had only a brief career and no success. She was the *Möwe*'s prize the *Yarrowdale* (4,652 tons), which was armed with five 15-cm guns, four 8.8-cm guns, and two torpedo tubes. The Germans apparently hoped to profit from the intelligence they had gleaned through wireless intercepts of the Northern Patrol's movements and dispositions. They did not succeed. The *Leopard* passed through the Little Belt on 7 March 1917 but had not yet taken any prizes when on 16 March in the waters between Scotland and Norway she was intercepted by the armored cruiser *Achilles* and the boarding vessel *Dundee* (2,187 tons) of the Northern Patrol. The latter sent a boat to examine the suspicious ship, which claimed to be Norwegian, but the British were cautious and escaped damage when the raider suddenly disclosed her identity and fired a torpedo. The Germans made no attempt to surrender, and after a hot fight the *Leopard* was sunk with all hands, including the British boarding party.[121]

The German raiders were a popular subject for authors in the 1920s. They seemed a romantic link with an earlier age, far removed from the grim slaughter and *spurlos versunkt*—sunk without a trace—activities of the U-boats. Their commanders also seem to have behaved chivalrously and have received a good press—particularly von

Luckner—and were usually well spoken of by their former prisoners. The losses they inflicted were nowhere near the losses inflicted by the U-boats. Nevertheless they were not negligible, for a 1940 study by the Admiralty points out the cruisers of 1914 and the auxiliary cruisers of 1916–17 had captured more than 620,000 tons of shipping. These losses were described as "very heavy" and were obscured only by the even greater success of the submarines. However, more than half of these losses were due to the early cruisers, such as the *Emden* and *Karlsruhe*. The three raiders of 1916–17 sank only about 268,000 tons. Given the worldwide shortage of shipping, these losses were painful; and the raiders also, as we have seen, tied down a large number of cruisers. Many of those Allied losses may have been unnecessary. The Admiralty study pointed out that the success of the raiders could have been drastically cut had the British and French resorted to convoys and employed the cruisers wasted on useless patrols as escorts. In addition the raiders would have been deprived of the coal they took from their prizes, which certainly would have curtailed their activities. In fact, as the Admiralty study pointed out, even if convoys had been confined to vessels carrying coal, the raiders "would very soon have been brought to a dead stop."[122] The raiders, though, were secondary. The real decision in the naval war would depend on the success or failure of the submarine campaign, and here the introduction of the convoy system was decisive.

THE HIGH SEA FLEET AND THE SUBMARINE CAMPAIGN

What of the High Sea Fleet during the U-boat campaign? The High Sea Fleet had the constant task of supporting the essential minesweeping activities that kept the vital *Wege* clear for the U-boats in the Bight. But could or would the great ships do anything more? Certainly the demands of the submarine service caused a constant drain on the personnel of the High Sea Fleet. The effects were especially felt among the officers. It was true that the submarine war was one of relatively junior officers, with little scope for the more senior, who had traditionally found employment in the big ships or staffs of squadron commanders. Nevertheless the submarines took the most experienced of the younger officers, who then had to be replaced, and their replacements were neither experienced nor, as events proved, as successful in relations with their men.[123] The first serious disturbances in the High Sea Fleet occurred in August 1917 and were dealt with harshly.[124]

In March 1917 Scheer planned a sortie by the High Sea Fleet into the Hoofden to attack convoy traffic between the east coast of England and the Netherlands where U-boat attacks on shipping were hampered by the presence of destroyer escorts. On a night when the moon would provide plenty of light German light cruisers and destroyer flotillas would sweep the convoy route with the battleships in direct support. The kaiser, on the advice of the deputy chief of the Admiralstab, Vice Admiral Koch, ruled that the sweep could only be undertaken if air reconnaissance was assured to counter the danger the Grand Fleet might receive intelligence of the German sortie in sufficient time to intercept the High Sea Fleet. Scheer protested that the often unreliable airship reconnaissance was not really necessary and resented the implied lack of trust in him that the kaiser's and Admiralstab's limitations implied. The controversy marked a definite rift between the High Sea Fleet commander and the Admiralstab, because Scheer, with great disgust, assumed they were reverting to the policy in which the fleet would be saved for peace or in the unlikely event the British would try to force the Belts. The decision was not changed, and consistently bad weather prevented air reconnaissance during the period when the phase of the moon was judged ripe for the operation. Scheer reluctantly dispersed his flotillas for exercises planned long in advance, well aware of the harmful effects the cancellation would have on morale.[125]

In the autumn of 1917, the Germans decided to support the submarine campaign with surface ships by striking at the Scandinavian convoys. Scheer wanted to terrorize the neutrals trading with the British and force the latter to divert ships from the antisubmarine campaign to protect the Scandinavian traffic. The light cruisers *Brummer* (Fregattenkapitän Leonhardi) and *Bremse* (Fregattenkapitän Westerkamp) were well suited for the task. They had originally been laid down as minelayers for the Russian navy and had proportionately high speed and a good radius of action. Moreover, they resembled British light cruisers, and the Germans repainted them a British-style dark gray to heighten the illusion.

On 17 October, about a half hour after dawn, the *Brummer* and *Bremse* attacked the westbound Scandinavian convoy of twelve ships approximately 70 miles east of Lerwick. They sank the escorting destroyers *Mary Rose* and *Strongbow* and nine neutral ships in the convoy. Two armed trawlers and three freighters escaped. The *Strongbow* was sunk before she could get off a wireless signal; the *Mary Rose* appears to have attempted one, but it was jammed by the Germans. Consequently, the British did not receive word of the attack until the Germans had gotten safely away. The Admiralty had, as usual, intelligence the Germans were preparing some move, but they did not know where. On the 15th strong light cruisers and destroyer patrols—a total of 3 cruisers, 27 light cruisers, and 54 destroyers—from the Grand Fleet and Harwich Force had been ordered to sea. The British, however, had not expected the Germans to operate so far to the north, and the British patrols were well south of the Scandinavian convoy route and not in the right place to intercept.[126]

There is evidence that the old excessive secrecy and watertight compartmentation between different departments played some role in the tragedy. Room 40 knew from the call sign that the *Brummer* was at sea and that she was a minelayer and assumed the mission involved minelaying. They had no information as to what British ships were at sea, for those positions were shown only on charts in the Operations Division. Had they seen the position of the convoys on their own charts, they might have guessed what the Germans were up to. It is difficult to understand why the Operations Division, which had the information on British positions, did not make the proper deductions about a possible threat to the convoy or send more timely information to Beatty, who reportedly was furious and subsequently paid an angry visit to the Admiralty.[127]

The British attempted to retaliate with a raid of their own into the Bight on 17 November. Their objective was the cruisers or battle cruisers, which they knew usually covered the minesweepers working to keep the *Wege* clear. The extensive British mining had by now forced the German minesweepers to work as far as 150 miles from the coast. The British striking force under Vice Admiral T. W. D. Napier consisted of the light battle cruisers *Courageous* (flag) and *Glorious* and two light cruiser squadrons (8 light cruisers) plus the indispensable destroyer screens. The *Courageous* and *Glorious* had been Fisher's idea for Baltic operations; they were large, very fast, armed with 15-inch guns, but very lightly armored. They were supported by Vice Admiral Pakenham—who commanded the whole operation—with six battle cruisers and nine destroyers. The First Battle Squadron with six dreadnoughts and eleven destroyers was a few hours steaming distance away. They hoped to catch and destroy the Germans before the High Sea Fleet could put to sea.

The British surprised the German minesweepers, which were covered by Rear Admiral von Reuter and the Second Scouting Group's four light cruisers. There were also two German dreadnoughts, the *Kaiserin* and *Kaiser*, out in support near Helgoland. Reuter engaged the British while the minesweepers fled, and then retired at high speed toward his battleship support behind dense clouds of smoke. The British assumed the Germans were using channels that were free of mines and followed, but the smoke provided them with few clear targets. Napier lost his chance to catch the Germans when he altered course on reaching the position his chart indicated was the limit of British minefields. The Germans had as usual made good use of smoke, and Napier could not be certain they had not altered course because of mines. When the smoke cleared sufficiently for Napier to realize the Germans had not changed course, he resumed the chase for another 12 miles until he reached a point his chart indicated as a dangerous mined area. He then turned back. The minefield actually referred to a British field laid in 1915 and was not shown on the charts in the two light cruiser squadrons; they continued the pursuit together with the battle cruiser *Repulse*, which Pakenham had detached to support the light cruisers. The *Repulse* and the light cruisers ended their pursuit when the dreadnoughts *Kaiserin* and *Kaiser* came in sight and opened fire on them. The British wisely retired without serious damage, but they had failed in their objective and had actually sustained more hits (7) than they scored (5). None of the damage was severe, although the cruiser *Calypso*'s captain was mortally wounded by a shell from the German light cruisers and a shell from the *Repulse* started a serious fire in the *Königsberg*. The Germans lost only a single armed trawler, overwhelmed at the start of the action.

The Helgoland Bight action turned out to be the last encounter between the big ships during the war. The affair, like so many other attempts to bring the Germans under the big guns of the Grand Fleet, proved frustrating. Napier was criticized for an error in judgment in pursuing the Germans at 25 knots rather than the 30 knots the *Glorious* and *Courageous* were capable of. In addition, poor staff work as revealed in the muddled situation regarding the minefields certainly contributed toward cheating the British of success. Excessive secrecy seemed to remain a problem. Had Napier possessed all the information on the minefields available to the Admiralty, he might have been able to anticipate much better the German movements as they retired and inflict more serious damage.[128]

In the meantime the success of the *Brummer* and *Bremse* against the hitherto successful Scandinavian convoy had prompted a review of the situation. The losses had been particularly embarrassing, because the convoy had been escorted by warships and the ships sunk were neutral Scandinavians whom the British had succeeded in persuading to defy German threats. One proposal involved lessening vulnerability by reducing the frequency of sailings. This, however, conflicted with British obligations to supply Norway with a stipulated amount of coal each month. On a purely tactical level, Beatty ordered destroyer captains in the event of attack by surface warships to scatter the convoy. Once it was scattered they could no longer protect it, but the destroyers were not to be risked uselessly and should avoid becoming engaged with superior forces. Their primary duty was to report the attack and enemy position immediately by wireless. A conference at Longhope on 10 December recommended that Methil in the Firth of Forth be used as a convoy assembly port instead of Lerwick farther to the north. This would have the advantage of shortening the voyage, which would help the British fulfill their commitment to the Norwegians to supply 250,000 tons of coal per month. The British deliveries of coal were less than half that amount in November. Beatty warned, however, that the new route was closer to the German bases and therefore more vulnerable. He proposed using as escorts the cruisers that served as oceanic escorts for the North Atlantic convoys.

The Germans struck again while these discussions were in progress. Scheer planned a two-pronged attack with the destroyers of the Second Flotilla (Korvettenkapitän Heinecke), the biggest and fastest the Germans had (1,116 to 1,350 tons, four 3.4-inch guns, six torpedo tubes, and more than 33 knots). The destroyers were escorted to the northeast end of Dogger Bank by the light cruiser *Emden*. They then separated. Heinecke with the Fourth Half-Flotilla was to attack convoy traffic in the war channel along the east coast of England north of Newcastle, whereas the four destroyers of the Third Half-Flotilla were to proceed north to attack the Lerwick-Bergen route. On 12 December Korvettenkapitän Hans Holbe in *G.101*, with *V.100*, *G.103*, and *G.104* of the Third Half-Flotilla, attacked the eastbound Scandinavian convoy approximately 25 miles off Bjornefjord. The six ships in the convoy were escorted by the destroyers *Partridge* and *Pellew* and four armed trawlers. The British had used cruisers, when available, to patrol near the route, and on this day the armored cruisers *Shannon* and *Minotaur* with four destroyers were out, but about 60 miles west of the convoys when the Germans attacked. Three of the German destroyers engaged the escorts while the fourth went after the convoy. The British escorts were caught in the leeward position, with their gunners blinded by spray, although the *Partridge* after being disabled still managed to hit *V.100* with a torpedo, which failed to explode. The Germans made good shooting, and in three-quarters of an hour succeeded in sinking the *Partridge*, the trawler escorts, and the six merchant ships of the convoy. Only the damaged *Pellew* escaped, probably saved by a rain squall. The *Shannon* and *Minotaur* arrived too late to catch the Germans, and the Third Light Cruiser Squadron (three cruisers), which had been patrolling to the south, also did not succeed in intercepting them, largely because the bad weather made the Germans decide to return via the Skaggerak and the Baltic instead of the Bight.

Heinecke's Fourth Half-Flotilla had less success on the east coast. The Germans were hampered by mist and the fact navigational lights were normally extinguished and lit only when required, but caught two stragglers from the southbound east-coast convoys. They sank one Danish steamer, later torpedoed but failed to sink a Swedish steamer, and subsequently sank by gunfire one of four small ships they encountered and erroneously believed was the convoy. They had, in fact, missed the real convoy and turned for home.[129]

The British maintained their intention to use Methil as the point of departure for the Scandinavian convoy, which would sail every three days. This was altered to every four days in March and every five days at the end of April. The longer intervals were to reduce the strain of providing continuous escorts for the convoys. There was also to be a daily convoy from the Humber to Methil. The fact that the route was now closer to the German bases also meant that a heavier supporting force always had to be at sea. Beatty at first used a battle squadron, which, as Newbolt comments in the official history, "was a great departure from the principle of rigid concentration which had dominated the organisation and employment of the Grand Fleet since the war began: it was illustrative of the extent to which the war against commerce had engaged our strength and resources." The covering force, in fact, was reduced to a light cruiser squadron by the end of June 1918, and to a pair of armored cruisers somewhat later. This dispersion was a calculated risk, for with it there was the possibility the Germans could achieve what they had always hoped to do and concentrate overwhelming force against a portion of the Grand Fleet. The British as a result became even more dependent on the quality of their intelligence and ability to detect German moves.[130]

The German successes against the Scandinavian convoys in late 1917 caused considerable discontent in Britain over the way the Admiralty conducted the war. It was undoubtedly one of the factors in the dismissal of Jellicoe as First Sea Lord in December. However, it should not obscure the fact that the major threat came from submarines, not from surface craft, and that, if anything, it was the Germans who failed to profit from the geographical conditions that gave their surface craft a good shot at the Scandinavian convoy. They might well have raided more often. Furthermore, the Scandinavian convoys themselves were a success, despite the 1917 losses. The postwar Admiralty statistical summary reveals that with the "old system" between 28 April 1917 and 18 January 1918, a total of 1,617 ships were convoyed eastbound, of which 17 were sunk by the Germans; and 1,806 ships were convoyed westbound and 23 sunk. Under the "new system" from 19 January 1918 to the end of the war, there were 2,045 ships in eastbound (OZ) convoys, of which only 3 were sunk; and in the westbound (HZ) convoys, 2,185 ships were convoyed and only 12 sunk. The grand total for the war was 7,653 ships convoyed and 55 lost, a loss rate of .72 percent. When the total for the east-coast convoys is added to that for the Scandinavian convoy, there were between April 1917 and November 1918 no less than 30,713 ships convoyed, of which 126 were sunk, yielding a loss rate of .41 percent.[131]

The situation at the end of 1917 was far from clear; the recent defection of Russia from the war and the threat of a major German offensive on the western front were disturbing. War weariness was evident among all the Allies. The prospect of final victory against Germany and her allies appeared distant, if not uncertain. As for the war at sea, losses to submarines remained disturbingly high, but it now seemed that the convoy system had turned the tide. It remained to be seen if the Germans would be able to alter this trend in 1918.

12

THE MEDITERRANEAN: 1915–1918

THE U-BOAT FLOTILLA

The Germans sent their first submarines to the Mediterranean in response to the Anglo-French expedition to the Dardanelles when it became apparent their Austrian allies could do little to affect the situation with their own small submarine force, however effective it might be in defending the Adriatic against superior Anglo-French forces. The German submarines *U.21, UB.7,* and *UB.8* achieved success in their initial appearance but ran into severe limitations in the vicinity of the Dardanelles, where the swarms of small craft and extensive netting and booms restricted their opportunities after the initial surprise. By the end of June 1915, the Germans had assembled another three UB boats at Pola, two of them destined for transfer to the Austrian navy.

The Germans also were assembling three UC minelayers at Pola, but in June the Admiralstab ordered them converted to transports to meet the pressing need to carry small quantities of critically needed supplies to Turkey. The Germans still had very little offensive capability in the Mediterranean. The UB boats were hampered by their lack of range and had difficulty mastering the Dardanelles currents. Moreover, in mid-July 1915 the redoubtable Kapitänleutnant Hersing's *U.21,* the only U-boat with a long radius of action, was damaged by a mine and likely to be immobilized at Constantinople for at least six weeks. The Mediterranean was attractive to the Admiralstab. A significant portion of British imports passed through the Mediterranean, which was obviously crucial to French and Italian trade, and submarines would be able to operate more effectively here when the autumn bad weather hampered operations in the Atlantic. Also, there were certain relatively narrow areas or focal points through which all traffic had to pass, notably the Suez Canal, Malta, Crete, and Gibraltar.

The Mediterranean had another advantage. There would be fewer problems with neutrals, especially as they were not likely to meet American ships and fewer U.S. citizens traveled through the Mediterranean compared to the waters around the British Isles. On 21 July the kaiser approved detaching the large submarines *U.34* and *U.35* from the Baltic. The submarines proceeded directly to Cattaro, and the Germans decided to make use of the Austrian bases rather than Constantinople. There were better supply and repair facilities in the Adriatic, and submarines could avoid the dangerous passage through the Dardanelles. In August the Germans added *U.33* and *U.39* to their Mediterranean forces, motivated by the desperate appeals from the German military attaché in Constantinople, who reported that the excellent close naval support provided by the Royal Navy was inflicting painful losses on the Turks at the beachheads.

A diplomatic problem existed. There was no state of war between Germany and Italy, but the Germans got around the difficulty by ordering their submarines to refrain from taking hostile action against Italian shipping in the eastern Mediterranean where the Italians might expect hostile action only from German submarines. When conducting cruiser warfare on the surface in the west up to the line of Cape Matapan, the Germans flew only the Austrian flag.[1]

The four German U-boats operating in the Mediterranean or on their way to Cattaro achieved noticeable, though not spectacular, results in September, sinking seven steamers and a small French auxiliary warship, representing more than 22,000 tons. It was only a harbinger of things to come. Kapitänleutnant Kophamel, then in command of *U.35*, noted that away from the swarm of light craft at the Dardanelles, Allied security and countermeasures were apparently very weak. Moreover, the submarines were operating under somewhat fewer restrictions in the Mediterranean. They could attack large merchant ships in the Aegean while submerged on the suspicion they were troop transports or auxiliary cruisers.[2]

The German submarine campaign in the Mediterranean would not have been possible without the use of the Austrian naval bases at Pola and Cattaro. But beyond providing bases, would the Austro-Hungarian navy be able to participate in the campaign? The k.u.k. Kriegsmarine had already used submarines most effectively in the defense of the Adriatic, but its ability to contribute to the submarine campaign outside of the Adriatic was limited. The Austrians would have liked to do so, but there were strong technical and political factors limiting them. The most obvious was a lack of suitable submarines, something the Germans had recognized when they transferred two of the UB boats assembled at Pola to the Austrians.

The marinekommandant Admiral Haus authorized the construction of additional submarines in March 1915, once he realized it was going to be a long war. The Austrians initially ordered somewhat unenthusiastically four of the *Havmanden* class, largely because the Whitehead yard at Fiume had built three for the Danish navy before the war. The Austrians immediately ran into a series of problems difficult to overcome, including the demand by the Hungarian government that Hungarian firms receive a significant share of the production. The result, after intricate negotiations, was a compromise in June by which the four submarines were to be partially built in Linz and

Pola and final assembly achieved at either Pola or Fiume. Hungarian firms received about two-thirds of the subcontracting work, Austrian firms about a third. The *Havmandens* did not actually enter service until August to November of 1917. They suffered from unreliable engines, were unhandy, and on the whole represented a prewar design that was largely obsolete by that date.

In the summer of 1915, Haus wisely opted for the German UB.II design, although the Germans were understandably reluctant to actually sell any of their own submarines to the Austrians or earmark any of their building capacity for Austrian purposes. The most they were willing to do was sell the UB.II plans to the Austrians for the construction of up to six submarines. The Austrian naval authorities then had the by-now familiar difficulty of allocating production between Austrian and Hungarian firms. After long and complicated negotiations, the Austrian firm Cantiere Navale received orders for two, and the Hungarian firm Danubius orders for four. The submarines were not laid down until the winter and spring of 1916, and the usual difficulties with subcontractors—who suffered from shortages of labor and materials—meant that the delivery dates were not met. The Austrian UB.IIs (*U.27* to *U.32*) did not enter service until the first half of 1917. In 1916 the Austrians also laid down another two UB.II boats, *U.40*, a gift from the Österreichischen Flottenverein, and *U.41*, a replacement for a submarine that had been lost.[3] The Austrians therefore had only a handful (6 to 8) of modern and reliable submarines. Even those were relatively short ranged, and when they finally entered service their use outside of the Adriatic tended to be restricted to the central Mediterranean routes between Malta and Crete. The patrols to the western and eastern portions of the Mediterranean remained the monopoly of the larger German U-boats. The Germans obviously had to carry on the overwhelming majority of submarine operations in the Mediterranean.

The German submarine campaign in the Mediterranean is generally considered to have begun in earnest in October 1915 when the Admiralstab ordered *U.33* and *U.39*, followed by *U.35* later in the month, to attack the approaches to Salonika and Kavalla. The Germans sank 18 ships in the Mediterranean in October, representing 63,848 tons. This was the major portion of the 83,714 tons sunk in all theaters the same month. The Admiralstab decided on further reinforcement for the Mediterranean, and a sixth large U-boat, *U.38*, sailed for Cattaro in mid-October. There were more far-reaching plans as well. The Admiralstab decided at the beginning of October the UB.II class would be ideal for the Mediterranean. They designated six of the class (*UB.42* to *UB.47*), but these submarines were too large to be shipped by rail in sections like the UB.Is, and the materials for their construction had to be shipped to Pola along with German workers to assemble them. This meant they could not be ready until spring 1916, and the absence of the workers from Germany meant a delay in completing U-boats for home waters. The decision seemed justified by the Mediterranean successes of November when submarines sank no fewer than 44 ships representing 152,882 out of the 167,043 tons sunk in all theaters. The total fell in December to 17 ships (73,741 tons) plus one ship sunk by submarine-laid mines (2,952 tons), but this still represented more than half the tonnage sunk in all theaters (107,735).

The Mediterranean submarines were formed into an independent U-boat flotilla at Cattaro, and a special command at Pola remained in charge of repair and assembly of new boats. U.35's commander, Kophamel, was designated senior U-boat commander in the Mediterranean, promoted to Korvettenkapitän, and given command of the flotilla at Cattaro. He was replaced in U.35 by Kapitänleutnant von Arnauld de la Perière, whose Mediterranean exploits later made him the most successful U-boat commander of the war.[4]

The German submarine campaign claimed, at least indirectly, another victim. The titular Allied commander in chief in the Mediterranean, Vice Admiral Boué de Lapeyrère, cabled the minister of marine on 10 October asking to be relieved of his command, ostensibly because his present state of health did not permit him to assure the responsibilities that had fallen on him in present circumstances. Lapeyrère undoubtedly was worn out; he had been in command of the major French naval force—the 1ère armée navale—since 1911 and had trained hard for the anticipated naval battle with the combined forces of the Triple Alliance. The war had turned into something entirely different when Italy defected from the Triple Alliance. He had been unable to get at the Austrian fleet in the Adriatic, and though theoretical Allied commander in chief in the Mediterranean, his real control of operations had been steadily whittled down. The Dardanelles campaign had been largely run by the British, and after Italy entered the war on the side of the Entente, operations in the Adriatic fell under Italian command. His responsibilities remained large, but the means at hand to counter the threat of German submarines were meager. He complained he had only 27 light cruisers and destroyers and 28 auxiliary gunboats and trawlers—a portion always under repair—to cover a line of communications of more than 1,900 miles in the Mediterranean outside the Adriatic and British zone of operations off the Dardanelles. Lapeyrère was forced to ask the Italians to return the French destroyers attached to Brindisi, so he could cover the movements to Greece.[5]

Lapeyrère's successor was Vice Admiral Dartige du Fournet, who was also unable to overcome the submarine menace, and who found himself more and more immersed in the problems of Greece. They eventually caused his downfall. As for the antisubmarine campaign, the French were indeed hampered by their relative poverty of small craft compared to the British. The British at the beginning of the war had been prepared to leave the Mediterranean to the French in order to concentrate on what they considered the decisive theater in the North Sea. They were, however, forced to play a steadily increasing role in the Mediterranean, where their interests were great, until in 1917 they assumed direction of Mediterranean antisubmarine operations. The theoretical French command in the Mediterranean became ever more theoretical.

The operations of Kapitänleutnant Max Valentiner and U.38 on his way from Helgoland to Cattaro were one of the reasons the sinkings by submarines had been so high in November. Valentiner sank 14 ships (47,460 tons) along the coast of North Africa but frustrated the hopes of the German naval leaders that they could avoid diplomatic

　　　　　A NAVAL HISTORY OF WORLD WAR I

complications in the Mediterranean. Fortunately, they had the Austrians to assume the blame. On 7 November *U.38* sank the Italian liner *Ancona* (8,210 tons) off Bizerte with a loss of more than 200 lives, among them approximately 20 Americans. The action had taken place on the surface, and as Germany was not at war with Italy, *U.38* had worn the Austrian flag.

The anticipated diplomatic storm soon followed. Haus was inclined to back his German allies strongly and from the very beginning. The Austrian Foreign Office was a bit hesitant, but finally agreed to the Germans replying to the Italian demands that the submarine that sank the *Ancona* was indeed Austrian. In case of future arbitration, *U.38* and its crew was retroactively entered into the k.u.k. List of Warships.

The United States pressed the Austrians very hard on the issue, and after what was virtually an ultimatum, the Austrians backed down. The Germans, who were anxious to avoid war with the United States, were particularly insistent they do so. The Austrians, without naming the specific submarine or officer involved, announced in a note of 29 December that the commander of the submarine had failed to take into sufficient consideration the panic that occurred among the *Ancona*'s passengers, which had rendered the embarkation more difficult, and he had been accordingly "punished" for exceeding his instructions. The Austrians promised to pay an indemnity. The Austrian ambassador in Berlin asked the Germans to refrain in the future from attacking neutral or enemy passenger liners while flying the Austrian flag. There is, however, considerable irony in the fact the United States had come close to breaking off relations with Austria-Hungary and possibly even declaring war over the conduct of submarine operations at a time when the k.u.k Kriegsmarine actually had little capacity to conduct those operations outside of the Adriatic.[6]

INEFFECTIVE ALLIED COUNTERMEASURES

The major British and French priority in the face of the submarine menace in the Mediterranean was the protection of troop transports. Unfortunately they did not have enough destroyers. Admiral Sir Henry Jackson, the First Sea Lord, admitted that "the demands on our resources are beyond our capabilities." He protested, "Everyone is screaming for destroyers, especially the French, & I have to harden my heart to all such requests."[7] Jellicoe, ever alert to demands on the Grand Fleet's resources, pointedly remarked that "charity begins at home," and that they should not risk weakening the Grand Fleet or losing command of the sea in home waters to satisfy their Allies in what was primarily a French sphere of action.[8]

The French commander in chief in the Mediterranean was fully conscious that British resources were stretched to the limit, but so were his own once the Salonika campaign began. The French played the major role in this expedition, but the heavy demands on destroyers to escort troop transports threatened to wear them out prematurely, particularly when the onset of bad weather in the winter of 1915–16 exacerbated the situation. By the end of November, 28 of 61 French destroyers had broken down or were under refit, a wastage of 46 percent.[9]

The British and French resorted to rough expedients. The British escorted troop transports through dangerous points where they also provided patrols, and they frequently varied the routes. They also armed vessels as rapidly as guns became available. The French, given their inability to give direct escort to all transports, tried to provide indirect protection by patrolling routes and hunting for suspected submarine supply bases. In late November the French also decided to completely separate the transport of men from the transport of matériel. Troops for Salonika were carried in six large, fast (minimum speed of 15 knots) passenger liners commanded by naval officers, armed as auxiliary cruisers with naval gun crews, and fitted with a powerful wireless. The liners sailed alone and without escort. Under these conditions tragedy was perhaps inevitable, and it came on 26 February. The fast Cie Générale Transatlantique liner *Provence (II)* (13,753 tons), now an auxiliary cruiser, was carrying more than two thousand troops to Salonika when Arnauld de la Perière in *U.35* torpedoed her south of Cape Matapan. The ship took on an immediate list and many lifeboats could not be used. She went down with close to one thousand men in one of the worst French disasters of the war.[10]

The Mediterranean was becoming a much more dangerous place for British shipping, and they were forced to order a partial rather than complete diversion of Mediterranean trade. On 9 March 1916 the Admiralty issued a notice through the Liverpool and London War Risks Insurance Association that on or after 15 March vessels proceeding to or from Atlantic ports and ports in the Far East or Australia would use the Cape route, whereas ships proceeding to or from ports in India would continue to use the Suez Canal.[11]

The Allies made a somewhat halting effort at collaboration in the Mediterranean with an agreement signed in Paris on 3 December 1915. The Mediterranean was divided into eighteen patrol zones, four British, four Italian, and ten French. The British zones were mostly adjacent to their possessions, that is, Gibraltar, Malta, and Egypt, as well as the Dardanelles. The Italian zones were off their own coasts and their Libyan colony. The French had the remainder of the Mediterranean coast as well as the Ionian Islands, but the zones were largely coastal and there was a sizable area that was unassigned in the central and eastern Mediterranean. Here each nation allotted what they could spare, the French to the west and the British to the east of Malta.[12]

Neither the British nor French authorities in the Mediterranean were particularly satisfied with the Paris agreement, which Commodore Keyes, chief of staff at the Dardanelles, termed "a ridiculous convention" that was "simply futile and impractical." Nevertheless the Admiralty decreed that they should give the plan a chance and not seek modifications until it had proven to be a failure after sufficient trial.[13] It was really the French who soon pushed for a new conference to examine a wider range of Mediterranean problems.

The Malta conference, 2–9 March 1916, covered a wide range of questions. Some were technical, such as the problem of regulating wireless traffic. De Robeck had termed

French wireless procedure "a positive danger." The most important decisions naturally concerned the antisubmarine war, and here the decisions of the conference were unfortunate. The Allies essentially accepted a British proposal to revise the Mediterranean patrol zones, which were enlarged and reduced in number from eighteen to eleven. The unassigned zone in the central and eastern basin disappeared, most of it going to the British, except for an extension of the French zone in the Ionian Sea. The British also assumed control of most of the Aegean, including the island of Crete. The Allied admirals decided that they lacked sufficient vessels to protect shipping by direct escort and opted for a system of patrolled routes. Escorts were to be reserved for special cases. There were a certain number of these patrolled routes prepared in advance for each journey and designated by letter. The commander in chief then merely ordered a ship to follow, for example, route B between two points in its voyage. There was a single route coming and going, with ships to move out 5 miles to starboard at night or in thick weather. The routes were the only ones patrolled and were kept as secret as possible. The French commander in chief and the French fleet also shifted their base from Malta, which was now becoming too crowded and was in the midst of a British zone. The French went first to Argostoli in Cephalonia where they would be better situated to intercept the Austrian fleet. They subsequently moved to Corfu where the large harbor, once it was properly netted, provided better scope for exercises and training.[14] The big French ships trained for an event that would never occur: an attempt by the Austrian fleet to break out of the Adriatic and into the Mediterranean.

The Allies following the Malta conference were unduly optimistic because of the fewer number of sinkings by submarines in the first quarter of 1916. This was due to the smaller number of submarines at sea because of refits and bad weather, and the restrictive orders against sinking passenger liners. It was certainly not the result of the ineffectual Allied countermeasures. This soon became evident in the second quarter of 1916. The UB.II boats being assembled at Pola also began to enter service, but it was really the large U-boats under experienced commanders such as Arnauld de la Perière that had the most notable results, particularly in the western portion of the Mediterranean and often in the underprotected Italian and French zones.

The British drifter patrol in the Strait of Otranto also proved no real obstacle. Submarines often could break through on the surface at night, passing between groups of drifters, and if spotted were usually able to outrun the surface craft. They might be compelled to submerge, particularly if a destroyer approached, but the patrols were not numerous enough to keep them submerged long enough to exhaust their batteries. Many submarines appear not to have been disturbed at all. From April to June of 1916, the Mediterranean U-boats sank either directly or through submarine-laid mines 100 ships representing 195,225 tons out of the 393,981 tons sunk by submarines in all theaters.[15]

The German successes continued through the summer of 1916, particularly in the western Mediterranean. The patrolled routes prescribed by the Malta conference proved a failure, not least because in late July the Germans learned which routes were patrolled through intercepted wireless messages. Moreover, by means of log books, maps, and other documents recovered from merchant ships before they were sunk, German intelligence gained a very good idea of what certain of those routes were as well as the instructions to move out 5 miles to the right or left of the route at night or in thick weather. By the end of August, the total tonnage sank by Mediterranean submarines had exceeded one million tons, an achievement for which Kophamel and the flotilla received a special telegram of congratulations from the kaiser. From 26 July to 20 August, Arnauld de la Perière and *U.35* enjoyed the most successful submarine cruise of any commander during the war; in the western Mediterranean he sank 54 steamers and sailing craft, representing more than 90,150 tons of shipping. Between July and September of 1916, Mediterranean U-boats sank directly or indirectly through submarine-laid mines 155 ships, or 321,542 tons, out of a worldwide total of 493,184 tons. The Mediterranean percentage of total sinkings by submarines had therefore risen from 49.6 percent in the second quarter of 1916 to more than 65 percent in the third quarter.

In the last quarter of 1916, and despite the onset of bad weather in the autumn, the tonnage sunk in the Mediterranean continued to rise. The submarines sank 129 ships or 427,999 tons out of 970,423 in all theaters, a respectable 44 percent.[16] The German losses in the Mediterranean were light. In 1916 they lost only two submarines in the Mediterranean, one, *UB.44*, disappeared, and another, *UC.12*, blew up on her own mines off Taranto.[17] The Mediterranean successes justified the dispatch of more submarines. As of 25 October 1916, the Mediterranean U-boat force numbered 10 large U-boats (including 1 in the Black Sea and 4 en route), 2 large minelayers, 5 UB.II boats (3 in the Black Sea), 1 small UB.I boat, and 8 UC small minelayers (including 4 preparing to leave Germany, 1 in the Black Sea, and 1 en route).[18]

By the end of the summer of 1916 German U-boats in the Mediterranean had also been freed from the obligation to operate under the Austrian flag when attacking Italian vessels while on the surface. On 28 August the Italian government declared war on Germany. Nevertheless the Germans and Austrians had to cover their past actions, and on 10 September agreed that the six large U-boats that had conducted operations against Italian ships would be formally and *retroactively* taken into the k.u.k. Kriegsmarine as of the moment they passed through the Straits of Gibraltar. This in no way altered the fact the U-boats were subordinate to the German Admiralstab, which had the responsibility for issuing their orders. The Germans and Austrians hoped these measures would avoid difficulties in prize courts, or if past incidents became the subject of international arbitration.[19]

Throughout 1915 and 1916, the German army high command and their Turkish allies periodically attempted to divert Mediterranean U-boats from the Admiralstab's primary mission—*Handelskrieg*. The Italian hold on their newly acquired colony of Libya after the Italo-Turkish war of 1911–12 had been tenuous at best, and even before Italy entered the war, the Italian military began pulling back to the coast. This had been the signal for a widespread uprising, and for most of the war the Italians considered themselves lucky to hold on to only a few coastal points in Tripolitania and Cyrenaica. The religious sect, the Senussi, had been particularly successful in Cyrenaica, and in the autumn of 1915 the German army general staff believed they were well armed with captured weapons and in a position to threaten the western frontier of Egypt. The navy was not happy, for at the beginning of 1916 they had been forced to employ and risk for a few weeks no less than three of the very limited number of submarines they then had available in the Mediterranean in order to delivery a piddling quantity of supplies.

The British defeated the Senussi invasion of Egypt from the west and by the end of March 1916 had succeeded in forcing them back from Sollum. The Turks, however, were anxious for submarines to continue transporting more men, matériel, and foodstuffs to Libya. They were backed as usual by the German army general staff. The navy would have been glad to wash its hands of these North African projects, but the German Foreign Office joined the army general staff in advocating them. The use of submarines to transport men and munitions to North Africa continued throughout the war, although in 1917 and 1918 the constant use of the converted UC.II-type minelayers *UC.20* and *UC.73* as transports represented a smaller proportion of the German submarine force.[20]

The Allies for most of 1916 responded to this steady hemorrhage of their shipping with antisubmarine tactics that were more of the same, adding whatever craft they could to the ineffective patrols on the patrolled routes while the admirals consistently overestimated the very few losses they actually were inflicting on the submarines. The submarine danger was so acute that in October the Admiralty prevailed on the War Office to agree to send troops going to or returning from Salonika and Egypt overland via Marseilles, which had the advantage of eliminating the long sea journey through the Bay of Biscay and western Mediterranean. Furthermore, as of 11 December the Admiralty prohibited insurance from being issued to ships entering the Mediterranean unless they were provided with a special license that was normally given only to ships carrying cargo to Mediterranean ports or using the Suez Canal while proceeding to ports in India west of Colombo. This had the effect of shifting shipping for Calcutta, Madras, Rangoon, and other Bay of Bengal ports to the Cape route. Once again, as with earlier measures shifting the Far East trade to the Cape, the disadvantages of reduced carrying capacity because of the longer route were offset by the reduced risk.[21]

There was dissent to the existing system. Rear Admiral Ballard, Limpus's successor at Malta, was disgusted with the system of patrolled routes and in October argued that unless they could put at least four times the present number of patrol vessels on the routes to ensure a submarine being brought to action whenever it appeared, they ought to give another system a trial. Ballard suggested convoys. The Admiralty were not prepared to accept convoys at this stage but eventually agreed on a scheme whereby "ports of refuge" would be established in the western basin of the Mediterranean. They would be protected by guns and nets, and ships would be directed to them during daylight hours when submarines were known to be active in the area. Ships would proceed at night to the next anchorage, keep as close to the coast as possible, and make full use of Spanish territorial waters. In contrast, in the eastern basin of the Mediterranean ships would be dispersed. After passing Cape Bon they would spread out on diverse routes to Malta, Alexandria, Port Said, and the Aegean. They would follow fixed routes in the Aegean and use the same procedure as in the western basin, anchoring in protected ports by day and proceeding by night.[22]

The British began to implement the plan for dispersion between Cape Bon and the Aegean on 11 January 1917 in advance of any formal agreement with the French. The result was confusion, for French authorities continued to use the old routes where they controlled movements, and British authorities at Alexandria sailed French as well as British ships under the new orders. In the end it took a major Allied naval conference at London, 23–24 January 1917, to straighten out the tangle. The conference decided on a trial of the two systems in the eastern basin of the Mediterranean. Coastal routes were to be used as much as possible in the western basin, although each country would decide if their ships should take the direct route patrolled by the French between Marseilles and Algiers. The British system of dispersion was to be used between Cape Bon and Port Said by British vessels and any Allied vessels that opted to join them, and ships proceeding to and from Salonika and the Aegean were to use the French system of fixed routes, frequently changed. The results of the two systems would be compared after an unspecified period of trial, and another conference would then decide on a permanent system. The British, however, had to promise that they would maintain their patrols on the French routes that ran through their zones, and that they would not divert any patrol craft from them to work on the dispersed routes. This did not bode well for the safety of ships on dispersed routes.[23] The adoption by the London conference of the hybrid system of dispersion together with the discredited fixed routes had disastrous results when the Germans began unrestricted submarine warfare.

THE BRITISH DIRECT THE ANTISUBMARINE WAR

The Allies had abandoned exclusive use of patrolled routes in the Mediterranean shortly before the Germans adopted unrestricted submarine warfare. The Germans declared the great majority of the Mediterranean a *Sperrgebiet* (prohibited area) except for the extreme western portion off Spain, including the Balearics, and initially, the 20-mile-wide corridor to Greek waters. The Austrians promised to assist the Germans outside of the Adriatic. Their smaller submarines as they became available would now operate against Allied shipping between Malta and Cerigo. In the early part of 1917, the situation in the Mediterranean was deceptively favorable to the Allies, for in January the greater part of the Mediterranean U-boat flotilla was under repair and refit at Pola and Cattaro after the heavy demands of 1916. In January sinkings fell to 78,541 tons, only 24 percent of the total of 328,391 tons sunk in all theaters. It was the lull before the storm, for by 10 February the Germans had 10 U-boats at sea in the Mediterranean, along with an Austrian submarine, and that month submarines sank 105,670 tons of shipping. This, however, represented only 20.3 percent of the 520,412 tons sunk in all theaters, for with the introduction of unrestricted submarine warfare, the Mediterranean percentage of total sinkings inevitably declined. The successes of the Mediterranean U-boat flotilla declined again in March to 61,917 tons, just under 11 percent of the total of 564,497 tons in all theaters. April 1917 turned into a record month for the Mediterranean flotilla, just as it was a record month for U-boats in all theaters. The Germans had 14 U-boats at sea at the beginning of the month, joined by 2 Austrians. They sank in the Mediterranean 254,911 tons (3,724 tons by submarine-laid mines), or 29.6 percent of the 860,334 tons sunk in all theaters. The Austrians contributed another 23,037 tons.[24]

The Admiralty were so alarmed by the heavy losses along the coast of Algeria, which they naturally attributed to the ineffectiveness of French patrols, that they ordered British shipping to abandon the coastal route in favor of hugging the Spanish coast from Gibraltar to Cape San Antonio and then use dispersed routes to Malta.[25] The French, however, complained that they were using more than eighty patrol craft of all sorts on their patrolled routes in the western Mediterranean whereas the British were escorting all British troopships or ships with valuable cargoes and following routes entirely different from the French. Furthermore, the French charged that the British used their destroyers to escort troopships, leaving trawlers on the patrolled routes through British zones. These trawlers often lacked wireless receivers and could not be counted upon to divert ships from threatened areas. Admiral Gauchet, now French commander in chief, described the situation on the Malta-Cerigo route as "every man for himself."[26]

Allied merchant ships deliberately made use of Spanish territorial waters. This proved to be correct, if not very heroic, and it naturally added to the length and duration of a voyage. German U-boat commanders were ordered to observe the Spanish 3-mile limit, and, in fact, to avoid mistakes they were normally to observe a 4-mile limit unless there was a particularly valuable target in the fourth mile and they were quite sure of their position.[27] On the whole, German U-boat commanders respected Spanish territorial waters and the Allies made extensive use of them. The Allies suspected the Germans were violating them, but careful analysis of sinkings generally established that the ships had strayed out of those waters when they were sunk. It was not hard to do; navigation so close to the coast could be difficult and hazardous, and merchant ship captains often were inclined to take a shortcut across the curve of a bay, which made them legitimate targets for the Germans. U-boat commanders were not angels; they obviously found more than enough targets in the Mediterranean without having to violate Spanish waters.

The Mediterranean situation could not be ignored by the Allied leaders by the spring of 1917. In early April General Sir William Robertson, chief of the imperial general staff, asked Jellicoe about a joint statement from the British naval leaders as to what reductions at Salonika would be necessary if the British were to continue the war in 1918. Jellicoe was a strong partisan of abandoning the Salonika expedition because of the strain on shipping and naval resources to support it. He recommended the immediate reduction or withdrawal of the British contingent, and he advocated a complete withdrawal if the cabinet expected the war to continue beyond 1917. This would then allow the British to recover a number of patrol craft for safeguarding commerce in home waters, free a large amount of shipping to build up a reserve of food and supply the French and Italians with coal and other necessities, and permit the British to give better protection to the sea communications with the army in Egypt.[28] The French could be expected to strongly oppose what in their eyes was a British attempt to abandon the Salonika expedition, where France was preponderant, in favor of the pursuit of imperial gains in Palestine. An Allied conference with the Italians at St. Jean de Maurienne on 19 April took no decision on Jellicoe's proposal, and one is inclined to believe that if the Allies did not succeed in mastering the submarine danger the issue was likely to be moot. It would then be a question of whether or not the British could continue the war.

The conflicting policies in the Mediterranean had made it obvious that another international conference was necessary. The Corfu conference took place during the crisis of the naval war. It was held in Gauchet's flagship *Provence* at Corfu 28 April to 1 May. The Allies unanimously decided they would not return to the discredited system of patrolled routes created at Malta in 1916. They would navigate only by night and along coastal routes whenever possible, and those coastal routes would be patrolled along with certain strategic straits. The conference made a major change in procedure: on routes that ran far from the coast, ships would be protected by convoys and escorts following dispersed routes, that is, routes chosen by a routing officer at the port of departure according to the circumstances of the moment.

The Corfu conference had really created a hybrid system rather than one of general convoys or ships sailing independently. All ships entering the Mediterranean were now required to stop at Gibraltar for instructions and formation into convoys before proceeding to Oran, although the authorities sometimes allowed ships to navigate independently without escort if there was no submarine danger. Ships followed the patrolled coastal route between Oran and Bizerte, but they were not necessarily escorted in those waters. Ships were formed into convoys again at Bizerte for the remainder of their voyage eastward. Ships bound from Gibraltar to Marseille or Genoa continued to follow Spanish coastal waters as long as the Germans respected them.

The most important decision of the Corfu conference as far as its implications for the future were concerned was the establishment of a "Direction Générale" at Malta, which was composed of officers delegated by the different navies and was charged with the direction of everything concerning transport routes and their protection. The idea was proposed by Admiral Gauchet, but the British managed to turn it to their own advantage, for they proposed that, without modifying the present system of a French commander in chief for all the Mediterranean, all the British naval forces be placed under a single commander. The British commander in chief would have an officer of flag rank charged with protecting transport routes who would be the British representative on the Direction Générale that Gauchet had proposed. The effect of this would be to give the British the predominant role in the antisubmarine campaign. Gauchet remained the theoretical commander in chief with the largest number of dreadnoughts, seemingly preoccupied with preparing for that major naval encounter with the Austrian fleet.

The French and the Italians had by far the preponderance in capital ships, but the real action in the Mediterranean by this date was the antisubmarine war, and here the balance had quietly swung decisively toward the British. In May 1917 the total of patrol vessels of all sorts in the Mediterranean, from destroyers to sloops, from trawlers to small torpedo boats, was: British, 429; French, 302; Italian, 119; and Japanese, 8.[29] The British had really learned that the Mediterranean was too important to be left to the French. British interests, whether they were shipping or overseas expeditions, were extensive, and they could not rely on others who, with the best will in the world, were apt to lack the resources to do the job. The British were forced to assume the leading part in the antisubmarine war.

The Japanese contribution needs a word of explanation. The British had long been anxious for Japanese assistance. The Japanese had been reluctant to send forces to European waters, although they had, as we have seen, provided considerable assistance in the opening months of the war and later in the search for the German raiders. In mid-April Rear Admiral Kozo Sato arrived at Malta with the Tenth and Eleventh Japanese destroyer flotillas, eight 650-ton *Kaba* class. Sato flew his flag in the cruiser *Akashi*, which served as headquarters ship. In August 1917 the Fifteenth Flotilla arrived with four of the new 850-ton *Momo* class and the armored cruiser *Idzumo*, which relieved the *Akashi*. The Japanese were nominally independent, but actually carried out whatever orders they received from the British commander in chief at Malta. The Japanese in fact worked very closely with the British, particularly in escorting troopships. They soon gained an excellent reputation. Their ships were new and well-handled, and the British paid them the ultimate compliment by turning over two of their own *H*-class destroyers to be renamed and manned by Japanese crews for the duration of the war. This Japanese contribution of fourteen destroyers at a critical moment in the war against submarines has been largely forgotten, but under the circumstances it was far from negligible.[30]

The decisions of the Corfu conference were only recommendations; they naturally had to be accepted by the respective governments. The Admiralty, however, acted fairly quickly, and the Malta-Alexandria convoy was introduced on 22 May with four ships escorted by four trawlers. It proved a success; only two ships were lost between 22 May and 16 July.[31] The French on 18 June formally established a special directorate for the submarine war. The Direction générale de la guerre sous-marine was to a large extent the result of pressure from the French parliament, where there were strong suspicions that the French naval staff had been too tradition-bound and had not paid enough attention to submarine warfare.[32]

Admiral the Honorable Sir Somerset Gough-Calthorpe, second son of the seventh Baron Calthorpe, was appointed British Mediterranean commander in chief. He had formerly commanded the Second Cruiser Squadron and had been second sea lord in 1916. Calthorpe was hardly one of the household names of the war and was deceptively mild mannered. He apparently had a certain amount of difficulty getting his authority accepted by the other commands, but he grew in assurance as time went on. He also possessed good judgment, although he was unfortunately somewhat backward about realizing the value of convoys. At the end of the war he was destined to play a considerable role in negotiating the armistice with the Turks and subsequently became high commissioner in Turkey and the Black Sea. One of his staff officers considered him a man who never sought greatness but had it thrust on him.[33]

The introduction of convoys into the Mediterranean proved difficult. The route structure was complex and the entire Mediterranean was considered a danger area, unlike the situation in the Atlantic where only about 350 miles required special protection for convoys. The British Isles naturally received priority in the allocation of escorts, and the Admiralty added to their own difficulties by insisting that convoys must remain small. There was also the problem of dealing with Allies, notably the Italians. The Italians proved extremely recalcitrant about contributing destroyers and escorts to the common cause, that is, convoys from Gibraltar, and Calthorpe really had no authority over their antisubmarine operations. The Italians insisted they were the only one of the Allies close to the enemy battle fleet, for Pola was only a few hours steaming distance from Venice. They therefore had to retain a significant destroyer force for the protection of Venice and needed their other antisubmarine forces for the protection of Italian traffic in the Tyrrhenian or on the routes to and from Albania and Libya.[34]

THE MEDITERRANEAN CONVOY SYSTEM

Near the end of the summer of 1917 there was still no organized convoy system in the Mediterranean as a whole, and the existing convoys tended to be disconnected and local. On 4–5 September another major Allied naval conference took place in London at which Admiral Mayo, commander in chief of the U.S. Atlantic Fleet, was present. Mediterranean affairs occupied only a small portion of the conference, but the Allies finally agreed on the relative priority of the convoys to be established. They gave precedence to establishing Gibraltar-Genoa convoys because of the Italian coal situation, followed by through convoys to Egypt via Bizerte, and convoys between France and her North African possessions.[35]

The U.S. Navy now made its appearance on the Mediterranean scene. In August the scout cruiser *Birmingham*, flagship of the Patrol Force of the U.S. Atlantic Fleet, arrived at Gibraltar. The U.S. Navy Department had been concerned over the submarine situation at the entrance to the Mediterranean and sent the light cruisers *Birmingham*, *Chester*, and *Salem*, seven old gunboats and Coast Guard cutters, and five ancient destroyers (which had to make the long voyage from the Philippines via Suez). The Americans initially worked on the Atlantic approaches to Gibraltar rather than in the Mediterranean itself. The cruisers were too vulnerable for escorting slow convoys and were used as ocean escorts, but the motley collection of small craft was soon operating in the Mediterranean.

The American forces at Gibraltar were distinctly different from those in the north. The destroyers at Queenstown were among the best in the U.S. Navy. The five destroyers at Gibraltar from the Philippines were the oldest in the navy, the 420-ton *Bainbridge* class. Rear Admiral A. P. Niblack, the commander of the American forces at Gibraltar, remarked in March 1918: "Every time they go out I feel a bit anxious until they get in again." The assorted gunboats and converted yachts were even older, some veterans of the Spanish-American War. There was, said Niblack, "a lot of junk here that has to be continuously rebuilt to keep it going." Naturally northern waters were given priority for new destroyers, and it was only in the summer of 1918 that the first pair of modern American destroyers, the *Dyer* and *Gregory*, arrived for work in the Mediterranean.[36]

The Mediterranean convoy system grew after mid-October when the British felt secure enough to introduce through convoys between the British Isles and Port Said. This enabled them to return Indian shipping from the Cape route to Suez with consequent and significant savings in tonnage by eliminating the time-consuming voyage around Africa. Ships would wait at Port Said for the through convoy to Gibraltar. The OE (outward eastern) and HE (homeward eastern) convoys ran at intervals of sixteen days and were restricted to ships that could maintain at least 10 knots. They were comparatively large with 16–20 ships, and timed to pass the relatively narrow waters between Sicily and Cape Bon during the hours of darkness.

Cooperation between the Allies always sounded much better at the numerous conferences than it proved to be in practice. There was never a real "pool" of Allied escorts, which was often talked about. There were escorts of different nationalities in some of the convoys, particularly the Gibraltar-Genoa route, but the Allies tended to concentrate on their own convoys and often had very different interests. The primary French concern was north-south, that is; communications with their North African possessions, although communications with the army at Salonika were also a major concern. The British were naturally more concerned with east-west communications, that is, the route from Gibraltar to Suez, and communications with their army in Egypt and Palestine.[37] Gibraltar was probably the most "international" of the bases and where cooperation between the Allies seemed better than at other points in the Mediterranean. The British commander in chief, Rear Admiral H. S. Grant, and his American counterpart, Rear Admiral Niblack, worked well together. Niblack wrote Sims: "If there should be a sudden lot of sinking around Gibraltar it would raise an interesting question as to who is responsible because every morning at 10 o'clock the British, American, Italian and French representatives gather around a table and plan for the day. It is the Allied Conference really working with all of the material available at the moment."[38]

Yet another navy joined the forces at Gibraltar in the closing days of the war. Brazil declared war on Germany on 26 October 1917, and the Brazilians decided to send a naval force to European waters. They experienced considerable difficulty making the ships ready for sea, and the Brazilian squadron, two scout cruisers, four destroyers, and a tender under the command of a rear admiral, did not sail until the spring of 1918 and then experienced a long delay at Freetown because of illness among the crews. There was some debate over how the squadron would have been employed. The Italians wanted them in the Mediterranean, the Americans wanted them to work closely with U.S. forces, and the French wanted them to protect traffic from South America to Europe along the African coast between Dakar and Gibraltar. The Allied Naval Council appeared to favor the latter, but the long delay in their arrival at Gibraltar and the end of the war made the question academic.[39]

The international nature of Gibraltar was often reflected in the convoys. A

British officer in the Flower-class sloop *Lychnis* described a 1918 convoy: "My most fantastic convoy from Genoa to Gibraltar consisted of my sloop as a fast escort (14½ knots!), a United States yacht, an Italian armed merchantman, a French trawler and a Portuguese trawler."[40] It would be naive to believe there were no problems; for example, an American officer in the gunboat *Paducah* recalled a squabble over responsibility for losses in a September 1918 convoy, but by Mediterranean standards things worked well. Moreover, the same officer emphasized how the attack in question came after Mediterranean submarines had become more wary and attacks and sinkings less numerous with things so quiet the last few months they thought nothing would happen.[41] This in itself was evidence of the success of the Mediterranean convoy system.

Whatever the difficulties, the convoy system worked in practice, and this is best reflected in the decline in tonnage sunk by submarines. There were months when the sinkings rose over the previous month, but the overall trend was down. It is important to remember, however, that no one could know this at that time and the spurts in losses were alarming. Ships were far safer in convoys, but they were never immune to losses, and convoys sometimes had only minimal protection. And there remained traffic which was neither in convoy nor well protected. The coasts of Algeria and Tunisia were particularly vulnerable. The Mediterranean tonnage sunk in May 1917 fell to 170,626 tons—plus 10,270 tons sunk by the Austrians—compared to the record 254,911 tons sunk in April. The first Mediterranean convoys began in late May, and in June the tonnage sunk fell to 164,299 tons plus 6,174 tons sunk by the Austrians.

In June 1917 the Germans replaced the Mediterranean Flotilla commander, Kophamel, with a higher ranking officer, Kapitän zur See Püllen, who assumed the title Führer der Unterseeboote (F.d.U.) im Mittlemeer and the rank of commodore. During the month of June the Germans had 18 submarines either on operations or about to be put to sea. Nevertheless the tonnage sunk by Mediterranean U-boats declined again in July to 90,334, plus 16,969 tons sunk by the Austrians, and there was another decline in August to 79,549 plus 38,823 tons sunk by the Austrians. This would be the best month of the war for the Austrians, both in tonnage sunk and in comparison to their German ally. The Austrian sinkings were, however, erratic. They sank no tonnage the following month, 12,663 tons in October, 4,016 tons in November, nothing in December, and had their second best month of the war with 26,020 tons in January 1918. The Austrians had only a small number of submarines, and the inevitable intervals these boats had to spend in dock tended to distort the results of Austrian operations.

The eastern Mediterranean was another unprofitable diversion forced on the Admiralstab throughout most of 1917 by the army high command at the request of their Turkish allies, who faced the advance of the British army in Palestine. The pickings were generally slim, conditions unfavorable, and the boats would have been much better employed in other areas. There was a concentration of three to four U-boats off the Syrian coast in November, and *UC.38* managed to sink the monitor *M.15* and destroyer *Staunch* off Gaza, forcing the withdrawal of the British squadron that had been bombarding the port. However, the real thrust of Allenby's offensive had been inland, and Gaza was captured, followed by Jerusalem a month later. The U-boats had been powerless to affect the course of the Palestine campaign, and the diversion to Syrian waters may have been responsible for the decline in tonnage sunk during November.[42]

The losses inflicted by the German U-boats jumped to 148,331 tons in December, the highest figure since the preceding June. The first through-Mediterranean convoys also suffered losses; OE.1 lost two ships and HE.1 lost three ships. It is not surprising that Calthorpe had doubts and feared that "this form of protection is not so efficacious as hitherto" and that convoys were a deterrent at best, not a reliable safeguard, and hampered in the Mediterranean by the restricted areas through which they had to pass. Calthorpe returned to the hoary old idea of making "offensive" operations primary, conducting the maximum effort in the Strait of Otranto and reducing numbers in the Aegean that were employed on minesweeping, blockade, and patrol. He also wanted to form hydrophone-equipped hunting flotillas in the Strait of Otranto. Calthorpe's remarks were sufficient to touch off another debate over convoys at the Admiralty where, incredible as it may seem, more than six months after the introduction of the convoy system following that disastrous April, the director of Operations Division, Rear Admiral Hope, could still suggest they might make better use of destroyers by reducing the numbers employed on escort duty and using those released to hunt submarines, working by divisions, and possibly using hydrophones. Fortunately, by this time the champions of the convoy system, such as Captain Whitehead, the director of mercantile movements, had accumulated enough evidence outside of the Mediterranean to refute the proposals. Moreover, the four subsequent OE convoys had arrived at Port Said without loss.[43]

A careful analysis of the Mediterranean situation would have revealed that the problem was not so much the convoys but the scale of escorts with which the British and their Allies were able to supply them. It was one thing to have a convoy system on paper, but its value was greatly diminished when the scale of protection was minimal, say, one sloop and three armed trawlers for an OE convoy. The trawlers might not be able to maintain the speed of the convoy, and if they had to fall back to assist a damaged ship, they might have insufficient reserve of power to catch up again.[44] Admiral Niblack estimated at the end of 1917 that there were only about two-thirds the number of ships necessary to furnish escorts for the convoys.[45]

Things were actually better for the Allies in the Mediterranean than they seemed, but this was hidden by what might be called the "fog of war." The Admiralstab had discovered in September that in terms of tonnage sunk per U-boat day their success was declining. The situation did not improve for the Germans in 1918, although they substantially reinforced their Mediterranean U-boats at the end of 1917 and in early 1918 with ten of the new UB.III class. As of 1 January 1918, the Mediterranean flotillas were also divided in two with the First Mediterranean U-boat Flotilla at Pola and the Second Mediterranean U-boat Flotilla at Cattaro.

These reinforcements were offset by the increasing difficulties the Germans faced in maintaining their submarines far from home in Austrian bases. The problem was a shortage of skilled labor. In January 1918 there was a backlog of submarines awaiting repair and refit that numbered as high as 17 on one day in Pola and 14 at Cattaro. The German difficulties were compounded in the fall of 1917 by the increasing scale of Allied air attacks on both Pola and Cattaro. These problems only increased in the course of 1918. By June the commander of the German U-boat station in the Gulf of Cattaro reported that frequent British air raids, primarily by DH.4s operating from bases in southern Italy, were affecting the submarine war by interrupting and delaying repairs and refits on submarines and exhausting the crews.[46]

In early 1918 there was renewed danger convoy escorts would be weakened in order to strengthen the Otranto barrage. On 16 January Calthorpe proposed a major reorganization of the barrage. The British commander in chief was seduced by the idea of bottling up the U-boats in the Adriatic and now wanted to deepen the barrage to cover sufficient depth from north to south so as to force submarines attempting to pass through the Strait to surface within sight or hearing of surface craft or aircraft. There would be new minefields, submarines on patrol north of the barrage, and kite balloon ships. Calthorpe envisaged lines of hunting craft equipped with hydrophones, which would force a submerged submarine to change course frequently, increase the distance it would have to travel, exhaust its battery, and thereby compel it to surface. The submarine would then be confronted by faster and more powerful craft than the trawlers and drifters the British had previously employed. Calthorpe proposed strengthening the destroyer force on the barrage, the destroyers to come from those on "defensive duties," that is, escorts and patrols. In more specific terms, Calthorpe proposed substituting sloops for destroyers in escorting the OE and HE convoys at the price of delaying and weakening other convoys in the Mediterranean. Calthorpe, in effect, regarded the Otranto barrage as "offensive" and wanted to strengthen it at the expense of the "defensive" convoys. He also for utmost efficiency wanted the British senior naval officer at Otranto to command the barrage. This required agreement among the Allies and was discussed at a naval conference in Rome, 8–9 February.

The British gained their major point at the conference—a British senior naval officer for the barrage—but at the cost of having to agree to the French scheme of continuing the construction of a "fixed" barrage of mines and nets. The British, after their own design for a fixed barrage had been destroyed by bad weather, preferred a "mobile" barrage with destroyers and drifters. The French and Italians favored a fixed barrage, and the former were particularly dubious about the efficacy of hydrophones. The French and Italians both insisted, and the British finally agreed, that escorts should not be weakened until the barrage had proven itself. In the long run, this may have been the most beneficial result of the Rome conference, for it was some time before the barrage could be completed, and in the meantime convoys would not be weakened and might continue to prove their value.[47]

The Americans offered a partial solution to the problem of where to find more small craft for the Mediterranean. Two squadrons of "submarine chasers" were expected in European waters. The Allies had recommended that they be divided equally between the Mediterranean and the Atlantic, with the first squadron of 36 going to the Atlantic.

The submarine chasers were 75-ton, 110-foot wooden-hulled craft, armed with a 3-inch gun and a small number of depth charges, and equipped with hydrophones. They were intended to work in groups of three or four, hunting for submarines with their listening devices. They were not, however, suited for escort work as they were too small and slow and could not keep up with even a slow convoy in any sort of sea. Furthermore, Admiral Benson and the Navy Department insisted they should be used "offensively" against submarines, and that meant hunting submarines, not other purposes. Calthorpe originally had wanted to use them on the Egyptian coast, but the Allies insisted they would be wasted here, and they were ordered to join the Otranto barrage.

The majority of the Mediterranean submarine chasers arrived at Corfu on 7 June under the command of Captain Charles P. ("Juggy") Nelson. The tender *Leonidas* accompanied them. The chasers were nicknamed the "splinter fleet" and manned by enthusiastic amateurs, a large proportion college graduates or undergraduates. The Americans were confident their listening devices were far superior to those employed by the British and expected great things from them. They went out on their first hunt 12–16 June and when the war ended they had conducted 37 hunts. Nelson believed they had achieved no fewer than 19 "kills." The truth is the chasers never achieved a single kill, and Admiral Sims at one point even admitted to a French officer that the Americans were using them "because we have them" although they were not very efficient for the purpose, because they had been designed before the difficulties of antisubmarine operations had been realized.[48]

The submarine chasers never fulfilled the hopes placed in them, but for that matter neither did the Otranto barrage. It accounted for only two confirmed kills in the course of the war, the Austrian *U.6* caught in the nets in May 1916 and the German *UB.53* mined in August 1918. The latter loss was due to the submarine commander's not realizing the mine net had been extended and thus striking a mine while surfacing in the belief he was clear. Had he known of the extension, he might have avoided it. The barrage *may* have been responsible for the Austrian *U.30* and the German *UB.44*, which disappeared without a trace, but even so, it would be scant return for the enormous efforts put into the undertaking.

There would have been even more effort had the war lasted longer. The Americans were engaged in the enormous Northern barrage mining project in the North Sea (see chapter 13) and had similar plans for the Mediterranean. The Americans expected to have a substantial number of minelayers available once the Northern barrage was completed and would also supply the majority of the material. A special Allied conference was held at Malta in early August with most of the discussions concentrating on the mining projects. The Allies recommended new projects off the Dardanelles, in the Aegean, and a second (Cape Cavallo–Saseno) Otranto barrage to be laid by the Americans. The Americans chose Bizerte as the site of their future minelaying base in the Mediterranean, but the war ended before any of these plans could be implemented.[49]

The submarine losses in the Mediterranean in the first half of 1918, although well below the peaks of 1917, remained high enough to cause alarm. The Germans, despite their difficulties with arranging refits, managed to keep an average 7 to 8 boats on operations all the time in January and an average 10 in March. The amount of tonnage sunk by the Mediterranean U-boat flotillas followed a seesaw pattern: 103,738 tons in January, 83,957 tons in February, 110,456 tons in March, 75,866 tons in April, 112,693 tons in May, and 58,248 tons in June. Sinkings by Austrian submarines remained erratic, from a high of 26,020 tons in January to nothing in February and June. The Allies might be said to have turned the corner after May 1918, for sinkings in the Mediterranean did not exceed 100,000 tons per month for the remainder of the war and showed a steady decline. The totals per month were: 76,629 tons in July; 65,377 tons in August; 35,856 tons in September; 28,007 tons in October; and 10,233 tons in November.

By the spring of 1918 the brunt of the U-boat war in the Mediterranean was carried on by the medium-sized boats of the UB.III class. The large U-boats that had been responsible for the outstanding successes of 1916 were not usually replaced if they were lost or returned to Germany for long refits. The Germans managed to keep up the number of U-boats; they still had twenty-eight in the Mediterranean in August. They also continued work on bombproof shelters at Pola, which could protect five submarines and would be finished by the spring of 1919. In August Commodore Grasshoff, one of the noted U-boat enthusiasts earlier in the war, became Befehlshaber der Unterseeboote (B.d.U.) im Mittelmeer.

The German submarines discovered that merchant ships were harder to find. The Allies developed an extensive network of direction-finding centers and stations in the Mediterranean. There were approximately 11 centers and 14 stations for the British, 20 stations for the Italians, and 14 stations for the French. Room 40 also sent a team of British cryptographers to Taranto, and later to Rome, in the spring of 1917. The Allies, as in northern waters, were therefore able to develop their ability to track U-boats and divert convoys and shipping away from danger areas.

The U-boats also found shipping much better defended, which was evident by U-boat losses. The Germans lost two U-boats in the Mediterranean in January, as many as in the entire year of 1917. Their worst month of the entire war came in May when they lost three U-boats and a fourth was heavily damaged and forced to take refuge in the Spanish port of Carthagena (where it was interned for the duration of the war).[50] Another loss was *UB.68*, which lost trim and broke the surface while attacking a convoy southeast of Malta on 4 October and was sunk by the gunfire of the sloop *Snapdragon*, trawler *Cradosin*, and steamer *Queensland*. The commander, Oberleutnant zur See Karl Dönitz, survived to become commander of German U-boats in the Second World War.[51]

The Allies were less successful in achieving unity of command for themselves. Consequently there was a substantial waste of capital ships employed watching the Austrian fleet because the French were unwilling to place their larger fleet under Italian command and the Italians would not consider anyone but an Italian C in C in the Adriatic. The British tried to get around the difficulty by suggesting Jellicoe as Mediterranean "admiralissimo," but the project failed.[52] Due to their inability to distribute assets rationally, and despite their paper superiority, for a time Allied naval supremacy in the

Aegean actually seemed to be threatened. This was due to the fear—unfounded as it turned out—that the Germans would acquire control of the Russian Black Sea Fleet (see chapter 8). In the summer of 1918 Gauchet sent four semidreadnought *Danton*s to the Aegean to join the potentially outgunned semidreadnoughts *Lord Nelson* and *Agamemnon*. This superiority entitled the French commander, Vice Admiral Amet, to command of the combined squadron to the annoyance of the British.[53]

The French predominance in the Aegean was only temporary. Once Bulgaria was knocked out of the war in September and it seemed likely Turkey would soon follow, neither Lloyd George nor the First Sea Lord Wemyss could consider the prospect of a French admiral leading an Allied squadron into the Dardanelles. The Admiralty ordered Calthorpe to proceed to the Aegean and hoist his flag in a battleship. Shortly afterward they ordered the dreadnoughts *Superb* and *Témeraire* to Aegean waters. Wemyss estimated that counting auxiliaries, 75 percent of the warships in the Aegean would now be British, and they could logically claim command. The claim caused bitter words between the French and the British, including a sharp exchange between the French premier, Clemenceau, and Lloyd George. Calthorpe, with Austria also on the verge of dropping out of the war, stripped the Otranto barrage of 16 British destroyers followed by 24 trawlers, 5 divisions of drifters, and all usable motor launches and prepared to support an advance by the British forces at Salonika along the northern Aegean coast toward Constantinople.

Relations between the British and French were exacerbated when the Turks began negotiations for an armistice at the end of October. The negotiations took place aboard the *Agamemnon,* and the armistice of Mudros was concluded on 30 October. Calthorpe rigidly excluded Amet from all the negotiations, for the Turkish negotiators had been accredited to negotiate only with the British. The Admiralty gave full approval to his conduct. With the *Superb, Témeraire,* and the destroyers from Otranto in Aegean waters, there could be no question of who was the predominant naval partner. Clemenceau accepted the fait accompli; it was Calthorpe, flying his flag in the *Superb,* who led the combined Allied fleet into the Dardanelles on 12 November after extensive sweeping. The following day the Allied fleet anchored off Constantinople.[54]

The submarine war in the Mediterranean ended in a less spectacular fashion. On 10 October the German command at Pola learned the Austrians had begun negotiations for an armistice, and German personnel began to evacuate Pola on the 28th. Nine U-boats were able to sail for Germany from Pola and three from Cattaro between 29 and 31 October. Ten U-boats that could not be made ready for the long voyage home were blown up or scuttled, seven off Pola and one each at Trieste, Fiume, and off Cattaro. The Allies made an attempt to catch the escaping submarines. A new group of American submarine chasers was diverted to Gibraltar on its arrival in European waters, and the British strengthened their patrols in the Straits of Gibraltar. The efforts were as unsuccessful as similar operations elsewhere during the war. One of the Mediterranean U-boats fired a parting shot shortly after passing through the Straits of Gibraltar. *UB.50* torpedoed and sank the old British battleship *Britannia* off Cape Trafalgar on 9 November.[55] The *Britannia* had the melancholy distinction of being the last British warship to be sunk during the war.

13

1918: THE SUBMARINE
THREAT CONTAINED

A NEW STRATEGY FOR
THE GRAND FLEET

On 24 December 1917 the first lord Sir Eric Geddes asked for and received Jellicoe's resignation as First Sea Lord. He was replaced by Admiral Sir Rosslyn Wemyss, the deputy chief of naval staff. Jellicoe's downfall was undoubtedly brought about by the disappointing action of 17 November and the two disasters to the Scandinavian convoy. By this time Jellicoe had been the subject of relentless attacks in the press and much criticism. He was not considered a success as First Sea Lord, and was certainly worn out by the strain of his immense responsibilities during more than three years of war.[1] In the final analysis, Lloyd George may have played the decisive role, for King George later wrote Beatty that the prime minister had "his knife into him for some time & wished for a change."[2]

Wemyss was not in office long before Beatty proposed a new strategy for the Grand Fleet that reduced the possibilities for offensive action by the big ships but clearly indicated the coast of Flanders as one of the few objectives for an attack. Beatty pointed out that it would be impossible for the British to force the Germans to an action at sea at a moment the British selected. In contrast, the German fleet could choose the propitious moment to sail and the British would then have to meet them with a sufficiently superior force. Beatty now had to reckon on the permanent detachment of those forces covering the Scandinavian convoys, for they likely would not be able to join him in the event of a fleet action. The British were clearly superior in battleships, although the Germans might whittle down that superiority by submarine and mine ambush on the avenues of approach. The situation was less favorable in regard to battle cruisers. The British had on paper nine to the Germans' six, but Beatty considered only three (the *Lion*, *Princess Royal*, and *Tiger*) fit to be in line against the Germans. The older *New Zealand*s and *Invincible*s were deficient in speed, protection, and armament, and the newer *Renown*s insufficiently armored. Here Beatty overestimated German capabilities, for he included the *Mackensen* in the German total. The *Mackensen* would indeed have been a formidable opponent, but although launched in April 1917, she was still about fifteen months from completion when stricken after the war. None of her three sister ships were ever completed.

Beatty cited other problems. The Grand Fleet had at best a very slim margin in light cruisers and destroyers because of the demands of convoy and antisubmarine work. There was also the question of British shells. They were inefficient and were not replaced by improved shells until the following summer. For now Beatty was forced to meet the enemy "under a most serious handicap." Beatty's conclusion was that "the correct strategy of the Grand Fleet is no longer to endeavour to bring the enemy to action at any cost, but rather to contain him in his bases until the general situation becomes more favorable to us." Beatty did not mean the British should avoid action if conditions favored them, nor should their role be passive or purely defensive. He recommended offensive minelaying in the vicinity of German bases and offensive operations against German bases on the Flemish coast, which, if successful and coupled with closing the Straits of Dover, might alter the whole situation in their favor and release needed light craft.[3]

The Admiralty approved the essence of Beatty's proposal on 17 January but insisted that the policy was "rendered necessary only by the exigencies of the present situation" and was to be regarded as "a purely temporary measure." They anticipated that within a few months the strength of both the British and U.S. navies in light craft would be considerably increased by the arrival of destroyers presently under construction—at which point the "temporary protective measures" could be abandoned and greater scope given to offensive schemes against the enemy fleet and bases.[4]

Beatty's proposals were not really new; he had followed essentially the same strategy throughout 1917. He was acutely conscious of the defects of British naval construction. In another paper of 29 December 1917 he pointed out that even the numerical superiority in battleships over the German fleet must be qualified by the fact the British battleships were "inferior in construction and protection," and that the improvements made since Jutland were at best "makeshift" and did not "compensate for radical defects in design," especially in regard to magazine protection. Beatty went so far as to write that should the Grand Fleet meet the High Sea Fleet under present conditions, "there may be a rude awakening for the Country."[5]

Beatty's superiority in battleships over the Germans had seemingly been enhanced beyond question in December 1917 when Battleship Division Nine of the U.S. Atlantic Fleet arrived at Scapa Flow on the 7th under the command of Rear Admiral Hugh Rodman. The American dreadnoughts became the Sixth Battle Squadron of the Grand Fleet and included the dreadnoughts *New York, Delaware, Wyoming,* and *Florida,* joined later by the *Texas.* The American ships were by British request coal burners, because coal was available in the British Isles, unlike fuel oil, which had to be imported. However, it took time before these ships were really integrated into the Grand Fleet. The British recognized that the Americans were keen—Rodman acknowledged they had a lot to learn—but at first Beatty was not impressed with their signaling or wireless, or the gunnery of some of the ships. The Americans had to adopt the British system of signaling and maneuvering and in some respects made remarkable progress. In early February when the Americans went out with the Grand Fleet, Beatty thought they "did very well, and will do better next time" and soon sent Rodman out on his own to cover the Scandinavian convoy. Nevertheless, there was no substitute for experience, and in June 1918, six months after their arrival, Rear Admiral Fremantle, the deputy chief of naval staff, reported Beatty still did not consider the American dreadnoughts had been assimilated well enough to be considered equivalent to British dreadnoughts—although for political reasons the Grand Fleet could not go to sea without them.[6] Beatty took care to conceal these thoughts, for most accounts report how well the British and Americans worked together. Rodman wrote in his memoirs: "In my year's service in the Grand Fleet there was never the slightest friction, petty jealousy, misunderstanding, or any serious personal obstacle to overcome." As for Beatty: "It was an honor and a pleasure to serve under him."[7] Rodman may have laid it on a bit thickly, but as friction among the Allies in the Mediterranean showed, it could easily have been very different. This in many ways reflects Beatty's success as a leader. He knew how to appeal to Americans and had the panache to be successful.

The darker thoughts and private doubts of Beatty concerning the design defects of his capital ships would also have been a surprise to most of the officers and men. The overwhelming majority were confident they had absorbed the lessons of Jutland and had few doubts what the result of another battle with the High Sea Fleet would be. It is another mark of Beatty's success that the morale of the Grand Fleet remained relatively high despite the lack of action and the uncomfortable conditions and dismal climate of its anchorage. The British worked hard at it, for in addition to the frequent exercises at sea, often under rugged conditions, there were organized sports and regattas for the men. The storeship *Gourko* was converted to include a theater where ships competed with one another in putting on entertainments. The British naval leaders gave the impression they cared about their men, and morale remained high and discipline good despite the frustrating conditions. Life was certainly no bed of roses, there were inevitable grumblings and discontents, but all in all the Grand Fleet was able to stand the strain of war far better than their German foes. The relationship between officers and men and the disciplinary situation in the German navy were quite different—with, as we shall see, significant consequences.[8]

THE DOVER STRAIT AND THE COAST OF FLANDERS

The Admiralty's desire to prevent the passage of submarines through the Straits of Dover made this area the focus of attention in home waters for the first few months of the new year. There were a number of reasons for this. The Admiralty believed that with the success of the convoy system in the open seas, the U-boats had shifted to attacking close to the shore in the Irish Sea and on the Channel coast where ships left convoys and proceeded to port independently. The British believed that the small UB boats of the Flanders Flotilla played a proportionately large role in these attacks, which could still cause painful losses, even if they came nowhere near the devastation of the preceding spring. If they could stop submarines from using the Dover Strait and force them to proceed north about the British Isles, they could reduce the amount of time U-boats could spend on station and thereby reduce shipping losses. There had been futile attempts to render the barrage effective earlier in the war, which provoked periodic and destructive raids by German destroyers (see chapter 11). The problem of how to proceed provoked a sharp dispute with Vice Admiral Bacon, commander of the Dover Patrol since 1915, which ended with Bacon's removal from his command. The controversy has also been termed "the catalytic cause" of Jellicoe's dismissal.[9]

In the autumn of 1917, Plans Division at the Admiralty was alarmed over reports from the director of Naval Intelligence that a substantial number of German submarines—reportedly 30 per month—were passing through the Dover Strait to take their toll on shipping in the Channel.[10] The mine-net barrage running from the southern tip of the Goodwin Sands to Snouw Bank off Dunkirk appeared to be ineffective. Roger Keyes, the dynamic chief of staff at the Dardanelles, had been appointed director of plans in September 1917, and in November the first lord appointed him chairman of the Channel Barrage Committee, charged with making the barrage more effective.[11] Bacon was aware of the barrage's limitations and earlier in 1917 had proposed augmenting it with a deep minefield running from Cape Gris-Nez to the Varne. The Admiralty had approved, but no work could be done until a sufficient stock of reliable mines was on hand. The British did not begin laying the minefield until November. Bacon had also found other schemes more attractive. A brilliant, if somewhat difficult, officer who was far from popular in the navy, he found himself in sharp disagreement with the proposals of the Channel Barrage Committee concerning the new barrage. The committee recommended that the minefield—later to be extended to Folkestone—should be swept by searchlights at night. The objective was to force submarines to dive into the deep minefield. The lights would be provided by destroyers with searchlights or drifters with flares closely patrolling the minefield, but ultimately the searchlights would be mounted in specially converted lightships that could be moored and would be capable of riding out heavy weather. Bacon opposed the lightships and the patrols burning lights, which he claimed would disclose the line of obstructions and would be vulnerable to German attack. He proposed a system of searchlights fixed on shore on both sides of the Channel, supplemented by three or four shallow-draft and specially bulged ships fitted with searchlights and guns, and moored at equal distances across the Strait. These special craft, not the patrols, would provide the illumination.

These proposals were unacceptable to the Barrage Committee; Keyes was adamant that they could not wait for specially constructed vessels. Keyes, characteristically, wanted immediate action in the face of continued losses to submarines. There were a host of controversies, including Bacon's desire to strengthen the old mine-net barrage and the committee's desire to scrap it as useless. There is no space here to enter into the details of the dispute or the different technical proposals. Both Keyes and Bacon have written at length about it.[12] Personalities also came to play an important role in the controversy. When Bacon delayed an Admiralty order of 14 December ordering him to institute a strong patrol in the vicinity of the deep minefield, the recalcitrant Admiral was ordered to the Admiralty for a special conference on the 18th, which ended with Jellicoe finally issuing a direct order to institute a thick, illuminated patrol of the deep minefield. Bacon complied the following night, and UB.56 was forced to dive into the minefield and was destroyed. The submarine's destruction convinced Geddes, the first lord, as well as Wemyss, then deputy First Sea Lord, that Keyes and the Plans Division had been correct. By this time the controversy also had convinced them they would have no satisfactory solution while Bacon remained in command. Jellicoe, however, strongly supported Bacon. The climax was Jellicoe's dismissal followed a few days later by that of Bacon. Keyes, his bitter critic, superseded him in command of the Dover Patrol.[13]

Keyes was now free to implement the proposals of the Channel Barrage Committee. The deep minefields were laid, strengthened, and replenished as fast as they could get mines. There were about seventy craft, mostly drifters, in line abreast, stemming the tide and keeping station on lit mooring buoys that formed a lane through the center of the minefield. All available old 30-knot turtleback destroyers, P-boats, and paddle minesweepers with searchlights were stationed on either side of the minefield, with trawlers between them burning flares throughout the night at brief intervals. Keyes hoped that as soon as anything on the surface got past the flare line, it would be silhouetted against the glare to the drifters. The drifters, armed at best with a six-pounder, usually would be outgunned by submarines, but their major objective was to force the submarines to dive into the deep minefield. Keyes described the situation on 18 January: "Folkestone to Gris Nez is a glare of light. So killing submarines is simply a question of mines."[14]

The new system demonstrated results, although as in everything connected with the submarine war, they were measured rather than spectacular. There was no miracle cure for the submarine. In addition to the first victim, UB.56 on 19 December, the Dover Strait minefields apparently claimed UC.50 on 8 January, U.109 on 26 January, UB.38 on 8 February, UB.58 on 10 March, UB.33 on 11 April, and UB.55 on 22 April. In addition, the destroyer Leven sank UB.35 with depth charges north of Calais on 26 January. To put this in perspective, prior to December 1917, only about two U-boats had been destroyed by mines in the Dover Strait during the entire war.[15]

The objective, however, was not merely to sink submarines but rather to stop the U-boats from using the Dover Strait. Did the British succeed? On the whole, the answer is yes. The new effectiveness of the Dover Strait barrage was an unpleasant development for the Germans, particularly the Flanders Flotilla at Bruges, for it undercut the geographical advantages of this forward base. The UB and UC boats of the Flanders Flotilla were the majority of submarines passing through the Strait. The Dover passage had been optional for commanders of the High Sea Fleet submarines—mostly the larger U-boats—during most of 1917. On 1 November 1917, Commodore Michelsen, the

Befehlshaber der U-Boote, made the Dover route mandatory, unless physical conditions such as full moon or fog imposed unacceptable risks. The new British measures and the reluctance of U-boat commanders to use the Dover Strait led the B.d.U. at the beginning of February to allow High Sea Fleet U-boats to use the northern route again. The last High Sea Fleet U-boat to use the Strait was *U.55*, which left Helgoland on 18 February, but returned via the north of Scotland.[16] This added six days to their passage, which meant that much less time in operational areas.

The smaller and handier Flanders boats were harder to stop and continued to pass through the Strait, although the overall trend in passages was down. Through wireless intercepts the British were able to discern this, even if they could not know of every passage or all the details. Naval Intelligence estimated total outward and homeward passages by submarines to have been: in December, 38 via Dover and 23 via the north; in January, 17 via Dover and 19 via the north; and in February, 12 via Dover and 29 via the north. Another estimate, apparently using a different basis, showed similar results, with 19 Dover and 17 northern passages in December, 5 Dover and 18 northern passages in January, and one Dover and 39 northern passages in February. The Strait was never completely closed; the Flanders U-boats attempted to use it in diminishing numbers, and suffered losses, during much of the remainder of the war. The last U-boat to attempt the Dover passage appears to have been *UB.103*, sunk by depth charges from 6 drifters off Cape Gris-Nez on 16 September. It is always difficult in submarine warfare to ascertain exactly when and where a submarine was destroyed. Keyes at the end of the war estimated they had sunk 26 submarines in or near the barrage, but a modern estimate based on information unavailable at the time places the correct figure at 14. The effect was the same; the Dover Strait was with but few exceptions for all practical purposes closed to German submarines.[17]

What was the German response to these measures, and what about the vulnerability of the patrols burning lights? Keyes relied for protection on two destroyer patrols, one on the eastern half of the barrage and the other on the western half. The destroyers patrolled the area between the Folkestone and Cape Gris-Nez minefields and the old Goodwin Sands–Snouw Bank barrage. The latter was tacitly abandoned and allowed to deteriorate. The British also relied on receiving advance warning of a potential German raid through wireless intercepts and the work of Room 40.

The serious attack on the new barrage came in mid-February. Marinekorps Flandern requested the High Sea Fleet destroy the new British light barrier in the Strait, which "made it very much more difficult" for the U-boats to get through unmolested and was "actually almost impassable." The German forces in Flanders admitted they were unable "to deal a sufficiently effective blow" and asked the High Sea Fleet for assistance.[18] Scheer sent the Second Flotilla under Korvettenkapitän Heinecke, who was to proceed to the attack directly from the German coast without calling at the Flanders base in order to achieve surprise. The destroyers were to refuel at Zeebrugge *after* the attack and immediately return to German waters.

The operation was postponed once because of bad weather, but on 13 February

Heinecke in *B.97* sailed with the Third and Fourth Half-Flotillas, eight large (1,700–1,800 tons) and powerful destroyers, although one was forced to drop out and return to Germany with condenser trouble the following day. Shortly after midnight on the night of 14–15 February, the German force split in two northeast of Sandettie Bank. Heinecke in *B.97* led the Fourth Half-Flotilla (*B.109* and *B.110*, reinforced by *V.100*) in an attack on the barrage west of the Varne and Colbart Bank. Kapitänleutnant Kolbe in *G.101* led the Third Half-Flotilla (*G.102* and *G.103*) in an attack to the east of the bank. The Germans achieved complete surprise, aided by the very dark night and, perhaps, the fact that it was the first destroyer attack on the Dover Strait patrols since April of 1917. Also, the British patrols committed errors that helped the Germans escape. They had been alerted by NID that a German submarine would attempt to break through the barrage on its way home. This may have assisted the Germans when firing first broke out, as the patrols assumed it was the drifters engaging the submarine trying to break through on the surface.

There were other serious lapses. The three destroyers of Kolbe's group on their way home encountered the four destroyers of the eastern barrage patrol. The *Amazon*, the last ship in the British line, saw the Germans passing astern, challenged, and received no reply. Nevertheless, her commander concluded they were friendly and passed the message down the line of ships to the senior officer in the *Termagant* that three of their destroyers had passed. The senior officer asked how the *Amazon* knew they were friendly, but by the time the messages passed up and down the line and he learned the destroyers had not responded to the challenge, it was too late to act and the patrol continued as normal. Kolbe had not opened fire on the British because his force was slowed by condenser trouble in *G.103* and he erroneously believed the British patrol numbered six destroyers. The senior officer on the minefield patrol in the monitor *M.26* also failed to promptly inform Keyes he had seen a green flare, the signal for "enemy surface craft," as opposed to white and red flares, the signal for a submarine on the surface.

The Germans got away unscathed, although *G.102* was mined on the approaches to Zeebrugge and unable to return to Germany with the flotilla until repairs were completed a few days later. The German destroyers sank by gunfire a trawler and seven drifters and severely damaged another trawler, a paddle minesweeper, and five drifters. Scheer claimed they had sunk more than thirty ships and that a reconnaissance by one of the torpedo boats of Marinekorps Flandern the following day revealed "the guard had been completely withdrawn." The German official history published in the 1960s repeated the claim that the following night the illumination of the Strait had been extinguished.[19]

Keyes wrote Beatty,"The murder of those gallant fishermen has made me feel very b—y minded," and called the German communique "a dirty lie" because the trawlers and drifters had gone out full strength the next night with "the usual number burning flares incessantly."[20] Keyes demanded action against those patrol officers who had let his command down. In the end the commander of the *Amazon* was court-martialed and sentenced to be severely reprimanded. Keyes considered this sentence excessively lenient. The officer was relieved of his command, as were the commanders of the *Termagant* and *M.26*. Keyes, for his part, rewrote the patrol orders to include the clear statements that suspicious vessels were to be regarded as enemy; excessive challenges were to be avoided; and if a challenge was not immediately answered, offensive action was to be taken without delay.[21] None of this should obscure the fact that given the technology of the time, it probably would have been impossible to avoid some loss to the ships burning flares: they were easy targets. Unpleasant as it may have seemed, the occasional loss of trawlers and drifters on the barrage might have been the price of maintaining control of the Strait. Under the circumstances, the courage of the auxiliary patrol who manned the little ships is all the greater. It is also significant that this turned out to be the last destroyer raid on the Dover Strait during the war. The Germans could not permanently shake the barrage and, as we have seen, the barrage was steadily growing more effective.

The German Flanders Flotilla did try to attack the Allied line of communications between Dunkirk and Nieuport where the railway line ran close to the sea. The attack on the night of 20–21 March by nine destroyers and six torpedo boats—with another four small *A*-class torpedo boats to mark the bombardment positions—coincided with the beginning of Ludendorff's major offensive on the western front. After Russia dropped out of the war, the Germans were able to shift troops to the western front, and employing their numerical superiority, as well as innovative tactics, they began a great attack on 21 March. In very broad terms, the Ludendorff offensive was a desperate gamble to achieve a decision on the western front before the American army could arrive in force. The naval accompaniment was puny. The German flotilla was divided into three bombardment groups, but their raid achieved little. They were promptly engaged by the monitor *Terror* anchored off the coast, and the flotilla leader *Botha*, British destroyer *Morris*, and French destroyers *Capitaine Mehl, Magon*, and *Bouclier* immediately put to sea from Dunkirk. The running battle that followed had all the confusion usual in a night action of this sort. The torpedo boats *A.19* and *A.7*, which had marked the positions through which the bombardment groups had to pass, were cut off, and the *Botha*, although slowed by damage from the guns of the German destroyers, managed to ram and sink *A.19*. Her fighting lights were, however, extinguished by damage to her electrical circuits. This led to a tragic mistake, for when the officer commanding the torpedo tubes in the *Capitaine Mehl* saw a large destroyer without fighting lights, he concluded she was German and fired a torpedo—striking the *Botha* in the after boiler room. In the meantime the French destroyers overwhelmed and sank *A.7* and then screened the *Morris*, which towed the crippled *Botha* back to port. The Flanders Flotilla had lost a pair of ships with little to show for it, and, although they conducted a fleeting bombardment farther to the east in the vicinity of La Panne on 9 April, the Flanders Flotilla was as incapable of seriously disturbing the seaward flank of the Allied armies as the High Sea Fleet was of permanently disrupting the blockade in the Dover Strait.[22]

THE ZEEBRUGGE AND OSTEND RAIDS

Zeebrugge, Ostend, and Bruges formed a triangle with Bruges as its apex. The submarine pens at Bruges, protected by massive concrete shelters from aerial attack, were connected to Zeebrugge by an 8-mile canal. A series of smaller canals also led from Bruges to Ostend. The base of the triangle was formed by approximately 12 miles of heavily fortified coastline between Zeebrugge and Ostend. Zeebrugge was also the location of a particularly active German naval air station. The shelter given by the mole generally provided smooth water for seaplanes to take off within the harbor, and throughout 1918 the Brandenburg W.12 and W.29 twin-float seaplanes—the W.29 a powerfully armed monoplane—earned considerable respect from their British opponents.

The German destroyers and submarines at Bruges were invulnerable to attack from the sea. British monitors had bombarded Zeebrugge and Ostend from the sea in operations requiring elaborate preparations and careful screening as well as seldom-achieved conditions of weather and tide. Bacon had hoped to cut off Bruges by damaging the lock gates to the canal at Zeebrugge. The German defenses necessitated long-range indirect bombardment, which, as the official history put it, required "hitting an invisible target ninety feet long and thirty feet wide from a distance of about thirteen miles," all the while under fire from the four 12-inch guns of the Kaiser Wilhelm II battery. The bombardments could not inflict permanent damage, and Bruges remained out of reach.[23]

Keyes was determined to block Zeebrugge and Ostend from the moment he became commander of the Dover Patrol. He recognized the potential threat to the barrage that the Flanders Flotilla represented: "At present it is an awful strain on my flotilla to keep up this constant watch on the Z[eebrugge] destroyers who have so many and such easy objectives within a short steam."[24] The success of the Dover barrage and the blocking of Zeebrugge and Ostend were linked, and offensive action of this sort was completely in line with Keyes's natural inclinations. Plans Division had studied the question well before Keyes replaced Bacon. The importance of Zeebrugge was evident. There had been separate proposals for an attack by others, including Bayly and Tyrwhitt in 1916 and 1917. Bacon too had elaborated various schemes, which Keyes and Plans Division dismissed as impractical.[25]

Keyes submitted the final plan for Operation Z.O. to the Admiralty on 24 February.[26] By then preparations were well under way. The basic plan was to simultaneously sink blockships in the entrance to the Zeebrugge-Bruges canal and the entrance to Ostend harbor. The blockships would be obsolete cruisers: the *Iphigenia, Intrepid,* and *Thetis* for Zeebrugge; the *Sirius* and *Brilliant* for Ostend. The blockships at Zeebrugge would have to pass the massive curved stone mole—1,840 yards long, 80 yards wide, and connected to the shore by a 300-yard viaduct—which formed the harbor and then proceed more than 3,400 feet to the entrance of the canal. There were batteries at the northern extremity of the mole that threatened the blockships, and the raiding force would therefore have to storm and temporarily occupy the northern part of the mole to neutralize the danger. The mole would be attacked from the seaward side by approximately 700 Royal Marines and 200 seamen carried in the specially modified old cruiser *Vindictive* and Mersey ferries *Daffodil* and *Iris II*. The *Vindictive* was fitted with machine guns, mortars, flame throwers, one 11-inch and two 7.5-inch howitzers for engaging the shore batteries, ramps, and specially hinged brows that would be lowered onto the mole for landing troops. The ferries, which the *Vindictive* would have to tow to the approaches to Zeebrugge, would carry 22-foot scaling ladders because even at high water their decks would be well below the mole.

The British planned to sacrifice CMBs—later altered to the obsolete submarines *C.1* and *C.3*—to blow up the viaduct connecting the mole to the shore, thereby preventing German reinforcements from reaching the mole. The plan also called for the extensive use of smoke screens, and aerial attacks and long-range bombardments of the coastal batteries near Ostend and Zeebrugge by monitors would serve as diversions. The bombardments would begin, weather permitting, in the weeks preceding the operation in order to lull the Germans into the belief they were routine. The crews of the blockships would abandon ship in boats and rafts and would be picked up by motor launches and CMBs. A grand total of 165 vessels of all types and 82 officers and 1,698 seamen and marines were allocated to the operation. Keyes flew his flag in the destroyer *Warwick*.[27] Many of the men had been specially picked from the Grand Fleet. There would have been no lack of volunteers: for many Operation Z.O. seemed to end a long period of frustration. At last the navy was really going to do something. Again, Keyes probably expressed the typical sentiment when he wrote Beatty: "The more I think of it the more confident I feel that—even if we don't absolutely achieve *all* we are setting to do—we will accomplish a good deal for the credit of the Service, and will give the enemy a bad night."[28]

The operation was originally scheduled to take place during the period in March when tide and moon conditions were right, but had to be postponed when the necessary amount of the essential smoke making chemicals could not be produced in time and the late arrival of some of the ships delayed their conversion. The expedition sailed the night of 11 April but when only about 16 miles from their objective Keyes discovered the wind had dropped to nothing and then shifted so that it was blowing from the south. This would have deprived the British of the benefits of the smoke screen and exposed the force to possible disaster. Keyes had no choice but to abort the operation and execute the far from easy task of turning the force about and returning to port. The feelings of all, especially keyed up for the operation, can only be imagined. The operation was canceled again on the 13th after the vessels had already raised steam because the wind had risen to the point where the sea was too rough for the small craft to operate or the boarding vessels to berth on the seaward side of the mole. The British now had to wait in great suspense for the next period of favorable conditions of tide and moon.[29]

The tidal conditions were right for the operation to take place the night of 22–23 April, although the moon itself was full. Keyes elected to take the risk rather than wait for the next dark period the following month. The date may have been auspicious; the 23d was St. George's Day—the patron saint of England. As dusk fell, Keyes made the general signal to the force: "St. George for England" and Captain Carpenter, command-ing the *Vindictive*, replied: "May we give the dragon's tail a damned good twist." The Zeebrugge operation might well have ended in disaster, given the scale of German defenses and the implacable conditions of modern warfare, which seemed to put a premium on firepower over human courage. Furthermore, the Germans were fore-warned. During the aborted attempt on the night of 11–12 April, a CMB had run aground off Zeebrugge and the Germans recovered an order with plans for the operation. They apparently acted in only the most desultory manner on the information with a general order for a higher degree of alert to some, but not the most important, sectors of the coast defense.[30]

The Germans reacted to the approach of the British about ten minutes before the *Vindictive* was due to reach the mole. Unfortunately, the British smoke screen here was rendered ineffective by a shift in the wind and the destruction of many of the smoke floats by German gunfire. The old cruiser was exposed to the German gunners in the light of star shells and searchlights. The *Vindictive*'s upper works were swept by heavy fire in the last 200 yards of her approach and casualties were heavy. The commander and second in command of the marine landing party were killed, along with the commander of the seamen landing party. Carpenter increased speed, but the final surge brought the *Vindictive* more than 340 yards farther along the mole than had been intended. This had unfortunate consequences, for it meant the guns at the end of the mole—her original objective—were too far for the landing parties to reach, her guns could not bear on the troops defending them, and she was now exposed to fire from shore batteries to the west of the mole. Other things went wrong. The special grapples with which she was equipped to anchor her to the mole failed to grip, and it required the *Daffodil* to push her against the mole before the special brows for landing troops could be dropped. By this time, only two—later increased to four—were serviceable. The *Daffodil* was forced to keep pinning the cruiser to the mole for the full fifty-five minutes the landing parties were on shore. The *Iris* was not able to anchor to the mole and had finally gone alongside the *Vindictive*'s starboard quarter to disembark her troops only to have the recall sounded.

The landing parties performed prodigious feats of valor, but they did not get very far, and it was physically impossible for them to reach the crucial guns on the mole extension, which were covered by machine guns. The *Vindictive*'s 11-inch howitzer was able to engage shore batteries, but one of the 7.5-inch guns was knocked out and the other never opened fire—two successive crews were killed by shell fire. Carpenter ordered the recall to be sounded once the blockships had been seen passing into the harbor. It seemed something of a miracle that any of the landing party could be reembarked and that the *Vindictive*, *Iris*, and *Daffodil* could get away without being sunk. The British were more successful at the viaduct. Although *C.1* had parted her tow and failed to arrive before the recall, *C.3* reached the viaduct and lodged between two piers. Her crew after setting the fuses escaped in a skiff under heavy fire. The explosion cut the viaduct.

What of the blockships themselves? The heavy fighting on the mole combined with smoke may have enabled the three blockships to approach and escape detection until they were almost on top of the batteries at the extension of the mole. They were then subjected to virtually point-blank fire, but the Germans seemed to concentrate on the *Thetis*, the lead ship. The *Thetis* was riddled but managed to break through the net defense at the entrance to the harbor. She was, however, repeatedly holed and sinking and grounded before reaching the canal entrance. The *Intrepid* and *Iphigenia* did succeed in reaching the entrance to the canal where they blew their charges and scuttled themselves. At this point, the raid seemed to have achieved at least partial success.

The attempt on Ostend was less dramatic and a complete failure. The wind shifted suddenly, ruining the smoke screen laid by the motor launches and exposing the calcium-light buoys the British had laid to mark the entrance to the harbor. They were sunk by German gunfire. The Germans had also shifted the light buoy marking the entrance to the harbor a mile to the east, and the result was that the blockships *Brilliant* and *Sirius* sank a mile to the east of the harbor entrance.

Keyes repeated the attempt on Ostend the night of 10–11 May with the battered *Vindictive* and old cruiser *Sappho* serving as blockships. The *Sappho* suffered a boiler accident that reduced her speed to only 6 knots and she had to drop out. The *Vindictive* at first had difficulty making out the harbor entrance in the fog and smoke, came under heavy fire, grounded, and was sunk by her crew in a position that, unfortunately, blocked only a third of the fairway. Keyes's flagship *Warwick* was mined while retiring with *Vindictive*'s crew, which she had embarked from the battered motor launch that had picked them up. The destroyer was lucky to avoid sinking and had to be towed back by the destroyer *Velox*.[31]

Keyes planned a third attempt for June, using the *Sappho* and the old battleship *Swiftsure*. The ships were fitted out and the crews exercised, but the Admiralty canceled the attempt as unnecessary for the moment as the Germans did not appear to be using Ostend for fear of British siege guns and monitor bombardments.[32] It is a minor footnote to history that the officer selected to command the *Swiftsure* in this desperate venture was Commander Andrew Browne Cunningham, the future Admiral of the Fleet Viscount Cunningham of Hyndhope, probably the most famous of Britain's naval leaders during the Second World War. Cunningham wrote more than thirty years later that he still thought it a pity the operation never came off.[33]

Notwithstanding the failure at Ostend, it seemed as if the raid had succeeded in blocking Zeebrugge. The cost had been high: 170 killed, 400 wounded, and 45 missing. The destroyer *North Star* had been sunk by the batteries at Zeebrugge along with two motor launches. It all seemed worth it to the British public. At last the navy had done something, acted offensively instead of reacting to some German initiative. Keyes was created a Knight Commander of the Bath, and eleven well-merited Victoria Crosses were awarded for the operation. The story of the raid was thrilling and cheered not only the British but the Allies as well. They needed cheering, for the apparent success and great gains achieved by Ludendorff's offensive on the western front had been alarming. There can be no doubt it was a gallant tale to which this sparse summary cannot do justice.[34] The reaction in the navy was similar, for many had the feeling that in the absence of great battles at sea they suffered in public opinion in comparison with the army. The comments of Captain William W. Fisher, then director of the Anti-Submarine Division and a future Mediterranean commander in chief (1932–35), are typical. He wrote Keyes: "You have earned the gratitude of the whole Navy. We feel vindicated. We can put up our heads again."[35]

But what were the real results of the raid? Aerial photographs seemed to confirm week after week that large German destroyers were bottled up in Bruges, and until mid-June large submarines also could be seen in the open, exposed to air attack and indicating the submarine shelters were full. Consequently Keyes believed—and would continue to believe for the remainder of his life—that the Zeebrugge-Bruges canal was blocked for a long period of time.[36] The real situation appears to be different. The Germans were apparently able to widen and deepen the channel between the stern of the blockships and the western side of the canal where they also removed two piers. The Germans claimed that within two days of the raid, small shallow-draft torpedo boats and submarines were able to use the canal, and that on 14 May four 950-ton destroyers were able to transit the Zeebrugge locks. The destroyers in aerial photographs may not have been the same ships. Furthermore, the author of the German official history has pointed out that in order for Operation Z.O. to have been successful the British would have had to block *both* Zeebrugge and Ostend, for ships could have proceeded via canal from Bruges to either place. It is also evident that NID knew of this situation soon after the raid, but understandably did not see any purpose in publishing the news.[37] The psychological impact of the raid far outweighed the importance of its actual results, although in the relevant volume of the British official history published more than a decade after the war there is a frank admission that the average number of submarines entering or exiting the Flanders bases did not decline until five weeks *after* the Zeebrugge raid.[38]

Another aftermath of Zeebrugge was an indication of future difficulties. Keyes requested four squadrons of aircraft to be placed under his direct orders to carry on an incessant attack against the destroyers and submarines the aerial photographs had revealed at Bruges. When Keyes assumed command of the Dover Patrol he had under his orders the Fifth Group of the Royal Naval Air Service consisting of five squadrons with approximately ninety aircraft based on airfields to the west of Dunkirk. On 1 April 1918, the Royal Flying Corps and Royal Naval Air Service were joined to form the Royal Air Force. Keyes therefore lost direct control of his aircraft and the Admiralty had to apply to the newly formed Air Ministry for assistance.[39] The air force reply was prompt, but Keyes received only a fraction of what he wanted and the British air attacks were neither sufficiently heavy nor sustained long enough for really effective results. The official history of the war in the air admits that "it is probably true to say that the Royal Air Force had contributed the most important part of its share in the enterprise before the event" in the form of reconnaissance and aerial photography.[40] The problem was that the Air Ministry had other priorities, for Field Marshal Sir Douglas Haig, the hard-pressed commander of the British Expeditionary Force in France, attached the greatest importance to heavy and continuous bombing of railway junctions, concentrations of troops, and German air fields.[41] Keyes believed that "golden opportunities were missed of inflicting heavy losses on the enemy."[42] The argument the aircraft were urgently needed elsewhere may not be valid. There had been a lull in fighting on the western front during May, and once again the official history of the air war admits that a temporary concentration "could, and should" have been made against Bruges.[43]

The actual tactical cooperation with the Royal Air Force—for example, reconnaissance and diversionary raids during the operation—had been good. The basic problem was one of establishing priorities, and in this case naval interests had come second.[44] It is not surprising that Keyes after retiring from the navy and entering Parliament spent much of his career fighting for the navy to regain control of its air service.[45]

The Zeebrugge-Ostend raid in the long run did contribute to the success of the Dover Patrol, for it might be viewed in conjunction with the Dover barrage and there was no doubt of the success of that. The British official history takes the view that "Zeebrugge was no longer as easy of access as a destroyer base must be if it is to be used as a starting and returning point for raiding forces. The stealthy exit, and rapid return of the raiders—which are the first necessities of such operations—were no longer possible." This is opposite to the assertion in the German official history—published much later—that the conduct of the war from Zeebrugge suffered "only minor and temporary restrictions."[46] However, neither the destroyers of the Flanders flotilla nor the High Sea Fleet repeated their raid on the Dover barrage, and we have seen how the number of submarines passing through the Dover Strait steadily declined to virtually nothing. Yet there was no further attempt to shake that barrage.

The losses of the Flanders U-boat flotillas rose. In the first quarter of 1918, the cruises ending in loss totaled 8 percent; in the second quarter, the loss rose to 33 percent; and in the third quarter, it rose still further to 40 percent. The success of the east-coast convoys and effective counterattacks by their escorts certainly contributed to this. In the summer of 1918, the east coast of Britain became as dangerous for submarines as the Straits of Dover. During 1918 six submarines were lost and one put out of commission in this area. The submarines and their bases also were subject to incessant pressure from aircraft. The decline in the effectiveness of the Flanders flotillas was therefore due to a number of factors, but with this decline the value of the German bases in Flanders was eroded. On 1 October there were only nine or ten effective submarines in the Flanders flotillas. When the bases in Flanders were threatened by the Allied advance into Belgium at the beginning of October, the few Flanders submarines at sea were ordered to return to Germany at the end of their cruises. Five submarines, either obsolete or damaged, were blown up along with a few torpedo boats, but the majority of the Flanders destroyers and torpedo boats were able to escape.[47] The German bases in Flanders, despite their strategic location in the "cockpit of Europe"—a position traditionally of great concern to the British—did not really fulfill their potential. The British may have been worried at times, but the lines of communication between Great Britain and France were never seriously threatened or disrupted for long. The British were simply too strong.

THE LAST SORTIE OF THE HIGH SEA FLEET

Although the great majority of operations in the first three months of 1918 concerned either submarines or small ships such as destroyers and torpedo boats, the High Sea Fleet remained a potential threat. The fleet-in-being can *always* act given the inherent mobility of ships, and the Grand Fleet, now joined by the Americans, *always* had to be ready to counter that action, conscious also of the fact that the High Sea Fleet could choose its most advantageous moment to sortie. There was at the beginning of 1918 concern that the German heavy ships might raid the Dover Strait and break out into the Channel with the objective of inflicting heavy losses on the forces making up the Dover barrage, disrupting communications between England and France, and, possibly, drawing the Grand Fleet southward into a mine and submarine ambush. The light cruisers and destroyers of Tyrwhitt's Harwich Force would not have been able to stop them. The British had the Third Battle Squadron stationed in the Swin—off the Thames estuary—but this only consisted of the *Dreadnought* and two predreadnoughts of the *King Edward VII* class. The latter were laid up at the end of March, their crews used for antisubmarine craft. They were not replaced by dreadnoughts, for Beatty consistently opposed any diversion of this sort. The Grand Fleet frequently had either a division (four) or squadron (eight) of battleships out to support the Scandinavian convoy, and these ships could not be relied upon all the time to join any concentration of forces. There were also four battleships continuously under refit. To detach three dreadnoughts to the Swin *might* therefore mean a reduction of the Grand Fleet by as many as eleven ships on the day the High Sea Fleet chose to do battle. The Germans might reduce their numbers still more by clever deployment of submarines and mines before a battle. Building on this "worst case scenario," Beatty concluded: "The combined reduction might well cause the Grand Fleet to be inferior in numbers of ships capable of lying in the line." Whatever force the British put into the Swin, the Germans could bring a superior force against them.[48]

There was another reason as well. The memory of Jutland was still a powerful one. As Beatty explained to his wife about a fortnight after the Ludendorff offensive had begun, the internal situation of Germany was an unknown quantity and Germany was ruled by a military party which had to obtain a great success or be discredited and might gamble on a naval victory. Beatty wrote:

With such in my mind one cannot afford to run the shadow of a risk, as an indecisive action on the sea with the main fleets, would amount to a German victory. Therefore, at all costs we must aim at annihilation. To obtain this is indeed a difficult problem. The North Sea is so small and the spread of ships so great, that in a few hours the beggars can retire behind minefields and submarine screens in their own waters. I often wonder what Nelson would have thought of it. His high spirit would have chafed him to death by this time.[49]

The strategic situation improved somewhat when the Grand Fleet was finally able to make its long-delayed move to Rosyth on 12 April, although the practice remained of detaching a squadron at a time to Scapa Flow for full-caliber gunnery and other exercises that could not be carried out in the south.[50]

The High Sea Fleet struck, but not toward the south. The Scandinavian convoy covered by a detached battleship force was an attractive target, and the Germans had demonstrated its vulnerability on two occasions the previous autumn (see chapter 11). It would have been quite possible for them to send a force superior in strength and overwhelm the British with battleships and battle cruisers instead of the light cruisers and destroyers used against the destroyer escorts in the autumn of 1917. The British were well aware of the danger, and in January the convoys were run at three-day intervals instead of daily in order to avoid having two convoys at sea at the same time. At the beginning of March, they shifted the interval of the convoys to four and at the end of April to five days. Unfortunately, the need for safety had to be balanced against the need to maintain the volume of traffic with Scandinavia. Longer routes and longer convoy intervals meant, in effect, some diminution of carrying capacity.[51]

Scheer explained his motives for the sortie of the High Sea Fleet in simple terms: Our U-boats had learnt that the steamers were assembled there [between England and Norway] in large convoys, strongly protected by first-class battleships, cruisers and destroyers. A successful attack on such a convoy would not only result in the sinking of much tonnage, but would be a great military success, and would bring welcome relief to the U-boats operating in the Channel and round England, for it would force the English to send more warships to the northern waters.[52]

The German chances for success were enhanced by the exceptional measures they took to conceal their departure, notably, strict wireless silence. This would nullify the advantage the British might hope to enjoy through the wireless intercepts and activities of Room 40. The German plan was for Hipper with the battle cruisers, light cruisers of the Second Scouting Group, and destroyers of the Second Flotilla to attack the convoy and its covering force on Wednesday, 23 April. All available ships of the High Sea Fleet, namely, the flagship (*Baden*) and three battleship squadrons (minus the *Markgraf*), the Fourth Scouting Group (minus the *Stralsund*), and four destroyer flotillas, would proceed to a position from which they could support Hipper if necessary. U-boats that had recently sailed on patrol were ordered for a 24-hour period to look for opportunities to attack off the Firth of Forth and report all sightings of warships and convoys. The Germans could only stay one day off the Norwegian coast, for the range of the destroyers and some of the light cruisers restricted them to a sortie of no more than three days.

The Germans assembled at Schillig Roads on the 22d, ostensibly to conduct maneuvers and exercises in the Helgoland Bight. They sailed at 6:00 A.M. on the 23d but immediately ran into heavy fog, which eventually forced them to anchor on reaching the edge of the minefields. There was sufficient visibility for them to proceed after half an hour, and Scheer thought the poor visibility actually helped them to avoid detection from the British submarines he assumed were deployed about the edges of the minefields on the approaches to the Bight. He was not completely correct. There were four British submarines on patrol, and one, *J.6*, stationed to the west of Horns Reef, spotted the

Germans on the evening of the 23d. Her commander, however, had been told there might be British ships in the area covering a minelaying operation and therefore made no report.

At 5:20 A.M. on the 24th, Hipper was approximately 60 nautical miles west of Egerö steering a northwesterly course with the High Sea Fleet approximately 80 nautical miles behind him. The Germans had been unreported and now seemed to have every chance of overwhelming the Scandinavian convoy and its escorts. There was, however, a fatal flaw in the German plan. Despite all the tactical skill in preparation and assuring the sortie had been undetected, Scheer was acting on faulty intelligence. He had assumed from U-boat reports that convoys usually sailed at the beginning and middle of the week and therefore chose Wednesday as the day for an attack. The intelligence was not correct. A convoy of 34 ships, escorted by the armed boarding steamer *Duke of Cornwall* (1,528 tons) and two destroyers, had left Bergen on the preceding day, the 22d, was about 140 miles east of the Orkneys when Scheer sailed, and would arrive at Methil in the late morning of the 24th. The convoy was covered to the south by the Seventh Light Cruiser Squadron and the Second Battle Cruiser Squadron (the *Australia, Indomitable, Inflexible,* and *New Zealand*). An eastbound convoy sailed from Methil at 6:30 A.M. on the 24th under escort of two destroyers. This meant that there was no convoy or its covering force for the Germans to intercept off the coast of Norway.

High winds prevented the Germans from undertaking airship reconnaissances on the 23d or 24th. There was good visibility on the 24th, and Hipper searched as far as 60° north and subsequently as far east as Utsire light before turning for home at 2:10 P.M. Several hours before the Germans had suffered another stroke of bad luck, which might have proved fatal because it forced them to break radio silence. At 5:10 A.M. the battle cruiser *Moltke* lost her starboard inner screw, which caused the turbine to race, and before the governor could cut off the supply of steam, a wheel on the engine turning gear disintegrated. Fragments of metal pierced the discharge pipe of an auxiliary condenser, several steam pipes, and the deck leading to the main switch room. The central engine room and main switchboard room were immediately flooded, the starboard engine room took on water, salt water entered the boilers, and the starboard and center engines were put out of action. The *Moltke* took on 2,000 tons of water before a diver managed to close the valves controlling the flow of water to and from the auxiliary condenser. Hipper signalled—visually—for the crippled ship to close on the main fleet and continued his search for the convoys. The *Moltke*'s situation steadily deteriorated, however, and at 6:43 she was forced to signal the flagship that she could only make 4 knots and at 8:45 that she was out of control. Scheer was obliged to close on her, and at 10:50 the battleship *Oldenburg* took her under tow. The High Sea Fleet turned for home, and by afternoon the port engines of the *Moltke* were able to run at least temporarily at half speed. The High Sea Fleet limped homeward at 10–11 knots.

The British had been on the alert for German movements because of the Zeebrugge raid the night of the 22d and unusual wireless traffic to the minesweepers in the Bight, but it was not until the *Moltke* broke wireless silence that they realized significant German ships were far out at sea. The first report placed the *Moltke* 12 miles inland, so it was not until somewhat more than an hour later that subsequent wireless interceptions persuaded Beatty to order the fleet to raise steam.[53] At 10:47 A.M. the Admiralty ordered Beatty to put to sea and concentrate east of the Long Forties. Beatty was proud that the Grand Fleet and its 31 battleships (4 of them American), 4 battle cruisers, 2 cruisers, 24 light cruisers, and 85 destroyers were able to get out of what he termed the "cul-de-sac" at Rosyth at top speed through dense fog within three hours.[54] It was too late to intercept the Germans; in fact, a study made in the interwar period concluded the Grand Fleet would have had to have sailed before midnight of the preceding night if it was to intercept the High Sea Fleet during daylight hours on the 24th. There was thick fog at the time, which would mean that even *J.6*'s failure to report probably had no real effect on the final outcome.[55]

The Germans might have suffered additional loss. *J.6* sighted them around 4:00 A.M. on the 25th, submerged but did not attack, and reported them after they had passed out of sight. The Germans were through the minefields, in which they lost *M.67*, one of their sweepers, when the *Moltke* was able to cast off her tow and limp homeward under her own power. She was approximately 40 nautical miles north of Helgoland when *E.42* managed to hit her with a torpedo near the port engine room. *E.42* was subjected to a depth charge attack, but escaped.[56] The *Moltke*—which had been torpedoed by *E.1* in the Baltic in 1915—took on another 1,730 to 1,760 tons of water but was able to limp home, another tribute to the stout construction of German ships.[57]

The operation of 24 April 1918 turned out to be the last sortie executed by the High Sea Fleet during the war. It was also the farthest, and, but for faulty intelligence, it might have inflicted heavy loss. Had Scheer sailed either the day before or a day later he probably would have caught the convoy and its covering force. The author of the British official history questions why Scheer relied on U-boat reports and wireless interceptions to estimate convoy sailing dates when he might easily have obtained more complete and reliable reports from civilian sources—the German consular agents. There is also a little-known footnote to these operations. On 16–18 April the covering force for the Scandinavian convoy had been the Sixth Battle Squadron (less the *Delaware*), that is, the American dreadnoughts under Rear Admiral Rodman. The Americans had therefore missed Scheer's sortie by little more than a week. The service of the American battleships with the Grand Fleet has traditionally been treated as a rather ho-hum affair, dull but necessary. One wonders about the effect on American public opinion had those battleships fallen in with the High Sea Fleet with a loss of three or four ships and a few thousand lives.[58]

The sortie of 23 April was also the last time the Grand Fleet would go to sea in strength seeking battle. There would not be another chance to catch the High Sea Fleet at sea and bring about the illusive classical naval action. The episode also convinced Beatty that he could not rely on Room 40 to always provide advanced warning of a German sortie. He realized that the Grand Fleet could not be at sea all the time and that there would always remain the possibility of disaster to what he termed "this cursed convoy supporting Force." Captain James, who served in Room 40 at the time, later wrote that despite all the marvelous new inventions that might assist, nothing could give the same assurance as a frigate off the enemy's coast. Indeed, Professor Marder believes it is perhaps fortunate Scheer did not attempt another raid on the Scandinavian convoys.[59]

Scheer provides no real explanation in his memoirs why he did not go after the Scandinavian convoy again. The High Sea Fleet became a declining factor during the remainder of the war, and the morale of its men declined. There had already been trouble, harshly suppressed, in the summer of 1917, and the use of a sizable number of capital ships in the Ösel expedition (see chapter 7) in the autumn of 1917 had been at least partially motivated by the desire to restore morale through activity. Morale did seem to improve noticeably with real activity, which effaced what a growing number of men regarded as unfair treatment or a lack of concern on the part of their officers. The German naval commanders seemed to lack the facility that the British had showed to sustain morale during the long months of relative idleness.[60] The results for the Germans would be disastrous when Scheer tried to use the fleet in the closing days of the war.

If one takes a broad view of the naval war, even if the High Sea Fleet struck at the convoy and sank a few dozen merchant ships and several large warships, in fact, even if the High Sea Fleet forced the suspension of the Scandinavian convoy, it would not necessarily by this date have affected the outcome of the war. That might only have been accomplished by submarines, particularly submarines working against the lines of communication across the Atlantic. The major question for 1918 was whether the submarines could regain the edge they had lost by the autumn of 1917 and succeed in breaking the "Atlantic bridge."

THE ATLANTIC BRIDGE

The really decisive submarine operations were apt to be those conducted by the German-based boats of the High Sea Fleet. There are even those who argue that the importance of the Flanders flotillas was overrated, and, by inference, the considerable efforts such as the Dover barrage and the Zeebrugge raid—not to mention the justification for the Passchendaele offensive of 1917—were not the crucial points of the naval war. The Flanders flotillas had been responsible for only about one-third of all losses; two-thirds of the losses were due to the submarines of the High Sea Fleet flotillas.[61] The antidote in 1917 had been the convoy. Could the Germans shake that system in 1918?

The Germans began the year 1918 with no fewer than 120 submarines of the so-called 1919 Program on order (see chapter 11). None were ever be finished. That was not apparent at the beginning of 1918, nor was the fact that the war would not last beyond the end of the year, and the Germans looked ahead to anticipated requirements for 1920 and 1921. In January they ordered another twenty-eight of the UF boats (UF.21 to UF.48), designed primarily for operations in the Channel and North Sea from Flanders bases. The simplified design enabled yards that had not formerly been engaged in submarine construction to be used. Some were switched from the construction of minesweepers, and in the winter of 1918 the Germans had no fewer than eleven yards building submarines. They were plagued by delays. The principal problem, as always, was the shortage of skilled labor, such as engine fitters, riveters, and caulkers. The problem was compounded in the winter of 1918 by strikes and, ominously for its future implications, the refusal of workers to work overtime because of their poor diet and high absenteeism during bad weather. The army was the only likely source of skilled labor, but the high command would not release men in the face of the massive requirements in manpower for Ludendorff's offensive in the west. Notwithstanding the difficulties, the U-Boat Office gave contracts for another 192 submarines in June 1918 including 16 large Ms boats (*U.213* to *U.228*). The latter, with a range of 10,000–12,000 miles at 8 knots would have had a higher surface speed (17–18 knots), which would have increased their chances for obtaining a favorable firing position when operating against convoys in the open seas.

How could these contracts ever have been fulfilled, given the shortages of labor? Ironically, the U-Boat Office in mid-August 1918 thought the final defeat of Ludendorff's offensive gave them an opportunity. The reasoning was simple. The German army was now on the defensive, the submarine war would be even more decisive than before, and the army would be obligated to release the men. They recommended drafting thousands of workers to yards and shifting construction of torpedo boats, minesweepers, and trawlers to yards in occupied Baltic territories in order to free German yards for U-boat construction. They even suggested drafting more than 10,000 workers in Austria to build up to 37 UB.III boats at the Austrian yards in Trieste, Fiume, and Monfalcone.[62] This suggestion certainly revealed little grasp of the reality of the situation in Austria-Hungary.

The idea of concentrating all efforts on submarine construction gained powerful support when Scheer on 11 August became head of Seekriegsleitung—generally referred to as SKL—with Captain von Levetzow, former operations officer in the fleet, his chief of staff. Holtzendorff, chief of the Admiralstab, and Cappelle, state secretary of the Reichsmarineamt, retired. The latter was replaced by Vice Admiral Ritter von Mann-Tiechler, the head of the U-Boat Office. Hipper assumed command of the High Sea Fleet. The reorganization was an effort to streamline the German naval command by creating a real supreme command similar to the one the army enjoyed and ending the fragmentation of authority between Admiralstab, naval cabinet, and the various naval commands such as the High Sea Fleet and Marinekorps Flandern. Ernst von Weizsäcker, a naval staff officer, had a more cynical and widely quoted interpretation: "When a headquarters staff is no longer in a position to lead its forces in the proper sense of the word, it sets about organising."[63]

Scheer moved to general headquarters at Spa to be in close touch with the kaiser and army supreme command. His first meeting with Hindenburg and Ludendorff took place on 12 August, just a few days after the successful British offensive at Amiens on the 8th, a day Ludendorff termed "the black day of the German army." According to Scheer, the army leaders admitted that their best hope now lay in the U-boat offensive, and Ludendorff promised to do his utmost to assist it despite the great lack of personnel. Scheer wanted to put the whole industrial power of Germany behind the construction of U-boats. The mere replacement of losses would not suffice; they must increase the total number of U-boats at sea. Scheer proposed to apply American methods of mass production with the German iron and engine industries supplying the necessary parts and the assembly of submarines taking place at special collecting yards in order to reduce the number of skilled workers needed in one place. The number of U-boats would be limited to a small number of different types with specialization and perfecting improvements subordinated to the need to speed construction.

The navy held discussions with a number of leading industrialists at the Reichsmarineamt on 19 September concerning the ways and means to implement the new large building program that, not surprisingly, was to be known as the "Scheer Program." The numbers were huge. There would have been 172 submarines delivered in 1919 according to the existing delivery timetable. The Scheer Program would have called for 333 in 1919 plus 79 added to the orders for 1920 for a total of 405 submarines.

The Scheer Program for 1919 would have required an additional 48,000 trained workers for new construction, 16,000 trained workers for U-boat repairs, and 5,000 trained workers for subcontract work within Germany. On 21 September Colonel Bauer of the army high command (OHL) indicated the navy might apply for 40,000 in November 1918 if the situation at the front permitted. That was a big if, for the situation had deteriorated to the point where after the collapse of the Bulgarian front on 29 September the supreme command advised the government that it was time to begin peace negotiations. The discussions on the Scheer Program assumed more and more an air of unreality, although paradoxically the prospect of a running down of operations on the western front led Colonel Bauer to speculate they might be able to release 15,000–20,000 men from the army. The end of war with the armistice on 11 November meant the end of the Scheer Program. It probably could not have been carried out in its entirety had the war continued, and Scheer, who probably realized this, might have pushed it more for psychological reasons.[64]

What of the performance of the submarines actually in service? The tonnage sunk by U-boats in 1918 showed no sign of climbing to the levels of the preceding year. The worldwide losses to shipping were: January, 295,630 tons; February, 335,202 tons; March, 368,746 tons; April, 300,069 tons; May, 296,558 tons; and June, 268,505 tons. Approximately 29 percent of this tonnage was sunk by U-boats of the Mediterranean flotillas. The exchange ratio had fallen from August 1917 to January 1918 to 16 ships sunk for every U-boat lost. In 1918 the exchange rate varied from 37 in March to 10 in May—the worst month for the Germans as far as submarine losses were concerned. In May for the first time since the introduction of unrestricted submarine warfare the British gained more tonnage (194,247 tons) than they lost (185,577 tons), although part of this was due to the transfer of ships from foreign registers rather than new construction. Worldwide shipping losses rose during the summer to 280,820 tons in July and 310,180 tons in August only to fall sharply to 171,972 tons in September, 116,237 tons in October, and 10,233 tons in November. The always troublesome Mediterranean flotillas sank 24.3 percent of this total.[65]

The Germans probed for a weak point. The success of the convoys on the high seas led the submarines in early 1918 to concentrate on attacks in coastal waters, the Channel, and Irish Sea. They found opportunities when ships were dispersed from convoys and proceeded to their final destinations, or before convoys could be formed. The antidote by now was obvious: the institution of a system of local convoys to complement the system of ocean convoys. At the beginning of 1918, the OZ and HZ Scandinavian convoys were complemented by a system of east-coast convoys, notably, daily UM (Humber to Methil), TM (Tyne to Methil), MT (Methil to Tyne), UT (Humber to Tyne), and TU (Tyne to Humber). The details of these convoys changed according to circumstances; for example, in March 1918 the direct UM (Humber to Methil) convoy was dropped as unnecessary because the majority of traffic for Scandinavia came from or via the Tyne, whereas in July the escorts of the UT and TU convoys were strengthened and the sailing times altered after heavy losses, which had usually taken place off Flamborough during hours of darkness and were due to submarines operating on the surface.[66] Eventually, because of the threat from the Flanders U-boats virtually all shipping between the Humber and the north was included in the convoys, which averaged 50 ships. One east-coast convoy, UT.18, had the distinction of being the largest oceanic or coastal convoy during the war. It numbered 73 ships and 18 escorts. Figures on losses tend to vary, but approximately 23,000 ships were convoyed in east-coast convoys during the war and 71, or .4 percent, were lost to enemy action. In 1918, 16,000 ships were convoyed and 35, or .22 percent, lost.[67]

The Irish Sea had been another trouble spot. In mid-October 1917 Vice Admiral C. H. Dare, commanding at Milford, recognized the ineffectiveness of the hunting flotillas equipped with hydrophones, which had been on patrol most of the year. Dare recommended escorting convoys to their ports of destination and forming coastal vessels into convoys escorted by drifters or small auxiliary patrol vessels. The hydrophone flotillas with their present instruments and the incessant bad weather were "a waste of useful ships." In December Dare began local convoys between Milford, Holyhead, Kingstown, and the south coast of Ireland. They were successful; 74 ships were convoyed in 12 convoys that month, with none lost or damaged.[68]

The fact that U-boats seemed to be conducting what amounted to an offensive in the Irish Sea and Bristol Channel in February caused the Admiralty to extend the ocean convoys to their terminal ports (see chapter 11). In June 1918 regular Irish Sea convoys were developed, and fairly late in the war in October, a system of NCC, or north Cornish coast, convoys began. Coastal convoys have attracted little attention, but coastal waters were what Professor Marder has termed "the weak link" in the convoy system. There was a somewhat hazy area where convoys had not yet been fully formed or protected, where escorts might be late in arrival, and where ships were vulnerable. It was usually between the port of departure and the convoy assembly point or the convoy dispersal point and the port of arrival, and the majority of shipping losses in 1918 occurred among ships sailing independently in coastal waters.[69]

Coastal traffic could benefit through aerial protection, and by 1918 aircraft and kite balloons played a steadily increasing role. The majority of maritime aerial patrols in

1915 and 1916 had been carried out by lighter-than-air, nonrigid airships, notably the S.S. (submarine scout) and C (coastal) types. These were more suitable for longer range patrols in the North Sea. In April 1917 the famous "spider-web" patrols had been instituted by flying boats based at Felixstowe. These patrols were centered on the North Hinder light vessel in the southernmost portion of the North Sea and were designed to detect submarines of the Flanders flotillas on passages to their operational areas. The objective was to force the submarine to submerge and keep it down for ten hours to exhaust its batteries. The number of seaplane and airplane stations around the coast continued to grow. On 1 January 1918, the British employed on antisubmarine duties in home waters a total of 291 seaplanes, 23 airplanes, and 100 airships. Near the close of the war on 1 November 1918 there were 285 seaplanes, 272 airplanes, and 100 airships. There were an average 310 aircraft ready for service each day during the last six months of the war with a monthly average of 13,000 hours on operations, 26 U-boat sightings, and 18 attacks.[70]

The number of aircraft were still well below the November 1917 estimates by the director of plans of the requirements in 1918 for antisubmarine aircraft in home waters. The initial estimate of 591 (525 seaplanes, 66 airplanes) had been revised upwards in early 1918 to 1,180 (459 seaplanes, 726 airplanes). However, we have seen that on 9 November there were only 557 seaplanes and aircraft. The targets were not met because the estimates had not been made sufficiently early and the conflicting demands for the army and newly formed Independent Air Force drew aircraft from antisubmarine work.

The British could expect some help from the Americans and would have had much more had the war not ended when it did. The strength of the U.S. Naval Air Service in European waters steadily increased after the first small contingent of 7 pilots and 122 mechanics without any aircraft of their own arrived in France in June of 1917. By the time of the armistice, there were 2,500 officers and 22,000 men with more than 400 seaplanes and aircraft. The Americans took over Killingholme Air Station near the mouth of the Humber, established four seaplane bases and a kite balloon station in Ireland, as well as six seaplane stations, three dirigible stations, and two kite balloon stations in France, and another two seaplane stations in the Adriatic. They were working on a large assembly and repair base at Pauillac near Bordeaux when the war ended. Killingholme was probably the most important strategic location. Operations began in July 1918 and by September there were 1,900 men and 46 aircraft flying regular patrols over the North Sea.

The Planning Section of Admiral Sims's staff decided to concentrate the principal American naval air effort in the Felixstowe-Dunkirk area.[71] They also intended to attack enemy bases and formed the Northern Bombing Group, based near Calais and Dunkirk. The force of naval and Marine Corps aircraft was independent as far as administration and internal organization were concerned, but operated under the control of the vice admiral commanding the Dover Patrol. There were originally to be 12 squadrons, divided equally into a day wing and a night wing, but production difficulties in the supply of aircraft forced a reduction to 8, half marines. The Americans, in default of aircraft of their own, ordered Caproni bombers from Italy for night operations, but deliveries fell way behind schedule and the type turned out to be unsatisfactory.

Deliveries of American manufactured DH.4s also lagged, and they were forced to obtain DH.9a's from the British. Operations did not really begin until the late summer of 1918, and when the war ended there were only 6 Capronis, 12 DH.4s, and 17 DH.9s out of a planned 40 Capronis and 72 DH.4s. The Northern Bombing Group made their objective the destruction of the submarine bases at Bruges, Zeebrugge, and Ostend, and there was a strong belief in the American navy that had the deliveries of aircraft equalled the readiness of the shore establishment and personnel the results might have been substantial. The American naval air effort was relatively small for much of 1918, but like so much of the American war effort, it seemed to snowball in the closing months of the war. It was yet another reinforcement to the antisubmarine campaign.[72]

The French contribution should not be forgotten either. The French naval air service grew from 8 aircraft and 32 pilots at the beginning of the war to 1,264 aircraft, 37 airships, 702 pilots, and 6,470 men at the time of the armistice. In a wide area from Dover to the Adriatic the French had 36 coastal bases, 6 centers for captive balloons, and 4 centers for dirigibles. Not surprisingly, much of the French effort was in the Mediterranean and Adriatic. The numbers at Dunkirk were relatively small, only three escadrilles or roughly 32 aircraft of different types in 1916. French seaplanes at Dunkirk suffered heavy losses in mid-1917, and the French clearly recognized that in the first half of the year German naval aircraft enjoyed air superiority. In September 1917 a German air raid virtually wiped out the French bomber escadrille at Dunkirk. The naval air war in the north was a predominantly British affair, but this was hardly surprising. The bulk of French naval forces operated in the Mediterranean and Adriatic, and the distribution of aircraft reflected this.[73]

The use of aircraft was severely limited by weather, and critics of aircraft could later point to lack of success in actually destroying submarines. A postwar technical study found that German submarines appear to have been surprised by the introduction of the "Large America" seaplanes in 1917, and consequently the new arm obtained excellent results. On the other hand, "the Germans progressed more rapidly both in appliances and tactics to avert attack from the air than we did in means for developing the attack." In 1918 U-boats were generally fitted with "altiscopes," which enabled them to check for aircraft in the vicinity before surfacing. The number of submarine sightings in 1918 increased over 1917, but not nearly in proportion to the increased number of hours flown.[74] Kite balloons were also controversial, since they might divulge the location of a convoy and could usually be seen by a submarine before they themselves could see it.

It is certainly true that the aircraft employed on antisubmarine duties in the First World War had little ability to actually "kill" a submarine. But their greatest contribution was probably the respect they instilled in submarines and the limitations they therefore placed on submarine operations. When aircraft could provide aerial cover for a convoy, the convoy was virtually immune. It is hard to quantify the number of submarine attacks on a convoy that did not take place and the number of ships saved because a submarine was kept down by aircraft and prevented from obtaining a favorable firing position.[75] In 1918 U-boats increasingly resorted to night attacks made on the surface. It has been estimated that toward the end of the war almost two-thirds of all attacks were made while surfaced at night. Coastal convoys reduced the effectiveness of the attacks in coastal waters. The aircraft coupled with coastal convoys had the effect of driving many German submarines out of coastal waters, and from May to July 1918 there was a sharp increase in the percentage of submarine attacks more than 50 miles from shore where the U-boat commanders hoped to be beyond the range of land-based aircraft. A post–World War II Admiralty study pointed out that the U-boats apparently preferred the difficulties of interception in the wider waters of the western approaches to the dangers of air attack inshore.[76]

Could the Germans defeat the convoys by a concentration of U-boats against them? We have seen that the Germans did not operate U-boats in concert the way they would in the "Wolf Pack" tactics of the Second World War (see chapter 11). They did attempt an apparent concentration against the convoy routes in the western approaches in May 1918, almost a year after the convoy system had begun. On 10 May the Germans had eight submarines in the danger area through which nine convoys had to pass. The Admiralty knew something of the concentration and diverted HG.73—an inbound Gibraltar convoy—to pass to the west of the positions of three U-boats. No attacks on convoys took place that day. The next evening *U.86* sank the *San Andres*, one of a pair of ships detached from HG.73 for the Bristol Channel under escort of two trawlers. At dawn the following day, the U-boats suffered disasters. The huge liner *Olympic*, escorted by four American destroyers, was near the Scillies when she spotted *U.103* on the surface. The *Olympic*'s captain promptly put his helm over and rammed and sank the submarine. Shortly afterward *UB.72* was sunk in Lyme Bay by the British submarine *D.4*.

The U-boats had little luck over the next few days. They either missed the convoys completely or their attacks failed. On the 17th the skillful *U.55* sank the *Scholar* (1,635 tons) in the well-protected Gibraltar convoy (HG.75), and shortly afterward the same boat sank the *Denbigh Hall* (4,943 tons) in the combined HL.33 and HJL.2 convoy despite efforts to divert the latter. Nevertheless, from 10 to 17 May the Germans, for a loss of two of their own, had managed to sink only three ships in convoy plus another two or three—there are minor inconsistencies between the text and detailed track charts—caught sailing independently. In that same period, 183 ships in inbound and 110 ships in outbound convoys had passed safely through the danger zone. The New Zealand Shipping Company's *Hurunui* (10,644 tons) was sunk by *U.94* 48 miles south by west of the Lizard on the 18th. On 23 May the armed merchant cruiser *Moldavia* (9,500 tons) was torpedoed in the Channel off Beachy Head by *UB.57* while escorting convoy HC.1. She was carrying American troops and 57–64—accounts vary—were lost. On the whole, however, German success remained small, and the apparent submarine concentration seemed to ease after the 25th.[77] The British official history, published in 1931, was vague about British intelligence, merely remarking that "the Admiralty had roughly located" the U-boat concentration. We now know more detail on how wireless intercepts by the French and British assisted them to follow or anticipate the movements of the U-boats.[78]

The Germans in 1918 also tried another variant in the U-boat war—the use of the large U-cruisers in waters far from the western approaches. The large submarines could undertake cruises of three months and included the merchant submarines of the *Deutschland* class, which had been converted for military operations. They were formed into the special U-Kreuzer-Verband. The unit's ten large U-cruisers, plus approximately five older boats attached from time to time, operated in two distinct theaters. In the Eastern Atlantic the U-cruisers operated in the vicinity of the Azores, the Canaries, and the coast of West Africa. In the Western Atlantic they brought the submarine war to the shores of North America.

The operations of the U-cruisers in the Eastern Atlantic from December 1917 through May 1918 could not really be termed a success. Certainly the new U-cruisers, commanded by successful veterans including some of the most famous aces from the Mediterranean, sank ships. *U.152* (Kapitänleutnant Kolbe) in a 117-day cruise sank 13 steamers and 4 sailing craft, or 30,580 tons; and *U.155* (Korvettenkapitän Eckelmann)— the former merchant submarine *Deutschland*—in a 111-day cruise sank 10 steamers and 5 sailing craft, a total of 50,031 tons. The successes included the Italian naval oil carrier *Sterope* (9,500 tons), sunk after a one-hour artillery duel on 7 April, and the British troop transport *Nirpura* (7,640 tons) torpedoed in a Gibraltar to England convoy on 16 April. *U.153* and *U.154* operated together for a time and sank the British Q-ship *Willow Branch* (3,314 tons) after a hot fight off Cape Blanco on 25 April. But their success against shipping was meager. Furthermore, *U.154* was torpedoed and sunk approximately 180 miles west of Cape St. Vincent by the British submarine *E.35* on 11 May. The British had acted on an intercepted wireless message arranging a rendezvous with *U.62* and had sent *E.35* from Gibraltar. *U.153* witnessed *U.154*'s destruction and was able to warn *U.62*.[79] When *U.153* returned to Germany after a cruise of 110 days, she had sunk only three steamers and one sailing craft, a total of 12,742 tons.

The score for the other U-cruisers was also unspectacular. *U.156* in 117 days sank only 21,484 tons; *U.157* in 135 days sank only 10,333 tons. *U.156* had been lucky to return at all. She was nearly the victim of an elaborate trap sprung by Admiral Hall and British Intelligence. The British had intercepted a message arranging a rendezvous between *U.156* and *U.157* and a Spanish brigantine loaded with wolfram at Ferro Island in the Canaries on 17 January. The submarines were to bring the precious ore back to Germany. The British submarine *E.48* was sent to the rendezvous and fired three torpedoes at *U.156*. One hit midships, but failed to explode.[80]

The submarine campaign was about sinking tonnage, and in the first half of 1918 a U-boat operating in the waters around the British Isles sank an average 280 tons per day, whereas the daily average for all the U-cruisers but *U.155* had been below this. *U.155* only just exceeded the average number of ships sunk per day, .15 to .13 in northern waters. In much of the same period, February to mid-April, no fewer than forty-two different convoys with 597 ships passed through a portion of the area where the U-cruisers were operating. Only one ship, the *Nirpura*, was sunk.[81] The operations of the U-cruisers were not, in contemporary terms, cost effective.

Could an attack on shipping off the North American coast have had a greater effect—in a sense bring home the war to the American people? Could the convoys be defeated and the Atlantic bridge broken on the other side of the ocean? The onslaught by German U-boats on shipping off the American coast in the early part of 1942 certainly caught the U.S. Navy unprepared and the Germans took a heavy toll. This was not the case in the First World War. The Germans had certainly demonstrated they were capable of reaching North American waters during the period of American neutrality with the voyages of the *Deutschland* and *U.53* in 1916, but the expected attacks had never materialized in 1917. The U-boats were obviously busy elsewhere. Sims had consistently advised Washington that regardless of what German submarines were capable of doing, or even if a few submarines reached the American coast, it would be a strategic mistake for the Germans to disperse their U-boat force for operations far from the critical area around the British Isles. A German submarine would have been able to make three or four patrols in the Eastern Atlantic for every patrol to North America and would find many more targets in the dense traffic of the shipping lanes around Britain and northern France. Sims was apprehensive that a few German submarines sent largely for propaganda purposes might arouse public opinion in the United States to the point where valuable antisubmarine craft would be retained in American waters rather than being sent to Europe where they were needed. He was confident they would have intelligence of German submarines departing for the Western Atlantic and would, if necessary, be able to divert antisubmarine forces from European waters, which would still arrive before the submarines.

The Americans were not to be deflected from the correct strategy. A special board appointed to study the defense of American waters took essentially the same line as Sims by recommending the dispatch of the maximum force to the active theater of the war while retaining a minimum force to parry a German offensive on the American coast. The special board and Admiral Benson, chief of naval operations, differed with Sims on an important point. Sims, reflecting the British viewpoint, believed American destroyers should be used to protect merchant traffic. Benson and the special board maintained priority should be given to the protection of American troop transports. Benson in February 1918 also opposed using American destroyers for screening duties with the Grand Fleet. They were to protect troop transports and mercantile traffic. Benson, reflecting his partiality toward protecting the buildup of American forces in France, also favored Brest rather than Queenstown as the primary port for American destroyers.[82] Brest in 1917 lacked the facilities to serve as a major American naval base, and Sims had been content to send less than a dozen converted yachts for antisubmarine duties.[83] In the face of the impending troop movements in 1918, the reluctant Sims was forced to divert forces to the French port, where Rear Admiral Henry B. Wilson became commander, U.S. naval forces in France, with his flag in the destroyer tender *Prometheus*. The Americans, characteristically, poured resources into Brest, constructing fuel tanks for example, and ultimately had more forces than at Queenstown when the major troop movements were taking place. There were no fewer than 36 destroyers, 12 armed yachts, and the usual complement of tenders, minesweepers, and tugs.[84]

These were not the only U.S. antisubmarine forces in northern European waters. There were also submarine chasers and submarines. Sub Chaser Detachment No. 1 (36 chasers and a tender) was at Plymouth and Sub Chaser Detachment No. 3 (about 30 chasers) at Queenstown. The submarines were 7 L class—given AL numbers to avoid confusion with the British L class—plus a tender and repair ship. They operated out of Berehaven on antisubmarine patrols.[85]

The question of whether to extend unrestricted submarine war to American waters produced considerable debate in Germany. By the spring of 1918, the converted merchant submarines of the *Deutschland* type were entering service along with the new large long-range U-cruisers. The arrival of these big boats was not without considerable technical difficulties, but now the Germans had the means to carry the war to the American coast. Holtzendorff in March 1918 proposed doing so in order to scatter the antisubmarine forces opposed to the Germans and because it was easier to interdict commercial traffic at well-known assembly points than at unknown destinations. Ludendorff and Hindenburg, anxious to stop the arrival of American troops, supported the move. The German Foreign Office was opposed, largely on the grounds it would inflame public opinion, bring neutrals into the war against Germany, and hamper possible peace negotiations on the basis of President Wilson's Fourteen Points. The kaiser equivocated, first approving of the plan in April but then advocating postponement in June and July on the grounds that the Germans did not have enough submarines to make it effective. The kaiser stood firm against the military. Furthermore, Scheer was also against such operations in principle, and when he became head of the Seekriegsleitung in August, the issue was not likely to be raised again. When German submarines began operating in American waters by the spring, they did so under the rules of *cruiser warfare* rather than unrestricted warfare.

There were some in the German navy who were not enthusiastic about any operations in American waters. Commodore Michelsen, Befehlshaber der U-Boote, was a leading example. He had opposed extending the prohibited zone to American waters after the large U-cruisers began to enter service. He considered the number of U-cruisers still too small, and, despite the success of *U.53* off Nantucket in 1916, the time required for the long passage to and from their operational zone and for overhaul in the yard after each cruise would mean the large submarines would not be able to equal the tonnage sunk by smaller U-boats even though they would cost more to build and require more men to operate.[86] In view of the lack of enthusiasm in the German government and navy—admittedly for different reasons—German submarine operations off the North American coast in 1918 were relatively limited in scope and less than what the Germans were capable of.

The first submarine to attack American waters, *U.151*, sailed from Kiel on 18 April and arrived off the American coast on 22 May. The submarine first laid mines off Chesapeake and Delaware bays, which claimed a 5,300-ton tanker (later salvaged) off Delaware. *U.151* then proceeded to sink a trio of generally small coastal sailing ships north of Norfolk on the 25th and another six steamers and sailing vessels south of New York and about 60 miles off the New Jersey coast on 2 June. The largest had been the New

York and Puerto Rico line's *Carolina* (5,093 tons).

The usual wireless interceptions had provided prior warning the submarine was on her way and shipping had been alerted, but Sims warned the American authorities in the strongest possible manner that nothing was to be done to give away the secret that they had advance notice of the submarines coming. The Navy Department drafted a circular letter, dated 4 May, which stipulated the steps to be taken to defend shipping (including convoys) should U-boats commence operations in coastal waters. Consequently, the American reaction was swift once survivors had been rescued and confirmation received a U-boat was actually operating off the U.S. coast. Coastal shipping was placed under the protection of the naval districts, and a series of special routings together with air and sea patrols was started. On 3 June the chief of naval operations ordered the four naval districts controlling the coast from Rhode Island and the eastern tip of Long Island to Cape Hatteras to institute coastal convoys, and a general wireless message was broadcast to all Allied merchant vessels to make port until further notice if they were not properly convoyed. The convoys were basically confined to the mid-Atlantic region, and traffic elsewhere had to hug the coast. The extent of the U.S. coast was naturally much greater than that of Britain, and the Americans were hampered in instituting patrols owing to an insufficient number of seaworthy patrol craft or aircraft and trained pilots. The American patrols also included substantial numbers of the 110-foot submarine chasers, which were not proving terribly effective in European waters. Nevertheless, Secretary of the Navy Daniels assured the chairman of the House Naval Affairs Committee that there was no necessity to recall any ships from European waters and that the navy's defense plans were "adequate."

The Americans also anticipated that the Germans might attack shipping from the Caribbean and Gulf of Mexico. The Gulf route was particularly important because oil supplies moved through these waters on their way to the east coast or transshipment to Europe. The navy established a force designated "American Patrol Force," with headquarters near Key West, and prepared to adopt convoys as soon as the Germans threatened those waters. They did not prove necessary.

The U-boats' activities created a sensation that is hardly surprising considering, for example, that one of the *Carolina*'s lifeboats drifted ashore at Atlantic City while a Shriners' parade was taking place on the boardwalk. There were even articles by eminent authorities in the press warning that seaplanes might be launched from submarines to bomb targets inland. This led the New York City Police to erect air-raid sirens every thirty blocks and prohibit the use of display lights at night. On 4 June a thirteen-night blackout began, lasting until the authorities decided the blacked-out area was even more conspicuous because it was surrounded by areas lighted as usual.[87]

It took several days for the system of convoys to go into effect, and *U.151*, which had moved south to the waters off Virginia, found numerous victims. When *U.151* returned to Germany in July after a 94-day cruise, she had sunk 23 vessels, most of them small, representing by German figures 51,336 tons, and had also cut the undersea cables between New York and Nova Scotia and New York and Colón. Her commander,

Korvettenkapitän von Nostitz und Jänkendorf, reported brisk traffic by vessels sailing alone and unescorted and favorable opportunities for submarines. The British organized a strong hunting patrol to try and intercept the boat on her way home. They had no success, although the submarine commander reported torpedoes had been fired at his boat north of the Hebrides on 13 July and in the Skaggerak on the 17th. The long voyage must have been a considerable strain, for U.151 was not ready to sail again until 17 October, only to be recalled by wireless within three days.[88]

The coastal convoys ran between New York and Norfolk with submarine chasers and other small antisubmarine craft serving as escorts. Vessels from the Third Naval District escorted ships from New York to Barnegat, where they were relieved by craft of the Fourth District, which brought the convoy to Winter Quarter light off Maryland where the Fifth District craft brought them to Norfolk. Ships were retained in port until there were sufficient numbers to make a convoy worthwhile, and every effort was made to have the escorts on their return journey pick up a convoy going in the opposite direction. If no reliefs were on hand, the escorts would have to take the convoy through to its port of destination. Apparently the submarine chasers had difficulty keeping up with the faster convoys. The Americans also formed a "naval hunt squadron," which worked out of Norfolk. It consisted of the destroyer *Jouett* (833 tons) and six submarine chasers. The chasers eventually received hydrophones, but, not surprisingly as the experience of war in European waters had shown, these methods achieved little success. The number of aircraft and dirigible patrols along the coast also increased. Secretary of the Navy Daniels soon sought to reassure America's allies and offset any German propaganda over the raids. He issued a statement for publication in London on 9 June that the German submarine raid would not in any way change the policy of the American government. The road to France would be kept open for the shipment of troops and supplies, and there would be no weakening of American naval forces in European waters.[89]

The second submarine destined for American waters, U.156, under the command of Kapitänleutnant Feldt, sailed on 16 June with orders to lay mines off New York and operate off New England, Nova Scotia, and Newfoundland. U.156's greatest success was undoubtedly on 19 July when the large American armored cruiser *San Diego* was sunk by a mine approximately 10 miles southeast of Fire Island off the Long Island shore. Fortunately the loss of life was small, only six, but the *San Diego* was the largest American warship lost during the war, ironically in American waters and close to the entrance to New York harbor. Sims had again provided advance warning of the departure of the submarine but not, of course, its operational area.

U.156's most brazen feat was to sink a tug (later salved) and her tow of four barges off Orleans on Cape Cod, and then survive an ineffective attack by four seaplanes—all in full view of bathers ashore. The tonnage involved was small, and the American government promptly took over the Cape Cod Canal for the duration of the war and placed it under the U.S. Railroad Administration. The move was partially to end the high toll charges that had forced the tug and its coal barges to take the longer and more dangerous open sea route. Furthermore, on 1 August the Allegheny region of the U.S. Railroad Administration diverted coal traffic from Port Richmond, Philadelphia, to Port Reading, New Jersey. This permitted coal traffic to New England to proceed by the East River, Long Island Sound, and Cape Cod Canal, a much more sheltered route.

On 20 August *U.156* captured the Canadian steam trawler *Triumph* (239 tons) about 60 miles south by west of Canso, Nova Scotia. The Germans manned and armed the vessel and, working in conjunction with the submarine, used it to capture and sink seven other fishing craft in the Grand Banks fishing area before scuttling their prize. *U.156* never returned to Germany. The submarine was probably mined and sunk on 25 September in the Northern barrage while attempting to return home. *U.156* sank approximately 9 steamers and 20 sailing craft, representing 29,150 or 33,582 tons.[90]

The third submarine to raid American waters was *U.140*, which sailed on 2 July under the command of Korvettenkapitän Kophamel, former leader of the Mediterranean U-boat flotilla. On 6 August the submarine destroyed the Diamond Shoal light vessel off the coast of North Carolina but narrowly escaped a depth-charge attack by the American destroyer *Stringham* on 10 August. The submarine had been chasing the Brazilian steamer *Uberaba* (6,062 tons), which had sent out a distress call. This was the sole encounter between a destroyer and submarine in American waters during the war; the depth-charge attacks opened leaks that left a trail of oil and made operations in coastal waters too dangerous. Kophamel was forced to curtail his cruise. *U.140* returned to Kiel after an 81-day cruise, having sunk a total of 30,004 tons.[91]

The fourth submarine to operate off the North American coast in August was the large new minelayer *U.117*, which sailed on 11 July. The submarine's first victims on 10 August were nine small craft of the swordfishing fleet on St. George's Bank, about 60 miles east of Nantucket. *U.117* laid four minefields between Barnegat and Wimble Shoal, North Carolina, but had to begin her return trip prematurely because of a leaking oil bunker. On a 74-day cruise *U.117* sank 23,724 tons of shipping. The mines took their toll long after the submarine had departed. On 29 September the predreadnought *Minnesota* struck a mine off the mouth of the Delaware but was able to reach the dockyard under her own power. Smaller merchant vessels were less fortunate. The *San Saba* (2,458 tons) was mined and sunk off Barnegat on 4 October, and the Cuban steamer *Chaparro* (2,873 tons) was sunk not far away on the 27th. The last victim of *U.117*'s mines was the Naval Overseas Transportation Service's freighter *Saetia* (2,458 tons), which was lost approaching the Delaware on 9 November.

The American hunting squadrons had little luck and, in fact, suffered casualties from their own side. On 27 August the subchaser *S.C.209* was sunk by gunfire from the armed steamer *Felix Taussig* 27 miles south of Fire Island lighthouse after being mistaken for a submarine. The U.S. Navy also used submarines on antisubmarine patrols, often accompanied by submarine chasers or other small patrol craft. They never encountered U-boats, and there were, perhaps inevitably, incidents when they were mistaken for the enemy. Fortunately, there were no losses. The U.S. Navy also experimented with its own form of decoy vessel. In September and October, a four-masted schooner, the *Robert H.*

McCurdy, was at sea off the mid-Atlantic coast accompanied by submarines. A similar decoy, the 693-ton *Charles Whittemore,* worked out of Newport, Rhode Island.[92] Aircraft also flew many hours of patrols, and on 14 August east of Cape May they and submarine chasers forced *U.117* to submerge. The bombs were ineffective, but the attack probably saved a passing tanker. Once again aircraft may not have been able to destroy a submarine, but they were able to force it to stay submerged, preventing it from obtaining a favorable firing position.

The last two submarines to raid the American coast, *U.155* and *U.152,* sailed on 11 August and 5 September, respectively. *U.155* after sinking relatively few ships and having been beaten off by the British *Newby Hall* (4,391 tons) was ordered by the Admiralstab on 11 October to leave the American coast and operate off the Azores. The next day the homeward-bound American transport *Amphion* (7,490 tons), the former North German Lloyd *Köln,* repelled the submarine after an artillery duel. *U.155* managed to torpedo and sink the American steamer *Lucia* (6,744 tons) in an eastbound convoy on the 17th, but was ordered home by the Admiralstab three days later. The score after a 96-day cruise was a disappointing 15,812 tons.

U.152, another converted merchant submarine, had even less success. The submarine proved too slow and unmaneuverable to approach or maintain contact with a convoy west of Ireland, the British steamer *Alban* (5,223 tons) was able to escape north of the Azores on 24 September, and the American tanker *George G. Henry* of the Naval Overseas Transportation Service eventually forced the submarine to break off the action after a long artillery duel on the 29th. The next day *U.152* attacked the Naval Overseas Transportation Service freighter *Ticonderoga* (5,130 tons), which had straggled from an eastbound convoy because of engine trouble. The *Ticonderoga* tried unsuccessfully to ram the submarine, whose shells repeatedly hit the freighter. The convoy's ocean escort, the cruiser *Galveston,* appeared in the distance, forcing the submarine to submerge, but the cruiser's commander did not want to distance himself from his convoy and did not close. The submarine was able to surface and completed the destruction of the crippled *Ticonderoga,* whose crew was compelled to raise a white sheet and abandon ship. The loss of life had been heavy, 213 out of 237 aboard. Proceeding westward, *U.152* met no opportunities to attack until ordered by the Admiralstab to leave American waters for the Azores on 11 October. On the 22d she received a wireless message for all U-boats to return to Germany. In the course of a 71-day patrol she had sunk only three ships, representing 7,975 tons.[93]

The German submarine offensive failed in its larger purpose. The six submarines working off the North American coast in 1918 sank from May to November (excluding those ships later salvaged) a total of 93 ships representing 166,907 gross tons. More than half (45) were American, but only 33 were actually steamers, the remainder mostly sailing vessels or small fishing craft.[94] The important convoys across the Atlantic were hardly disturbed, and losses in convoys remained small, generally stragglers.

It is also to the credit of the American leaders that despite the shock of having the war brought to the very doorstep of the United States, and despite the inevitable

A NAVAL HISTORY OF WORLD WAR I

rumblings in Congress or vocal public opinion, they never lost sight of the big strategic picture. The war would be won or lost on the European continent, and American warships were not pulled back from European waters and the convoys continued to sail without interruption. Secretary of the Navy Daniels in his annual report termed German submarine operations against the American coast "one of the minor incidents of the war."[95]

The transport of American troops to Europe was the responsibility of Rear Admiral Albert Gleaves, who had been designated the American commander of convoy operations in the Atlantic and subsequently commander of the Cruiser and Transport Force. The liners in the American merchant marine suitable to carry troops across the Atlantic were relatively limited in number. Few of the larger passenger liners before the war had flown the American flag. However, there were 18 large German ships that had been interned in American ports and were promptly seized by the American government. In some ships the Germans had attempted to sabotage machinery, whereas others suffered from the long years of lay-up. It took considerable work to bring the ships back into service by the end of the year, but the effort was certainly justified. The 18 ships represented 304,270 tons and were estimated to have a carrying capacity of 68,600 troops.[96] The former German ships received new American names, when appropriate, and included the largest liner in the world, the Hamburg-Amerika line's *Vaterland* (54,282 tons), which became the *Leviathan*. The *Leviathan* was really in a class by herself. She carried 7,250 troops on her first voyage in December and more than 10,000 in subsequent voyages. The huge liner is estimated to have carried one-tenth of all American troops transported to Europe. She required special handling; for example, she could only dock at Liverpool on a full moon tide, and Brest therefore became her usual destination. The *Leviathan* usually sailed alone because of her speed, although she was sometimes accompanied by the Great Northern Steamship Company's (8,255 ton) *Great Northern* and *Northern Pacific*. These two new (1915) liners were the fastest in the American merchant marine and had been built for the west-coast route from San Francisco to Portland, Oregon. Despite their smaller size, some considered them to be the best of the transports in U.S. service, and from 1921 to 1922 the *Great Northern*, renamed *Columbia*, served as flagship of the U.S. Atlantic Fleet.[97]

The Americans ran their own troop convoys directly from New York to the Bay of Biscay. These were in addition to the HX and HC mercantile convoys and were controlled and escorted by the U.S. Navy, but coordinated with the routing charts at the Admiralty. Nevertheless American resources even with the addition of the former German ships were nowhere near sufficient for the job, and the majority of American troops were carried in British or British-controlled vessels. As of 24 August 1918, 1,454,941 American troops had arrived in Europe, 770,928 of them (52.9 percent) carried in British or British-controlled ships, 663,764 (45.6 percent) in American ships, 18,596 (1.3 percent) in French ships, and 1,653 (.1 percent) in Italian ships.[98] By the end of the war 2,079,880 American troops had been carried to Europe, 51.25 percent in British or British-leased ships, 46.25 percent in American ships, and 2.5 percent in other vessels, notably French and Italian. The Americans furnished the escorts for most of their troops; 82.75

percent were carried under American escort, 14.125 percent under British escort, and 3.125 percent under French escort. The number of American troops transported each month began to rise sharply in March 1918, passed 120,000 in April, exceeded 247,000 in May, and did not drop below this figure until October. The largest number of Americans, more than 311,000, crossed in July.[99]

The Royal Navy manned and operated the former White Star liner *Olympic* (45,324 tons) and Cunard liners *Mauretania* (31,938 tons) and *Aquitania* (45,647 tons) as troopships. In 1918 they were exclusively employed in the transport of American troops. The Admiralty considered that their great speed and ability to maintain it in almost all weather conditions made it safer for them to proceed on their own, and a regular ocean escort would not have been able to keep up with them. They were usually met at the 15th meridian by an escort of four destroyers and escorted to their destination. The British liners had a smaller troop capacity than the *Leviathan*. Their record for the number of troops carried in a single voyage was: the *Olympic*, 6,148; the *Aquitania*, 6,090; and the *Mauretania*, 5,162. The *Leviathan* carried a record 10,860. These great ocean liners were, like the *Queen Mary* and *Queen Elizabeth* in the Second World War, valuable assets. The Admiralty calculated that of the 1,037,116 American and Canadian troops carried to Britain in 1918, no fewer than 135,467 (13 percent) had been carried in the four so-called monster transports.[100]

The huge logistical needs of the American forces in France were handled by the Naval Overseas Transportation Service, which was established on 9 January 1918 to operate the growing number of cargo ships and transports that had been acquired since the United States entered the war. There were already at this date 73 vessels. The maximum number of ships operated at any one time was 378.[101]

The really large movements of American troops began in April, but it was not until August that the Navy Department became sufficiently worried about the possibility of some action by German surface raiders to take measures to add to their security. The older cruisers that furnished the ocean escorts would not have lasted long against a powerful raider such as a battle cruiser. The U.S. Navy therefore stationed Battleship Division Six at Berehaven, Ireland, where it would be well situated to furnish protection to a convoy. Battleship Division Six consisted of the battleships *Utah* (flag), *Nevada,* and *Oklahoma* under the command of Rear Admiral T. S. Rodgers. The *Nevada* and *Oklahoma* were oil burners, armed with 14-inch guns, and the Americans also sent an oiler and tug to service them. The full division was on station by 10 September but was never needed. There were no German raiders.[102]

The troopship convoys suffered relatively few losses, although they were not unscathed. In the British-controlled convoys from New York and Halifax, the *Tuscania* (14,348 tons) in Halifax convoy HX.20 carrying 2,000 American and Canadian troops was torpedoed and sunk by *UB.77* on 5 February, 7 miles north of Rathlin Island light vessel off the northern Irish coast—166 troops and 44 crew were lost. The armed merchant cruiser *Moldavia* also had been carrying troops when she was sunk in May while escorting convoy HC.1 in the English Channel. Not all losses were due to enemy action.

The armed merchant cruiser *Otranto* (12,124 tons) was carrying troops while escorting New York convoy HX.50. On 6 October, while in the Irish Sea, she was rammed by the P&O liner *Kashmir* (8,985 tons), also carrying American troops, whose steering had broken down. The *Otranto*, sinking, grounded off the Isle of Islay, but 362 troops and 69 crew lost their lives.

The American-controlled convoys enjoyed better luck. The losses tended to be where routes converged on the approaches to French ports. All were westbound ships returning for more troops and, consequently, more lightly protected than on their troop-laden voyage eastbound. German submarines torpedoed five American troop transports, of which three sank. The smaller, former Southern Pacific Railway Company New York–New Orleans steamer *Antilles* (6,800 tons) was torpedoed and sunk, 17 October 1917, the former Hamburg-Amerika liner *President Lincoln* (18,162 tons) on 31 May 1918, and the former Hamburg-Amerika liner *Cincinnati*, now the transport *Covington* (16,339 tons), on 1 July. The two liners torpedoed by submarines that managed to make port were the former Red Star liner *Finland* (12,222 tons), torpedoed 28 October 1917, and the former North German Lloyd liner *Kronprinzessin Cecilie*, now the *Mount Vernon* (19,503 tons), torpedoed 5 September. The American convoys had their share of mishaps, including fire at sea and collisions in convoy, usually when a ship's steering failed. They also evaded or beat off submarine attacks. The loss of life in the ships torpedoed was mostly among crew rather than troops and, tragic as it might have been, was trifling compared to the vast number of men moved across the Atlantic. The losses caused by the great influenza epidemic of 1918 were much worse. There were probably close to 15,000 cases of influenza and pneumonia that developed during the Atlantic voyages, which are estimated to have claimed more than 2,000 lives, more than 700 of them soldiers. The situation grew serious enough for the War Department to reduce the number of troops embarked on each liner by 10 percent.[103]

The last word on the Atlantic bridge might be given to a young British naval officer, Sub-Lieutenant G. M. Eady, who had been first lieutenant in the sloop *Hollyhock* in the Mediterranean for more than a year. The *Hollyhock* was one of those hard-worked, ubiquitous Flower-class sloops that did yeoman service in the antisubmarine war and that had paid off at Gibraltar for a long refit. Eady was on his way home through France for leave in mid-October 1918 and described how his train made such slow progress and with frequent halts so that it was possible to get out and walk without fear of being left behind:

The chief cause of our delays were the movements of huge numbers of Americans across France. In fact we scarcely saw any Frenchmen in the country, all the soldiers were Americans, and more than half the rolling stock and Red Cross trains were also from America. The whole of France seemed to have been bought up by the Yank. He had built his own camps, railways, stores, everything. It was a pity some of the German submarine commanders could not see the stuff that was slipping by them.[104]

There could be no clearer testimony to the final failure of the U-boat offensive.

THE NORTHERN BARRAGE

The Northern barrage was a major—one is tempted to say prodigious—effort to bar exit from the North Sea to submarines by means of minefields laid between the Orkney Islands and Norwegian territorial waters in the approaches to Hardanger Fjord to the south of Bergen. It was similar to the effort to bar the Straits of Dover but on a much larger scale. The idea of a great North Sea minefield was advanced by the Bureau of Ordnance in Washington shortly after the American entry into the war. Sims had been opposed; they needed all the surface craft they could assemble for the convoy system, and "to have started the North Sea barrage in the spring and summer of 1917 would have meant abandoning the convoy system"—which would have been "sheer madness." The idea nevertheless had strong support in Washington and surfaced again at an inter-Allied conference in London in September 1917 at which Admiral Mayo, commander of the U.S. Atlantic Fleet, was present. The General Board of the U.S. Navy was won over to the project, and Benson, who was originally opposed, became a strong advocate when he visited London later in the fall.[105] The Northern barrage was agreed to in principle, but its execution was contingent on the availability of sufficient patrol craft, minelayers, and, of course, reliable mines. Jellicoe estimated its completion would require 100,000 mines, and as British factories were fully committed, American industry would have to be used. The Northern barrage became for the U.S. Navy what one historian terms "the one naval effort of its own devising that it succeeded in merchandising to the western coalition."[106] The technical preparations, however, took considerable time, and the British did not commence laying the first fields in the western section (Area B) until 3 March 1918.

There were three areas. The largest, Area A, was approximately 130 miles long and would be laid by the U.S. Navy. The western sector, the approximately 50-mile-long Area B, and the eastern sector, the approximately 70-mile-long Area C, would be laid by the British. In practice the Americans joined the British in laying Areas B and C, partially to take advantage of the greater minelaying capacity of the American minelayers. The minefields in the three sectors differed. Area B had deep minefields and strong patrols to force submarines to dive into those fields. The large Area A had only a shallow field laid in successive lines and, presumably, did not require strong patrols. Area C was considered too far away for patrols and therefore had both deep and shallow mines.

The American force, commanded by Rear Admiral Joseph Strauss, commander of the Mine Force, required an immense logistical effort. The Americans developed a new type of "antenna" mine as opposed to the "contact" mines in service. The antenna mine exploded when a ship brushed a long copper antenna rising to the surface from whatever depth the mine was laid. This eliminated the need for a ship to contact the mine itself and, in theory, reduced the number of mines necessary to make an effective field. The mines were brought from factories to a loading depot at St. Julien's Creek, Virginia, near the Norfolk Navy Yard where a fleet of 21—some accounts say 24—Lake-class cargo ships brought them to ports on the west coast of Scotland. The Lakes were another wartime development. The Naval Overseas Transportation Service operated about 67 of the class. They were standardized small—approximately 2,300 tons—ships built by yards on the Great Lakes, their size limited by the necessity of passing through the Welland Canal at Niagara Falls.[107] The mines they carried were hauled from the west coast of Scotland by rail and canal to special assembly plants established at Invergordon and Inverness. The actual minelaying force, Mine Squadron One of the U.S. Atlantic Fleet under the command of Captain Reginald R. Belknap, consisted of the old cruisers *San Francisco* (flag) and *Baltimore*, converted to minelayers before the U.S. entry into the war, and eight other converted merchant vessels, generally coastwise steamers. The large ships were capable of laying 5,500 mines in a four-hour operation. The Americans began minelaying in the central Area A simultaneously with British activity in Area C on 8 June.[108]

The British had grave doubts about the reliability of the American mines. British patrols consistently reported hearing what they considered to be premature explosions in the American minefields and doubted that American mines laid as deep as 85 feet would seriously harm a submarine passing on the surface. The Americans, in turn, did not believe the British gave their wholehearted support to the barrage or really fulfilled their promises regarding their contribution. Beatty was, indeed, dubious and believed the Admiralty had committed themselves to doing too much. He would have preferred much smaller minefields laid in the Kattegat, Fair Island Channel, and northern and southern entrances to the Irish Sea. The reported premature explosions of the American mines led Beatty to charge in August that the Admiralty had foolishly accepted the American claims the mines would do what they were claimed to do, with the result that they had wasted valuable vessels, time, and material "in planting the North Sea with stuff which debars us from using it and can do no harm to the enemy." Wemyss sought to mollify him, but hardly displayed great enthusiasm when he explained that the decision about the American mines had been reached when the submarine campaign overshadowed everything and that "drastic measures necessitating the whole-hearted operations of the Americans were required, and this, I believe, it was only possible to obtain by agreeing to the use of their mines."[109] Wemyss was also anxious to avoid giving offence to Sims, although in fact Sims was never an enthusiastic supporter of the barrage. The commander of American naval forces in European waters remained a staunch supporter of the convoy system as the most effective means of fighting the U-boats.[110]

Given Beatty's state of mind, it is not surprising there was a major difference of opinion between the allies in August when the Americans proposed to supplement the deep mines in the western Area B with shallow mines. The proposal was based on intelligence that German submarines had been avoiding the central and eastern areas and passing through either Area B or Norwegian territorial waters. Beatty insisted that a 10-mile gap should be left east of the Orkneys to permit the Grand Fleet to cut off any German raiders that might force the barrage in an attempt to attack the Scandinavian convoys. Beatty also opposed the Admiralty's desire to mine the 3 miles of Norwegian territorial waters at the eastern edge of the barrage, with or without the consent of the Norwegians, should the latter decline to mine it themselves with British-supplied mines.

The leads between the islands and the Norwegian coast would still be open, and a British violation of Norwegian neutrality would certainly cause the Germans to do the same. This would mean an interruption of traffic bound for Britain, which proceeded through coastal waters around the south of Norway before being formed into convoy at Bergen. Beatty found the whole idea of coercion of a small friendly neutral repugnant. In the end Beatty and the Americans compromised: a 3-mile gap in the minefields was maintained. As for the Norwegians, diplomacy eventually prevailed, and in late September the Norwegian government declared that as of 7 October the Northern barrage would be extended through their territorial waters in the vicinity of Utsire. The war ended before any of the mines were actually laid.[111]

While the British and Americans were laying the barrage in July, the British continued to waste considerable time and effort "hunting" submarines with hydrophones in the western sector north of the barrage. Following intelligence that a large U-cruiser would be homeward bound, there was a major sweep in the area between the Shetland and Faeroe Islands 12–14 July. The hunting force consisted of a destroyer leader, two destroyers, three sloops, and five divisions of trawlers. They were in contact with a submarine, but after a sixteen-hour chase had nothing to show for their efforts.[112] British hydrophone hunting was no more successful than the efforts of the American submarine chasers.

The strong force of the northern patrol, which had participated in these fruitless hunts, was suddenly shifted to Buncrana by the Admiralty in August. The move was caused by an apparent increase in German submarine attacks on convoys in the northwestern approaches to the northern entrance to the Irish Sea. The northern patrols were now in a position to assist the convoys, but the move had, in effect, nullified a certain portion of the plan for the Northern barrage. The submarines were supposed to be driven into the deep minefields by the strong patrols on the surface, similar to the operations in the Straits of Dover. The Northern barrage became, in the words of the official British historian, "more a dangerous obstacle than a death-trap into which our surface forces were to drive the German submarines."[113]

There is something typically American about the Northern barrage that foreshadowed American performance in the Second World War. There was tremendous effort, great enthusiasm, much money, and considerable ingenuity directed toward implementing a bold project, huge in scale. By the time of the armistice there had been thirteen American and twelve British minelaying excursions on the barrage, the last on 24 October. The barrage had been thickened in places to a depth of 35 miles. A grand total of 70,263 mines had been laid, of which 56,611 were American. The cost had been approximately $40 million—and these were 1918 dollars.[114] There is, however, the nagging question of whether it was worth it. This immense effort and expense had been undertaken in the last six months of the war when the convoy system had proved itself. Furthermore, the barrage actually accounted for very few submarines. American writers believed eight submarines were destroyed, and possibly as many more damaged and a great strain imposed on the submarine crews in the short life of the barrage. The number must be revised downward. There were probably six submarines claimed by the barrage and possibly a seventh. Two or three may have been damaged. Had the war lasted longer—and those backing the barrage seemed to think it would—more mines would have been laid, and, undoubtedly, more submarines would have been destroyed. But would the results ever have been in proportion to the effort?[115]

NAVAL AVIATION IN THE FINAL MONTHS

In the last few months of the war, aviation had become a weapon to be taken seriously, rather than the annoyance it had been at the beginning. We have already seen how both land planes and flying boats were extensively used in the antisubmarine campaign. The British had also steadily increased the number of aircraft with the Grand Fleet by fitting platforms to turrets from which aircraft could be flown off, but not recovered. By the close of the war, the Grand Fleet when it put to sea could actually put up an air umbrella—on a one time basis—of approximately 110 aircraft.[116] These were used for scouting and defensive missions. But what of actually carrying war to the enemy? Beatty, influenced by air-minded officers in the Grand Fleet such as Captain Richmond, had this in mind in August 1917 when he proposed at a conference with the First Sea Lord in the *Queen Elizabeth* that a dawn attack by Sopwith T.1 Cuckoo torpedo planes be used to strike the High Sea Fleet in its German bases. There would be 121 torpedo planes, flown in flights of forty, which would be transported to within range by carriers. The torpedo planes might be accompanied by long-range H.12 ("Large America") flying boats, operating independently from the carriers from their bases in England.[117] In the absence of suitable carriers, Beatty suggested using eight merchant vessels fitted with flying-off platforms. Unfortunately the material to execute a plan like this was not available in 1917. The Admiralty also claimed the torpedo-carrying aircraft, the Sopwith Cuckoo, would not be available in quantity until the following summer—in fact only a little more than ninety had been delivered by the time of the armistice—the torpedo it could carry too small, and the tactics for torpedo attacks on warships still unpracticed to justify diverting badly needed merchant ships and dockyard facilities for conversion work. The dawn attack by torpedo aircraft would have to wait until the technical means were available.[118]

There had been air raids with seaplanes launched by seaplane carriers earlier in the war in both the North Sea and the Black Sea. The results had been meager; the weight and drag of floats imposed performance penalties on seaplanes and the process of launching and recovering them in the open sea was difficult, particularly in North Sea conditions. The British worked doggedly at launching land aircraft from ships and the much more difficult task of recovering them. There is no space to describe this fascinating story here, but by the summer of 1918 they were close to introducing true aircraft carriers. The battle cruiser *Furious* had originally been designed as one of Fisher's light battle cruisers for the Baltic project. She had been something of a freak with a primary armament of only two 18-inch guns. The design was altered and *Furious* joined the fleet as a fast seaplane carrier in the summer of 1917 with the forward 18-inch turret replaced by a flight platform. She originally embarked five Sopwith Pups and three Short 184 seaplanes. On 2 August 1917 a Sopwith Pup flown by Squadron Commander E. H. Dunning landed on board, the first time an aircraft had landed onto a moving ship. Dunning succeeded with a second attempt, but on the third trial on 7 August, his engine stalled, the aircraft was blown over the side, and he was killed. Between November and March, the *Furious* went through another conversion, and the after turret was also replaced by a flight deck and hangar with fore and aft elevators for aircraft. Unfortunately, the experiments at landing aircraft proved to be a failure because of eddies and air currents caused by the midships superstructure and funnels. After the war the *Furious* was reconstructed as a true aircraft carrier with a long flight deck, but in the summer of 1918 she could launch her complement of approximately sixteen aircraft but not recover them. Land aircraft still had to ditch when they rejoined the carrier after an operation.

The *Vindictive* was another carrier under construction. She was actually a converted light cruiser, originally named the *Cavendish* but renamed in honor of the cruiser expended in the Zeebrugge-Ostend raids. The *Vindictive* was fitted with a hangar, flying-off deck forward, and flying-on deck aft. She was designed to carry six reconnaissance aircraft and has been described as a miniature *Furious,* but did not join the fleet until the closing days of the war.

The *Argus* was the most interesting and potentially the most useful of the carriers under construction in the summer of 1918. She was originally laid down in June 1914 as the Lloyd Sabaudo liner *Conte Rosso,* but construction halted after the beginning of the war. The ship was acquired by the Admiralty in 1916 for conversion into a seaplane carrier. The work went slowly, hampered by repeated design changes in what was still a very experimental field. The *Argus* was eventually completed with a flush deck unobstructed by superstructure or funnels as well as a pilothouse charthouse that could be lowered during flying operations. She did not commission until September 1918, but soon completed a series of successful takeoffs and landings with Sopwith 1 1/2 Strutters. She was capable of carrying 20–21 aircraft. In October she embarked a squadron of Sopwith T.1 Cuckoo torpedo planes that were to be used to attack the High Sea Fleet in Wilhelmshaven. The squadron pilots were still gaining experience in carrier operations when the war ended a few weeks later.[119]

The carrier operations actually carried out in the summer of 1918 were far more modest than Beatty had wanted, although they are not without interest. The *Furious* played a prominent role. The carrier would proceed to the edge of the Helgoland Bight minefields and launch reconnaissance aircraft. The British hoped to trap a Zeppelin, and on one occasion, 17 June, she was bombed twice by German seaplanes. The *Furious* launched two Sopwith Camels, but they failed to catch the first attackers and had to ditch. The *Furious* launched another pair of Camels to counter a second German attack, and a German seaplane was forced down. The British decided to attack the Zeppelins in their base at Tondern, and at dawn on 19 July, after earlier attacks had been aborted because

A NAVAL HISTORY OF WORLD WAR I

of weather, the *Furious* launched two flights of Sopwith Camels—seven aircraft—each carrying two 50-pound bombs. The *Furious* was screened by the First Light Cruiser Squadron, with a division of the First Battle Squadron and the Seventh Light Cruiser Squadron out in support. She was approximately 80 miles northwest of the German base. The British succeeded in destroying one of the sheds, along with Zeppelins *L.54* and *L.60*. One Camel had been forced down by engine trouble before reaching the target, three had to land in Denmark, one pilot was drowned, and two made it back to their ships to be picked up by a destroyer after ditching. The raid was the first conducted by land planes flown off a carrier and was the most successful carrier launched operation of the war.[120]

The Grand Fleet and Harwich Force carried aircraft for defensive purposes, particularly against Zeppelins, which shadowed British squadrons on their sweeps. Naturally the pilots would have to ditch after each operation. In the North Sea on 21 August 1917 the light cruiser *Yarmouth* launched a Sopwith Pup flown by Lieutenant B. A. Smart, who shot down Zeppelin *L.23*. This success led to a number of light cruisers being fitted with flying-off platforms on their turrets. There was another variation: destroyers towed lighters carrying flying boats and then experimented with land planes. On 11 August 1918, a Sopwith Camel took off from a lighter towed by the destroyer *Redoubt* of the Harwich Force, and the pilot, Lieutenant S. D. Culley, succeeded in shooting down Zeppelin *L.53* off Terschelling.[121]

Culley's victory occurred shortly after a stunning success by German seaplanes during the same operation. Tyrwhitt with four light cruisers and thirteen destroyers of the Harwich Force was on a reconnaissance sweep of the southwestern exits of the Helgoland Bight minefields. Three of the destroyers towed lighters carrying flying boats, and two towed lighters with aircraft, one of them Culley's. When the British reached a point approximately 25 miles northwest of the island of Vlieland, six shallow-draft coastal motorboats armed with torpedoes were detached to cross the minefields and proceed to the mouth of the Ems with orders to attack any German minesweepers or their supporting forces they encountered. The CMBs should have had air cover, but there was no wind that morning, and the flying boats were unable to take off.

The CMBs kept about a mile outside of Dutch territorial waters and had just passed Terschelling when they were attacked by six, later increased to eight (German sources say nine), German aircraft of the Kampstaffel V and Kampstaffel I from the Borkum naval air station. A running battle developed as the flotilla closed up to concentrate the fire of their Lewis guns and continued eastward at 30 knots for about half an hour, the airplanes dropping a few bombs but relying mostly on their machine guns. The Germans gained the advantage when the CMBs turned to the west to rejoin the Harwich Force when they were abeam of Ameland lighthouse. The German aircraft now had the sun behind them. Four (German sources say five) more German aircraft from Kampfstaffel Norderney joined the fight, and the CMBs were riddled as they ran out of ammunition or their guns jammed. The German aircraft were all seaplanes, either the older Friedrichshafen FF.49C or the more modern Brandenburg W.12 and W.29. The CMBs managed to shoot down one of the Brandenburg W.29s, but eventually all but

CMB.41 were dead in the water. Three CMBs were sunk, *CMB.41* managed to reach the Dutch shore, and two others, crippled, drifted into Dutch territorial waters and were towed to port by a Dutch torpedo boat.[122]

An entire naval force had been eliminated by aircraft the same morning that a reconnaissance Zeppelin had been destroyed by a plane launched by a naval force. The actions on 11 August gave a striking demonstration of the new dimension in naval warfare. At the same time, the *Argus* was nearing completion and there were plans for an air attack on the German fleet. The carrier-launched attack never took place before the war ended, but the development of the *Argus* along with the events of 11 August pointed the way toward the future course of naval warfare to those who paid attention.

DER TAG: THE END OF THE WAR

By the beginning of autumn, the Allied armies were advancing steadily in France and Flanders, and the end of the war was much closer than those engaged in the daily routine of naval operations probably realized. Despite all the emphasis on submarines and aircraft, the war might well have ended with a classic naval action, the same type of action that had been anticipated at the beginning in 1914. The Germans evacuated their Flanders bases between 29 September and 3 October. Eleven destroyers, 13 torpedo boats, 7 submarines, and 33 seaplanes escaped to German waters. Those ships that were not ready for sea or could not make the journey were blown up or scuttled. They included 5 destroyers, 3 submarines, and 12 torpedo boats. Tyrwhitt had been standing by to intercept and believed the Admiralty had been "caught napping" and had not expected the Germans to break out so soon. Consequently, the Harwich Force put to sea five hours behind the Germans and was further slowed when its destroyers could not keep up in a full gale. The Germans also benefited from the moonless nights and their ability to slip out at high water through the channels in the sand banks off the Scheldt, which kept the British flotillas from closing.[123]

On 29 September the news that Germany's ally Bulgaria had concluded an armistice led the German high command to advise the kaiser to seek an immediate armistice. On 3 October Prince Max von Baden became German chancellor and immediately appealed to President Wilson for an armistice. Wilson's terms included the evacuation of enemy soil by German armies and the end of submarine attacks on passenger vessels. On 20 October Prince Max accepted Wilson's demands that submarine attacks on passenger ships cease. Scheer had been opposed to this while fighting was still in progress, for it would be tantamount to ending the submarine campaign. Nevertheless, on 21 October the U-boats were recalled. The German naval leaders, however, were not willing to end the war quietly. In Scheer's eyes the end of the submarine campaign released the U-boats for service with the High Sea Fleet. The navy could not remain inactive while fighting continued on the front, and a success at sea would obtain more favorable peace terms. The High Sea Fleet would choose its point of attack wisely, and even if it suffered losses, the enemy losses would be in proportion and the Germans would still have sufficient strength to protect the submarine campaign in the North Sea should it have to be resumed. On 21 October Scheer's chief of staff Captain von Levetzow secretly brought the order to Hipper: "The forces of the High Sea Fleet are to be made ready for attack and battle with the English Fleet." Scheer apparently did not inform either the kaiser or the chancellor.[124]

Hipper was well aware he might receive such an order. He had discussed the possibility of a final battle with his staff earlier in the month, and on 10 October his own chief of staff, Rear Admiral von Trotha, had given him the draft of a plan for a bombardment of the British coast, the interruption of the supply lines between Britain and the Continent, and a battle with the British fleet. The objective was to relieve pressure on the right flank of the German army. The element of "honor" was also not lacking. As Trotha's memorandum presented it: "As to a battle for the honor of the fleet in this war, even if it were a death battle, it would be the foundation for a new German fleet of the future if our people were not altogether defeated; such a fleet would be out of the question in the event of a dishonorable peace."[125]

This point has been widely cited, although a recent biographer of Hipper argues this motivation was one of many and not necessarily decisive in planning the operation. The German plan was more than just a suicide mission into the jaws of the Grand Fleet. There was some military rationale behind it, possibly even some chance of success, and Hipper insisted on some leeway in choosing the moment for its execution. Certainly Hipper was also well aware that with the exception of the destroyers and U-boats, the German crews were now unreliable, and that the fleet had been weakened by the widespread disappearance of experienced middle rank officers.[126]

Hipper's plans for the sortie of the High Sea Fleet were contained in Operations Plan No. 19 of 24 October. The High Sea Fleet would leave the Bight by day and remain out of sight of the Dutch coast. The fleet would proceed into the Hoofden—the southern part of the North Sea—and attack the Flanders coast and Thames estuary at daylight on the second day of the operation. The commander of destroyers with 3 cruisers and the Second Destroyer Flotilla (10 destroyers) would attack the Flanders coast, and the commander of the Second Scouting Group with 4 cruisers and the Second Destroyer Half-Flotilla (5 destroyers) would attack the mouth of the Thames. The High Sea Fleet (18 dreadnoughts) would cover the Flanders attack; the 5 battle cruisers of the First Scouting Group would cover the attack on the Thames estuary. The retirement of the German fleet would be arranged so as to arrive at the most advantageous place to give battle off Terschelling one or two hours before dark on the evening of the second day. The commander of the Fourth Scouting Group (6 light cruisers), reinforced by the cruiser-minelayer *Arkona*, the auxiliary cruiser *Möwe*, and the Eighth Destroyer Flotilla (10 destroyers), would be responsible for mining the routes by which the Grand Fleet might be expected to approach. In case there had been no encounter with the British by the night of the second to third day, the commander of the flotillas would execute an offensive sweep in the direction of the Firth of Forth with the destroyers starting from Terschelling light vessel.

The Germans intended to use, if possible, 7 Zeppelins for reconnaissance. Submarines were an even more important part of the plan. There would be approximately 25 U-boats deployed in six lines on British approach routes from the east coast of Scotland to Terschelling to cover the retirement of the High Sea Fleet and attack British forces before and after the battle. The U-boats had orders to concentrate on warships, refrain from attacks on cargo ships, make use of even unfavorable firing opportunities, and in the case of battleships and battle cruisers as far as possible fire salvoes of three torpedoes. They were not to economize on the expenditure of torpedoes. The operational orders were issued on 27 October with the operation to take place on the 30th. The submarines left for their designated positions the next day; the High Sea Fleet would concentrate in Schillig Roads on the 29th under the usual cover that "exercises" were scheduled for the 30th.[127]

The debate over the *Flottenvorstoss* has usually become involved with controversy over Scheer's and the navy's underhanded behavior and refusal to submit to civilian control, and the plan is usually seen in the light of the mutiny it provoked. The social and political repercussions are well known. The question here might be framed in narrower terms. Did the plan make sense and was there any chance of success? The British were alert to the possibility of some German action before the end of the war. They were also aware the Germans might seek to decoy the Grand Fleet to the south, and the concern the Germans might try to draw them over a line of submarines or mines had been a source of worry throughout the war. The wireless interception and directional-finding stations also were able to ascertain an apparent concentration of six U-boats off the Firth of Forth. There also was evidence of unusual activity in the Bight, particularly minesweeping, always the signal for an operation. The Admiralty did not, however, expect the Germans to strike *during* armistice negotiations. They anticipated the blow might fall *after* the armistice terms had been settled.[128] The Germans might therefore have achieved at least some surprise.

It is also probable that Beatty had abandoned the cautious strategy evident at the beginning of the year. With the convoy system a success, he could afford to take more chances. He was chagrined that the war might end before the Grand Fleet had a chance to come to grips with the High Sea Fleet. "It is terrible to think that it is possible after all these weary months of waiting, we shall not have an opportunity of striking a blow," he wrote to his wife on 22 September.[129] It seems certain he would have rushed to meet Scheer.[130] The results of such an action will never be known. Would the submarines have inflicted losses on the dreadnoughts, moving at high speed and screened by destroyers? What of mines? Air reconnaissance? The weather? The Germans might have inflicted some losses. Light craft, patrols, and cargo ships in the southern part of the North Sea might all have suffered. What if the Grand Fleet had met the Germans off Terschelling? What of the lessons of Jutland? Fire control? British shells? The weather and conditions of light? There are simply too many variables to give definite answers. Certainly the British and Americans would have suffered losses, but surely the Grand Fleet would not have been eliminated as an effective fighting force. What would have happened to the

German fleet? It might have suffered as many or perhaps more losses, but probably not annihilation. What of German difficulties in moving through their own minefields? British submarines? The list of unanswerable questions grows. The problem is well suited for war gamers with their computers, but of course those games can only say what might have happened, not what would have happened.

On a far broader scale, would it really have mattered by this date? The American army was now in France in great numbers. The convoys were moving vast quantities of supplies with relative safety to the British Isles and France. The German army was in full retreat. What if traffic in the southern North Sea and Dover Strait was temporarily disrupted, or a few British or American warships were lost? The tide would not have turned, and the German sailors would have lost their lives in vain. Undoubtedly they sensed this, and without entering into detail a mutiny in various degrees took place, mostly in the large German ships. Ratings refused to rejoin their ships or weigh anchor, demonstrated for peace, and cheered President Wilson. Hipper was forced to cancel the operation, and he then dispersed the fleet, the First Squadron to the Elbe, the Third to Kiel, and the Fourth to Wilhelmshaven. This served only to spread the disorders to the naval ports. The kaiser's brother Prince Heinrich fled from Kiel on 5 November, reportedly in a truck flying the red flag. The disorders spread, and on 9 November Scheer advised the kaiser that the navy could no longer be relied on. The kaiser uttered the bitter words, "I have no longer a Navy," the last words Scheer ever heard from his emperor.[131] The kaiser abdicated the same day and left for exile in the Netherlands. The Germans signed the armistice on 11 November. There would be a different *Der Tag* than many had anticipated at the beginning of the war.

The discussions among the Allies over the Armistice terms had been acrimonious. The Admiralty at first had no idea how deeply the rot had spread in the German fleet. Beatty had been anxious for the surrender of all but eight or nine capital ships—the latter number equivalent to the British capital ships he anticipated losing should there have been a general engagement. This would have meant the surrender of two of the three German battle squadrons and all battle cruisers. The British naval proposals were opposed by the politicians and some of the Allied military. They did not want to push the Germans too hard, and few really wanted to face a fifth winter of renewed war. There is no space here to enter into the detail of these negotiations, but in the end the British naval proposals were watered down. The American naval representative in the Allied Naval Council, the reportedly anglophobe Admiral Benson, was against the surrender as opposed to mere internment of the German fleet, suspecting the British would eventually get their hands on most of the German ships. The German ships would not be surrendered but merely interned, their eventual disposition left to a peace conference.

It is not without significance that it was the First Sea Lord, Admiral Wemyss, who represented the Allied navies alongside Marshal Foch, representing the Allied armies, at the signature of the armistice in the railway car near Compiègne on 11 November. The naval terms of the armistice specified that 10 German dreadnoughts; all 6 battle cruisers; 8 light cruisers, including 2 minelayers; and 50 of the most modern destroyers would be interned under care and maintenance parties at a designated Allied port. In December the Germans also had to agree to substitute the fleet flagship *Baden* for the battle cruiser *Mackensen*, whose construction was not sufficiently advanced to permit her to put to sea or be towed. All submarines would be surrendered, all Russian warships captured in the Black Sea would be returned, and the blockade would remain in force until the signature of a peace treaty.[132]

There was no neutral nation willing to accept the interned German fleet, and the Allied Naval Council quickly accepted the British proposal of Scapa Flow as a suitable location. On the evening of 15 November, the light cruiser *Königsberg* arrived off May Island in the Firth of Forth with Rear Admiral Meurer, Hipper's representative, to discuss the details of the internment. In a series of coldly correct, if not frigid, meetings that evening and the following day with Beatty and his officers in the flagship *Queen Elizabeth*, it was arranged that the submarines would surrender to Admiral Tyrwhitt at Harwich, and the surface ships would surrender to Beatty in the Firth of Forth and later proceed to Scapa Flow for internment until their final fate was decided by the peace treaty.[133]

Tyrwhitt and the Harwich Force met the first group of twenty submarines at sea on 20 November and escorted them into port. Tyrwhitt had given strict orders that there should be no cheering or demonstration, and the surrender of what had been for so long the largely unseen enemy had a curious air of unreality, with the British at action stations until the last minute. The Royal Naval ensign was hoisted over each submarine and the crews quickly repatriated. The U-boats continued to trickle in over the next eleven days, and by 1 December a total of 114 had been surrendered. This by no means represented all German submarines, and an Allied Control Commission that visited Germany in December discovered no less than 62 still seaworthy, with another 149 under construction. The Allies ordered the Germans to immediately surrender all seaworthy boats, towing those that could not proceed under their own power. All boats on the stocks were to be broken up and no new construction undertaken. Eventually 176 submarines were surrendered to the British. Another seven foundered en route to Harwich, a number of old unseaworthy craft were broken up in Germany, and eight were eventually recovered from neutral ports where they had taken refuge. One U-boat (*UC.48*) was scuttled by her crew at Ferrol in March 1919 to prevent the Spanish from handing her over. The former German submarines were divided among the victorious Allies and, no doubt, carefully studied.[134]

The surrender of the U-boats, which were Germany's most deadly weapon at sea and the greatest threat to the British, had been curiously anticlimactic. The big spectacle was provided by what had become the lesser threat in 1918, the German surface ships. The symbolism, though, was immense. Operation ZZ—the arrival of the German fleet in the Forth—took place on 21 November. Many British and Americans sarcastically referred to it as *Der Tag*, only instead of giving battle, the Germans came to surrender. The Germans were under the command of Rear Admiral von Reuter. Hipper had informed the state secretary he did not feel up to the job. He watched the big ships leave

Schillig Roads with the thought, "My heart is breaking with this; my time as fleet commander has come to an inglorious end." Shortly afterward he asked to be placed on the inactive list and retired.[135]

Beatty in the *Queen Elizabeth* met the Germans at sea with the Grand Fleet and representatives from the other naval commands, reportedly 370 ships. The Americans were represented by the five dreadnoughts of the Sixth Battle Squadron, Admiral Sims in the flagship *New York*. The French navy was represented by Rear Admiral Grasset in the old armored cruiser *Amiral Aube*, accompanied by two destroyers. The day, though, really belonged to the Royal Navy. The British fleet formed into two columns of thirteen squadrons, and the light cruiser *Cardiff* led the German fleet between the two immense columns. The British turned 180° and escorted them to port. Von Reuter arrived in *Friedrich der Grosse,* one of 9 dreadnoughts, 5 battle cruisers, 7 light cruisers, and 49 destroyers—numbers somewhat less than those specified in the armistice terms. The battleship *König* and cruiser *Dresden* were in dock and joined later, and one destroyer had been sunk by a mine in the Bight. The British ships wore their battle ensigns and were at action stations in case the Germans tried something, although the German ships were supposed to have been de-munitioned and without their breech blocks. Nevertheless, after four years of bitter war the British simply did not trust the Germans. The British guns were empty, but the ammunition cages were up and loaded, ready to be rammed home. The directors were trained on the Germans and correct range and deflection kept continuously on the sights. The ships' companies of the Grand Fleet were fascinated by this close look at the enemy, although to British eyes the German ships looked dirty and unkept. For the commander in chief and many of the British officers there were mixed emotions, for they would have preferred a naval victory like Trafalgar instead of the peaceful surrender in what more than one described as a funeral procession. The Germans reached their assigned anchorage in the middle of the Firth without incident, and the fleet cheered Beatty as the *Queen Elizabeth* proceeded to her anchorage. After the flagship had been secured, Beatty briefly addressed the ships' company. He was about to leave the quarterdeck when he stopped, turned, and to the delight of the men said: "Didn't I tell you they would have to come out?" At approximately 11:00 A.M. Beatty made the general signal: "The German flag will be hauled down at sunset to-day, Thursday, and will not be hoisted again without permission." That evening Beatty held a service of Thanksgiving.[136] The naval war was over.

MAPS

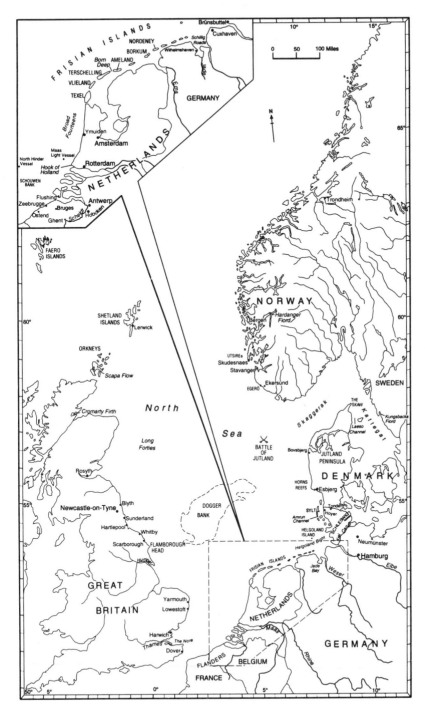

1. THE NORTH SEA

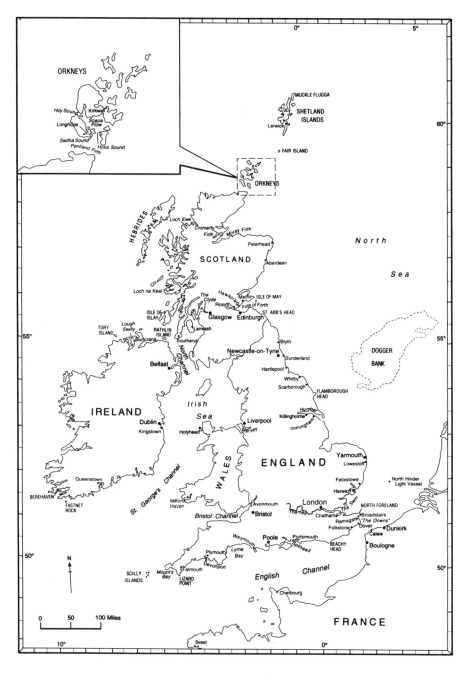

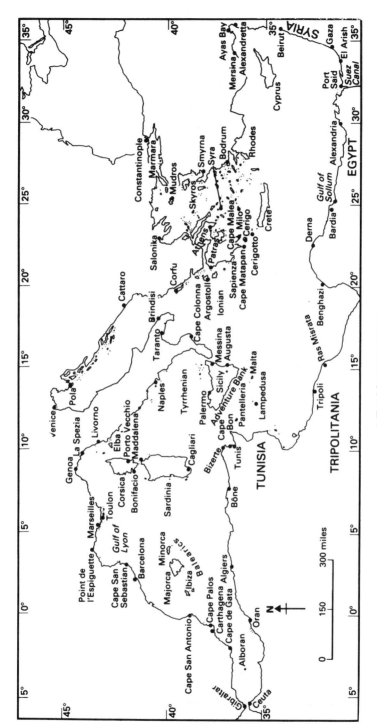

3. THE MEDITERRANEAN

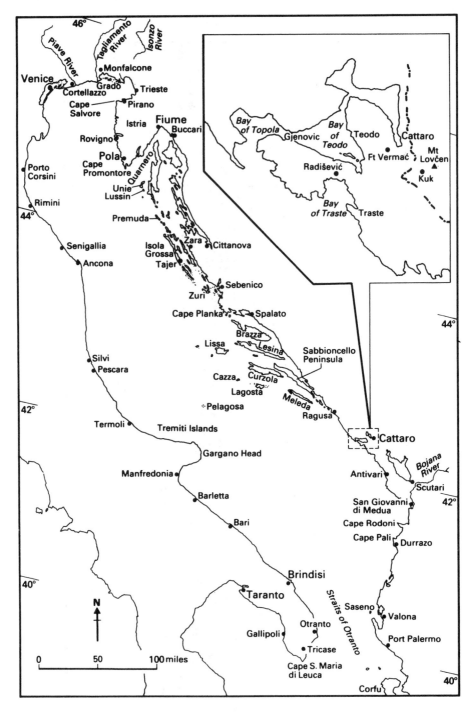

The following labels appear on the map:

46°

Piave River

Tagliamento River

Isonzo River

Monfalcone

Venice

Grado

Cortellazzo

Trieste

Cape Salvore

Pirano

Istria

Fiume

Buccari

Rovigno

Pola

Cape Promontore

Quarnero

Unie Lussin

Porto Corsini

Rimini

44°

Premuda

Senigallia

Ancona

Isola Grossa Tajer

Zara

Cittanova

Sebenico

Zuri

Cape Planka

Spalato

Brazza

Silvi

Pescara

Lissa

Lesina

Sabbioncello Peninsula

42°

Cazza

Curzola

Lagosta

Meleda

Pelagosa

Ragusa

Termoli

Tremiti Islands

Gargano Head

Cattaro

Manfredonia

Antivari

Bojana River

Scutari

Barletta

San Giovanni di Medua

42°

Bari

Cape Rodoni

Cape Pali

Durrazo

Brindisi

40°

Taranto

N

Saseno

Valona

Otranto

Straits of Otranto

Port Palermo

Gallipoli

Tricase

Cape S. Maria di Leuca

Corfu

40°

0   50   100 miles

Inset map labels:

Bay of Topola

Bay of Teodo

Teodo

Cattaro

Gjenovic

Ft Vermać

Mt Lovćen

Radišević

Kuk

Bay of Traste

Traste

44°

4. THE ADRIATIC

5. The Aegean

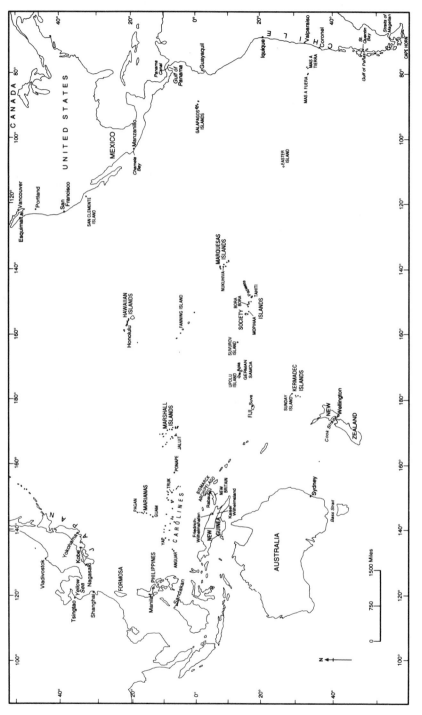

6. THE PACIFIC

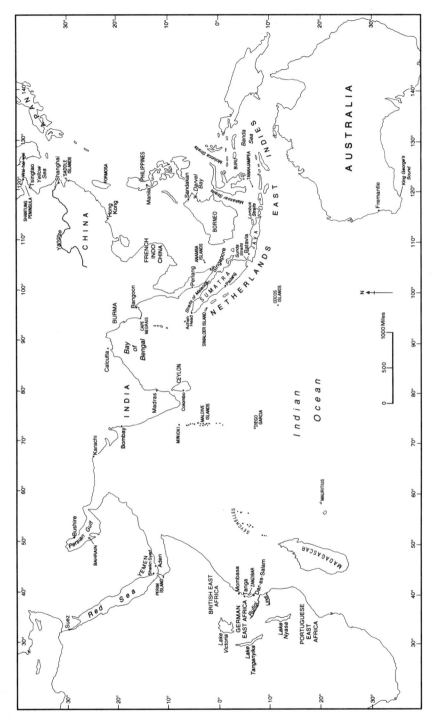

7. THE INDIAN OCEAN

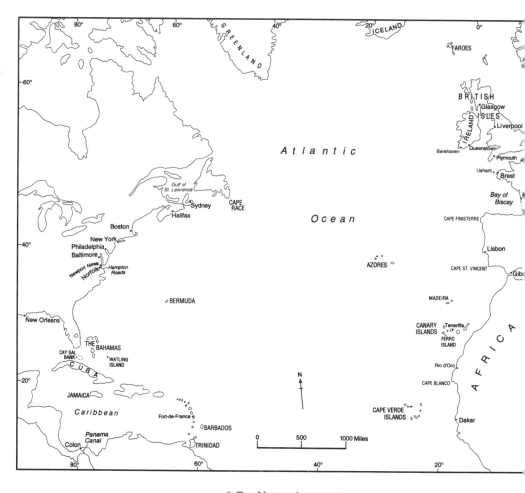

8. THE NORTH ATLANTIC

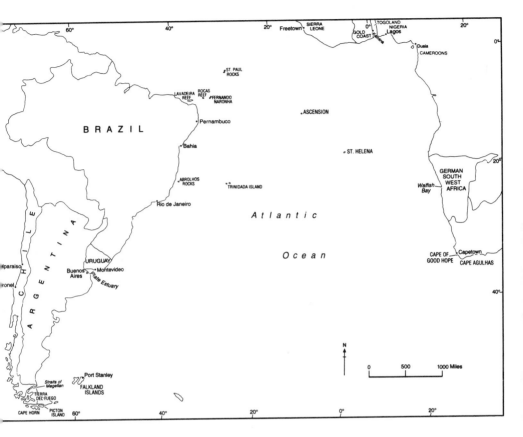

9. THE SOUTH ATLANTIC

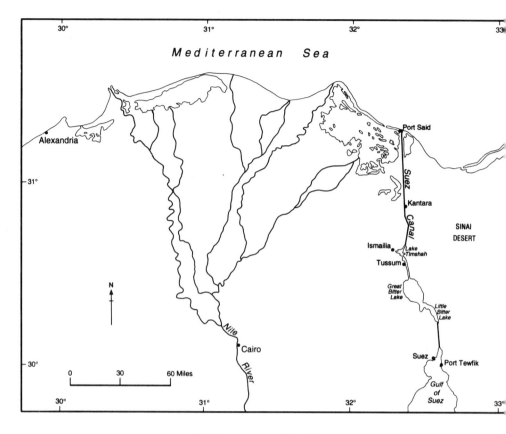

Mediterranean Sea

Alexandria

Port Said

Suez Canal

Kantara

SINAI
DESERT

Ismailia
Lake
Timshah

Tussum

Great
Bitter
Lake

Little
Bitter
Lake

Nile

Cairo

River

N

0   30   60 Miles

Suez   Port Tewfik

Gulf
of
Suez

10. EGYPT AND THE SUEZ CANAL

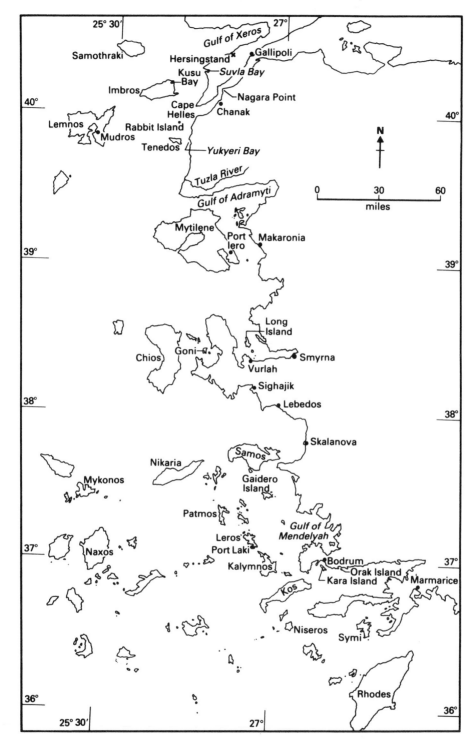

11. Aegean coast of Asia Minor and approaches to the Dardanelles

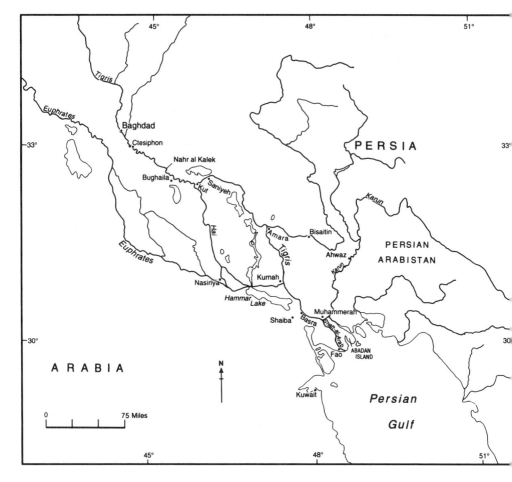

45°　　　　　　　48°　　　　　　51°

Tigris

Euphrates

33°　　　　　　　　　　　　　　　　　　　　　　　　　　33°

Baghdad

Ctesiphon

PERSIA

Nahr al Kalek

Bughaila

Saniyeh

Kut

Hai

Karun

Euphrates

Amara

Tigris

Bisaitin

PERSIAN

Ahwaz

ARABISTAN

Karun

Nasiriya

Kurnah

Hammar Lake

Muhammerah

30°　　　Shaiba　　Basra　_Shatt-al-Arab_　　　　　　30°

A R A B I A

N

Fao

ABADAN
ISLAND

Kuwait

Persian

Gulf

0　　　　　　75 Miles

45°　　　　　　　48°　　　　　　51°

12. MESOPOTAMIA

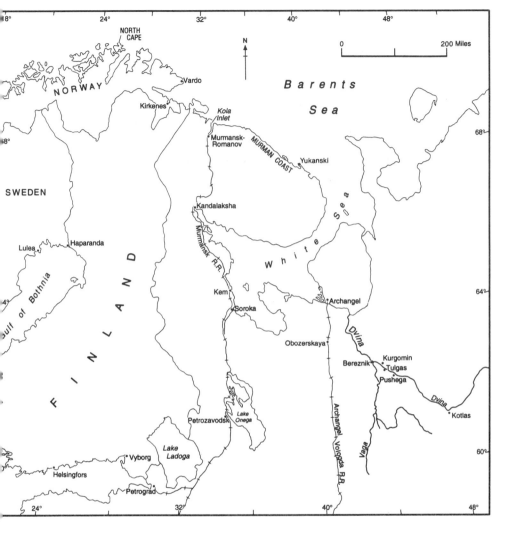

13. NORTH RUSSIA

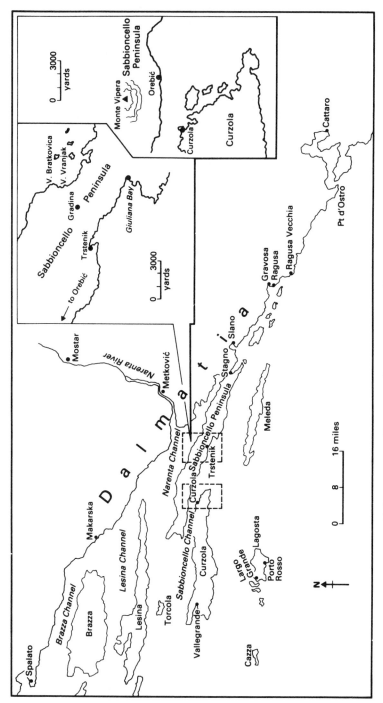

14. SABBIONCELLO PENINSULA, CURZOLA, AND THE DALMATIAN COAST

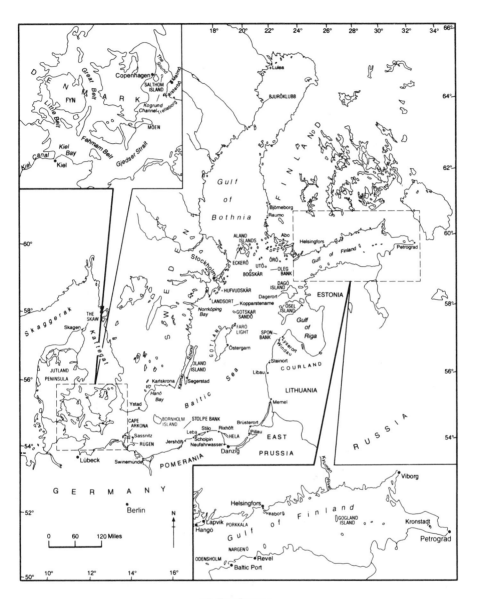

15. THE BALTIC

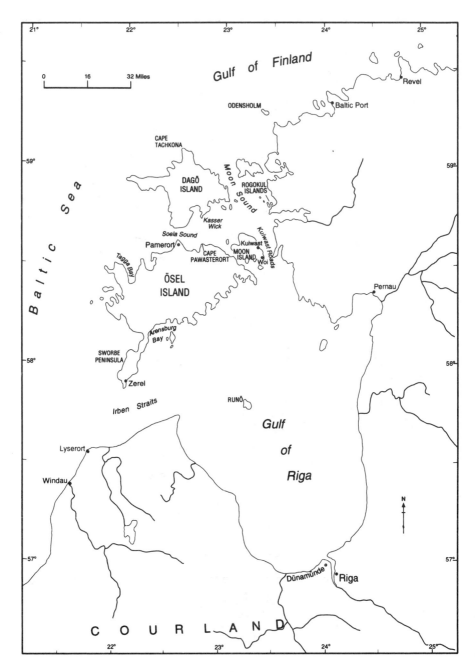

16. GULF OF RIGA

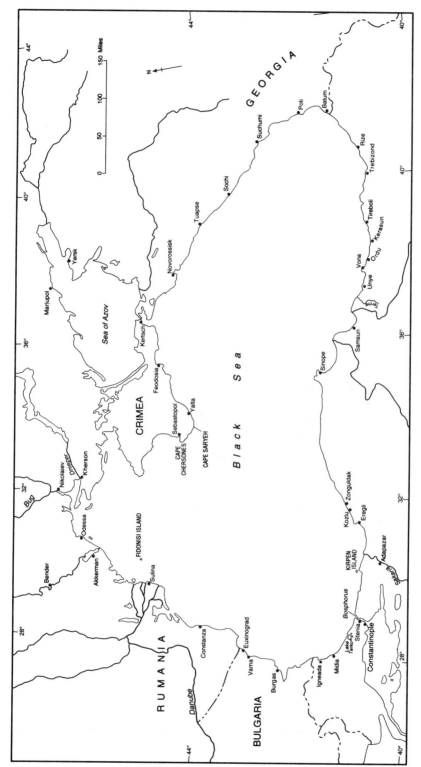

17. THE BLACK SEA

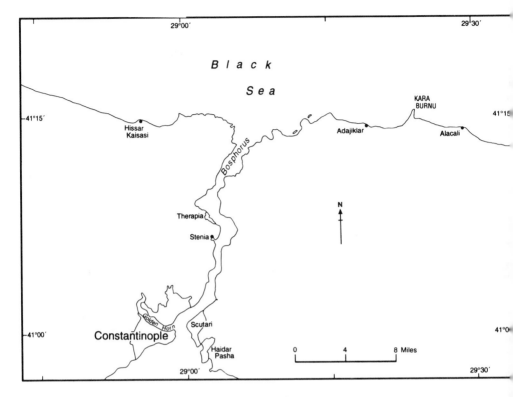

18. The Bosphorus and vicinity

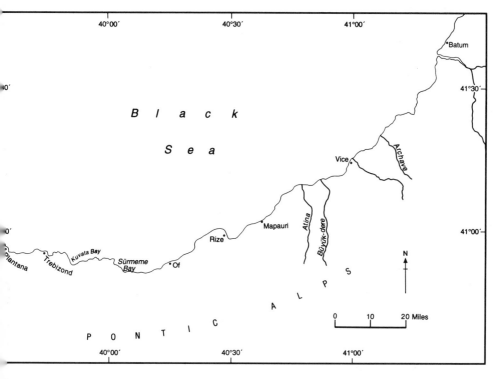

19. Lazistan coast

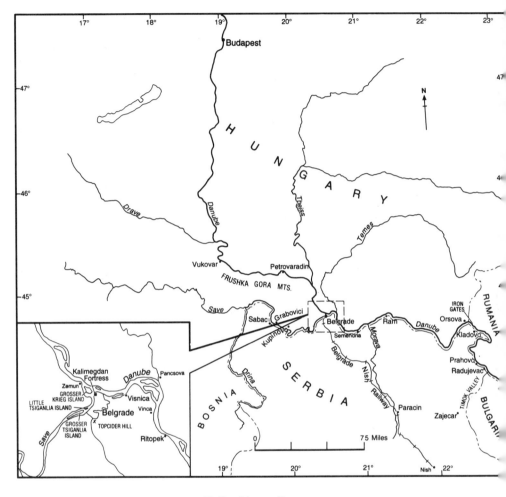

20. THE MIDDLE DANUBE

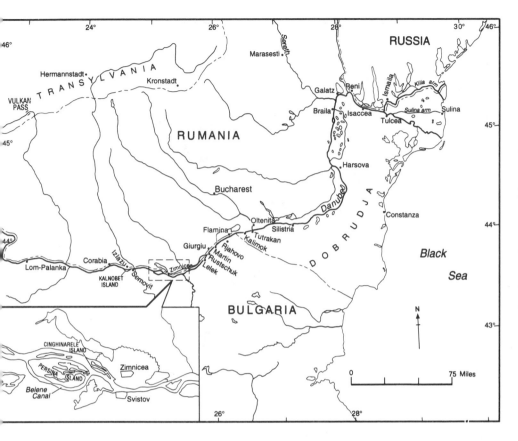

21. THE LOWER DANUBE

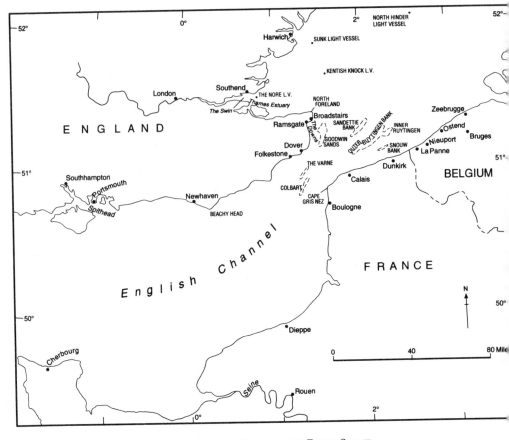

22. THE ENGLISH CHANNEL AND DOVER STRAIT

A NAVAL HISTORY OF WORLD WAR I

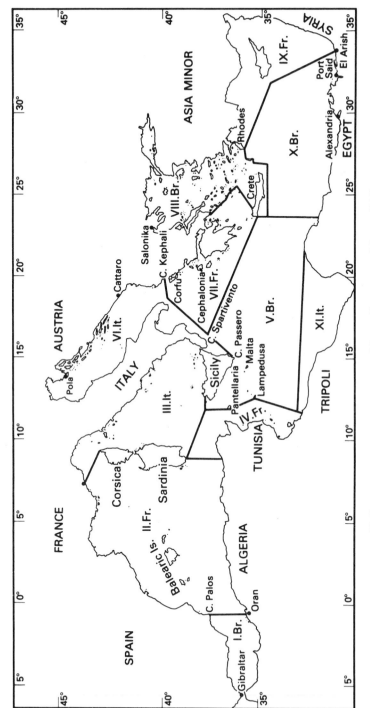

23. PATROL AREAS ESTABLISHED BY THE MALTA CONFERENCE (MARCH 1916)

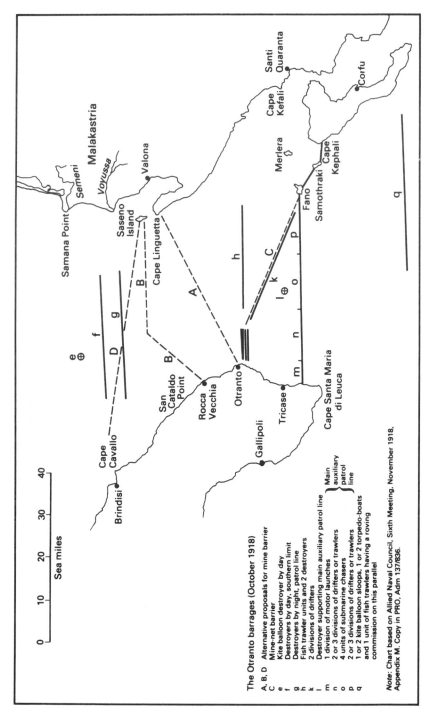

The Otranto barrages (October 1918)

A, B, D   Alternative proposals for mine barrier
C   Mine-net barrier
e   Kite balloon destroyer by day
f   Destroyers by day, southern limit
g   Destroyers by night, patrol line
h   Fish trawler units and 2 destroyers
k   2 divisions of drifters
l   Destroyer supporting main auxiliary patrol line
m   1 division of motor launches
n   2 or 3 divisions of drifters or trawlers
o   4 units of submarine chasers
p   2 or 3 divisions of drifters or trawlers
q   1 or 2 kite balloon sloops, 1 or 2 torpedo-boats
          and 1 unit of fish trawlers having a roving
          commission on this parallel

Note: Chart based on Allied Naval Council, Sixth Meeting, November 1918,
Appendix M. Copy in PRO, Adm 137/836.

24. THE OTRANTO BARRAGES (OCTOBER 1918)

A NAVAL HISTORY OF WORLD WAR I

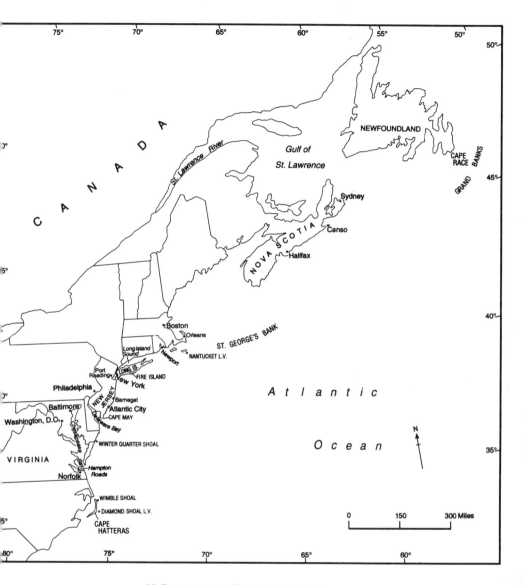

25. East coast of Northern America

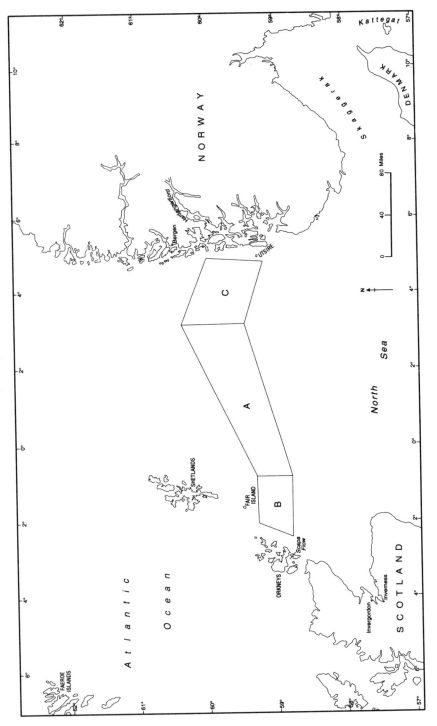

26. THE NORTHERN BARRAGE

Notes

1. The Naval Balance in 1914

1. An excellent introduction to the subject remains "The New Navalism," in William L. Langer, *The Diplomacy of Imperialism*, 2d ed. (New York: Knopf, 1951); see also Kennedy, *British Naval Mastery*.

2. This period is well covered in Marder, *Anatomy of British Sea Power* and Ropp, *Development of a Modern Navy*.

3. The most complete recent study is Kennedy, *Anglo-German Antagonism*.

4. Historians generally complain there is no adequate biography of Tirpitz. He and his projects can be studied through Jonathan Steinberg, *Yesterday's Deterrent*; Volker Berghahn, *Der Tirpitz-Plan* (Düsseldorf: Droste Verlag, 1971) and his more convenient shorter work in English, *Approach of War*; Weir, *Building the Kaiser's Navy*; and Herwig, *"Luxury Fleet,"* chap. 3.

5. Summary of the Tirpitz program based on Berghahn, *Approach of War*, 32–42; and Steinberg, *Yesterday's Deterrent*, 208–23.

6. Cited by Berghahn, *Approach of War*, 29. This interpretation is particularly associated with Eckart Kehr, *Schlachtflottenbau und Parteipolitik, 1894–1901* (Berlin: E. Ebering, 1930).

7. Membership figures cited in Wilhelm Deist, *Flottenpolitik und Flottenpropaganda: Das Nachrichtenbureau des Reichsmarineamtes, 1897–1914* (Stuttgart: Deutsche Verlagsanstalt, 1976), 157.

8. Cited by Berghahn, *Approach of War*, 40.

9. Berghahn, *Approach of War*, 38; Herwig, *"Luxury Fleet,"* 42–43.

10. For surveys of the diplomatic history, see Christopher Andrew, *Théophile Delcassé and the Making of the Entente Cordiale* (London: Macmillan, 1968); Zara Steiner, *Great Britain and the Origins of the First World War* (London: Macmillan, 1977); George L. Monger, *The End of Isolation* (London: Thomas Nelson, 1963); and on the Anglo-French staff talks, Williamson, *Politics of Grand Strategy*.

11. On Fisher as first sea lord, see especially Marder, *Dreadnought to Scapa Flow*, vol. 1; Ruddock F. Mackay, *Fisher of Kilverstone* (Oxford: Clarendon Press, 1973).

12. On Scott, see Padfield, *Aim Straight* and *Guns at Sea*; and Admiral Sir Percy Scott, *Fifty Years in the Royal Navy* (London: John Murray, 1919).

13. On development of the dreadnought type and battle cruiser, see Parkes, *British Battleships*, chaps. 80–81, 83–84; Burt, *British Battleships*, 19–33, 39–45.

14. On this point, see Sumida, *Defence of Naval Supremacy*, 27–28, 37–41, 51–61.
15. This point is stressed by Charles H. Fairbanks, Jr., "The Origins of the *Dreadnought* Revolution: A Historiographical Essay," *International History Review* 13, no. 2 (May 1991): 264.
16. Sumida, *Defence of Naval Supremacy*, 160–61, 330–34. See also Sumida, "British Capital Ship Design and Fire Control in the *Dreadnought* Era: Sir John Fisher, Arthur Hungerford Pollen, and the Battle Cruiser," *Journal of Modern History* 51 (June 1979): 205–30; and Sumida, *The Pollen Papers*. On the importance of the *Dreadnought* and gunnery developments as part of a system for increasing the combat capability of fleets, see Karl Lautenschläger, "The *Dreadnought* Revolution," 121–36.
17. On Churchill as first lord, see Randolph S. Churchill, *Winston S. Churchill*, vol. 2, *Young Statesman, 1901–1914* (London: Heinemann, 1967); Gilbert, *Challenge of War*; Marder, *Dreadnought to Scapa Flow*, vol. 1, chaps. 10–11; and Churchill, *The World Crisis*.
18. On the 1912 redeployment, see Halpern, *Mediterranean Naval Situation*, chap. 2.
19. On the naval race and diplomacy of the period, see Kennedy, *Anglo-German Antagonism*, chap. 20; Herwig, "*Luxury Fleet*," chaps. 4–5.
20. March, *British Destroyers*, 165.
21. The figures have been culled from various authorities (who naturally differ): *Conway's All the World's Fighting Ships, 1906–1921*; Marder, *Dreadnought to Scapa Flow* 1:439–42; H. M. Le Fleming, *Warships of World War I* (London: Ian Allan, n.d.); Taylor, *German Warships*.
22. There were also thirty to thirty-three modern oil-burning destroyers at Harwich. The exact number of destroyers that would have accompanied the High Sea Fleet is difficult to establish. On British destroyers, see March, *British Destroyers*, 162.
23. Figures given vary widely. The ones cited here are gathered from Corbett and Newbolt, *History of the Great War* 1:12 n. 2, 438–40; Goldrick, *The King's Ships*, 48–50; Weyer, *Taschenbuch der Kriegsflotten*, 424.
24. On these subjects, see Cowie, *Mines, Minelayers and Minelaying*, chaps. 4–5; Campbell, *Jutland: An Analysis*, 369–72, 385–88.
25. For full discussions of these points, see Marder, *Dreadnought to Scapa Flow*, vol. 1, chaps. 12 and 13; Roskill, *Strategy of Sea Power*, 108–10; Goldrick, *The King's Ships*, chaps. 2–3; Philbin, *Hipper*, 22–26; Herwig, "*Luxury Fleet*," chap. 7; and Herwig, *German Naval Officer Corps*.
26. These questions are covered at length in Halpern, *Mediterranean Naval Situation*, passim.
27. On the naval law of 1900, see Ropp, *Development of a Modern Navy*, 329–36. On the pre-1914 French navy, Walser, *France's Search for a Battle Fleet*; Halpern, *Mediterranean Naval Situation*, chap. 3; and Le Masson, "La politique navale française," *Propos maritimes*, 181–239.

28. French figures drawn from Thomazi, *L'Adriatique*, 213–16; and Halpern, *Naval War in the Mediterranean*, 3–5.

29. On the Italian navy, see Halpern, *Mediterranean Naval Situation*, chap. 7; Halpern, *Naval War in the Mediterranean*, 5–7; Ropp, *Development of a Modern Navy*, 181–84, 198–201; and the detailed study published by the Ufficio Storico, Gabriele and Friz, *La politica navale italiana*. The Ufficio Storico is also responsible for a magnificent series of studies, "Le navi d'Italia," on different types of Italian warships.

30. On the Austro-Hungarian navy, see Halpern, *Mediterranean Naval Situation*, chap. 6; Sokol, *Austro-Hungarian Navy*; Sokol, *Des Kaisers Seemacht*; and Lawrence Sondhaus, *The Habsburg Empire and the Sea: Austrian Naval Policy, 1797–1866* (West Lafayette, Ind.: Purdue University Press, 1989).

31. On the Triple Alliance Naval Convention, see Halpern, *Mediterranean Naval Situation*, chaps. 8–9; and the very detailed study published by the Ufficio Storico, Gabriele, *Le convenzioni navali della triplice*.

32. On the Balkan naval race, see Halpern, *Mediterranean Naval Situation*, chap. 11.

33. A recent survey of the Russo-Japanese War is J. N. Westwood, *Russia Against Japan, 1904–05: A New Look at the Russo-Japanese War* (London: Macmillan, 1986). Discussions of the Russian navy on the eve of the war are in Saul, *Sailors in Revolt*, chap. 1; Halpern, *Mediterranean Naval Situation*, 295–313; and Greger, *Die Russische Flotte*, 9–14. An important source for data on ships is Watts, *The Imperial Russian Navy*.

34. The most convenient source for summaries of the smaller naval powers is now *Conway's All the World's Fighting Ships, 1906–1921*. On Spanish warships, see Alfredo Aguilera, *Buques de Guerra Españoles, 1885–1971* (Madrid: Editorial San Martin, 1980).

35. There is a good summary on the Japanese navy in *Conway's All the World's Fighting Ships, 1906–1921*; and much detail in Hansgeorg Jentschura, Dieter Jung, and Peter Mickel, *Warships of the Imperial Japanese Navy, 1869–1945* (London: Arms & Armour Press, 1977).

36. Representative surveys include Knox, *United States Navy*, chaps. 29–34; William Reynolds Braisted, *The United States Navy in the Pacific, 1897–1909* (Austin: University of Texas Press, 1958); idem, *The United States Navy*; and James R. Reckner, *Teddy Roosevelt's Great White Fleet* (Annapolis, Md.: Naval Institute Press, 1988).

37. Information on the U.S. Navy may be found in Silverstone, *U.S. Warships*; Reilly and Scheina, *American Battleships*; Friedman, *U.S. Battleships*; and *Conway's All the World's Fighting Ships, 1906–1921*, 105–33.

2. Northern Waters: The First Six Months

1. King-Hall, *North Sea Diary*, 43.
2. Marder, *Dreadnought to Scapa Flow* 1:370–73.
3. Ibid. 356–68, 388–93; on the continental commitment and historic C.I.D. meeting see also Williamson, *Politics of Grand Strategy*, 188–93.
4. Groos, *Krieg in der Nordsee* 1:54–57; for exhaustive studies of German plans see Lambi, *German Power Politics*, 400–401.
5. Lambi, *German Power Politics*, 404–5.
6. Kennedy, "German Naval Operations Plans," 184–88; Lambi, *German Power Politics*, 422–23; Groos, *Krieg in der Nordsee* 1:54.
7. Cited by Herwig, "The Failure of German Sea Power, 1914–1945: Mahan, Tirpitz and Raeder Reconsidered," *International History Review* 10, no. 1 (February 1988): 81.
8. Jellicoe, *The Grand Fleet*, 12–13. On Jellicoe himself and the circumstances of his assumption of command, see Marder, *Dreadnought to Scapa Flow* 1:433–34; ibid. 2:10–11; Patterson, *Jellicoe*, 56–58; and Goldrick, *The King's Ships*, 21–27.
9. Jellicoe, *The Grand Fleet*, 13–15.
10. On the initial deployments, see Goldrick, *The King's Ships*, 26–30; Corbett and Newbolt, *Naval Operations* 1:11–14, 31, 37–38.
11. Thomazi, *Guerre navale dans le nord*, 33–38. On the prewar agreements, see ibid., 30–31; and in more detail (including map), Williamson, *Politics of Grand Strategy*, 320–25.
12. For a brief synopsis of the auxiliary patrol, see Dittmar and Colledge, *British Warships*, 141–48; on French trawlers, see Thomazi, *Guerre navale dans le nord*, 65, 79.
13. Details on German deployment are in Groos, *Krieg in der Nordsee* 1:40–41, Scheer, *Germany's High Sea Fleet*, 13–16, 20–21, 26–27; and Goldrick, *The King's Ships*, 46–51.
14. Jellicoe, *The Grand Fleet*, 29–31; Groos, *Krieg in der Nordsee* 1:45; Jellicoe to Battenberg, 18 August 1914, in Patterson, *The Jellicoe Papers* 1:52.
15. Scheer, *Germany's High Sea Fleet*, 11, 25; German text in Groos, *Krieg in der Nordsee* 1:54.
16. Goldrick, *The King's Ships*, 64–69; Groos, *Krieg in der Nordsee* 1:65–72; Corbett and Newbolt, *Naval Operations* 1:38–39.
17. On Norwegian policy, see Riste, *The Neutral Ally*, 33–37; on British operations, see Goldrick, *The King's Ships*, 59–60, 70–71; and Corbett and Newbolt, *Naval Operations* 1:38, 77–78.
18. Details of the transport are in Corbett and Newbolt, *Naval Operations*, vol. 1, chap. 4; Scheer, *Germany's High Sea Fleet*, 63–64; and Groos, *Krieg in der Nordsee* 1:78–82.
19. Goldrick, *The King's Ships*, 69–73; Keyes, *Naval Memoirs* 1:69; Groos, *Krieg in der Nordsee* 1:72–78, 251; Jellicoe, *The Grand Fleet*, 16–17.

20. Jellicoe, *The Grand Fleet*, 29, 77, 92; Marder, *Dreadnought to Scapa Flow* 2:67–69.

21. On the use of submarines with the fleet, see Marder, *Dreadnought to Scapa Flow* 4:36–37, 85; Hezlet, *The Submarine and Sea Power*, 74–75; and Everitt, *The K Boats*.

22. The best recent account is Goldrick, *The King's Ships*, chap. 5. For further detail, see Marder, *Dreadnought to Scapa Flow* 2:50–54; Corbett and Newbolt, *Naval Operations* 1:100–120; Keyes, *Naval Memoirs*, vol. 1, chap. 4; Halpern, *The Keyes Papers* 1:11–22; Patterson, *Tyrwhitt*, chap. 2.

23. For the German side, see Groos, *Krieg in der Nordsee*, vol. 1, chap. 5.

24. Chatfield, *The Navy and Defence*, 124–25; see also Beatty's dispatch reproduced in Chalmers, *Life and Letters of Beatty*, 148–49.

25. King-Hall, *North Sea Diary*, 59.

26. Patterson, *Tyrwhitt*, 62; Keyes to Goodenough, 5 September 1914, in Halpern, *The Keyes Papers* 1:19.

27. Görlitz, *The Kaiser and His Court*, 25, 228; Tirpitz, *My Memoirs* 2:92; Philbin, *Hipper*, 85–86; Scheer, *Germany's High Sea Fleet*, 55–56; Goldrick, *The King's Ships*, 114–16.

28. Corbett and Newbolt, *Naval Operations* 1:163, 165, 172–77; Goldrick, *The King's Ships*, 120–22, 123–35; the account of Sturdee's remarks on the Broad Fourteens is in Keyes to Richmond, 4 June 1936, Halpern, *The Keyes Papers* 2:353.

29. Corbett and Newbolt, *Naval Operations* 1:239–46; Jellicoe, *The Grand Fleet*, 149–52; Goldrick, *The King's Ships*, 139–42; Schmalenbach, *German Raiders*, 16, 18, 45–46.

30. Jellicoe, *The Grand Fleet*, 19; Dittmar and Colledge, *British Warships*, 105–7; Marder, *Dreadnought to Scapa Flow* 2:72–74, 77–81. The remark about "lavatory attendants" is quoted in ibid., p. 73, n. 24. Statistics and a very full account of mine warfare are in Taffrail, *Swept Channels*.

31. Corbett and Newbolt, *Naval Operations*, vol. 1, chaps. 15–16; Thomazi, *Guerre navale dans le nord*, 54–56; Goldrick, *The King's Ships*, 147–49, 152.

32. Marder, *Dreadnought to Scapa Flow* 2:88–89.

33. Beatty to his wife, 2 November 1914, reproduced in Chalmers, *Life and Letters of Beatty*, 160; Keyes, *Naval Memoirs* 1:130.

34. Mackay, *Fisher of Kilverstone*, 464–68, 475–76, 490–91, 493–95; Marder, *Dreadnought to Scapa Flow* 2:93–97.

35. The fullest account is now Beesly, *Room 40*, 3–7; on the *Magdeburg* episode, see Mäkelä, *Das Geheimnis der "Magdeburg."*

36. On these points, see Beesly, *Room 40*. See also the older and more circumspect biography of Hall: James, *Admiral Sir Reginald Hall*.

37. Jellicoe to Admiralty, 30 October 1914, in Patterson, *The Jellicoe Papers* 1:75–77.

38. Jellicoe, *The Grand Fleet*, 153, 168–69, 170, 174, 186–87; Patterson, *The Jellicoe Papers* 1:77–79, 83–86, 88–89, 94, 96–98, 102–3.

39. Tirpitz to Chief of the Naval Staff, 16 September 1914, reproduced in Tirpitz, *My Memoirs* 1:95–96. The full version of the letter is in Tirpitz, *Deutsche Ohnemachtspolitik im Weltkrieg*, 104–6.

40. Tirpitz, *My Memoirs* 2:99–102; Philbin, *Hipper*, 87–91; Corbett and Newbolt, *Naval Operations* 2:249–53; the best account in English by far is Goldrick, *The King's Ships*, 159–66.

41. Goldrick, *The King's Ships*, 174–76; for the exchange between Jellicoe and the Admiralty over the move, see Patterson, *The Jellicoe Papers* 1:93–95.

42. Hipper's plan of 12 November 1914 is reproduced in Philbin, *Hipper*, 92–95.

43. The best modern account is Goldrick, *The King's Ships*, chap. 8; see also Marder, *Dreadnought to Scapa Flow* 2:132–47; a recent account of Hipper's role is in Philbin, *Hipper*, 98–101; Room 40's role is analyzed in Beesly, *Room 40*, 49–56.

44. Beatty to Jellicoe, 20 December 1914, in Patterson, *The Jellicoe Papers* 1:110–11.

45. German operations may be followed in Robinson, *The Zeppelin in Combat*, 40–46; on the British side, see Goldrick, *The King's Ships*, 221–26; the operation is studied in detail in Layman, *The Cuxhaven Raid*.

46. Goldrick, *The King's Ships*, 229–37; Marder, *Dreadnought to Scapa Flow* 2:98–100. The British also lost the predreadnought *Bulwark* on 26 November as a result of an internal explosion, probably caused by excessive temperatures in the ammunition passages igniting loose cordite.

47. Good accounts of the battle are in Goldrick, *The King's Ships*, chap. 11; Bennett, *Naval Battles*, chap. 8; fresh material on Hipper's role is in Philbin, *Hipper*, 103–12.

48. Beatty to Keyes, 10 February 1915, reproduced in Keyes, *Naval Memoirs* 1:163.

49. Quotations from Müller taken from Görlitz, *The Kaiser and His Court*, 60–62. The circumstances surrounding Ingenohl's replacement are well covered in Goldrick, *The King's Ships*, 289–94.

50. Memorandum by Tirpitz, 25 January 1915 reproduced in Görlitz, *The Kaiser and His Court*, 58–60.

51. Text published in Gibson and Prendergast, *German Submarine War*, 27–28.

52. King-Hall, *North Sea Diary*, 94–97.

53. The extremely detailed official history is in Bell, *Blockade of Germany*.

54. A highly readable account is Chatterton, *The Big Blockade*.

55. This account and statistics drawn from Tupper, *Reminiscences*; De Chair, *The Sea Is Strong*; Hampshire, *The Blockaders*; and Brocklebank, *Tenth Cruiser Squadron*.

56. Quoted in Tupper, *Reminiscences*, 217–18.

57. De Chair, *The Sea Is Strong*, 191; Tupper, *Reminiscences*, 264.

3. THE MEDITERRANEAN: 1914–1915

1. On this point see Halpern, *Mediterranean Naval Situation*, 275–76.
2. Lorey, *Krieg in den türkischen Gewässern* 1:2–3; Berghahn, *Approach of War*, 188–89; Souchon to his wife, 1, 2 August 1914, BA/MA, Nachlass Souchon, N156/10.
3. Revel to Salandra, 1 August 1914, ACS, Carte Salandra 2/16; for detail see Halpern, *Naval War in the Mediterranean*, 5–6, 8–9.
4. Halpern, *Naval War in the Mediterranean*, 14–15; Bayer von Bayersburg, *Unter der k.u.k. Kriegsflagge*, 7 ff.; Sokol, *Des Kaisers Seemacht*, 239–41; Aichelburg, *Die Unterseeboote Österreich-Ungarns* 1:65; Kontreadmiral Erich Heyssler, "Erinnerungen," (Graz, 1936, typescript in private possession), 388.
5. See Halpern, *Naval War in the Mediterranean*, 17, 19–20; Conrad, *Aus Meiner Dienstzeit* 4:174–75, 178–79; Sokol, *Österreich-Ungarns Seekrieg*, 73–74.
6. Halpern, *Naval War in the Mediterranean*, 17–22; Sokol, *Österreich-Ungarns Seekrieg*, 70–74. For the account of the German naval attaché in Vienna, see "Aufzeichnungen des Marineattachés in Wien in der Zeit vom 5–16 August 1914," and "Niederschrift über einen mündlichen Bericht des Korvettenkapitän Freiherr von Freyberg vom 14 Oktober 1914" in NARS, T-1022, Roll 537, PG 69132. An Austrian defense is in Admiral Khuepach, "Warum hat Admiral Haus der deutschen Mittelmeerdivision sein Hilfe versagt?" Kriegsarchiv, Vienna, Nachlass Khuepach, B/200, Fasc. 6, no. 11.
7. On Lapeyrère, see Taillemite, *Dictionnaire des marins français*, 41–42; De Belot and Reussner, *La puissance navale* 3:26; and Halpern, *Naval War in the Mediterranean*, 22.
8. Halpern, *Mediterranean Naval Situation*, 135 ff.
9. French accounts are in Thomazi, *L'Adriatique*, 21–31; Salaun, *La Marine française*, 144–49; Laurens, *Commandement naval*, 31–45; and Dartige du Fournet, *Souvenirs de guerre*, 4.
10. On prewar limitations, see Halpern, *Mediterranean Naval Situation*, 128–30.
11. Lumby, *Policy and Operations*, 146, 157.
12. Corbett and Newbolt, *Naval Operations* 1:67–68; Marder, *Dreadnought to Scapa Flow* 2:31–41; Churchill, *The World Crisis* 1:269–75; Roskill, *Strategy of Sea Power*, 113; and Gilbert, *Churchill* 3:42.
13. Lorey, *Krieg in den türkischen Gewässern* 1:6–7; Trumpener, "Escape of the *Goeben*," 175–77.
14. Marder, *Dreadnought to Scapa Flow* 2:33–36. The transcript of the Troubridge court-martial is in Lumby, *Policy and Operations*, pt. 3.
15. Commission de la Marine de Guerre (Députés), *Rapport sur l'affaire du 'Goeben' et du 'Breslau' presenté par M. Abel, Député*, 14 May 1918, p. 35, SHM, Carton Ed-76; Cabinet du Ministre, "Les operations navales en Méditerranée de 3 au 8 Âout 1914," enquête fait par M. Chaumet (Sept. 1917), ibid., Audition de M. Augagneur,

Commission de la Marine de Guerre, 18 July 1917, pp. 18–19, SHM, Carton Ed-76bis. The attack on Lapeyrère is in Bienaimé, *La guerre navale*. For a short summary of the controversy, see Halpern, *Naval War in the Mediterranean*, 24–26.

16. Lorey, *Krieg in den türkischen Gewässern* 1:31; Trumpener, *Germany and the Ottoman Empire*, 30–32, 40–43.

17. Halpern, *Naval War in the Mediterranean*, 48.

18. Trumpener, "Escape of the *Goeben*," 171.

19. Protocole de convention passés entre l'Amirauté Britannique et l'État-Major Général de la Marine Française, 6 August 1914, SHM, Carton Es-11.

20. Naval Staff, *The Mediterranean*, 49–50; Corbett and Newbolt, *Naval Operations* 1:86–88.

21. Thomazi, *L'Adriatique*, 36–40; Marine to Armée Navale, 13 August 1914, SHM, Carton A-31; Augagneur (possibly Pivet) to Lapeyrère, 13 August 1914, SHM, Carton Ed-80; Le Comte, "L'affaire de la *Zenta*," 1254–59; Sokol, *Österreich-Ungarns Seekrieg*, 80–84.

22. On prewar plans, see Halpern, *Mediterranean Naval Situation*, 131–35.

23. Docteur, *Carnet de bord*, 15; Halpern, *Naval War in the Mediterranean*, 28–29; Thomazi, *L'Adriatique*, 41.

24. Haus to Kailer, 6 September 1914, Kriegsarchiv, Vienna, Nachlass Kailer; Kailer to Haus, 10 September 1914, Kriegsarchiv, Vienna, Nachlass Haus.

25. Extraits du rapport du Monsieur le Contre-Amiral de Bon sur sa mission au Montenegro, 27 October 1914, pp. 89, 93–94, SHM, Carton Es-18; Lapeyrère to Augagneur, 8, 25 September, 18 October 1918, SHM, Carton Ed-83; Thomazi, *L'Adriatique*, 52–57; Laurens, *Commandement naval*, 52–56.

26. Joffre, *Mémoires* 1:484–86; Halpern, *Naval War in the Mediterranean*, 31–32, 34–37.

27. Lapeyrère to Augagneur, 25 October, 4 November 1914, SHM, Carton Ed-83; Sokol, *Österreich-Ungarns Seekrieg*, 91–96; Thomazi, *L'Adriatique*, 53–56.

28. Summarized in Halpern, *Naval War in the Mediterranean*, 37–39, 69–76.

29. Ibid., 102–5; Sokol, *Österreich-Ungarns Seekrieg*, 164–69; Sieche, "Die diplomatischen Aktivitäten rund um das Haus-Memorandum vom März 1915," *Marine—Gestern, Heute* 9, no. 3 (Sept. 1982): 93–98, 102–5.

30. Greger, *Austro-Hungarian Warships*, 68–72; Aichelburg, *Unterseeboote Österreich-Ungarns* 1:69, 2:63–64, 70–76; Halpern, *Naval War in the Mediterranean*, 39–41; Sokol, *Österreich-Ungarns Seekrieg*, 118–20, 135–42; Thomazi, *L'Adriatique*, 67–69.

31. Halpern, *Naval War in the Mediterranean*, 93–95; Thomazi, *L'Adriatique*, 70–72, 74–79; Sokol, *Österreich-Ungarns Seekrieg*, 100–5, 143–46, 147–51.

32. Trumpener, "Escape of the *Goeben*," 171.

33. Halpern, *Naval War in the Mediterranean*, 48–50; Souchon to his wife, 12, 15 August, 27 September 1914, BA/MA, Nachlass Souchon N156/10, N156/11; Trumpener, *Germany and the Ottoman Empire*, 42–43; Souchon to Tirpitz (?), 27 August 1914, NARS, T-1022, Roll 1261, PG 60055; Lorey, *Krieg in den türkischen Gewässern* 1:36–38.

34. Lorey, *Krieg in den türkischen Gewässern* 1:36, 2:4–10; Trumpener, *Germany and the Ottoman Empire*, 35–36; Souchon to his wife, 9, 20 September 1914, BA/MA, Nachlass Souchon, N156/11.

35. Gilbert, *Churchill* 3:204, 207–9; Churchill to Grey, 17 August 1914, in Lumby, *Policy and Operations*, 454–55; Admiralty to Rear Admiral, *Indefatigable*, 27 August 1914, in Lumby, *Policy and Operations*, 448; Battenberg to Limpus, 19 November 1914, National Maritime Museum, Greenwich, Limpus MSS.

36. Admiralty to Marine, Bordeaux, 20 September 1914, in Lumby, *Policy and Operations*, 454–55; Admiralty to SNO, *Indefatigable*, 25 September 1914, in Lumby, *Policy and Operations*, 455; Gilbert, *Churchill* 3:209, 212–13. On the importance of the Straits for Russian trade, see Alan Bodger, "Russia and the End of the Ottoman Empire," in *The Great Powers and the End of the Ottoman Empire*, ed. Marian Kent (London: Allen & Unwin, 1984), 83–84.

37. Details of the Turkish decision for war are in Trumpener, *Germany and the Ottoman Empire*, 54–62; Frank G. Weber, *Eagles on the Crescent: Germany, Austria and the Diplomacy of the Turkish Alliance, 1914–1918* (Ithaca, N.Y.: Cornell University Press, 1970), 72–86; Lorey, *Krieg in den türkischen Gewässern* 1:45; Souchon to Kaiser Wilhelm, 3 November 1914, BA/MA, Nachlass Souchon, Nl56/3. On Turkish motives, see Feroz Ahmad, "The Late Ottoman Empire," in Kent, *The Great Powers*, 15–18.

38. Lorey, *Krieg in den türkischen Gewässern* 1:47–50; Greger, *Die Russische Flotte*, 45; Pavlovich, *The Fleet* 1:284–90.

39. Souchon to his wife, 29 October 1914, BA/MA, Nachlass Souchon, N156/3.

40. Corbett and Newbolt, *Naval Operations* 1:359–64; Gilbert, *Churchill* 3:216–17; Admiralty to Admiral Superintendent, Malta, 1 November 1914, Carden to Admiralty, 14, 22 November 1914, in Lumby, *Policy and Operations*, 456–59, 460–61.

41. On this point, see Gilbert, *Churchill* 3:218; and Marder, *Dreadnought to Scapa Flow* 2:201.

4. Sweeping the Seas

1. Figures from Fayle, *Seaborne Trade* 1:6, 14.

2. Fayle, *Seaborne Trade* 1:21–22.

3. Raeder and Mantey, *Der Kreuzerkrieg* 1:20–23. The activities of the Tsingtau *Etappe* are discussed in Burdick, *Siege of Tsingtau*, 40–41.

4. Burdick, *Siege of Tsingtau*, 209, n. 24. Burdick was informed by the current Bundesarchiv-Militärarchiv that the records of the service were burned for security reasons in 1919.

5. Admiralty (O.U. 6337 [40]), *Review of German Cruiser Warfare*, 29–31. Copy in Naval Library, Ministry of Defence.

6. Fayle, *Seaborne Trade* 1:35–43, 197–99, 284–85. See also Doughty, *Merchant Shipping and War*, 115–21.

7. Discussions on the defense of trade are in Hurd, *The Merchant Navy* 1:212–13, 222–23, 240–41; Corbett and Newbolt, *Naval Operations* 1:15; Marder, *Dreadnought to Scapa Flow* 2:102–3.

8. On arguments against convoys, see Hurd, *The Merchant Navy* 1:212–15, 241–43; and the excellent discussion in Winton, *Convoy*, chap. 1.

9. Fayle, *Seaborne Trade* 1:143; Corbett, *Naval Operations* 1:15.

10. Nish, "Admiral Jerram," 413–14.

11. Nish, "Admiral Jerram," 411–13; Naval Staff, *The Eastern Squadrons*, (Naval Staff Monographs [Historical], Vol. 5, April 1922), 33–38, 40–42, 45.

12. Naval Staff, *The Eastern Squadrons*, 43, 55.

13. German movements summarized from Raeder and Mantey, *Der Kreuzerkrieg* 1:61–67; see also Burdick, *Siege of Tsingtau*, 26–27, 38–41; Bennett, *Coronel and the Falklands*, 55–57.

14. Raeder and Mantey, *Der Kreuzerkrieg* 1:68–72; see also Bennett, *Coronel and the Falklands*, 56–57.

15. Raeder and Mantey, *Der Kreuzerkrieg* 1:79–82; on supply ships from Tsingtau, see Assmann, *Die Kämpfe der Kaiserlichen Marine*, 37–39; Burdick, *Siege of Tsingtau*, 40–41.

16. Excerpts from Jerram's letter to his wife reproduced in Nish, "Admiral Jerram," 417–18; quotations from his official report in Naval Staff, *The Eastern Squadrons*, 38–39.

17. Jerram's operations in Naval Staff, *The Eastern Squadrons*, 40–44; Corbett and Newbolt, *Naval Operations* 1:137–44; on the responsibility of the Admiralty, see Roskill, *Churchill and the Admirals*, 38–39; Bennett, *Coronel and the Falklands*, 50–52.

18. The best account in English is Burdick, *Siege of Tsingtau*. For the role of the German navy see official history: Assmann, *Die Kämpfe der Kaiserliche Marine*.

19. Information on the Royal Netherlands Navy in the East Indies provided by the Afdeling Maritieme Historie, Ministerie van Defensie, The Hague, letter of 8 April 1988.

20. Summary of *Emden*'s career taken from Naval Staff, *The Eastern Squadrons*; Raeder and Mantey, *Der Kreuzerkrieg*, vol. 2; and relevant portions of Corbett and Newbolt, *Naval Operations*, vol. 1; Hurd, *The Merchant Navy*, vol. 1; and Fayle, *Seaborne Trade*, vol. 1. A convenient synopsis is Friedrich Forstmeier, "SMS *Emden*: Small Protected Cruiser, 1906–1914," in *Warships in Profile*, ed. Anthony Preston (Windsor: William Murrow, 1974), 3:1–24.

21. The career of the *Emden* is the basis of a minor publishing industry. Among the useful works: Van der Vat, *Gentlemen of War*; and the memoirs of two participants, Franz Joseph, Prince of Hohenzollern, *Emden*; and Mücke, *The "Ayesha."* A detailed account of the engagement is in Jose, *The Royal Australian Navy*, chap. 7.

22. The circumstances of Müller's imprisonment changed for the worst in October 1916

when he was removed from Malta, where the *Emden* survivors had been confined, and without explanation taken to England. He was exchanged for internment in the Netherlands in January 1918 because of his poor health (malaria) and repatriated to Germany in October 1918. Van der Vat, *Gentlemen of War*, 181–84.

23. For examples, see Corbett and Newbolt, *Naval Operations* 1:288, 294–95, 298–99, 385; Fayle, *Seaborne Trade* 1:272–73, 332.

24. Fayle, *Seaborne Trade* 1:272–73.

25. Admiralty (O.U.6337 [40]), *Review of German Cruiser Warfare*, 26.

26. Raeder and Mantey, *Der Kreuzerkrieg* 2:122–24.

27. On the operations against *Königsberg*, see Corbett and Newbolt, *Naval Operations* 2:236–39; 3:63–67.

28. Corbett and Newbolt, *Naval Operations*, 296–97, 338–39, 374–75; Fayle, *Seaborne Trade* 1:276; Admiralty (O.U.6337 [40]), *Review of German Cruiser Warfare*, 8–9; the best case for *Königsberg*'s accomplishments is, not surprisingly, Raeder and Mantey, *Der Kreuzerkrieg* 2:206–10.

29. The thorough German record is in Raeder and Mantey, *Der Kreuzerkrieg*, vol. 2, pt. 3; Admiralty (O.U. 6337 [40]), *Review of German Cruiser Warfare*, 9–10; Corbett and Newbolt, *Naval Operations* 1:45–51, 320–30, 372–74; Fayle, *Seaborne Trade* 1:265–66.

30. Raeder and Mantey, *Der Kreuzerkrieg* 1:409–10; Admiralty (O.U.6337 [40]), *Review of German Cruiser Warfare*, 1, 6; Fayle, *Seaborne Trade* 1:221–22, 225–26; Bennett, *Coronel and the Falklands*, 76–78; Chatterton, *The Sea Raiders*, 56–64.

31. Fayle, *Seaborne Trade* 1:163–64; Corbett and Newbolt, *Naval Operations* 1:145–46; Admiralty (O.U.6337 [40]), *Review of German Cruiser Warfare*, 1, 6; Bennett, *Coronel and the Falklands*, 82–83.

32. Admiralty (O.U.6337 [40]), *Review of German Cruiser Warfare*, 11–13; Corbett and Newbolt, *Naval Operations* 1:304, 306–8, 339. Detailed German records are in Raeder and Mantey, *Der Kreuzerkrieg*, vol. 3. On the career of the *Cormoran*, see Burdick, *Frustrated Raider*; on *Cap Trafalgar*, Colin Simpson, *The Ship that Hunted Itself*.

33. Corbett and Newbolt, *Naval Operations* 1:133–35; Admiralty (O.U.6337 [40]), *Review of German Cruiser Operations*, 1, 11; Raeder and Mantey, *Der Kreuzerkrieg* 3:11–22; Chatterton, *The Sea Raiders*, 31–34; Schmalenbach, *German Raiders*, 136–37.

34. Admiralty (O.U.6337 [40]), *Review of German Cruiser Warfare*, 1, 12–13; Schmalenbach, *German Raiders*, 136–37; Chatterton, *The Sea Raiders*, chaps. 9–10, 11.

35. Corbett and Newbolt, *Naval Operations* 1:129–30.

36. Cited by French, *British Strategy and War Aims*, 27.

37. Corbett and Newbolt, *Naval Operations* 1:130–31; French, *British Strategy and War Aims*, 27–28; Louis, *Great Britain and Germany's Lost Colonies*, 36–37; Guinn, *British Strategy and Politics*, 40–41.

38. Corbett and Newbolt, *Naval Operations* 1:275, 316–17, 331–32, 407–8; 2:234–35; see also the section on the Cape Squadron in Naval Staff, *The Eastern Squadrons*.

39. The naval aspects can be followed in relevant portions of Corbett and Newbolt, *Naval Operations;* on German activities in East Africa, see also Assmann, *Die Kämpfe der Kaiserlichen Marine,* pt. 2. An overall survey is in Dane, *British Campaigns in Africa and the Pacific.*

40. Corbett and Newbolt, *Naval Operations* 4:81–85. The operations are the subject of Shankland, *The Phantom Flotilla.* See also John Mackenzie, "The Naval Campaigns on Lakes Victoria and Nyasa, 1914–1918," *Mariner's Mirror* (1985): 169–82.

41. Jose, *The Royal Australian Navy,* 59–62, 70–73.

42. This subject is covered in exhaustive detail in Mackenzie, *The Australians at Rabaul.*

43. Account of the Australian–New Zealand convoy drawn from: Naval Staff, *The Eastern Squadrons,* 8–26; Corbett and Newbolt, *Naval Operations* 1:287, 299–302, 332, 380–81; Jose, *The Royal Australian Navy,* 150–64, 409–13.

44. Details of Indian, South African, and Mediterranean convoys summarized from: Naval Staff, *The Eastern Convoys;* Naval Staff, *The Mediterranean;* and Corbett and Newbolt, *Naval Operations* 1:155, 280–81, 378–79.

45. Wemyss quoted in: Lady Wemyss, *Lord Wester Wemyss,* 178, 182.

46. Corbett and Newbolt, *Naval Operations* 1:203–5, 210–12. The convoy arrived safely at Plymouth on 14 October after having been diverted from Southampton because of German submarine activity in the Channel.

47. Pochhammer, *Before Jutland,* 106–8.

48. Randier, *La Royale* 1:220–21; Pochhammer, *Before Jutland,* 110–12; Jose, *The Royal Australian Navy,* 558–59.

49. Naval Staff, *The Eastern Squadrons,* 77–78.

50. Corbett and Newbolt, *Naval Operations* 1:278.

51. On these points, see Louis, *Great Britain and Germany's Lost Colonies,* chap. 2.

52. Naval Staff, *The Eastern Squadrons,* 78, 87–88.

53. Hirst, *Coronel and After,* 15, 94, 97, 103–4; Hickling, *Sailor at Sea,* 21–22; Bennett, *Coronel and the Falklands,* 19–21.

54. Bennett, *Coronel and the Falklands,* 24.

55. A very clear discussion is in Bennett, *Coronel and the Falklands,* 78–79, 94–98; see also Hirst, *Coronel and After,* 97; Marder, *Dreadnought to Scapa Flow* 2:105–12.

56. Hirst, *Coronel and After,* 111. Similar sentiments are in Hickling, *Sailor at Sea,* 46–51. Clear accounts of the battle are in Bennett, *Coronel and the Falklands,* chap. 1, and Corbett and Newbolt, *Naval Operations,* vol. 1, chap. 25; a vivid German perspective is Pochhammer, *Before Jutland,* chap. 8.

57. Bennett, *Coronel and the Falklands,* 110.

58. Bingham, *Falklands, Jutland and the Bight,* 49.

59. United States regulations cited by Corbett and Newbolt, *Naval Operations* 1:371–72.

60. Naval Staff, *The Eastern Squadrons,* 178–86.

61. Japanese deployments covered in Naval Staff, *The Eastern Squadrons,* 108–9.

62. Jose, *The Royal Australian Navy,* 123.

63. Ibid., 111, 125–27.
64. Details in Raeder and Mantey, *Der Kreuzerkrieg* 1:233–39; a synopsis is in Hirst, *Coronel and After*, 155–58.
65. Raeder and Mantey, *Der Kreuzerkrieg* 1:253–54; Tirpitz, *My Memoirs* 2:83–85.
66. Raeder and Mantey, *Der Kreuzerkrieg* 1:241, 270–73.
67. Bennett, *Coronel and the Falklands*, 135.
68. The Admiralty later presented Mrs. Felton a gift of silver plate. Hirst, *Coronel and the Falklands*, 204.
69. Detailed accounts of the action are in the respective official histories: Corbett and Newbolt, *Naval Operations*, vol. 1; Raeder and Mantey, *Der Kreuzerkrieg*, vol 1. An excellent general account is Bennett, *Coronel and the Falklands*; and for the view from individual ships, see Pochhammer (*Gneisenau*), *Before Jutland*; Bingham (*Invincible*), *Falklands, Jutland and the Bight*; Hirst (*Glasgow*), *Coronel and After*; Spencer-Cooper (*Cornwall*), *Battle of the Falkland Islands*; Dixon (*Kent*), *The Enemy Fought Splendidly*; and Buchan, *Log of H.M.S. "Bristol,"* 78–83.
70. The officer was Lieutenant Canaris, the future head of Abwehr, the German intelligence organization in the Second World War. Bennett, *Coronel and the Falklands*, 174–76.
71. Bennett, *Coronel and the Falklands*, 71.

5. THE OVERSEAS CAMPAIGNS

1. Gilbert, *Churchill* 3:19–21; Mackay, *Fisher of Kilverstone*, 455–56; Marder, *Dreadnought to Scapa Flow* 2:178–81; on a similar scheme by Churchill to seize the northern portion of Sylt, see ibid., 187–88.
2. Marder, *Dreadnought to Scapa Flow* 2:182–84; Jellicoe, *The Grand Fleet*, 129–30; Jellicoe to Admiralty, 24 September 1914, in Patterson, *The Jellicoe Papers* 1:69, doc. 45; Patterson, *Tyrwhitt*, 69.
3. Churchill to Fisher, 4 January 1915, reproduced in Gilbert, *Churchill* 3:236; Churchill to Jellicoe, 4 January 1915, in Patterson, *The Jellicoe Papers* 1:118–19, doc. 95.
4. Gilbert, *Churchill* 3:225–26; Marder, *Dreadnought to Scapa Flow* 2:184–87; Churchill to Fisher, 21, 22 December 1914, Marder, *Fear God and Dread Nought* 3:105, 107.
5. Kaarsted, *Great Britain and Denmark*, 53.
6. Gilbert, *Churchill* 3:241–43.
7. Richmond Diary, 4, 19 January 1915, in Marder, *Portrait of an Admiral*, 134–35, 138–39; Marder, *Dreadnought to Scapa Flow* 2:188–90.
8. On the battle cruisers, see Parkes, *British Battleships*, 608, 618–22; on monitors, see Buxton, *Big Gun Monitors*, 12, 26.
9. Churchill's remarks in Churchill, *The World Crisis* 2:27–28; Marder, *Dreadnought to*

Scapa Flow 2:191–96; and on extensive argument the Baltic was a talking point, Mackay, *Fisher of Kilverstone*, 456–57, 459–61, 463–65, 467–68, 472–73.

10. Cited in James, *A Great Seaman*, 138.

11. Jellicoe, *The Grand Fleet*, 154–55; Marder, *Dreadnought to Scapa Flow* 2:197–98; Mackay, *Fisher of Kilverstone*, 473; Marder, *Fear God and Dread Nought* 3:93; Gilbert, *Churchill* 3:241–42, 270–71, 275.

12. Corbett, *Naval Operations* 3:148–54.

13. Described in detail in Bacon, *The Dover Patrol*; and for a differing view, from Bacon's successor at Dover, see Keyes, *The Naval Memoirs*, vol. 2; see also Patterson, *Tyrwhitt*, 182–84.

14. James, *A Great Seaman*, 138.

15. David French, *British Strategy and War Aims*, 47; on French projects for a Syrian expedition and suspicions of the British at this time, see Andrew and Kanya-Forstner, *The Climax of French Imperial Expansion*, 65–70 and Tanenbaum, *France and the Arab Middle East*, 7–8. Turkish rail communications are discussed in Macmunn and Falls, *Egypt & Palestine* 1:19–21, 26–27.

16. Corbett and Newbolt, *Naval Operations* 1:73–78; Macmunn and Falls, *Egypt & Palestine* 1:28, 34–36, 41.

17. Corbett and Newbolt, *Naval Operations* 1:111–12; Thomazi, *Méditerranée*, 77; Macmunn and Falls, *Egypt & Palestine* 1:28–29. The most detailed account is in the relevant chapters of the Naval Staff monograph, *The Mediterranean, 1914–1915*.

18. Corbett and Newbolt, *Naval Operations* 1:114–17; Macmunn and Falls, *Egypt & Palestine* 1:40–43, 48–49; Thomazi, *Méditerranée*, 80–81.

19. Macmunn and Falls, *Egypt & Palestine* 1:63–64, 71, 89; Corbett and Newbolt, *Naval Operations* 1:366–69. On German attempts at mining, see Lorey *Krieg in den türkischen Gewässern* 1:246–47.

20. Corbett and Newbolt, *Naval Operations* 2:223–26; Macmunn and Falls, *Egypt & Palestine*, vol. 1, chaps. 7–8. Many details on the *Tara* episode are in Davies, *The Sea and the Sand*.

21. A succinct discussion of the origins of the Dardanelles campaign is in French, *British Strategy and War Aims*, 68–74. More detailed accounts are in Marder, *Dreadnought to Scapa Flow*, vol. 2, chap. 9; Gilbert, *Churchill*, vol. 3, chaps. 6, 8–10; and Cassar, *The French and the Dardanelles*, chap. 3.

22. On Fisher's role, see Mackay, *Fisher of Kilverstone*, 480, 488–90.

23. Vice Amiral Aubert, "Note pour le Ministre sur l'action aux Dardanelles," 7 February 1915, SHM, Carton Ed-109. On the French role, see Halpern, *Naval War in the Mediterranean*, 56–60; Cassar, *The French and the Dardanelles*, 56–60, 62–66; Laurens, *Le commandement*, 75–76, 80–82.

24. Churchill, *The World Crisis* 2:547–50.

25. Souchon to his wife, 6 January 1915, BA/MA, Nachlass Souchon, N156/12; There were similar doubts at the Admiralty, see: Admiral Sir H. B. Jackson, "Note on forcing the passages of the Dardanelles and Bosphorus. . . ," 5 January 1915, PRO,

Adm 137/1089; see also Richmond, "Remarks on Present Strategy," 14 February 1915, reproduced in Marder, *Portrait of an Admiral*, 142–45.

26. Hankey to Balfour, 10 February 1915, British Library, London, Balfour MSS., Add. MSS. 49703, f.165.

27. Gilbert, *Churchill* 3:288, 292–97; Cassar, *The French and the Dardanelles*, 73–75; Thomazi, *Dardanelles*, 64.

28. Keyes to his wife, 8 March 1915, in Halpern, *The Keyes Papers* 1:103–4.

29. Wemyss to Limpus, 4 March 1915, National Maritime Museum, Greenwich, Limpus MSS; Rear Admiral Hugh Miller, unpublished autobiography, 136. Microfilm copy at Imperial War Museum, London, PP/MCR/16.

30. French, *British Strategy and War Aims*, 80–82; Gilbert, *Churchill* 3:320–22, 332–35. The Russians had also vetoed Greek participation in the campaign, see: ibid., 220–21, 281, 287, 315–16, 328–29; Corbett and Newbolt, *Naval Operations* 2:103, 123–25.

31. Halpern, *Naval War in the Mediterranean*, 65, 77.

32. Churchill to Kitchener, 20 January 1915, reproduced in Gilbert, *Churchill* 3:267–68; Halpern, *Naval War in the Mediterranean*, 66.

33. Corbett and Newbolt, *Naval Operations* 2:195–200, 209–10; Naval Staff, *The Mediterranean, 1914–1915*, 118–24; Halpern, *Naval War in the Mediterranean*, 67–68.

34. Authorities differ in their details of the (inevitably) still mysterious affair. See: Captain G. R. C. Allen, "A ghost from Gallipoli," *The Royal United Service Institution Journal* 108, no. 630 (May 1963): 137–38; letter by Admiral Sir William James, 7 September 1963, in ibid. 108, no. 632 (November 1963): 374–75; see also James's, *The Eyes of the Navy*, 60–64; Gilbert, *Churchill* 3:358–60; Beesly, *Room 40*, 80–82.

35. Churchill to Carden, 11 March 1915, reproduced in Gilbert, *Churchill* 3:337; Marder, *Dreadnought to Scapa Flow* 2:242–45, 263–65; Keyes, *Naval Memoirs*, vol. 1, chap. 12; Keyes to his wife, 15, 17 March 1915, in Halpern, *The Keyes Papers* 1:108–10.

36. Marder, *Dreadnought to Scapa Flow* 2:245–50; Corbett and Newbolt, *Naval Operations* 2:213–23; Keyes, *Naval Memoirs*, vol. 1, chap. 13; Keyes to his wife, 21 March 1915, in Halpern, *The Keyes Papers* 1:110–15; Bush, *Gallipoli*, 51–64.

37. For the arguments, see Keyes, *Naval Memoirs* 1:185–86; Churchill, *The World Crisis*, vol. 2, chap. 13; Marder, *Dreadnought to Scapa Flow* 2:259–65; Marder, "The Dardanelles Revisited: Further Thoughts on the Naval Prelude," in *From the Dardanelles to Oran*, 1–32.

38. Souchon to his wife, 19 March 1915, BA/MA, Nachlass Souchon, N156/13.

39. On 28 March the major batteries of the Dardanelles defenses reported 46 shells (8 modern, 38 old) for each of the five 35.5-cm cannon; 62 shells (12 modern, 50 old) for each of the three 24-cm cannon; 120 high-explosive shells for each of the thirty-two 15-cm howitzers; 230 shells (30 armor piercing, 200 practice) for each of the three British 15-cm cannon; and 140 shells for each of the five 15-cm Krupp cannon. Bachmann to Kaiser Wilhelm, 31 March 1915, microfilm copy of German naval records in NARS, T-1022, Roll 587, PG 68126.

40. Halpern, *Naval War in the Mediterranean*, 69–70, 106.

41. Ibid., 71–75, 107–8.

42. Good accounts of the landings are in: James, *Gallipoli*; Moorehead, *Gallipoli*; Aspinall-Oglander, *Military Operations: Gallipoli*; Keyes, *Naval Memoirs*, vol. 1, chap. 17; Bush, *Gallipoli*.

43. Wemyss to Limpus, 6 September 1915, National Maritime Museum, Greenwich., Limpus MSS.

44. Keyes, *Naval Memoirs* 1:335–77; Churchill, *The World Crisis* 2:350–51; Gilbert, *Churchill* 3:117–18; Guépratte, *L'Expédition des Dardanelles*, 147.

45. Keyes, *Naval Memoirs* 1:338.

46. Lorey, *Krieg in den türkischen Gewässern* 1:138–44; Corbett and Newbolt, *Naval Operations* 2:406–8.

47. Marder, *Dreadnought to Scapa Flow* 2:276–86, 286–91; Gilbert, *Churchill* 3:422–29, 433–45, chap. 14; Churchill, *The World Crisis* 2:380 ff.; Mackay, *Fisher of Kilverstone*, 496–505.

48. Halpern, *Naval War in the Mediterranean*, 107–12; Lorey, *Krieg in den türkischen Gewässern* 1:149–51; Otto Hersing, *U.21 rettet die Dardanellen*, 43–47.

49. De Robeck to Limpus, 16 May 1915, reproduced in Halpern, "De Robeck," 448–50.

50. Corbett and Newbolt, *Naval Operations* 3:28–31; Lorey, *Krieg in den türkischen Gewässern* 1:151–55; Halpern, *Naval War in the Mediterranean*, 116–17; 148–57.

51. Bush, *Gallipoli*, 225; Lorey, *Krieg in den türkischen Gewässern* 2:149–50; Edwards, *We Dive at Dawn*, 182; Corbett and Newbolt, *Naval Operations* 2:302–4, 374–75; 3:32–35; 75–79, 100–102, 114–19; Keyes, *Naval Memoirs* 1:288–89, 347–50; other accounts of the submarines at the Dardanelles are: Brodie, *Forlorn Hope 1915*; Shankland and Hunter, *Dardanelles Patrol*.

52. On the Suvla landings, see Corbett and Newbolt, *Naval Operations* 3:68–70, and chap. 5; Aspinall-Oglander, *Military Operations: Gallipoli*, vol. 2; Keyes, *Naval Memoirs*, vol. 1, chap. 22; James, *Gallipoli*, chaps. 10–11; Bush, *Gallipoli*, chap. 20.

53. On the French plans and Sarrail, see Tanenbaum, *General Maurice Sarrail*, 56–65; King, *Generals and Politicians*, chap. 4; Cassar, *The French and the Dardanelles*, chap. 8. Numerous documents on this obscure plan may also be found in Ministère de la Guerre, État-Major de l'Armée—Service Historique, *Les Armées Français dans la Grande Guerre*, Tomb 8-1er vol., Annexes—1er vol. (Paris, 1924).

54. Proposal by Keyes for a renewal of the naval attack on the Dardanelles and de Robeck's comments, 17 August 1915, in Halpern, *The Keyes Papers* 1:188–92; Memorandum by Captain Godfrey, 13 September 1915, Keyes to de Robeck, 23 September 1915, in ibid., 194–204; Keyes's memorandum of 18 October 1915 printed in Keyes, *Naval Memoirs* 1:440–43.

55. Keyes Diary, 17 October–10 November 1915, in Halpern, *The Keyes Papers* 1:216; de Robeck to Jackson, 20 October 1915, ibid., 232–33; de Robeck to Balfour, 20 October 1915, in idem., "De Robeck," 478–79.

56. On Keyes in London, see Keyes Diary, 29 October–9 November 1915, in Halpern, *The Keyes Papers* 1:219–31; Balfour to Keyes, 1 November 1915, ibid., 234–35; Memorandum by Keyes, n.d. [6 November 1915], ibid., 235–40; Keyes to Jackson, 11 November 1915, ibid., 241–42; Jackson to de Robeck, 7 November 1915, in idem., "De Robeck," 480. For the French role, see also Cassar, *The French and the Dardanelles*, 212–16.

57. De Robeck to Limpus, 9 November 1915, in Halpern, "De Robeck," 480–81; Limpus to de Robeck, 12 November 1915, ibid., 481–83.

58. Halpern, *Naval War in the Mediterranean*, 185–87; on the argument the Ayas Bay project was a mere diversion, see James, *Gallipoli*, 329–31; and as a desirable alternative to other campaigns, see Barker, *The Bastard War*, 409–11.

59. The decision to evacuate is discussed in Aspinall-Oglander, *Military Operations: Gallipoli*, vol. 2, chaps. 28–30; James, *Gallipoli*, 321–32; Marder, *Dreadnought to Scapa Flow* 2:309–29.

60. Wemyss to de Robeck, n.d. (probably 29 November 1915) in Halpern, *The Keyes Papers* 1:257–58; Wemyss to Jackson, n.d. (late November, early December 1915), ibid. 1:268–69; Keyes, *Naval Memoirs* 1:473–75.

61. On the evacuations, the very detailed account is in Aspinall-Oglander, *Military Operations: Gallipoli*, vol. 2, chaps. 21, 32. See also Keyes, *Naval Memoirs*, vol. 1, chap. 26; James, *Gallipoli*, 339–42, 344–47; Bush, *Gallipoli*, 300–306.

62. Naval operations are covered in Corbett and Newbolt, *Naval Operations* 1:375–78, 388–95; Nunn, *Tigris Gunboats*, chaps. 1–3; and detail on all aspects of the expedition in Moberly, *The Campaign in Mesopotamia*. See also Naval Staff, *Mesopotamia and the Persian Gulf*.

63. French, *British Strategy and War Aims*, 137.

64. Corbett and Newbolt, *Naval Operations* 2:11–13; Nunn, *Tigris Gunboats*, 78–85. Operations in Persia are covered in detail in the recently released 1928 confidential publication: Moberly, *Operations in Persia*, chap. 2.

65. Corbett and Newbolt, *Naval Operations* 3:15–23; Nunn, *Tigris Gunboats*, chap. 6; Barker, *The Bastard War*, 65–69.

66. Corbett and Newbolt, *Naval Operations* 3:185–88; Nunn, *Tigris Gunboats*, chap. 7; Barker, *The Bastard War*, 69–76.

67. Full details in Moberly, *Operations in Persia*, chap. 3; see also: Corbett and Newbolt, *Naval Operations* 3:189–90; Barker, *The Bastard War*, 135–39.

68. On the decision to advance, see French, *British Strategy and War Aims*, 144–46; Corbett and Newbolt, *Naval Operations* 3:181–82, 188–99; Barker, *The Bastard War*, 77–80, 93–99.

69. Nunn, *Tigris Gunboats*, 200, 202, 211–12; Corbett and Newbolt, *Naval Operations* 3:197, n. 1.

70. Nunn, *Tigris Gunboats*, chaps. 9–10; Corbett and Newbolt, *Naval Operations* 3:226–69; Barker, *The Bastard War*, chap. 5.

71. Corbett and Newbolt, *Naval Operations* 4:87–91; Barker, *The Bastard War*, 225–27; Nunn, *Tigris Gunboats*, chaps. 12–13.

72. For Wemyss's comments, see Lady Wemyss, *Lord Wester Wemyss*, 281–86; on the administrative reorganization, see Barker, *The Bastard War*, 266–70, 272–73; Moberly, *The Campaign in Mesopotamia* 3:31–35.

73. A thorough discussion of British strategy is in Moberly, *The Campaign in Mesopotamia* 3:37–55; for a succinct summary, see Guinn, *British Strategy and Politics*, 157–58, 217–20.

74. Moberly, *The Campaign in Mesopotamia* 3:193–96; Nunn's vivid account is in his *Tigris Gunboats*, 259–67; see also Barker, *The Bastard War*, 310–11. The relatively small German role in Iraq is described in Lorey, *Krieg in den türkischen Gewässern* 1:248–60, 350–58; and Köppen, *Die Überwasserstreitkräfte*, chap. 18.

75. Moberly, *The Campaign in Mesopotamia* 4:140–41. In July 1918 a naval party from the *Moth* and *Mantis* was sent to the Caspian in a complex effort to gain control of that sea following the Bolshevik Revolution and withdrawal of Russia from the war, a tangled subject far beyond the scope of this book. See ibid., 202, 329–30.

76. See Thomazi, *Méditerranée*, 92–94, 102–3, 115–17.

77. On the Anatolian cattle raids, see Halpern, *Naval War in the Mediterranean*, 290–93; documents concerning the raids are in Halpern, *Royal Navy in the Mediterranean*, doc. 66–69, 71, 73, 76–77, 82, 85, 87, 90, 95, 97; see also Taffrail, *Endless Story*, 95–100; Usborne, *Blast and Counterblast*, 99–100; and Myres, *Commander J. L. Myres*.

78. Fremantle to Admiralty, 30 December 1917; Minutes by Naval Staff; Calthorpe to Admiralty, 21 January 1918, *Royal Navy in the Mediterranean*, 329–41.

79. Marder, *Portrait of an Admiral*, 250–51, 388; Halpern, *Naval War in the Mediterranean*, 421–22.

80. For a study in depth of this relationship, see Keith Neilson, *Strategy and Supply: The Anglo-Russian Alliance, 1914–1917* (London: Allen & Unwin, 1984).

81. Fayle, *Seaborne Trade* 2:118–23, 212, 350–51. See also: Naval Staff, *A History of the White Sea Station, 1914–1919* (February 1920).

82. Details about *Meteor* from Schmalenbach, *German Raiders*, 16, 32, 46–49, 71, 132, 136–37. *Meteor* did not survive her second patrol in August to lay mines off the Scottish coast. Although she surprised and sank the armed boarding steamer *Ramsay* southeast of Pentland Firth on the 8th when the latter lowered a boat to examine the innocuous-looking steamer flying Russian colors, the British spread a wide net and she was caught off Horns Reef by Tyrwhitt's cruisers the following day and scuttled to avoid capture. Details in Corbett and Newbolt, *Naval Operations* 3:122–26.

83. Fayle, *Seaborne Trade* 2:123–24; Corbett and Newbolt, *Naval Operations* 3:48–50; Hurd, *The Merchant Navy* 2:67–69; ibid. 3:240; Russian accounts differ sharply from the British on the amount of Russian assistance provided, see Pavlovich, *The Fleet*, 513–17.

84. Gibson and Prendergast, *The German Submarine War*, 111–12, 117; Hurd, *The Merchant Navy* 2:262, 345–47; Spindler, *Handelskrieg mit U-Booten* 3:232–37, 257–58.

85. Fayle, *Seaborne Trade* 2:350.

86. For a full discussion of the Petrograd Conference, see Neilson, *Strategy and Supply*, chap. 6. On Arctic forces, see Corbett and Newbolt, *Naval Operations* 5:303; Gibson and Prendergast, *The German Submarine War*, 112; Greger, *Die Russische Flotte*, 42; Pavlovich, *The Fleet*, 549–50; Naval Staff, *History of the White Sea Station*, 8–9.

87. Spindler, *Handelskrieg mit U-Booten* 4:42, 84–85, 275–76; Naval Staff, *History of the White Sea Station*, 9–10; Fayle, *Seaborne Trade* 3:238–39.

88. John W. Wheeler-Bennett, *Brest-Litovsk: The Forgotten Peace* (1938; reprint, New York: St. Martin's, 1966), 380, 406.

89. Fayle, *Seaborne Trade* 3:358–60. The ships, most of whose owners were anti-Bolshevik, were run under the British flag.

90. On this point, see remarks by the British senior naval officer on the Dvina: Altham, "The Dwina Campaign," 230.

91. Holger H. Herwig, "German Policy in the Eastern Baltic Sea in 1918: Expansion or Anti-Bolshevik Crusade?" *Slavic Review* 32, no. 2 (June 1973): 344 ff.

92. The literature is large. Standard works are: George F. Kennan, *Soviet-American Relations, 1917–1920*, vol. 2: *The Decision to Intervene* (Princeton: Princeton University Press, 1958); Richard H. Ullman, *Anglo-Soviet Relations, 1917–1921*, vol. 1: *Intervention and the War* (Princeton: Princeton University Press, 1961). A succinct account on the naval aspect is in: Roskill, *Naval Policy Between the Wars*, vol. 1, chap. 3.

93. Outline of naval operations drawn from Corbett and Newbolt, *Naval Operations* 5:323–32; Altham, "The Dwina Campaign," 231–40.

94. For memoirs by the commanders of the Murmansk and Archangel forces, respectively, see Maynard, *The Murmansk Venture*; Ironside, *Archangel, 1918–1919*. On U.S. involvement, see Beers, *U.S. Naval Forces in North Russia*.

95. See Bennett, *Cowan's War*.

6. THE ADRIATIC

1. Thaon di Revel, "Promemoria No.1. Esame di operazioni di guerra nell'Adriatico," Sept. 1914, USM, Cartella 354/3. Excerpts are printed in the official history: Ufficio Storico, *Marina italiana* 1:312–23; see also Halpern's *Mediterranean Naval Situation*, 208–11 and *Naval War in the Mediterranean*, 85–86.

2. Biographical studies are: Ferrante, *Paolo Thaon di Revel* and Po, *Thaon di Revel*. See also the entry in Cannistraro, *Dictionary of Fascist Italy*, 532–35.

3. Revel, "Nuovo esame di operazioni di guerra nell'Adriatico," 5 January 1915, printed with slight changes in Ufficio Storico, *Marina italiana* 1:325–58. See also Ferrante, *La grande guerra in Adriatico,* 29–33.

4. A worthwhile biography, emphasizing his explorations, is Dainelli, *Il Duca degli Abruzzi.* See also the entry in Cannistraro, *Dictionary of Fascist Italy,* 489–90.

5. On Abruzzi's proposals, see Ferrante, *La grande guerra in Adriatico,* 33–36.

6. Discussion of Italian war plans in Halpern, *Naval War in the Mediterranean,* 84–92. The general Italian war plan is printed virtually in full in Viale [Minister of Marine], "Piano generale delle operazioni in Adriatico," 18 April 1915, Ufficio Storico, *Marina italiana* 1:331–41.

7. Short accounts in English are: Zeman, *Gentlemen Negotiators,* chap. 1; Bosworth, *Italy and the Approach,* chap. 6.

8. "Agreement between the Three Powers and Italy," 26 April 1915, PRO, Cab 37/128.

9. On the naval convention, see Halpern, "Anglo-French-Italian Naval Convention," 106–29; and Gabriele, "Le convenzione navale italo-franco-britannica del 10 maggio 1915," *Nuova antologia* 1:492–94, fasc. 1972–73 (April–May 1965).

10. L. Aldovandi Marescotti, *Nuovi ricordi e frammenti di diario* (Milan: Mondadori, 1938), 222. See also Halpern, *Naval War in the Mediterranean,* 93, 96–101.

11. For a good summary in English of the crisis over intervention, see Seton-Watson, *Italy from Liberalism to Fascism,* 443–47.

12. The differing national viewpoints are in Sokol, *Österreich-Ungarns Seekrieg,* chap. 7; Ufficio Storico, *Marina italiana,* vol. 2, chaps. 1–2; a summary in Admiral Vittoria Prato, "La nostra entrata in guerra nel 1915 e le prime operazioni in Adriatico," *Rivista marittima* 98, no. 5 (May 1965): 42–47.

13. Abruzzi, "Schema generale del piano di guerra in Adriatico," enclosed in Abruzzi to Revel, 21 May 1915, Abruzzi to Vice Admiral Presbitero (commander in chief, II Squadra), 20 May 1915, USM, Cartella 354/3.

14. Thursby to Admiralty, Report of Proceedings, 4 June 1915, and minute by Balfour, 20 July, PRO, Adm 137/780.

15. Lapeyrère to Augagneur (minister of marine), 26 May 1915, SHM, Carton Ed-83; Lapeyrère to Augagneur, 19 May 1915, SHM, Carton A-75.

16. On these points, see Halpern, *Naval War in the Mediterranean,* 173, 206–7, 209–11, 240, 271–72.

17. Events summarized from Ufficio Storico, *Marina italiana* 2:83–90, 116–18; Sokol, *Österreich-Ungarns Seekrieg,* 228–30; Ufficio del Capo di Stato Maggiore della Marina, "Relazione generale sull'opera svolta dal 1 Aprile al 1 Ottobre 1915," 158–59, copy in ACS, 1° Aiutante di Campo Generale di S.M. il Re, Sezione Speciale, Filza 24; Richmond Diary, 26 June 1915, in Marder, *Portrait of an Admiral,* 178.

18. Plans summarized in Halpern, *Naval War in the Mediterranean,* 130–31.

19. Ufficio Storico, *Marina italiana* 2:109–10, 120–28; Spindler, *Handelskrieg mit U-booten* 2:196–97; Aichelburg, *Die Unterseeboote Österreich-Ungarn* 1:121, 133–34, 2:318–19, 337.

20. Ufficio Storico, *Marina italiana* 2:171–75; Richmond Diary, 12, 18, 23 June, 9, 13 July 1915 in Marder, *Portrait of an Admiral*, 169, 173, 175, 181, 183; Daveluy to Lapeyrère, 26 July 1915, SHM, Carton Ed-91.

21. Ufficio Storico, *Marina italiana* 2:178–85; Sokol, *Österreich-Ungarns Seekrieg*, 233–35; Revel to Abruzzi, 27 (?) July 1915, ACS, Carte Brusati/12 (VIII-17-61); Revel to Abruzzi, 17, 27 July 1915, USM, Cartella 363/1.

22. Summary discussion in Halpern, *Naval War in the Mediterranean*, 134–39; in addition to the Ufficio Storico's *Marina italiana*, there is a very detailed study of the Pelagosa occupation in Ufficio Storico, *Occupazione dell' Isola di Pelagosa*.

23. Richmond Diary, 18 August 1915, in Marder, *Portrait of an Admiral*, 192.

24. Halpern, *Naval War in the Mediterranean*, 131–32, 139–40.

25. Revel to Abruzzi, 30 July, 27 August 1915, USM, Cartella 356/3; Villarey (Italian naval attaché) to Admiralty, 26 August 1915, with minutes by Oliver and Wilson, PRO, Adm 137/1140.

26. These British operations are well covered in: Kemp and Jung, "Five Broken Down B Boats," 10–29.

27. On the Italian navy in this period, see Halpern, *Naval War in the Mediterranean*, 141–47.

28. Daveluy to Lapeyrère, 30 August 1915, SHM, Carton Ed-91.

29. Summary in Halpern, *Naval War in the Mediterranean*, 205–11. See also Thomazi, *L'Adriatique*, 108–9; Corbett and Newbolt, *Naval Operations* 4:101–2; Naval Staff, *The Mediterranean*, 210–11; Sokol, *Österreich-Ungarns Seekrieg*, 242–43, 246–49. The subject is treated at length in Ufficio Storico, *Marina italiana*, vol. 2, chaps. 11–13.

30. Summary in Halpern, *Naval War in the Mediterranean*, 212–14; more detailed accounts from the respective national points of view are in Corbett and Newbolt, *Naval Operations* 4:106–17; Naval Staff, *The Mediterranean*, 216–25; Ufficio Storico, *Marina italiana*, vol. 2, chap. 15; Sokol, *Österreich-Ungarns Seekrieg*, 250–63; Thomazi, *L'Adriatique*, 110–14.

31. Thursby to Jackson, 20 February 1916, in Halpern, *Royal Navy in the Mediterranean*, 108.

32. The most detailed study with statistics: Ufficio Storico, *Marina italiana*, vol. 2, chaps. 16–18, and Appendix 10, pp. 615–18; see also Halpern, *Naval War in the Mediterranean*, 215–16; Sokol, *Österreich-Ungarns Seekrieg*, 271–72; Corbett and Newbolt, *Naval Operations* 4:118–25; and for current sensitivity over the subject, see Ferrante, *La Grande Guerra in Adriatico*, 55–58.

33. See the discussions in Halpern, *Naval War in the Mediterranean*, 216–18; Sokol, *Österreich-Ungarns Seekrieg*, 286–87; Bayer von Bayersburg, *Die Marinewaffen im Einsatz*, 29; Sokol, *Austro-Hungarian Navy*, 116–18; and Baumgartner, "Österreich-Ungarns Dünkirchen?"

34. Naval Staff, *The Mediterranean*, 203–7; Thursby to Limpus, 28 September, 17 October, 8 November 1915, in Halpern, *Royal Navy in the Mediterranean*, 24–27, 32–34. Several chapters on the drifters in the Adriatic are in Chatterton, *Seas of Adventures*.

35. Lejay (French liaison officer with Italian fleet) to Lacaze, 23 July 1916, SHM, Carton

Ed-93; Kerr to Admiralty, 18 November 1916, and Kerr, "Situation in the Mediterranean," 30 November 1916, British Library, London, Jellicoe MSS, Add. MSS 49035.

36. Halpern, *Naval War in the Mediterranean*, 278–80.

37. Thomazi, *L'Adriatique*, 138–39; Ufficio Storico, *Marina italiana* 3:300–303, 520–33; Sokol, *Österreich-Ungarns Seekrieg*, 360, 367–75.

38. The *Carroccio* (1,657 tons) was the former German *Choising* that had brought the *Emden*'s landing party across the Indian Ocean after they had scuttled the schooner *Ayesha*.

39. Summary in Halpern, *Naval War in the Mediterranean*, 357–66; full accounts in Corbett and Newbolt, *Naval Operations* 4:297–306; Ufficio Storico, *Marina italiana*, vol. 4, chap. 20; Sokol, *Österreich-Ungarns Seekrieg*, 376–93; Thomazi, *L'Adriatique*, 147–53; and the analysis in Lukas, "Das Gefecht in der Otrantostrasse."

40. Ufficio Storico, *Marina italiana* 3:215–20. The issue of sabotage in these cases remains difficult to prove; see Ferrante, *La grande guerra in Adriatico*, 62–63.

41. On these points, see Halpern, *Naval War in the Mediterranean*, passim. The old B-class submarines had been recalled from Venice in October 1916 after the arrival of four W-class submarines sold by the British to the Italians. Two 12-inch gunned monitors remained with the Italian naval forces in the upper Adriatic.

42. Halpern, *Naval War in the Mediterranean*, 265–68.

43. Most of the relevant correspondence is printed in Sokol, *Österreich-Ungarns Seekrieg*, 394–400. See also Halpern, *Naval War in the Mediterranean*, 285–87.

44. On the changes, see Halpern, *Mediterranean Naval Situation*, 310–11, 333–36.

45. Air operations are covered in detail in Sokol, *Österreich-Ungarns Seekrieg*, chaps. 10, 18, 27; and Schupita, *Die k.u.k. Seeflieger*. See also Thomazi, *L'Adriatique*, 122; Ufficio Storico, *Marina italiana* 3:167–68.

46. Ufficio Storico, *Marina italiana* 3:50–55; a short summary of their characteristics is in Fraccaroli, *Italian Warships*, 129 ff. Exhaustive detail in Bagnasco, *I Mas e le motosiluranti italiane*.

47. Thomazi, *L'Adriatique*, 126–27; Ufficio Storico, *Marina italiana* 3:371–74, 394–97; Sokol, *Österreich-Ungarns Seekrieg*, 422–24.

48. For a brief description, see Ferrante, *Il grande guerra in Adriatico*, 82–88.

49. Ufficio Storico, *Marina italiana* 6:431–35; Sokol, *Österreich-Ungarns Seekrieg*, 621–23. Substantial extracts from Rizzo's report are printed in Ferrante, *Il grande guerra in Adriatico*, 91–93, 171–73. A short account in English is in Winton, *Below the Belt*, 123–25.

50. The most detailed account in print is Plaschka, *Cattaro—Prag*. See also his "Phänomene sozialer"; and Sokol, *Österreich-Ungarns Seekrieg*, chap. 30; Ufficio Storico, *Marina italiana*, vol. 7, chap. 5.

51. Halpern, *Naval War in the Mediterranean*, 449–50; Horthy, *Memoirs*, 88–89.

52. For a full discussion of the U.S. Adriatic plans, see Halpern, *Naval War in the Mediterranean*, 434–41.

53. Ferrante, *Il grande guerra in Adriatico*, 106–9; Sokol, *Österreich-Ungarns Seekrieg*, 624–27; Ufficio Storico, *Marina italiana* 7:364–70, and chap. 7.

54. Sokol, *Österreich-Ungarns Seekrieg*, 627–30; Bagnasco, *I mas e le motosilurante italiane*, 619–27; Ufficio Storico, *Marina italiana*, vol. 7, chap. 20; Winton, *Below the Belt*, 126. On Austrian measures, see Halpern, *Naval War in the Mediterranean*, 451–52; Greger, *Austro-Hungarian Warships*, 65–67; and Bilzer, *Torpedoboote der k.u.k. Kriegsmarine*, 136 ff.

55. Corbett and Newbolt, *Naval Operations* 5:287–88; Sokol, *Österreich-Ungarns Seekrieg*, 550–51. British reports of the action are printed in Halpern, *The Royal Navy in the Mediterranean*, 450–59.

56. Halpern, *Naval War in the Mediterranean*, 452–53, 537; Heyssler to Keyes, 1 March 1921, in Halpern, *The Keyes Papers* 2:52; Trapp, *Bis zum letzten Flaggenschuss*, 126.

57. Sokol, *Österreich-Ungarns Seekrieg*, 553–63; Ufficio Storico, *Marina italiana*, vol. 7, chap. 29; Rizzo's report is reproduced in Ferrante, *La grande guerra in Adriatico*, 110–13, 177–79; see also Halpern, *Naval War in the Mediterranean*, 501–2; Tomicich, "Die Versenkung."

58. Halpern, *Naval War in the Mediterranean*, 516–18; Italian military operations in Albania are covered in detail in Stato Maggiore dell'Esercito, Ufficio Storico, *Le Truppe Italiane in Albania (Anni 1914–20 e 1939)* (Rome: Ufficio Storico [Esercito], 1978), chap. 4.

59. Halpern, *Naval War in the Mediterranean*, 556–58; Sokol, *Österreich-Ungarns Seekrieg*, 636–45; Ufficio Storico, *Marina italiana* 8:380–97. Although the action is omitted in Corbett and Newbolt's *Naval Operations*, the British reports are printed in Halpern, *Royal Navy in the Mediterranean*, 557–66.

60. Sokol, *Österreich-Ungarns Seekrieg*, chap. 31; Ufficio Storico, *Marina italiana* 8:509–19; short accounts are in Halpern, *Naval War in the Mediterranean*, 566–67; Winton, *Below the Belt*, 126–28; the reports of Rossetti and Paolucci are printed in Ferrante, *La grande guerra in Adriatico*, 183–201.

61. Greger, "Wussten die Italiener davon?"; Ferrante, *La grande guerra in Adriatico*, 116–20.

7. THE BALTIC

1. A good survey of Russian naval plans is in the translation of the Soviet official history: Pavlovich, *The Fleet* 1:48–49. Unfortunately the translation is poor, if not at times almost unintelligible.

2. For comments on Essen, see Pavlovitch, *The Fleet* 1:60; Graf, *The Russian Navy*, 31–32, 34–36.

3. Graf, *The Russian Navy*, 36.

4. Pavlovich, *The Fleet*, 50–53, 55, 57–59; see also Monasterev, *Sur Trois Mers*, 12–13.

5. Firle, *Krieg in der Ostsee* 1:2–3, 2 n. 1, 5.

6. Ibid. 1:29.

7. Prince Heinrich had been chief of the High Sea Fleet from 1906 to 1909 when he was described as being "forced" to leave his post. See Gemzell, *Organization, Conflict and Innovation*, 197–98.

8. Görlitz, *The Kaiser and His Court*, 15.

9. Görlitz, *The Kaiser and His Court*, 15; Gemzell, *Organization, Conflict and Innovation*, 198.

10. Firle, *Krieg in der Ostsee* 1:48–51; Görlitz, *The Kaiser and His Court*, 16.

11. "La Sauvegarde de la neutralité du Danemark par la flotte danoise pendant la guerre mondiale" (Extract from a brochure published by the Society of Naval Lieutenants, *Flotte ou Police du Mer*), annexed to report from French Military Attaché in Denmark, 26 January 1925, SHM, Carton Ea-174.

12. Admiral Scheer, *Germany's High Sea Fleet*, 60.

13. Pavlovich, *The Fleet*, 72.

14. Monasterev, *Sur Trois Mers*, 18–20. The story leaked out after the war. There is an account in the files of the French naval staff based on Swedish publications reported in the *Berliner Tageblatt*, 17 May (year illegible), "Un amiral veut agir," SHM, Carton Ea-163. The incident is not in Pavlovich, *The Fleet*.

15. Commander H. Grenfell (naval attaché, Petrograd) to Sir George Buchanan (British ambassador), 6 November 1914, PRO, Adm 137/271, ff. 274–75.

16. These operations can be followed in detail on the German side in Firle, *Krieg in der Ostsee*, vol. 1, chaps. 3, 5–6. For the Russian perspective, see Pavlovich, *The Fleet*, 74–76. A convenient summary of events is in Greger, *Die Russische Flotte*, 15.

17. A very detailed account of these events is in Mäkelä, *Das Geheimnis der "Magdeburg."*

18. Greger, *Die Russische Flotte*, 15–16.

19. Monasterev, *Sur Trois Mers*, 27–29; a more detailed account with some differences is in the Italian translation: Monasterev, *La Marina Russa*, 38–58.

20. The loss of the cruiser made Admiral von Pohl glad that he had advised the kaiser to reject a plan by the chief of the High Sea Fleet and Prince Heinrich to use the Second Battle Squadron (8 Deutschland class) to bombard Libau. Letter of 17 November 1914, in Pohl, *Aufzeichungen und Briefen*, 88–89.

21. Firle, *Krieg in der Ostsee* 1:285–86; Pavlovich, *The Fleet*, 113, 118, 123. The account of Baltic operations has been summarized from these two sources supplemented by Greger, *Die Russische Flotte* and Monasterev, *La Marina Russa*.

22. Commodore (S) to Commander in Chief, Grand Fleet, 10 October 1914, PRO, Adm 137/271. For details see Keyes, *Naval Memoirs* 1:116–18; Halpern, *The Keyes Papers* 1:39–41; and Wilson, *Baltic Assignment*, 16–19, 25–26.

23. Sir H. Lowther (British minister at Copenhagen) to Sir Edward Grey, 31 December 1914, Copy in PRO, Adm 137/271, ff. 520–22.

24. Naval Staff, *The Baltic*, 17–24; Wilson, *Baltic Assignment*, chap. 3.

25. Grenfell to Buchanan, 6 November 1914, PRO, Adm 137/271, ff. 268–77.

26. Naval Staff, *The Baltic*, 22–23, n. 4, 24–28.

27. Ibid., 29–35; Wilson, *Baltic Assignment*, 53–56.

28. Excerpts from "Denkschrift des Oberbefehlshabers der Ostseestreitkräfte" [Prince Heinrich], 25 March 1915, in Rollman, *Krieg in der Ostsee*, vol. 2, *Das Kriegsjahr 1915* (Berlin, 1929), 26–27.

29. Pavlovich, *The Fleet*, 129–35.

30. Graf, *The Russian Navy*, 32.

31. Wilson, *Baltic Assignment*, 62–66.

32. The debate is given in detail in: Rollmann, *Krieg in der Ostsee* 2:88–94, 101.

33. Diary of Admiral Richard F. Phillimore, 11 November 1915, Imperial War Museum, London, Phillimore MSS. 75/48/2. See also similar report from the British naval attaché in Buchanan to Foreign Office, 8 February 1916, PRO, Adm 137/1248, ff. 135–37.

34. See the convenient summary in Norman Stone, *The Eastern Front*, 171–72, 184 ff.

35. See, for example, the criticisms in Pavlovich, *The Fleet*, 145–47. German comments are in Rollman, *Krieg in der Ostee* 2:45, 48, 188–94.

36. Cited in Waldeyer-Hartz, *Hipper*, 176.

37. Hoffmann, *War Diaries* 1:77.

38. See the discussion in Rollman, *Krieg in der Ostsee* 2:280–85.

39. Pavlovich, *The Fleet*, 156. Similar charges are repeated for other occasions during the war.

40. Scheer, *Germany's High Sea Fleet*, 91.

41. Grenfell to Buchanan, 9 June 1915, and minutes by Oliver (COS), 29 June, Jackson (first sea lord), 1 July, and Balfour (first lord), 3 July, PRO, Adm 137/271, ff. 295–300; Laurence to S. S. Hall, 30 June 1915, ibid., ff. 378–80; Buchanan to Foreign Office, 17 August 1915, and minute by Oliver, 18 August 1915, ibid., ff. 353–54. See also Wilson, *Baltic Assignment*, 78–81.

42. Minutes by Oliver, 28 November, H. W. Wilson (?), 29 November, H. B. Jackson, 30 November, and Balfour, 26, 29 November 1915, PRO, Adm 137/1247, ff. 31–35.

43. Wilson, *Baltic Assignment*, 81–85; Corbett and Newbolt, *Naval Operations* 3:135–36; Rollman, *Krieg in der Ostsee* 2:311–12.

44. Wilson, *Baltic Assignment*, 89–96.

45. See remarks in *Conway's All the World's Fighting Ships, 1906–1921*, 316.

46. Capitaine de frégate Gallaud to Minister of Marine, 22 December 1914, 6 June 1915 (with endorsement by Paléologue, the French ambassador), SHM, Carton Ed-60.

47. Jonquières to Favereau, 30 June 1915, Favereau to Jonquières, 13 July 1915 (with covering letter and report from Chief of flotilla division, 7 July), ibid.

48. Jonquières, Rapport au Ministre, 20 July 1915, and Augagneur, Decision du Ministre, 26 July 1915, ibid.

49. Wilson, *Baltic Assignment*, 107–8; Pavlovich, *The Fleet*, 162–63.

50. Rollman, *Krieg in der Ostsee* 2:323–24, 329; Groos and Gladisch, *Krieg in der Nordsee* 4:339–45.

51. Rollman, *Krieg in der Ostsee* 2:325–26.

52. Ibid. 2:336.

53. Marder, *Dreadnought to Scapa Flow* 2:417–19; Schoultz, *With the British Battle Fleet*, 47–53, 64–69, 357–59.

54. Admiralty Memorandum (probably by Oliver), 26 February 1916, PRO, Adm 137/1247, ff. 192–98.

55. The story is well told in Wilson, *Baltic Assignment*, 148–57, 160.

56. Gagern, *Krieg in der Ostsee* 3:7–8, 54–55. On Prince Heinrich's intervention see: Ganz, "'Albion'—The Baltic Islands Operation," 92.

57. Gagern, *Krieg in der Ostsee* 3:29–30, 36.

58. Cromie to S. S. Hall, letters of 29 May, 17 June 1916, 10 October 1917, reproduced in Anonymous, *Letters on Russian Affairs from Captain F. N. A. Cromie* (n.p., 1919), 1–2, 9, 81.

59. Compare the tables in Greger, *Die Russische Flotte*, 26, 36–37, and Gagern, *Krieg in der Ostsee* 3:37, 46, 49–50.

60. The Russian and German accounts differ more widely than usual. See Pavlovich, *The Fleet*, 193–97; Gagern, *Krieg in der Ostsee* 3:31–33; Graf, *The Russian Navy*, 83–85.

61. Historical Section Summary, PRO, Adm 137/1248, f. 563. See also Talpomba to Minister of Marine, n.d. (c. 3 August 1916) and 17 September 1916, SHM, Carton Xk-1; Gagern, *Krieg in der Ostsee* 3:44.

62. Gagern, *Krieg in der Ostsee* 3:130–31.

63. Consett, *The Triumph of Unarmed Forces*, esp. 79–85, 97–98, 105. For an interesting survey, see also Franklin D. Scott, "Gustav V and Swedish attitudes towards Germany, 1915," *Journal of Modern History* 39, no. 2 (June 1967): 113–18. On the importance of Swedish sources to the German navy, see Weir, *Building the Kaiser's Navy*, 136, 159.

64. McKercher and Neilson, "'The Triumph of Unarmed Forces,'" 178–99. See also McKercher, *Esme Howard*, 162–71.

65. The Swedish prince was probably William, Duke of Södermanland (1884–1963), second son of King Gustav V. See Statements by the Masters of the *Thelma* (23 November 1915), *F. D. Lambert* (29 January 1916), and *Gitano* (5 February 1916). Howard to Grey, 7 February 1916, PRO, Adm 137/1125, ff. 390–92, 401–7, 417–18, 422–24; Shipping Intelligence Officer, Newcastle to Admiralty, 6 July 1916 (case of *Penmount*), Adm 137/1247, ff. 452–56; T. Holliday to Messrs. B. J. Sutherland & Co., Ltd. (case of *Dunrobin*), 11 June 1916, ibid., ff. 470–71. Norwegian torpedo boats gave similar protection in Norwegian waters.

66. Historical Section Summary, PRO, Adm 137/1248, f. 563; Fayle, *Seaborne Trade* 2:334–36, 3:152; Bell, *Blockade of Germany*, 531–32, 534, 608; Koblik, *Sweden: The Neutral Victor*, 65–66, 72; and an exhaustive study on Swedish-German relations:

Justus-Andreas Grohmann, *Die deutsch-Schwedische Auseinandersetzung um die Fahrstrassen des Öresunds im Ersten Weltkrieg* (Boppard am Rhein: H. Boldt, 1974).

67. Attaché Navale to Minister of Marine, Paris, 1 September 1916, SHM, Carton Ea-160; Cromie to Hall, 13/26 September 1916, *Letters on Russian Affairs*, 18–19. See also Monastarev, *Sur Trois Mers*, 85.

68. Gagern, *Krieg in der Ostsee* 3:92–98; Frantz Wietling, "Action des torpilleurs dans la Baltique," in Mantey, *Les Marins Allemands*, 77–84.

69. Two excellent modern studies are Saul, *Sailors in Revolt* and Mawdsley, *Russian Revolution*. For the perspective of émigré officers, see Graf, *The Russian Navy* and White, *Survival through War and Revolution*. For the Bolshevik viewpoint, see the memoir Raskolnikov, *Kronstadt and Petrograd*. The impressions of a British naval officer later murdered in the embassy at Petrograd are in Cromie, *Letters on Russian Affairs*.

70. Tschischwitz, *Conquest of the Baltic Islands*, 4–5, 22. For a good short account, see Ganz, "'Albion'—The Baltic Islands Operation," 93–97.

71. Scheer, *Germany's High Sea Fleet*, 295; Gagern, *Krieg in der Ostsee* 3:166–68.

72. Ludendorff, *My War Memories* 2:506; Hindenburg, *Out of My Life*, 281–82; Hoffmann, *War Diaries* 2:186–87.

73. Gagern, *Krieg in der Ostsee* 3:169; Görlitz, *The Kaiser and His Court*, 301; Hopman, *Das Kriegstagesbuch eines deutschen Seeoffiziers*, 240–42; Hopman to Tirpitz, 4 October 1917, cited in Holger Herwig, "The Dynamics of Necessity: German Military Policy during the First World War," in *Military Effectiveness*, vol. 1, *The First World War*, edited by Allan R. Millett and Williamson Murray (Boston: George, Allen & Unwin, 1988), 113, n. 96.

74. Tschischwitz, *Conquest of the Baltic Islands*, 34.

75. Ibid., 52, 55, 69; *Conway's All the World's Fighting Ships, 1906–1921*, 148–49; Hopman, *Kriegstagebuch*, 246.

76. Tschischwitz, *Conquest of the Baltic Islands*, 20–21, 147.

77. *Conway's All the World's Fighting Ships, 1860–1905*, 184; Breyer, *Battleships and Battle Cruisers*, 389 n. 2.

78. The operations of the British submarines are difficult to follow in the German and Russian accounts; see Wilson, *Baltic Assignment*, 191–98.

79. Buchanan to Foreign Office, 17, 18 October 1917, Minute by Oliver, 18 October 1917, Memorandum by Naval Staff (Operations Division), 20 October 1917, PRO, Adm 137/1249, ff. 399, 434–36, 438, 443–44.

80. Figures gathered from Tschischwitz, *Conquest of the Baltic Islands*, 239, 248–49; Pavlovich, *The Fleet*, 257.

81. Herwig, "Luxury Fleet," 236–37.

82. Tschischwitz, *Conquest of the Baltic Islands*, 188.

83. Ibid., iv.

84. Admiralty Memorandum for the War Cabinet, "Naval Situation in the Baltic," 22 November 1917, PRO, Adm 137/1249, ff. 421–30.

85. Memorandum for War Cabinet by First Lord of the Admiralty, 28 December 1917, ibid., ff. 492–96.

86. Herwig, "German Policy," 339–43; Gagern, *Krieg in der Ostsee* 3:354–61.

87. Herwig, "German Policy," 342–43; Graf, *The Russian Navy*, 175–76.

88. Lt. Downie to Commodore (S), 5 May 1918, PRO, Adm 137/1570, ff. 369–70; Wilson, *Baltic Assignment*, 209–11.

8. THE BLACK SEA

1. For a full discussion of Black Sea war plans, see Pavlovich, *The Fleet*, 272–76, 279–82; on the prewar naval balance, see Halpern, *Mediterranean Naval Situation*, 295–303, 307–10.

2. Pavlovich, *The Fleet*, 281–82.

3. On the failure to catch the *Goeben* in the minefield, see Pavlovich, *The Fleet*, 288–90; more details were given later in the war to the British officer attached to Russian Imperial Headquarters, Phillimore to Admiralty, 6 June 1916, PRO, Adm 137/1389, ff. 280–81.

4. Souchon to Kaiser Wilhelm, 3 November 1914, BA/MA, Nachlass Souchon N156/3.

5. Souchon to Chef des Admiralstabes, 29 November 1914, NARS, Microfilm Publication, T-1022, Records of the German Navy, 1850–1945, Roll 788, PG 75239.

6. Pavlovich, *The Fleet*, 291–92; Greger, *Die Russische Flotte*, 46.

7. Lorey, *Der Krieg in den türkischen Gewässern* 1:62–63, 66–67.

8. Russian and German versions of the encounter are in Pavlovich, *The Fleet*, 296–300; Lorey, *Krieg in den türkischen Gewässern* 1:64–66; Greger, *Die Russische Flotte*, 46.

9. Souchon to his wife, 18 November, 26 December 1914, cited in Halpern, *Naval War in the Mediterranean*, 54.

10. Souchon to his wife, 23 August 1914, cited in Halpern, *Naval War in the Mediterranean*, 49; Lorey, *Krieg in den türkischen Gewässern* 1:67–68.

11. Greger, *Die Russische Flotte*, 46–47; Lorey, *Krieg in den türkischen Gewässern* 1:70–73; Pavlovich, *The Fleet*, 301–5; Monasterev, *La Marina Russa*, 257–65. Pavlovich differs from the other accounts in a number of details, among them that *Oleg* was not sunk by *Breslau* but rather was scuttled along with the other blockships. Monasterev has *Oleg* damaged, but not sunk, by torpedo boats rather than the *Breslau*.

12. Mäkelä, *Auf den Spuren der Goeben*, 76; Breyer, *Battleships and Battle Cruisers*, 270. Repairs to the port side were completed by the end of March, and the *Goeben* could then make at least 20 knots and was used for Black Sea operations in April. Lorey, *Krieg in den türkischen Gewässern* 1:93, 100.

13. Lorey, *Krieg in den türkischen Gewässern* 1:72–73, 80–82.

14. Grand Duke Nicholas's memorandum is summarized in Buchanan to Grey, 25 January 1915, reproduced in Churchill, *The World Crisis* 2:155–56.

15. Pavlovich, *The Fleet*, 318; on Russian promises to the British, see Gilbert, *Churchill* 3:315, 344.

16. Lt. Comdr. G. W. Le Page (British observer with Black Sea Fleet) to Grenfell, 10 April 1915, PRO, Adm 137/754, ff. 52–53. See also Pavlovich, *The Fleet*, 318–19.

17. Pavlovich, *The Fleet*, 318–20; Monasterev, *La Marina Russa*, 269–70. On British promises to Russia over Constantinople, see Gilbert, *Churchill* 3:217, 320–21.

18. As usual, the German and Russian accounts differ widely. Lorey claims the bombardment was not directed at the Bosphorus fortifications and was insignificant from the military point of view, *Krieg in den türkischen Gewässern* 1:93. Pavlovich names the fortifications fired on and claims hits were scored; see *The Fleet*, 321–22.

19. Lorey, *Krieg in den türkischen Gewässern* 1:93–100; Pavlovich, *The Fleet*, 322–24.

20. Lorey, *Krieg in den türkischen Gewässern* 2:126–27.

21. Ibid. 1:129–33; Pavlovich, *The Fleet*, 327–29; Greger, *Die Russische Flotte*, 49.

22. Souchon to his wife, 10, 16 April 1915, cited in Halpern, *Naval War in the Mediterranean*, 114.

23. Pavlovich, *The Fleet*, 327.

24. Souchon to his wife, 15 May 1915, cited in Halpern, *Naval War in the Mediterranean*, 114.

25. Souchon to his wife, 16 May 1915, cited ibid., 115. On the coal problem, see Lorey, *Krieg in den türkischen Gewässern* 1:133–38.

26. Greger, *Die Russische Flotte*, 49–50; Monasterev, *La Marina Russa*, 279–81; Lorey, *Krieg in den türkischen Gewässern* 1:166–67.

27. Greger, *Die Russische Flotte*, 50, 165; Lorey, *Krieg in den türkischen Gewässern* 2:127–29; Pavlovich, *The Fleet*, 337–39. Pavlovich (and Monasterev) incorrectly claim the *Krab's* minefield was responsible for damaging the *Breslau*.

28. Lorey, *Krieg in den türkischen Gewässern* 2:174–76; Greger, *Die Russische Flotte*, 50.

29. Lorey, *Krieg in den türkischen Gewässern* 1:176–77, 193–95, 203–5.

30. Firle, Kriegstagebuch, 5 and 9 September 1915, cited in Halpern, *Naval War in the Mediterranean*, 163.

31. Le Page to Grenfell, 23 September, 7 November, 15 December 1915, with comments by DNI (W. R. Hall), 31 October, 17 December 1915, 18 January 1916, PRO, Adm 137/754; Phillimore to Admiralty, 3 November 1915, ibid., Adm 137/1389, ff. 46–47.

32. Pavlovich, *The Fleet*, 338, 341.

33. Greger, *Die Russische Flotte*, 51; Pavlovich, *The Fleet*, 343–45; Lorey, *Krieg in den türkischen Gewässern* 1:195–98.

34. Phillimore to Admiralty, 3 November 1915, PRO, Adm 137/1389, ff. 45–47; see also Phillimore Diary, 29 October 1915, IWM, Phillimore MSS, 75/48/2.

35. Greger, *Die Russische Flotte*, 53; Lorey, *Krieg in den türkischen Gewässern* 1:222.

36. Pavlovich, *The Fleet*, 393–94.

37. As usual the Russian and German accounts differ, Lorey identifying the *Imperatritsa Ekaterina* as the *Imperatritsa Maria*. See Pavlovich, *The Fleet*, 394–95; Lorey, *Krieg in den türkischen Gewässern* 1:212–16; Greger, *Die Russische Flotte*, 52–53; Monasterev, *La Marina Russa*, 289–90.

38. Le Page to Grenfell, 20 January 1916 and note by NID, 16 February 1916, PRO, Adm 137/754. See also Pavlovich, *The Fleet*, 341–42. On coal for Turkey, see Lorey, *Krieg in den türkischen Gewässern* 1:217–18.

39. Allen and Muratoff, *Caucasian Battlefields*, 550–52.

40. The Caucasus campaigns can be studied in detail in Allen and Muratoff, *Caucasian Battlefields* and Larcher, *La Guerre Turque*.

41. Minutes by NID (W. R. Hall), 10 February, 5 March 1916, PRO, Adm 137/754; technical details from *Conway's All the World's Fighting Ships, 1906–1921*, 322.

42. The various accounts of these operations have maddening discrepancies in detail. See Pavlovich, *The Fleet*, 355–66; Allen and Muratoff, *Caucasian Battlefields*, 369–72; Greger, *Die Russische Flotte*, 52–53; Monasterev, *La Marina Russa*, 297–304.

43. Lorey, *Krieg in den türkischen Gewässern* 1:216–25.

44. Pavlovich, *The Fleet*, 369. With the irritating inconsistency which bedevils Black Sea accounts, both Lorey and Greger report it was the *Imperatritsa Maria*.

45. Le Page to Grenfell, 9 April 1916, PRO, Adm 137/754, f. 304.

46. Ibid.

47. Standard accounts, all differing in detail, are Pavlovich, *The Fleet*, 366–73; Greger, *Die Russische Flotte*, 53–54; Allen and Muratoff, *Caucasian Battlefields*, 378–82; Lorey, *Krieg in den türkischen Gewässern* 1:225–30; Monasterev, *La Marina Russa*, 305–14.

48. Russian operations summarized from Pavlovich, *The Fleet*, 374–77; Greger, *Die Russische Flotte*, 54–55. German operations from Lorey, *Krieg in dem türkischen Gewässern* 1:232–33, 236–40.

49. The submarine also landed another five agents on the Georgian coast, sank a steamer off Suchumi, and on 8 July torpedoed and sank the small hospital ship *Vpered* (858 tons) off Hopa on the Lazistan coast.

50. Pavlovich is highly critical of the handling of the fleet, *The Fleet*, 424–28; Greger, *Die Russische Flotte*, 57. On German movements, see Lorey, *Krieg in den türkischen Gewässern* 1:260–62.

51. Phillimore to Admiralty, 1, 22 July 1916; PRO, Adm 137/1389; Le Page to Grenfell, 9 August 1916, Minutes by DID (W. R. Hall), 2 July, 8 September, 2 October 1916, ibid., Adm 137/754.

52. Le Page to Grenfell, 24 July 1916, PRO, Adm 137/754, f. 381; Pavlovich, *The Fleet*, 377.

53. Pavlovich, *The Fleet*, 421; Greger, *Die Russische Flotte*, 59.

54. Capitaine de vaisseau Dumesnil to Minister of Marine, 20 November 1916, SHM, Carton Ea-157.

55. Greger, *Die Russische Flotte*, 56; Lorey, *Krieg in den türkischen Gewässern* 1:263–67; Pavlovich, *The Fleet*, 428–30.

56. Pavlovich, *The Fleet*, 410.

57. Greger, *Die Russische Flotte*, 57–60, 65–69; Lorey, *Krieg in den türkischen Gewässern* 1:280–86, 290, 295–96, 298.

58. Halpern, *Naval War in the Mediterranean*, 247–48. The Russians acknowledge the loss to German submarines in 1916 of 6 transports, 2 hospital ships, a steamer, and 13 sail and auxiliary motor-sailing ships. Another 4 transports and 2 steamers were damaged., Pavlovich, *The Fleet*, 440.

59. See especially Westwood, "The End of the *Imperatritsa Mariia*."

60. Pavlovich, *The Fleet*, 430, 438. Details on the journey are in Phillimore to Admiralty, 7 July 1916, PRO, Adm 137/1389. See also: Snook, "British Naval Operations" 1:40–44, 4:343–44, 355.

61. Pavlovich, *The Fleet*, 481.

62. Pavlovich, *The Fleet*, 483–85; Greger, *Die Russische Flotte*, 61.

63. Le Page to Grenfell, 3 April 1917, PRO, Adm 137/940. Similar views were expressed by the British naval attaché in 1912. Cited in Halpern, *Mediterranean Naval Situation*, 301.

64. On conditions in the Black Sea Fleet, see especially the series of reports: Le Page to Grenfell, 29 April, 7, 11, 17, 23 May 1917, PRO, Adm 137/940.

65. For information on German minesweeping at the Bosphorus, see Lorey, *Krieg in den türkischen Gewässern* 1:303–4; Köppen, *Die Überwasserstreitkräfte und ihre Technik*, 268–69.

66. Greger, *Die Russische Flotte*, 61–62; Pavlovich, *The Fleet*, 458–60; Lorey, *Krieg in den türkischen Gewässern* 1:305. Once again, accounts differ in many details. Pavlovich reports the accident occurring on the first night, with a second explosion sinking the launch after her survivors had been transferred, and the Russians returning the next night to successfully lay mines.

67. A full account is in Le Page to Grenfell, 30 May 1917, PRO, Adm 137/940.

68. Le Page to Grenfell, 23 June 1917, PRO, Adm 137/940. On Kolchak, see also White, *Survival Through War*, 150–52.

69. Greger, *Die Russische Flotte*, 62; Lorey, *Krieg in den türkischen Gewässern* 1:305–11. Pavlovich, *The Fleet*, 460–64.

70. Landing operations discussed in Pavlovich, *The Fleet*, 481–86. See also Greger, *Die Russische Flotte*, 63.

71. Lorey, *Krieg in den türkischen Gewässern* 1:320–22; Greger, *Die Russische Flotte*, 64; Pavlovich, *The Fleet*, 469–70, 470 n. 1.

72. Lorey, *Krieg in den türkischen Gewässern* 2:328–29.

73. Halpern, *Naval War in the Mediterranean*, 421–25.

74. A summary of events is in Halpern, *Naval War in the Mediterranean*, 542–46.

75. Halpern, *Naval War in the Mediterranean*, 547–55. Details of the fate of the ships gleaned from *Conway's All the World's Fighting Ships, 1906–1921* and Greger, *Die Russische Flotte*.

9. THE DANUBE

1. Full details are in Pawlik, Christ, and Winkler, *Die k.u.k. Donauflottille*, and Greger, *Austro-Hungarian Warships*. For a short history of the flotilla, see Rauchensteiner, "Austro-Hungarian Warships," 153–73.
2. Wulff, *Donauflottille*, 13. Wulff served in the flotilla throughout the war.
3. A succinct and convenient discussion of the reasons for this failure may be found in Rothenberg, *Army of Francis Joseph*, chap. 12.
4. Details on Russian assistance to Serbia in Pavlovich, *The Fleet*, 305–8, 346–47. As usual when dealing with Russian sources, there are discrepancies. A British intelligence officer in May 1915 reported the Russian forces at Kladovo as two small river steamers (the *Tiraspol* and *Agrafena*) and a 60-foot diesel launch with torpedo tube and machine guns, and a double row of observation mines laid just above Kladovo. They numbered about fifty, including an officer and nine military engineers. He reported nothing about artillery batteries or booms. There were another twenty men at Prahovo, with the passenger steamer *Sveti Sergi* and a launch. See Report by Captain L. S. Amery, 24 May 1915, PRO, Adm 137/1141, f. 205.
5. Ibid., ff. 198–202. Rear Admiral Troubridge, the head of the British Mission to Serbia, was far less sanguine over the capabilities of the Serbian rail system than Amery.
6. Pavlovich, *The Fleet*, 305–8, 346–47. See also Fryer, *Royal Navy on the Danube*, 19.
7. Wulff, *Donauflottille*, 24; Pawlik, Christ, and Winkler, *Die k.u.k. Donauflottille*, 52, 122.
8. Cardale to Troubridge, 10 March 1915, PRO, Adm 137/1141, ff. 212–14; Fryer, *Royal Navy on the Danube*, 21–24; Wulff, *Donauflottille*, 45.
9. Wulff, *Donauflottille*, 49, 53–54; Fryer, *Royal Navy on the Danube*, 35–36, 39–40.
10. Fryer, *Royal Navy on the Danube*, 61; Fitch, *My Mis-Spent Youth*, 136–37.
11. A full discussion of Troubridge's appointment is in Fryer, *Royal Navy on the Danube*, 54–59.
12. Wulff, *Donauflottille*, 48–49.
13. There are differences over the exact sequence of events and cause of *Belgrade*'s loss. See Wulff, *Donauflottille*, 54–55; Fryer, *Royal Navy on the Danube*, 90; Fitch, *My Mis-Spent Youth*, 140–41.
14. Gilbert, *Churchill* 3:252–53.
15. Lord Hankey, *Supreme Command* 1:270–75; Gilbert, *Churchill* 3:272, 274–75.
16. Kemp, *Die Royal Navy*, 44, 83, 90. Details of the class are in *Conway's All the World's Fighting Ships, 1906–1921*, 99–100. On the service of the Insect-class in Mesopotamia, see chap. 4.
17. Gilbert, *Churchill* 3:302, 308, 318.
18. Admiral H. B. Jackson, "Notes on the Transport of Military Forces to Serbia," 25 March 1915, PRO, Adm 137/1141, ff. 151–55; J. F. Parry (hydrographer), *Report on the River Danube from Budapest to Braila*, 26 March 1915, ibid., ff. 160–63.

19. Admiralty to Troubridge, 3 April 1915, ibid., ff. 166–68.

20. Major Gossett (War Office) to Admiral Sir Douglas Gamble (with copies of the reports), 11 June 1915, ibid., ff. 180–97.

21. Troubridge to Admiralty, 14 May 1915, ibid., ff. 171–79.

22. Captain L. S. Amery, "Notes on a Visit to Galatz and Braila . . . ," 20 April 1915, ibid., ff. 181–84; Amery, "Notes on the Iron Gates and Cataract Section of the Danube," 21 May 1915, ibid., ff. 194–97; Amery, "Notes on the Prahovo Line &c," 24 May 1915, ibid., ff. 198–202.

23. Troubridge to Admiralty, 10 July 1915, PRO, Adm 137/1141, f. 299; Troubridge Diary, 8 July 1915, Imperial War Museum, London, Troubridge MSS.

24. See the full discussion in Fryer, *Royal Navy on the Danube*, chap. 8. Fryer's speculation the British monitors might not have been able to pass through the Iron Gates is unfounded; three did in 1919. See Kemp, *Die Royal Navy*, 92–93.

25. Troubridge Diary, 11 October 1915, Troubridge MSS.

26. Information on Serbian vessels is scanty, but by September they apparently had the armored motor boats *Dalmatia* (1–37-mm revolver cannon, 1-mitrailleuse); *Pobeda* (1–37-mm revolver cannon), the latter under command of a Russian lieutenant; and *Sveti George*; tug *Timok*; and motorboats *Galeb* and *Yadar*. A Russian boat, *Sloboda*, is also mentioned. Translation of report by Major Milan Nikolitch, Engineering Adviser on Staff of Defence of Belgrade to (Serbian) Headquarters, 20 September 1915, PRO, Adm 137/1141, ff. 362–64.

27. Cardale to Troubridge, 10 March 1915, Troubridge to Admiralty, 8, 26 April 1915, PRO, Adm 137/1141. See also Fitch, *My Mis-Spent Youth*, 138–40, 144–46.

28. The incident is discussed at length in Fryer, *Royal Navy on the Danube*, 100–102; see also Wulff, *Donauflottille*, 55–57; Pawlik, Christ, and Winkler, *Die k.u.k. Donauflottille*, 103–4; Csikos, "Der Schienmonitor der k.u.k. Donauflottille."

29. Troubridge to Admiralty, 10 July, 21 August 1915, and remarks by Admiral Gamble, 6 September, and Admiral H. B. Jackson, 7 September 1915, PRO, Adm 137/1141, ff. 299–301, 305, 313–15.

30. Details of the plan of campaign from General von Falkenhayn, *German General Staff*, 179–87.

31. Hermann Schmidtke, *Völkerringen um die Donau*, 50, 57–58. The author served with the German motorboats on the Danube. See also Wulff, *Donauflottille*, 71.

32. The action of the monitors is summarized in Wulff, *Donauflottille*, 63–71. On the action of the Allied naval missions, the best account is Fryer, *Royal Navy on the Danube*, chap. 13. Unfortunately, Fryer's very useful attempt to reconcile conflicting Allied and Austrian reports is hampered by his having relied on the earlier (1918) work of Wulff, written during the war, rather than the fuller and more balanced work of 1934.

33. Troubridge to Admiralty, 9 January 1916, PRO, Adm 137/1141, ff. 409–10.

34. The most complete accounts of the land operations are Glaise-Horstenau, *Österreich-Ungarns Letzter Krieg* 3:187–342; and Reichsarchiv, *Der Weltkrieg*, vol. 9, chap. 3.

35. Described in detail in Fryer, *Royal Navy on the Danube*, chaps. 14–15; see also Fitch, *My Mis-Spent Youth*, chap. 15.

36. Wulff, *Donauflottille*, 73–74, 77–78; Schmidtke, *Völkerringen um die Donau*, 51, 53–54; Pavlovich, *The Fleet*, 347–48.

37. Parry, *Report on the River Danube*, PRO, Adm 137/1141, ff. 161–62; DDSG (Donau-Dampfschiffahrts-Gesellschaft), *Von Wien zum Schwarzen Meer* (Vienna, n.d.), 104–5.

38. Fregattenkapitän Gabor von Döbrentei, "Die Donauhandelsflotte im Kriege," in Wulff, *Donauflottille*, 204–7. The Russians took the *Vaskapu* to southern Russia where the Austrians eventually recovered her in 1918.

39. On the planning around Romania's entry into the war, see Larcher, *La Grande Guerre*, 134–42.

40. For accounts by the Austrian and German commanders, see Arz, *Zur Geschichte des Grossen Krieges*, 102–20; Falkenhayn, *Der Feldzug der 9. Armee*.

41. Falkenhayn, *German General Staff*, 316–21; Falls, *The Great War*, 227–28; Stone, *The Eastern Front*, 264–65.

42. *Conway's All the World's Fighting Ships, 1906–1921*, 421–22; Alexandrescu, "Kämpfe der rumänischen Kriegsmarine."

43. The former commander of the Romanian Danube Flotilla gives his version of events in Negresco, *Comment on fit la Guerre sur le Danube*, 30–34.

44. Wulff, *Donauflottille*, 82–86; Alexandrescu, "Kämpfe der rumänischen Kriegsmarine," 395, 397.

45. The most detailed accounts are in Reichskriegsministeriums, *Der Weltkrieg*, vol. 11, chap. 4; and Glaise-Horstenau, *Österreich-Ungarns Letzter Krieg* 5:223–358, 449–628; a standard monograph is Kabisch, *Der Rumänienkrieg*.

46. A short account of Russian participation in the Romanian campaign is in Stone, *The Eastern Front*, chap. 12.

47. Phillimore to Admiralty, 30 October, 7 November 1916, PRO, Adm 137/1389, ff. 463–64, 473–74. Phillimore naturally reflects the Russian point of view. Romanian activities are explained in exhaustive detail in Negresco, *Comment on fit la Guerre sur le Danube*, chaps. 3–7.

48. The Austrian mining detachment used light boats to launch mines in the Danube current to drift down to the Romanian lines, and on 20 October claimed to have sunk a patrol boat. This was probably the river torpedo boat *Maracineanu*, which the Romanians acknowledge as having been mined and sunk with all hands. Wulff, *Donauflottille*, 96–97; Alexandrescu, "Kämpfe der rumänischen Kriegsmarine," 399.

49. Phillimore to Admiralty, 30 October, 7 November 1916, PRO, Adm 137/1389, ff. 463–64, 476.

50. Ingénieur principal du Génie Maritime Mercier and Lieutenant de Vaisseau de Breda, "Rapport complémentaire au sujet d'une mission à l'armée du Danube," 29 September–4 October 1916, SHM, Carton Ed-115.

51. Regele, *Kampf um die Donau 1916*, 76–80. Regele used Romanian literature published in the interwar period.

52. Wulff, *Donauflottille*, 88–92; Regele, *Kampf um die Donau 1916*, 81–82; Glaise-Horstenau, *Österreich Ungarns Letzter Krieg*, vol. 5, pt. 2, pp. 328–33; there is more emphasis on the importance of German air attacks in Reichskriegsministerium, *Der Weltkrieg* 11:208–12.

53. A very detailed study of the operation is in Regele, *Kampf um die Donau, 1916*, chap. 4. Mackensen's reactions are in Wolfgang Foerster, *Mackensen: Briefe und Aufzeichnungen* (Leipzig: Bibliographisches Institut, 1938), 290–92.

54. Wulff, *Donauflottille*, 93–95. A Romanian source describes a Romanian garrison of 238 sailors, infantry, and artillery defending Cinghinarele against about 5,000 attackers. Averescu, "Kämpfe der rumänischen Kriegsmarine," 398.

55. Capitaine de frégate de Belloy to Minister of Marine, 18 October, 2 November 1916, Capitaine de vaisseau Zarine and de Belloy, "Considerations sur la position stratégique du Danube Octobre 1916," n.d. (c. 17 October 1916), "Note sur la Mission Navale Française (Groupe des secteurs fluviaux)," n.d. (2 November 1916), SHM, Carton Ed-115. The memorandum is also reproduced in Negresco, *Comment on fit la Guerre sur le Danube*, annex I, 365–72.

56. Wulff, *Donauflottille*, 100–103; Schmidtke, *Völkerringen um die Donau*, 82–90. An exhaustive study is in Regele, *Kampf um die Donau*, chap. 5.

57. Schmidtke, *Völkerringen um die Donau*, 68, 90, 110–13. They were later commanded by the famous Kapitänleutnant von Mücke, who had escaped with part of the *Emden*'s crew in the schooner *Ayesha*. See above, chapter 4.

58. Capitaine de vaisseau de Belloy to Minister of Marine, 22 March 1917, Lieutenant de vaisseau de Breda, "Travaux de la Mission Navale Française sur le Danube (Mois de Mai-Juin-Juillet 1917)," 3 August 1917, SHM, Carton Ed-115.

59. An interesting and detailed report was furnished to the Admiralty by the British liaison officer with the Russian Black Sea Fleet Engineer Commander Le Page to Rear Admiral Stanley, 13 November 1917, PRO, Adm 137/940 (pt. 1). Russian operations are summarized in Pavlovich, *The Fleet*, 470–73.

60. Berthelot's journal has recently been published. See Glenn E. Torrey, *General Henri Berthelot and Romania: Mémoires et Correspondance, 1916–1919* (Boulder, Colo.: East European Monographs, 1987).

61. Pawlik, Christ, and Winkler, *Die k.u.k. Donauflottille*, 105–6.

62. Pawlik, Christ, and Winkler, *Die k.u.k. Donauflottille*, 107–10; Wulff, *Donauflottille*, 153–69.

63. Louis Cordier, *Victoire éclair en Orient* (3d ed., Aurillac: U.S.H.A., 1969), 244, 245 n. 3; Ducasse, *Balkans 14–18*, 230–35.

64. Wulff, *Donauflottille*, 168–88, 226–32; Schmidtke, *Völkerringen um die Donau*, 152–57.

10. From Dreadnoughts to Submarines: 1915–1916

1. Groos and Gladisch, *Krieg in der Nordsee* 4:41–42.
2. Scheer, *Germany's High Sea Fleet*, 87–88.
3. See chapter 2. The dreadnought *Vanguard* was also destroyed by an internal explosion at Scapa Flow in November 1917.
4. Pohl to Bachmann, 7 April 1915, cited in Groos, *Krieg in der Nordsee* 4:58–59. Translation by NID in Naval Historical Library, London.
5. Trotha to Tirpitz, 31 March 1915, ibid., 45–46.
6. Lans to Tirpitz (and enclosure), 13 September 1914, reproduced in Tirpitz, *Deutsche Ohnemachtspolitik*, 85–89; see also Gemzell, *Organization, Conflict and Innovation*, 146–47.
7. Wegener, "Reflections on Our Maritime Situation," 1 February 1915, reproduced in Wegener, *Naval Strategy*, 133–44. On Wegener, see Herwig's introduction, ibid., xv–xxx. For Tirpitz's reaction and the original memorandum, see Tirpitz, *Deutsche Ohnemachtspolitik*, 208–13.
8. Wegener, "Can We Improve Our Situation?" 12 July 1915, *Naval Strategy*, 184.
9. Ibid., 195–97.
10. Ibid., 162–63. On German war aims and the United States, see especially Herwig, *Politics of Frustration*, 133–38.
11. See Herwig's introduction to Wegener, *Naval Strategy*, xxx ff.
12. Herwig, "*Luxury Fleet*," 161.
13. Tirpitz to von Pohl, 16 September 1914, cited in Groos, *Krieg in der Nordsee* 2:89–90.
14. Memorandum by Tirpitz, 26 January 1915, reproduced in Groos, *Krieg in der Nordsee* 3:248–49.
15. Tirpitz to Trotha, 10 March 1915, quoted in Groos, *Krieg in der Nordsee* 4:42. Translation by NID.
16. Herwig, "*Luxury Fleet*," 158–61.
17. See Groos and Gladisch, *Krieg in der Nordsee*, vols. 1–5; Tirpitz, *Deutsche Ohnemachtspolitik*; and von Pohl, *Aus Aufzeichnungen und Briefen*. For the Müller diaries see Görlitz, *The Kaiser and His Court*, and on the "Tirpitz-line" in the official history, see Bird, *German Naval History*, 27–30.
18. Spindler, "Submarine in Naval Warfare," 837.
19. Gemzell, *Organization, Conflict and Innovation*, 440 n. 6; Captain A. Gayer, "German Submarine Operations," 622.
20. Michelsen, *La Guerre sous-marine*, 15; Gayer, "German Submarine Operations," 625.
21. Gemzell, *Organization, Conflict and Innovation*, 142; Stegemann, *Die Deutsche Marinepolitik*, 22–23.

22. For full details and exhaustive discussion, see the volume produced by the Historical Section of the Committee of Imperial Defence: Bell, *Blockade of Germany*. Shorter works are Guichard, *Histoire du Blocus Naval;* Parmelee, *Blockade and Sea Power;* and Siney, *Allied Blockade of Germany*. The German outlook is in Vincent, *Politics of Hunger*, esp. chap. 2.

23. Fayle, *Seaborne Trade* 1:285.

24. Gibson and Prendergast, *German Submarine War*, 15.

25. Hurd, *The Merchant Navy* 1:270–71.

26. Gemzell, *Organization, Conflict and Innovation*, 142–44; Stegemann, *Die Deutsche Marinepolitik*, 23–26; Herwig, "Luxury Fleet," 163–64; Scheer, *Germany's High Sea Fleet*, 222–24; Müller, *The Kaiser and His Court*, 62–63.

27. Text in Scheer, *Germany's High Sea Fleet*, 225–27.

28. From the monthly analysis of U-boat gains, losses, and total strength given in Tarrant, *U-Boat Offensive*, 15–18; Gayer, "German Submarine Operations," 626. Not surprisingly, different authorities cite different figures, but the general import is the same: the number of submarines available was small.

29. Rössler, *The U-Boat*, 38–40, 44–47, 50.

30. Tarrant, *U-Boat Offensive*, 163; Grant, *U-Boat Intelligence*, 182.

31. Rössler, *The U-Boat*, 47–49.

32. Tirpitz, *My Memoirs* 2:139–47. See also Michelsen, *La Guerre sous-marine*, 24–25; Lundeberg, "German Naval Critique," 107–9.

33. May, *World War and American Isolation*, 123–28; Scheer, *Germany's High Sea Fleet*, 229–31; Tarrant, *U-Boat Offensive*, 14.

34. Fryatt merits an entire chapter in Hurd, *The Merchant Navy*, vol. 2, chap. 15, 307–36.

35. Hezlet, *The Submarine and Sea Power*, 30–31, 44–48; Tarrant, *U-Boat Offensive*, 17–19; on the unsuccessful Folkestone–Cape Gris-Nez barrage, see Bacon, *The Dover Patrol* 2:391–93.

36. Groos, *Krieg in der Nordsee* 2:290–92; 4:24–28; Michelsen, *La Guerre sous-marine*, 66.

37. Groos, *Krieg in der Nordsee* 4:121–22; Tarrant, *U-Boat Offensive*, 16, 19–20; Gayer, "German Submarine Operations," 627–28.

38. Corbett and Newbolt, *Naval Operations* 2:274, 385–86; Fayle, *Seaborne Trade* 2:12, 27, 30; Scheer, *Germany's High Sea Fleet*, 231–32.

39. Hurd, *The Merchant Navy* 2:308–12; May, *World War and American Isolation*, 146–47; Fayle, *Seaborne Trade* 2:93.

40. Gayer, "German Submarine Operations," 631–32; Michelsen, *La Guerre sous-marine*, 29.

41. This is substantially the conclusion of the most balanced of the recent surveys, Bailey and Ryan, *The Lusitania Disaster*, esp. 331.

42. May, *World War and American Isolation*, 148–59, 205–10; the diplomatic negotiations are recounted in detail by Bell, *Blockade of the Central Powers*, 423 ff. On the conflict within the German government, see Ritter, *The Sword and*

the Scepter 3:128–50; Görlitz, *The Kaiser and His Court*, 77 ff.; and summaries in Tarrant, *U-Boat Offensive*, 20–22; and Herwig, "Luxury Fleet," 164–65.

43. Figures culled from Spindler, *Handelskrieg mit U-Booten* 5:362–63; and Tarrant, *U-Boat Offensive*, 21, 163. On further U-boat construction, see Rössler, *The U-Boat*, 49–50, 53.

44. Ritchie, *Q-Ships*, 25, 39–41, 167–68; Grant, *U-Boats Destroyed*, 25–27. Much useful and fascinating information on Q-ships can be obtained from the old classics: Chatterton, *Q-Ships and Their Story* and Campbell, *My Mystery Ships*.

45. Ritchie, *Q-Ships*, 58–66.

46. Ibid., 55.

47. Görlitz, *The Kaiser and His Court*, 104–5; the memorandum is reproduced in Tirpitz, *Deutschlands Ohnemachtspolitik*, 419–20.

48. May, *World War and American Isolation*, 218–27; Ritter, *The Sword and the Scepter* 3:147–50; Bell, *Blockade of Germany*, 441–46. There are numerous documents relating to the *Arabic* affair in Tirpitz, *Deutschlands Ohnemachtspolitik*, 382 ff.

49. Gayer, "German Submarine Operations," 634.

50. Görlitz, *The Kaiser and His Court*, 121–22.

51. Herwig, "Luxury Fleet," 158–59. The terminology was widespread enough to reach the chief of the Mittelmeerdivision in distant Constantinople. Souchon to his wife, 3 October 1916, Nachlass Souchon, N156/18.

52. Hezlet, *The Submarine and Sea Power*, 48; Fayle, *Seaborne Trade* 2:26, 37–38.

53. Hezlet, *The Submarine and Sea Power*, 53–54; Fayle, *Seaborne Trade* 2:127–29, 167–69; Spindler, *Handelskrieg mit U-Booten* 5:362–63.

54. Stegemann, *Die Deutsche Marinepolitik*, 32; Hezlet, *The Submarine and Sea Power*, 54.

55. Gayer, "German Submarine Operations," 635.

56. Tarrant, *U-Boat Offensive*, 25–26; Scheer, *Germany's High Sea Fleet*, 234–37; Michelsen, *La Guerre sous-marine*, 37–40; Bell, *Blockade of Germany*, 585–90; German policy is followed in detail in May, *World War and American Isolation*, chap. 11; on Kophamel, see also Halpern, *Naval War in the Mediterranean*, 201–2.

57. Halpern, *Naval War in the Mediterranean*, 202–3; Görlitz, *The Kaiser and His Court*, 133–44; May, *World War and American Isolation*, 236, 246–49.

58. Operational totals cited by Tarrant, *U-Boat Offensive*, 26–27; details on U-boat orders and Admiralstab memorandum from Rössler, *The U-Boat*, 53–59, 63–65.

59. May, *World War and American Isolation*, 249–52; Tarrant, *U-Boat Offensive*, 29–30; Ambrose Greenway, *A Century of North Sea Passenger Steamers* (London: Ian Allan, 1986), 97–98, 102, 105; Ritter, *The Sword and the Scepter* 3:172–77; Scheer, *Germany's High Sea Fleet*, 242.

60. Spindler, *Handelskrieg mit U-Booten* 5:362–63. These figures include the Baltic and Black Sea, but the sinkings in these areas were few and have little effect on the total. British figures from Fayle, *Seaborne Trade* 2:268–69, 3:465.

61. Fayle, *Seaborne Trade* 2:269, 271.

62. Losses from Grant, *U-Boat Intelligence*, 183; Ritchie, *Q-Ships*, 81.

63. Lundeberg, "German Naval Critique," 110–12; Gayer, "German Submarine Operations," 640–41; Tarrant, *U-Boat Offensive*, 30.

64. Schmalenbach, *German Raiders*, 46–49, 71, 132, 137; Corbett and Newbolt, *Naval Operations* 3:266–72; Fayle, *Seaborne Trade* 2:253–57. Full details of each voyage in Raeder and Mantey, *Der Kreuzerkrieg*, vol. 3. Details on the *Greif*'s interception in Hezlet, *Electronics and Sea Power*, 111.

65. Scheer, *Germany's High Sea Fleet*, 242–43.

66. Groos, *Krieg in der Nordsee* 5:27–32; Scheer, *Germany's High Sea Fleet*, 96–103.

67. Corbett and Newbolt, *Naval Operations* 3:275–76; Scheer, *Germany's High Sea Fleet*, 107.

68. Scheer, *Germany's High Sea Fleet*, 113–17; Hezlet, *Electronics and Sea Power*, 110–11; Corbett and Newbolt, *Naval Operations* 3:288–89.

69. Jellicoe to Balfour, 25 January 1916, Patterson, *The Jellicoe Papers* 1:203; Hezlet, *Aircraft and Sea Power*, 49. Details on *Vindex* in Layman, *Before the Aircraft Carrier*, 50–51.

70. Hezlet, *Aircraft and Sea Power*, 50; Corbett and Newbolt, *Naval Operations* 3:273–74, 290–96; Scheer, *Germany's High Sea Fleet*, 118–19.

71. Jellicoe to Jackson, 12 April 1916, in Patterson, *The Jellicoe Papers* 1:232–34; Jellicoe to Beatty, 11 April 1916, reproduced in Ranft, *The Beatty Papers* 1:301–2.

72. Beatty to Jellicoe, 14 April 1916, in Ranft, *The Beatty Papers* 1:302–4. A shorter version is also printed in Patterson, *The Jellicoe Papers* 1:235–37.

73. Corbett and Newbolt, *Naval Operations* 3:301–9, 316–17; Scheer, *Germany's High Sea Fleet*, 124–29; Patterson, *Tyrwhitt*, 156–59.

74. Jellicoe, *The Grand Fleet*, 47–48, 78–79; Marder, *Dreadnought to Scapa Flow* 2:432–35.

75. Hezlet, *Aircraft and Sea Power*, 51–52; Corbett and Newbolt, *Naval Operations* 3:309–11; Marder, *Dreadnought to Scapa Flow* 2:427–28.

76. Rival plans discussed in Marder, *Dreadnought to Scapa Flow* 2:443–45; Scheer, *Germany's High Sea Fleet*, 134–35; Corbett and Newbolt, *Naval Operations* 3:320–23.

77. On the misinterpreted signal, see especially Beesly, *Room 40*, 152–56; Roskill, *Beatty*, 152–54; and Marder, *Dreadnought to Scapa Flow* 3:46–48. All subsequent references to volume 3 are from the second revised edition.

78. Marder, *Dreadnought to Scapa Flow* 3:50–51.

79. Roskill, *Beatty*, 154–55.

80. Campbell, *Jutland*, 39; Roskill, *Beatty*, 157–58. In general my account of the battle is based on Campbell, Roskill, and Marder, *Dreadnought to Scapa Flow*, vol. 3. The role of aircraft is from Hezlet, *Aircraft and Sea Power*, 56–57.

81. Detailed discussion in Campbell, *Jutland*, 64–67.

82. Ibid., 106.

83. Cited by Marder, *Dreadnought to Scapa Flow* 3:88 and n. 69.

84. There is a very full discussion of the pros and cons in Marder, *Dreadnought to Scapa Flow* 3:100–108.

85. Campbell, *Jutland*, 155.

86. The debate is well summarized and, indeed, continued in Marder, *Dreadnought to Scapa Flow* 3:120–26; and Roskill, *Beatty*, 172–73.

87. Scheer, *Germany's High Sea Fleet*, 155; Groos, *Krieg in der Nordsee* 5:310–12; see also Marder, *Dreadnought to Scapa Flow* 3:126–29.

88. Weizsäcker, *Memoirs*, 33.

89. Philbin, *Hipper*, 130.

90. For extensive detail, see Marder, *Dreadnought to Scapa Flow* 3:132–40.

91. Roskill, *Beatty*, 178–79; Campbell, *Jutland*, 256.

92. Jellicoe to Jackson, 5 June 1916, Patterson, *The Jellicoe Papers* 1:271.

93. Hezlet, *Electronics and Sea Power*, 121–22.

94. Roskill, *Beatty*, 182. See also Marder, *Dreadnought to Scapa Flow* 3:185–86.

95. Roskill, *Beatty*, 186.

96. Beesly, *Room 40*, 159–62.

97. Casualty figures from Campbell, *Jutland*, 338–41.

98. Görlitz, *The Kaiser and His Court*, 170–71; Herwig, "Luxury Fleet," 187–88. For the views of the German official history, see Groos, *Krieg in der Nordsee* 5:6, 444–45, 450, 452–54.

99. On the Jutland controversy, see Roskill, *Beatty*, chap. 15; on battleship names, Marder, *Dreadnought to Scapa Flow* 3:248.

100. Jellicoe to Beatty, 13 June 1916, Ranft, *The Beatty Papers* 1:338.

101. Campbell, *Jutland*, 337. For abundant material on the commander's dispatches, reactions, and measures taken after the battle, see Ranft, *The Beatty Papers*, vol. 1, pt. 5; and Patterson, *The Jellicoe Papers* 1:285–308, 2:20–31, 47–61, 95–98. Part 4 of vol. 2 is devoted to the postwar Jutland controversy, and the controversial "Harper Report" on the battle is printed as an appendix.

102. Marder, *Dreadnought to Scapa Flow* 3:127–28, nn. 47–50.

103. Campbell, *Jutland*, 369 ff.; see also Campbell's perceptive comparison of British and German battle cruiser design in his *Battle Cruisers*.

104. Campbell, *Jutland*, 385–87; for the shell problem, see Lord Chatfield, *The Navy and Defence*, chap. 16; on the post-Jutland revolution, see Roskill, *Beatty*, chap. 9, and Marder, *Dreadnought to Scapa Flow*, vol. 3, chap. 7.

105. A. P. P. [Comdr. Anthony Pellew], "'Something Wrong with Our Bloody Ships,'" *Naval Review* 64, no. 1 (January 1976): 17–21.

106. On these points, see especially Sumida, *Defence of Naval Supremacy*, 299–305.

107. Scheer, *Germany's High Sea Fleet*, 168–69.

108. Görlitz, *The Kaiser and His Court*, 171–72; Herwig, "Luxury Fleet," 189–90.

109. Marder, *Dreadnought to Scapa Flow* 3:237 n. 10.

110. The account when not otherwise noted is essentially based on Scheer, *Germany's High Sea Fleet*, 179–86; and Marder, *Dreadnought to Scapa Flow* 3:289–96.

111. Gladisch, *Krieg in der Nordsee* 6:30. On British intelligence, see Beesly, *Room 40*, 165–66.

112. Robinson, *The Zeppelin in Combat*, 161–62.

113. Quoted in Patterson, *Tyrwhitt*, 171–72. Tyrwhitt's navigation officer reported that when the moon rose on their way back, it was indeed as bright as day. Quoted in Marder, *Dreadnought to Scapa Flow* 3:296.

114. Naval Staff, *Home Waters—Part VII*, 124.

115. Jellicoe to Admiralty, 24 August 1916, and Admiralty to Jellicoe, 9 September 1916, Patterson, *The Jellicoe Papers* 2:61–65.

116. Beatty to Jellicoe, 6 September 1916, and Jellicoe to Admiralty, 14 September 1916, Remarks by Oliver, n.d., Admiralty to Jellicoe, 25 September 1916, in Patterson, *The Jellicoe Papers* 2:71–76; Naval Staff, *Home Waters—Part VII*, 129–31.

117. Spindler, *Handelskrieg mit U-Booten* 3:222–25.

118. Scheer, *Germany's High Sea Fleet*, 186–87, 190.

119. Hezlet, *The Submarine and Sea Power*, 73. On the German "E-Dienst" (*Entzifferungsdienst*), or decrypting service, at Neumünster, see Beesly, *Room 40*, 32–33, 167.

120. Gladisch, *Krieg in der Nordsee* 6:147–48.

121. Naval Staff, *Home Waters—Part VII*, 196–98; Corbett and Newbolt, *Naval Operations* 4:67–68; Scheer, *Germany's High Sea Fleet*, 191–94; Hezlet, *Electronics and Sea Power*, 137.

11. THE SUBMARINE CRISIS: 1917

1. Hezlet, *The Submarine and Sea Power*, 63–64. Submarine sinkings from Spindler, *Handelskrieg mit U-Booten* 5:362–63.

2. Hurd, *The Merchant Navy* 2:350–51, 357–58; Gibson and Prendergast, *German Submarine War*, 116, 133; Corbett and Newbolt, *Naval Operations* 4:251–52.

3. For a full account see Messimer, *The Merchant U-Boat*.

4. Admiral Scheer, *Germany's High Sea Fleet*, 264–67. The British official history makes much of the American reaction; an American diplomatic historian rather downplays it. See Corbett and Newbolt, *Naval Operations* 4:249–50; and May, *World War and American Isolation*, 337–38.

5. Hezlet, *The Submarine and Sea Power*, 63, 65–66. Trotha's remark cited by Scheer, *Germany's High Sea Fleet*, 245.

6. The German viewpoint is given in Spindler, *Handelskrieg mit U-Booten* 3:361–71; and Reichskriegsministeriums, *Der Weltkrieg*, vol. 11, chap. 11 (pt. A). An extremely detailed diplomatic account is in Birnbaum, *Peace Moves and U-Boat Warfare*.

7. Herwig, "Luxury Fleet," 194–97. The English-speaking reader can follow the crisis within the German government in detail in Ritter, *The Sword and the Scepter*, vol. 3, chap. 8.

8. Scheer, *Germany's High Sea Fleet*, 248–52. An apparently earlier (January 1915) paper by Professor Levy is reproduced in Spindler, *Handelskrieg mit U-Booten* 1:225–26.

9. Müller's firsthand account is in Görlitz, *The Kaiser and His Court*, 228–31. For a succinct summary, see also Tarrant, *U-Boat Offensive*, 44–47.

10. Spindler, *Handelskrieg mit U-Booten* 4:2–3.

11. Rössler, *The U-Boat*, 75–76; see also Gayer, "German Submarine Operations," 653.

12. Quoted in Rössler, *The U-Boat*, 78.

13. Ibid.

14. Details from *Conway's All the World's Fighting Ships, 1906–1921*, 149–50, 155–56.

15. Naval Staff, *Home Waters—Part VIII*, 174–75; Gibson and Prendergast, *German Submarine War*, 137–38 (and chart).

16. Halpern, *Naval War in the Mediterranean*, 307–8.

17. The sequence of events may be followed in May, *World War and American Isolation*, chap. 19. On the Zimmermann telegram, see Beesly, *Room 40*, chap. 13.

18. Major-General Lord Edward Gleichen, ed., *Chronology of the Great War* (3 vols., London: 1918–20; reprinted [3 vols. in 1], London: Greenhill, 1988), 179, 185, 195. The United States did not declare war against Austria-Hungary until 7 December 1917.

19. Spindler, *Handelskrieg mit U-Booten* 5:364–65.

20. Hezlet, *The Submarine and Sea Power*, 88–89; Grant, *U-Boat Intelligence*, 184–85; Fayle, *Seaborne Trade* 3:92–93.

21. Corbett and Newbolt, *Naval Operations* 4:385.

22. Fayle, *Seaborne Trade* 3:42–45.

23. Waters, "Notes," par. 17., Copy in Naval Historical Branch, Ministry of Defence, London.

24. Naval Staff, *Home Waters—Part VIII*, 24–25.

25. Technical History Section, *TH 30. Control of Mercantile Movements*, 6.

26. Jellicoe, *The Submarine Peril*, 2–10. Jellicoe's memorandum on the submarine menace (29 October 1916) is reproduced in Patterson, *The Jellicoe Papers* 2:88–92.

27. Ritchie, *Q-Ships*, 115–18, 125–28.

28. P-boats were 613-ton, 244-foot patrol boats equipped with twin screws and capable of 20 knots. They were handy craft with a low silhouette, fitted with a ram bow of hardened steel. Their armament included a 4-inch and 2-pounder gun and two torpedo tubes, later replaced by depth charges. The 44 P-boats served at Dover, the Nore, and Portsmouth. Details from Dittmar and Colledge, *British Warships*, 98.

29. For a very detailed account see Hackmann, *Seek & Strike*, chaps. 2–4.

30. Naval Staff, *Home Waters—Part VIII*, 107.

31. Naval Staff, *Home Waters—Part VIII*, 107–9; Beatty to Admiralty, 31 January 1917, Ranft, *The Beatty Papers* 1:394–97; Marder, *Dreadnought to Scapa Flow* 4:87 and n. 28.

32. Jellicoe to Beatty, 4 February 1917, Patterson, *The Jellicoe Papers* 2:142–43.

33. Marder, *Dreadnought to Scapa Flow* 4:87–88; Naval Staff, *Home Waters—Part VIII,* 87–88, 390.

34. Naval Staff, *Home Waters—Part VIII,* 389–90; Naval Staff, *Home Waters—Part IX,* 131; Grant, *U-Boats Destroyed,* 49–54; Grant, *U-Boat Intelligence,* 72–79; Beesly, *Room 40,* 267–68.

35. Grant, *U-Boats Destroyed,* 74; Spindler, *Handelskrieg mit U-Booten* 4:504–6.

36. Scheer, *Germany's High Sea Fleet,* 187–89; Gladisch, *Krieg in der Nordsee* 6:147–48, 219–20.

37. Corbett and Newbolt, *Naval Operations* 4:55–63. The missing bow of the *Nubian* was later replaced by that of another Tribal-class destroyer, the *Zulu,* which had lost her stern to a mine, the combined ship named *Zubian.*

38. Quoted in Corbett and Newbolt, *Naval Operations* 4:64.

39. Marder, *Dreadnought to Scapa Flow* 3:308–11; Naval Staff, *Home Waters—Part VII,* 189–90; Corbett and Newbolt, *Naval Operations* 4:66–67.

40. Scheer, *Germany's High Sea Fleet,* 189; Corbett and Newbolt, *Naval Operations* 4:69–70; Marder, *Dreadnought to Scapa Flow* 4:311–12.

41. Corbett and Newbolt, *Naval Operations* 4:73–79; Patterson, *Tyrwhitt,* 176–80; Beesly, *Room 40,* 275.

42. Corbett and Newbolt, *Naval Operations* 4:352–55; Beesly, *Room 40,* 275; Naval Staff, *Home Waters—Part VIII,* 190–92.

43. Corbett and Newbolt, *Naval Operations* 4:361–68.

44. Gladisch, *Krieg in der Nordsee* 6:239–40, 291–93.

45. Naval Staff, *Home Waters—Part VIII,* 394–95; Corbett and Newbolt, *Naval Operations* 4:372–78; Marder, *Dreadnought to Scapa Flow* 4:107–8; Reginald Pound, *Evans of the Broke* (London: Oxford University Press, 1963). The Germans attempted to continue the attacks on Dunkirk and on the night of 24–25 April sank the small French destroyer *Etendard* but were frustrated in their next raid on the night of 20 May by four French destroyers off Nieuport. They then ceased raids on Dunkirk for the next few months. See Thomazi, *Guerre navale dans le Nord,* 177–79.

46. Marder, *Dreadnought to Scapa Flow* 4:73–74; Grant, *U-Boats Destroyed,* 44–49. Of the six U-boats sunk, two were rammed by patrol destroyers, two torpedoed by patrol submarines, one stranded, and only one was mined: ibid., 58

47. For an exhaustive account, see Bacon, *The Dover Patrol;* a short account is in Corbett and Newbolt, *Naval Operations* 5:36–41, 45–48, 118–19; and Jellicoe, *The Submarine Peril,* 83–87.

48. Memorandum by Jellicoe for the War Cabinet on a project for attacking Ostend and Zeebrugge, June 1917, Patterson *The Jellicoe Papers* 2:171–72; Jellicoe to Beatty, 30 June 1917, ibid., 173.

49. Marder, *Dreadnought to Scapa Flow* 2:203–5; Patterson, *Jellicoe,* 185–86.

50. Gladisch, *Krieg in der Nordsee* 6:336.

51. On this point, see Roskill, "The U-Boat Campaign."

52. See the excellent survey in Winton, *Convoy,* 12–16, chap. 2.

53. Patterson, *Tyrwhitt*, 168.

54. Corbett and Newbolt, *Naval Operations* 5:29–32; Naval Staff, *Home Waters—Part VII*, 63–64; Marder, *Dreadnought to Scapa Flow* 4:138.

55. Fayle, *Seaborne Trade* 3:473.

56. Naval Staff, *Home Waters—Part VII*, 243–44; Naval Staff, *Home Waters—Part VIII*, 30–33; Corbett and Newbolt, *Naval Operations* 5:27–29; Fayle, *Seaborne Trade* 3:99, 149, 473.

57. Naval Staff, *Home Waters—Part VIII*, 69–73, 180–82.

58. Naval Staff, *Home Waters—Part VIII*, 359–66; see also Roskill, *Beatty*, 219–20.

59. Naval Staff, *Home Waters—Part VIII*, 370–76; see also Corbett and Newbolt, *Naval Operations* 4:382–83, 5:15–17.

60. Naval Staff, *Home Waters—Part VIII*, 184–85.

61. Naval Staff, *Home Waters—Part VIII*, 184–85; Waters, "Notes," par. 14–15. See also Marder, *Dreadnought to Scapa Flow* 4:119–22; and the stimulating discussion in McKillip, "Undermining Technology by Strategy," 18–37.

62. Report of meeting held at the Admiralty, 23 February 1917, Patterson, *The Jellicoe Papers* 2:149–50.

63. Naval Staff, *Home Waters—Part VIII*, 186–87, 187 n. 2.

64. Cited in Marder, *Dreadnought to Scapa Flow* 4:127.

65. Jellicoe, *The Submarine Peril*, 101–2, 111. For a critique of Jellicoe's attitude, see especially Marder, *Dreadnought to Scapa Flow* 4:145 n. 43.

66. Naval Staff, *Home Waters—Part VIII*, 377–78; Marder, *Dreadnought to Scapa Flow* 4:150–52.

67. Naval Staff, *Home Waters—Part VIII*, 378–80.

68. Herwig, *Politics of Frustration*, 128–29.

69. Trask, *Captains & Cabinets*, 44–45.

70. In 1910 Sims had been reprimanded by President Taft for an indiscreet speech at the Guildhall in London that implied that in the event of an Anglo-German war, the United States and Great Britain would be allies.

71. See, for example, Trask, *Captains & Cabinets*, 131–32.

72. The quotation is from Sims's 1920 testimony before the congressional committee investigating the naval conduct of the war. Cited ibid., 55.

73. On Benson's views, see especially Klachko, *Benson*, 57–60. See also: General Board to Daniels, 5 April 1917, in Simpson, *Anglo-American Naval Relations*, 19–20. Unfortunately this excellent work appeared too late to be fully cited.

74. Sims, *The Victory at Sea*, 3–4; Morison, *Sims*, 339–41.

75. Klachko, *Benson*, 63–65; Trask, *Captains & Cabinets*, 62–65.

76. Sims, *The Victory at Sea*, 6–7.

77. Cable of 14 April 1917 reproduced in Sims, *The Victory at Sea*, 374–76; Trask, *Captains & Cabinets*, 65–68.

78. Marder, *Dreadnought to Scapa Flow* 5:121–23; Taussig gives his account in a four-part article, "Destroyer Experiences." Bayly's own interesting memoirs are in *Pull*

Together! See also the Naval Historical Foundation's pamphlet: DeLany, *Bayly's Navy.*

79. Klachko, *Benson,* 67–68; Taussig quotation in Sims, *The Victory at Sea,* 58. A slightly different version is in Taussig, "Destroyer Experiences," *Proceedings,* vol. 48, no. 12 (December 1922): 2036.

80. Morison, *Sims,* 354–55; Taussig, "Destroyer Experiences," *Proceedings,* vol. 49, no. 1 (January 1923): 53, 57, 58.

81. Roskill, *Hankey* 1:355–58. Substantial portions of the memorandum are printed in Corbett and Newbolt, *Naval Operations* 5:10–14 and in Lord Hankey, *Supreme Command* 2:646–47.

82. Minute of Rear Admiral A. L. Duff, 26 April 1917, Memorandum by Jellicoe to the First Lord, Sir Edward Carson, 27 April 1917, Patterson, *The Jellicoe Papers* 2:157–62; Roskill, *Hankey* 1:379–84. There is an exhaustive discussion of the subject in Marder, *Dreadnought to Scapa Flow,* vol. 4, chap. 6.

83. Corbett and Newbolt, *Naval Operations* 5:43–44; Naval Staff, *Home Waters—Part VIII,* 385.

84. Morison, *Sims,* 356–57.

85. Naval Staff, *Home Waters—Part VIII,* 385; Naval Staff, *Home Waters—Part IX,* 155; Fayle, *Seaborne Trade* 3:129–30.

86. Winton, *Convoy,* 67.

87. Naval Staff, *Home Waters—Part IX,* 156–59; further details in Winton, *Convoy,* 80–82; Beesly, *Room 40,* 264–65.

88. Naval Staff, *Home Waters—Part IX,* 160.

89. Technical History Section, *TH 14. Atlantic Convoy System,* 22.

90. Trask, *Captains & Cabinets,* 88–89.

91. Cited in Klachko, *Benson,* 71. See also Allard, "Anglo-American Naval Differences," 76.

92. Paper prepared by Jellicoe for the War Cabinet on the influence of the Submarine upon Naval Policy and Operations, 18 November 1917, Patterson, *The Jellicoe Papers* 2:226–29.

93. Details on convoys taken from Technical History Section, *TH 14. Atlantic Convoy System,* 21–29; description of "Commissioned Escort Ships" from Corbett and Newbolt, *Naval Operations* 5:58.

94. For a U-boat commander's view of the problems caused by convoys, see the classic report of Kapitänleutnant Saalwächer of *U.94,* 6 August 1917, in Spindler, *Handelskrieg mit U-booten* 4:224–25. See also Doenitz, *Memoirs,* 4.

95. Technical History Section, *TH 14. Atlantic Convoy System,* 23–25, 28; Technical History Section, *TH 15. Convoy Statistics,* 21. See also Corbett and Newbolt, *Naval Operations* 5:101–3.

96. Technical History Section, *TH 15. Convoy Statistics,* 23–25.

97. Spindler, *Handelskrieg mit U-Booten* 5:364–65.

98. Grant, *U-Boat Intelligence*, 185–86; Grant, *U-Boats Destroyed*, 67–69.

99. Hezlet, *The Submarine and Sea Power*, 95–97.

100. Hezlet, *The Submarine and Sea Power*, 96–97. There are detailed accounts in Fayle, *Seaborne Trade*, vol. 3, and the account by the former chairman of the Allied Maritime Transport Executive, Salter, *Allied Shipping Control*.

101. Cited in Marder, *Dreadnought to Scapa Flow* 5:192.

102. Beatty to his wife, 19 June 1917, Ranft, *The Beatty Papers* 1:443.

103. Remarks by Beatty on Operation BB, 6 July 1917, PRO, Adm 137/875, ff. 206, 259; minutes by Oliver, Duff, Fisher, Hope, and Jellicoe, ibid., passim. Printed accounts are in Naval Staff, *Home Waters—Part IX*, 162–69; and Corbett and Newbolt, *Naval Operations* 5:54–55.

104. Naval Staff, *Home Waters—Part IX*, 173–74; Corbett and Newbolt, *Naval Operations* 5:121–23.

105. Beatty to his wife, 7 July 1917, Ranft, *The Beatty Papers* 1:445–46.

106. Beatty to Admiralty, 17 October 1917, and minutes by naval staff, PRO, Adm 137/876; Corbett and Newbolt, *Naval Operations* 5:145–49; Grant, *U-Boats Destroyed*, 50–53.

107. Spindler, *Handelskrieg mit U-Booten* 4:386–91; Gerald Feldman, *Army, Industry and Labor in Germany* (Princeton: Princeton University Press, 1966), 362–63.

108. Spindler, *Handelskrieg mit U-Booten* 4:39–40; see also Lundeberg, "German Naval Critique," 115–16.

109. Michelsen, *La Guerre sous-marine*, 90.

110. Tarrant, *U-Boat Offensive*, 55–56; Waters, "Notes," par. 31.

111. Fayle, *Seaborne Trade* 3:251–54; Technical History Section, *TH 14. Atlantic Convoy System*, 32–33; Technical History Section, *TH 8. Scandinavian Convoy*, 11–15.

112. Cited in Historical Section, *The Defeat of the Enemy Attack*, 1A:5.

113. Herwig, "Luxury Fleet," 228; Spindler, *Handelskrieg mit U-Booten* 4:395–97.

114. Rössler, *The U-Boat*, 78–80.

115. The authoritative German official history of these operations is Raeder and Mantey, *Der Kreuzerkrieg*, vol. 3.

116. Details from Schmalenbach, *German Raiders*, 137–38; Corbett and Newbolt, *Naval Operations* 4:176–91; Admiralty, *Review of German Cruiser Warfare*, 14–16. See also the *Möwe*'s captain's wartime account: Dohna-Schlodien, *Der Möwe*.

117. Corbett and Newbolt, *Naval Operations* 4:216–17.

118. Figures from Schmalenbach, *German Raiders*, 47, 71, 138, 140; Admiralty, *Review of German Cruiser Warfare*, 17–21; Corbett and Newbolt, *Naval Operations* 4:209–26. The standard monograph is Alexander, *The Cruise of the Raider "Wolf."*

119. Luckner, *Seeteufel*; Thomas, *Count Luckner*. Luckner's image tarnished somewhat when he toured Australia and New Zealand in 1938 and was regarded by some as an apologist for the Nazi regime. See the interesting Carl Rühen, *The Sea Devil: The Controversial Cruise of the Nazi Emissary von Luckner to Australia and New Zealand in 1938* (Kenthurst, Australia: Kangaroo Press, 1988).

120. Schmalenbach, *German Raiders*, 47, 71, 138; Admiralty, *Review of German Cruiser Warfare*, 21–22; Corbett and Newbolt, *Naval Operations* 4:195–206.

121. Schmalenbach, *German Raiders*, 34, 71; Corbett and Newbolt, *Naval Operations* 4:191–95; Admiralty, *Review of German Cruiser Warfare*, 22–23.

122. Admiralty, *Review of German Cruiser Warfare*, 2–3.

123. Scheer, *Germany's High Sea Fleet*, 280.

124. Horn, *German Naval Mutinies*, chap. 4.

125. Gladisch, *Krieg in der Nordsee* 6:248–55.

126. Ibid. 7:44–51; Scheer, *Germany's High Sea Fleet*, 309–10; Corbett and Newbolt, *Naval Operations* 5:149–56; Marder, *Dreadnought to Scapa Flow* 4:294–99.

127. Marder, *Dreadnought to Scapa Flow* 4:295 n. 3. See also the full discussion in Beesly, *Room 40*, 276–79.

128. Marder, *Dreadnought to Scapa Flow* 4:299–308; the detailed official histories are: Corbett and Newbolt, *Naval Operations* 5:164–77; and Gladisch, *Krieg in der Nordsee* 7:55–87; a small collection of documents is in Patterson, *The Jellicoe Papers* 2:230–38; intelligence matters in Beesly, *Room 40*, 280.

129. Scheer, *Germany's High Sea Fleet*, 311–14; Corbett and Newbolt, *Naval Operations* 5:156–59, 184–94.

130. Corbett and Newbolt, *Naval Operations* 5:194; Marder, *Dreadnought to Scapa Flow* 4:313–15.

131. Technical History Section, *TH 8. Scandinavian Convoy*, 26–27.

12. THE MEDITERRANEAN: 1915–1918

1. On the German decision to reinforce their Mediterranean submarines, see Halpern, *Naval War in the Mediterranean*, 148–53. See also Spindler, *Handelskrieg mit U-Booten* 2:197–201.

2. Halpern, *Naval War in the Mediterranean*, 157–58; Spindler, *Handelskrieg mit U-Booten* 2:202–5.

3. Austro-Hungarian submarine construction described in detail in Aichelburg, *Unterseeboote Österreich-Ungarns* 1:92–100, 110–17. See also Halpern, *Naval War in the Mediterranean*, 158–59.

4. Halpern, *Naval War in the Mediterranean*, 190–91, 194; Spindler, *Handelskrieg mit U-Booten* 3:10, 24–26, 37. Tonnages from ibid., 388, 390.

5. Lapeyrère to Augagneur, 4 October 1915, SHM, Carton Ed-83.

6. On the *Ancona* affair, see Halpern, *Naval War in the Mediterranean*, 194–98; Lansing, *War Memoirs*, 87–92, 94; Link, *Wilson*, 62–63, 66–72; Link, *Papers of Woodrow Wilson* 35:208–9, 282, 286–89, 364–66, 368–70, 378–80.

7. Jackson to Jellicoe, 1, 21 November, 1915, British Library, London, Jellicoe MSS, Add. MSS 49009.

8. Jellicoe to Jackson, 8 November 1915, Jellicoe to Balfour, 23 February 1916, reproduced in Patterson, *The Jellicoe Papers* 1:186, 189.

9. Dartige to Lacaze, 6 December 1915, SHM, Carton Ed-84.

10. Halpern, *Naval War in the Mediterranean*, 230–33. Details on the loss of the *Provence* in Thomazi, *Méditerranée*, 169–70.

11. Halpern, *Naval War in the Mediterranean*, 237–38; see also Fayle, *Seaborne Trade* 2:257–59.

12. Report by Captain H. W. Grant, n.d. (c. 7 December 1915) and Agreement of 3 December 1915, PRO, Adm 137/499.

13. Halpern, *Naval War in the Mediterranean*, 234–35; Keyes to his wife, 30 December 1915, reproduced in Halpern, *The Keyes Papers* 1:299.

14. Halpern, *Naval War in the Mediterranean*, 238–42. The Procès Verbaux and General Report of the conference may be found in PRO, Adm 137/499.

15. Spindler, *Handelskrieg mit U-Booten* 3:388, 390.

16. Details of *U.35*'s cruise and tonnages are in Spindler, *Handelskrieg mit U-Booten* 3:161–63, 388, 390; Halpern, *Naval War in the Mediterranean*, 250–53.

17. Grant, *U-Boat Intelligence*, 183–84. They lost four in the Black Sea.

18. Figures from Holtzendorff, Immediatvortrag, 25 October 1916, NARS, T-1022, Roll, 803, PG 75267.

19. Halpern, *Naval War in the Mediterranean*, 251–52; In 1916 Austrian submarines did not usually operate outside the Adriatic and in *Handelskrieg* sank only sixteen ships, mostly small coastal steamers or sailing craft. On Austrian operations see Aichelburg, *Unterseeboote Österreich-Ungarns* 1:172–85, 2:90–91, 302–3, 356–58.

20. Submarine communications with Libya are discussed in Halpern, *Naval War in the Mediterranean*, 191–93, 245–48, 250, 313, 535; Gibson and Prendergast, *German Submarine War*, 76; and Spindler, *Handelskrieg mit U-Booten* 3:25, 32–34, 43–44, 46–47; 4:188; 5:168–69, 206–8.

21. Correspondence regarding transporting troops overland to Marseilles is in PRO, Adm 137/1221; correspondence regarding shifting more trade to the Cape route is in ibid., Adm 137/2894.

22. Ballard's proposal (14 October 1916) and ensuing Admiralty minutes and memoranda are reproduced in Halpern, *Royal Navy in the Mediterranean*, 178–82, 197–202.

23. For a summary of the arguments over dispersion and the London conference, see Halpern, *Naval War in the Mediterranean*, 326–33. The agenda, minutes, and conclusion of the conference are in PRO, Adm 137/1420.

24. Halpern, *Naval War in the Mediterranean*, 307–12; German figures from Spindler, *Handelskrieg mit U-Booten* 5:388, 390; Austrian figures from Aichelburg, *Unterseeboote Österreich-Ungarns* 2:490–91.

25. The events can be followed in Spindler, *Handelskrieg mit U-Booten* 4:160, 170–72, 180, 185; Moraht, *Werwolf der Meere*, 56–62; Gibson and Prendergast, *German Submarine*

War, 240–44; Corbett and Newbolt, *Naval Operations* 4:276–86; Thomazi, *Méditerranée*, 58, 185–88; and Ufficio Storico, *Marina italiana* 4:181–84, 236–37.

26. Gauchet to Lacaze, 10 March 1917, SHM, Carton Ed-85.

27. Holtzendorff to Admiralstab, 18 May 1917, Admiralstab to U-Flotilla, Pola, 29 May 1917, NARS, T-1022, Roll 731, PG 75298.

28. Robertson to Jellicoe, 6 April 1917, and Jellicoe, "Protection of Shipping in the Mediterranean," 17 April 1917, PRO, Adm 137/1413.

29. On the Corfu conference and its background, see Halpern, *Naval War in the Mediterranean*, 338–49. Figures on Allied patrol vessels from Report of Sub-Committee, Minutes of Corfu Conference, Annex I, PRO, Adm 137/1421.

30. Naval Staff, *Mediterranean Staff Papers*, 21. The Americans, as usual, were particularly interested in Japanese naval activity. See: ONI, "Japanese Naval Operations during European War," n.d., NARS, RG 38, U-4-b, No. 11083; Train (U.S. naval attaché in Italy) to Sims, 26 June 1917, and Train to ONI, 21 August 1917, ibid., RG 45, OT File, Box 335.

31. Gibson and Prendergast, *German Submarine War*, 256, 258.

32. Summary in Halpern, *Naval War in the Mediterranean*, 340–41; see also: Laurens, *Commandement naval*, 267–69; Thomazi, *Guerre navale dans la Méditerranée*, 193–94; Salaun, *La Marine Française*, 263–64.

33. Halpern, *Naval War in the Mediterranean*, 369–72, and 447 n. 47. On Calthorpe, see especially Godfrey, *Naval Memoirs* 2:96, 99–100. The first Mediterranean C-in-C designate was Vice Admiral Wemyss, then C-in-C Egypt and East Indies. Wemyss was called to the Admiralty in August as Second Sea Lord and eventually replaced Jellicoe as First Sea Lord in December.

34. The Italian question is dealt with in Halpern, *Naval War in the Mediterranean*, 375–86, 403–8.

35. The voluminous minutes, reports, and conclusions of the conference are in PRO, Adm 137/1420.

36. Niblack to Sims, 28 March 1918, NARS, RG 45, TD File, Box 553. See also "The American Effort in the Mediterranean," n.d. (postwar), ibid., OD File, Box 308; Sims, *The Victory at Sea*, 160–63.

37. Naval Staff, *Mediterranean Staff Papers*, 59–61, 67; Fayle, *Seaborne Trade* 3:184–85; Halpern, *Naval War in the Mediterranean*, 386–90.

38. Niblack to Sims, 19 January 1918, NARS, TD File, Box 553.

39. Halpern, *Naval War in the Mediterranean*, 444–46. See also Robinson, "The Brazilian Navy."

40. "Yamew," "Mediterranean Convoys," 242.

41. Anthony Morse, Sr., "When ASW Was Young," *Naval History* 4, no. 2 (Spring 1990): 72–74.

42. Halpern, *Naval War in the Mediterranean*, 311–16, 394–95, 398–99; Corbett and Newbolt, *Naval Operations* 5:79–81; Spindler, *Handelskrieg mit U-Booten* 3:388, 390;

ibid. 4:376–77, 476–77, 479–84; 496–97; Aichelburg, *Unterseeboote Österreich-Ungarns* 2:490–92.

43. Calthorpe to Admiralty, 27 November 1917, with minutes by naval staff, in Halpern, *Royal Navy in the Mediterranean*, 313–19; Halpern, *Naval War in the Mediterranean*, 390; Corbett and Newbolt, *Naval Operations* 5:81–82.

44. Naval Staff, *Mediterranean Staff Papers*, 69.

45. Niblack to Sims, 19 January 1918, NARS, TD File, Box 553.

46. Michelsen, *La Guerre sous-marine*, 70–71, 171–72; Halpern, *Naval War in the Mediterranean*, 453–56. On the Cattaro air raids, see Raleigh and Jones, *The War in the Air* 6:321–22.

47. Barrage proposals are in Calthorpe to Admiralty, 16 January 1918, and Admiralty minutes, in Halpern, *Royal Navy in the Mediterranean*, 367–73, 383–88. Rome conference and its background in Halpern, *Naval War in the Mediterranean*, 409–10, 426–31. French ideas on the fixed barrage are in Thomazi, *L'Adriatique*, 142–43, 164–65, 179–81.

48. Sims to Ratyé, 16 August 1918, NARS, RG 45, TD File, Box 553. See also the very full postwar account in Nelson to Sims, 16 December 1919, ibid., OD File, Box 310. For published accounts, see Halpern, *Naval War in the Mediterranean*, 433–34, 503–8; Sims, *The Victory at Sea*, chap. 6; and Moffat, *Maverick Navy*.

49. Halpern, *Naval War in the Mediterranean*, 508–13, 518–21, 565; Grant, *U-Boats Destroyed*, 132–33, 162–63; Spindler, *Handelskrieg mit U-Booten* 5:201. The voluminous reports of the Allied Conference on Mediterranean Minelaying, August 1918, are in PRO, Adm 137/836. For U.S. plans, see also Allied Naval Council Memorandum No. 203, "Minelaying Operations, Mediterranean," 11 September 1918, ibid.

50. Halpern, *Naval War in the Mediterranean*, 453–57, 534–39; Spindler, *Handelskrieg mit U-Booten* 5:364–65; Aichelburg, *Unterseeboote Österreich-Ungarns* 2:492–93. For cryptography and direction finding, see especially Naval Staff, *Mediterranean Staff Papers*, 32, 110–20; Grant, *U-Boat Intelligence*, 134–42; Beesly, *Room 40*, 178–80; and Hezlet, *Electronics and Sea Power*, 142–45.

51. Gibson and Prendergast, *German Submarine War*, 272, 274; the view from *Lychnis* is in "Yamew," "Mediterranean Convoys," 243; Dönitz's account is in Doenitz, *Memoirs*, 1–4; see also Padfield, *Dönitz*, 83–89.

52. The question of the Mediterranean admiralissimo is discussed in detail in Halpern, *Naval War in the Mediterranean*, 457–87, 522–34; a series of documents on the subject are printed in Halpern, *Royal Navy in the Mediterranean*, 474–96, 523–24, 537–40, 545–47, 549–55. A summary of Revel's arguments and the Italian position is in Ufficio Storico, *Marina italiana* 7:424–25. See also Roskill, *Hankey* 1:558–59; Lord Hankey, *Supreme Command* 2:811–12; Freidel, *Franklin D. Roosevelt*, 350–51, 362–64; and Charles-Roux, *Souvenirs Diplomatiques*, 314–16.

53. Halpern, *Naval War in the Mediterranean*, 498–501. The British and French squadron in the Aegean was also reinforced by the Greek armored cruiser *Averoff* and four

Greek destroyers. The Greek fleet had been either disarmed or (the light craft) sequestered in October 1916 because of the equivocal conduct of King Constantine. After King Constantine was forced to abdicate in June 1917 and Greece entered the war on the side of the Allies, the French somewhat reluctantly returned the Greek ships, which were slowly manned as reliable crews became available. Older Greek destroyers and torpedo boats also worked as escorts, primarily in the Aegean. See ibid., 293–300, 367–69.

54. Halpern, *Naval War in the Mediterranean*, 558–65. See also Lloyd George, *War Memoirs* 2:1974; Godfrey, *Naval Memoirs* 2:116. A series of documents, including the Clemenceau–Lloyd George exchange, on the end of the war with Turkey are printed in Halpern, *Royal Navy in the Mediterranean*, 568–86.

55. Halpern, *Naval War in the Mediterranean*, 567–68; Corbett and Newbolt, *Naval Operations* 5:359–60. Spindler, *Handelskrieg mit U-Booten* 5:195–97, 214–15, 226–28. In addition four U-boats on operations were ordered by wireless to return to Germany, one (*UC.74*) lacked sufficient fuel and was interned in Barcelona, and another (*U.34*) disappeared.

13. 1918: THE SUBMARINE THREAT CONTAINED

1. On the dismissal of Jellicoe, see especially Roskill, "The Dismissal of Admiral Jellicoe." Patterson, *Jellicoe,* chap. 8; and Marder, *Dreadnought to Scapa Flow,* vol. 4, chap. 12. Jellicoe's account of the circumstances leading to his dismissal is in Patterson, *The Jellicoe Papers* 2:240–45.

2. King George V to Beatty, 10 February 1918, reproduced in Ranft, *The Beatty Papers* 1:511.

3. Beatty's memorandum of 9 January 1918 is substantially quoted in Marder, *Dreadnought to Scapa Flow* 5:132–34; see also Corbett and Newbolt, *Naval Operations* 5:205–7. Details on the *Mackensen* from Gröner, *German Warships* 1:57–58.

4. Admiralty Memorandum of 17 January 1918 quoted in Marder, *Dreadnought to Scapa Flow* 5:135–36.

5. Beatty's paper, "The Situation in the North Sea," 29 December 1917, quoted in Marder, *Dreadnought to Scapa Flow* 5:133–34 nn. 10, 12.

6. Beatty to his wife, 5 February 1918, *The Beatty Papers* 1:508; Roskill, *Beatty,* 243–44; Chalmers, *Beatty,* 299–301; Chatfield, *The Navy and Defence,* 163–64; Marder, *Dreadnought to Scapa Flow* 5:124–26.

7. Rodman, *Yarns of a Kentucky Admiral,* 266–67.

8. Roskill, *Beatty,* 245–48; Marder, *Dreadnought to Scapa Flow* 5:128–31; Chalmers, *Beatty,* 305–8.

9. Marder, *Dreadnought to Scapa Flow* 4:322.

10. Submarine losses and use of the Strait are discussed in Grant, *U-Boats Destroyed*, 44–49, 74–79; Grant, *U-Boat Intelligence*, 79–81. See also Beesly, *Room 40*, 281–82.

11. Keyes, *Naval Memoirs* 2:115–19.

12. Keyes, *Naval Memoirs* 2:118–26, 135–47; Bacon, *The Dover Patrol* 2:401–13; Bacon, *Concise Story of the Dover Patrol*, 158–66; Bacon, *From 1900 Onward*, 260–62, 291–96. A number of documents on the subject are printed in Halpern, *The Keyes Papers* 1:416–39.

13. Full accounts of the controversy are in Corbett and Newbolt, *Naval Operations* 5:178–83, 204; Marder, *Dreadnought to Scapa Flow* 4:315–22, 347–48. See also Lady Wemyss, *Wemyss*, 365–67.

14. Keyes to Beatty, 18 January 1918, *The Keyes Papers* 1:443–44. See also Chatterton, *The Auxiliary Patrol*, 194–97.

15. Grant, *U-Boat Intelligence*, 79–88; Marder, *Dreadnought to Scapa Flow* 5:41; Corbett and Newbolt, *Naval Operations* 5:209–10.

16. Michelsen, *Guerre sous-marine*, 114; Grant, *U-Boats Destroyed*, 79–80, 83; Tarrant, *The U-Boat Offensive*, 61–62; Gayer, "German Submarine Operations," 652–55.

17. Tables in Grant, *U-Boat Intelligence*, 85–86, 94, 95; see also Chatterton, *The Auxiliary Patrol*, 301.

18. Scheer, *Germany's High Sea Fleet*, 314–15.

19. British accounts are Corbett and Newbolt, *Naval Operations* 5:211–19; Keyes, *Naval Memoirs* 2:174–79; the standard German account is Gladisch, *Krieg in der Nordsee* 7:189–95; and Scheer, *Germany's High Sea Fleet*, 315–18.

20. Keyes to Beatty, 19 February 1918, Halpern, *The Keyes Papers* 1:458.

21. Keyes, *Naval Memoirs* 2:176–81; Marder, *Dreadnought to Scapa Flow* 5:43–44.

22. Corbett and Newbolt, *Naval Operations* 5:223–37; Keyes, *Naval Memoirs* 2:193–96; Gladisch, *Krieg in der Nordsee* 7:236–37; Thomazi, *Guerre navale dans le Nord*, 191–92.

23. For the bombardments of May and June 1917, see Corbett and Newbolt, *Naval Operations* 5:36–41, 45–48. Bacon, not surprisingly, provides great detail in Bacon, *The Dover Patrol*, vol. 1, chap. 4.

24. Keyes to Beatty, 18 January 1918, Halpern, *The Keyes Papers* 1:447.

25. Keyes, *Naval Memoirs* 2:127–34; Keyes to Beatty, 5 December 1917, Halpern, *The Keyes Papers* 1:423; Patterson, *Tyrwhitt*, 181–83; a review of previous plans is in Corbett and Newbolt, *Naval Operations* 5:241–43; for Bacon's plans in detail, see Bacon, *The Dover Patrol*, vol. 1, chaps. 8 and 10.

26. Plan for Operation Z.O. and Remarks by Sea Lords printed in Halpern, *The Keyes Papers* 1:460–78. See also Keyes, *Naval Memoirs*, vol. 2, chaps. 17–19.

27. A good summary is in Corbett and Newbolt, *Naval Operations* 5:244–51.

28. Keyes to Beatty, 10 February 1918, Halpern, *The Keyes Papers* 1:452.

29. Keyes, *Naval Memoirs* 1:249–56.

30. Gladisch, *Krieg in der Nordsee* 7:267.

31. Very detailed accounts in Keyes, *Naval Memoirs*, vol. 2, chaps. 22–26; Corbett and Newbolt, *Naval Operations* 5:252–73.
32. Keyes, *Naval Memoirs* 2:337–39; Keyes to Beatty, 16 June 1918, Halpern, *The Keyes Papers* 2:500–501.
33. Viscount Cunningham, *A Sailor's Odyssey*, 92–94.
34. Although the conclusions are wrong, an excellent account is Pitt, *Zeebrugge;* see also Carpenter, *The Blocking of Zeebrugge.*
35. Captain W. W. Fisher to Keyes, 23 April 1918, Halpern, *The Keyes Papers* 1:484.
36. Keyes, *Naval Memoirs* 2:319–20, 337; see also Roger Keyes, *Amphibious Warfare and Combined Operations* (Cambridge: At the University Press, 1943), 69–70. This view is reflected in Keyes's biographer, Aspinall-Oglander, *Keyes*, 247; as well as Pitt, *Zeebrugge*, 206–10.
37. Gladisch, *Krieg in der Nordsee* 7:265–69; Marder, *Dreadnought to Scapa Flow* 5:59–65; Beesly, *Room 40*, 282–83.
38. Corbett and Newbolt, *Naval Operations* 5:274–75.
39. Raleigh and Jones, *The War in the Air* 6:380–83.
40. Ibid., 385.
41. Admiralty to Air Ministry, 3 May, and Air Ministry to Admiralty, 16 May 1918, Roskill, *Naval Air Service* 1:666–67; Admiralty to Air Ministry, 22 May 1918, ibid., 672–73; Air Ministry to War Office and Admiralty, 22, 23 May, 1918, ibid., 673–75; Vice-Admiral Dover to Admiralty and Admiralty reply, 30 May 1918, ibid., 675.
42. Keyes, *Naval Memoirs* 2:341; Keyes reproduces extracts from his letter to the Admiralty of 28 May on the disadvantages resulting from the loss of the RNAS, ibid., 406–8, Appendix 4. See also Marder, *Dreadnought to Scapa Flow* 5:64–65.
43. Raleigh and Jones, *The War in the Air* 6:392. For full detail of air operations see ibid., 384–96.
44. On this point, see Hezlet, *Aircraft and Sea Power*, 98.
45. On Keyes's later career, see Aspinall-Oglander, *Keyes* and Halpern, *The Keyes Papers*, vol. 2.
46. Corbett and Newbolt, *Naval Operations* 5:275; Gladisch, *Krieg in der Nordsee* 7:265.
47. Grant, *U-Boats Destroyed*, 93–96.
48. The subject is discussed in Wemyss to Beatty, 28 January, 7 February, 30 March 1918, and Beatty to Wemyss, 1 April 1918, Ranft, *The Beatty Papers* 1:506–7, 508–9, 523–26.
49. Beatty to his wife, 7 April 1918, ibid., 527.
50. Marder, *Dreadnought to Scapa Flow* 5:144.
51. Technical History Section, *TH 8. Scandinavian Convoy*, 15; Fayle, *Seaborne Trade* 3:254. A succinct account is in Marder, *Dreadnought to Scapa Flow* 5:145–47.
52. Scheer, *Germany's High Sea Fleet*, 318. See also Gladisch, *Krieg in der Nordsee* 7:217–18.
53. The question of Room 40 and wireless intelligence is examined in Beesly, *Room 40*, 285–89.

54. Beatty to Keyes, 28 April 1918, Halpern, *The Keyes Papers* 1:486.

55. The study was contained in a lecture given at the Staff College in 1931 by Commander John Creswell. Cited by Marder, *Dreadnought to Scapa Flow* 5:153.

56. The sortie may be followed in Gladisch, *Krieg in der Nordsee* 7:218–25; Corbett and Newbolt, *Naval Operations* 5:230–39; Scheer, *Germany's High Sea Fleet*, 318–23; and Marder, *Dreadnought to Scapa Flow* 5:148–56.

57. Campbell, *Battle Cruisers*, 25.

58. Corbett and Newbolt, *Naval Operations* 5:239–40. The report of the operation by the U.S. battleships is in Rodman to Beatty, 20 April 1918, PRO, Adm 137/877, f. 67.

59. Beatty's comment (in a letter to Wemyss, 26 April) and Admiral James's postwar comments (1936) are cited in Marder, *Dreadnought to Scapa Flow* 5:155–56.

60. These points are discussed at length in Horn, *German Naval Mutinies*; for a summary discussion, see Herwig, "Luxury Fleet," 230–35, 241–42.

61. Roskill, "The U-Boat Campaign."

62. Full details in Rössler, *The U-Boat*, 80–81, 330.

63. Weizsäcker, *Memoirs*, 36. Scheer states his case in Scheer, *Germany's High Sea Fleet*, 324–29. See also Herwig, "Luxury Fleet," 245.

64. Exhaustive detail in Rössler, *The U-Boat*, 81–87; See also Scheer, *Germany's High Sea Fleet*, 333–37, 341–44; Herwig, "Luxury Fleet," 245; Weir, *Building the Kaiser's Navy*, 172–78.

65. Figures from Spindler, *Handelskrieg mit U-Booten* 5:364–65. Data on British tonnage from Corbett and Newbolt, *Naval Operations* 5:277. On the exchange rate, see Hezlet, *The Submarine and Sea Power*, 95–101.

66. Full details in Technical History Section, *TH 8. Scandinavian Convoy*, 16–18.

67. Waters, "Notes," pars. 2.22–2.26.

68. Corbett and Newbolt, *Naval Operations* 5:195–97.

69. Marder, *Dreadnought to Scapa Flow* 5:104; Waters, "Notes," pt. 2, table 3, p. 72; Fayle, *Seaborne Trade* 3:251–52, 288–89, 309; see also Technical History Section, *TH 39. Miscellaneous Convoys*.

70. Historical Section, *Defeat of the Enemy Attack*, 1A:6–10. See also Hezlet, *Aircraft and Sea Power*, 90–92, 100–101; and Price, *Aircraft versus Submarine*, chap. 1. There is a mine of information centered on Great Yarmouth in Gamble, *North Sea Air Station*.

71. Extracts from U. S. Navy Planning Section Memorandum No. 12, 15 February 1918, reproduced in Roskill, *Naval Air Service* 1:624–32.

72. On U.S. naval aviation in World War I, see Turnbull and Lord, *United States Naval Aviation*, chaps. 11–13; Edwards, "The U.S. Naval Air Force"; Van Wyen et al., *Naval Aviation in World War I*, 84–87; Raleigh and Jones, *The War in the Air* 6:383–84; and Sims, *The Victory at Sea*, chap. 11.

73. Randier, *La Royale* 2:245–49; Thomazi, *Guerre navale dans le Nord*, 155–66, 220–21; Salaun, *La Marine Française*, 237–39, 262–63, 289–90.

74. Technical History Section, *TH 4. Aircraft v. Submarine*, 15.

75. Ibid., 19.
76. Historical Section, *Defeat of the Enemy Attack,* 1A:9; Marder, *Dreadnought to Scapa Flow* 5:91–95.
77. Corbett and Newbolt, *Naval Operations* 5:278–81; ibid., vol. 5 (Maps), 25–27. Newbolt does not mention the loss of the *Moldavia,* possibly because it occurred in the Channel and not in the area of the U-boat concentration in the Western Approaches. Note on the *Moldavia* from Technical History Section, *TH14. Atlantic Convoy System,* 27.
78. Grant, *U-Boat Intelligence,* 46–49; Grant, *U-Boats Destroyed,* 116–18.
79. Grant, *U-Boats Destroyed,* 119; Grant, *U-Boat Intelligence,* 147–49.
80. Beesly, *Room 40,* 191–200; Grant, *U-Boat Intelligence,* 147–48; Spindler, *Handelskrieg mit U-Booten* 5:241–42.
81. Corbett and Newbolt, *Naval Operations* 5:283–84; Spindler, *Handelskrieg mit U-Booten* 5:232–46; Gibson and Prendergast, *German Submarine War,* 296–98.
82. Sims, *The Victory at Sea,* 310–16; Klachko, *Benson,* 71, 107–11; Trask, *Captains & Cabinets,* 89–90. See also Allard, "Anglo-American Naval Differences," 76–77.
83. See Breckel, "The Suicide Flotilla"; Rose, *Brittany Patrol;* and Paine, *The "Corsair."*
84. Sims, *The Victory at Sea,* 349–50; Taussig, "Destroyer Experiences," *Proceedings,* vol. 49, no. 3 (March 1923): 392–408.
85. Knox, *United States Navy,* 412, 414–15; Sims, *The Victory at Sea,* 215–28, 279–81; an account of operations at Plymouth is in Moffat, *Maverick Navy;* on the submarines at Berehaven, see Carroll Storrs Alden, "American Submarine Operations," *Proceedings,* vol. 46, no. 7 (July 1920): 1013–48.
86. Herwig, *Politics of Frustration,* 142–45; Michelsen, *Guerre sous-marine,* 56, 90–91. See also Scheer, *Germany's High Sea Fleet,* 331–32; and Görlitz, *The Kaiser and His Court,* 375–76.
87. Clark, *When the U-Boats Came,* 21–22, 63–65, 78–79. An extremely detailed official account is Navy Department, *German Submarine Activities.*
88. Spindler, *Handelskrieg mit U-Booten* 5:232–33, 251–53; Grant, *U-Boat Intelligence,* 151–53; *U.151's* raid is recounted in detail in Clark, *When the U-Boats Came,* 315.
89. Clark, *When the U-Boats Came,* 94–97, 104–5.
90. Spindler, *Handelskrieg mit U-Booten* 5:258–60; Clark, *When the U-Boats Came,* chaps. 10–11, 13, 16, and p. 178; Grant, *U-Boat Intelligence,* 152–56. There are discrepancies in the total tonnage credited to the submarine, probably because many of the victims were small fishing craft and the submarine did not survive the cruise.
91. Spindler, *Handelskrieg mit U-Booten* 5:262–64; Clark, *When the U-Boats Came,* chap. 12; Grant, *U-Boat Intelligence,* 153–55.
92. These operations as well as the little-known American submarine patrol around the Azores are described in Alden, "American Submarine Operations," *Proceedings,* vol. 41, no. 6 (June 1920): 811–50.

93. Details of the cruises from Spindler, *Handelskrieg mit U-Booten* 5:253–58, 261–62, 264–65; Clark, *When the U-Boats Came,* chaps. 14, 17–20, and pp. 294–95, 303–7; Grant, *U-Boat Intelligence,* 154–59; Clephane, *Naval Overseas Transportation Service,* 173–77.

94. Clark, *When the U-Boats Came,* 309–10, 320.

95. Navy Department, *Annual Report, 1918,* 16–17.

96. Sterling, "The Bridge," 1669–77; and for great detail Gleaves, *Transport Service;* and Crowell and Wilson, *Road to France,* vol. 2, chap. 23, and pp. 410–12. Crowell was assistant secretary of war and director of munitions, 1917–20. The authors list 20 German passenger liners, but have included the *Princess Alice* (10,000 tons), interned in the Philippines, and the Austro-America's *Martha Washington* (8,000 tons), wrongly identified as German.

97. Frothingham, *Naval History* 3:131–34, 200–3; Silverstone, *U.S. Warships,* 246, 261, 263.

98. Capt. Byron T. Long (Convoy Operations Section), Memorandum for Admiral Sims, 24 August 1918, NARS, RG 45, TT File, Box 565.

99. Navy Department, *Annual Report, 1919,* 206–7. Slightly different figures are shown on the chart in Frothingham, *Naval History* 3:205. A list of American convoys is printed in Crowell and Wilson, *Road to France* 2:603–20, Appendix G.

100. Technical History Section, *TH 14. Atlantic Convoy System,* 26–27, 116–17. The Admiralty figures do not always match those of the Americans, largely because they are based on troop movements to the British Isles rather than France and include Canadian and Australian troops as well as American.

101. Clephane, *Naval Overseas Transportation Service,* xix.

102. Sims to Admiralty, 10, 19 August 1918, PRO, Adm 137/1622, ff. 234–48. See also Frothingham, *Naval History* 3:245. Detailed plans in case of a raid are printed in Technical History Section, *TH 14. Atlantic Convoy System,* 59–61.

103. Summarized from Crowell and Wilson, *Road to France,* vol. 2, chap. 29.

104. Eady, "Experiences in a Mediterranean Convoy Sloop, 1917–1918," 124, IWM, Eady MSS.

105. Sims, *The Victory at Sea,* 291; Trask, *Captains & Cabinets,* 88, 151, 153–56; Klachko, *Benson,* 92–93. The British official history creates the erroneous impression that the proposal was pushed by Jellicoe: Corbett and Newbolt, *Naval Operations* 5:131–32.

106. Trask, *Captains & Cabinets,* 216–17.

107. Clephane, *Naval Overseas Transportation Service,* 120, a list of Lake ships in NOTS service is printed in ibid., 226–30.

108. The most detailed account, although from the American point of view, is Navy Department, *The Northern Barrage.* See also Belknap, "The Yankee Mining Squadron." Shorter accounts are in Corbett and Newbolt, *Naval Operations* 5:131–32, 229–30, 334–35; Marder, *Dreadnought to Scapa Flow* 5:66–67; and Sims, *The Victory at Sea,* chap. 9.

109. Allard, "Anglo-American Naval Differences," 70; Corbett and Newbolt, *Naval Operations* 5:229; Beatty to Wemyss, 10 August 1918, Wemyss to Beatty, 15 August 1918, Balfour [foreign secretary] to Robert Cecil [minister of blockade], 22 August 1918, in Ranft, *The Beatty Papers* 1:535–36, 538–40.
110. Trask, *Captains & Cabinets*, 217; Morison, *Sims*, 415–16.
111. Marder, *Dreadnought to Scapa Flow* 5:67–72; Corbett and Newbolt, *Naval Operations* 5:348–49. The issues are discussed in Wemyss to Beatty 23, 30 August, 2 September 1918, Beatty to Wemyss 1 September 1918, and Balfour to Cecil, 22 August 1918, in Ranft, *The Beatty Papers* 1:540–49.
112. Corbett and Newbolt, *Naval Operations* 5:339–42.
113. Corbett and Newbolt, *Naval Operations* 5:339–44; Marder, *Dreadnought to Scapa Flow* 5:72.
114. Knox, *United States Navy*, 417–19; Morison, *Sims*, 415–16. The Navy Department study gives slightly different figures: 56,760 American and 16,300 British mines for a total of 73,060. Navy Department, *The Northern Barrage*, 121.
115. Grant, *U-Boat Intelligence*, 101–9. See also the discussion in Marder, *Dreadnought to Scapa Flow* 5:73; and Lundeberg, "Undersea Warfare," vol. 1, no. 2, pp. 65–67.
116. Hezlet, *Aircraft and Sea Power*, 83–84.
117. On the Cuckoo and H.12 "Large America," see Thetford, *British Naval Aircraft*, 80–81, 310–11.
118. On Beatty's plans, see Roskill, *Beatty*, 233–34; Marder, *Dreadnought to Scapa Flow* 4:237–40; Marder, *Portrait of an Admiral*, 268–69; extracts of the plan and the Admiralty's reply are in Beatty to Admiralty, 11 September 1917, and Admiralty to Beatty, 25 September 1917, in Roskill, *Naval Air Service* 1:541–43, 549–54.
119. Short accounts are in Layman, *Before the Aircraft Carrier*, 58–71; Kemp, *Fleet Air Arm*, 86–92; for a most complete account, see Friedman, *British Carrier Aviation*, chap. 3.
120. Raleigh and Jones, *The War in the Air* 6:363–67; Corbett and Newbolt, *Naval Operations* 5:347.
121. Friedman, *British Carrier Aviation*, 54; Raleigh and Jones, *The War in the Air* 6:372–73; Corbett and Newbolt, *Naval Operations* 5:346–47; Robinson, *The Zeppelin*, 338–39.
122. The sources differ in detail: see Corbett and Newbolt, *Naval Operations* 5:344–47; Patterson, *Tyrwhitt*, 201–4; Raleigh and Jones, *The War in the Air* 6:570–75; Gladisch, *Krieg in der Nordsee* 7:308–10. Gladisch identifies individual aircraft numbers and pilots, but does not identify type. The latter may be culled from Imrie, *German Naval Air Service*, which has a photograph of the action.
123. Gladisch, *Krieg in der Nordsee* 7:332–33; Tyrwhitt to Keyes, 1 October 1918, *The Keyes Papers* 1:509; Patterson, *Tyrwhitt*, 205–6; Corbett and Newbolt, *Naval Operations* 5:362–63.
124. Scheer's apologia is in Scheer, *Germany's High Sea Fleet*, 348–55. See also the succinct account in Herwig, "Luxury Fleet," 247–48.

125. Cited in Philbin, *Hipper*, 155. See also Horn, *German Naval Mutinies*, 204–5; and Gladisch, *Krieg in der Nordsee* 7:340–41.

126. Philbin, *Hipper*, 145–47, 154–57, 159–63.

127. The plan and German order of battle is printed in Gladisch, *Krieg in der Nordsee* 7:344–47; a short English summary is in Marder, *Dreadnought to Scapa Flow* 5:171.

128. Marder, *Dreadnought to Scapa Flow* 5:171–72; Corbett and Newbolt, *Naval Operations* 5:369–70; Grant, *U-Boat Intelligence*, 160–65; Beesly, *Room 40*, 293–97. See also Beatty to Wemyss, 18 October 1918, Wemyss to Beatty, 19 October 1918, Fremantle (DCNS) to Beatty, 29 October 1918, all in Ranft, *The Beatty Papers* 1:556–59.

129. Beatty to his wife, 22 September 1918, Ranft, *The Beatty Papers* 1:554.

130. On this point both Roskill and Marder agree. See Roskill, *Beatty*, 260–61, 271–72; Marder, *Dreadnought to Scapa Flow* 5:172 n. 11.

131. A very full account in English is in Horn, *German Naval Mutinies*. Short accounts are in Philbin, *Hipper*, 163–73; Herwig, "*Luxury Fleet*," 249–53; and Marder, *Dreadnought to Scapa Flow* 5:172–75.

132. Accounts of the negotiations of the naval terms from different perspectives are in Corbett and Newbolt, *Naval Operations* 5:370–77, 413–18; Marder, *Dreadnought to Scapa Flow* 5:175–87; Trask, *Captains & Cabinets*, chap. 9; Klachko, *Benson*, 120–26; Roskill, *Beatty*, 269–75; Lady Wemyss, *Wemyss*, 383–95.

133. A detailed account conveying the atmosphere is in Roskill, *Beatty*, 276–79. See also "Procedure regarding carrying out of naval terms of armistice," n.d. (November 1918), and Beatty to Eugénie Godfrey-Faussett, 26 November 1918, in Ranft, *The Beatty Papers* 1:562–69, 572–74.

134. Corbett and Newbolt, *Naval Operations* 5:380–81; Patterson, *Tyrwhitt*, 209–10; Gibson and Prendergast, *German Submarine War*, 330–33; Tarrant, *U-Boat Offensive*, 77; Rössler, *The U-Boat*, 88.

135. Quoted in Philbin, *Hipper*, 174–76.

136. Good descriptions are in Marder, *Dreadnought to Scapa Flow* 5:190–94; Lord Chatfield, *The Navy and Defence*, 173–77. Chatfield was Beatty's flag captain; Herwig, "*Luxury Fleet*," 254–55; and Chalmers, *Beatty*, 346–49. Chalmers reproduces Beatty's orders for Operation ZZ, 440–45, appendix v.

Select Bibliography

Unpublished Materials

A broad survey such as this must by its very nature be based largely on published sources. There are, however, a number of places where archival material has been used and cited in the notes.

Archivio Centrale dello Stato, Rome (cited as ACS).

British Library, London.

Bundesarchiv-Militärarchiv, Freiburg im Breisgau (cited as BA/MA).

Imperial War Museum, London (Cited as IWM).

Kriegsarchiv, Vienna.

National Archives and Records Service, Washington, D.C. (cited as NARS). In addition to American records, the National Archives contain Microfilm Publication T-1022, Records of the German Navy, 1850–1945.

National Maritime Museum, Greenwich, England (cited as NMM).

Naval Historical Branch, Ministry of Defence, London.

Public Record Office, London (cited as PRO).

Service Historique de la Marine, Vincennes, France (cited as SHM).

Ufficio Storico della Marina Militare, Rome (cited as USM).

British Naval Staff Studies and Technical Histories

Copies of these studies may be found at the Naval Historical Branch, Ministry of Defence, London.

Historical Section. *The Defeat of the Enemy Attack on Shipping, 1939–1945.* 2 vols. (1956).

Naval Staff, Gunnery Division. *Grand Fleet Gunnery and Torpedo Memoranda on Naval Actions, 1914–1918* (April 1922).

Naval Staff, Training and Staff Duties Division. Historical Monographs. *Mediterranean Staff Papers Relating to Naval Operations from August 1917 to December 1918* (January 1920); *Naval Operations in Mesopotamia and the Persian Gulf* (July 1921); *The Eastern Squadrons, 1914* (April

1922); *The Baltic, 1914* (August 1922); *The Atlantic Ocean: From the Battle of the Falklands to May 1915* (October 1922); *The Mediterranean, 1914–1915* (March 1923); *Home Waters.* 9 vols. (1924–39).

Review of German Cruiser Warfare, 1914–1918 (1940).

Technical History Section, Admiralty. *TH 4. Aircraft v. Submarine. Submarine Campaign, 1918* (March 1919); *TH 7. The Anti-Submarine Division of the Naval Staff, December 1916–November 1918* (July 1919); *TH 8. Scandinavian and East Coast Convoy Systems, 1917–1918* (July 1919); *TH 14. The Atlantic Convoy System, 1917–1918* (October 1919); *TH 15. Convoy Statistics and Diagrams* (February 1920); *TH 30. Control of Mercantile Movements. Part I. Text* (August 1920); *TH 39. Miscellaneous Convoys* (June 1920).

Waters, D. W. "Notes on the Convoy System of Naval Warfare, Thirteenth to Twentieth Centuries." Part 2: "First World War, 1914–1918" (March 1960).

AUSTRIA-HUNGARY

Aichelburg, Wladimir. *Die Unterseeboote Österreich-Ungarns.* 2 vols. Graz: Akademische Druck-u. Verlagsanstalt, 1981.

Aichelburg, W., L. Baumgartner, F. F. Bilzer, G. Pawlik, F. Prasky, and E. Sieche. *Die 'Tegetthoff Klasse: Österreich-Ungarns grösste Schlachtschiffe.* Vienna: Arbeitsgemeinschaft für Österreichische Marinegeschichte, 1979.

Baumgartner, Lothar. "Österreich-Ungarns Dünkirchen? Ein Gegenüberstellung von Berichten zum Abtransport der serbischen Armee aus Albanien im Winter 1915/16." *Marine— Gestern, Heute* 6, no. 2 (June 1982): 46–53.

Baumgartner, Lothar, ed. *Denn Österreich lag einst am Meer: Das Leben des Admirals Alfred von Koudelka.* Graz: H. Weishaupt Verlag, 1987.

Bayer von Bayersburg, Heinrich. *Unter der k.u.k. Kriegsflagge, 1914–1918.* Vienna: Bergland Verlag, 1959.

———. *Österreichs Admirale und bedeutende Persönlichkeiten der k.u.k. Kriegsmarine, 1867–1918.* Vienna: Bergland Verlag, 1962.

———. *'Schiff verlassen!', 1914–1918.* Vienna: Bergland Verlag, 1965.

———. *Die Marinewaffen im Einsatz,1914–1918.* Vienna: Bergland Verlag, 1968.

Bilzer, Franz F. *Die Torpedoboote der k.u.k. Kriegsmarine von 1875–1918.* Graz: H. Weishaupt Verlag, 1984.

———. *Die Torpedoschiffe und Zerstörer der k.u.k. Kriegsmarine, 1867–1918.* Graz: H. Weishaupt Verlag, 1990.

Csikos, Stefan. "Der Schienmonitor der k.u.k. Donauflottille." *Marine—Gestern, Heute* 7, no. 4 (December 1980): 148–51.

Glaise-Horstenau, Edmund von, et al. *Österreich-Ungarns Letzter Krieg, 1914–1918.* 7 vols. and 10 supplements. Vienna: Verlag der Militärwissenschaftlichen Mitteilungen, 1930–38.

Greger, René. *Austro-Hungarian Warships of World War I.* London: Ian Allan, 1976.

————. "Wussten die Italiener davon?" *Marine Rundschau* 76, no. 7 (July 1979): 445–76.

Horthy, Admiral Nicholas. *Memoirs*. London: Hutchinson, 1956.

Lukas, Karl von. "Das Gefecht in der Otrantostrasse am 15 Mai 1917: Versuch einer kritischen Betrachtung." *Marine—Gestern, Heute* 4, no. 2 (June 1977): 34–40.

Martiny, Nikolaus von. *Bilddokumente aus Österreich-Ungarns Seekrieg, 1914–1918*. 2d ed. 2 vols. Graz: Akademische Druck-u. Verlagsanstalt, 1973.

Oedl, Franz. "50 Jahr Otranto." *Österreichische Militärische Zeitschrift* (1967): 244–48.

Pawlik, Georg, and Lothar Baumgartner. *S.M. Unterseeboote: Das k.u.k. Unterseebootswesen, 1907–1918*. Graz: H. Weishaupt Verlag, 1986.

Pawlik, Georg, Heinz Christ, and Herbert Winkler. *Die k.u.k. Donauflottille, 1870–1918*. Graz: H. Weishaupt Verlag, 1989.

Plaschka, Richard Georg. *Cattaro—Prag: Revolte und Revolution*. Graz and Cologne: Böhlau, 1963.

————. "Phänomene sozialer und nationaler Krisen in der k.u.k. Marine 1918." In Militärgeschichtliches Forschungsamt, Freiburg im Breisgau (ed), *Vorträge zur Militärgeschichte*. Vol. 2: *Menschenführung in der Marine*, 50–68. Herford and Bonn: E. S. Mittler, 1981.

Rauchensteiner, Manfred. "Austro-Hungarian Warships on the Danube: From the Beginning of the Nineteenth Century to World War I." In *Southeast European Maritime Commerce and Naval Policies from the Mid-Eighteenth Century to 1914*, edited by Apostolos E. Vacalopoulos, Constantinos D. Svolopoulos, and Béla K. Király, 153–73. Boulder, Colo.: Social Science Monographs, 1988.

Schupita, Peter. *Die k.u.k. Seeflieger: Chronik und Dokumentation der Österreichisch-ungarischen Marineluftwaffe*. Koblenz: Bernard & Graefe Verlag, 1983.

Sieche, Erwin. *Die 'Radetzky' Klasse: Österreich-Ungarns letzte Vor-Dreadnoughts*. Graz: H. Weishaupt Verlag, 1984.

Sokol, Anthony E. *The Imperial and Royal Austro-Hungarian Navy*. Annapolis, Md.: U.S. Naval Institute, 1968.

Sokol, Hans Hugo. *Österreich-Ungarns Seekrieg*. 2 vols. Vienna: Amalthea Verlag, 1933. Reprint. Graz: Akademische Druck-u. Verlagsanstalt, 1967.

Sokol, Hans Hugo. *Des Kaisers Seemacht: Die k.k. Österreichische Kriegsmarine, 1848 bis 1914*. Vienna: Amalthea Verlag, 1980.

Tomicich, Edgar. "Die Versenkung des k.u.k. Schlachtschiffes *Szent István* am 10 Juni 1918." *Marine—Gestern, Heute* 6, nos. 1 and 2 (March and June 1979).

Trapp, Georg von. *Bis zum letzten Flaggenschuss: Erinnerungen eines Österreichischen U-Boots-Kommandanten*. Salzburg and Leipzig: Verlag Anton Pustet, 1935.

Wagner, Anton. "Der k.u.k. Kriegsmarine im letzten Jahr des Ersten Weltkrieges." *Österreichische Militärische Zeitschrift* (1968): 409–15.

Wagner, Walter. *Die Obersten Behörden der k.u.k. Kriegsmarine, 1856–1918*. Vienna: Ferdinand Berger, 1961.

Winterhalder, Konter-Admiral Theodor. *Die Österreichisch-Ungarische Kriegsmarine im Weltkrieg*. Munich: J. F. Lehmanns Verlag, 1921.

Wulff, Olav. *Österreich-Ungarns Donauflottille in den Kriegsjahren 1914–1916*. Vienna: Verlag von L. W. Seidel, 1918.

Wulff, Vizeadmiral Olaf Richard. *Die Österreichisch-ungarische Flottille im Weltkrieg, 1914–1918*. Vienna and Leipzig: Wilhelm Braumüller, 1934.

FRANCE

Auphan, Amiral. *L'Honneur de servir: mémoires*. Paris: Editions France-Empire, 1978.

Béarn, Hector de. *Souvenirs d'un marin*. Geneva and Paris: La Palatine, 1960.

Bienaimé, Vice-Amiral. *La Guerre navale, 1914–1915: fautes et responsabilités*. Paris: Jules Tallandier, 1920.

Blois, Hubert de. *La Guerre des mines dans la marine française*. Brest and Paris: Editions de la Cité, 1982.

Cassar, George H. *The French and the Dardanelles*. London: Allen & Unwin, 1971.

Christienne, Charles, and Pierre Lissarague. *A History of French Military Aviation*. Translated by Francis Kianka. Washington, D.C.: Smithsonian Institution Press, 1986.

Coutau-Bégarie, Hervé. *Castex, le stratège inconnu*. Paris: Economica, 1985.

———. *La puissance maritime: Castex et la stratègie navale*. Paris: Fayard, 1985.

Dartige du Fournet, Vice-Amiral. *Souvenirs de guerre d'un amiral, 1914–1916*. Paris: Plon, 1920.

Debat, Georges. *Marine oblige*. Paris: Flammarion, 1974.

Decoux, Jean. *Adieu Marine*. Paris: Plon, 1957.

Docteur, Amiral Jules Théophile. *Carnet de bord, 1914–1919*. Paris: La Nouvelle Société d'Edition, 1932.

Dousset, Francis. *Les Navires de guerre français de 1850 à nos jours*. Brest and Paris: Editions de la Cité, 1975.

———. *Les Porte-avions français des origines (1911) à nos jours*. Brest and Paris: Editions de la Cité, 1978.

Ducasse, André. *Balkans 14–18 ou le Chaudron du Diable*. Paris: Laffont, 1964.

Dumas, Robert, and Jean Guiglini. *Les Cuirassés français de 23,500 tonnes*. 2 vols. Grenoble: Editions des 4 Seigneurs, 1980.

Forget, Contre-Amiral, et al. *En patrouille à la mer*. Paris: Payot, 1929.

France, Ministère de la Guerre, État-Major de l'Armée, Service Historique. *Les Armées françaises dans la grande guerre*. Tomb 8, 1er vol. Annexes. Paris: Imprimerie Nationale, 1924.

Guépratte, Vice-Amiral P.-E. *L'Expédition des Dardanelles, 1914–1915*. Paris: Payot, 1935.

Guerre navale racontée par nos amiraux, La. 4 vols. Paris: Schwarz, n.d.

Guichard, Louis. *Au large (1914–1918)*. Paris: La Renaissance du Livre, 1919.

Joffre, J. J. C. *Mémoires du Maréchal Joffre*. 2 vols. Paris: Plon, 1932.

King, Jere Clemens. *Generals and Politicians*. Berkeley and Los Angeles: University of California Press, 1951.

Labayle-Couhat, Jean. *French Warships of World War I*. London: Ian Allan, 1974.

La Bruyère, René. *Notre marine marchande pendant la guerre.* Paris: Payot, 1920.

Laurens, Adolphe. *Le Commandement naval en Méditerranée, 1914–1918.* Paris: Payot, 1931.

Le Comte, J. "L'affaire de la Zenta." *Revue maritime*, no. 204 (November 1963): 1254–59.

Le Masson, Henri. *Histoire du torpilleur en France.* Paris: Academie de la Marine, [1966].

———. *Du Nautilus (1800) au Redoutable.* Paris: Presses de la Cité, 1969.

———. *Propos maritimes.* Paris: Editions Maritimes et d'Outre-Mer, 1970.

Masson, Philippe. *La Marine française et la Mer Noire (1918–1919).* Paris: Publications de la Sorbonne, 1982.

———. *Histoire de la marine.* 2 vols. Paris: Lavauzelle, 1982–83.

Moreau, Laurent. *À bord du cuirassé "Gaulois": Dardanelles-Salonique, 1915–1916.* Paris: Payot, 1930.

Randier, Jean. *La Royale: l'éperon et la cuirasse.* Brest and Paris: Editions de la Cité, 1972.

Raphael-Leygues, Jacques. *Georges Leygues: Le "Père" de la marine.* Paris: Editions France-Empire, 1983.

Ropp. Theodore. *The Development of a Modern Navy: French Naval Policy, 1871–1904,* edited by Stephen S. Roberts. Annapolis, Md.: Naval Institute Press, 1987.

Roux, Louis. *La Marine marchande.* Paris: Payot, 1923.

Salaun, Vice-Amiral. *La Marine française.* Paris: Les Editions de France, 1934.

Taillemite, Étienne. *Dictionnaire des marins français.* Paris: Editions Maritimes et d'Outre-Mer, 1982.

———. *L'Histoire ignorée de la marine française.* Paris: Librairie Académique Perrin, 1988.

Tanenbaum, Jan Karl. *General Maurice Sarrail, 1856–1929.* Chapel Hill: University of North Carolina Press, 1974.

Thomazi, A. *La Guerre navale dans la zone des Armées du Nord.* Paris: Payot, 1924.

———. *La Guerre navale dans l'Adriatique.* Paris: Payot, 1925.

———. *La Guerre navale aux Dardanelles.* Paris: Payot, 1926.

———. *La Guerre navale dans la Méditerranée.* Paris: Payot, 1929.

Walser, Ray. *France's Search for a Battle Fleet: Naval Policy and Naval Power, 1898–1914.* New York: Garland, 1992.

GERMANY

Alexander, Roy. *The Cruise of the Raider "Wolfe."* New Haven: Yale University Press, 1939.

Assmann, Kurt. *Die Kämpfe der Kaiserlichen Marine in den Deutschen Kolonien.* Berlin: E. S. Mittler, 1935.

Bauer, Hermann. *Als Führer der U-Boote im Weltkrieg.* Leipzig: Koehler & Amelang, 1943.

———. *Reichsleitung und U-Bootseinsatz 1914 bis 1918.* Lippoldsberg: Klosterhaus Verlag, 1956.

Bergen, Claus, ed. *U-Boat Stories: Narratives of German U-Boat Sailors.* London: Constable, 1931.

Berghahn, Volker R. *Germany and the Approach of War in 1914.* New York: St. Martin's Press, 1973.

Burdick, Charles. *The Frustrated Raider: The Story of the German Cruiser Cormoran in World War I.* Carbondale: Southern Illinois University Press, 1979.

Chatterton, E. Keble. *The Sea-Raiders.* London: Hurst & Blackett, 1931.

Doenitz, Admiral Karl. *Memoirs: Ten Years and Twenty Days.* Cleveland and New York: World Publishing, 1959.

Dohna-Schlodien, Nikolaus Burggraf und Graf zu. *Der Möwe zweite Fahrt.* Gotha: Verlag Friedrich Andreas Perthes, 1919.

Falkenhayn, Erich von. *General Headquarters and Its Critical Decisions.* London: Hutchinson, 1919.

Firle, Rudolph, Heinrich Rollman, and Ernst von Gagern. *Der Krieg in der Ostsee.* 3 vols. Berlin (Vol. 3 Frankfurt-on-Main): E. S. Mittler, 1922–64.

Gagern, Ernst von. *See* Firle, Rudolph, *Der Krieg in der Ostee.*

Gayer, A. "Summary of German Submarine Operations in the Various Theaters of War from 1914 to 1918." *United States Naval Institute Proceedings* 52, no. 4 (April 1926): 621–59.

———. *Die Deutschen U-Boote in ihrer Kriegführung, 1914–1918.* Berlin: E. S. Mittler, 1930.

Gemzell, Carl-Axel. *Organization, Conflict and Innovation: A Study of German Naval Strategic Planning, 1888–1940.* Lund: Esselte Studium, 1973.

Gladisch, Walther. *See* Groos, Otto, and Walter Gladisch, *Der Krieg in der Nordsee.*

Görlitz, Walter, ed. *The Kaiser and His Court: The Diaries, Note Books and Letters of Admiral Georg Alexander von Müller, Chief of the Naval Cabinet, 1914–1918.* London: Macdonald, 1961.

Gröner, Erich. *German Warships, 1815–1945.* Vol. 1, *Major Surface Vessels.* Rev. Eng. ed. Annapolis, Md.: Naval Institute Press, 1990.

Groos, Otto, and Walther Gladisch. *Der Krieg in der Nordsee.* 7 vols. Berlin (Vol. 7 Frankfurt-on-Main): E. S. Mittler, 1920–65.

Hase, Commander Georg von. *Kiel & Jutland.* London: Skeffington & Son, [1921].

Hersing, Otto. *U.21 rettet die Dardanellen.* Zurich, Leipzig, and Vienna: Amalthea Verlag, 1932.

Herwig, Holger H. *The German Naval Officer Corps: A Social and Political History, 1890–1918.* Oxford: Clarendon Press, 1973.

———. *The Politics of Frustration: The United States in German Naval Planning, 1889–1941.* Boston: Little, Brown, 1976.

———. *"Luxury Fleet": The Imperial German Navy, 1888–1918.* London: Allen & Unwin, 1980.

Herzog, Bodo. *60 Jahre Deutsche U-Boote, 1906–1966.* Munich: J. F. Lehmanns Verlag, 1968.

Herzog, Bodo, and Günter Schomaekers. *Ritter Der Tiefe—Graue Wölfe: Die erfolgreichsten U-Boot-Kommandanten der Welt des Ersten und Zweiten Weltkrieges.* Munich: Verlag Welsermühl, 1965.

Hohenzollern, Joseph, Prince of. *Emden: My Experiences in S.M.S. Emden.* London: Herbert Jenkins, 1928.

Hopman, Admiral. *Das Kriegstagebuch eines deutschen Seeoffiziers.* Berlin: August Scherl, [1925].

Horn, Daniel. *The German Naval Mutinies of World War I.* New Brunswick, N.J.: Rutgers University Press, 1969.

Hubatsch, Walther. *Die Ära Tirpitz: Studien zur deutschen Marinepolitik 1890–1918.* Göttingen: Musterschmidt Verlag, 1955.

———. *Die Admiralstab und Die Obersten Marinebehörden in Deutschland, 1848–1945.* Frankfurt-on-Main: Bernard & Graefe Verlag, 1958.

Imrie, Alex. *German Naval Air Service.* London: Arms and Armour, 1989.

Jeschke, Hubert. *U-Boottaktik: Zur deutschen U-Boottaktik, 1900–1945.* Freiburg: Verlag Romach, 1972.

Kennedy, Paul M. "The Development of German Naval Operations Plans against England, 1896–1914." In *The War Plans of the Great Powers, 1880–1914,* edited by Paul M. Kennedy. London: Allen & Unwin, 1979.

Kopp, Georg. *Two Lone Ships.* Eng. trans. London: Hutchinson, 1931.

Köppen, Paul. *Die Überwasserstreitkräfte und ihr Technik.* Berlin: E. S. Mittler, 1930.

Lambi, Ivo Nikolai. *The Navy and German Power Politics, 1862–1914.* Boston: Allen & Unwin, 1984.

Lochner, R. K. *The Last Gentleman-of-War: The Raider Exploits of the Cruiser Emden.* Annapolis, Md.: Naval Institute Press, 1988.

Lorey, Hermann. *Der Krieg in den türkischen Gewässern.* 2 vols. Berlin: E. S. Mittler, 1928–38.

Luckner, Felix Graf von. *Seeteufel: Abenteuer aus meinen Leben.* Leipzig: Koehler, 1922.

Lundeberg, Philip K. "The German Naval Critique of the U-boat Campaign, 1915–1918." *Military Affairs* 27, no. 3 (Fall 1983): 105–18.

Mäkelä, Matti E. *Souchon der Goebenadmiral.* Braunschweig: Vieweg, 1936.

———. *Auf den Spuren der Goeben.* Munich: Bernard & Graefe Verlag, 1979.

———. *Das Geheimnis der 'Magdeburg.'* Koblenz: Bernard & Graefe Verlag, 1984.

Mantey, Vice Amiral E. von. *Les Marins allemands au combat.* Paris: Payot, 1930.

Messimer, Dwight R. *The Merchant U-Boat: Adventures of the Deutschland, 1916–1918.* Annapolis, Md.: Naval Institute Press, 1988.

Michelsen, Andreas. *La Guerre sous-marine (1914–1918).* Paris: Payot, 1928.

Moraht, Robert. *Werwolf der Meere: U.64 jagt den Feind.* Berlin: Vorhut Verlag Otto Schlegel, 1933.

Mücke, Kapitänleutnant Hellmuth von. *The 'Ayesha': Being the Adventure of the Landing Squad of the Emden.* Boston: Ritter & Co., 1917.

Niezychowski, Alfred von. *The Cruise of the Kronprinz Wilhelm.* Garden City, N.Y.: Doubleday, Doran, 1931.

Philbin, Tobias R. *Admiral von Hipper: The Inconvenient Hero.* Amsterdam: B. R. Grüner, 1982.

Pohl, Admiral Hugo von. *Aus Aufzeichnungen und Briefen während der Kriegszeit.* Berlin: Karl Siegismund, 1920.

Raeder, E., and Eberhard von Mantey. *Der Kreuzerkrieg in den ausländischen Gewässern.* 3 vols. Berlin: E. S. Mittler, 1922–37.

Reichskriegsministeriums. *Der Weltkrieg, 1914–1918.* 15 vols. Berlin: E. S. Mittler, 1925–42.

Ritter, Gerhard. *The Sword and the Scepter: The Problem of Militarism in Germany.* 4 vols. Coral Gables: University of Miami Press, 1969–73.

Ritter, Paul. *Ubootsgeist: Abenteuer und Fahrten im Mittelmeer.* Leipzig: Verlag K. F. Koehler, 1935.

Robinson, Douglas H. *The Zeppelin in Combat: A History of the German Naval Airship Division, 1912–1918.* 3d ed. Seattle: University of Washington Press, 1980.

Rollman, Heinrich. See Firle, Rudolph, *Der Krieg in der Ostee.*

Rössler, Eberhard. *The U-Boat: The Evolution and Technical History of German Submarines.* Eng. trans. London and Melbourne: Arms and Armour Press, 1981.

Ruge, Friedrich. *In vier Marinen.* Munich: Bernard & Graefe Verlag, 1979.

Scheer, Admiral. *Germany's High Sea Fleet in the World War.* London: Cassell, 1919.

Schmalenbach, Paul. *German Raiders: A History of Auxiliary Cruisers of the German Navy, 1895–1945.* Cambridge: Patrick Stephens, 1979.

Schmidtke, Hermann. *Völkerringen um die Donau.* Berlin: Alfred Marchwinski, 1927.

Schulz, Paul. *In U-Boot durch die Weltmeere.* Bielefeld and Leipzig: Velhagen & Klasing, 1931.

Spindler, Rear Admiral Arno. "The Value of the Submarine in Naval Warfare." *U.S. Naval Institute Proceedings* 52, no. 5 (May 1926): 835–54.

———. *Der Handelskrieg mit U-Booten.* 5 vols. Berlin (Vol. 5 Frankfurt-on-Main): E. S. Mittler, 1932–66.

Stegemann, Bernd. *Die Deutsche Marinepolitik, 1916–1918.* Berlin: Duncker & Humblot, 1970.

Steinberg, Jonathan. *Yesterday's Deterrent: Tirpitz and the Birth of the German Battle Fleet.* London: Macdonald, 1965.

Taylor, John C. *German Warships of World War I.* London: Ian Allan, 1969.

Thomas, Lowell. *Count Luckner: The Sea Devil.* Garden City, N.Y.: Doubleday, Page, 1927.

———. *Raiders of the Deep.* Garden City, N.Y.: Doubleday, Doran, 1928.

Tirpitz, Admiral Alfred von. *My Memoirs.* 2 vols. New York: Dodd Mead, 1919.

———. *Deutsche Ohnemachtspolitik im Weltkriege.* Hamburg and Berlin: Hanseatische Verlagsanstalt, 1926.

Trumpener, Ulrich. "The Escape of the *Goeben* and *Breslau*: A Reassessment." *Canadian Journal of History* 6 (1971): 171–87.

Valentiner, Max. *Der Schrecken der Meere: Meine U-Boot Abenteuer.* Zurich, Leipzig, and Vienna: Amalthea Verlag, 1931.

Van der Vat, Dan. *Gentlemen of War: The Amazing Story of Captain Karl von Müller and the S.M.S. Emden.* New York: William Morrow, 1984.

Waldeyer-Hartz, Hugo von. *Admiral von Hipper.* London: Rich & Cowan, 1933.

Wegener, Vice Admiral Wolfgang. *The Naval Strategy of the World War.* Translated by Holger H. Herwig. Annapolis, Md.: Naval Institute Press, 1989.

Weir, Gary E. *Building the Kaiser's Navy: The Imperial Naval Office and German Industry in the von Tirpitz Era, 1890–1919.* Annapolis, Md.: Naval Institute Press, 1992.

Weizsäcker, Ernst von. *Memoirs of Ernst von Weizsäcker.* Chicago: Henry Regnery, 1951.

GREAT BRITAIN

Aspinall-Oglander, Cecil F. *History of the Great War, Military Operations: Gallipoli.* 2 vols in 4. London: Heinemann, 1929–32.

———. *Roger Keyes.* London: The Hogarth Press, 1951.

Bacon, Admiral Sir Reginald. *The Dover Patrol, 1915–1917.* 2 vols. London: Hutchinson, 1919.

———. *The Concise Story of the Dover Patrol.* London: Hutchinson, 1932.

———. *From 1900 Onward.* London: Hutchinson, 1940.

Bayly, Admiral Sir Lewis. *Pull Together! The Memoirs of Admiral Sir Lewis Bayly.* London: Harrap, 1939.

Beesly, Patrick. *Very Special Admiral: The Life of Admiral J.H. Godfrey, CB.* London: Hamish Hamilton, 1980.

————. *Room 40: British Naval Intelligence, 1914–1918.* London: Hamish Hamilton, 1982.

Bell, A. C. *A History of the Blockade of Germany and of the Countries Associated with Her in the Great War, Austria-Hungary, Bulgaria and Turkey.* London: HMSO, 1937 (released to the public, 1961).

Benn, Captain Wedgwood. *In the Side Shows.* London: Hodder & Stoughton, 1919.

Brocklebank, Joan, ed. *Tenth Cruiser Squadron Northern Patrol: From the diaries and letters of Captain H.C.R. Brocklebank, CBE, RN.* Affpudle, Dorset: Privately printed, 1974.

Brodie, C.G. *Forlorn Hope 1915: The Submarine Passage of the Dardanelles.* London: W.J. Bryce, 1956.

Burt, R. A. *British Battleships of World War One.* London: Arms & Armour, 1986.

Buxton, Ian. *Big Gun Monitors.* Tynemouth, Northumberland: World Ship Society and Trident Books, 1978.

Campbell, Rear Admiral Gordon. *My Mystery Ships.* London: Hodder & Stoughton, 1928.

Chalmers, Rear Admiral W. S. *The Life and Letters of David, Earl Beatty.* London: Hodder & Stoughton, 1951.

Chatfield, Admiral of the Fleet Lord. *The Navy and Defence.* London: William Heinemann, 1942.

Chatterton, E. Keble. *Q-Ships and Their Story.* London: Sidgwick & Jackson, 1922.

————. *The Auxiliary Patrol.* London: Sidgwick & Jackson, 1923.

————. *The Big Blockade.* London: Hurst & Blackett, [1932].

————. *Danger Zone: The Story of the Queenstown Command.* London: Rich & Cowan, 1934.

————. *Seas of Adventures: The Story of the Naval Operations in the Mediterranean, Adriatic and Aegean.* London: Hurst & Blackett, 1936.

————. *Fighting the U-Boats.* London: Hurst & Blackett, 1942.

————. *Beating the U-Boats.* London: Hurst & Blackett, 1943.

Churchill, Winston S. *The World Crisis.* 5 vols. in 6. New York: Scribner's, 1923–31.

Corbett, Julian S., and Henry Newbolt. *History of the Great War: Naval Operations.* 5 vols in 9. London: Longmans, Green, 1920–31.

Cork and Orrery, Admiral of the Fleet, Earl of. *My Naval Life, 1886–1941.* London: Hutchinson, 1942.

Cronin, Dick. *Royal Navy Shipboard Aircraft Developments, 1912–1931.* Tonbridge, Kent: Air Britain, 1990.

Cunningham of Hyndhope, Viscount. *A Sailor's Odyssey.* London: Hutchinson, 1951.

De Chair, Admiral Sir Dudley. *The Sea Is Strong.* London: Harrap, 1961.

Dewar, Vice Admiral K. G. B. *The Navy from Within.* London: Gollancz, 1939.

Dittmar, F. J., and J. J. Colledge. *British Warships, 1914–1919.* London: Ian Allan, 1972.

Doughty, Martin. *Merchant Shipping and War: A Study in Defence Planning in Twentieth Century Britain.* London: Royal Historical Society, 1982.

Edwards, Lieutenant Commander Kenneth. *We Dive at Dawn.* London: Rich & Cowan, 1939.

Elliott, Peter. *The Cross and the Ensign: A Naval History of Malta, 1798–1979.* Cambridge: Patrick Stephens, 1980.

Fairbanks, Charles H., Jr. "The Origins of the *Dreadnought* Revolution: A Historiographical Essay," *International History Review* 13, no. 2 (May 1991): 246–72.

Fayle, C. Ernest. *Seaborne Trade.* 3 vols. London: John Murray, 1920–24.

Fitch, Harry. *My Mis-Spent Youth: A Naval Journal.* London: Macmillan, 1937.

Fremantle, Admiral Sir Sydney Robert. *My Naval Career, 1880–1928.* London: Hutchinson, 1949.

French, David. *British Strategy and War Aims, 1914–1916.* London: Allen & Unwin, 1986.

Friedman, Norman. *British Carrier Aviation: The Evolution of the Ships and Their Aircraft.* Annapolis, Md.: Naval Institute Press, 1988.

Gamble, C. F. Snowden. *The Story of a North Sea Air Station.* London: Oxford University Press, 1928. Reprint. Neville Spearman, 1967.

Gilbert, Martin S. *Winston S. Churchill.* Vol. 3: *The Challenge of War, 1914–1916.* Boston: Houghton Mifflin, 1971.

Godfrey, J. H. *The Naval Memoirs of Admiral J. H. Godfrey.* 7 vols. in 10. Hailsham: Privately printed, 1964–66.

Goldrick, James. *The King's Ships Were at Sea: The War in the North Sea August 1914–February 1915.* Annapolis, Md.: Naval Institute Press, 1984.

Goodenough, Admiral Sir William E. *A Rough Record.* London: Hutchinson, 1943.

Gretton, Vice Admiral Sir Peter. *Winston Churchill and the Royal Navy.* New York: Coward-McCann, 1969.

Guinn, Paul. *British Strategy and Politics, 1914–1918.* London: Oxford University Press, 1965.

Hackmann, Willem. *Seek & Strike: Sonar, Anti-Submarine Warfare and the Royal Navy, 1914–54.* London: HMSO, 1984.

Halpern, Paul G., ed. *The Keyes Papers.* Vol. 1, *1914–1918.* Publications of the Navy Records Society, Vol. 117. London: Navy Records Society, 1972. Reprint. London: Allen & Unwin, 1979.

———, ed. *The Keyes Papers.* Vol. 2, *1919–1938.* Publications of the Navy Records Society, Vol. 121. London: Allen & Unwin, 1980.

———, ed. "De Robeck and the Dardanelles Campaign." In *The Naval Miscellany, Volume V,* gen. ed. N. A. M. Rodger, 439–98. Publications of the Navy Records Society, Vol. 125. London: Allen & Unwin for the Navy Records Society, 1984.

———, ed. *The Royal Navy in the Mediterranean, 1915–1918.* Publications of the Navy Records Society, Vol. 126. Aldershot: Temple Smith for the Navy Records Society, 1987.

Hampshire, A. Cecil. *The Phantom Fleet.* London: William Kimber, 1960.

———. *The Blockaders.* London: William Kimber, 1980.

Hankey, Lord. *The Supreme Command, 1914–1918.* 2 vols. London: Allen & Unwin, 1961.

Hunt, Barry D. *Sailor-Scholar: Admiral Sir Herbert Richmond.* Waterloo, Ont.: Wilfred Laurier University Press, 1982.

Hurd, Archibald. *The Merchant Navy.* 3 vols. London: John Murray, 1921–29.

James, Admiral Sir William. *The Sky Was Always Blue*. London: Methuen, 1951.

——. *The Eyes of the Navy: A Biographical Study of Admiral Sir Reginald Hall*. London: Methuen, 1955.

——. *A Great Seaman: The Life of Admiral of the Fleet Henry F. Oliver*. London: Witherby, 1956.

Jellicoe, Admiral of the Fleet, Earl. *The Grand Fleet, 1914–16: Its Creation, Development and Work*. London: Cassell, 1919.

——. *The Crisis of the Naval War*. London: Cassell, 1920.

——. *The Submarine Peril*. London: Cassell, 1931.

Kemp, Lieutenant Commander P. K. *Fleet Air Arm*. London: Herbert Jenkins, 1954.

Kennedy, Paul M. *The Rise and Fall of British Naval Mastery*. New York: Scribner's, 1976.

Kenworthy, Lieutenant Commander, Hon. J. M. *Sailors, Statesmen—And Others: An Autobiography*. London: Rich & Cowan, 1933.

Kerr, Admiral Mark. *Land, Sea and Air*. London: Longmans, Green, 1927.

——. *The Navy in My Time*. London: Rich & Cowan, 1933.

Keyes, Roger. *The Naval Memoirs*. 2 vols. London: Thornton Butterworth, 1934–35.

King-Hall, Commander Stephen. *A North Sea Diary, 1914–1918*. London: Newnes, [1936]. Originally published under pseudonym Etienne as *A Naval Lieutenant, 1914–1918*. London: Methuen, 1919.

Leslie, Shane. *Long Shadows*. London: John Murray, 1966.

Lloyd George, David. *War Memoirs of David Lloyd George*. 2d ed. 2 vols. London: Odhams, [1936].

Lumby, E. W. R., ed. *Policy and Operations in the Mediterranean, 1912–1914*. Publications of the Navy Records Society, Vol. 115. London: Navy Records Society, 1970.

Mackay, Ruddock F. *Fisher of Kilverstone*. Oxford: Clarendon Press, 1973.

Mackenzie, Compton. *Gallipoli Memories*. London: Cassell, 1929.

March, Edgar J. *British Destroyers: A History of Development, 1892–1953*. London: Seeley Service, 1966.

Marder, Arthur J. *The Anatomy of British Sea Power: A History of British Naval Policy in the Pre-Dreadnought Era, 1880–1905*. New York: Knopf, 1940. Reprint. Hamden, Conn.: Archon Books, 1964.

——. *From the Dardanelles to Oran*. London: Oxford University Press, 1974.

——. *From the Dreadnought to Scapa Flow: The Royal Navy in the Fisher Era, 1904–1919*. 5 vols. London: Oxford University Press, 1961–70.

——. *Portrait of an Admiral: The Life and Papers of Sir Herbert Richmond*. London: Cape, 1952.

——, ed. *Fear God and Dread Nought: the Correspondence of Admiral of the Fleet Lord Fisher of Kilverstone*. 3 vols. London: Cape, 1952–59.

Myres, J. N. L. *Commander J. L. Myres, RNVR: The Blackbeard of the Aegean*. London: Leopard's Head Press, 1980.

Padfield, Peter. *Aim Straight: A Biography of Admiral Sir Percy Scott*. London: Hodder & Stoughton, 1966.

Parkes, Oscar. *British Battleships*. 2d ed. London: Seeley Service, 1966.

Patterson, A. Temple. *Jellicoe: A Biography*. London: Macmillan, 1969.

———. *Tyrwhitt of the Harwich Force*. London: Macdonald, 1973.

———, ed. *The Jellicoe Papers*. 2 vols. Publications of the Navy Records Society, Vols. 108 and 111. London: Navy Records Society, 1966–68.

Plumridge, John H. *Hospital Ships and Ambulance Trains*. London: Seeley Service, 1975.

Poolman, Kenneth. *Armed Merchant Cruisers*. London: Leo Cooper, 1985.

Popham, Hugh. *Into Wind: A History of British Naval Flying*. London: Hamish Hamilton, 1969.

Raleigh, Sir Walter, and H. A. Jones. *The War in the Air*. 6 vols. Oxford: Clarendon Press, 1922–37.

Ranft, B. M., ed. *The Beatty Papers*. Vol. 1, *1902–1918*. Publications of the Navy Records Society, Vol. 128. Aldershot: Scolar Press fror the Navy Records Society, 1989.

Ritchie, Carson I. A. *Q-Ships*. Lavenham, Suffolk: Terence Dalton, 1985.

Rodger, N. A. M. *The Admiralty*. Lavenham, Suffolk: Terence Dalton, 1979.

Roskill, Stephen W. *Churchill and the Admirals*. London: Collins, 1977.

———. "The Dismissal of Admiral Jellicoe." In *1914: The Coming of the First World War*, edited by Walter Laqueur and George L. Mosse, 204–28. Reprint. New York: Harper & Row, 1966.

———, ed. *Documents Relating to the Naval Air Service*. Vol. 1, *1908–1918*. Publications of the Navy Records Society, Vol. 113. London: The Navy Records Society, 1969.

———. *Earl Beatty: The Last Naval Hero*. London: Collins, 1980.

———. *Hankey: Man of Secrets*. Vol. 1, *1877–1918*. London: Collins, 1970.

———. *Naval Policy Between the Wars*. Vol. 1, *The Period of Anglo-American Antagonism, 1919–1929*. London: Collins, 1968.

———. *The Strategy of Sea Power*. London: Collins, 1962.

———. "The U-Boat Campaign of 1917 and Third Ypres." *Journal of the Royal United Service Institution* 104, no. 616 (November 1959): 440–42.

Salter, J. A. *Allied Shipping Control: An Experiment in International Administration*. Oxford: Clarendon Press, 1921.

Samson, Air Commodore Charles Rumney. *Fights and Flights*. London: Ernest Benn, 1930.

Schoultz, Commodore G. von. *With the British Battle Fleet*. London: Hutchinson, [1925].

Simpson, Michael, ed. *Anglo-American Naval Relations, 1917–1919*. Publications of the Navy Records Society, Vol. 130. Aldershot: Scholar Press for the Navy Records Society, 1991.

Sueter, Rear Admiral Murray F. *Airmen or Noahs*. London: Putnam, 1928.

Sumida, Jon Tetsuro. *In Defence of Naval Supremacy: Finance, Technology and British Naval Policy, 1889–1914*. Boston: Unwin Hyman, 1989.

———, ed. *The Pollen Papers, 1901–1916*. Publications of the Navy Records Society, Vol. 124. London: Allen & Unwin for the Navy Records Society, 1984.

Taffrail [Captain Taprell Dorling]. *Endless Story: Being an Account of the Work of the Destroyers, Flotilla Leaders, Torpedo-Boats and Patrol Boats in the Great War*. London: Hodder & Stoughton, 1931.

———. *Swept Channels: Being an Account of the Work of the Minesweepers in the Great War*. London: Hodder & Stoughton, 1935.

Thetford, Owen. *British Naval Aircraft since 1912.* 4th rev. ed. London: Putnam, 1977.

Tupper, Admiral Sir Reginald. *Reminiscences.* London: Jarrolds, [1929].

Tweedie, Admiral Sir Hugh. *The Story of a Naval Life.* London: Rich & Cowan, 1939.

Usborne, Vice Admiral C. V. *Blast and Counterblast: A Naval Impression of the War.* London: John Murray, 1935.

————. *Smoke on the Horizon: Mediterranean Fighting, 1914–1918.* London: Hodder & Stoughton, 1933.

Weldon, L. B. *"Hard Lying": Eastern Mediterranean, 1914–1919.* London: Herbert Jenkins, 1925.

Wester Wemyss, Admiral of the Fleet, Lord. *The Navy in the Dardanelles Campaign.* London: Hodder & Stoughton, 1924.

Wester Wemyss, Lady. *The Life and Letters of Lord Wester Wemyss.* London: Eyre & Spottiswoode, 1935.

Winton, John. *Convoy: The Defence of Sea Trade, 1890–1990.* London: Michael Joseph, 1983.

————. *Jellicoe.* London: Michael Joseph, 1981.

"Yamew." "Mediterranean Convoys, 1918." *Naval Review* 53, no. 3 (July 1965): 241–45.

Young, Filson. *With Beatty in the North Sea.* Boston: Little, Brown, 1921. British edition titled *With the Battle Cruisers.*

ITALY

Bagnasco, Erminio. *I Mas e le Motosiluranti italiane, 1906–1966.* Rome: Ufficio Storico della Marina Militare, 1967.

Bargoni, Franco. *Esploratori, fregate, corvette ed avvisi italiani.* Rome: Ufficio Storico della Marina Militare, 1970.

Bernotti, Romeo. *Cinquant'anni nella marina militare.* Milan: Mursia, 1971.

Bravetta, Ettore. *La grande guerra sul mare.* 2 vols. Milan: Mondadori, 1925.

Caraccioli, Mario. *L'Italia e i suoi alleati nella grande guerra.* Milan: Mondadori, 1932.

Dainelli, Giotti. *Il Duca degli Abruzzi: le imprese dell'ultimo grande esploratore italiano.* Turin: Unione Tipografico, 1967.

Ferrante, Ezio. *Il Grande Ammiraglio Paolo Thaon di Revel.* Supplement to *Rivista Marittima* 8/9. Rome: *Rivista Marittima,* 1989.

————. *Il Mediterraneo nella coscienza nazionale.* Supplement to *Rivista Marittima* 5. Rome: *Rivista Marittima,* 1987.

————. *La Grande Guerra in Adriatico: nel lxx anniversario della vittoria.* Rome: Ufficio Storico della Marina Militare, 1987.

Fioravanzo, Giuseppe, C. M. Pollina, G. Riccardi, and F. Gnifetti. *I cacciatorpediniere italiani, 1900–1966.* Rome: Ufficio Storico della Marina Militare, 1969.

Fraccaroli, Aldo. *Italian Warships of World War I.* London: Ian Allan, 1970.

Gabriele, Mariano. *Le convenzioni navali della Triplice.* Rome: Ufficio Storico della Marina Militare, 1969.

Gabriele, Mariano, and Guiliano Friz. *La politica navale italiana dal 1885 al 1915*. Rome: Ufficio Storico della Marina Militare, 1982.

Giamberardino, Oscar di. *L'Ammiraglio Millo*. Livorno: Società Editrice Tirrena, 1950.

Giorgerini, Giorgio. *Gli incrociatori italiani, 1861–1964*. Rome: Ufficio Storico della Marina Militare, 1964.

Giorgerini, Giorgio, and Augusto Nanni. *Le navi di linea italiane (1861–1961)*. Rome: Ufficio Storico della Marina Militare, 1962.

Manfroni, Camillo. *Storia della marina italiana durante la guerra mondiale, 1914–1918*. 2d ed. Bologna: Nicola Zanichelli, 1925.

———. *Nostri alleati navali: ricordi della guerra Adriatica, 1915–1918*. Milan: Mondadori, 1927.

Morabito, Nicola. *La marina italiana in guerra, 1915–1918*. Milan: Omero Maranzoni, 1934.

Pieri, P. *L'Italia nella prima guerra mondiale*. Turin: Einauldi, 1965.

Po, Guido. *Il Grande Ammiraglio Paolo Thaon di Revel*. Turin: S. Lattes, 1936.

Pollina, Paolo M. *I sommergibili italiani, 1895–1962*. Rome: Ufficio Storico della Marina Militare, 1963.

———. *Le torpediniere italiane, 1881–1964*. Rome: Ufficio Storico della Marina Militare, 1964.

Ufficio Storico. *Occupazione dell'Isola di Pelagosa*. Chronistoria Documentata della Guerra Marittima Italo-Austriaca, 1915–1918. Collezione: L'impiego delle Forze Navali-Operazioni, Fascicolo 8. (Rome, June 1922).

Ufficio Storico dell R. Marina. *La marina italiana nella grande guerra*. 8 vols. Florence: Vallecchi, 1935–42.

Ufficio Storico della Marina [Ammiraglio di Squadra Giuseppe Fioravanzo]. *La marina militare nel suo primo secolo di vita (1861–1961)*. Rome: Ufficio Storico della Marina Militare, 1961.

RUSSIA

Arbeitskreis für Wehrforschung. *Das deutsche Bild der russischen und sowjetischen Marine*. Beiheft 7/8 der *Marine Rundschau*. Frankfurt-on-Main: E. S. Mittler, 1962.

Basily, Nicolas de. *Memoirs: Diplomat of Imperial Russia, 1903–1917*. Stanford, Calif.: Hoover Institution Press, 1973.

Cromie, F. N. A. *Letters on Russian Affairs from Captain F.N.A. Cromie*. Privately published, 1919.

Crosley, Pauline. *Intimate Letters from Petrograd*. New York: E. P. Dutton, 1920.

Giorgerini, Giorgio. *Cenni di Storia e Politica Navale Russa*. Supplement to *Rivista Marittima*. 2d rev. ed. Rome: *Rivista Marittima*, 1986.

Graf, H. *The Russian Navy in War and Revolution*. Munich: Oldenbourg, 1923.

Greger, René. *Die Russische Flotte im Ersten Weltkrieg, 1914–1917*. Munich: J. F. Lehmanns Verlag, 1970.

Mawdsley, Evan. *The Russian Revolution and the Baltic Fleet*. New York: Barnes & Noble, 1978.

Monasterev, N. *Sur Trois Mers (La marine russe dans la guerre mondiale d'après les documents officiels et les récits des combattants)*. Tunis: E. Saliba, 1932.

Monasterev, N. *La marina russa nella guerra mondiale, 1914–1917*. Florence: Vallecchi, 1934.

Nekrasov, George. *North of Gallipoli: The Black Sea Fleet at War, 1914–1917*. Boulder, Colo.: East European Monographs, 1992.

Pavlovich, Rear Admiral Professor N. B., ed. *The Fleet in the First World War*. Vol. 1, *Operations of the Russian Fleet*. Eng. trans. New Delhi: Amerind Publishing for the Smithsonian Institution and National Science Foundation, Washington, D.C., 1979.

Polmar, Norman, and Jurrien Noot. *Submarines of the Russian and Soviet Navies, 1718–1990*. Annapolis, Md.: Naval Institute Press, 1991.

Raskolnikov, F. F. *Kronstadt and Petrograd in 1917*. Eng. trans. London: New Park, 1982.

Saul, Norman E. *Sailors in Revolt: The Russian Baltic Fleet in 1917*. Lawrence: Regents Press of Kansas, 1978.

Watts, Anthony J. *The Imperial Russian Navy*. London: Arms & Armour, 1990.

Westwood, John N. "The End of the *Imperatritsa Mariia*: Negligence or Sabotage?" *Canadian Slavonic Papers* 21, no. 1 (March 1979): 66–75.

White, D. Fedotoff. *Survival through War and Revolution in Russia*. Philadelphia: University of Pennsylvania Press, 1939.

Wilson, Michael. *Baltic Assignment: British Submariners in Russia, 1914–1919*. London: Leo Cooper, 1985.

Woodward, David. *The Russians at Sea*. London: William Kimber, 1965.

UNITED STATES OF AMERICA

Alden, Carroll Storrs. "American Submarine Operations in the War." *United States Naval Institute Proceedings* 46, nos. 6 and 7. (June–July 1920): 811–50, 1013–48.

Alden, John D. *Flush Decks & Four Pipes*. Rev. ed. Annapolis, Md.: Naval Institute Press, 1989.

Allard, Dean C. "Anglo-American Naval Differences During World War I." *Military Affairs* (April 1980): 75–81.

Beers, Henry P. *U.S. Naval Forces in North Russia (Archangel and Murmansk), 1918–1919*. Washington, D.C.: Office of Records Administration, Navy Department, 1943.

Belknap, Captain Reginald R. "The Yankee Mining Squadron or Laying the North Sea Barrage." *United States Naval Institute Proceedings* 45, no. 12; 46, nos. 1 and 2 (December 1919–February 1920): 1973–2009, 5–32, 197–230.

Braisted, William Reynolds. *The United States Navy in the Pacific, 1909–1922*. Austin: University of Texas Press, 1971.

Breckel, Lieutenant H. F. "The Suicide Flotilla." *United States Naval Institute Proceedings* 53, no. 6 (June 1927): 661–70.

Celephane, Lewis P. *History of the Naval Overseas Transportation Service in World War I*. Washington, D.C.: Naval History Division, 1969.

Clark, William Bell. *When the U-Boats Came to America.* Boston: Houghton Mifflin, 1929.

Coletta, Paolo E. *Admiral Bradley A. Fiske and the American Navy.* Lawrence: Regents Press of Kansas, 1979.

Cronon, E. David, ed. *The Cabinet Papers of Josephus Daniels, 1913–21.* Lincoln: University of Nebraska Press, 1963.

Crowell, Benedict, and Robert Forrest Wilson. *The Road to France: The Transportation of Troops and Military Supplies.* 2 vols. New Haven: Yale University Press, 1921.

DeLany, Vice Admiral Walter S. *Bayly's Navy.* Washington, D.C.: Naval Historical Foundation, 1980.

Dorwart, Jeffrey M. *The Office of Naval Intelligence: The Birth of America's First Intelligence Agency, 1865–1918.* Annapolis, Md.: Naval Institute Press, 1979.

Edwards, Lieutenant Commander W. Atlee. "The U.S. Naval Air Force in Action, 1917–1918." *United States Naval Institute Proceedings* 48, no. 11 (November 1922): 1863–82.

Freidel, Frank. *Franklin D. Roosevelt: The Apprenticeship.* Boston: Little, Brown, 1952.

Friedman, Norman. *U.S. Battleships: An Illustrated Design History.* Annapolis, Md.: Naval Institute Press, 1985.

———. *U.S. Destroyers: An Illustrated Design History.* Annapolis, Md.: Naval Institute Press, 1982.

Frothingham, Thomas G. *The Naval History of the World War.* 3 vols. Cambridge, Mass.: Military Historical Society of Massachusetts, 1924–26. Reprint. Freeport, N.Y.: Books for Libraries Press, 1971.

Gleaves, Vice Admiral Albert. *A History of the Transport Service.* New York: George H. Doran, 1921.

———. *The Admiral: The Memoirs of Albert Gleaves, USN.* Pasadena, Calif.: Hope Publishing House, 1985.

Hurley, Edward N. *The Bridge to France.* Philadelphia: J. B. Lippincott, 1927.

Klachko, Mary (with David F. Trask). *Admiral William Shepherd Benson: First Chief of Naval Operations.* Annapolis, Md.: Naval Institute Press, 1987.

Knox, Dudley W. *A History of the United States Navy.* 2d ed. New York: G. P. Putnam's Sons, 1948.

Leighton, John Langdon. *Simsadus: London.* New York: Henry Holt, 1920.

May, Ernest R. *The World War and American Isolation, 1914–1917.* Cambridge: Harvard University Press, 1959. Reprint. Chicago: Quadrangle Books, 1966.

Melia, Tamara Moser. *"Damn the Torpedoes": A Short History of U.S. Naval Mine Countermeasures, 1777–1991.* Washington, D.C.: Naval Historical Center, 1991.

Millholland, Ray. *The Splinter Fleet of the Otranto Barrage.* London: Cresset Press, [1936].

Moffat, Alexander W. *Maverick Navy.* Middletown, Conn.: Wesleyan University Press, 1976.

Morison, Elting E. *Admiral Sims and the Modern American Navy.* Boston: Houghton Mifflin, 1942.

Navy Department. *Annual Report of the Secretary of the Navy for the Fiscal Year 1918.* Washington, D.C.: Government Printing Office, 1918.

Navy Department. *Annual Report of the Secretary of the Navy for the Fiscal Year 1919.* Washington, D.C.: Government Printing Office, 1919.

Navy Department, Office of Naval Records and Library. *German Submarine Activities on the Atlantic Coast of the United States and Canada.* Washington, D.C.: Government Printing Office, 1920.

Navy Department, Office of Navy Records and Library. *The Northern Barrage and Other Mining Activities.* Washington, D.C.: Government Printing Office, 1920.

Nutting, William Washburn. *The Cinderellas of the Fleet.* Jersey City, N.J.: Standard Motor Construction Co., 1920.

Paine, Ralph D. *The Corsair in the War Zone.* Boston and New York: Houghton Mifflin, 1920.

Reilly, John C., and Robert L. Scheina. *American Battleships, 1886–1923: Predreadnought Design and Construction.* Annapolis, Md.: Naval Institute Press, 1980.

Rodman, Hugh. *Yarns of a Kentucky Admiral.* London: Martin Hopkinson, 1929.

Rose, H. Wickliffe. *Brittany Patrol: The Story of the Suicide Fleet.* New York: W. W. Norton, 1937.

Silverstone, Paul H. *U.S. Warships of World War I.* London: Ian Allan, 1970.

Sims, Rear Admiral William Sowden. *The Victory at Sea.* Garden City, N.Y.: Doubleday Page, 1921. Reprint. Annapolis, Md.: Naval Institute Press, 1984.

Sprout, Harold, and Margaret Sprout. *The Rise of American Naval Power, 1776–1918.* Rev. ed. Princeton, N.J.: Princeton University Press, 1966. Reprint. Annapolis, Md.: Naval Institute Press, 1990.

Sterling, Captain Yates. "The Bridge Across the Atlantic." *United States Naval Institute Proceedings* 51, no. 9 (September 1925): 1669–83.

Still, William N. *American Sea Power in the Old World: The United States Navy in European and Near Eastern Waters, 1865–1917.* Westport, Conn.: Greenwood Press, 1980.

Taussig, Captain J. K. "Destroyer Experiences during the Great War." *United States Naval Institute Proceedings* 48, no. 12; 49, nos. 1–3 (December 1922–March 1923).

Trask, David F. *Captains and Cabinets: Anglo-American Naval Relations, 1917–1918.* Columbia: University of Missouri Press, 1972.

Turnbull, Archibald D., and Clifford L. Lord. *History of United States Naval Aviation.* New Haven: Yale University Press, 1949.

Van Wyen, Adrian O., et al. *Naval Aviation in World War I.* Washington, D.C.: Chief of Naval Operations, 1969.

Weir, Gary E. *Building American Submarines, 1914–1940.* Washington, D.C.: Naval Historical Center, 1991.

CAMPAIGNS AND ACTIONS

Agar, Captain Augustus. *Baltic Episode.* London: Hodder & Stoughton, 1963.

———. *Footprints in the Sea.* London: Evans, 1959.

Alexandrescu, Vasile. "Kämpfe der rumänischen Kriegsmarine im Ersten Weltkrieg." *Marine Rundschau* 77, no. 7 (July 1980): 394–99.

Allen, W. E. D., and Paul Muratoff. *Caucasian Battlefields: A History of the Wars on the Turco-Caucasian Border, 1828–1921.* Cambridge: Cambridge University Press, 1953.

Altham, Captain E. "The Dwina Campaign." *Journal of the Royal United Service Institution* 68, no. 2 (May 1923): 228–53.

Bailey, Thomas A., and Paul B. Ryan. *The Lusitania Disaster: An Episode in Modern Warfare and Diplomacy.* New York: Free Press, 1975.

Barker, A. J. *The Bastard War: The Mesopotamian Campaign of 1914–1918.* New York: Dial Press, 1967.

Bennett, Geoffrey. *The Battle of Jutland.* London: Batsford, 1964.

———. *Cowan's War: The Story of British Naval Operations in the Baltic, 1918–1920.* London: Collins, 1964.

———. *Coronel and the Falklands.* New York: Macmillan, 1962.

———. *Naval Battles of the First World War.* Rev. ed. London: Batsford, 1968. Reprint. London: Pan, 1983.

Bingham, Commander, Hon. Barry. *Falklands, Jutland and the Bight.* London: John Murray, 1919.

Burdick, Charles B. *The Japanese Siege of Tsingtau.* Hamden, Conn.: Archon Books, 1976.

Bush, Captain Eric Wheler. *Gallipoli.* London: Allen & Unwin, 1975.

Campbell, N. J. M. *Jutland: An Analysis of the Fighting.* London: Conway Maritime Press, 1986.

Carpenter, Captain A. F. B. *The Blocking of Zeebrugge.* London: Herbert Jenkins, 1922.

Chatterton, E. Keble. *The 'Konigsberg' Adventure.* London: Hurst & Blackett, 1932.

Dane, Edmund. *British Campaigns in Africa and the Pacific, 1914–1918.* London: Hodder & Stoughton, 1919.

Davies, William. *The Sea and the Sand: The Story of HMS Tara and the Western Desert Force.* Caernarfon, Gwynedd: Gwynedd Archives and Museums Service, 1988.

Dixon, F. B. *The Enemy Fought Splendidly.* Poole, Dorset: Blandford Press, 1983.

Falkenhayn, Eric von. *Der Feldzug der 9. Armee gegen die Rumänien und Russen 1916/17.* 2 vols. Berlin: E. S. Mittler, 1921.

Frame, T. R., and G. J. Swinden. *First In, Last Out: The Navy at Gallipoli.* Kenthurst, N.S.W.: Kangaroo Press, 1990.

Fryer, Charles E. J. *The Royal Navy on the Danube.* Boulder, Colo.: East European Monographs, 1988.

Ganz, A. Harding. "'Albion'—The Baltic Islands Operation." *Military Affairs* (April 1978): 91–97.

Gwatkin-Williams, Captain R. S. *Under the Black Ensign.* London: Hutchinson, n.d.

Hadley, Michael L. *U-Boats against Canada: German Submarines in Canadian Waters.* Kingston and Montreal: McGill-Queens University Press, 1985.

Hadley, Michael L., and Roger Sarty. *Tin-Pots and Pirate Ships: Canadian Naval Forces and German Sea Raiders, 1880–1918.* Montreal: McGill-Queens University Press, 1991.

Herwig, Holger H. "German Policy in the Eastern Baltic Sea in 1918: Expansion or Anti-Bolshevik Crusade?" *Slavic Review* 32, no. 2 (June 1973): 339–57.

Hickling, Vice Admiral Harold. *Sailor at Sea.* London: Kimber, 1965.

Hirst, Paymaster-Commander Lloyd. *Coronel and After.* London: Peter Davies, 1934.

Hough, Richard. *The Pursuit of Admiral Graf Spee.* London: Allen & Unwin, 1969.

Ironside, Edmund. *Archangel, 1918–1919.* London: Constable, 1953.

James, Robert Rhodes. *Gallipoli.* New York: Macmillan, 1965.

Kabisch, Ernst. *Der Rumänienkrieg 1916.* Berlin: Vorhut Verlag Otto Schlegel, 1938.

Kemp, Paul, and Peter Jung. "Five Broken B Boats: British Submarine Operations in the Northern Adriatic, 1915–1917." *Warship International* 26, no. 1 (1989): 10–29.

Layman, R. D. *The Cuxhaven Raid.* London: Conway Maritime Press, 1985.

Macintyre, Captain Donald. *Jutland.* London: Evans, 1957.

Mackenzie, John. "The Naval Campaigns on Lakes Victoria and Nyasa, 1914–1918." *Mariner's Mirror* 71, no. 1 (February 1985): 169–82.

Mackenzie, S. S. *The Australians at Rabaul: The Capture and Administration of the German Possessions in the Southern Pacific.* "The Official History of Australia in the War of 1914–1918, Vol. 10," 4th ed. Sydney: Angus and Robertson, 1942.

Macmunn, Lieutenant General Sir George, and Captain Cyril Falls. *Military Operations: Egypt & Palestine.* 2 vols. London: HMSO, 1928.

Maynard, Major General C. *The Murmansk Venture.* New York: Arno Press & The New York Times, 1971.

Middlemas, Keith. *Command the Far Seas: A Naval Campaign of the First World War.* London: Hutchinson, 1961.

Moberly, Brigadier General F. J. *The Campaign in Mesopotamia.* 4 vols. London: HMSO, 1923–27.

———. *Operations in Persia, 1914–1919.* London: HMSO, 1987.

Moorehead, Alan. *Gallipoli.* New York: Harper, 1956.

Negresco, Contre-Amiral N. *Comment on fit la Guerre sur le Danube.* Bucharest: Imprimerie Nationale, 1938.

Nish, I. H. "Admiral Jerram and the German Pacific Fleet, 1913–15." *Mariner's Mirror.* 56, no. 4 (November 1970): 411–21.

Nunn, Vice Admiral Wilfrid. *Tigris Gunboats.* London: Andrew Melrose, 1932.

Pitt, Barry. *Zeebrugge: St. George's Day 1918.* London: Cassell, 1958.

Pochhammer, Captain Hans. *Before Jutland: Admiral von Spee's Last Voyage.* London: Jarrolds, 1931.

Regele, Oskar. *Kampf um die Donau 1916.* Potsdam: Ludwig Voggenreiter Verlag, 1940.

Reuter, Vice Admiral Ludwig von. *Scapa Flow: The Account of the Greatest Scuttling of All Time.* London: Hurst & Blackett, 1940.

Ruge, Vice Admiral Friedrich. *Scapa Flow 1919: The End of the German Fleet.* London: Ian Allan, 1973.

Shankland, Peter. *The Phantom Flotilla: The Story of the Naval Africa Expedition, 1915–1916.* London: Collins, 1968.

Shankland, Peter, and Anthony Hunter. *Dardanelles Patrol.* London: Collins, 1964.

Snook, David. "British Naval Operations in the Black Sea, 1918–1920." *Warship International* 26, nos. 1 and 4 (1989): 36–50, 331–56.

Sokol, Hans. "Der Krieg auf der Donau, 1914–1918." *Marine Rundschau* 65, no. 6 (December 1968): 403–11.

Spencer-Cooper, Commander H. *The Battle of the Falkland Islands.* London: Cassell, 1919.

Tschischwitz, Lieutenant General von. *The Army and Navy during the Conquest of the Baltic Islands in October 1917.* Eng. trans. Fort Leavenworth, Kans.: Command and General Staff School Press, 1933.

Van der Vat, Dan. *The Grand Scuttle; The Sinking of the German Fleet at Scapa Flow in 1919.* London: Hodder & Stoughton, 1982.

Wilson, Michael. *Destination Dardanelles: The Story of HMS E7.* London: Leo Cooper, 1988.

GENERAL

Belot, R. de, and André Reussner. *La Puissance navale dans l'histoire.* Vol. 3, *De 1914 à 1959.* Paris: Editions Maritimes et d'Outre-Mer, 1960.

Birnbaum, Karl E. *Peace Moves and U-Boat Warfare.* Stockholm: Almqvist and Wiksell, 1958.

Breyer, Siegfried. *Battleships and Battlecruisers, 1905–1970.* Garden City, N.Y.: Doubleday, 1973.

Campbell, N. J. M. *Battle Cruisers: The Design and Development of British and German Battlecruisers of the First World War Era.* London: Conway Maritime Press, 1978.

Castex, Amiral. *Théories stratégiques.* 5 vols. Paris: Société d'Editions Maritimes, Géographiques et Coloniales, 1929–35.

Chack, Paul, and Jean-Jacques Antier. *Histoire maritime de la première guerre mondiale.* 3 vols. Paris: Editions France-Empire, 1969–74.

Coletta, Paolo E. *Sea Power in the Atlantic and Mediterranean in World War I.* Lanham, Md.: University Press of America, 1989.

Compton-Hall, Richard. *Submarines and the War at Sea, 1914–1918.* London: Macmillan, 1991.

Consett, Rear Admiral M. W. W. P. *The Triumph of Unarmed Forces (1914–1918).* Rev. ed. London: Williams and Norgate, 1928.

Conway's All the World's Fighting Ships, 1860–1905. London: Conway Maritime Press, 1979.

Conway's All the World's Fighting Ships, 1906–1921. London: Conway Maritime Press, 1985.

Cowie, Captain J. S. *Mines, Minelayers and Minelaying.* London: Oxford University Press, 1949.

Friedman, Norman. *Submarine Design and Development.* Annapolis, Md.: Naval Institute Press, 1984.

Gibson, R. H., and Maurice Prendergast. *The German Submarine War, 1914–1918.* London: Constable, 1931.

Grant, Robert M. *U-Boats Destroyed: The Effects of Anti-Submarine Warfare, 1914–1918.* London: Putnam, 1964.

Grant, Robert M. *U-Boat Intelligence, 1914–1918.* London: Putnam, 1969.

Gray, Edwyn. *The Killing Time: The U-Boat War, 1914–1918.* New York: Scribner's, 1972.

Guichard, Louis. *Histoire du blocus navale.* Paris: Payot, 1929.

Halpern, Paul G. "The Anglo-French-Italian Naval Convention of 1915." *Historical Journal* 13, no. 1 (March 1970): 106–29.

———. *The Mediterranean Naval Situation, 1908–1914*. Cambridge: Harvard University Press, 1971.

———. *The Naval War in the Mediterranean, 1914–1918*. London and Annapolis: Allen & Unwin and Naval Institute Press, 1987.

Hewison, W. S. *This Great Harbour Scapa Flow*. 2d ed. Kirkwall: Orkney Press, 1990.

Hezlet, Vice Admiral Sir Arthur. *Aircraft and Sea Power*. London: Peter Davies, 1970.

———. *Electronics and Sea Power*. New York: Stein and Day, 1975.

———. *The Submarine and Sea Power*. London: Peter Davies, 1967.

Hough, Richard. *The Great War at Sea, 1914–1918*. London: Oxford University Press, 1983.

Jane, Fred T., ed. *Jane's Fighting Ships, 1914*. London: Sampson Low, Marston, 1914. Reprint. Newton Abbot, Devon: David & Charles, 1968.

Jane's Fighting Ships, 1919. Edited by O. Parkes and Maurice Prendergast. London: Sampson Low, Marston, 1919. Reprint. Newton Abbot, Devon: David & Charles, 1969.

Jose, Arthur W. *The Royal Australian Navy, 1914–1918*. "The Official History of Australia in the War of 1914–1918, Vol. 9," 11th ed. Sydney: Angus and Robertson, 1943. Reprint. St. Lucia: University of Queensland Press in association with the Australian War Memorial, 1987.

Kaarsted, Tage. *Great Britain and Denmark, 1914–1920*. Odense: Odense University Press, 1979.

Kahn, David. *The Code Breakers: The Story of Secret Writing*. New York: Macmillan, 1967.

Kennedy, Paul M. *The Rise of the Anglo-German Antagonism, 1860–1914*. London: Allen & Unwin, 1980.

Koblik, Steven. *Sweden: The Neutral Victor*. Lund: Läromedelsförlagen, 1972.

Larcher, Commandant M. *La Guerre turque dans la guerre mondiale*. Paris: Etienne Chiron and Berger-Levrault, 1926.

Laurens, Adolphe. *Histoire de la Guerre Sous-Marine Allemande (1914–1918)*. Paris: Société d'Editions Géographiques, Maritimes et Coloniales, 1930.

Lautenschläger, Karl. "The *Dreadnought* Revolution Reconsidered." In *Naval History: The Sixth Symposium of the U.S. Naval Academy*, edited by Daniel M. Masterson, 121–36. Wilmington, Del.: Scholarly Resources, 1987.

Layman, R. D. *Before the Aircraft Carrier: The Development of Aviation Vessels, 1849–1922*. Annapolis, Md.: Naval Institute Press, 1989.

Leon, George B. *Greece and the Great Powers, 1914–1917*. Thessaloniki: Institute for Balkan Studies, 1974.

Lundeberg, Philip K. "Undersea Warfare and Allied Strategy in World War I." *Smithsonian Journal of History* 1, nos. 1 and 2 (1966–67): 1–30, 49–72.

McKercher, B. J. C. *Esme Howard: A Diplomatic Biography*. Cambridge: Cambridge University Press, 1989.

McKercher, B. J. C., and Keith E. Neilson. "'The Triumph of Unarmed Forces': Sweden and the Allied Blockade of Germany, 1914–1917." *Journal of Strategic Studies* 7, no. 2 (June 1984): 178–99.

McKillip, Robert W. H. "Undermining Technology by Strategy: Resolving the Trade Protection Dilemma of 1917," *Naval War College Review* 44, no. 3 (Summer 1991): 18–37.

Padfield, Peter. *The Great Naval Race: The Anglo-German Naval Rivalry, 1900–1914.* New York: David Mckay, 1974.

———. *Guns at Sea.* London: Hugh Evelyn, 1973.

Parmalee, Maurice. *Blockade and Sea Power: The Blockade, 1914–1919, and Its Significance for a World State.* New York: Thomas Y. Crowell, 1924.

Preston, Anthony. *Battleships of World War I.* New York: Gallahad Books, 1972.

Price, Alfred. *Aircraft versus Submarine: The Evolution of Anti-submarine Aircraft, 1912 to 1972.* London: William Kimber, 1973.

Riste, Olav. *The Neutral Ally: Norway's Relations with Belligerent Powers in the First World War.* Oslo and London: Universitetsforlaget and Allen & Unwin, 1965.

Robinson, Walton L. "The Brazilian Navy in the World War." *United States Naval Institute Proceedings* 62, no. 12 (December 1936): 1712–20.

Siney, Marion C. *The Allied Blockade of Germany, 1914–1916.* Ann Arbor: University of Michigan Press, 1957.

Tarrant, V. E. *The U-Boat Offensive, 1914–1945.* Annapolis, Md.: Naval Institute Press, 1989.

Terraine, John. *Business in Great Waters: The U-Boat Wars, 1916–1945.* London: Leo Cooper, 1989.

Vincent, C. Paul. *The Politics of Hunger: The Allied Blockade of Germany, 1915–1919.* Athens: Ohio University Press, 1985.

Weyer, B., ed. *Taschenbuch der Kriegsflotten, 1914.* Munich: J. F. Lehmanns Verlag, 1914. Reprint. 1968.

Williamson, Samuel R. *The Politics of Grand Strategy: Britain and France Prepare for War, 1904–1914.* Cambridge: Harvard University Press, 1969.

Winton, John. *Below the Belt: Novelty, Subterfuge and Surprise in Naval Warfare.* London: Conway Maritime Press, 1981.

INDEX

Admiralty (*continued*)
and Helgoland action (1917), 378; and
Mediterranean, 386, 389, 391, 393–94,
397; and Aegean, 401; and Ostend,
414; and Air Ministry, 415; and large
liners, 436; and Northern barrage,
439, 440; and German evacuation of
Flanders, 444; and armistice with
Germany, 446, 447
Adriatic: and French operations, 59–62;
and French assistance to Italians, 139;
geographic features of, 139, 140;
submarines cause stalemate in, 151–52,
168; and assistance to Serbia, 153–54,
155, 157–58; and action of 29 December
1915, 156–57; and British drifters, 158,
159; and action of 15 May 1917, 162–65;
and question of command, 166–67,
175; naval guerrilla war in, 168–69,
172–73; in American plans, 171–72;
and action of 23 April 1918, 173;
sinking of *Szent István* in, 174–75; and
bombardment of Durazzo, 175–76; and
situation after armistice, 177–78
Aegean: Greco-Turkish naval race in, 15,
16; and British operations, 59, 133;
mining projects in, 399; reinforced by
Allies, 401, 529n. 53
Agadir crisis (1911), 22
airships, British, 425
Åland Islands, 191, 221, 222
Albania, 153, 155, 159, 175. *See also*
Durazzo; San Giovanni di Medua;
Valona
Albion, Operation, 213–21, 421
Albrecht, Korvettenkapitän Conrad, 349
Alexandretta, 107, 113, 122, 123. *See also*
Ayas Bay
Allenby, General Edmund H. H., 396
Allied Naval Council, 172, 395, 447, 448
Altham, Captain E., 137

Amedeo di Savoia, Duke of Aosta, 141
Ameland, island, 101, 102
Amery, Captain Leopold S., 269, 270
Amet, Vice Admiral Jean-François-
Charles, 401
Anatolia, 132, 133
Ancona, 144, 172
Anglo-French Entente (1904), 4–6, 25, 70
Anglo-French-Italian Naval Convention
(1915), 117, 143–44
Anglo-French Mediterranean
Convention (1914), 58, 144
Anglo-German naval race, 2–7, 10–11
Anglo-Japanese Agreement (1902), 4
Anglo-Persian Oil Company, 124
Anglo-Russian Entente (1907), 5
Antivari, 153
Antwerp, 35
ANZAC. *See* Australian and New
Zealand Army Corps
Apia (German Samoa), 83–85, 88, 92
Arbuthnot, Rear Admiral Sir Robert
Keith, 42, 321
Archangel, 134–37
Argostoli, 146, 387
Armistice (11 November 1918), 447–48
Arnauld de la Perière, Kapitänleutnant
Lothar von, 384, 386–88
Arz von Straussenberg, General Arthur
Baron, 276, 278
Asquith, Herbert Henry, 83, 103, 117
Assmann, Korvettenkapitän Kurt, 349
Aston, Major General Sir George, 101
Augagneur, Victor, 57, 110, 202
Australia, 83–85, 88
Australian and New Zealand Army
Corps (ANZAC), 85, 87, 111, 116
Australian Squadron, 84, 90, 96. *See also*
Patey
Austria-Hungary, 385, 341, 401
Austria-Hungary, Armeeober-

Caspian Sea, 496n. 75
Castelorizo, island, 132
Cattaro, gulf: Austrian base at, 14, 154; French operations against, 60; in Italian plans, 142, 151, 167; and British air attacks, 168, 398; and mutiny in Austrian fleet, 170–71; in U.S. plans, 171; and German submarines, 384, 397, 401
Caucasus, mountains, 110, 131
Channel Barrage Committee, 406, 407
Channel Fleet, 21, 22, 24, 44, 87
Chatfield, Captain Alfred Ernle Montacute, 31, 32
Chaumet, Charles, 57
Childers, Erskine, 21
China Squadron, 85
China Station, 70
Churchill, Winston Spencer: as First Lord, 6, 7, 16, 23, 25; and Helgoland action, 30, 32; opposes mining, 34; and Antwerp, 35; and Fisher, 36; and Limpus, 63; and *Emden*, 73; and Coronel, 92, 94; and North Sea projects, 101–6, 109; and Dardanelles campaign, 109–11, 113, 114, 117, 229; and Alexandretta, 113; and Sabbioncello, 167, 171; and Danube, 268; and *Lusitania*, 299; and Q-ships, 300; names battleships in World War II, 326
Clemenceau, Georges, 401
codes and code books, 36–37, 185. *See also* Room 40
Combes, Emile, 11
Conrad von Hötzendorf, General Baron Franz, 53, 154, 167, 168
Consett, Rear Admiral M. W. W. P., 210
Constantine I, King of Greece, 529n. 53
Constantinople, 230, 401
Constanza, 247, 248, 278

convoys: neglected, in favor of dispersion, 69–70; and major troop movements in 1914, 69, 75–76, 78, 82, 84, 86–88, 90, 95; as real antidote to cruiser warfare, 76–77, 372, 375; in Baltic, 204, 207–8; debate over, at Admiralty, 343, 355–56; and Dutch trade, 351; and French coal trade, 351–52; Scandinavian, 352–53, 379, 405, 417; objections to, 353–55; general system of, introduced, 360–64, 434; and percentage of loss, 364–65, 379–80; threat to, in coastal waters, 369, 405–6, 424, 426; German raids against Scandinavian, 376, 378–79, 403, 418–21; in Mediterranean, 385, 392–98, 400; protected by aircraft, 426; German concentration against routes of, 427; in U.S. coastal waters, 431, 432; and American troop ships, 435–37; and Northern barrage, 438–40; mentioned, 344
Corbett, Sir Julian, 90, 104
Corfu, island: French base on, 146, 166–67, 387; and Serbian army, 158, 160, 274; and U.S. submarine chasers, 171; naval conference at (1917), 392–93
Coronel, battle of, 38, 92–93, 95–97, 100
Corsi, Vice Admiral Camillo, 140, 152, 167
Cowley, Commander Charles H., 130
Cox, Sir Percy, 125
Cradock, Rear Admiral Sir Christopher, 79, 91–93, 95
Crampton, Captain Denis B., 156
Cromarty, 10, 29
Cromie, Lieutenant Commander Francis N. A., 201–3, 208
cruiser warfare: and *Emden*, 74–76; and *Königsberg*, 77–78; and *Karlsruhe*, 78–79; and *Dresden* and

Ferrarini, Capotimoniere, 170
Finland, 221, 222
Firle, Kapitänleutnant Rudolph, 117, 235
Firman, Lieutenant Humphrey O. B., 130
Fisher, Admiral of the Fleet, 1st Baron
(John Arbuthnot Fisher): as First Sea
Lord, 5, 6; prewar strategy of, 21;
recalled as First Sea Lord, 36;
building program of, 36, 120, 129; and
pursuit of Spee, 38, 93–94, 100; and
Baltic/North Sea projects, 103, 104,
105, 110, 187, 377, 441; and
Dardanelles campaign, 110, 111, 114,
117
Fisher, Captain William W., 343, 367,
415
Fiume, 141, 142
Flanders flotillas: development of, 297;
operations of, 304, 329, 335; role of,
disputed, 351, 406, 421; strength of,
306; and Dover barrage, 407–8, 410–
11, 416; evacuated, 416, 444; mentioned, 105, 308, 309
Flottenverein, 3
Foch, Marshal Ferdinand, 141, 447
Fox, Captain Cecil, 35
France: and Macedonian campaign, 106;
interested in Syria, 107, 113, 132; and
Dardanelles campaign, 110–11, 116,
120, 121; and Salonika, 392
France, Army (units): XIXème Corps, 55;
7th Infantry Division, 285; 227th
Infantry Regiment, 285
France, Ministry of Marine, 54–55
France, Ministry of War, 54–55
France, Navy: as challenge to British,
1; and Mediterranean, 6–7, 11, 58;
building program of, 11–12;
strength of, 12–13; and Goeben, 15;
role of, in northern waters, 25, 26;
and repatriation of troops from

North Africa, 54–55; and lack of
colliers and oilers, 59; and naval
convention with Italy, 143–44;
provides assistance to Italians, 146,
153–55; and Salonika, 153–54, 385–
86; and command in Adriatic, 167,
400; shifts base to Corfu, 146, 387;
considers submarines for Baltic,
201–2; and mission to Serbia, 265–
66, 273; and mission to Romania,
282, 284; and coal trade convoys,
352; and search for German
raiders, 371; and shortage of light
craft for escorts, 384–86; patrols
in Mediterranean, 391, 395;
establishes *Direction générale de la
guerre sous-marine*, 393; and Otranto
fixed barrage, 398; and Greek fleet,
529n. 53. *See also* Augagneur; Boué
de Lapeyrère; Dartige du Fournet;
Gauchet
France, Navy (formations): 1ère Armée
Navale, 12, 13, 54, 384; 2ème Escadre
Légère, 25
Franchet d'Esperey, General Louis-Félix,
175
Franz Ferdinand, Archduke, 11, 14, 71
Franz Joseph I, Kaiser, 14, 60, 171
Fremantle, Rear Admiral Sydney R.,
133, 405
French, David, 125
French, General Sir John D. P., 105
Fryatt, Captain Charles A., 296, 351
Fuss, Dr. Richard, 337

Gallipoli, 116, 118, 119, 121, 122. *See also*
Cape Helles; Dardanelles, campaign
Gallwitz, General Max von, 271, 272
Gansser, Kapitänleutnant Konrad, 241
Gauchet, Vice Admiral Dominique-
Marie, 164, 167, 391–92, 401

Gayer, Kapitänleutnant Albert, 294, 309
Geddes, Sir Eric Campbell, 50, 403, 404
George V, King, 403
Germany: and trade with Sweden, 199,
    208–10; and submarine blockade of
    Great Britain, 293, 298, 299; and
    Baralong affair, 301; and decision for
    unrestricted submarine warfare, 338;
    and the United States, 356–57; and
    Italy, 382, 385, 388; signs armistice, 447
Germany, Army: high command of, and
    Danube route, 267; and Serbian
    campaign, 271–73; and Salonika, 274;
    and Romanian campaign, 276, 278–
    79, 283; requests that the navy
    support the Turks with submarines,
    388–89, 396
Germany, Army (units): Armeegruppe
    Lauenstein, 191, 194; Eighth Army,
    214; Ninth Army, 278; Eleventh
    Army, 152, 271, 273; Niemen-Armee,
    194; XXII Reserve Corps, 272; 42nd
    Infantry Division, 214; 217th Infantry
    Division, 283; 2nd Infantry Cyclist
    Brigade, 214; Donauwachtflottille,
    284, 286; Kaiserliches
    Motorbootkorps, 272–73, 383–84
Germany, Navy: as challenge to British,
    2, 6, 8, 9; organization of, 2; building
    program of, 2–3, 4, 7; bases of, 10;
    prewar strategy of, 22–23; inability of,
    to hinder transport of BEF, 28–29; use
    of submarines by, 29, 33, 40, 47; and
    Mediterranean, 61, 109, 116; and
    forces abroad (1914), 66; use of
    auxiliary cruisers by, 66–68, 87; and
    North Russia, 135, 136; and
    submarines at Pola, 145; and Italy,
    148; and Cattaro mutiny, 171; and
    Baltic, 180–84, 187, 193, 195–99, 205,
    207, 211–12; antisubmarine methods

of, in Baltic, 203–4, 207–8; and
    Operation Albion, 220; and Black Sea,
    256–57; presence of, on Danube, 283,
    513n. 57; search for strategy by, 287–
    91; submarine campaign of, 291–94,
    296, 298–300, 302, 304, 306–8, 310,
    338–39; submarine construction
    program of, 294–95, 306–7, 339–40,
    370, 421–23; and reappearance of
    surface raiders, 309–10, 370–75;
    minesweeping operations of, 345,
    349, 378; and Flanders, 346, 348–49;
    and support of Senussi, 388–89;
    operations of, in North American
    waters, 430; and armistice terms, 447–
    48. *See also* Admiralstab; High Sea
    Fleet; submarines, German
Germany, Navy (formations): First
    Scouting Group, 44, 196, 315, 323–24,
    329–30, 445; Second Scouting Group,
    31, 44, 196, 214, 315, 320–21, 330, 377,
    418, 445; Fourth Scouting Group, 192,
    418, 445; First Squadron, 26, 196, 288,
    447; Second Squadron, 26, 315, 330,
    502n. 20; Third Squadron, 26, 199,
    214–15, 217, 289, 315, 319–20, 322–23,
    330, 333, 347; Fourth Squadron, 185,
    192, 195, 214–15, 255, 289, 447;
    Seventh Battleship Division, 192;
    Second Destroyer Flotilla, 324, 378,
    408, 418, 445; Third Destroyer Flotilla,
    322, 333, 346–48; Sixth Destroyer
    Flotilla, 347–49; Ninth Destroyer
    Flotilla, 333, 346–47; Tenth Destroyer
    Flotilla, 211; Second Destroyer Half-
    Flotilla, 445; Third Destroyer Half-
    Flotilla, 378, 409; Fourth Destroyer
    Half-Flotilla, 333, 378–79, 409; First
    Zeebrugge Half-Flotilla, 348; Second
    Zeebrugge Half-Flotilla, 348; Eighth
    Torpedo Boat Flotilla, 196, 445; First

Submarine Flotilla, 29; Mediterranean U-boat Flotilla, 384, 390; First Mediterranean U-boat Flotilla, 397; Second Mediterranean U-boat Flotilla, 397; U-Kreuzer-Verband, 428; Danube Half-Flotilla, 283. *See also* East Asiatic Cruiser Squadron; Flanders flotillas; High Sea Fleet; Mittelmeerdivision

Germany, U-boat Inspectorate, 294–95, 306, 339

Germany, U-boat Office, 370, 422

Gibraltar, 6, 58, 394–96, 401

Giolitti, Giovanni, 144

Gleaves, Rear Admiral Albert, 435

Glossop, Captain John, 76

Godfrey, Captain William Wellington, 121

Goltz, Generalmajor Rüdiger Graf von der, 221, 283

Goodenough, Commodore William E.: and Helgoland action, 30–32; and Scarborough raid, 40–41; and Dogger Bank action, 45; and Jutland, 319

Goodhart, Lieutenant Commander F. H. J., 200, 203

Gough-Calthorpe, Admiral Hon. Sir Somerset Arthur, 393–94, 397–99, 401

Grand Fleet: strength of, 6–9, 25–26, 38; rigid battle orders of, 10; prewar strategy of, 22; deployment of, 24, 27, 47–48; and Scarborough raid, 40–42; and Canadian convoy, 86–87; is reinforced, 95; and assistance to Russians, 199, 206, 219–20, 312; strategy of, 287, 311, 332–33, 403–4; and German raid on Lowestoft, 313; moves base to Rosyth, 314, 317; and Jutland, 315–27; changes in, after Jutland, 327–28; and operations of 19 August 1916, 330–31; destroyer requirements of, 347, 356, 363, 385;

fuel stocks of, 362; submarine hunting operations of, 366–68; and Scandinavian convoy, 376, 379, 403, 417, 420; and action of 17 November 1917, 377; is joined by U.S. battle-ships, 404–5; morale in, 445; and aviation, 441, 443; in Scheer's plans, 445–46. *See also* Beatty; Jellicoe

Grant, Rear Admiral Heathcote S., 395

Grasset, Rear Admiral Maurice-Ferdinand-Albert, 358, 449

Grasshoff, Kapitän zur See Kurt, 337, 400

Great Britain, Air Ministry, 415

Great Britain, Army (units): Duke of Cornwall's Light Infantry, 70–71; Third Army, 120; 29th Division, 111, 116

Great Britain, Board of Trade, 352

Great Britain, Foreign Office: and Mediterranean, 7; opposes mining, 34; and blockade, 49; vetoes Limpus's appointment, 63; and Churchill's North Sea plans, 101; opposes Alexandretta landing, 107; and Scandinavian convoys, 352

Great Britain, Ministry of Shipping, 355, 360, 361

Great Britain, Navy: nineteenth-century supremacy of, 1; and German challenge, 2–4, 7–9; gunnery of, 6, 9, 328; bases of, 9–10; prewar strategy of, 21–22, 101; and transport of BEF, 28; use of submarines by, 30; and mine warfare, 34, 344–45; expeditions by, against German colonies, 82, 83; and Dardanelles, 116; and Persian Gulf, 124; and operations on Tigris-Euphrates, 125–29, 130–31; and Anatolia cattle raids, 132–33; and supplies to North Russia, 133–37; and convention with Italians, 143–44; and

Haldane, 1st Viscount (Richard Burdon Haldane), 7
Hall, Commodore Sidney Stewart, 200
Hall, Captain William Reginald, 10, 37, 114, 428. *See also* Room 40
Hamilton, General Sir Ian, 112, 120
Hankey, Colonel Maurice P. A., 111, 268–69, 360
Hartlepool, 40, 41
Hartog, Kapitän zur See, 323
Harwich Force: deployment of, 24; opening moves of, 27; and Scarborough raid, 40–41; and Dogger Bank action, 45; operations of, against German sorties, 311; and raid on Lowestoft, 313; and Jutland, 316; and operations of 19 August 1916, 330; and German destroyer raids, 347–48; and Dutch convoys, 351; use of aircraft by, 443; and German evacuation of Flanders, 444; receives surrender of U-boats, 448; mentioned, 376, 417. *See also* Tyrwhitt
Haun, Fregattenkapitän, 80
Haus, Admiral Anton: meets Revel, 15, 140; and Constantinople, 53; and assistance to *Goeben*, 54, 57; is suspicious of Italy, 60; justifies defensive strategy, 61; strikes first blow at Italians, 144–45; and Serbian campaign, 154–56, 159; and action of 29 December 1915, 157; and Conrad, 167–68; death of, 168; and submarine construction, 382–83; supports German submarine warfare, 385; mentioned, 151, 175
Hayes-Sadler, Captain Arthur, 124, 255, 256
Heimburg, Oberleutnant zur See Heino von, 118, 119, 148
Heinecke, Korvettenkapitän, 378–79,

408–9
Heinrich, Admiral Prince of Prussia: given Baltic command, 26, 182–83; and Mischke, 184; and operations in Baltic, 185, 190, 192, 198, 211–12; and Libau, 193, 502n. 20; and British submarines, 203–4, 207; and Gulf of Riga, 207; and Operation Albion, 214; mentioned, 447, 502n. 7
Heinrich, Kapitän zur See Paul, 182, 214, 216, 219
Helgoland, action (1914), 30–32
Helgoland, action (1917), 377–78, 403
Helgoland, island, 10, 101, 102, 106
Helsingfors, 180, 181, 221–22
Henderson, Commander Reginald Guy, 355, 360
Hentsch, Lieutenant Colonel Richard, 267
Herbert, Lieutenant Commander Godfrey, 301
Hersing, Kapitänleutnant Otto, 33, 118, 292, 381
Herwig, Professor Holger, 337
Hezlet, Vice Admiral Sir Arthur, 296, 303, 324, 336, 365
High Sea Fleet: strength of, 5, 7, 9, 25–26, 39; bases of, 10; strategy of, 23, 27; and Scarborough raid, 40–42; morale in, 47, 375, 421; and Baltic, 203, 214–15; operations of (1916), 304, 311–13; and Jutland, 315–27; and sortie of 19 August 1916, 330–31; and support of submarine operations, 333, 421; weight of, as "fleet-in-being," 356, 417; operations of (1917), 375–77; and assistance to Flanders flotillas, 408, 410, 416; and Scandinavian convoy, 418–21; attacked by British carrier aircraft, 441–42, 444; and plans for *Flottenvorstoss* (1918), 444–46; mutiny

High Sea Fleet (*continued*)
in, 447; arrives for internment, 448–
49. *See also* Germany, Navy; Ingenohl;
Pohl; Scheer

Hindenburg und Benckendorff, Field
Marshal Paul von: and Operation
Albion, 214; and submarine
construction, 339; and submarine
warfare, 368, 430; mentioned, 326,
337, 422

Hipper, Rear Admiral Franz: commands
scouting group, 26, 38; and
Helgoland action, 32; bombards
Yarmouth, 39; and plans for Atlantic
sortie, 40, 87; raids Scarborough and
Hartlepool, 40–42; and Dogger Bank
action, 44–45; in Baltic, 196–98; and
Jutland, 315, 317–21, 323; and
Scandinavian convoy, 418–19;
assumes command of High Sea Fleet,
422; and plans for *Flottenvorstoss*
(1918), 445, 447; and internment of
High Sea Fleet, 448–49; mentioned, 313

Hoffman, Colonel Max, 198

Holbrook, Lieutenant Norman D., 119

Holtzendorff, Admiral Henning von:
and North Russia, 136; becomes chief
of Admiralstab, 302; and submarine
warfare, 304–6, 308, 329, 335, 368, 430;
and memorandum of 22 December
1916, 337–38; retirement of, 422;
mentioned, 303, 322

Hood, Rear Admiral Hon. Horace L. A.,
35, 315, 320, 321

Hope, Rear Admiral George P. W., 397

Hopman, Rear Admiral Albert: and
Baltic operations, 191, 193, 195, 212;
and Operation Albion, 214, 217, 219;
as head of NATEKO (Black Sea), 257

Hornby, Rear Admiral R. S. Phipps, 86,
87, 94

Horthy de Nagybánya,
Linienschiffskapitän Nikolaus: raids
drifters (July 1916), 161; and action of
15 May 1917, 162–64, 166; becomes
Flottenkommandant, 171; and plans
for offensive against Otranto barrage,
174–75; mentioned, 173, 177

Horton, Lieutenant Commander Max
K., 33, 188, 192, 195, 203

Howard, Esme, 210

Howe, Admiral of the Fleet Richard,
Earl, 326

Huguet, Rear Admiral A. L. M., 70

Hungary, 382, 383

Hutier, Lieutenant General Oskar von,
214

hydrophones: as antisubmarine device,
343–44, 367, 424, 440; in Strait of
Otranto, 397, 398; and U.S. Navy, 399,
432

India, Army, 86, 106

India, Army (units): 6th Division, 124,
127; Fortieth Pathans, 71

India, Government of, 124, 125, 130

Indian Ocean: and German cruisers, 72,
75–78, 373; and Japanese navy, 90,
373

Ingenohl, Admiral Friedrich von:
strategy and deployment of, 23, 26,
39; and raids on British coast, 40–42;
and Dogger Bank action, 44; is
relieved, 47; and submarine warfare,
293; mentioned, 287, 288

insurance, marine, 68, 303

Irben, strait, 195, 197, 199, 206, 213–17

Irish Sea, 424

Italo-Turkish War (1911–1912), 15, 109,
388

Italy: and Triple Alliance, 11, 140;
declares neutrality, 52, 73; negotiates

Jerram, Vice Admiral Sir Thomas Henry Martyn, 70, 72–75, 85, 91, 321

Jeune École, 1, 11

Joffre, General Joseph-Jacques-Césaire, 35, 60, 105, 111, 120

Jonquières, Vice Admiral Marie-Pierre-Eugène de Fauque de, 201, 202

Jutland, battle of: German destroyer strength at, 27; preliminaries to, 314–17; battle cruiser action at, 318–19; main and night action at, 320–25; losses at, 325–26; aftermath of, 326–28; mentioned, 9, 312, 314, 329, 340, 348, 404–5, 417

Kahle, Fregattenkapitän, 349

Kanin, Vice Admiral B. A., 193, 208, 211

Karl I, Kaiser, 171, 177, 286

Karpf, Commodore Hans von, 194, 195

Kathen, Lieutenant General von, 214

Keal, Loch na, 29, 33

Kelly, Captain William A. Howard, 56

Kemp, Commodore Thomas W., 135

Kerber, Vice Admiral L. F., 186, 193, 204

Kerillis, Rear Admiral Henri de, 70

Kerr, Lieutenant Commander Charles L., 266, 271

Kerr, Rear Admiral Mark, 160, 161

Keyes, Commodore Roger John Brownlow: as Commodore (S), 24, 29, 188; and Helgoland action, 30, 32; warns of patrol by *Bacchante*, 33; on Fisher, 36; and Scarborough raid, 41–42; and Cuxhaven raid, 43; and Dogger Bank action, 45, 46; at Dardanelles, 112, 115–17, 120–22; opposes evacuation, 121–23; criticizes Allied Mediterranean agreement, 386; and Channel Barrage Committee, 406–7; and Dover Patrol, 408–10; and Zeebrugge raid, 411–15; and control

of naval aircraft, 415–16

Khomenko, Rear Admiral, 243

Kiel: visited by British squadron, 10–11; and project for British attack, 102, 103

Kiel Canal, 10, 101, 179

King-Hall, Rear Admiral Herbert G., 77, 95

King-Hall, Commander Stephen, 47, 48

Kitchener, Field Marshal 1st Earl (Horatio Herbert Kitchener): and Borkum project, 103; and Belgian coast landing, 105; favors Alexandretta scheme, 107, 113, 122; and defense of Egypt, 108; and Dardanelles campaign, 111, 117, 121–23; and Danube, 268; death of, 329

Knorr, Korvettenkapitän Wolfram von, 97, 241, 246

Koch, Vice Admiral Reinhard, 375

Kogrund Channel, 211

Köhler, Fregattenkapitän Erich, 78, 79

Kolbe, Kapitänleutnant Constantin, 428

Kolbe, Kapitänleutnant Hans, 378, 409

Kolchak, Rear Admiral Alexander V., 183, 209, 245–47, 251–52

Kophamel, Korvettenkapitän Waldemar: commands Mediterranean U-boat flotilla, 305, 384, 388, 396; commands *U35*, 382; commands *U140*, 433

Kövess von Kövessháza, General Hermann Baron, 271

Kress von Kressenstein, Colonel Friedrich, 107

KuK Kriegsmarine. *See* Austria-Hungary, Navy

Kungsbacka Fjord, Sweden, 101

Kurosch, Vice Admiral A. P., 209

Kut, 128–31

Lacaze, Rear Admiral Marie-John-Lucien, 121, 155

Marder, Professor Arthur J., 322, 324, 330, 421, 424

Marinekorps Flandern, 297, 333, 346, 408–9, 422

Marmara, sea: and Allied operations, 111, 113, 116, 121, 122; and Allied submarine operations, 119

Maude, Lieutenant General Sir Stanley, 131

Mauve, Rear Admiral Franz, 315

Maxwell, General Sir John, 108

Maynard, Major General Sir Charles, 137

Mayo, Admiral Henry Thomas, 394, 438

Mediterranean: and 1912 redeployment, 6–7; naval race in, 11, 13–15; and Japanese destroyers, 18, 393; and Anglo-French convention (1914), 58; appearance of German submarines in, 104, 132, 381; failure to achieve unified command in, 141, 400; favorable opportunities for German submarines in, 302, 305, 309, 335–36, 381–82; declared *Sperrgebiet*, 340, 390; German submarine campaign in, 383–85, 387–88, 390–91, 397, 399–401, 423; and Paris agreement (December 1915), 386; and Malta conference (March 1916), 386–87; failure of antisubmarine measures in, 389–90; and London conference (January 1917), 390; and Corfu conference (April 1917), 392–93; and London conference (September 1917), 394; convoy system in, 394–97

Mediterranean Expeditionary Force, 112

Merchant Marine, British: volume of, 65; effects of submarine campaign on, 303, 308–9, 336, 341–42; in Holtzendorff's memorandum (22 December 1916), 337–38; and convoy system, 364–65, 423

merchant ships, American: *Algonquin*, 341; *Amphion*, 434; *Antilles*, 437; *Carolina*, 431; *Covington*, 437; *Cushing*, 298; *Felix Taussig*, 433; *Finland*, 437; *George G. Henry*, 434; *Great Northern*, 435; *Gulflight*, 298; "Lake" class, 438–39; *Leviathan*, 435, 436; *Lucia*, 434; *Mount Vernon*, 437; *Nebraskan*, 299; *New York*, 358; *Northern Pacific*, 435; *Pass of Balmaha*, 373; *President Lincoln*, 437; *Saetia*, 433; *San Saba*, 433; *Ticonderoga*, 434

merchant ships, Austro-Hungarian: *Baron Call*, 176; *Belgrade*, 267; *Croatia*, 285; *Locrum*, 169; *Martha Washington*, 534n. 96; *Odessa*, 285; *Sarajevo*, 169; *Trinitas*, 267; *Vaskapu*, 274; *Wien*, 177

merchant ships, Belgian: *Samland*, 371

merchant ships, Brazilian: *Uberaba*, 433

merchant ships, British: *Alban*, 434; *Aquitania*, 436; *Arabia*, 335; *Arabic*, 301, 302; *Brussels*, 296, 351; *Cymric*, 308; *Denbigh Hall*, 427; *Dunrobin*, 210; *Falaba*, 298; *F. D. Lambert*, 210; *Glitra*, 292; *Glyndwr*, 193; *Hesperian*, 302; *Hurunui*, 427; *Julnar*, 129, 130; *Kashmir*, 437; *Laconia*, 341; *Lusitania*, 298–302; *Malachite*, 292; *Marina*, 335; *Mauretania*, 298–99, 436; *Merion*, 118; *Minieh*, 371; *Moorina*, 109; *Newby Hall*, 434; *Nicosian*, 301; *Nirpura*, 428; *Olympic*, 34, 427, 436; *Otaki*, 371; *Patagonia*, 235; *Penmount*, 210; *Primo*, 292; *Queen*, 346; *Queen Elizabeth*, 436; *Queen Mary*, 436; *Queensland*, 400; *Royal Edward*, 118; *Saint Theodore*, 371; *San Andres*, 427; *Scholar*, 427; *Teiresias*, 108; *Thelma*, 210; *Turritella*, 372; *Tuscania*, 436; *Vienna*, 134; *Yarrowdale*, 371, 374 merchant ships, Canadian: *Triumph*, 433

merchant ships, Cuban: *Chaparro*, 433

merchant ships, Danish: *N. J. Fjord*, 317

merchant ships, Dutch: *Batavier V*, 307; *Katwijk*, 298; *Mecklenburg*, 307; *Medea*, 298; *Palembang*, 307; *Princess Juliana*, 307; *Tubantia*, 307; *Zaanstroom*, 307

merchant ships, French: *Amiral Ganteaume*, 292; *Carthage*, 118, 119; *Portugal*, 242; *Sussex*, 307, 308

merchant ships, German: *Ahlers*, 91; *Ayesha*, 76, 500n. 38; *Baden*, 91, 100; *Belgravia*, 309; *Choising*, 76, 500n. 38; *Cincinnati*, 437; *Corcovado*, 62; *Dora Hugo Stinnes*, 193; *Fortuna*, 374; *General*, 62; *Germania*, 202, 204; *Guben*, 310; *Hedwig von Wissmann*, 84; *Holsatia*, 91; *Koenig*, 77; *Köln*, 434; *Kronprinzessin Cecilie*, 437; *Lissabon*, 210; *Markomannia*, 72, 75; *Präsident*, 78; *President Lincoln*, 437; *Princess Alice*, 534n. 96; *Pungo*, 309; *Rio Negro*, 79; *Santa Isabel*, 100; *Seydlitz*, 100; *Syria*, 208; *Titania*, 71, 72, 88, 96, 97; *Vaterland*, 435; *Wachtenfels*, 372; *Walküre*, 89; *Worms*, 210

merchant ships, Greek: *Ellispontos*, 298; *Pontoporos*, 75

merchant ships, Italian: *Ancona*, 385; *Carracio*, 500n. 38; *Conte Rosso*, 442

merchant ships, Japanese: *Fukoku Maru*, 71

merchant ships, Norwegian: *Belridge*, 297; *Bergensfjord*, 49

merchant ships, Romanian: *Dacia*, 276; *Imparatul Traian*, 276; *Regele Carol I*, 276; *Rumania*, 276

merchant ships, Russian: *Athos*, 228; *Kornilov*, 240; *Lazarev*, 240; *Oleg*, 228, 506n. 11; *Rjasan*, 72, 76; *Sloboda*, 511n. 26; *Sveti Sergi*, 510n. 4; *Vpered*, 508n. 49

merchant ships, Spanish: *Igotz Mendi*, 373

merchant ships, Swedish: *Hanna*, 297; *Nike*, 202

merchant ships, Turkish: *Carmen*, 237; *Irmingard*, 237, 238, 248; *Rodesto*, 248

Mesopotamia, campaign: origins of, 124; and capture of Kurnah, 125; psychological dimensions of, 125, 126; and advance on Baghdad, 126–29; and siege of Kut, 129–30; War Office assumes control of, 130; and capture of Baghdad, 131–32; cost of, 132; mentioned, 106, 123

Meurer, Rear Admiral Hugo, 221, 222, 448

Michelsen, Kapitän zur See Andreas, 346, 369, 407–8, 430

Miller, Rear Admiral Hugh, 112

Milne, Vice Admiral Sir Archibald Berkeley, 56, 57

Mischke, Rear Admiral Robert, 183, 184, 200

Mittelmeerdivision: establishment of, 15; and action on outbreak of war, 51–52, 53; and Turkish fleet, 62; misleading name of, 225; new opportunities for, 256. *See also* Souchon

Mola, Rear Admiral, 176

Monro, General Sir Charles C., 120–23

Montecuccoli, Vice Admiral Rudolph, Graf, 14

Montenegro, 61, 153, 157

Montgelas, Oberleutnant zur See Graf von, 200

Moon Sound, 181, 191, 196–98, 206; 214–19

Moore, Rear Admiral Sir Archibald G. H. W., 30, 46

Moriyama, Captain, 96

Moroccan crisis (1905), 5

Mücke, Kapitänleutnant Helmuth von, 76, 513n. 57

Mudros, 112, 116, 118, 258, 401

Muhammerah, Sheik of, 125, 126

Müller, Admiral Georg Alexander von: and Ingenohl, 46, 47; and Baltic command, 182; and Denmark, 183; and submarine warfare, 293, 302, 337; and Tirpitz, 303; and Jutland, 326; mentioned, 303

Müller, Fregattenkapitän Karl von, 71, 72, 74–76, 489n. 22

Murmansk, 134–37

Myres, Lieutenant Commander John L., 133

Nakhimov, Operation, 254

Napier, Vice Admiral T. W. D., 377

Nasmith, Lieutenant Commander Martin E., 119, 188

NATEKO (Nautisch-Technische Komission für Schwarze Meere), 257

Naval Air Service, American, 425, 426

Naval Air Service, British: and Cuxhaven raid, 43; and Zeebrugge and Bruges, 415; and seaplane raids on zeppelin bases, 311–12, 314, 441; and development of carriers, 442, 443

Naval Air Service, French, 426

Naval Air Service, German, 42–44, 411, 443–44

Naval Staff, British, 102. *See also* Admiralty

Nelson, Captain Charles P., 399

Nelson, Vice Admiral, 1st Viscount (Horatio Nelson), 46, 184, 417

Nemits, Rear Admiral, 254

Nepenin, Vice Admiral A. J., 211, 212

Nerger, Korvettenkapitän Karl-August, 372, 373

Netherlands: and friction with

Germany, 298, 302, 307; possible entry into war of, 337; mentioned, 347, 447

Netherlands, Navy, 18, 74–75, 102, 444

Netherlands East Indies, 74, 75

Newbolt, Sir Henry John, 341, 372, 379, 533n. 77

New Guinea, 83, 85, 88, 89

New Zealand, 78, 83–85

Niblack, Rear Admiral Albert Parker, 394, 395, 397

Nicholas, Grand Duke, 110, 113

Nicholas II, Tsar, 184, 185

Nixon, General Sir John, 126–30

Njegovan, Vice Admiral Maximilian, 168, 169, 171

Norges Rederforbund, 352

Northern barrage, 399, 433, 438–41

Norway: declares neutrality, 28, 179; territorial waters of, used by Allied shipping, 135, 504n. 65; in Wegener's plans, 289; heavy shipping losses of, 352, 353; British obligated to supply coal to, 378; British proposals to mine territorial waters of, 439–40

Nostitz und Jänkendorf, Korvettenkapitän von, 432

Novorossisk, 256, 257

Nunn, Captain Wilfred, 127, 129, 131

Odessa, 63, 231, 256, 285

Oliver, Rear Admiral Sir Henry F.: opposes mining, 34; and Room 40, 37; and Churchill's Baltic schemes, 104–5; on Helgoland, 106; and assistance to the Russians, 219; and Jutland, 316; meets with Jellicoe and Beatty, 331–32, 344; and Scandinavian convoy, 352; objections of, to convoys, 353–54

Ösel, island. *See* Albion, Operation

Ostend: Germans develop base at, 35,

105; as outlet for submarines, 297, 346; bombarded by monitors, 350, 411; attempts to block, 411–12, 414–15; as target of U.S. Northern Bombing Group, 426

Otranto, strait: French blockade of, 61, 62; and British drifters, 159–61, 387, 397, 401; fixed barrage of, 160–61; raided by Austrians, 161, 173; and action of 15 May 1917, 162–66; and U.S. submarine chasers, 171, 399; and Horthy's planned offensive, 174–75; and Calthorpe's proposed reorganization, 398; and ineffectiveness of barrage, 399

Pagano di Melito, Tenente di vascello, 169

Page, Walter Hines, 359

Pakenham, Vice Admiral Sir William C., 377

Palestine, campaign, 106, 392, 395–97

Palladini, Rear Admiral, 176

Panama Canal, 94, 357

Paolucci, Tenente di vascello Raffaele, 177

Papeete (Tahiti), 85, 89, 92

Passchendaele, battle of, 350, 421

Patey, Rear Admiral Sir George E.: and Australian expeditions, 84, 85, 88; and pursuit of Spee, 89, 91, 95, 96

Peirse, Rear Admiral Richard H.: and Emden, 75; and defense of Egypt, 107, 109; and operations at Smyrna, 113–14

Pelagosa, island, 147–51

Pellegrini, Tenente di vascello Mario, 172

Pelletan, Camille, 11–12

Persia, 125, 128

Persian Gulf, 106, 110, 124, 128

Persian Gulf Expeditionary Force

("Force D"), 124

Pfundheller, Kapitän zur See Hans, 33

Piave, river, 169

Picot, Lieutenant de vaisseau Edouard, 265–66

Pohl, Admiral Hugo von: as Chief of Admiralstab, 23; strategy of, 39, 40, 287–88, 290; replaces Ingenohl, 47; and Spee's squadron, 97; and Baltic, 183, 199, 502n. 20; and submarine warfare, 293, 295, 302; and Flanders flotillas, 217; death of, 305; mentioned, 291

Pola: and German submarines, 116, 118, 145, 382–84, 387, 397; as Austrian base, 140; attacked by Italy, 172–73, 177; as target of air raids, 398, 400; Germans evacuate, 401

Pollen, Arthur Hungerford, 6, 9, 328

Poole, Major General Sir Frederick C., 137

Premuda, island, 174

Prölss, Kapitänleutnant Eduard, 330

Püllen, Kapitän zur See, 396

Pustkuchen, Oberleutnant zur See Herbert, 307

Q-ships: employed by Germans in Baltic, 204, 208; used by British, 300, 301, 309; decline in effectiveness of, 343; mentioned, 363, 428

Queenstown, 359, 362, 394, 429

Rabaul (New Britain), 84, 85

Rebeur-Paschwitz, Vice Admiral Hubert, 255

Red Sea, 86

Regia Marina. See Italy, Navy

Reichsmarineamt, 2, 339, 423

Reuter, Rear Admiral Ludwig von, 377, 448, 449

operations in North Russia, 135; and operations affected by climate, 179–80; and submarines, 201, 202, 205; and mining offensive, 204–5; mine and coast defenses of, 206–7; prewar Black Sea plans of, 223–24; and Danube, 262–64, 273–74, 278–79, 282, 284, 510n. 4. *See also* Black Sea Fleet; Essen; Russia, Baltic Fleet

Russo-Japanese War (1904–1905), 5, 16, 18, 21, 34, 91, 180

Ryan, Commander Cyril Percy, 343

Sabbioncello peninsula, 142, 147, 167, 171–72

Sablin, Vice Admiral N. P., 256

Salandra, Antonio, 52

Salonika: Anglo-French landing at, 120, 152; troop movements to, 146, 154, 389; and German plans, 274; Jellicoe recommends withdrawal from, 360, 391–92; and the French, 385–86, 395; British forces advance toward, 401. *See also* Macedonia, campaign

San Giovanni di Medua, 153–55, 157

Sarrail, General Maurice Paul Emmanuel, 120, 274

Saseno, island, 153

Sato, Rear Admiral Kozo, 393

Save, river, 262–63, 265–66, 272

Scapa Flow, 10, 24, 29–30, 288, 418, 488

Scarborough, 40–42

Scheer, Admiral Reinhard: on British strategy, 27; fails to impede transport of BEF, 28–29; complains of minefields in Belts, 183; favors more offensive strategy, 207, 310–12; and Operation Albion, 213–14; and submarine warfare, 293, 295, 305, 308–10; raids Lowestoft, 313; and Jutland, 314–16, 318–20, 322–28;

advocates resumption of unrestricted submarine warfare, 328–29, 332, 336–37; and sortie of 19 August 1916, 329–31; defends use of *Moltke* to support submarines, 334; and destroyers for Flanders flotillas, 347–49, 408; and submarine construction, 370, 422–23; plans sortie (March 1917), 375–76; and Scandinavian convoy, 376, 378, 418–21; and submarines in American waters, 430; plans *Flottenvorstoss* (November 1918), 444, 446, 447; mentioned, 288

Scheidt, Rear Admiral, 192

Schmidt, Vice Admiral Ehrhard, 185, 192, 195–98, 214, 217

Schneider, Kapitänleutnant Rudolf, 301

Schoultz, Captain G. von, 206

Schröder, Vice Admiral Ludwig von, 297, 346

Schwerer, Capitaine de vaisseau Zéphirin-Alexandre-Antoine, 58

Schwieger, Kapitänleutnant Walter, 299, 302, 308

Scott, Captain Percy, 5

Sebastopol, 17, 63, 256–58

Seekriegsleitung (SKL), 422, 430

Seitz, Linienschiffskapitän Heinrich, 154–57

Senussi, 109, 128, 388, 389

Serbia: resists Austrians, 110, 115; is overrun, 120, 152, 271–74; supplies for, 153–54, 263; importance of, for Dardanelles campaign, 232, 236–37, 267; improvised naval forces of, on Danube, 262, 270, 511n. 26; British naval mission to, 270–71

Serbia, Army, 152, 155, 157–58

Serbian Relief Committee, 153–54

Seymour, Lieutenant Commander Ralph F., 41, 46

trade, British: plans for defense of, 69; and cruiser warfare, 76–77; effect of submarine campaigns on, 303, 308–9, 336, 341–42; and convoy system, 364–65, 369, 424–25; and German raiders, 309–10, 370–75; and Mediterranean, 384, 386–87, 389–97, 400. *See also* convoys

Trafalgar, battle of (1805), 326, 449

Trapp, Linienschiffsleutnant Georg, Ritter von, 62, 149, 174

Trieste, 141, 142, 170

Triple Alliance, 4, 7, 11, 384

Triple Alliance Naval Convention (1913), 15, 51–53, 140

Tripolitania, 388

Trotha, Kapitän zur See Adolf von: and Russian Baltic Fleet, 221; favors more aggressive fleet policy, 288, 310; on Scheer, 327; and submarine warfare, 336–37; and plan for *Flottenvorstoss*, 445

Troubridge, Rear Admiral Ernest Charles Thomas: and escape of *Goeben*, 56, 57; supports Lapeyrère, 59; at Dardanelles, 63; and naval mission to Serbia, 266, 271, 273–74; comments on proposals for Danube operations, 269–70

Trukhachev, Vice Admiral, 209

Tschischwitz, Lieutenant General, 220, 221

Tsingtau, 66, 71, 72, 74

Tsuchiyama, Rear Admiral M., 90

Tsushima, battle of (1905), 184

Tupper, Rear Admiral Reginald G. O., 50

Turkey: concludes alliance with Germany, 52, 57; enters war, 58, 62, 64, 86, 224; sultan of, proclaims *jihad*, 106; attacks Suez Canal, 107, 108; and offensive in Caucasus, 110; and ammunition supplies, 114, 115; protests cattle raids, 133; claims part of Black Sea Fleet, 257; concludes armistice, 258, 401; vital supplies brought by submarine to, 381, 388–89

Turkey, Army (units): Fourth Army, 106, 107; VIII Corps, 107

Turkey, Navy: acquires dreadnoughts, 15–16, 224; strength of, 62, 106; deficiencies of, 225; and mine-sweeping at Bosphorus, 251; and 1918 sortie of *Goeben* into Aegean, 255; acquires *Goeben*, 258. *See also* Mittelmeerdivision; Souchon

Tyrwhitt, Commodore Reginald Yorke: commands Harwich Force, 24; and Helgoland action, 30–32; warns of patrol by *Bacchante*, 33; and Scarborough raid, 40, 41; and air raid on Cuxhaven, 43; and Dogger Bank action, 45; opposes Baltic projects, 102–3; and Zeebrugge, 105, 411; operations of, 311, 313, 316, 330–31, 347–48; and Dutch convoys, 351; and German evacuation of Flanders, 444; receives surrender of German submarines, 448; mentioned, 417, 443. *See also* Harwich Force

U-boats. *See* submarines, German

Ukraine, 256–57, 284

United States: and Panama Canal, 94; in Wegener's plans, 290; competition for sympathy of, 292; and submarine warfare, 295, 298, 305, 306, 335–36; and *Lusitania* affair, 299; and *Arabic* affair, 301–2; and *Sussex* affair, 307–8; in Holtzendorff's memorandum of 22 December 1916, 338; and war with Germany, 340–41, 356; seizes

About the Author

Paul G. Halpern was born in New York in 1937 and is a graduate of the University of Virginia. He served as an officer in the U.S. Army from 1958 to 1960 and received a Ph.D. from Harvard University in 1966. He joined the faculty at Florida State University in 1965 and is now a professor of history.

He is the author of *The Mediterranean Naval Situation, 1908–1914,* and *The Naval War in the Mediterranean, 1914–1918.* He has also edited the three-volume *Keyes Papers: Selections from the Private and Official Correspondence of Admiral of the Fleet Baron Keyes of Zeebrugge* for the Naval Records Society as well as another volume of documents, *The Royal Navy in the Mediterranean, 1915–1918.* He is currently working on a biography of Admiral Anton Haus, chief of the Austro-Hungarian navy.

Professor Halpern has served on the council of the Naval Records Society and as a visiting professor in the strategy department of the Naval War College. He is a fellow of the Royal Historical Society.

❧

The Naval Institute Press is the book-publishing arm of the U.S. Naval Institute, a private, nonprofit, membership society for sea service professionals and others who share an interest in naval and maritime affairs. Established in 1873 at the U.S. Naval Academy in Annapolis, Maryland, where its offices remain today, the Naval Institute has members worldwide.

Members of the Naval Institute support the education programs of the society and receive the influential monthly magazine *Proceedings* and discounts on fine nautical prints and on ship and aircraft photos. They also have access to the transcripts of the Institute's Oral History Program and get discounted admission to any of the Institute-sponsored seminars offered around the country.

The Naval Institute also publishes *Naval History* magazine. This colorful bimonthly is filled with entertaining and thought-provoking articles, first-person reminiscences, and dramatic art and photography. Members receive a discount on *Naval History* subscriptions.

The Naval Institute's book-publishing program, begun in 1898 with basic guides to naval practices, has broadened its scope in recent years to include books of more general interest. Now the Naval Institute Press publishes about one hundred titles each year, ranging from how-to books on boating and navigation to battle histories, biographies, ship and aircraft guides, and novels. Institute members receive discounts of 20 to 50 percent on the Press's nearly six hundred books in print.

Full-time students are eligible for special half-price membership rates. Life memberships are also available.

For a free catalog describing Naval Institute Press books currently available, and for further information about subscribing to *Naval History* magazine or about joining the U.S. Naval Institute, please write to:

Membership Department
U.S. Naval Institute
291 Wood Road
Annapolis, MD 21402-5035
Telephone: (800) 233-8764
Fax: (410) 269-7940
Web address: www.usni.org